HAYDEN

An Autobiography

To Dallas,
my constant companion through
the best and the worst that life has offered.

CONTENTS

We are all shaped by our lifetime experiences. The lessons these provide are stored in our personal memory banks, the data functioning like invisible navigation signals, instinctively guiding our responses and ambitions through life when certain stimuli engage them. It would seem that a great deal of the shaping of our character is rather much in place by our twelfth year. That is why I commence this work with the biggest initial influences on my life, my early home life and the Great Depression. These things defined much of what I became and how and why I reacted to various later experiences in public life in the way in which I did.

Then, while still young and impressionable, my experiences in the Queensland Police Force were important influences shaping my values. The work of a policeman can make one suspicious and conservative in many respects; it can also encourage compassion as a result of sharing in so much of other people's tragedy and suffering. You have to do more than just fulfil the bare, formal requirements of the job on hand when your fellow humans are in distress. When someone has experienced one of life's terrible injustices and found their heart and soul torn into painful little strips, natural instincts prevent you from walking away and leaving them in a mess of uncomprehending despair. Giving that help can be nourishing for the soul. You also learn an important degree of tolerance for others, for their differences and quirks; you learn to respect the nobleness of ordinary people's character and yet recognise the base impulses which are capable of tripping up any of us. It is these very imperfect materials which bind human communities together. And if we do not have a sense of community, a commitment to a degree of co-operation, especially in shared adversity, then brutishness can undermine the important virtues which make a civilisation.

My early years in Canberra as a member of parliament were, in some respects, wide-eyed, credulous ones, too often guided by a set of well-meant, ideological values which I came to recognise could be impediments to consistently logical, open-minded analysis. And there was, in those early days, the occasional disillusionment with a hero, someone who appeared to have risen above personal disadvantage to become a respected leader of the working class, a fighter for just causes in the face of formidable odds. It was sometimes painful to discover that someone I admired suffered in private a fickleness of purpose. So I learnt to admire some people for their finer attributes but I forsook the indulgence of heroes, for we should make our own decisions as acts of reasoned, free will. Received wisdom can be deceptive.

As a late maturer, and a university student, my studies gave me more than a formal degree as I concurrently beavered away at the many-faceted role of a parliamentarian. They helped me prise open dark little boxes of prejudice cloistered in corners of my mind, letting the light of knowledge and understanding from the liberal humanities flow in. Through this exposure I gained a wider appreciation of humanist values and a better sense of community obligation by which to guide my efforts in public office.

These matters, and many more, are the foundations on which I built my commitments as Minister for Social Security, Treasurer, and then, following the abject and demoralising defeat for Labor after the 1975 and 1977 elections, as Labor Leader of the Opposition. They are also the material on which I later built my role as Minister for Foreign Affairs and then Foreign Affairs and Trade. In these offices I learnt much that was new, about the limits to change imposed by a savvy community, about striving for practical achievements as distinct from responding to fuzzy wish lists which some sought to have me adopt or to impose on me. I continued to develop a sense of good and fair public policy, of the need to protect my own intellectual integrity, and to exercise my own free will in choosing between courses of action, so that I could discharge my duties and obligations as honestly as possible. There were many happy experiences, some even gave the feeling of triumph, just as there were hurtful buffetings and set-backs. They all went together to create a richly woven tapestry representing my life. Some have commented publicly on a natural caution and suspicion in my character which they have interpreted as a form of paranoia. Well, one of the great lessons of public life for me has been to discover that it is distinctly dangerous in politics not to have a little paranoia. If you drop your guard when it should be up, that's when your enemies will get you.

And last of all in that long career in public life, spanning thirty-five continuous years, my wife, Dallas, an underground coal miner's daughter from Ipswich, and I, the product of an extremely humble background in South Brisbane, between us discharged the many public duties, in Australia and overseas, of head of state and spouse. In spite of our modest backgrounds our occupying these elevated roles was accepted by the community generally as quite normal in this very fair-minded, egalitarian country of ours.

Acknowledgments

I am extremely grateful to Mr Warren Horton, Librarian, Australian National Library, Canberra, and his staff, and to Mr John Templeman, National Parliamentary Librarian, and his staff, in particular the ever helpful and diligent Mrs Dianne Hawke, for the library resources which were so generously made available for my personal researches. I am similarly grateful to Mr Des Stevens, Chief Librarian, Queensland State Library and especially his staff at the Oxley Memorial Library for helpful assistance in conducting my researches there. The Departments of Prime Minister and Cabinet, Treasury, Foreign Affairs and Trade and Social Security assisted greatly by facilitating access to innumerable documents. Many hours spent at the Australian Archives, Mitchell Repository, Canberra, fossicking through historical documents, notably in connection with the early history of ANZUS, also proved rewarding.

Some of us need minders, from time to time, to protect us from the consequences of our own excessive enthusiasms. Barrister Michael Sexton filled that role marvellously with respect to certain legal considerations which arose from the original manuscript. Professor Geoffrey Bolton was kind enough to cast a professional historian's eye over an earlier draft of the manuscript and make some helpful suggestions on points of fact. Incidentally, the final form of the manuscript is solely my responsibility. I should thank Louise Adler who first suggested this undertaking to me and whose good humoured goading finally got me started on something I was not all that keen about initially. By the time I was well into this work I realised my first instincts were correct, but by then it was too late to retreat. My publisher Angelo Loukakis, his deputy Clare Forster, and Lisa Mills were wonderfully forbearing with me and their professional assistance was and is admired. Nonetheless, my sometimes temperamental nature, without the redeeming quality of being even faintly a creative *artiste*, must have frequently left them wishing I had stuck with my first instincts about embarking on this task. Most of all I should acknowledge my debt to episodic bouts of insomnia which provided me with the opportunity to work long stretches, undistracted, in the quiet, small hours of so many pitch-black Canberra mornings.

PART I

GROWING UP, GETTING ANGRY

Back to Basics

I was born at Brisbane on 23 January 1933. The second-worst year of the Great Depression had barely commenced. Families were being ejected from their homes, farms sold up, businesses closed down and even banks failed as a large slab of the economy was pitilessly dragged under by international economic collapse.

The unemployed trudged the streets in a futile search for work. Many walked the bush 'track' or 'jumped the rattler',[1] desperately looking for employment of any kind, anywhere. A scarce job, as humble as that of a navvy, could, as likely as not, provoke a frantic scramble among despairing men, or be the cause of a fight. It was, after all, the difference between eating and starving. During that social and economic catastrophe, a few days' 'relief work' of the most menial and unskilled type was a prize worth pursuing, even by professionally qualified and middle-class men.

Single men, at least in Queensland, had to walk 30 miles (50 kilometres) each week, to a different destination to that of the previous week, to collect government food coupons for basic rations. The coupons were issued from police stations. My father periodically related an anecdote to me as a youngster. On one occasion men made their way to Booval Police Station, at Ipswich. Some managed to get a 'lift' with a truck. The police sergeant mustered and addressed them along the lines of, 'Some of youse is lucky beggars. Youse got er ride all the way ter 'ere on a truck. Give the poor buggers what 'ave walked all the way a break. Stand to one side so's we can look after them first. There's enough 'ere for all entitled to rations'. Unwisely, several did as proposed. The policeman said to them accusingly, 'Youse is not entitled ter rations. Youse 'ave gotta walk 30 miles; not bludge a ride!' How did they handle it? Notch up the belt a bit tighter I expect. There was no other way left for them, except begging and crime. The philosophy of the State Government was diabolically simple and harsh. If it kept men on the move, it believed, they would be prevented from coming together on a more permanent basis. Thus, rabble-rousing Bolshevik agents would be denied the opportunity of redirecting the discontent of the unemployed into radical, even revolutionary, action.

This was a time of 'soup kitchens', of 'free meals for the unemployed', of moving on, of forever shuffling on in the hopeless pursuit of a job. A time when the human casualties of this economic calamity had little chance of any personal dignity. Shanty camps of flimsy sapling wood and waste sheet iron structures sprang up on public lands. Survival came ahead of pride. Pawnshops, the *monts-de-piété,* charity, even begging, became a central focus for so many of those who were suffering. These were tough, mean times and they made so many men and women hard and bitter about a system which ruthlessly cast them aside. They were the victims, not the cause, of this vast economic failure. Yet, among those in the community who were warm, comfortable and secure, were some who condemned the unemployed for their shiftlessness, their slackness, for being 'work-shy'. These responses were not new and can still be heard today.

Unemployment stood at 31.3 per cent in 1933, an improvement on the 35 per cent of the year before. Unemployment in the United States of America reached 25 per cent, Canada 19 per cent, and Britain 14 per cent in that devastating global economic failure.[2] In Australia '. . . the Great Depression lasted longer and caused more misery than in most countries . . .'[3] This was a time of single pay-packet families, low workforce participation rates, and no unemployment benefits. As cruel as the experience of unemployment was during any of the post World War II recessions, in particular the harsh one of the early nineties, that of the Great Depression was far, far fiercer.

I was a child of that Great Depression. My parents were 'busted' by it. My father was foreclosed in a small musical instrument and repair shop in Rockhampton. He never fully recovered his self-respect from the shock of failure and the humiliation of being dispossessed. He and my mother hated a system which had treated them, and legions more, so villainously. Their hate and distrust were my legacy. Messages of human anguish coming from the Great Depression were probably the greatest single influence shaping my personal and political values, igniting a burning resentment at the injustice of it all during my formative years. So much of what I did, later, in public life, the conceptual framework within which I sorted out my value judgments, were responses to that legacy.

My framework was built on notions of social justice and public duty; of redistribution from the 'haves' to the 'needy'; of social egalitarianism and equality of opportunity; of the right to personal self-respect and the defence of human dignity; of freedom of speech and freedom from want and fear. With social engineering and economic planning the cruel excesses of the recurrent 'boom and bust' of the capitalist business cycle would be avoided. Public enterprise, which by obvious definition meant common ownership by the people, would replace the exploitation of the private profit motive. In this way class oppression, inherent in the capitalist system, would be eliminated and the inevitable tendency towards private monopoly capital halted. The perfectibility of humankind could be achieved within a decent environment which was co-operative and caring rather than competitive and only concerned to reward the winners.

Government—big government—would be the mechanism for the transformation of society to a creative, caring and secure association of people. People would at last be free! If they resisted this liberation, if they were determined to stay unfree then there was little else for it but for us to make them free, to do so in their own interests. The goal of a free, democratic socialist society was too important, many of us felt back then, to be obstructed by ignorance.

It was a simple, sustaining creed, shared by many whose politics were of the left. It was also dangerously deceptive in many of its elements. It can be seen that in those early years I had the potential for becoming a rather unpleasant little autocrat. Fortunately, with maturation and the experience and responsibility of handling so much of the public's affairs, during thirty-five years in public office, I progressively shed this clumsy ideological baggage. My Democratic Socialist values were supplanted by Social Democratic ones, which in turn I have sought to further develop and refine. I would now describe myself as a secular liberal humanist.

I started my involvement in active political life with the conviction that I had the formula to re-create society so as to make it just and secure. I ended my days restrained by the humbling knowledge that there are clear limits as to what society, in its well-founded wisdom, will allow us to impose as the pace of its transformation. More than that, it is rare for change to occur in the form of a major and total departure from what went before. The mood of the community has to be receptive to change and such a disposition mostly does not develop overnight.

It was the height of callow hubris to presume, as I did, that such extensive social and economic transformation of society as I had in mind could be effected in less than one man's lifetime. Equally immature was the implicit presumption that the new-found social and economic arrangements would prove infinitely durable, requiring only periodic tinkering to keep them ticking over smoothly and well. Of course it was Utopian and impractical, but it should be recalled that the affairs of many nations were regulated by such thinking in our own lifetimes, mostly with dreadful consequences. To presume that a functioning social system can reach a level of perfection, that there is no requirement for further evolution, is to wish decay and death upon it, for an indisputable constant of life is change. Social organs, like biological ones which also serve humankind, need to constantly evolve in response to their ever changing environment. To fail to adapt leads to atrophy and extinction.

Antecedents

My father, George, was born in 1881 in Oakland, California, of Irish parents from Cork. He 'climbed over the wall', absconding from a seminary where he was training to become a Catholic priest. George became a merchant seaman, left his ship while in Australia, became an illegal immigrant and never changed that status. It was not without irony that years later, as Foreign Minister, I had to make complicated judgments about illegal migrants; but in the days when I was a police officer I had to deal with such people on a number of occasions and mine was a simple approach. It was mostly a matter of, to put it crudely but accurately, 'Piss off and if I see you again you'll be in real strife'. I never saw any again. Most were deserters from British merchant ships who, I presume, like my father, eventually became good Australian citizens.

My mother's paternal grandparents, the Newberrys, arrived here in 1852 from County Tyrone, Ireland, where they were illiterate farm workers. They were Church of England and among that 30 per cent of our Irish immigrants who were non-Catholics. They became successful farmers near Cundletown, not far from Taree in New South Wales. My mother's maternal grandfather, Denis Byrne, arrived on the *Hotspur* in 1861 from County Louth, Ireland, where he had been a bootmaker. His wife, Ann Jane Hammill, a domestic from County Meath, had disembarked a few years earlier. Both were Catholics. They conducted a pub, one of fourteen I am told, at Wyrallah, also on the Northern Rivers of New South Wales. (In extenuation I hasten to add the Irish were not the only ones to import a good thirst to this country. They just put a more determined effort into catering for it!)

My mother's mother eloped to Queensland with my mother's father without worrying at all about formalities, for there were some difficulties about marrying across the religious divide; a divide now largely gone. They failed as cane farmers at Babinda, North Queensland, and her father ended up a bush worker around Longreach, settling there later as a blacksmith. In the early years of her first marriage my mother, Vi, was widowed. With an infant to raise and no social security benefits then, she took one of the few jobs available to a woman in those times, as a barmaid at Longreach. She was determined to make her own way in life. Our background, plainly, was absolutely bog-Irish. The sharp smells of peat, potatoes and poteen hang heavily upon the family lineage, a lineage we share with many generations of Australian battlers. It is one of which I am immensely proud.

My father had known the simple pleasures of a few good times just as he was run down by more than a fair share of bad ones. For his generation and at his station in life his experience was probably not unusual. As a merchant seaman, at the turn of the century and a little later, he travelled widely but never well. Beached merchant seamen in those times, on miserable wages at sea and destitute soon after being paid off in foreign ports, borrowed, or more likely begged and stole, to exist until another berth was obtained. They dossed where they could at night and in winter in some ports it could be an awful experience. Anywhere that gave a cover overhead and held the cold at bay, even slightly, was regarded as a stroke of good fortune. Those men, in those hard times, could be plunged so deeply into despair that the protection of a public convenience was better than nothing.

George had been an active member of the Industrial Workers of the World (IWW), an anarcho-syndicalist working-class movement.

The Wobblies, as they were called, believed in the 'great national strike' as a weapon for paralysing the capitalist system, establishing the latent power of the working-class as a prelude to replacing capitalism with a humane, enlightened system of government by the common people. But when Churchill brought to an end the English National Strike of 1926, 'arming' the police in the process as the mythology of the event misleadingly has it, my father never forgave him. However, he was wise enough thereafter to acknowledge that as an industrial tactic national strikes were a pipedream—too many compromising union officials for it to work and too much naked power within the State to allow it to succeed, was his view.

The anarcho-syndicalists, of course, were not without their 'grand plan'. Syndicates of workers, deriving their strength from trade unions and federations of such, would manage the industries in which they worked and form the nucleus of worker participatory government. The State was an instrument of despotism, according to that movement, and State socialism and State capitalism gave the same result. Parliamentary government was a sham which forged the shackles of bondage to the State. At the same time, my father completely distrusted the Communists, condemning them for treachery to the working-class movement; the cause was vague but there appeared to have been some industrial–political struggle in America in which he was personally involved and perhaps the IWW was bested by less than scrupulous tactics by the Marxists, or perhaps it was by Marxist tactics which were even less scrupulous than those of their opponents.

That he had unpleasant encounters with the police in the course of his IWW activism was clear. The Pinkertons, a private detective service in America, were frequently described as a ruthless strike-breaking organisation not the least averse to 'verballing', as we would describe it these days, union officials. Railway guards, whose job it was to manhandle unemployed 'bums' off freight cars, often when trains were moving fast, were mentioned with contempt. The police forces of the world were instruments of repression in the hands of the ruling class of the State. That was a view not without its irony for me later.

On some occasions, at a merry moment in the evening, he would recite with gusto some coarse doggerel remembered from his American past:

Early in the morning,
Before the sparrow farts,
The bum arises from his nest
And gazes all around,
Hallelujah I'm a bum, hallelujah bum again.

It was a derisive protest against authority, as I recall it. The defiance of someone down but who refuses to acknowledge he is out. Yet my father was constantly fearful that his illegal immigrant status might be discovered. He accordingly sought to keep away from the eye of authority. There was no militant activism of any sort for George in Australia; for that was far too risky!

On occasions, primed to talk, he would recount experiences at sea, which were all wondrous to small ears. At other times he would denounce injustice in general and racism in particular. From within this experience, I am sure, were sown small, fertile germs of humanist values in an impressionable mind. 'In the tramcars of San Francisco there were signs towards the rear which read "This section reserved for our coloured patrons" ', he would recall angrily, or else with equal anger mention that 'In Shanghai there is a sign in a public park which says "Dogs and Chinamen not allowed entry" '. (I saw the sign for myself when I visited Shanghai in 1976. It stood in a nondescript little park as a reminder of those leisurely, gracious years of colonialism when the advantages of civilisation were brought to the 'lesser breeds', as it was once said, with gunboats imposing the 'benefits' of opium on the 'ungrateful' Chinese.) He flared at the injustice of it. He would condemn conspiracy theories depicting Jewish bankers as controlling international finance: 'The Presbyterians control this country's wealth . . . look no further than the Vatican for real wealth and conspiratorial power'. My father was nothing if not ecumenical.

One of George's best friends was a Maori, Ted Pickering, a large, well-built, strong man, who was a professional wrestler—one of the many things to which he turned his hand in order to earn an honest shilling. Yet he seemed altogether too much a gentle, thoughtful person to have engaged in such a violent occupation. The times, however, left little room for a fastidious choice of work. As long as it was lawful it had to be tried. He also became friendly with a non-conforming Jew, Harry Portrait as I recall the name, who operated a small clothing factory in South Brisbane. They, Harry and George, had a common bond. They had had similar experiences as they canvassed for business in the course of their different occupations: the rude rejections, false hopes of a deal, accounts never paid, the debtor who did a 'moonlight flit'; it was all very dispiriting.

My father tuned and repaired pianos, pianolas and organs. He canvassed door to door through the suburbs, leaving early in the mornings and returning late in the evening, in a persistent search for work. He worked under our rented home, a typical small, but well-worn Queensland timber cottage. Its condition then reflected the impecunity of those who lived in it. Many times he would come home late in the evening, tired and depressed after a long day of door knocking, looking for work. 'That was for Kathleen Mavourneen today,' he often said with resignation. 'Why does he do so much work for Mrs Mavourneen, Mum?' 'Shh, Billy. Don't upset him, he's been working hard. It means he doesn't expect to get paid.' A work life of finger pecking at keys repetitiously—pling, pling, pling—hammering into his brain like a high-pitched automatic percussion drill. A lifetime of tapping a metal tuning fork and testing by ear the mellowness of the felt hammer striking the piano wire against the resonance of the humming fork—ting, ting, ting—it was relentless. Constant fine adjustments of pegs which tightened, or loosened, the piano wire, searching for a fine pitch for the instrument—ping, ping, ping; ting, ting, ting—it went on without respite. So much repetition, so much tedium, so much reason to have felt driven to distraction with tasks which left an obviously intelligent man less than fulfilled.

No wonder he became depressed, and little wonder that he drank to escape, unfortunately in periodic excess. He justified his drinking with a hollow little maxim. He only drank beer, brandy and rum and accordingly would never be an alcoholic. Beer was not a spirit, brandy was for medicinal purposes, and rum, although a spirit, was a pure one! Suddenly, in the course of one of these bouts the normalcy of the home could explode into violence and be engulfed by a frightening din. On one occasion he chased my mother with a carving knife, hurling abuse as he went. He crashed down the high back stairs as he pursued her. There was an audible crack as though a bone had been broken when his arm struck one of the stair treads. My mother, no longer in danger, helped him to his feet and supported his return to the bedroom, full of solicitation. I still find her concern incomprehensible, and after happening so often in different guises, before and after this incident.

I was quite young and greatly excited the first time I can recall my father taking me 'to town', as we used to say when we visited the Brisbane CBD. To share his company in this way was a rare treat for he was usually too busy to allow for social excursions. At some point of the day's activities he left me outside the public bar of the Daniel Hotel in George Street while he had a beer. I waited and waited as time excruciatingly dragged its leaden feet along. I periodically peeped into the bar and there he was, in the distant corner, the centre of much *bonhomie* entertaining several other drinkers, complete strangers I suspect, with his engaging salesman's personality. (He would have been described, I expect, as a good bloke, a real man's man, by his drinking companions.) Then suddenly, with one peep, he was not there! I was terrified! I was crying when an older woman with a younger female, most probably her daughter, who had been watching me from the Adelaide Street tram stop approached inquiring about my distress.

At home I was repeatedly enjoined to tell outsiders nothing about our family's private affairs, and so I refused to communicate. The women went away, came back later, went away and a little later came back again with a rather grave young policeman. As a concerned confabulation about me developed between these three, one in which I resolutely refused to engage, my father suddenly materialised. He reassured these three that I was in good care and said he was going back into the pub for another beer; he patted me on the head, and then was as good as his word. The three strangers dispersed, and the two women, whose faces I still recall with some clarity after all these years as soft and kindly, were distinctly unimpressed.

Eventually my father and I boarded a tram for home. As we journeyed he teased me about my crying outside the hotel. 'Never grow into a real man if you cry over nothing!' he assured me. But that was not the whole story and years later my mother filled me in on the rest of what had happened. He had actually arrived home without me, but 'with more than half a cargo of booze on board'. He had forgotten about me! A brief blazing row followed and he quickly scampered back to the city by tram to retrieve me—not, however, before a few more pots in the pub.

I recall another experience—I was about fourteen—when I heard my mother desperately call for help, and went to find he was beating and verbally abusing her in the tiny lounge room. I was terrified. I hit him, more a push than a blow, and over he went, no doubt unbalanced by the effects of alcohol more than anything else. For days after I felt terrible, dismal, like a mortal sinner who had violated a sacred sanction. If I had understood Greek mythology then I would have probably thought of metaphorically tearing out my eyes. What I did was right but, strangely, it filled me with self-disgust. On a later occasion, on a 'brandy bender' he went to sleep smoking. The cigarette fell into the bedclothes and set the bedroom on fire. There was pandemonium as the flames leapt and spread. He rushed about, stupefied, trying to quell the savage flames with saucepans of water from the kitchen. The heavy, choking crimson smoke flooding the little dining room—where I slept on a well-worn settee—left me disoriented as I tried to work out where I was and what was happening. I brought in the garden hose but it made little difference. Fortunately the fire brigade and police arrived. At the time our mother was in hospital recovering from major bowel surgery.

Then there were the periodic long, late evening family walks led by mother, fleeing our residential 'haven' for a few hours in a desperate effort to escape domestic violence and to allow George to lay down and 'sleep it off'. Ah! the memories of childhood linger, the bitter and the sweet! I daresay it was unsurprising that Vi frequently deplored her fate, declaring to me with asperity, 'Men are mongrels . . . all of them . . . useless mongrels . . . '. For all that, she more often restated the Catholic creed about the indissolubility of marriage and parents' duty to their children and a wider community. That is how she lived out her life, even though she frequently mouthed contradictory declarations about women's rights, including divorce. Her deep superstitious faith in the Church might have left her room to express these yearnings but it permitted no leeway in which to do anything about them.

For all his problems with life, George stayed with the task of working; thank goodness, for the family grew from one to four children. A normal working week was seven days. Up at 5 a.m. to start, he would work away under the draughty house. After the war finished he had his old army greatcoat for added warmth in winter. There was much that was noble in his endeavours. He knew the system had whipped him but he would not say surrender.

Nonetheless, as a matter of principle he refused to accept 'government handouts' while he was capable of getting work. Somehow he held this principle intact through the Great Depression and beyond. It was sometimes a case of living on 'thin gruel' to survive, but in his contrary, independent way he made it. When at fifty-one years of age he married Vi, twenty-four years his junior, he accepted certain family responsibilities. He never shirked them. He was still working when he dropped dead at the age of seventy-two years, literally with tools of his trade in his hands. The work never stopped until he stopped, finally, *finis*.

If this last sounds like a relatively generous testament to my father, it is also a relatively new one. For most of my life I hated him and his memory. Apart from the unforgivable violence to my mother, there was a lack of rapport between us. I felt like a micro-satellite circling within the compulsive gravitational field of a powerful parental universe, but rarely being noticed by it. There was another matter. What seemed to me to be minor infractions of household discipline resulted in, effectively, whippings about the legs with thin rubber tubing used in organs and pianolas. In spite of the presumed cruelty of this I can clearly recall having a passionate dispute—which resulted in fisticuffs—with a boy, named Jones I think, from the flats for transients next door. His father, like so many fathers of the times, belted his son with a broad, cut-throat razor strop. The argument, involving perverse pride, was as to whose father was more effective at giving hidings and which of us received the more painful discipline! Those, however, were times when corporal punishment was common and young boys were expected to become men by stoically accepting the pain of beltings. It was the sort of toughening that made good footballers and soldiers, so we were assured. Only sissies cried.

In a sad sort of way George Hayden's struggle to exist and provide for others bore some of the pathos of Willy Loman, Arthur Miller's chief character in his memorable play *Death of a Salesman*.

George had been an outstanding salesman and won several State awards as such. The tragedy of Loman, who failed to adjust to major change, was very much George's experience, from the bust of the Great Depression right up to his funeral service. Even the funeral service had uncanny similarities to that of Loman. For all that he would so often invoke the name of this or that business friend, none came to see him off. Just the mourning family and a couple of supportive neighbours. The militant atheism of his life was over-ridden by our mother in his death. He might have been a heretic alive but he was not going to be pushed across the darkening Styx without the protection of the sacred cross. The local Catholic priest could not be asked to conduct the service. She intended to honour George's wish for a cremation and Catholic priests, then, could not preside over cremations. No matter, he did receive some of the decencies due to a Catholic, even a failed one: the priest came to the home to give extreme unction to the dead body under the house. Vi felt some reassurance at that. The principle of necessity meant that a Protestant minister was commissioned for the funeral service.

Vi had a different temperament to that of her husband and was more optimistic by nature. There was an Irish sentimentality and a fervid Irish nationalism to her nature. She had never been to Ireland but to hear her talk of it, especially of Post Office Square, Dublin, Easter Friday 1916, one could have been forgiven for concluding otherwise. Hers was a version of history looked at with a marked squint in one eye, a mythologised account that improved for the Irish with each telling. Everything good that happened in Ireland had been the work of the Irish. The bad was caused by the English occupiers, especially the hated 'black and tans'. She lived this part of her life elementally and by myth rather than by reason and reality. We all do that to a greater or lesser extent.

I visited Ireland in 1987; the colours of the countryside, of the waters and the sky, so soft and comforting. A gentle and generous beauty abounded and the folk were so hospitable and kind. While there I also made an important personal discovery—Vi would be the last of the great Irish nationalists in her family line. Ireland for me was beautiful but foreign. The ethos of Australia and its sun-drenched, rough and craggy countryside have too thoroughly saturated my veins to ever allow me to look elsewhere for inspiration or comfort, and least of all exile. There is in my personality, nonetheless, an elemental thing which can provoke an unwise, impulsive defiance, a compulsive stubbornness in the face of unanticipated challenge. I suspect it is some of the emotional, sentimental baggage which many Irish are condemned to bear through life. That is why, I expect, the hackles at the back of my neck rise whenever I read brave Robert Emmet's defiant address in 1803 as he impatiently and impudently strode the dock, immediately after he had been condemned to being hung, drawn and quartered by a judge with a foreign accent. His offence? Attempting a futile insurrection. No surrender there. I still find it pulse-quickening to read that brave, foolish, defiant proclamation penned by Patrick Pearse in 1916 whose triumph was born from failure: 'IRISHMEN AND IRISHWOMEN: In the name of God and of the dead generations from which she receives her old tradition of nationhood, Ireland, through us, summons her children to her flag and strikes for her freedom'.

If only the wise, cautionary views of Mary Hayden, his tweedy, academic friend, had prevailed.[4] Then, perhaps, there would have been no Easter Friday rebellion, no glory from the graves of the martyrs, no martyrs indeed, no reason for deep hatred towards England, for independence would have continued its inexorable advance as an act of grace from the colonial power; but this is too dreadful to contemplate! The Irish live a fuller life with a good enemy at hand. Peter Hayden of Boleycarrigen, County Wicklow, a captain of the insurgents in Lord Edward Fitzgerald's 1798 rebellion, would have been a preferred inspiration. He was killed with thirty-five other prisoners by the yeomanry in those 'troubles'. The Irish sustained themselves through centuries of adversity by burnishing their folklore history with tender, loving care, a heritage they implanted in, and which was thereafter cherished by, Labor as part of its own traditions.

Australian culture, too, resonates with its unmistakable Irish influences; a rebelliousness, a suspicion of authority, a touchy cockiness, a testy combativeness, self-deprecating humour. There is another curious Irish inheritance of ours; we take from the Irish their penchant for admiring noble heroes who sacrifice themselves to lost causes. This is understandable, for the Irish cherish so many causes fought with passion and conviction, but lost in the engagement. This is central to the Australian psyche. We have an extraordinary capacity to venerate flawed folk heroes. Think of Ned Kelly, Les Darcy, Phar Lap. Or even dwell upon the heroic legend-making from Gallipoli. Anzac Day is, essentially, our sacred national day on which, unlike any other country in the world, we commemorate a major military defeat as our national apotheosis. We are myth-makers with a tendency towards conspiracy theories as we rationalise setbacks to hopes fondly embraced. The significant factor in all of this is that a setback becomes the spur for a fresh assault later in pursuit of a great objective. This is no defeatist psychology. It is, fundamentally, the personality of a true fighter for causes deeply believed in. We all recognise that element in the Australian make-up. These were, indeed, essential qualities for perseverance against overwhelming adversity faced by the early settlers of this country. Their sacrifices forged a legend by which we live. Pluck, perseverance and resourcefulness in the face of adversity are an important part of the national heritage they left for us.

Growing up at South Brisbane

At the time of my birth Vi and George lived in a rooming house at Gotha Street, Fortitude Valley. Sister Heaven (yes, that was her name) presided over the birth at the Lady Bowen Hospital nearby. Later they got around to marrying, an unusually casual attitude for such narrow-minded, censorious times. (The first I learnt of this was as a young teenager seeking a copy of my birth certificate at the office of the Registrar of Births, Deaths and Marriages. The records officer persisted in asserting an extract from the certificate would be enough. I insisted on my rights and was finally handed the full certificate. On it was plastered 'illegitimate', as the government sanctioned terminology of those times put it.)

Vi and George moved on to another rooming house in Spring Hill, a suburb rather removed from top drawer billing and in which the police commonly foot-patrolled in groups of four. (When I walked the beat there in the early fifties we still walked it in pairs and occasionally there would be three of us.) Vi's ineffable social pretensions, however, finally won through. They rented a house, but a much more modest one than my mother preferred. It was at 48 Mabel Street, a gravel surface street that slid to a dead end at the bottom of a sharp rise. Little timber houses, mostly perched high on stilts, as southerners like to call the stumps, crowded in on one another. Number 48 was a mean, well-worn little dwelling. To the rear of this house there was a paddock with an open gully serving as an industrial dry-fill dump, where I spent many contented hours fossicking out wonders from the waste, allowing free rein to a fertile imagination and playing in old car bodies and other industrial refuse.

Neighbours knew each other, for better or worse. Mondays were special: washing day. I would rouse at 5 a.m., chop firewood, light up the wood under the boiler, and have it merrily bubbling away by 6 a.m. when my mother would start the weekly washing. Splendid arabesques of flame danced about in the belly of the cast iron boiler stand like abandoned sprites, firing my imagination with the most delightful daydreams. Soon I would be off, lost in a make-believe land, far away from where I was. Adventures, kindness, pleasures, happiness—they were all experienced there before the fire.

Down the backyards would be seen pretty much the same bustling activity of housewives washing clothes, hand-wringing washed garments, stringing the washing out on lines mostly elevated by wooden props. These clothes props were hawked about the streets for sale on the back of a horse-drawn cart. The vendor, always wearing a battered fedora sharply tilted to one side of the head, would be heard calling out, "lothes props . . . rabbitos'. The drudgery of the washing chore out of the way, housewives engaged in gossipy conversation across side and back fences. 'Holding up the fence' was how this was described in those more innocent times, times blithely unaware of the sins of chauvinism and sexism. (I daresay it seems rather archaic, and worse, to some today.) These relaxed, gossipy moments were priceless for they continually crafted, reshaped, and cemented again, the sense of community between the inhabitants of the street and nearby.

The values Vi imparted concerned matters of specific principle rather than abstract philosophy. 'There's room for all types in the world. Live and let live.' Much of her endearing, instinctive liberalism was spun out in fine golden threads of wisdom like this. It so happened that young Larry, who lived close by and who made a habit of running hard against the rough face of life, was in trouble with his parents. He had stolen a litter of pigs and sought to palm them off to his parents as Fox Terrier pups. Vi, as a good family friend, was brought in for advice. 'Better get them back to where they came from before the police arrive.' With much protestation and a stream of genuine tears Larry was on his return trip.

But meanwhile, the pride of the Woolloongabba Police Station duly arrived. It was a Ford Tourer with a spanking new canvas hood, a car which needless to say tended to be kept quite busy. A lean, impatient constable was out of the driving seat in a thrice and heading towards Larry's front door. His companion, a portly, florid sergeant, his neck bulging over his uniform mandarin collar, moved with more circumspect deliberation. Vi was at the front fence as those lofty custodians of law and order approached. One of her extraordinary talents was an ability to easily engage complete strangers in extended conversation. The big policeman quickly settled into a gossip over the fence. Yes, he had served at Blackall where Vi had been a barmaid. In fact he had enjoyed 'a few beers' in that very pub on occasion. Common ground was quickly established. As he withdrew empty-handed, Vi assured the older policeman that Larry was 'really a very good boy' who would never do anything wrong. Although I fully expected it to, her voice did not give her away when she told this 'whopper'. Nor was the sky rent with a thunderbolt from heaven for such patent dissimulation.

There is a brief but pathetic sequel to the story of Larry. With World War II, Larry advanced his age and joined the army and was then shipped off to the Middle East. He was no jingo, there were no heroics, certainly no bombast about Empire and so on. For him, like most young men who went to war voluntarily, it was an adventure. He was, as are most young men in their estimation, indestructible. I came home from prep school one day to find my mother crying. She had seen the telegram boy go to Larry's home earlier. She did not have to inquire about his mission. There were too many give-away signs in his manner and demeanour. Larry had been killed in action with his infantry unit.

My mother had another little bit of potted wisdom of inestimable value, namely that 'Boys aren't born bad, it's what happens to them as children that makes them bad'. This underpinned her numerous prescriptions for making society a better place to avoid boys becoming bad. A lot of it flowed from her natural love and affection. I still recall warmly her soft, ample breast, her reassuring embrace, the pain a motherly kiss could quickly overcome. I daresay that Vi's kind of wisdom has had its fashion, although I confess to being unable to shrug it off completely. The defect of oversimplification aside, a view such as hers is preferable to me than the intolerant condemnation of young people who run into trouble with the law as 'born troublemakers'. Vi was an instinctive determinist, and determinism helpfully explains much about the cause of some of our social pathology. But it is of no use to the victims of violent crimes and can squib the issues of offenders' responsibility and accountability—nor does it satisfactorily explain white collar crime and corruption in high places.

Of the various individuals living nearby in those days, probably the most colourful was a reclusive old widower, 'Digger' Halliday. As his nickname signals, he was a veteran of World War I, and from the trenches at the Western Front no less. Once a fortnight he would collect his war pension. On the way home he would slake a compounded thirst long and well at one of the wayside 'watering holes'. Then we would be subjected to a virtuoso performance as he came down the hill, walking stick acting as a stage prop. There was a family at the top of the hill with a name he presumed to be German—Hummerdross. They would get an earful as he turned rifles, machine guns and cannon on the Germans, and them in particular, his walking stick scything the air as he railed away. The Hummerdross family was good and respected. This did not discourage neighbours from enjoying the street theatre, but from the discreet safety of blinds and other screens. The slightest noise would redirect Digger's abusive salvo to that source and an unbroken flow of fully primed imprecations would be lobbed on the hapless householder. No-one ever complained. For the other thirteen days of the fortnight Digger quietly minded his own business and enjoyed the respect of the street.

Such characters were always a welcome diversion to the main game for me, namely school. How I loathed it! It was like setting out for prison each day. Oh, God! I hated the place with a vengeance! The daily prospect of punishment, the dread of dull repetition and the despair of tedium was ever present as I reluctantly dragged my feet towards the school. 'A like an apple;

B like a bat and ball; C like . . . ???', and the sonorous, discordant chant soon had me drifting off into the rich adventures of another daydream. The cool, endless vault of blue outside, above the classroom windows, was always there beckoning me. One could escape into flights of fancy leaving the dreary atmosphere of the grey classroom with its dusty, dull, bare board floors far behind. There, beyond the planets, way past the infinity of space, a million miles from the daily primitive, forced march across stony, parched land ploddingly imposed by the education system, there I was free!

My first school was St Ita's Convent conducted by the Ursuline Order of Sisters at Dutton Park. We learnt much there, such as the appealing advice that it was easier for a camel to pass through the eye of a needle than for a rich man to enter the portals of heaven. Was it not true after all, that behind every large fortune there was almost certainly a big crime? We were also told a poor woman who put her few coppers quietly into the plate was more important than the rich man who ostentatiously rattled his golden coins into the collection receptacle. As most of us came from poor homes, that made us feel a lot better. Yet there was a large and showy SP bookie whose daughter attended our school. He lived near us and by our standards he was rich. He wore a spruce grey homburg hat and smoked large, fat cigars which left a heavy, aromatic scent on the fine, light air of a winter's night as his fleshy bulk floated past. He donated to school and church with a practised public flourish. Much fuss was made of his periodic appearance at school and more regular attendance at church. Thus the seeds of scepticism took root. In real life the quiet widow's copper coins were not noted but the clear ring of the rich man's gold caused much exuberance.

It so happened one day we were fallen in for early morning parade. A nun announced the death of a man whose copious family attended the school and whose wife had been a casual cleaner of the school and church. He had borne a proud Irish name. He rarely attended church but his poor wife, a timid soul, did so regularly, no doubt praying to God to save her from his next beating. He was a wastrel.

The good nuns adopted simplified descriptions of Heaven and Hell in a hard-hitting effort at trying to terrify a little conscience and holiness into us infant heathens. Heaven shone with its own indescribably beautiful glory. Hell was an infernal region of permanent torment. Then there was Purgatory, seemingly reserved for the lucky ones, the culprits of minor league wickedness in this world. Purgatory appeared to function as a form of Sinners Anonymous where feckless Catholics, otherwise in good standing with the faith, could dry out for a while, through a process of spiritual contemplation about, and atonement for, their past wrongs. Then they moved on to Heaven. This easy option was not available for pagans and Protestants.

The Mother Superior solemnly enjoined us children to 'pray for his soul so that his stay in Purgatory will be brief before he goes to Heaven'. My thoughts were in instant revolt. 'Strike a light, talk about rigging the system as a favour! Anyone else would go straight to Hell.' This inflicted another dent in my religious belief, but only a small one for somewhere around my twelfth year I was suddenly fired with a burning ambition to become a priest. I attended church with an unhealthy regularity. I was jealous of the special status of the altar boys, one of whom I could never become because by then I attended a State school. I wanted to share as a priest—not any priest but as *the* priest—in the mystical, sublime moment of transubstantiation when the holy wine and the host are mingled and become the blood and body of Christ.

Unfortunately, the inspiration to serve did not last. Among other subversive distractions I started to discover girls. Priests and girls do not go together; or at least they should not, according to the rules. In that painful, confused, conscience-stricken, masturbatory period of early teenage, I was overwhelmed by the most terrifying of premonitions. If this could be so much fun by myself, how much more delightful it would be with the company of a girl! But what if I got killed in an accident before I found out? It was too horrifying to dwell upon! Afterwards, the insistent masturbatory demand met, I would be lashed by my conscience. Would God strike me down as an unregenerate sinner? The mounting evidence of pimples was a dead give-away of what I was doing in private. Lord Baden-Powell's handbook for us callow Scouts sternly enjoined that we should sleep with bedroom windows open and on our sides. With ample fresh air and this posture in bed we would avoid 'bad dreams'. We were also advised to avoid rich foods but in our household this was obviously not a problem. By now I slept on an open verandah, winter or summer, where fresh air flooded in, often at a low winter's temperature. I painfully contorted my body to stay on my side as much as possible, but I was still plagued with nocturnal emissions, sometimes in multiples. Oh, God: save me! I was heading for Hell on a fast track.

'Catholic dogs just like frogs drinking holy water,' the jeer rang out, in doggerel fashion, across the road from St Ita's Convent School. Several children from nearby Dutton Park State School were giving the 'Micks' a 'bit of what for', as the pupils of St Ita's were trooping homeward. Stones were heaved almost as fiercely as the epithets. Ironically, Dutton Park State School was the next school I attended. This followed a blazing row between my father and the convent school authorities because the school authorities decided school piano work would be carried out by a large, central city piano firm. 'If they couldn't stick by one of their own they couldn't be trusted on anything,' was roughly his rationalisation, and a rather breathtaking one for an avowed atheist who was openly hostile to the Church. It was only through my mother's insistence that my sister Pat and I had been enrolled at a Catholic school in order to get a 'good Christian' education. Thus, accompanied by the fury of my father at the backsliding of the Catholic Church, I was shipped off to this new school.

The head teacher of the prep school was a certain Miss MacLeod, a tyrant with tight, thin lips, drained of the blood of simple humanity. For the first few weeks after my arrival she would delight in making regular visits to the classroom to check on my progress. I suspect she would have been plunged into an inordinately bleak pit of despondency had there been any improvement on the regular report that I was well behind the other children in the level of my education. These grim reports gave her a chance to click her tongue deprecatingly, move her head from side to side negatively and murmur, but sufficiently loud for the whole class to hear her say, '. . . those people [being the Catholics] are a disgrace'. . . It seemed that Catholic schools were a scandal, and Catholics by nature no better. Even now, when I think of her, I visualise a scene where bagpipes are gearing up like tomcats having a spat in a kerosene can. I can see her in her Sunday best, pinning an orange ribbon to her bodice as she moves to the head of the procession honouring King Billy and the Battle of the Boyne every 12 July, the pipes and drums swirling.

There at Dutton Park State School, each day was commenced with a sea of doleful faces mouthing the most boring cant designed to brainwash them, making them good little jingos and dutiful forelock tuggers for the future: 'I love God, Honour my King, country and flag, Cheerfully obey my parents, teacher and the law'.

With a screech and a thump, a shrill and uneven fife band, perpetually offbeat with the big drum, would then strike up.

The school grounds were pivotally sited. On one side they snuggled up to Boggo Road prison and the Loch Venereal Diseases Hospital for Women. This latter was a place of treatment for females, who, in having provided essential services and comfort for the fighting men of Australia and our allies—more enthusiastically to some of our allies as a matter of fact for they had more money to spend—had become casualties of the war effort. In front there was an extraordinarily busy highway with scarcely a day passing by without at least one long convoy of military vehicles moving along it. Established on the other side was an interstate and suburban railway system. Great black, and sometimes huge bottle-green, steel monsters with roaring flames in their bellies, spewing smoke, belched and whistled their way along the interstate track, drawing carriages full of young soldiers, a blur of cheerful faces going to war. Where did they go, after leaving behind the boisterous cheers of us young urchins who swirled across the gravelly playground to wave farewell? Oh, Holy Mary, Mother of God! Your son should have protected those poor boys. They were hurtling forth at breakneck speed into the very jaws of death—to die in Changi, or at Lae, to be destroyed on the Burma Railway, or any of the other hellholes of World War II, was where they went.

Years later Dallas and I witnessed some of the mute testimony to this prodigious waste of human life when we visited Kanchanaburi War Cemetery, near Hell Fire Pass, in Thailand. There were a staggering 1362 Australian war graves. And the number of Dutch graves was surprisingly greater at 1896. I was embarrassed to have forgotten the valiant contribution of those troops. What a shock then for us to have been confronted with the huge number of British graves, nearly 3500 of them. In spite of the peril faced by Britain from Europe, in the Middle East and the Mediterranean, and despite the great cost to her war effort in those theatres as a result of over-extending herself into our region, she did not leave us completely abandoned, as some popular Australian folklore has it.

But for Dutton Park State School, I have the fondest memories. Its style was in harmony with its environment of South Brisbane. Perhaps unpromising in appearance to an outsider in those days, but the repository of rich nuggets of learnt wisdom about life, about give and take, about forgiving and forgetting, about getting up and having another go in the face of adversity. I learnt much there about tolerance and sympathy for others—values already acquired at home, the other major prop of my impressionable infancy.

The house in which we lived was undoubtedly humble, but it radiated a warmth and security. A mother who clucked about us children like a mother hen, was always around to care for us. Always washing, always down on her knees scrubbing modestly priced congoleum squares, or moving along on a foam rubber knee pad, rubbing wax floor polish into the congoleum with a piece of waste cotton material. Then it was rub, rub, rub, the buffing of a polish onto the floor-covering by hand. There was, early on, ironing of clothing with a heavy, solid block of iron heated over an antique and faulty wood stove in a fairly primitive kitchen; this method later replaced with a small, electric iron. On that same cantankerous stove nutritious meals were produced and wonder of wonders, against all the physical laws, Vi would turn out magnificent, well-risen sponges from the unevenly tempered oven. If they failed to rise, out they went to the fowl yard without sentiment and another attempt was made.

The round of chores seemed endless in its punitive repetition. The residence was decidedly no mansion, and it desperately required extensive, basic maintenance, an undertaking which the thrifty landlord resolutely resisted. My mother consoled her sense of disappointment at the rather shabby exterior of the structure and the faded internal walls by maintaining a spotlessness inside and with our personal dress. 'We may never be rich but by golly no-one can ever say we're not clean and tidy. That's more important in life.' Cleanliness was next to godliness. It would have seemed, too, that regularity rated just as highly as cleanliness among the list of important simple virtues. I have vivid impressions still of youngsters huddled about, chattering good naturedly, as the latest infant was treated with a homemade soap suppository coated in oil, then hoisted aloft by its haunches above a chamber pot by Vi, to be thus 'potty trained'. The procedure was quite a ceremony and the seriousness with which it was undertaken registered its importance as another experience in the moulding of a human being: regularity, punctuality, predictability! Good disciplining for future fresh inputs into the capitalist system of production.

The 'dripping tin', a large, used treacle can, filled with an accumulation of cooking fats, the residue from pots and pans after each meal was cooked, did silent, sentinel duty at the end of the stove. It contained a rich harvest of tastes that lingered in the fats which ran off a variety of meats cooked on the ancient stove. A large dollop of the warm dripping, embracing all the piquant, savoury tastes which had blended themselves within the tin over time, like a medieval monastery soup for weary travellers, would be slapped onto a slice of bread, then spread across it. The next step was to liberally lace it with salt and pepper. It was a superb delicacy that was heaven to taste. Rich, oozy, black treacle spread across the face of a piece of bread straight was pleasant, but a very poor second place to the heady ambrosia of dripping, salt and pepper on a plain slice of bread. Threepence or sixpence worth of soup bones from the butcher's, generously laced with vegetables from the backyard garden, simmered steadily in a large pot towards the end of the stove top, or a baked chicken from the family 'chook yard', richly brown, with a mouth-watering glint as it came out of the oven, supplemented a practical diet. A threepenny bag of broken biscuits, from Webster's cake and biscuit factory in Annerley Road, was a treasure trove of delicate flavours. The bag seemed not just big but absolutely huge to a small boy. We were of course rather poor, as many families of those times were. As we had not met any social workers to that point, who by their ingrained disposition would have helped us to recognise our condition and become dependent upon them, we did not know about it; nor for that matter, worry about it. Life tended to have its simple pleasures. There was a quiet nobility of character among so many we knew and we had our sense of personal dignity.

There were also the frugal virtues of the less well-off. Furniture was purchased within budget, often from any of several second-hand stores at nearby Woolloongabba. Times are much harder now. There are no longer any second-hand furniture shops for the 'battlers', only antique stores and outlets for 'preloved' items at hideously inflated prices to cater to the tastes of the new age middle classes. I slept on the open front verandah in a bed with such a badly sagging wire mattress that it was more like a hammock. There were no sheets— they were too expensive—just blankets. In that moody, rainy, monsoon season straddling the Christmas–New Year period it was delightful lying in bed at night, the persistent, heavy rain drumming down on the corrugated iron roof above, like a mob of horses' hooves cantering across a parched, open plain out west. A lone frog croaking in the roof guttering, his steady, regular bass amplified by the metal walls around him. It was all so drowsy, dreamy and reassuring. A young boy's vivid imagination would soar out, above and beyond the limitations of our modest existence. There was no wretchedness there, out in the boundless land of make-believe.

Learning more about life

'They also serve who sit and wait,' or so one war effort slogan had it for the good females who stayed at home knitting socks or whatever for their menfolk away at the front. Undeniably, some who stayed at home 'did their bit' to help the war effort, quite enthusiastically in fact. In case of enemy attack there were slit trenches in the nearby Boggo Road prison yard. The excavated spoil was heaped at the shoulders of the trenches. In the way of so many working-class communities of the time, home discipline could swing between extremes of laxity and severity. A small group of noisy, squabbling scamps, among whom I was included, was wandering the streets one night, well after the respectable hour for youngsters from better regulated homes. We were taking advantage of the pendulum swing on the lax arc of domestic discipline.

An American soldier and his girlfriend, for that night, both rolling gently from the pleasantly suffusing effects of a good cargo of booze, weaved their way to the trenches and climbed in. In an instant, like well-disciplined Kulkadoon hunters, silence descended on our little group as the quarry had suddenly come into view. We knew what to do. After all we had done it before. After a few minutes we silently moved forward and then, at the edge of the trench, with a whoop and a bellow, furiously pushed the loose spoil on top of the copulators. The effect was electrifying! We were off like gunshots. So was the soldier—but unfortunately, with his pants at less than half-mast, his progress was greatly impeded. We departed under a hail of epithets and lumps of earth. In retrospect it was a damn mean and petty thing to have done, but at the time we thought it a great night. We had a grudging respect for the soldier. A good soldier, as the aphorism has it, dies with his boots on. This one might not have cared all that much to confront the final resolution of his life, but he was prepared to go a good bit of the way toward it. He at least made love with his boots on.

Meanwhile, as the Japanese embarked on the war in the Pacific our propaganda machine, in all of its crude ramifications, was churning out its indoctrination with voices of hate and it was being swallowed whole by most people. Remarks such as, 'The Japs . . . loathsome! four-eyed, stunted monsters, fiends and rapists, barbarians and yellow to boot!' were frequently heard. The woman next door announced one day: 'I'm smashing all of my Japanese crockery. Don't want anything to do with the Japs,' the good neighbour added sententiously and in sympathy with the popular sentiment. She fixed Mum with a beady eye. 'Me too,' said Mum. She was too shrewd to be outdone in the jingoism stakes at a time when softness towards the enemy could be regarded as sympathy for them. 'Whacko'. . . I said to myself and tore off to the kitchen. There I piled up the crockery in anticipation of making a contribution to the war effort *and* having a morning of huge fun. But Mum came into the kitchen in a troubled rush. 'What are you up to, you young beggar? Billy, leave that crockery alone . . . ' 'But Mum, you said . . . '

'I know what I said to that old battleaxe next door . . . I don't trust her . . . but that's all the crockery we've got and we can't afford any more.' The conversation ended on that clear, decisive note and with a sharp clip on the back of my head. 'Ouch!'

There was a whole other 'war effort' going on in a home not far from where we lived. Our family was friendly with the family who lived there. The lady of that house, sometimes with the help of a close female relative, provided what might be delicately described as at-home hospitality services for American servicemen—for a suitable fee of course. I suspect she became involved in this enterprise initially, not so much as a business undertaking, but rather as a hobby, for she had a bubbly personality and a generous disposition. Then, in the way of these things I daresay, she discovered she had a natural flair for what had started out as a recreational interest. Like many people today who embark on a handicraft as a pastime, discover they are rather naturally skilled at what they are doing and then proceed to go commercial, she decided to turn what had been an avocation, into something a little more serious. Whenever clients called, and there was a steady business conducted there, the 'man' of the house, who seemed to have no gainful occupation away from the home, would retreat to the chook pens in the backyard. There he would proceed to clean and tidy those fowl yards. With so little for him to do otherwise, that house had the tidiest and cleanest chook yards I have ever seen, before or since.

Greater Brisbane was a huge garrison city during World War II. There were many thousands of Australian and American troops, but there were also Dutch, Indonesian, Filipino, and goodness knows what other nationalities represented in military uniforms about the city, and its river was crammed with almost as great a variety of military and merchant ships. The number of military personnel in and around Brisbane nearly equalled the civilians living there.[5] Their presence was reassuring, for in the immediate lead-up to the allied conflict with Japan, Australians, in particular those in the north, felt at great risk. Shortly before the declaration of war in the Pacific, in December 1941, an American naval flotilla berthed at the Hamilton and Newstead wharves in Brisbane. Thousands of people stood on the banks of the Brisbane River, just looking at the wonderful sight and breathing a bit more freely because the American warships were there. I can still recall my father, who took me to see these visitors, saying in subdued tones, 'We're saved, the Americans will save us'.

Even with the massed presence of foreign troops after the declaration of war, there was a jumpiness, a mounting sense of terror in our community that invasion by the apparently invincible Japanese Imperial Armed Forces was in prospect. This public fear was thoroughly understandable. The War Cabinet, briefed by its military advisers, shared that apprehension and it was added to with loose talk of a Brisbane Line as a fall back position from which to make a last ditch defence of the country.[6] Invasion of Australia was in fact an option preferred by the Japanese Navy but one, fortunately, over-ridden by the more practical Japanese Army. Nonetheless, if Eisenhower's initial Euro-centred thinking had persisted after the fall of South-East Asia to the Japanese, we could have been isolated and perhaps reduced by attrition to an irresistibly vulnerable target of conquest.[7] Claims that Australian troops on the Kokoda Trail and at Milne Bay single-handedly put a stop to the inexorable advance of the Japanese forces are understandable, but somewhat unfair to the Americans. It is indisputable that Australian troops fought magnificently in halting the Japanese forces in Papua New Guinea. The national pride resonating from this statement tends to blur a more comprehensive and accurate appreciation of related events. The heroic American assault against Guadalcanal, at the same time as the battles of Kokoda and Milne Bay, forced the Japanese Army to split its forces to fight the three major battles on two quite separate fronts when their forces were only adequate to fight effectively on one of those fronts. Without Guadalcanal the pitched battles in Papua New Guinea would have been considerably more difficult for us, and vice versa of course.

In Brisbane, meanwhile, there were many American Negro servicemen, who were racially segregated by the USA military authorities. They were restricted to South Brisbane where their major recreation centre was the Dr Carver Club, a converted hotel. My father railed at this discrimination when at home, for by now he was in the army. Early in the war he put his age down so he could join the forces. He was sixty but solemnly declared he was much younger. He was delighted for one over-riding reason. It was the first regular job, with a secure income of six shillings and six pence per day, he had since the Depression galloped over him with its cloven hooves. Because of his physical condition he was put in a works company.

A saucy rumour reached the little push of urchins with whom I fraternised. It was that a white woman was hanging about with Negro servicemen at the Carver Club. By itself that was of no interest, but the account that she dressed in slacks and an unbuttoned blouse, fully exposing her breasts, caused a lot of excited blood to thump up our necks and across our foreheads, not to mention the obvious palpitations in our groins. The chance to see how a woman was really made was too good to pass up. At last we saw her on the footpath talking with an American Negro serviceman. On noting our salacious interest in her mammary glands she exposed them further, tilting them provocatively in our direction. And were they exciting! Whacko! We were all snickering and giggling as we walked by, totally preoccupied with one of the great mysteries of life at last fully revealed to us, when I walked slap bang into a power pole at the edge of the footpath. The woman and her companion made some inaudible comments and laughed. I took off, helter-skelter, nursing my embarrassment as I went. But it was worth it, that we all agreed. Most exciting thing any of us had ever done. We went back several times but she had disappeared. We speculated that perhaps the 'cops 'ad got 'er', or more likely those tough hombres of the USA Military Police who swaggered about with big night sticks and huge .45 pistols strapped to their waists. In fact she may well have been taking enforced rest and recovery leave at the Loch Hospital for Women. She was, after all, in a high-risk wartime occupation and no doubt suffered the equivalent for her profession of combat stress.

The American servicemen were impressive. With the cut and quality of their clothes superior to those of the Australian troops, they certainly looked dashing. They had large colourful shoulder patches and their paratroopers wore leather boots running up well above the ankle, encasing the bottoms of their trousers. Centrally sited buildings were commandeered and generously converted to serve as recreational centres for them and their female 'companions' whom they entertained expansively for they were much better paid than the Australians. The Australians were mostly dressed in undistinguished but thoroughly serviceable fighting uniforms of rough cotton, jungle-green in colour. They wore heavy leather boots and broad-brimmed hats in the style of a farmer's hat with small felt patches on the hat bands signifying their battalions. The men themselves were generally a uniform yellow in skin and eye colour, the consequence of taking Atebrin, an anti-malarial prophylactic; mostly these were combat zone soldiers either from the front in New Guinea or preparing to go there.

One day a number of us youngsters discovered a long line of interstate railway carriages which had been shunted into a siding just down from Dutton Park State School. This, it turned out, was a hospital train full of young wounded men; though most of them seemed in good spirits, it was nonetheless a sobering experience. Then as mysteriously as it had arrived, a day or two later it was gone without trace. On another occasion, ever looking for fresh experiences, some of us entered a large, enclosed storage shed at Clapham Junction near Moorooka. There were women army nurses busily at work, a few men who were perhaps doctors, and lots of young wounded Australian soldiers on stretchers. They were in far worse condition than those we saw on the train and were disconcertingly subdued. There were occasional groans, a pained call for attention. All seemed heavily bandaged. The paraphernalia of medical aid seemed erected everywhere. Some of the wounded slept, others smoked, nearly all of those awake just stared emptily at blank walls. None looked comfortable. The beautiful animal spirits of youth had been cruelly scourged from them forever. A special sort of manhood had been cauterised into their souls in an instant with the fierce heat of enemy bullets. It was terrifying! As youngsters we tended to think of the war as exciting with invincible, indestructible Australian soldiers resolutely routing the enemy. One day, we fondly imagined, we would be there too upholding the great national warrior heritage. This grave, shocking moment in our lives illustrated war's awfulness. A voice of authority was suddenly bellowing, 'Get those bloody kids out of here and keep the bloody doors shut!'. My father, who was frequently in charge of an army works company at this yard, subsequently told me wounded troops from the north were often transferred to interstate trains at Clapham Junction in circumstances designed to avoid public attention. Propaganda had to concentrate on victories and troops in high spirits; while attention to the personal calamities which are an inescapable part of war might demoralise the public.

In March 1944, when I was fully eleven years of age, my mother entered the Brisbane Mothers' Hospital for several days. The birth of my younger sister Joan was imminent. Our father was away in army camp. It fell to me to run the house; cooking, washing and ironing, cleaning the house and looking after my sister Pat, a year younger than me, and brother John, three years younger. We grew up in a house where we were expected to pull our weight with domestic chores and accordingly we were well practised in the tasks before us. It never occurred to us that we were rather young for this sort of responsibility and, in particular, being left to ourselves. There were no relatives with whom we could have been boarded.

Nevertheless, an anonymous source soon reported our 'abandonment' to the State Children's Services Department. As the mills of the bureaucracy ground but slowly, by the time inspectors arrived our mother had returned home. In response to their intrusive pressure, our mother attempted pleasant reasonableness. That was unsuccessful. Then she adopted a firmer, more direct, but courteous approach. That failed too. Then she gave them a 'touch of the blow torch'. You see, where we lived, well down in the social pile, you learnt that in extremis you had to fight. Now that did work and the measured invocation of Vince Gair's name, our local member and a minister of the State Government, reinforced the message. Not that old Vince knew anything about the good use to which his name had been put.

I expect that I was an attractive youngster, an asset which quickly wasted as I proceeded to early manhood no doubt—but as a paper boy (earning a penny a dozen papers sold and thus accumulating some spending money) I would be periodically accosted by what we urchins selling newspapers called 'dirty old men'. This was at Clarence Corner near the Mater Hospital or sometimes further along at the Vulture Street intersection. We would be solicited with offers of threepence or lollies or story books to read if we went to their nearby rooms. 'Garn, I'll tell the police about you,' usually had them quickly moving on. I clearly remember one gent, however, responding with anger and threats, waving a fine, carved walking stick intimidatingly, telling me what an 'ungrateful little gutter snipe' I was and how I failed to appreciate him as a 'good friend to young boys'. He had been pestering me and others over the previous two or three evenings. The newspaper agency vendor, who presumably had been watching, suddenly materialised telling him unceremoniously to 'piss off' or he would call the police. The old codger stood his ground, giving every bit as good as he got and threatening legal action for this abuse of his reputation. He behaved as though one of his fundamental rights, the right to solicit young boys I daresay, had been violated and he was outraged. Perhaps he was merely somewhat ahead of his time.

My family was unable to afford holidays away. Not many could where we lived. Once, however, I went on a cub camp way out in the unspoilt bushlands bordering the Pine River. The area since then has long been saturated with suburban housing. It was great fun. Games around a large and jolly camp fire followed by cooking scrumptious spuds in their jackets after burying them deep in piles of red hot embers. The stars above were flawlessly beautiful. And so to the land of nod, comfortably settled into our sleeping bags. Suddenly a rustle. Something coming under the tent flaps! Apprehension for those of us disturbed by the movement. We had seen our first snake earlier in the day. A big black thing that sent us scampering in some fear. No snake that. It was a scout master. A very popular one, making his way to the sleeping bag of a particular boy who displayed no surprise at the unorthodox arrival of his nocturnal visitor. A menacing command to 'get back to sleep,' from the scout master soon followed. We all pretended to but every sense was strained as we sought to gauge the nature of this intrusion. Whispering, giggling, quiet movement in the sleeping bag now occupied by two and suddenly the trusty scout master was departing. I slept only fitfully after that.

South Brisbane threw together this hodge-podge of influences, at home and in the neighbourhood, which went to work on me, helping me shape my values and define my objectives in later public life. In this respect a critical local influence, like that of our home, was that South Brisbane was overwhelmingly Labor; for that party stood by the battlers just as the unions defended the workers from exploitative bosses. The intensity of local support for Labor was exemplified on the death of wartime Prime Minister John Curtin in 1945. I remember this event quite vividly for I witnessed a remarkable thing that day. I was walking along a street where poky Queensland timber houses huddled together on 'stilts', as the funeral service was being broadcast. It seemed every house was playing the doleful radio broadcast of the service and I could see so many women sitting on their verandahs. They were openly crying, displaying deeply felt grief at the passing of, I think, the only national leader to have captured so much respect, trust and affection. His patent honesty, genuine commitment to the people, his modesty in high office, and his determination in the face of great adversity had become an agent of national bonding at a time of crisis. For all of that, I suspect he would have been less successful as a peacetime national leader and I now have some uncertainties about his wartime performance, in particular virtually surrendering Australian authority over our forces in the Pacific to General Macarthur.[8]

The exciting buzz of a military garrison community where movement, action and a breakdown of the more restrictive conventions of a peacetime society were exciting constants, even for a youngster, was tempered with certain, inescapably dull routines. School was the most hated of them. The thought always uppermost in my mind was how to escape this chamber of horrors. Suddenly I made my big break-out. It was discovered that the chronic constipation, the headaches, bouts of nausea, occasional fainting spells and other symptoms, were not feigned after all. My mother, with a quack-like faith had tried to treat these ailments for years. She had accepted them as evidence of anaemia on the advice of a local doctor. Thenceforth I was fed daily on a serving of Arnott's arrowroot biscuits mashed in a bowl of compounded Nestlé Vi-Lactogen. This lay treatment was associated with regular, but ineffectual doses of vile-tasting Epsom salts, varied from time to time with a teaspoon of execrable castor oil. The human plumbing system was relentlessly purged but bodily illness was not scourged.

Eventually, my mother, who was becoming desperate at the mounting persistence of the symptoms, took me for medical tests at the 'free' Brisbane General Public Hospital. Lead poisoning was diagnosed through blood testing. Thereafter followed years of sharp, painful pricks to the fingertip for regular blood testing and daily doses of an absolutely revolting, arsenic-based medicine. The remedy brought its own delayed after-effects. In recent years Bowen's disease has been diagnosed, accompanied by an outbreak of skin carcinomas which require medical attention. Lead poisoning was a common enough ailment in those times among Queensland children. Homes were painted with lead-based paint to better withstand the blistering Queensland summer sun. The paint surface was always poisonous, especially for children who incautiously came in contact with it. I was fascinated by small water drops after rain which hung on the underside of the front verandah railing. They were so cool, perfectly semi-hemispheric, pure looking. They were irresistible. So I would suck at them. With each lick went an ingestion of lead; handling lead-based painted railings and other timbers at any time meant further ingestions of the noxious substance. Once my medical condition was established to my teacher's satisfaction, no questions were raised if I reported ill. Then off to the 'sick room', an uninviting storeroom whose only virtue was it carried, higgledy-piggledy, stocks of out-of-date magazines and a few old books through which I could contentedly amble. Meanwhile the torture chamber of the classroom was reserved for others. I thought I was lucky. In fact I was very foolish.

For God, King and country: with the navy

My first job was as a junior clerk with the Queensland Public Service at the State Stores Board, a place to which the less promising recruits to the public service were directed. It was housed in old convict barracks on the Brisbane River. Even the original whipping triangle was still in place. I sometimes reflected being strapped to the triangle would be a better fate than the drudgery to which I had been condemned. My daily task was to ensure that each bundle of order forms of 1000 was in numerical order, then break the bundle up into four separate lots of 250, then pin hard covers to each of these smaller bundles. This massively demanding intellectual task completed, I then had to inscribe some record of the order numbers contained within each cover on the spine of the book thus created and, after that, place the bound bundles in numerical order on shelves. This had been a full-time job for the person who held it before me. He had been promoted to a better role after twelve months of loyal and diligent service to this task. With faithful service I, too, could look to a long, and very slowly moving future ahead of me. I soon understood why so many of the long-serving staff drank during lunch breaks—at least a few also hid bottles at their workplace—and topped themselves up well after work.

I could complete my daily quota in a few hours, in spite of slow coasting to spin the job out. Then I would disappear into the storage warehouse, recline on soft bales, read, daydream or chatter to others who happened to be about. The public service was the pits. There was a senior buyer there, Hefferan I think was his name, who was forever rolling his own cigarettes, lighting them, flicking the match up and down then tossing it in the wastepaper basket. He was sometimes ineffective in extinguishing the match and the wastepaper basket would ignite. These were entertaining diversions from the grim, humdrum routine of the office. One day I added a bit of flair to this performance. As the wastepaper basket erupted into flames and staff ran about delightedly at the prospect of casting off the oppressive shackles of office work for a few minutes, I hauled down a large red fire extinguisher and gave the flaming basket a thorough drenching. There was chemical extinguisher foam everywhere. Suddenly delight turned to alarm then to recrimination. This time I had gone too far, it seemed.

I was in strife and soon paraded before the manager, Wrench by name and sour by nature. His deputy, Lyons, stood by him deprecatingly regarding my presence. In summary, I was told with great deliberation that I was squandering a splendid opportunity to succeed in a great career, I was a disruptive influence, lacked commitment, and the way I was going I was unlikely to amount to anything in the workplace. My probationary period as a junior clerk would be extended to see if I just might have the right stuff to become a good public servant. Lyons warmed to me later, when he discovered I rowed competitively, a sport he much liked.

Lyons made a practice of checking correspondence, recently completed by the stenographers, to ensure there were no mistakes. I would be asked to assist by going to his office where I would be given a carbon copy of a freshly typed letter, the original of which he held and from which he read aloud. It was my job to follow, on the copy, his reading from the original and let him know if there were any mistakes compared to the original. Quite a bundle of correspondence would be checked in this rather eccentric way. It occurred to me that if I was not careful, with perseverance, and perhaps a helpful lobotomy, I could become a successful public servant and end up like Wrench, Lyons or Hefferan. I was starting to get frightened.

At least I was earning a wage and that did not go astray at home. Our residence was, to put it gently, more than a little frayed at the edges. I bought materials, and commenced painting the internal walls of the dining room. I still recall the first night after painting that room. We were eating our dinner. My father would stop eating every now and again and soberly gaze at the wall. It was an unusual, almost perplexed, look on his face. It was as though the freshly painted wall was symptomatic of something and perhaps he was not quite sure what. Thus, progressively, the roof was repaired and painted, I built in the front verandah where my brother and I slept, and later also enclosed part of the back verandah, installing a new bathroom and, with the help of an apprentice friend of my brother, the plumbing was installed. No more cold showers, summer and winter, in a galvanised metal bathtub set in a makeshift room under the house. Thus my early wages were going towards a good cause. We were starting to see some material improvement. The reward was seeing how pleased Mum was with each advance in this handiwork.

At eighteen, deprived of any say on the matter, I was 'persuaded' to accept the 'King's shilling', as it used to be described. I was conscripted into the navy. I totally objected to being told, without any consultation, that I had to do something which infringed on my freedom as an individual. I consequently even contemplated joining the Communist Party in protest and to have it defend my civil rights (which testifies as to just how callow I was). With this purpose in mind I attended what was billed as a 'huge' protest rally at the Brisbane Trades Hall organised by the CP. As it turned out, it was attended by fewer than a score of people and no-one took any notice of me. I was still smarting about this autocratic compulsion as a matter of principle when I completed my training. I found myself in an awful bind for I thoroughly enjoyed my navy training and did not want it to end. In a perverse way I wanted to object about this too!

The highlight of this experience, or at least higher authority seemed to think so, was a visit to Flinders Naval Depot, Victoria, where we were training, by the Chief of the Navy Staff, Vice-Admiral Sir John Collins. The distinguished old salt was the first Australian to command the Australian Navy, having reached that exalted rank in 1947 after several decades of British Admirals striding the bridge of authority over our nation's navy. We conscripts, the first to be called up in an expensive and totally wasteful political stunt by the reigning Menzies Government, were assembled to hear Collins speak. At the conclusion of his brief address the Admiral elegantly inquired, with disarming casualness, 'Any complaints?' Not a sound, not even the whiffle of a low-level, after-lunch fart. He asked again, with mild but mock surprise. The silence resonated with its own emptiness.

Collins turned to the officer in command of us, 'No complaints . . . most unusual for a group of sailors, eh, Commander?'. 'Most unusual, Sir,' the Commander responded with crisp agreeableness and, no doubt, with a calculated eye on his next promotion. They exchanged the knowing grins, or were they smirks, of ringmasters who knew when they had broken a team of fractious young colts to the hard bit. Rather hesitatingly I raised a hand and said, 'Please, Sir . . . we're . . . cold!'. 'COLD!' he echoed in amplification. The great man stared at me in dissimulated surprise; that such a thing could be! He had obviously chosen to forget that when the winter winds blow across those foggy foreshores at Flinders Naval Depot, they come straight off the frozen glaciers of the nearby Antarctic icecap. The old seadog addressed the Commander with synthetic concern. 'Oh, I think we can do something about that, can't we Commander?' There was the hint of mockery as he said that. 'We certainly can, Sir,' the ever agreeable Commander chimed back.

The distinguished senior naval person departed in a black limousine, bequeathing us a cloud of dust, while we hapless youngsters were fallen in and double marched. We were double marched, and double marched, and double marched again. All this occurred to an accompaniment of rising mutterings, unkindly directed at me by my colleagues. We were halted. 'Are yer warm now?' the Chief Petty Officer in charge demanded, without any feigned concern for our feelings. 'Yes, Chief!' Not even the King's College Choir performing at its best could have struck such perfect harmony, nor rendered such a clear high C. 'Good; well just to be sure we stay warm . . . SQUAD . . . at the double . . . MARCHHH!' I soon discovered how fickle the quality of some friendships could be when creature comforts were placed at risk.

There was an experience during which I felt, fleetingly, I just might be destined for greater things. I was happily sitting on my lashed, swinging hammock in a dormitory block, when some colleagues nearby, unable to resolve an argument, drew me into their dispute. 'Do women have orgasms like men or don't they?' it was impatiently demanded. Why on earth they would have asked me to adjudicate on such a thing was incomprehensible—I was then fully eighteen, and at such an advanced age for a male, in that boldly macho age, secretly conscious that I was an utter failure. I was completely, but not as a preferred state, chaste; furthermore, my ignorance of women's biology and physiology was abysmal. I had to fence this one carefully. I could not afford to confess my great deficiency as a robust young male of the times. I pondered sagely for a few seconds and gave my judgment in studied fashion, 'Naw, women aren't like men. They don't have orgasms'. My judgment was accepted. The fifties was a period notable for its ignorance, intolerance and narrow-mindedness to which, with this uninformed comment, I made my own contribution.

The navy was deeply committed to 'Honour God, King and Country', an injunction which seemed to be inscribed everywhere. At the end of our first week of training we were briefed about church service on Sundays. Belief was a matter for the individual and attending church was not compulsory. No more than half-a-dozen or so of us non-believers and backsliders watched one day as the true Christians marched off to church. Then we prepared to settle into a pleasant, lazy Sunday morning. Suddenly a petty officer appeared. This looked menacing. 'Fall in!' he commanded. There were muttered objections regarding our free choice and so on. 'Church is vulantree . . . youse is right . . . but if youse choose not to go to church, youse does galley duty. Fall in! . . . Double march . . .' I stuck with my principles for two Sundays. I soon discovered the discomfort of swabbing galley floors, cleaning cooking utensils, and forbearing the hectoring complaints about the quality of our work from the perpetually dissatisfied ratings of the regular navy. Pragmatism triumphed over principle.

Minor infractions of discipline were punished with ratings double marching around the parade square for lengthy periods, holding a .303 rifle above the head with arms fully extended and bayonet scabbard bouncing uncomfortably on one's backside. In less than a minute the rifle felt like a tonne of lead. To lower the arms provoked abuse, even added punishment. For slightly more serious offences the penalty was duck-walking or frog-marching with a rating's hammock straddled over his shoulders. The pain in the thighs after a few minutes of this unnatural contortion was diabolically cruel. Deserters were marched through accommodation blocks between guards with uniform badges torn off and ships' ribbons removed from caps. It was all so disgustingly primitive. However, there was a small but brief piece of revenge. All officers had to be saluted according to the discipline of naval tradition and most officers rode bicycles around the grounds. We conscripts would string out, going to and from meals, each saluting as a procession of officers came past, each officer having to return the salute hanging on to their bicycle with one hand and slightly unbalancing its steering as the other hand briskly swung upwards. In a short time a new naval tradition was coined—no saluting of officers on pushbikes.

Soon, the mainly enjoyable experience of National Service Training was over. I was back home and into the rut again. Each evening, as I trudged my way home from the tram stop, I would pass a near neighbour on her way to work, a woman who lived about one-and-a-half streets away from us. She was slim, skinny really, with very pale skin colouring and totally grey hair; she was about fifty years of age. She always walked at a smart pace, looked straight ahead and gave no encouragement for conversation. Vi, however, was not put off by her demeanour. In her inimitable way she would frequently engage this lady in gossipy exchanges and was able to report she was a 'good woman', an office cleaner who had raised a boy on her own. Vi held her in high respect. Later I got to know her, briefly.

A policeman's lot is not an 'appy one

I may not have known much in those days but I reckoned I knew a lot about how exciting the life of a policeman was. Dick Tracy had been a childhood hero, always besting crooks like Big Boy, Flat Top, The Brow and his cruel 'spike machine'. Good and bad were clear cut, and good always triumphed after a deal of drama and real excitement. Tess Goodheart was a bit of a bore though. Could not stand people who were all virtue and no flaw—then or now. I knew all about J. Edgar Hoover and his men at the FBI relentlessly hunting down wrongdoers, from picture cards attached to G-Man chewing gum. Police work, as I saw it, offered great personal freedom of judgment and authority to do good. Suddenly I made the dash for this exciting new lifestyle. I left the humdrum cares of office work behind and became a member of Queensland's finest, a constable of the State police force. My father obviously fretted at this step but said little. He died while I was training. There was, by my standards, a considerable pay improvement over that available to me in the public service and with his death the extra help this could contribute at home became more important.

In a short time I had a problem. One night before falling in to go on night duty at the now demolished Roma Street Police Station, I was taken to one side by the duty senior sergeant, O'Donoghue I recall was his name. He was about my height but he was huge. In fact he was almost spherical in shape with a high florid colouring to his face—the cost of maintaining this must have fully extended his pay cheque. He wanted to know if I was a Communist and, if not, why I was receiving copies of communist magazines in the mail. These were glossy, pictorial productions entitled *USSR* and *Soviet Union*, I believe, illustrating the joys of the workers' paradise in the then USSR, a place where the past worked but only just, as we now know.

Complimentary subscriptions had been arranged as a farewell thought by a workmate at the State Stores Board, Merv Young, an active member of the Communist Party. We used to have long political discussions, with Young always assuring me that the workers' revolution was only ten years away. After a few years of this I pointed out to him that, if his timetable was reliable, it should have been by then only eight years away. A bit of throat clearing and he got on to the more important subject of what the dictatorship of the proletariat would mean. Making deserts blossom was one goal. O'Donoghue advised me, between his perpetual wheezing—I suspect he suffered from emphysema for he was a compulsive, smelly and messy cigarette smoker—that I had better cancel the mailings. He reminded me that according to police regulations an officer could be sacked at any time within the first twelve months of service. No reasons for dismissal had to be provided and the termination was not appealable.

I pondered the matter in the course of a long, boring night of plod and decided that while I was not keen about this new occupation being ended almost before it started, on the other hand I had rights and we had a State Labor Government dedicated to protecting the rights of workers and individuals. This was 1953, the year before the Labor 'split' in Victoria and four years before an equally nasty split in Labor in Queensland, which goes to show how naive I was about the internal condition of the Labor Party. Heresy hunting anti-communism was the fashion within the controlling clique in the Labor Party in Queensland. Catholic Action was directing the relentless scourging of Communists, fellow-travellers and people marginally suspected of being sympathisers, in unions and the workplace. The State Public Service, in particular the police force, was being infiltrated by agents for Catholic Action as part of this cleansing process. I did nothing, which, with the benefit of hindsight, was potentially riskier than I had imagined.

Then, later, I became aware that the publications had ceased arriving in the mail. I let the matter lie as I had been long uninterested in the publications, rarely removing them from their wrappers. But very suggestively, when the Labor 'split' came, our mailman (Jackie Bourke, of national sporting fame in his youth as a boxer) became an outspoken activist for the breakaway Queensland Labor Party, the political front for Catholic Action in the State. I have often wondered if there was any connection.

I had some mild revenge on the portly O'Donoghue later, in the aftermath of a disturbance at the brothel then in Margaret Street in the city. By way of background, prostitution was tolerated then so long as it was restricted to designated brothels, the 'girls' underwent weekly medical examinations at the State Health Department, and provided no 'bludgers' attached themselves to the women. These establishments were generally out of the way of the main concourse of public activity. It seemed to work tolerably well. People who were opposed to prostitution could pretend it did not happen because they did not see it under their noses. And those frequenters of the bordellos who preferred to moralise against the practice in public could retain their 'respectability', as they were unlikely to be spotted.

Only a couple of smart, fashionably dressed young detectives who reported directly to Inspector Frank Bischoff, head of the CIB, visited the brothels regularly to check them out. For Bischoff was alert to the temptations of vice and corruption to which general police might be exposed with any loosely managed arrangement. Later it was revealed, rather sensationally, that Bischoff had natural entrepreneurial instincts and was an outstanding organiser. He had established a structured system of corruption throughout the State. There was flair to the man. He would not use just anyone as his bagman, not if a commissioned officer was available, and he believed in sharing the spoils, paying a generous commission to his bagmen.[9] No wonder he was widely admired, and similarly, that some traditions in Queensland have long antecedents.

For the rest of us, duty visits to brothels only occurred when we were directed to go in emergencies. On the night of the incident mentioned, I interviewed the 'madam' or perhaps, in this woman's case, the 'house mother', while the sergeant flirted outrageously but harmlessly with the working girls, causing them great mirth, a happy way for them to finish a long night's hard work. But then, no matter how trivial an incident the police department required a report, in fact as a bureaucratic monster it loved consuming paper endlessly and often pointlessly. Reports were standardised. They always commenced, 'I have the honour to report . . . '. What I eventually filed roughly went: 'Sir, I have the honour to report I called at the Margaret Street brothel during duty hours last night. I observed some especially interesting people working there . . . '. Actually, as I look back on it, it was a bit laboured, but it was effective. O'Donoghue came storming out of his office, roaring as he made his way, his high colouring turning an even darker red as his porcine figure swelled larger with rage. He made some comments about 'smart alecs' and demanded a redraft. Happy to comply, I felt rather full of myself as I went home that morning.

There was one slightly discordant note to the episode: the house mother. It had given me a jolt, recognising her. She was the 'cleaning lady' around the corner from where we lived. The experience of interviewing her was surreal. We both looked at one another as the interview took place—it was all quite formal and detached—but neither gave the slightest hint that one knew the other. Afterwards when I would see her, which was irregularly for I now worked varying shifts, I would greet her as we passed in the street. She always responded impersonally, as she always had. If she was talking to my mother when I came along, or anyone else for that matter, she would quickly move away, which is what she had always done. If she worried about me disclosing my discovery, she gave no hint of it.

It would be wrong of me to leave any impression I might believe in the notion of the harlots with their golden hearts. The lifestyle of the prostitute can make them tough, cynical, unscrupulous, suspicious; and nowadays, with drug addiction thrown in as a major cause of prostitution, a new and complex element is added to the tragedy. Some, with good reason, are also quite hateful of men. They are often associates of criminals and at the same time sources of information to the police on the activities of those same criminals, as I learned at first hand. As a young detective I was at the Boggo Road prison gates at 6 a.m. one day, with a more senior detective, waiting for a prisoner's release. There was some unfinished business we wished to talk to him about. Out first came a petty criminal who had been sent down for six months for 'bludging' on a prostitute. She was there and rushed over enfolding him in her meretricious embrace, gushing, 'I'll never forgive the copper bastards for sending you off'. . . It was all a bit much. My colleague had 'pinched' the bludger at her request and did so as a favour because she was a good source of information, a 'dog' as police argot then had it. She wanted the bludger out of circulation as she had a new 'fancy'. That did not last. No matter, she remained, in the terminology of the day, a good 'dog'.

By trudging along this grotty margin of society there is always an occupational risk of developing a jaundiced view of life. I worked night shift briefly with a senior detective who had a remarkable memory for faces, names and aliases, dates and offences. He would identify people, sometimes lots of them, in large crowds, such as theatregoers leaving the cinema, with 'form'. At a certain point he would spit out with disgust, 'I wonder if there's anyone in Brisbane without form?'. When an officer's outlook becomes as unbalanced as this, and likely to affect his judgment, it is time for him to go—not of course that many of them ever did.

From Roma Street Station I was transferred to Woolloongabba Station. The far end of the area in the Woolloongabba district, in South Brisbane, covered some rough precincts near the old Victoria Bridge. It was a shabby area of urban decay and social blight, much of which has since been rehabilitated as part of the elegant new South Bank cultural and recreational zone.

The now demolished Palace Hotel on the corner of Stanley and Melbourne Streets, directly opposite a police call box where we were required to 'swing corners' on beat duty, was something of a bloodhouse. Especially so on Friday and Saturday nights, mostly around closing time, 10 p.m., which was when the night shift came on duty. My first few experiences of weekend night duty quickly taught me something important. The more senior constable working with me would solicitously offer to walk his beat first, allowing me a 'blow' as I held the corner. Inevitably this first run over the beat would take an inordinately long time during which I would be confronted with any disturbances at the pub opposite. I soon amended these arrangements.

On one night, as a colleague and I arrived at the call box (having hitched a free ride on the running board of a council tram, which was standard practice then for police transport was extraordinarily scarce), we found a sizeable brawl in full swing outside the Palace Hotel. We were soon having a rough time and collecting plenty of loose 'haymakers'. My colleague, who had obviously been drinking before commencing duty, suddenly drew a large, ugly .45 automatic pistol and started waving it about and threatening the brawlers. This inflamed them. I feared the fool was intoxicated sufficiently and stressed enough to pull the trigger. God alone knew what tragedy might have occurred then. With difficulty I wrestled his arm down and got him to put the gun away. In the meantime we were peppered with a lot of loose punches. Eventually the disturbance subsided. I expected my colleague would be grateful for my intervention when he sobered up. Instead he became increasingly surly and threatening towards me and remained that way until he disappeared on transfer.

Walking the beat in the infant hours of morning in the wet season—wearing a heavy waterproof cloak which reached to the ankles and had attached a wide shoulder to hip shawl which buttoned down the front, standard issue boots encased in galoshes, cap covered with a waterproof protector including a flap drooping down the back of the neck, the steady light rain forming a thin, grey mist, the small, soft raindrops sensually flicking my face—stimulated reveries. One night a torch flashed several times from St Helen's Private Hospital situated just past the dilapidated shelter for homeless men conducted by the Salvation Army, the latter out of necessity on a shoestring budget. I investigated and met the sister in charge that night who was finding the night a drag. She offered a cup of tea.

The very next night we made love on a small office table—an event, given the size of that table, that was at least a triumph for the power of lust. She, Miriam[10], was married with two children, and at thirty-four years of age was about fourteen years older than me. She worked fairly consistent night work so she could be with her children during the day while her husband, who also worked, cared for them at night. I became besotted with her. I was, for the first time in my life, deeply in love. It was an unsurpassably delicious experience the thought of which was my constant companion. It would not be the last time I fell irretrievably in love and was disconsolately broken-hearted when the affair fell apart. We sometimes met during the day when the children were at infants school and kindergarten. There was always a fresh, clean smell about her body. She was soft and refreshingly cool to embrace, her touch gentle and caressing. When I looked into her peerless eyes, almost the colour of champagne, or nuzzled her flaxen hair, I knew there were only two people in all the world. Miriam taught me much about lovemaking, for my limited experience had left me operating like a rapid fire piston driver to that point; 'be gentle . . . think of me too . . . slower . . . '

I seriously spoke of my love for her but she always gently deflected it. Her duty to her children rose above all other considerations. Then one day she announced a disaster. She told me she and her family were moving interstate to take up a career opportunity for her husband, an engineer. She left my life as suddenly as she had entered it. I was inconsolable privately although I managed to conceal it. The persistent, cruel, exquisite pain in my chest felt as if it would crush me. A little later I was listlessly picking at my breakfast sandwiches in the Woolloongabba Station duty meal room. Two colleagues were engaged in the usual scatological talk which machismo police officers enjoyed only marginally less than discussion of sport in those times. 'Miriam's left town.' 'Yeah. She was a great bird. One of the best f . . . s I ever had.' 'Yeah. Make the butterflies swarm out of your a . . . e when you came. Hadn't had one as good as her in a long time.' And so the noisy snickering continued. I left for the ablution block. I felt dreadfully ill. My true love was a painted woman! a Jezebel! a whore! I felt like a cuckold! How could she possibly have cheated on me! As I left I heard one say to the other, 'What's wrong with Hayden? Moody bugger lately'. Soon I was rescued from my dreadful fate. Another great love of the century rose on the ruins of my shattered faith. Followed by another case of my heart being broken.

While I was learning these lessons from and about life, my instincts concerning human behaviour were being sharpened by experience. A young couple turned up at the police station one morning to report that the female had been raped. The culprit was, allegedly, the 'star boarder' living with them, a young Australian of Greek background who worked on the wharves. It just had the wrong ring to it. The complainant conceded this as investigations proceeded. What had happened was that in the midst of a disagreement the previous night, when both husband and wife had consumed too much liquor, a nasty argument had broken out. Her revenge, as she fielded heavy clouts about the body, was to bitterly declare that she had been pleasuring the boarder in the matrimonial bed during the day. Next morning, sober, contrite and aware of the potential damage to their rather elementally bonded marriage, she changed her story to rape. We were able to sort the matter out. They left, going their different ways. Before there had been two very happy men and one doubly happy woman in the world. Now the stock of that happiness was considerably diminished; a shame really.

After a while, there was not much that happened that really shocked, no matter how depraved, debased or complicitous. I could only do the best I could in a very flawed world. A retarded girl, frequently chained to a heavy metal bed-end in an isolated home in the bush 'for 'er own good', was reported as an incest victim by her mother, who also appeared a little retarded. The father, a mean, shifty little man, was the alleged offender. The incestuous conduct had been occurring for some time so our suspicion was that a family dispute with a component of vindictiveness had provoked the complaint, rather than any high-minded moral concern. After a solicitor had a talk with the family, the mother advised the investigating police that her husband was not the father of the girl. The girl was the issue from an affair with a travelling salesman, and she could not remember anything much else about him. That was the end of that case.

Some human behaviour is incomprehensible. Friday nights were the ones we most dreaded; most often the same addresses and the same experiences. I arrested a man one Friday night to prevent him continuing to beat his wife in her home. The wife-beater was subdued rather roughly out of necessity as he was extremely belligerent. Also, every time I handled one of these incidents I tended to see my mother. I dragged the basher out onto the footpath and charged him with offences in a public place, for legislated provisions covering these occurrences were rather thin in those days and arrests in the house difficult to sustain in court. The wife was abundantly grateful for our intervention. A sergeant at the lockup, however, warned me that there might be trouble from the wife. He had a 'feeling' about the woman. Sure enough she arrived at the lockup next morning, the signs of having been battered overnight quite evident. In behaviour that might seem incomprehensible to some, she roundly condemned the police, meaning me, and wanted to lodge a complaint. The older sergeant cleverly calmed her down, for, although it does not always work, police do develop psychological techniques for handling difficult people.

On another occasion when a sergeant and I were having a hard time subduing a violent wife-beater, the wife suddenly picked a pan from the stove top and commenced beating the sergeant, who was closer to her. These women and many more like them resumed cohabitation with their wife-beating spouses within a day or two of these sorts of incidents, mostly next day in fact. To say that it was economic dependence—and of course there is sometimes much to that—misleadingly simplifies the relationship between many women and men. There is undoubtedly something to the current politically correct vogue for describing males as abusing their power over women and treating them as chattels. But I am convinced that the relationship between male and female has deep emotional, psychological and biological influences to it also and these are much more profound than fashionable politically correct explanations. I saw my mother's conduct after a stormy night too often to accept those sorts of interpretations alone. Over-simplifying the basis of these relationships in the way in which the new 'violence industry' does—an industry which spawns a lot of well-paid community jobs for politically correct activists, while they can keep expanding the ambit and nature of the industry—can trivialise the complexity of a human relationship and cause us to try the wrong remedies.

There was another facet to police work which revealed itself at times, a face with ugly, disfigured features, otherwise concealed behind the acceptable image of public responsibility and care at CIB Headquarters on George and Elizabeth streets, which was, incongruously, a former Anglican Church. At least there was a thread of continuity in the community services being provided from the building. Confessions were still being heard but the techniques for obtaining them had changed with the more recent tenants. Another young detective and I entered the duty senior sergeant's office in the early morning hours, returning from a smash and grab near Roma Street Railway Station. The senior sergeant was swinging the sawn-off, lighter end of a pick handle which had a lanyard attached to it. He was explaining to some other detectives, with evident gusto, smacking the billet resoundingly against the palm of one hand, how he had used the deadly implement to flatten the 'Commie' Fred Patterson. This had happened on St Patrick's Day, 17 March 1948, in Brisbane. Patterson was the only member of the Communist Party to be elected to the Queensland Legislative Assembly. He was passing a group of striking unionists marching along Edward Street, from the now demolished old Trades Hall. Suddenly police, who reputedly had been drinking, charged the amiable picketing workers, laying many low with batons. When the one-sided affray was over Patterson was picked up from the road, unconscious with a severe skull fracture. He never fully recovered from this violence. He had been felled by the piece of pick handle in the hands of this senior sergeant. And what was worse, the police violence had the sanction of law invoked by the Hanlon Labor Government, the workers' government![11] This same Senior Sergeant then turned his attention to my colleague and me. He wanted to know if we had brought back evidence from the crime scene for later court use. He explained, in response to our perplexity, that we should have collected fragments of glass, price tags, even something more substantial which could be conveniently located on a suspect 'in case he's a f . . . ing liar'. Strangely, he was regarded as a good citizen in his suburb and was held in high standing by his church.

I did not care much for police work in the city. Much was mundane, too much impersonal, and it could be dreadfully boring. Early in my service I was transferred to Mackay, North Queensland. As a young single man I spent most of my time on relief duty at small stations in sugar cane farming communities in that region. These were the blue and gold carefree years of a young man which, now recalled, seem impossibly lustrous. The police work load was often slight so I took on manual cane cutting, scrub clearing, truck driving and a number of other rural occupations. The extra income was handy but the main attraction was the sheer delight of doing these tactile things, of being involved with people in a different way. My durable memories are of the lush, heady smell of burnt cane, of the gorgeous scent of molasses richly saturating the atmosphere, of horse-drawn windlass arms used as a mechanism for raising cane loads on simple mechanical cranes at railway loading yards, of the steady, noble tread of the beast as it strutted in repetitive circles winding up the windlass. The load was swung out, high over railway wagons and released to suddenly fall into one of the wagons. There would be a crash and a great submissive shudder would run through the ribbon of linked wagons. In the evenings great tongues of flame flared into the darkening sky, and raced and crackled through selected fields of cane, burning the crop in preparation for the cut of the next day. It was breathtakingly spectacular and the cool, fresh evening became seductive with the fragrance of molasses.

Much later I made a dreadful mistake. As Governor-General I visited some of those small villages. I wanted to recapture those happy, happy days of years ago, before they got lost in a fading memory. I nearly destroyed the magic of it all. Those villages which once sparkled with human activity looked so tiny, nondescript and drab. Earlier, there were people who gave so much gaiety to life. I still recall fondly what had caused the mirth and fun, even though on my return I discovered we now had little in common. The fault, of course, was exclusively mine. In old age one should never return to those places of precious memory from one's youth. Old eyes lose the capacity to distinguish the delicate balance of light and the brilliant colours that compose a blue and gold day, and old minds are wary of making new friends easily.

Life is never a continuous run of unalloyed happiness. There are the grim troughs, the pain-ridden stumbles. No black hole was worse than the obligation, as a policeman, of advising a wife and mother that her husband had been killed. No amount of rehearsing what to say when delivering the bad news helped, especially if you knew the family, which was almost a certainty in a small country town. You would climb the stairs, feet leaden with sadness, stand awkwardly on the top step. The knock was different, and before you could utter a word the widow read the message on your face as she opened the door. The widow's worst fears confirmed, inevitably the first question she would utter was, 'What's going to become of me and the children . . . ?'. After a few experiences like this I recognised the question was not a reflection of a selfish preoccupation. Remember, this was forty years ago. These women were wives, mothers, homemakers; and that was as much as the prevailing culture allowed them. A husband's death was a tragedy beyond contemplation.

There were those experiences, but there were others too: the problem of my mother's lack of independence, and the state of her marital relationship (a situation she shared with many women like her with whom I became acquainted in the course of police duties); the problems of single mothers being forced to adopt out their infants by parents more concerned about their own fragile moralistic outlook than the welfare of their daughter and grandchild; the bleak existence of chronic drunks with their poor nutrition and emaciated condition, their filthy clothing and personal neglect, and the lack of accommodation and care available to them; of Eugene Ebzrey, who then held the world record for convictions for drunkenness, chasing after me in the freezing cold hours of an early, dark winter's morning at North Quay begging to be locked up to escape the cold. All of these led me to feel a great anger at the injustices some people had to bear.

My resentment at such an uncaring system fed upon itself, insistently declaring something should be done about this unfairness. But by whom? And how would they? Eventually something major was done, although it took a couple of decades. With the election of the Whitlam Government in 1972 and my appointment as Minister for Social Security, I set about attending to that great register of social injustices I had been accumulating from childhood, through my police years, into the Parliament. I confess, however, the thought that one day I would take substantial steps to resolve those sorts of injustices by direct personal action had never crossed my mind in those earlier times.

Back in Brisbane I was becoming restless, unsettled. For while I enjoyed much of my police service, the future looked dismal. In those days it took twenty-eight years to reach the quite junior rank of Sergeant Second Class. I topped the State in my First Class Constable's law examination with the highest mark recorded to then. It meant little. Police officers who were senior in service to me, some who had failed the test for years and who just scraped across the pass line that year or in later years resumed their position ahead of me on the seniority list. In important respects life as I lived it was becoming dull. There had to be something more to life than emptying drunks' pockets at the watch-house. The sectarian struggle in the police force between Catholics and Masons, always being waged, was tiresome. In retrospect, I acknowledge now that it was a case of late maturity. The days of coasting along, of day-dreams, of throwing myself wholeheartedly and unreflectively into competitive sports like rugby, rowing, wood chopping, of carousing and chasing after interesting women were coming to an end.

The more serious I became about my future the more unsettled I became about the purpose of life. There had to be more to it than copulation, procreation and extinction. Existence on such a basis was pointless, meaningless. A large part of my problem was, still is I expect, an uncomfortable tendency towards deep bouts of depression. Sometimes they were brief but often they could run for a few weeks. They were also associated with difficulties about self-worth and I was periodically plagued by a strange, unsettling experience of apprehension. The thought that I had to end it all would hover about morbidly. I'd experience a feeling of impending disaster, as though some black grotesque Minotaur, stamping impatiently in the dark recesses of the unconscious, was waiting for the opportunity to charge, to smash me down, to trample over me. If only I could cling to the buoyant straw of faith in all this turbulence; to accept that 'the heart has its reasons which reason knows nothing of'. In moments of solitude I keep finding that this is something, I regret, I cannot do. I sometimes feel I have imposed my own sentence and condemned myself to be alone. There have been many times in my life when I have wished I could let my heart lead my head.

I was transferred to Ipswich from Redbank, a village then between Brisbane and Ipswich. I commenced studying through the State Secondary Correspondence School and matriculated. I had been loafing along for too long. I had a lot of leeway to make up. I would stuff papers inside my tunic before going out on the beat, and after briefly plodding my allotted course, disappear into the meal room for porters and cleaners at the city railway station. There I would study for a period, walk the beat and return. I was held in good standing by the railway workers once it was discovered I had strong Labor and trade union sympathies. Small but symbolically important favours like cups of tea were extended to me.

I did something else, the single most intelligent thing I have ever done. After a courtship of more than a year, in which I frequently despaired that she would accept me, I married Dallas. Perhaps it seems rather corny, but for me it was a case of love at first sight. I saw her walking in the street at Ipswich one day and decided in that instant she was the woman I wanted to marry. She was so beautiful—slim, erect, strong calves, her hair in a bun, she walked like a ballet dancer, and she had the most remarkably clear blue eyes. Later, I started flirting with her. I rather recall, with some embarrassment, the style was clumsy, *gauche* even, in a manner of which I would sternly disapprove if adopted by some suitor of our young daughters.

Our affair is something that has endured for more than thirty-five years. Without our marriage I would have been a much lesser person, for this marriage and a family gave me reason to exist beyond the narrow, self-centred confines by which I had lived to that point. This responsibility to others was a major incentive to succeed in life. I would sometimes tease Dallas—good-humoured family fun, especially when the children were about and younger— and suggest that the thing which really made me want to marry her were the rich strawberry cream sponges her mother, Vera Broadfoot, regularly baked for us. The children would shriek their delighted approval of granma's unsurpassable baking. Dallas and I had bushwalked and picnicked a lot in the countryside when we were courting, always with one of those scrumptious sponge cakes. After years of living mostly by myself in rough police barracks, eating simple fare at cheap hotels or cooking the basics for myself, those large cream sponges were a sybaritic delight. But the companionship of my future wife was the most delightful experience of all. Indeed, I remain eternally indebted to her for many things. Not least an amount of money I borrowed from her in our courting days, when I was in one of my impecunious states, to buy books with which to study for matriculation by correspondence. To this day I have not repaid her but I must, soon. Her quiet trust and confidence in me have been boundless and sustaining and her belief in what I could achieve has exceeded my own self-confidence.

And along the way something else happened too. In 1961 I was elected to the House of Representatives. This was quite a shock for quite a number of people, not a few of them being in the local Labor

Party. Some of the latter suddenly realised that if they had risked their arm and become the candidate, they would now be the local member. And without a doubt, a much better one than me . . . I should also confess I was foremost among those astonished by that result.

PART II

CANBERRA
BOUND

Take-off

Suddenly I was Canberra bound, lolling back in the cushioned comfort of a Trans-Australia Airlines aircraft. The seat was fully reclined. I felt like a voluptuary. It was a standard of luxury to which I was distinctly unaccustomed. 'Seat-backs upright for take-off' was the order snapped with ringing authority by a female cabin attendant as she moved down the aisle with clinical detachment, never doubting for a second that all would meekly comply and on the instant. Ah! here again was manifested my insignificance as a common mortal before the omnipotence of real power! It was 7 a.m. on Sunday, 19 February 1962 and I was departing from the Brisbane airport.

I had never been on an aircraft before, let alone travelled first class. I soon discovered I had a natural flair for quickly adjusting to the small but better things in life. Moving up to occupy a more comfortable berth in our social order is easy. Being pushed back down because you have lost your foothold in the system is what causes the pain. I would discover that too. My greatest task of the moment was to restrain the excitement welling up inside. I had to appear outwardly relaxed, to convey a sufficient impression of *savoir-vivre*. Poise, nonchalance, a relaxed worldliness which comes unforced from vast experience of the finer things in life, these were the qualities I needed to reflect casually, to make it clear I naturally belonged in these surroundings. Once aloft, a cheerful female cabin attendant inquired if I wanted breakfast. With studied calmness I responded, 'No thanks, I've already eaten, but I'll settle for some tea and toast'. 'Whatd'yerthinkthisis? . . . the Ritz?' she inquired good humouredly and to the mild entertainment of those nearby. Not a propitious start for what I expected would probably be a short journey, but which ended up a marathon event running over more than thirty-five years.

Dallas was otherwise engaged when I left—at the Ipswich Maternity Hospital, preparing for the birth of the second of our four children, Georgina. Michaela preceded Georgina and Ingrid and Kirk followed. It was as well Dallas followed her doctor's advice to go to the hospital then. Georgina was delivered at 1 a.m., 22 February 1962, less than twelve hours after I had been sworn in as the representative for the Federal Division of Oxley in the House of Representatives.

So I was heading to Canberra. It was all a big surprise, and not just for me. Bob Menzies, the Prime Minister, confessed as much publicly. He came within one seat of a hung parliament. Jim Killen's legendary 'close shave' in Moreton, where he scraped in with a handful of preference votes, saved Menzies' Government that year. It was said thereafter, of Killen and the Menzies Government, that both had been saved by the preference votes of the Communist Party candidate, Max Julius. Menzies was meant to have been so delighted with Killen's having 'saved his bacon' that he anointed him publicly, declaring 'Killen, you are magnificent!'. The comment became firmly established in our political folklore. Years later Killen confessed, *sotto voce,* that it was the sort of comment Menzies *would* certainly have made if he had thought about it; but as he had not actually said it, Killen decided to do so on Menzies' behalf. Perhaps the intention was to protect Menzies from any later embarrassing accusations of forgetfulness, or even ungratefulness.

Arthur Calwell, Labor's leader, was pleasantly stunned with his party's close run result. Most of the credit however belonged with his deputy, Gough Whitlam. Whitlam dazzled the Queensland electorate. On a platform of northern development he mesmerised the northerners with visions of rivers being turned inland and running backwards, of dams and roads littering the vast and sparsely populated top end of the country. Forget the economics, it is the votes which count and Queensland gave Labor a 10 per cent swing as against a national swing of 5.3 per cent. Here at last was someone who understood the State, who was capable of thinking the way Queenslanders did. Thereafter Queensland loved Whitlam. Whitlam's economics might have been fractured but his vision was perfect. It was that vision which helped get me elected.

In charting this course Whitlam was scarcely plumbing waters dark and unknown to other political parties. These were the years of unashamed political pork-barrelling. Menzies conjured up a trifecta for the occasion. First, he promised the Chowilla Dam for South Australia, Victoria and New South Wales. He concurrently earmarked £20 million for a further stage of the Snowy Mountains Hydro-electric Scheme and, unsure whether that was sufficient to bribe enough votes, he offered another £115 million for the scheme over five years. With exemplary tactical timing he had the page one lead of the *Sydney Morning Herald* screaming, 'Huge Iron Ore Deposits Discovered in Western Australia' within days of the election.[1]

This was an election when, unusually, the Fairfax dynasty and its Chief Executive Officer and Svengali, 'Rags' Henderson, smiled fondly on Calwell. The *Herald* transformed him from a party hack to someone 'Growing in Stature . . .', while on another occasion the page one lead trumpeted 'Calwell Challenge to Menzies on State of Economy'. Menzies was out of favour with the scions of the Fairfax family. His campaign opening was described as a 'Policy Speech Without a Policy'. The late Max Newton, then of the *Herald*'s staff, was allocated the task of writing speeches, in particular on economic matters, and press statements for Calwell. The press statements were often printed before Calwell had even seen them. This munificence was rather bewildering to a raw novice like me.

The press barons were supposed to be our natural enemies. Later, Calwell confided in me that he had promised the Fairfax organisation another television licence if Labor won government. I thought he said in Melbourne, but there was another view that it was for Newcastle. No matter, the Fairfax cup of simple gratitude overflowed. Curiously, perhaps, the 1961 national election 'was the first time the *Herald* had ever advocated the election of a Labor government, either Federal or State.'[2]

The geographic area contained within Oxley had not been represented by Labor since 1906. From 1949 the Federal Division of Oxley steadfastly held the Labor vote at a low 40 to 42 per cent. To win it required a swing of something like 8 per cent. In fact there was a 14 per cent swing on a two party preferred basis. I would have to confess, drawing on all the years of experience I have had in political life since 1961, if some young person came to me now proposing to contest an electorate with a similar geographic sprawl, of comparable socio-economic break-up, with a highly respected local member like the man I beat, with the voting pattern over time consistently adverse to Labor as it was in Oxley, I would be inclined to advise them not to try. Yet, the brash confidence of the young sometimes achieves things which experience and common sense suggest cannot be done. Meanwhile, I was travelling to Canberra on a Member of Parliament's travel pass and I really needed an excess luggage voucher to carry my overload of personal joy and happiness.

Initially I nominated for preselection to represent Labor in Oxley accepting the local party wisdom that it was unwinnable for our party. To me, nonetheless, it seemed a marvellous opportunity to gain some practical experience in political campaigning, for once I matriculated I wished to study law at university. One of the elective units I wished to undertake was political science. In my abysmal innocence I thought that if a university described a subject as a science then it had to be just that. Once embarked on university studies, however, I was quickly disabused of this grotesquerie.

'Something done half-heartedly should not have been attempted at all,' was another of my late father's homilies. In following this advice I threw myself into the preselection campaign wholeheartedly. I won 393 votes to 133. By contemporary standards, blighted with mega-scale branch stacking to fiddle preselection outcomes, that was not a large vote. For the times, however, and in particular for Oxley, it was impressively large. The preselection was 'pretty rough', as the late Dr Denis Murphy, Labor historian, has recorded. An official 'rort' was put in operation against me. I was regarded as being too close to the 'left', too comfortable with a number of Communists and certain radical causes. I had been investigated by a commissioned police officer, following a formal complaint lodged by an undivulged source, for writing a longish, impassioned letter of denunciation of the Sharpeville massacre in South Africa in 1960, published in the *Queensland Times,* Ipswich. Queensland police were of course supposed to be non-political. The Queensland Police Special Branch had collected photographs of me publicly involved in such radical action as marching for peace and others even worse, of me in the company of Communists.[3] I saw mine as a rather mild degree of radicalness but apparently it was more than some could stomach in those narrow-minded days immediately after the 'split' of 1957 and in the midst of the Cold War and McCarthyism. The right wing Australian Workers' Union (AWU) threw its considerable support behind my opponent. This gave his supporters the advantage of cutting out facsimile ballot papers printed in the AWU organ, the *Worker,* and attaching union right-to-vote vouchers to them, accumulated through dodgy practices by AWU organisers. My opponent's supporters had a mass voting machine instantly available to them. I did not. Thus I entered the contest with a heavy penalty weight.

I applied common sense, a bit of fight fire with fire. Necessity dictated the prevailing principles. The Miners' Union gave me membership voting authorisations which allowed their members to vote in ALP plebiscites, as the preselections were named in Queensland. That was handy. I distributed them to the people to whom they were made out and encouraged them to postal vote. A subtle sounding out of voting inclination was first undertaken—no point in doing leg work for your opponent. There was a large workforce at the Goodna Psychiatric Hospital, Ipswich. With the help of friends we canvassed there, and elsewhere, regularly, accumulating a huge postal vote from this source. All of this was in flagrant violation of the very unbalanced party rules as they then stood. The clear advantage of AWU support enjoyed by my opponent, moreover, may have been offset a little due to the Dinmore branch polling booth being set up in an empty front room of the house Dallas and I were renting in New Chum Road. The presiding officer was one of my best friends as was the only scrutineer on duty. I seem to recall reports of an unusually heavy run of voting there during a normally quiet part of the late afternoon.

Later I was to be one of those instrumental in progressively cleaning up rorts of this sort, including the AWU's facsimile voting racket. This culminated with National Executive intervention in the Queensland branch in 1980, when I led Labor as Leader of the Opposition. I preferred an aboveboard system, not one which forced candidates into vote racketeering. In the meantime, primitive political man had to fight with the crude weapons available to him. When the votes were counted I held my breath. No need to have done so. No-one noted the huge postal vote for me, the overwhelming preference of miners for my candidature, nor the impressive vote at little Dinmore.

To backtrack a little, my entry into politics on the Labor side owes a lot to a couple of men in particular. On arriving at Redbank Village, as it then was, to become one of the two local police officers there, on transfer from Brisbane, I stopped the first person I saw, and sought his directions to the police station. That man was Jack

Eustace, a devout Catholic and an equally committed Labor man. We became lifelong friends. Eustace introduced me to one of his best friends, Jack Penning, as deeply committed a Labor man as Eustace and as faithful to the Masonic Lodge as Jack was to his Church. Again, I made another lifelong friendship. Eustace was the job delegate for his union at the Goodna Psychiatric Hospital laundry. I need scarcely spell out the obvious benefits which accrued to me in the later plebiscite through that connection. It was through Eustace and Penning, both long passed on now regrettably, that I joined the Labor Party; but not before they had put a discreet but rigorous 'tape measure' over me to ensure that there were no 'Grouper' tendencies on my part. The Split had just taken place in the Queensland branch of the Labor Party. My attempts to join the Party in earlier years, especially at South Brisbane which was territory held by fire-eating Groupers, had been frustrated. I was subsequently advised that my father's radical views and certain comments of mine to 'reliable' sources within the Labor Party had me listed locally on the political equivalent of the Vatican's 'Index Librorum Prohibitorum' as unacceptable for party membership.

For Eustace, a Catholic endeavouring to be faithful to his religion and at the same time loyal to the Labor Party, the experience could be awful. Every Sunday he and his wife Vera and their four children would make their way to mass via train to the next village of Goodna. They would be shunned by many of the parishioners and subjected to fiery sermons denouncing the Labor Party; even the Eustace brothers divided over the issue of the Split. People of frailer heart would have given up one or the other, Church or Labor, or in some cases both, as many did. Not the Eustaces, nor thousands like them throughout this country. It was and remains the fact that it is the ordinary foot soldiers, people like the Eustaces, who were and are the heroes of the Labor Party.

In the Labor Party in Ipswich I witnessed the personal abuse and intimidation which came in the wake of the Split. To gain or maintain control, numbers were crudely stacked at meetings. Party veterans arrived at ordinary branch meetings with the rule book and standing orders in one hand and provocatively drafted resolutions in the other. The Groupers, if you supported the Split, or the 'dupes' or 'Coms', if you did not, would be sorted out with bare-knuckle debating tactics, crude resolutions, and Divisions called on the slightest pretext. I was actively on the side of the anti-Groupers. It was not a period for neutrality. Once the Split opened up the Party, one was either for or against. People who tried to take the middle ground were trampled into the dust. I confess with embarrassment now that I enjoyed the elemental conflict then as a conflictive rationalist, something of a narrow bigot in many ways, even a sectarian anti-Catholic. There was a lot of like-minded company about. In my defence, at least I commenced to realise earlier than most how much damage this shoddy, public donnybrook was causing for the Party. More than that, I became uneasy at the way decent people were being traduced merely because they were Catholics. Things came to a head later when, unwisely, I got into a punch-up at the back of the Racehorse Hotel at Bundamba one night defending the political reputation of my mate Jack Eustace, an event which forced me to sort out some of my contradictory views and to slag off much of the dross of sectarian prejudice.

Campaigning methods were rather slapdash back in 1961 when I first contested the Federal Division of Oxley. Party members relied on hunches or instincts and drew heavily on partisanship and prejudice in developing their campaign strategies. The State Office of the Party, without any appreciation of the high risk involved, depended on electorate intelligence coming from Party members in the various electorates to guide it in its overall campaign planning. One weekend, after I had won the preselection, I sat down with a large wad of tables covering several previous elections in Oxley. I made a few startling discoveries. The prevailing wisdom, that

Ipswich would look after itself as a Labor area but the country had to be won over, and that therefore most of the effort should go into the country while Ipswich could be taken for granted, was plain wrong. Over time this strategy had made little detectable impact on country voting. On the other hand, the Federal Labor vote in Ipswich was notably less than the combined Labor vote for the sitting Labor State parliamentarians representing that city. If we were able to capture their vote, then the big deficit we had to overcome was markedly reduced. There was agonised resistance to the new tactic of putting the major effort into Ipswich; I was squandering the wisdom of a generation.

The Oxley Federal Division embraced 18 000 square kilometres and was heavily populated with numerous large country centres. Effective campaigning was going to be demanding. Firstly, branches had to be formed in the country for all previously existing branches there had been destroyed by the Split. In Ipswich, too, a number of new branches had to be established for similar reasons, but more often to countervail the considerable negativity towards me which was seeping out of some existing branches. In a few branches, where key members included flotsam and jetsam from the old Grouper organisation, attitudes towards me bordered on the poisonous because of my friendships with 'lefties' and 'Coms'.

Throughout the twelve-month campaign Dallas regularly accompanied me, cradling our first born, Michaela, in her arms. By the time we were late into the campaign Dallas was well advanced in her second pregnancy. Her faith in what I would achieve never flagged, while I went through cyclical periods of doubt. We travelled in our second-hand frog-green FJ Holden, a cantankerous lump of metal and machinery sullenly spitting out an oily spume of exhaust smoke everywhere we went. In that eminently retirable thing, we covered the electorate. Dallas would clamber up on the bonnet, helping me nail election posters to trees or power poles, or would rummage in the boot, dragging out a rather antiquated public address system which we would set up at pig and calf and cattle sales, or on street corners in country towns. In this process contacts were made, the 'good Labor' men and women were identified and bit by bit we strung together our organisation. Ipswich party supporters rostered themselves to accompany us on these forays. A tremendous *esprit* developed. We all knew the odds were against us but everyone was determined to give it a go, to keep firing their best shots. Eventually we felt the excitement mix with hope, and then, in the way of these campaigns, a late but cautious confidence started to set in.

Somewhere at the midpoint of our campaign Gough Whitlam arrived in the course of a whistlestop tour of part of the State by motor car. We were near the end of his punishing itinerary and he was near the end of his rather short fuse. The public address system broke down as he was about to speak and we were treated to a pyrotechnic display of the Whitlam temper! We were all impressed at the imaginative effect to which he could put the English language, especially its basic Anglo-Saxonisms. My supporters desperately wanted him to declare Labor would win the Oxley Division. Gough was too cagey for that. He had studied the voting figures. He was confident that history would note his record closely, much as it did that of Alexander the Great, and so accordingly, any prognostications from him had to be the sober comment of a statesman. 'There is no doubt,' he said with careful measure, 'you have put in a magnificent campaign' [modest cheers]. 'I am confident Labor will win government' [unselfconscious cheers]. 'Labor winning Oxley will certainly guarantee we form a Labor government' [enthusiastic cheering]. The troops were ecstatic. 'Yer 'ear 'im Bill? He reckons we'll win in Oxley, whacko'. . . He might not have exactly said that, but it would have been imprudent to have disabused them in their enthusiasm.

Early Saturday morning, 9 December 1961, election day, and I was sitting on the edge of our bed in the gerontrified timber home we rented at Dinmore. What seemed to have been an infinity of tiring, tedious activity was over. My outward exuberant optimism which had helped spark and keep alive local enthusiasms, crumpled. Stark reality took over. We were in deep personal debt. Our car, necessary for mobility because of where we lived, was on its last few gasps before giving up the ghost completely. I could not eat. My stomach felt empty and squeamish. I was panicky. It was a strange sensation.

I recall, as I sat on the bed, thinking that I had over-reached myself, that someone with my sort of background had been grossly presumptuous to think of seriously deposing the sitting member, Dr Donald Cameron. He was Minister for Health, from a long-established local family; his grandfather was principal of the Ipswich Grammar School between 1875 and 1900. It was the first secondary school in Queensland, founded in 1863. Donald Cameron himself was properly respected for his numerous acts of charity and even more so his wife, Rhoda, who, with a few other people of social conscience, pioneered Aboriginal welfare rights long before it became fashionable. Dr Cameron was chieftain of the highland pipe bands, for one of which Dallas' father had been a piper and later a pipe major. Most of her several uncles and even more numerous cousins had been members of the band. In the fifties these were extremely important community links. To top it off Dr Cameron had been Dallas' family doctor and had even delivered her. Clearly the seat had been ready to move to Labor for some time. It was Cameron's great personal appeal and poor campaigning strategy by Labor which delayed its transfer to Labor.

The night, tired and old, was about to pass away. The vote coming in showed we had a chance, then we were ahead. My great fear that we could be toppled as the country vote registered was unjustified and, although Whitlam had been wrong and Menzies formed the government, I went to bed that night the new Member for Oxley. Dallas had been magnificent throughout the campaign. Her energies never flagged. Nor did her personal support and confidence wane. That night, as we went to bed, we embraced as an expression of love and mutual support. The uncertainty had exhausted itself as it had nearly depleted us. Dallas put the palm of my hand on her distended tummy to feel the baby kicking. New life, new hope, another generation, an added reason for wanting to succeed in life. Then Dallas suddenly buried her face into my neck and wept. She, too, had been apprehensive but had better self-discipline than I. There is sturdy material in the inner core of her personality that comes, I suspect, from her Scottish-Presbyterian background.

The splits of the fifties

The 1961 national election was an extraordinary turnaround for Labor so soon after the crippling splits of the fifties. During this period, there had been a great schism in the Labor Party, first in Victoria in 1954, followed by Queensland in 1957, which split the party wide open throughout Australia. A shadowy Catholic organisation called the Movement, which had powerful church backing, had been set up earlier to combat communism. It did this in workplaces by operating secretly, organising cells known as Industrial Groups (the members of which became known derogatively as 'groupers') to counter communist influence, in particular in trade unions. Paradoxically, the Movement, in its concept and functioning, applied Leninist techniques to fight Marxism-Leninisn in the community. With the splits of 1954 and 1957 those people who remained faithful to the objectives of the Industrial Groups, including many from the Labor Party and the trade unions, formed breakaway anti-Communist Labor Parties (as they were described by their members) in the various states. These vigorously assailed Labor which, in turn, attacked them with equal asperity.

The Movement reputedly had plans to take control of various institutions in the community, like the public services, police forces and justice systems, by having people faithful to it appointed to key offices, and in this way have the objectives of Catholic social theory implemented as general policy. Control of the Labor Party, as the political element capable of legislating for such policies, when in government, was essential to this strategy. Accordingly, its struggle within the Labor Party, which was ultimately about power over and control of the party, led the Movement into aggressive conflict with many party members who were not communist but who resisted this encroachment. This struggle also spilled over into the affiliated trade union movement. These forces exploded into the Labor splits of the fifties. The splits were avoidable and, moreover, I am quite convinced that the degree of influence available to and the level of encroachment achieved by the Movement were much exaggerated, sometimes by those with a sectarian motive for doing this.

The device which set off these fissionable forces within the Party was a public statement of October 1954 by Dr H. V. Evatt, then Labor Opposition Leader. He made it without consultation in a desperate and inexcusably selfish effort to save his sagging leadership.[4] Not for the first or last time in his career Evatt put his personal ambitions ahead of any other interests, such as those of the Labor Party. He might have saved his leadership in 1954, but he bequeathed Labor a legacy of more than two decades of internal division and self-evisceration, keeping it trapped in Opposition.

Much can be made, justifiably, of Evatt's formidable contribution to the creation and formulation of the United Nations, however, a considerable part of the effort was self-serving.[5] His incommensurable defence of basic individual rights in, effectively, single-handedly stomping the country to defeat Menzies' draconian 1951 Communist Party Dissolution referendum cemented his reputation as a civil libertarian. His first instinct, though, had been to allow the Bill to pass uncontested as he feared a forthcoming national election. The Labor Party Parliamentary Executive forced him to change ground and oppose the Bill.[6] Evatt's approach was always uneven: as an historian he ignored Premier Holman's ruthless treatment of Industrial Workers of the World activists; as Attorney-General, he detached himself from the oppressive government treatment of the hapless, harmless and benighted members of the Australia First Movement in the 1940s, a pro-Aryan, anti-Semitic, anti-Communist, nationalist organisation which was markedly unpopular, uninfluential, and totally ineffective with the Australian public. The harmless if eccentric Inky Stephensen, one of the founders of the Movement, whose main offence seemed to be a degree of ratbaggery, was interned for three-and-a-half years. He was only released when John Burton, Evatt's Department Secretary, forged Evatt's signature on the release document which Evatt had held indecisively for three months.[7] No wonder Hasluck concluded that the conduct of the matter, '. . . was undoubtedly the grossest infringement of individual liberty made during the war and the tardiness in rectifying it was a matter of shame to the democratic institution and to the authorities concerned'.[8] There was, and has been, no evidence produced that the Australia First Movement was a risk to our national security during World War II. Evatt's position contrasted emphatically with his staunch defence of the basic rights of the detained Communists Ratliff and Thomas the year before in 1941.[9]

For the Labor Party Evatt's positive contributions to the United Nations and in the field of civil liberties are, nonetheless, more than negated by the characteristically impulsive, wilful, self-serving behaviour he showed in 1954. The remarkable thing is that for having left a legacy of political ruin and desolation, where he was supposed to have created a government, he became canonised as another martyred hero of Labor, an enduring party icon. At an obscure book launch in Sydney on 5 October 1954, and reported graphically on the front page of the Sydney Morning Herald the next day, he made what was accurately reported as a 'bitter attack' against what he described as a 'small minority group' whom he accused of 'disloyal and subversive actions'. They were guilty of '[a]dopting methods which strikingly resemble Communist and Fascist infiltration of larger groups'. . . . The cognoscenti read 'Communist' to mean trade union official, Victorian State Labor Secretary, and former Communist Party member, Dinny Lovegrove. For 'Fascist' they read Bob Santamaria, mastermind of the Church-backed Catholic Social Studies Movement, or Movement, as it was known in the vernacular. To label Santamaria in this way may have been politically convenient, in a sectarian and racist fashion, because of his alleged Italian and Spanish family lineage. It was, however, not one of Evatt's more charitable acts in those less ethnically tolerant times.

Lovegrove's ineffable sin was, having become disaffected with the corrupt and sometimes physically vicious tactics within trade unions of the Communist Party, to become an apostate of this faith, exposing and denouncing its excesses. He did this at a time when too many among us—I was one—artlessly thought we saw a workers' paradise in the thicket of Marx's tendentious bombast. Of course, true democracy would only come with the 'dictatorship of the proletariat'; and of course, nothing could be more obvious nor just! That some of us, like me, could so readily believe the catchphrases of tyrants and their more numerous dupes, is a testament to how little we knew and how naive we were.

Santamaria meanwhile was, and remains, an implacably romantic distributivist. This does not make him a fascist, as some have claimed. Distributivism is a radical, if impractical, alternative to capitalism, not a handmaiden of it. As an ideology or philosophy, its aims are to break up large concentrations of wealth, while resisting human bondage to the machines of industrialism, as well as to invoke the revival of small-scale family farming, and small units in trade and industry, while giving encouragement to the craftsman.[10] In its nature it stands to the left of the prevailing market force ideology of recent Labor governments in Canberra, as Santamaria's regular newspaper commentaries demonstrate. At the same time that many on the left of the political spectrum were denouncing these 'decadent' political tendencies, there were among their number quite a few extolling the simple humanism of G. D. H. Cole and his Guild Socialism. This was merely a variation on the theme of the distributivists. Jim Cairns of the left, scion of good causes, was one such. Through the ages people have sought to escape from the rigorous imperatives of technical progress by smashing machines. Santamaria's vision may have been one of bucolic escapism, indisputably based on defective economics. Nonetheless, I suspect history will treat him not uncritically but more kindly than the detractors in his time. He was more correct on the nature of communism than a great number of them, including me at an earlier age. His flaw was zealotry, which always distorts attempts at credible analysis of the forces and weaknesses of postwar communism.

The fact is the activities of the Industrial Groups were scarcely a surprise to Evatt or any other senior official in the Labor Party by late 1954. The Industrial Groups enjoyed official recognition and formal support within the Labor Party from about 1945. Evatt excoriated Santamaria and his organisational tactics in October 1954, but only six months earlier had sought Santamaria's electoral support in a manner which was self-abasing. Evatt twice invited him to Canberra to assist in writing the 1954 election policy speech. He sought to woo Santamaria with the promise of making Keon, one of only two members of the Movement in Caucus, a minister in the event of winning the election.[11] He attempted to draw Santamaria into a conspiracy to depose Pat Kennelly, a Catholic opposing the Industrial Groups and Federal Secretary of the Labor Party, replacing him with either of two known Groupers. Archbishop Mannix believed Evatt's 'support for the Groups, however motivated, was important'.[12] In a desperate but clumsy effort to shore up his failing position as Opposition Leader he asked Lovegrove (leader of the Victorian Industrial Groups, among the many active roles he formally discharged within the Labor Party), whether Lovegrove 'could arrange for the Victorian executive [of the Labor Party] to pass a vote of confidence in [Evatt's] leadership'. Lovegrove's reply was reputedly unprintable but amounted to 'no'.[13] Clyde Cameron, former left wing Member of the House of Representatives, post-Split supporter of Evatt, of Presbyterian background with instinctive dark suspicions of Catholics, believes that 'had Evatt won the 1954 election he would have been a Grouper himself. He would have done whatever Santamaria told him to do.'[14]

Evatt was in deep trouble within the Party at the time he precipitated the Split and it was all his own work. His unilateral inclusion in the 1954 election policy speech of a number of uncosted, extravagant and distributively regressive promises provoked justifiable outrage on the part of many Caucus members. A little later, before the Royal Commission into Espionage that followed the defection of a Soviet MVD agent and his wife in Australia, the Petrovs, Evatt's strange behaviour left many wondering whether there was evidence of some symptom in his behaviour of an intellectually corrosive disability. His letter to the Foreign Minister for the USSR, Molotov, in the course of the Royal Commission hearing, inquiring whether the Soviet Union really did have spies in Australia and Molotov's 'reassuring' denial, exposed him to widespread ridicule. In the Caucus a vote of confidence resolution in Evatt's leadership was put on 20 October 1954. Evatt survived the challenge, but not before he and some of his more belligerent supporters irrevocably rent the rotting fabric of Caucus solidarity. Eddie Ward, the East Sydney 'firebrand', demanded a division so that the 'backsliders' would have to declare themselves. Evatt clambered onto the Caucus table to better identify friend from foe, shouting 'Get their names, get their names!'. Meanwhile Ward, in an ostentatious and threatening manner, recorded the names of those who voted for the resolution. Several New South Wales members, including Fred Daly, were moving across the room to vote against the resolution when they became so appalled by this heavy-handed intimidation that they wheeled about and voted affirmatively. It was theatre Grand Guignol, played out passionately but unedifyingly. Next day the newspapers of the nation carried all the names of those who voted in support of the resolution against Evatt. This vindictive 'leak' was designed to cause difficulties for the named among their branch members. It worked in most cases.

The atmospherics of that meeting, especially its unbridled anti-Catholicism from some quarters with obviously deeper roots than the specific issue before the Caucus, can be gauged from the following exchanges:

> Eddie Ward: 'Why don't you name the men who will stab Dr Evatt in the back later?'
>
> Keon: 'You're one!'
>
> Ward: 'That's a deliberate lie! . . . And now you're threatening Evatt with a writ if he tells the truth about you. You denied Ben Chifley in the Parliament when he told the truth about the corruption of popes in the Middle Ages. Now you're carrying out a campaign of political terrorism and branding those who won't stoop to your level as being anti-Catholic. Your sole aim is to exterminate the Coms and you'll use the methods of Communism to do it. You'll lie, you'll smear, and you'll destroy every decent Labor principle to win your way. There's nothing in the Bible, that I know of, to defend what you're doing. You and your mates are more in line with Menzies and his mob than with the great ideals of the Labor Party . . . Your mob take your orders from News Weekly and Pope Santamaria.'[15]

The Catholics were not reluctant to give as good as they got:

> Bill Bourke: 'You [Evatt], the anti-Catholic sectarian smearer that you are, phoned Santamaria to get his view on the nature of your policy speech . . .'[16]

There was a National Executive inquiry into Evatt's rather thin and poorly substantiated allegations. The flimsy official record shows this to have been a travesty of due processes and natural justice if ever there was one.[17] Evatt's position was upheld but his allegations were unsubstantiated. This was followed by a National Executive meeting which did some prodigiously unusual things. The Victorian State Executive of the Party was the heartland of Movement-manipulated opposition to Evatt. If these Groupers could be cleaned out, control of the Party would tip into the hands of the anti-Groupers who were more interested in achieving this than protecting Evatt. Evatt was merely a handy tool in this process. Thus he became an icon within the Party, not because of any inherent greatness, but because it was political convenience to some to have him seen as such. An instant increase in the Victorian Party membership was arranged through a narrow decision of the National Executive. Thus the Grouper Victorian Executive was suddenly under serious challenge. But while in Melbourne this executive was expelling people disloyal to it, the new anti-Grouper executive, with the endorsement of the National Executive, was doing exactly the same to other people, in another part of town. Each executive was thus claiming to be the authentic Labor Executive. The outcome of that dispute was critical to legitimacy in the eyes of the foot soldiers in the Party and to control of the Party through the National Conference.

Clyde Cameron's inestimable and often unorthodox organising abilities were spectacularly successful in this process. Cameron discovered through a confidential contact that certain 'cast iron' delegations to National Conference were going to split open as some delegates had secretly decided to flaunt their State Executive's instruction to endorse the anti-Grouper executive at Conference. These defectors, with other delegates, would give a combined majority vote endorsing the Grouper Victorian delegation. In turn, with this majority vote, the actions of the Grouper Victorian Executive and the role of the Movement could have been upheld, while Evatt would have been destroyed. Cameron arranged for a special National Executive meeting to be held immediately before the 1955 National Conference in Hobart where the anti-Grouper Victorian delegation was endorsed as the legitimate representative of that State. This was a gross and blatant violation of party rules, usurping the supreme authority of National Conference over all other organs of the Party.

The Premier of Queensland, Vince Gair, was furious. He recognised he had been outsmarted by an unscrupulous misuse of rules by someone else. He sought to storm into the conference chamber with the Victorian Grouper delegation. That would have been a disaster, for the Grouper delegation would have mustered enough numbers to have the interventionists repudiated by Conference. And so followed some rough counter measures, typical of those less fastidious times. Cameron arranged for Gair and his cronies to be locked out of the conference hall by the doorkeeper, Bill Ramsay. Gair marched off in high dudgeon with his seventeen delegates and the six Victorian Grouper delegates to convene a boycott conference of their own. This gave control of conference to the interventionists who with only thirteen delegates were short of a quorum but with the six anti-Grouper delegates from Victoria added could muster a quorum and determine all votes.

The process was not precise as to scruple but was undeniably effective. Cameron and his interventionist colleagues accordingly controlled Conference and thus determined the destiny of Labor over the next couple of decades. In one of those great ironies which characterise politics, a little over a decade-and-a-half later Cameron, at last responsibly confronting the intolerable damage done to the Party by the sustained sectarianism of the Victorian anti-Grouper Executive, would work unrelentingly to scourge it from office.[18] Cameron, if he ever stopped to think about these two contradictory roles, must have felt like an infanticide. He was, however, a man for action rather than one who dallied over abstractions.

Evatt was judged winner of this tactical battle, but he lost the larger strategic struggle. At the 1954 national election Labor won 50.5 per cent of the two party preferred vote, but because a high proportion of its votes were heavily concentrated in certain regions, it narrowly missed out on government. Next year, with Evatt as leader again, his 'victory' over the Groupers and his extraordinary tactics in relation to the Petrov Royal Commission still fresh in the minds of everyone, the Labor vote slumped dreadfully to 46.5 per cent, two party preferred. This great doctrinal schism was unnecessary. Functioning through secret cell structures according to Leninist principles, the Movement and its minions the Groupers, had achieved only modest success in wresting control of unions from the Communists. With limited achievement of its own and the Communist threat in the trade unions receding by attrition from other sources, the Industrial Groups membership contracted. In the trade union and Labor movements non-Communist members had been fighting back successfully against the Movement's grander plans to take over unions and State branches of the ALP more generally. Catholic Action was on the defensive. Catholic unionists and Party members were deserting the Industrial Groups. They were appalled by the Groups' over-zealous pursuit, not so much of Communists, but of imagined fellow-travellers whose main offence was not to collaborate with the Groups. Determined action from within would have defeated it without crippling the Labor movement over the long term.

One notable Grouper victory against the Communists was Laurie Short's gaining control of the key heavy industry Ironworkers' Union from Ernie Thornton and the Communist Party. Short's success was greatly assisted by a rising Sydney industrial solicitor, Jim McClelland. McClelland recounted to me on a number of occasions how he had helped 'bankroll' Short's campaign and how he had directed much of that successful activity. Thereafter, according to McClelland's accounts, he remained close to Short, and his legal firm was consistently briefed by the Ironworkers' Union—a most propitious outcome all round, tangibly so for McClelland.

Part of the McClelland team, in the battle for the Ironworkers' Union, was an emerging industrial advocate of the Sydney Bar, later to become much excoriated as Governor-General, John Kerr. According to claims made to me by McClelland—after Kerr's appointment as Governor-General, but before the lead-up to and the fateful events of 11 November, 1975—the former had warmly pressed Kerr's appointment on Labor Prime Minister Gough Whitlam, in spite of Whitlam's initial reservations. McClelland was influential as a loyal but often unsteady lieutenant of Whitlam's (especially after dinner). Ironically, after the 1975 constitutional crisis which destroyed the Whitlam Government, McClelland spent much time publicly denouncing Kerr, no doubt to appease the guilt he sometimes privately confessed over his role, as he described it to me, in influencing Kerr's appointment. It has to be said that McClelland was too harsh on himself privately, just as he was too fierce towards Kerr publicly.

In spite of the instructive example of the Victorian Split, the Queensland branch of the Labor Party lumbered inexorably on to its own appointment with calamity. In 1957 a schism opened up between the State Members of Parliament and the trade union movement. It was ostensibly about issues of principle, such as three weeks' annual leave for the workforce, opposition to the government's intention to back an independent oil distributor in an effort to break the oligopoly of established oil suppliers, and defending the independence of the University of Queensland. The first was understandable on the part of trade unions, although the Brisbane *Courier-Mail* hectored and lectured the government about the economic irresponsibility of conceding on this proposition. For the trade union movement to have become a sort of paladin in defence of the oil companies at that time reeked of political opportunism. The synthetic alarm of the trade unions on the third score, no matter how justified it was otherwise in principle, was best summed up by the Premier, Vince Gair, who challenged a union official with, 'I'll bet twenty quid you can't even spell academic!'. Gair was not out of pocket by a brass razoo as a result of the wager.

At this point a power broker of earthy charm and of enormous and relentless ambition, Jack Egerton of the Boilermakers' Union, was emerging within the party structure. He struck up an otherwise unlikely alliance of convenience with Schmella and Bukowski of the Australian Workers' Union. The craft unions and the huge AWU distrusted one another, the former regarding the latter as an industrial scavenger of union membership which, in a great number of cases, they believed should belong to them. Hitherto, the AWU had fairly much set the political agenda for Queensland through its effective control of the selection of most of the Parliamentary Labor Party membership. With Gair, a Labor leader capable of impetuous displays of abrupt, arrogant and stubborn behaviour, the AWU suddenly found its influence dismissed, especially in regard to a long-running and raggedly conducted industrial dispute within the shearing industry. A coalition of dissent against the State Labor Government was securely, if briefly, welded together between many formerly incompatible groups.

After some false starts the Queensland Central Executive, as the State executive council was then known, in April 1957 called on Gair to show cause why he should not be expelled from the Party for failing to follow the directions of that august and omnipotent body. Gair was conflictive and intransigent. The *Courier-Mail* vigorously barracked for him. Within a matter of weeks Gair, his cronies and the State Labor Government were history; the last State Labor government for thirty-three years. If Gair had been a little bending, even only slightly adroit, he might have avoided the split which occurred when he marched out of the Labor Party with most of his Ministry to form the Queensland Labor Party. The fact is, however, there were forces, directed by Jack Doherty of the AWU in collaboration with Joe Chamberlain of the left in Western Australia, and using Brisbane-based AWU officer Joe Bukowski as the hatchet man, who were determined to drive Gair from the party. After Gair's apostasy at Hobart in 1955 and his increasingly confrontationist attitude towards certain union leaders who were used to compliance from 'their' State parliamentarians, there was a fear he would undermine their control of the National Executive and Conference of the Party. Simply stated, Gair had to go!

The incoming Liberal–Country Party government quickly legislated for three weeks' annual leave. The economy did not turn belly-up as predicted by the newspapers, in fact the *Courier-Mail* seemed to have been struck instantly with acute laryngitis on the subject. Egerton went on to become State President of the Queensland Trades and Labour Council and State President of the Queensland branch of the Labor Party—a truly meteoric rise. Henceforth Egerton's handy, if not necessarily faithful, allies in the AWU were quickly scourged from the Party, their political usefulness spent. Over the numerous sterile, dismal years of Opposition following that Split, purges of non-conforming State parliamentarians were not uncommon.

The splits in Victoria and Queensland removed from the party the narrow, intolerant influences of Catholic Action and the Movement. These were replaced with a large dose of sectarian anti-Catholicism masquerading as 'principled left wingism'. A new form of intolerance was substituted for the old. A surprising number of the new leaders, like Egerton and Milliner, were Masons, just as a large number of those deposed had been Catholics. In the meantime the reputation of Evatt within Labor suffered no great harm, if indeed any at all. The 'Doc', as he was affectionately known by the trusting foot soldiers in the Party, was seen as a statesman of consistently high principle but rather too unschooled in the ways of devious politicians. He was characterised as a victim of the conspiracies and back-stabbing of others. This was and remains an utter misreading not only of his enormous capacity for crafty, self-serving conduct, but the flaws in his political judgment, and the general problem of a perhaps faltering personality. He was the cause of one of Labor's greatest and longest running disasters and he should be held accountable for that.

In spite of all the contumely heaped upon their heads, generally most Catholics stuck with Labor. Even at the crest of the success of the DLP, the so-called Catholic party, two out of three Catholics were voting against it. There is an important postscript to all this. The reverberations from Labor's various splits reached out well beyond the Party. None of the major institutions touched by the splits remained unchanged. Certainly not the Party itself, which went through a series of convulsions, culminating in National Executive intervention in Victoria in 1970 and Queensland in 1980 in the interests of re-establishing a healthier equilibrium.

New South Wales was the most successful State branch in warding off the impact of the splits. Cardinal Gilroy, Bishop J. Carroll and Labor Premier Cahill had observed the harmful, divisive effects of crude, reactive sectarianism directed against Church and Labor in 1922. Then, an over-confident but disastrous Catholic electoral drive in the guise of the Democratic Party resulted in the complete repudiation of that party, the decimation of Labor which was seen as Catholic-dominated, and the election for three years of the Fuller Government which 'was not just Protestant; it was militantly Protestant and anti-Catholic'.[19] Gilroy, Carroll and Cahill successfully warded off the splits of the fifties in New South Wales to preserve Church and Labor. A consequence was that, whereas old-style Irish tribal politics were cleansed from Labor's stables in Victoria and Queensland as a result of the splits, they were and remain preserved in New South Wales. As a distinct political style, with its brassy, 'corner cutting', and clubby backroom dealings, it is very much in harmony with the general personality of Sydney, but never much likely to succeed elsewhere. In all important respects, it should be remembered, Sydney remains faithful to its roots, set down so deeply with its foundation in 1788—Sydney, as the larrikin capital of Australia, is consistently truer to its colourful past than any other part of Australia.

Curiously, however, the Liberal Party was not immune from the aftershock of the Labor Split either. With the exception of the near-run results of the 1961 election, Menzies was never really stretched in holding government. Even 1961 had more to do with a clumsy and ill-timed credit squeeze than bold or imaginative tactics adopted by Labor. As was the case with other advanced economies, Australia enjoyed sustained economic growth and prosperity during the first quarter century after the war, that period now rather pretentiously termed the 'Menzies era'. Our success was derivative and due more to good luck than masterful management of the Australian economy. It was the happy product of real growth elsewhere. Government was sponging off wool, wheat, meat and mineral booms to maintain national prosperity indefinitely. Further, other countries were extracting better and more lasting benefits and accordingly better growth prospects from sustained postwar international prosperity than was Australia.

The structural defects in our economy and its narrow export base, comprised of items for which growth in demand was less than growth in world trade, was already becoming evident with the terms of trade progressively turning against us. No matter, Menzies took the credit for our good fortune and left the good times to keep rolling along with their own momentum, as if they were an entirely reasonable gift from heaven. In any event, post-Split Labor was too preoccupied with political self-mutilation to really train its attention on Menzies and the wider political processes. It was too easy for Menzies to win elections. He would concoct a threat to the national security, and then Labor would ritually over-react, isolating itself from the few who were more thoughtful in the community and the more numerous who were timorous. Coalition backbenchers would boisterously take up an anti-Communist chant orchestrated by Menzies. The breakaway DLP would deliver preference votes in marginal seats to these good little exorcists of communism—the degree of goodness being measured according to the volume of anti-Communist din and puffery they generated—and there was nothing else those people needed to do to win or hold seats. The reward for these Communist bounty hunters was DLP preference votes. Easy success fostered indolence among the coalition partners and with laziness came feebleness. Menzies' practice of shipping off to distant places strong ministers who might become competitors further enfeebled his party. A form of institutionalised decay had set in. Any knack for creative policy thinking among the Liberals slowly atrophied over the years. When Menzies departed the parliamentary scene, the cost of this attrition to creative and organisational energies became progressively apparent, glaringly so by 1972. Even now, the Liberal Party is still floundering in a desperate search for direction and regeneration. The fact is, Menzies more or less exclusively controlled his party's political development, effectively stifling its healthy evolution with the imposition of the values of his generation, a generation whose time had come and gone.

This process of political decay was accelerated in the sixties and onwards by the alienation of a younger, better educated and more independent generation of Australians. The generation which abhorred and repudiated Australian involvement, and in particular conscription for service, in the Vietnam War also rejected avuncular authority and no longer thoughtlessly accepted anything *ex cathedra*. The Liberal Party lost a large part of a political generation through this social trend. The Liberals' problems were further exacerbated by the great spiritual void at the core of Liberalism. Liberals existed dominantly because of what they opposed; in the words of Menzies their founder, they were, 'an instrument to combat communistic and socialistic [read Labor] influences which daily are making inroads into the lives of the people'.[20] If Menzies could make this form of negative identification sit very well, his successors were less capable. The negative appeal once offered by the Liberals now exists as an empty, irrelevant husk after thirteen years of successful Labor administration during which people have come to feel comfortable with a more competitive society, a moderate, sustained and successful foreign policy enjoying bipartisan support, their money safe in the banks, and so on. More than that, Labor has control of the political middle ground and—because of the genius of its factional structure and operations—a good swathe of the political territory to the immediate left and right of that middle ground. By continually returning to the past in an attempt to refresh itself, the Liberal Party is in danger of terminal collapse.

The social trends which served to undermine the Liberal Party also adversely affected the Catholic Church. Taking a prominent political role during the Labor splits, the Church was equally aggressive and intolerant later in support of Australian involvement in the Vietnam conflict. The adverse consequences were profound and long-term. The simple Irish rustic values of much of the priesthood, their tendency towards autocracy in dealing with the parish faithful, their presumption that as intermediaries between God and humankind they had authority to deliberate on matters well beyond their theological charter, merely exasperated and estranged much of a rising generation of young, educated Catholics. Priests thundered sermons in direct conflict with the resolution of the 1969 Catholic Bishops' Conference defending the right of conscientious objection, including to a particular war. This did little except add to the confusion and alienation in the parishes. Lay people reacted and the domineering power of the bishops was broken. There was more to this process than alienation over the Vietnam War, but that conflict acted as the catalyst for much lay disenchantment with the Church and is another reason why a good deal of the *social* direction of the Church is now in the hands of lay people, frequently quite radical in their social values.

The greatest loser in this complex process was the Australian community. With Labor so debilitated and the political process so easy to manipulate, Menzies more or less adopted a comfortable armchair attitude towards governing the country. There was no pressure from Labor for him to perform, to confront mounting challenges, such as the increasingly evident uncompetitiveness of Australian industry other than the farming and mining sectors. There was a limit to how long he could prudently allow large slices of the profitability of the mining and farming industries to be carved off through protection to subsidise economically inefficient, labour-intensive manufacturing industries, an area where we had distinct comparative disadvantages. That limit has long been exceeded and is a major factor in explaining why Australia has plummeted from eighth among the developed countries of the world on a per capita national income basis in 1950 to sixteenth today. The human and material strain and pain of our past decade, as government has struggled hard to make the Australian economy more efficient and able to survive in a keenly competitive world, is a cost for which the Menzies Liberal governments have much to answer.

But in the same era Labor, too, was culpable, for it went on indulging its internal discontent and accordingly failed to make the conservatives accountable for their neglect. And Labor was as boldly protectionist as any of Menzies' governments, while its notion of welfare policy was, like Menzies', almost limited to bidding for votes with an offer of an extra 'few bob' for pensioners. In fairness to the record, Menzies notched up some important national achievements over that very long period he held office. The community became better housed and much better educated because of his policies. He introduced a voluntary, national health insurance scheme, although it was designed more to meet the ideological and income expectations of the medical profession rather than the best interests of the public. All these favoured higher income groups and were notably regressive in their redistributional impact.[21] For instance, after tax subsidies, health insurance contributions were increasingly cheaper the higher one went up the income scale. The inescapable conclusion is that Menzies was an ardent practitioner of middle-class welfarism.

While the early postwar global economy was bountiful for Australia, and the domestic economy then less complex to manage than now, the Menzies governments, with a couple of notable exceptions, were cautious economic managers and tended to equivocate instead of acting decisively as economic difficulties loomed.[22] Menzies managed an effective public service administrative system, building on the substantial foundations he inherited from Chifley, and consolidating its independence. In this regard he retained many earlier Labor appointees in spite of opposition from within his party. Most significantly, he upheld the principles by which the Westminster Parliamentary system functioned, respecting the forms and procedures according to which the House worked. Sadly, there have been lapses in these standards at times in the succeeding years. In particular the rights of the Opposition were largely respected and most notably, in contrast to developments since Menzies, question time generally moved along at a quick and productive pace with sharp observations *ad hominem* rather rare. His style was distinguished and seignorial, but perhaps a little 'stagy' and dated, at least when I entered Parliament in 1961. In my earlier years much was made of his being well connected with the rich and powerful. Yet, having forsaken a successful and rewarding practice as a King's Counsel for a long career in public life, he proved on retirement to be a man of modest means.

The long trudge to government begins

In spite of the disarray of Labor following the trials, tribulations and devastation of the still recent Split in Queensland, there I was, standing in the Labor Opposition Caucus room, in the national Parliament. It was a sparkling, bright morning in Canberra,

Monday, 20 February 1962. The clarity of that best of all mornings was blinding, the freshness of the day exhilarating. I do confess I was more than a tad excited, so much so that events whirred along episodically. It was all very much a blur, the action jerky and disjointed, like the play of an old-fashioned movie reel.

Icons of the Hayden household, heroes of Labor, came and went as tangible, corporeal people. There was Arthur Calwell, architect and first manager of the massive postwar immigration programme which positively transformed the cultural mindset of this country. Feisty Eddie Ward, the man admired at home for never backing away from a fight with the class enemy, sauntered nearby, shaking hands casually in passing. In my innocence and excitement, however, it would be some time before I came to understand that there were dark, ugly sides to these two very public personas. Driven by ambitions even larger than their not inconsiderable talents, they had frequently harried Prime Minister Curtin at a time when he was more than fully extended organising the national war effort. Both objected to the reasonable adoption of conscription for defence of Australian security within a perimeter extraordinarily close to the Australian mainland. It was, presumably, acceptable for American conscripts to fight in defence of interests, including major Australian ones, a long way from their country and close to Australia. Fair burden sharing was not a principle of much interest to them. Calwell's pejorative epithet, spat across the Caucus meeting room, that Curtin would end up 'leading a government from the other side', devastated Curtin. The implication was of gross disloyalty. The defections of Hughes and Lyons, acts of the greatest treachery in Labor's eyes, or more cruelly, the acts of Labor 'rats', were still raw in Caucus members' minds. Curtin withdrew from the Caucus, demanding that Calwell openly recant and Caucus repudiate his scandalous statement.[23] Calwell, humbled, had complied.

That first Monday was spent with innumerable procedural matters, most important of which was the election of a shadow

Cabinet, more properly described as the Federal Parliamentary Labor Party Executive. Most of us newly arrived members were unknown quantities as to our factional disposition. The formal extra-parliamentary structure of such things, at least in the smaller States in those days, was almost non-existent. We were generously fêted in the Members' Tea Room. Lashings of coffee or tea, toasted or plain sandwiches, even cakes if one's tastes ran to sweet things. Ah, it was wonderful; what was more, people really seemed to enjoy my clumsy attempts at anecdotal humour and appreciate reflective insights on the state of the nation, raw recruit though I was. Regrettably, it was not destined to last. By late morning this brittle adulation was flagging. By lunchtime it was stone dead. As soon as a person's factional disposition was established those of another inclination decided to waste no more time (even more importantly, money), on a hopeless case. Those of a similar factional position did not need to.

The balloting proceeded according to an exhaustive majority system. A candidate had to obtain 50 per cent plus one of the valid vote cast to be elected. There would be endless rounds of voting and with each round a few candidates would be elected, then a few more and so on. Procedurally, it was an exhaustive business. It was also physically exhausting. The voting continued until about 3 a.m. A long-serving Caucus member, his political soul pickled through extended immersion in cynicism, casually pointed out to me that the scrutineers were mostly the 'biggest blokes in Caucus'. 'That's so they can watch how you vote. If you deviate from the left or right ticket and you belong to that group, well, they'll make you pay for it. If you vote middle-of-the-road, they'll both roll over you. You'll get nothing.' Ballot papers were filled out on a long, open table on a verandah then next to the Caucus room. Scrutineers hovered about the shoulders of voters, peering intently at the ballot papers. No confidentiality there. Then more wisdom: 'Know why this process takes so long but is preferred? Between each round the left and right horse trade. On the basis of their aggregate vote they divvy up the positions and vote each other in. If you're not with one of them you get nothing'.

I initially proposed voting cubicles for privacy. There was stunned disbelief among the factions' barons. 'How could I have so little faith and confidence in my comrades? Didn't we all struggle for the same thing? Great matters of trust were at stake here.' In private I was told by Tom Uren, who could be a rather intimidating conversationalist, that I was a 'trouble-making little c . . . '. He was a big man with broad, strong shoulders, and a face that had blocked a hundred punches as a professional heavyweight boxer. When he set his angry features not more than a few centimetres from yours to let you know bluntly what he thought of you for failing to support one of his pet projects, he was quite capable of causing a mild quake—at least in the pit of the tummy. What to do? As luck had it I struck on a line which stopped him dead. 'Why is it big blokes like you always seem to enjoy bullying little fellows like me?'

Over the years and used sparingly, a comment such as this often had the required effect, for Uren saw himself consistently as few others did who dealt with him: kind, patient, considerate, receptive to other people's ideas, and above all else a lover of his fellow man. The tactic became to put both hands behind my back, tilt my jaw up slightly, and earnestly make the same remark or one similar. Henceforth, with a comment such as this Uren would lapse into a mess of apologies, with profuse assurances that I had misunderstood him.

In spite of our differences, I mostly liked Uren. He had a homespun faith in his simple democratic socialist beliefs (although he could become very aggressive with people who disagreed with him). But despite that he was very much against class systems, he often related a story that sometimes made me wonder, a story of how he fought for the British Empire Heavyweight Championship at Earl's Court Garden, London, just after the war. To get his chance, he had worked his way to London on a coal-burning tramp steamer as a stoker, punishingly hard work by any measure. 'Billy,' he would say (for when I was in favour he would use the diminutive and when I was out of favour he would snarl 'You'), 'Billy, it was the most memorable thing in my life. When I was introduced to the packed crowd the MC called out "My Lords, Ladies and gentlemen." Just imagine Billy; Lords and Ladies coming to see me, an ordinary old pick and shovel bloke like me, fight'. So it would go, and the innocent gleam in his eyes as he related this experience revealed he savoured this in itself as a kind of triumph. But it seems on that occasion Uren was reaching above his class, in more ways than one. He went on to lose the fight.

Over time we drifted further apart, for Uren put too much innocent trust in Moscow, and later Beijing, for my comfort. That aside, I had a number of unpleasant experiences defending him against charges, mainly from members of the NSW Right, that he was a Stalinist. Much as I was able to repudiate the claim, I do recall one tricky moment in the men's urinal on the top floor of the old Parliament House. I was standing beside the late Frank Stewart there one night in a most levelling, democratic fashion. It was sometime after dinner and as was Stewart's usual style at this hour, he was in a dark and belligerent mood, while his comments were hard to follow. I was defending Uren against a standard attack that Uren was a Stalinist. Stewart, who was zipping up his fly, was becoming heated. Suddenly his fist came up off the toggle on his fly, straight towards my jaw. I drew back and took off. Though Stewart was shorter than Uren, he was every bit as physically compact and tough—as for myself, it was a case of the triumph of discretion over valour.

Shortly after the debates on voting cubicles, I pursued the notion of preferential voting. I was part of a new generation moving into the Caucus; the old shellbacks felt uncomfortable with us but could not resist the influence of these new ideas. Despite considerable hostility, the proposals caught on and cubicles and preferential voting were eventually adopted. Such is human genius that these changes, predicted as disasters, proved an even more efficient process for sustaining the power brokers' control of the system. For example, when deals were made across factions the night before a ballot, each voter was paired with another member of the same faction. These then inspected each other's completed ballot paper. Failure to show was tantamount to deviation from the ticket and punishment could be swift and firm.

New Labor members were invited to join the Clerk of the House of Representatives, Mr Allan Turner, in his tiny office. A tall, lean, desiccated man of pale appearance, he looked positively ancient, with a face drained of the slightest hint of humour (a condition no doubt brought on by years of poring over the House Standing Orders and May's *Parliamentary Practice*, a lifetime's journey about as exciting as watching paint dry). I rather clumsily deprecated Menzies and more generally his party. Turner pondered my views for what seemed some time, accompanied by audible throat clearing as if something unpleasant was caught near his epiglottis. Then it came: 'Mr Hayden, Ben Chifley was one of the greatest men to go through this Parliament. He always said that not all of the best bowlers are in one team'. More audible throat clearing. I took a beady eye fix on him and mentally registered: 'Ideologically unsound . . . needs watching'. I recall the incident, very properly, with embarrassment.

Then came the big day, the formal opening of Parliament. The ceremony in the House of Representatives fascinated me. I was, nonetheless, shocked. There was Menzies, of whom I had heard so much but whom I had never seen before, sitting opposite me. I felt let down. He looked so disappointingly human. Not a hint of cloven hooves nor horns, let alone a hand-held red hot trident. The style of his suit in design could have been described as 'advanced obsolescence', a crumpled, double-breasted blue pinstripe. Now, I did not approve of *my* prime ministers dressing in crumpled suits! After some formalities, the members of the House of Representatives prepared to troop off to the Senate. There, the Parliament was formally opened with a speech by Viscount De L'Isle, the Governor-General. De L'Isle was dressed in the full ceremonial vice-regal rig. A cocked hat sprouted a feathered plume from the crest. There was gold on his mandarin collar, his epaulettes, aiguillette, his belt and sword; he seemed to be covered in gold. If anything he looked like an exile from a suburban Gilbert & Sullivan company. I recall thinking for the first, but certainly not the last, time: 'Gawd, who'd put up with a job like that!'. As I sauntered out of the chamber heading towards the Senate I fell in comfortably beside Arthur Calwell. In turn he introduced me to Menzies who was walking beside him. Menzies warmly greeted me and the three of us chatted agreeably. Suddenly, 'Hssst! You don't do that!'. A Labor colleague, his face distorted with annoyance, glared at me grimly. I was moving ahead too fast, rising above my proper station. That was frowned on in some parts of our society. I fell back into the pack.

Whitlam was there, towering physically over everyone except Malcolm Fraser (on whom he looked down intellectually in any case). He carried himself with a natural grace, was well-suited, and overflowed with self-confidence. His upper middle-class credentials were impeccable. A graduate in law and the classics, a barrister by profession, he came from a well-established professional home and was a High Anglican to boot. These things, regrettably, did not advantage him with some. Certain Liberals resented him as a class turncoat. Others, Labor people, felt he could not be genuinely Labor, presumably because, *inter alia*, he kept his fingernails clean. The late Les Haylen, who wrote pseudonymously for Jack Lang's spiteful rag, *The Century*, dubbed Whitlam as 'White Tie and Tails Whitlam'. Whitlam apparently wore that kit to a formal social function at Parliament House which celebrated its opening after his first election. He was never allowed to forget that violation of working-class political correctness, the latter, of course, as interpreted for the workers by middle-class 'lefties'.

Jim Cairns was there too, moving about effortlessly among Government and Opposition members. An unassuming, handsomely boyish man in his forties, with a good, fit athletic figure, a genuinely warm personality, admired for his moral courage and his fearless defence of left wing principles. He was widely respected. I esteemed him greatly; too much so in those early years for I sometimes allowed his views to over-ride mine, as did many others. It was his feet. We should have looked at them from the start. Clay! The tale of Cairns is Greek tragedy for me and it still causes pain.

There are no heroes in real life. Just ordinary men and women, inevitably flawed because they are human. And it is perhaps the more dazzling ones who have to be watched more carefully. Dazzle can often blind us to a lack of intellectual rigour, depth and truth and discourage us from thinking for ourselves. Better to be honestly wrong through your own conclusions and with an open mind. The exercise of moral judgment is too important to surrender to someone else.

Suddenly Menzies had us in the grip of a 'khaki' election. Typical, for he loved nothing more than maintaining a continuous state of phoney tension about national security, something he was able to do for most of his prime ministership.[24] (Given his own background on active military matters, in particular his support for Chamberlain's 'appeasement' into World War II when he said publicly, 'I thoroughly agreed with what Chamberlain did at Munich and I still agree with what he did',[25] he was extraordinarily belligerent on such issues in the postwar period.) Yet I confess to liking, even admiring the earlier Menzies: the man who privately opposed sending Australian troops to the Middle East in 1939; who worried about the loss of young Australian lives at the front and who confronted Churchill over the security of Australian forces used in the Greek Campaign; who stood up to him in the Imperial War Cabinet when Churchill's own ministers and Chiefs of Staff were unwisely submissive; who faced down Churchill's hostility to the Irish to open up dialogue with Ireland's Prime Minister, De Valera on the question of Ireland's neutrality during the war, and indeed sought to develop that dialogue further; the public figure who openly supported Chamberlain because he saw (excusably, given the level of knowledge of Hitler's Third Reich at that time) Chamberlain's efforts as an honourable undertaking to avoid the horrors of war.[26]

There is much personal principle and moral courage in Menzies' record. We in the Labor movement successfully denied him popular recognition for these good things, largely out of genuine beliefs based on ignorance of that record, as a great deal of it occurred in secret confines. Also, I suspect, because we feared him as a formidable and successful foe. His own party was no help to his reputation. They were too timorous, and I suspect indolent also, to recognise the record we were damaging should have been fiercely defended as part of a valuable heritage on which they would need to draw for political sustenance in the future. That is something 'old' Labor would never have allowed to happen to its political patrimony. Was he too deferential to the English? I think so. But like all of us he was a product of his generation and his family background. It was, after all, a British born Labor Prime Minister, Andrew Fisher, who set the tone of these things by declaring during World War I that Australia would back England 'to the last man and the last shilling': a revered war time Labor Prime Minister, Curtin, who cemented the ties of empire by appointing a British Royal, the Duke of Gloucester, as our Governor-General in 1945: and that celebrated Australian Labor nationalist, H. V. Evatt, who described Australia's British roots as, '. . . the tie of brotherhood and kinship, which transcends all material links and baffles definition'.[27]

Many years later when I was Governor-General, Menzies' son-in-law, Peter Henderson, told me at a function at Government House that Menzies used to say to his family, 'You've got to be firm with the English. If you allow yourself to be used as a doormat they will trample all over you.' Perhaps he was less deferential than some of us had suspected.

In 1963, when President Sukarno of Indonesia was in diabolical trouble at home, and making threatening noises about the region, seeking to divert internal dissension to external issues, Menzies latched onto a God-given political opportunity. He began to tub-thump threateningly about Indonesia's demand for Dutch West New Guinea. However, when the Americans told him he was on the wrong tram, he quietly got off it. Not so Calwell. He took his advice from Rags Henderson of the Fairfax press empire. Thus Calwell maintained the rage against Sukarno's territorial ambitions. His written speeches were crafted masterfully as was his commentary to the press, which always seemed to be covered generously in the Fairfax newspapers. Once again, the late Max Newton was beavering away at their Broadway headquarters, producing this material for Calwell who, as before, often did not see it before its publication. No matter, Rags Henderson would have approved it beforehand.

Meanwhile Labor generally, and the Left in particular, misguidedly regarded Sukarno as some sort of romantic hero of the down-trodden Third World. They reversed Calwell's hostile stand. I recall being crushed by Cairns and others, in the course of this reversal, when I said over coffee one night that I could see little difference in principle if brown colonialism replaced white colonialism; it was still colonialism. The late Gordon Bryant was the only person to support me. Now, with fewer of the innocent ideals of my youth cluttering my thinking and much more practical experience behind me, I acknowledge the Realpolitik of the situation. The Dutch could not have lingered as colonisers. Dutch West New Guinea, or Irian Jaya as it came to be called, could not stand alone. That would have been seriously unsettling to the territory and destabilising for the region. As it has turned out, what happened was for the best, but more because of Suharto. That, however, was not the thinking of the Left. Sukarno was on the 'left', therefore he deserved support. He did not—he was a corrupt, incompetent, tinpot dictator.

Menzies continued to beat the jingo drum, speculating loudly on vaguely defined external threats which everyone knew to mean Indonesia. He pushed the panic button, urgently buying the F111 swing-wing strategic bomber, which was at that stage only a revolutionary design concept. What a non-nuclear power like Australia would do with strategic bombers was never explained. There were other issues: the contract was flawed, no firm pricing formula had been negotiated. No matter, the ploy worked. The community tingled with apprehension. Fear of the 'Yellow Hordes', that Pavlovian response from our insecure past surfaced again, was the perfect reaction for a politician like Menzies. That the aircraft did not arrive for another decade to deter this supposedly imminent security threat, and then at vastly inflated cost, was immaterial. In spite of the brouhaha over this fabrication, Menzies quietly reduced defence spending as a proportion of GDP through the first half of the 1960s. All that counted was safely getting over the finishing line ahead of Labor, and that contest was only months away. The years ahead could look after themselves.

Menzies played his trump card masterfully. He announced that an Australian–United States joint communication base would be established at North West Cape, Western Australia. Labor convened a special National Conference and produced a thoroughly defensible policy which stated that Australia should exercise its sovereign authority over such a potentially sensitive strategic war-fighting capability as that base. Menzies ridiculed this caution, accusing Labor of a lack of faith in 'great and powerful allies' and questioned its patriotism. Menzies also neglected to mention that his Defence Minister, Townley, and External Affairs Minister, Barwick, shared somewhat similar reservations but had been over-ruled by him.[28] The way Labor went about this decision-making, however, was indefensible. Thirty-six conference delegates—six from each State—convened in closed session at Canberra in March. Calwell and Whitlam were locked out of the meeting. They were not delegates in spite of being Leader and Deputy Leader of the Parliamentary Party respectively. They loitered about the footpath, pathetically alone while momentous policy-making was taking place elsewhere, decisions which would be binding on them and their publicly elected colleagues. They literally cooled their heels on the footpath through midnight and beyond. A photograph of their lonely exclusion was featured in the late Sir Frank Packer's *Daily Telegraph,* with the evocative lead: 'Waiting for Instructions . . . From Their Bosses'. Breathlessly the article added, '. . . 36 virtually unknown men . . . were deciding a question of international importance'.[29] The public was unhappy at the way elected representatives were pushed out of the way by non-accountable party officials.

Menzies quickly took his cue. That election was conducted around his charge that Labor was controlled by '36 Faceless Men'. Much of Labor's response was couched in a way easily represented as anti-Americanism, and this in an electorate otherwise overwhelmingly well-disposed to the Americans. Menzies primed the damaging epigrams, and Packer, and others, kept firing them. Little wonder Menzies later said appreciatively that Packer '. . . has been more than fair to me and left me deeply in his debt'. This was a Packer tradition after all. Billy McMahon himself confessed that Packer had been the 'decisive influence' in saving the Menzies Government in 1961.[30] The fact is that our political opponents and the media barons did not concoct these stories; the press certainly embellished them, but the raw material was provided by our ineffable stupidity.

I was standing outside the Brisbane City Hall on the night Calwell delivered his 1963 campaign speech there. A large crowd was exiting in leisurely fashion. A big, nay quite porcine, plain-clothes policeman from the Special Branch came to talk with me. His standard policeman's issue of suspicious features had softened when I greeted him by name. I said with puckish intent, 'Whatever are you doing for a livelihood these days? There are so few Coms left I thought you blokes would be out of a job by now?'. The eyes narrowed, there was silence. He was thinking seriously about this opening gambit. 'Na, na, not at all. They're popping up all the time. New ones off foreign ships in port and the like . . . 'id be some in your audience tonight.' Perhaps I lacked a proper sense of faith in his well-tried and proven system for discovering Communists. 'However do you identify them, like tonight in a large crowd of strangers?' His head continually swivelling left and right as he carefully surveyed the passing parade of people, he leant forward confidentially: 'When yer've been in the job as long as I 'ave yer can smell 'em. Believe me yer can smell 'em'. But if I thought my policeman friend's 'sniff test' for detecting the enemies of the people was simplistic and backward, much the same could be said of those times in general.

Dallas woke me early on the morning of 23 November, the last week of the election. I had returned from campaigning in distant country parts of my electorate somewhere about 2 a.m. after a long drive. 'President Kennedy has been assassinated,' she informed me. I was stunned at such a wicked act. Then, after a few minutes, I said to her, 'Well, that's done it. If we had any chance of winning, it's gone now. People will vote for the status quo for reassurance'. The 1963 national election was a debacle for Labor for a number of reasons, including Kennedy's assassination.

The general feeling in the party was that this was about as bad as it could get. By our own undivided efforts, however, 1966 was much worse, one of the worst defeats ever. In the course of arriving at that election, in October 1964 in fact, Menzies was delivering a statement to the House on defence. His style of delivery could be rather orotund, and was even more so this time. As for me, I found it irritating that he spoke so much about defence but did so relatively little. With some impatience I interjected that this was Menzies' thirteenth defence review. He flushed with anger and hotly retorted, 'That's right. You know all about a Cabinet, you poor little ignoramus'.[31] There was great delight among the Labor ranks. The unknown lightweight from Ipswich had thrown the national political heavyweight right off balance. Menzies had the grace to remove the interjection and retort from the Hansard. (I mention this because I did toy with the idea of entitling this memoir: *The Inexorable Rise of the Poor Little Ignoramus*.)

Well before that 1966 election we had locked ourselves into a passionate denunciation of Western involvement in the Vietnam War. This emotional opposition was intensified with the introduction of conscription to send further fighting forces there from Australia. Menzies, followed by Holt, exploited the nation's deep-seated sense of insecurity in the region and its underlying discomfort with Asians. 'Better to fight them there than here . . . The downward thrust of Chinese Communism . . . If Vietnam goes the rest of South-East Asia falls like dominoes, all the way to our shore'. . . It seemed our political opponents were only a breath away from invoking the 'Yellow Hordes'. This subliminal appeal to racism was generally applauded by media commentators as high-minded statesmanship on the part of Menzies. If so, it was incommensurably short sighted in its vision of our future in the region, just as it was remarkably devoid of rigorous historical and political analysis.

A violation of the provisions of the Geneva Accords of 1954—providing for a temporary separation between the North and the South as part of a settlement process of the colonial war between France and the Viet Minh—by the United States, abetted by Australia, was insupportable. An independently monitored election held in both North and South Vietnam to determine the future of the country was junked when President Eisenhower was advised by the CIA that Ho Chi Minh, the Communist-nationalistic leader of the North, could win as much as 80 per cent of the total vote.[32] Eisenhower's earlier view was the more realistic one, namely that France should withdraw from the Indochina countries giving them their independence and 'then let them fight their own war'.[33] Had that view prevailed, North and South Vietnam would have been united as they are now. The difference for us would have been that the sons of tens of thousands of American families and five hundred young Australians would still be alive today. And the drawn-out, ignominious conclusion of the war for the United States and its allies would also have been avoided. It was a war that demoralised the Australian Government, a government which, according to Billy Snedden, 'lacked courage and commitment to the Vietnam cause, and would not even discuss it. As soon as the matter came up in Cabinet, for some reason or other everybody would think of other subjects to discuss'.[34]

I was amongst the earliest and most passionate opponents of the war. In 1965, on my way back from a Queensland State Labor Party Conference at Townsville, I was talking to Whitlam about the immorality of Western intervention and the need for wholehearted Labor opposition. During a brief stopover at Mackay airport I predicted to him that the Australian public would rise in moral indignation against Western involvement. He meditated briefly, then said; 'No, Comrade, no. I'm afraid it's not like that. History shows the public like a good war. When the military bands start playing they'll all fall into step behind them. We'll have to be careful how we handle this one'. I was appalled. I subsequently learnt he was right. A more careful handling of our opposition, without jettisoning principle, would still have lost us seats in the 1966 election, but not as many as we did lose. Whitlam would then have had fewer electorates to win and less of the vote to make up in 1969. As it was he managed to gain 50.2 per cent of the two party preferred vote that year. With a better 1966 base to work from it is entirely feasible that he could have won government in 1969. In that case Australia would have been out of the war, and the ending of conscription would have come sooner instead of dragging on as it did. On the other hand, if the Government had used professional soldiers and avoided conscription it would have evaded much of the subsequent opposition, and perhaps even the defeat of 1972. It was, initially, as Whitlam predicted, a very popular war.

Shortly before the 1966 election, when the Parliament had been sitting into the small hours of the morning, I was walking along the lobby, approaching the office of Opposition Leader Calwell. There was a small knot of right wing Labor members congregated there, surrounding Calwell and aggressively hectoring him over his failure to endorse the United States' involvement in Vietnam. One was the late Pat Galvin who, for some reason, disliked me and was none too subtle in making that dislike known. 'What's up, Arthur,' I inquired genuinely enough, for I liked Calwell. Galvin turned on me, savagely declaiming, 'You mind your own bloody business'. With that incontestably sound advice he unleashed a haymaker from somewhere down near the linoleum floor runner. He was wide of his mark, perhaps due to his having taken a leisurely detour via the Members' Bar earlier. I retaliated. As I let loose a vigorous uppercut, Freddy Daly moved in between us. The punch landed four square on the side of Fred's head sending his spectacles for a sixer. Poor Fred, he did not deserve that. Noel Beaton from Victoria, who stood about 195 centimetres high, moved in and held us apart with his long arms, our flailing punches pounding the air harmlessly.

After every big night there is a bleak morning. I scoured the newspapers. Thank goodness, not a word about the silly affray. On to Ipswich for the weekend where I was warmly greeted by Dallas and the children, all solicitous about my welfare after the rigorous demands of another parliamentary week. I had a migraine and an attack of dyspepsia, partly the products of worrying about what might happen if the press got the story, but also partly due to a hangover from the night before. The telephone at home rang. I froze. It was the Brisbane *Sunday Truth*. The vultures of the press were hovering. How I excoriated them in the tumult of my thoughts! On the phone I bluffed and blustered. I talked about legal action. All rather predictable stuff from a politician caught misbehaving. As I hung up I realised I had been too high-pitched, too jumpy, panicky even. And although I managed to palm off Dallas' perplexed inquiries, from then until Sunday morning I lived on the sharp edge of a deep chasm of worries. I was out early to collect the newspapers. Not a word . . . . Phew! that was close. I resolved there and then that I had had my last drink! I kept the resolution for a whole week.

Labor had its own problem. It was clear the Party was its own worst enemy, and following the setback of 1963 Whitlam courageously embarked on a campaign to tell us just that. But that was only part of it; his larger mission was to reform the Party, make it more appealing to the public in its composition and conduct, and establish its relevance to contemporary society by developing appropriate policies. Calwell was the product of an older generation and felt distinctly uncomfortable with Whitlam's brash approach. Calwell was prepared to forbear the indignity of being locked out of the National Conference, and all the damage which could attend that exclusion. That, as with so many other things he unwisely tolerated, was the way things had been done during his generation. He felt comfortable with what he knew and never questioned it. Whitlam was part of the new middle class, was about greater individualism, of position and status based on merit. He was outraged, his anger directed at those established power structures which were a liability. Labor wanted to hang onto the past but Whitlam would not let it. He was reaching for the future. Labor was like a haggard old political crone, droning on about virtue but lacking appeal or conviction with most of the community. Virtue is easy for those who no longer tempt because of self-inflicted disfigurement. Me? I was young, I wanted to taste a bit of living in the fast political lane, like being a minister in a Labor government and being part of a sweeping social and economic reform process. Yes, I was inexorably moving towards Whitlam and I would get there, but not immediately. The disastrous 1966 election results left all of us shaken and most of us reassessing our attitudes and performance.

A personal tragedy

The 1966 election was less than five weeks away. We all knew it was going to be a disaster. A subsequent public opinion poll showed that we had been unable even to persuade our own supporters to endorse our policy. While 39 per cent of Labor voters opposed the involvement of outside military forces in Vietnam, 45 per cent believed the effort should be increased or stay as it was.[35] In the course of the last week of the sittings, Labor members were sombrely discussing their chances of remaining in the Parliament with the conclusion of the forthcoming election. There were more than a few anticipating an involuntary departure.

On Sunday, 23 October 1966 I was attending a party meeting. It was an electorate campaign organising meeting in Esk, a session to work on our election campaign. It was while I was there, in that small country town in the Brisbane Valley about fifty kilometres north of Ipswich, that Dallas and I experienced our most awful personal tragedy. A message was brought across from a local pub that the Ipswich Police Inspector was on the telephone and wished to speak to me. There was instant inner turmoil. As soon as I heard his voice, and before he had explained his mission, I knew there had been a fatality. My first thought was that it must have been Dallas. Panic welled up and so did pain. Now I was experiencing what all those poor people had experienced when, as a young policeman, I had trudged up their front steps with similar terrible news for them.

Our eldest child, Michaela, then five years old, had been struck by a car as she and her two sisters, excitedly but heedlessly, the way infants often do, ran across a road near our Ipswich home to obtain a lift home with a neighbour. They had just left Sunday School at a local dissenting Protestant church. In her excitement, poor little Michaela had run into the path of an oncoming car. Once certain things were in place—the car, the direction it was travelling, its moderate speed, the other car across the road, the timing of the infant's impulsive rush, and a whole series of other associated circumstances—the result had been determined. The fatality was unavoidable. The poor man driving the car was devastated but there was nothing he could have done to have averted it. There was an awful inevitability about the tragedy, given those circumstances,which came together at that exact moment.

The reason I mention this very personal matter briefly is to convey a message to a small group of people: to those parents who have lost a child and who feel desolately alone and not understood. For how could anyone else ever understand those very distinctive, wretched experiences which come with the loss of a loved youngster? Yet many do. They know the long, painful loneliness of the nights following the death, the nights of emotional torture that you curse because they seem to never end. Days when your sanity is in doubt. In my case I became obsessed with a dream world, a place I would enter in my mind and which at the same time would envelop me. In this desperate, recurring fantasy in which the experience was so close to being palpable that it seemed reality, I had gone off and wandered the world, forever it almost seemed. There one day, suddenly, I would come across her, Michaela, a handsome, mature young woman walking in a crowd, to nowhere in particular, in a strange city, in another part of the world. We were reunited. Neither of us ever doubted it would happen. She had been waiting and growing up. She was merely surprised it had taken so long for us to be reunited. I knew the report of her death was a mistake, that I would find her, still alive. It was all a terrible misunderstanding. She was merely lost; temporarily. In my despair, I expect, I was trying to deny reality with these images.

For Dallas the experience was far worse. She was breast-feeding our youngest, Kirk. The flow of milk dried up on the instant. She suffered the most excruciating distress, of a kind, I believe, only a mother could fully understand, for part of her had been violently torn away and destroyed. We felt as if we could never recover from the shock, indeed, felt as if we did not want to, that what we wanted far more was for it all to end for us too. But a sense of responsibility managed to maintain its weak flicker in our souls. There were others, the other children, who had to be considered. You eventually recover, but you never forget and when you read of the tragic death of some parents' child you remember and your sympathy reaches out to them. You literally pause in whatever you might be engaged at that time to let the plight of those unfortunate people occupy your mind, to enter your soul, to be embraced by compassion and understanding. You know what that night is like, the one they will now experience, and the nights that will succeed it for them. We were fortunate. Dallas and I were too devastated to do much. An extended family network came into operation quickly. Dallas' coal mining relatives, in particular the women, rostered themselves to be on hand at our home to quietly receive mourners. It was all done carefully and discreetly, for underground coal mining families, regrettably, learn how to handle tragedy as part of their existence.

Letters of condolence arrived. Some actually hurt, unintentionally no doubt, but they still provoked pain. They usually said something like: 'As difficult as this experience is, remember it is God's wish taken in His wisdom . . .'. Their effect made me rage that this God of the Christians, this Moloch! destroyed innocent little children randomly! Such letters were well meant but they were painful. The sympathy was welcome but not the manner of expression. Many other letters which arrived came from parents who had been through what we were suffering and they helped greatly. With them we discovered we were not alone, that this was not a unique experience, that sometime, perhaps far off, we would recover and the sentiments of those correspondents helped give a little buoyancy to our very depressed spirits. By writing on this subject, on something I have steadfastly refused to discuss for nearly thirty years, I hope in turn this may help a little somewhere.

In my sheer desperation I went to the Catholic presbytery, to call on a young priest with whom I had become friendly. We were both rather new in our respective business; both young, full of ideals about how we would change things for the better. In the conceited manner of youth, we thought that alone we were going to make a big difference to the destiny of humankind. (The priest probably has; my contribution falls well short of what I thought it was going to be.) I felt I could talk to him. In the event we talked at length. Just being with him and having his understanding but unsentimental support was sustaining. Then he said, 'I will pray for Michaela, Dallas and you and your family. You can join me if you wish. That is entirely a matter for you'. He knew of my non-belief. If ever I was going to believe, it would surely be at this time and in particular at that moment, for I desperately wanted a prop on which to lean. I desperately wanted to believe. This experience felt too big to handle alone. He prayed in a low tone, working the rosary beads gently through his fingers. I was grateful and I was embarrassed. The gratefulness I felt for the quiet personal strength he offered me was overwhelmed by embarrassment, for I found I could not move from the chair to my knees to join my friend. To do so, at that time, would have been one of the most inauthentic things I could have done. I discovered that reason would not let me make the leap of faith which my heart so desperately yearned for at that moment. It would have mocked religious belief, which I respected, and profaned the memory of our daughter. I felt it was irrational to believe in the unknowable. I was condemned by my choice to be alone. This was unfortunate for it is every bit as irrational to trust in the certainty of reason and reality; one frequently fails and the other is often deceiving. I regret my atheism, for it seems to me those people of deep, gentle, religious conviction are able to sustain themselves at times of tragedy by drawing on great wellsprings of inner faith. They are truly blessed. I am no militant rationalist, but rather an unbeliever.

I spent days pacing about pointlessly in our lounge room. There was no sense in doing it but I had to keep moving. It was as if physical movement could subordinate abstract thought. Every atom of my existence was in pain and distress; I felt bitter resentment at a wicked injustice I could not comprehend. I became aware of a sudden sense of dread and intrusion. Then I saw out of the large lounge room glass doors what I had hoped, rather unrealistically, was never going to happen. The mourning cars, bleak and final in the message their unmistakable blackness radiated, had quietly reversed up the drive. They had come to a silent halt. The boot of one was rocking slightly, noiselessly, with the momentum of the suddenly stopped vehicle. With that shuddering halt any semblance of self-confidence crumbled. This was the moment of finality. The point when reality intruded and dominated. There could be no more false hope, no more escaping into deceptive imaginings. Michaela was dead and life would go on.

Nature of course has no sense of the mood of such a moment. As I reflect on it now, the day of Michaela's funeral was what I would have described, in normal circumstances, as a glorious October day. There were, I believe, clear blue skies, sparkling green shrubbery, the joyful shriek of children at play somewhere nearby, traffic rumbling along the not too distant highway. Yes, that was it. You become acutely aware of individual noises at a time like this, especially during the depths of the dark mornings. Roosters crowing long before the sun is ready to rise, a lone car scurrying along an empty street, a dog barking, the living sounds of an empty, eternal pre-dawn morning. You hear noises which normally are lost in the blur, the helter-skelter of existence. It was as though existence had moved into a painful slow-motion and every last sound was registering.

Very soon the election began to close in on us, not to mention a university examination in statistical mathematics (for which I had been unable to get a deferment to the new year). Before the recent dreadful event I felt I had good reason for expecting a solid distinction or better as I had found the course congenial and the weekly tests a breeze. I managed a credit, which was a surprise, for such was my constant distress and confusion after this tragedy that I had experienced great difficulty in concentrating on and absorbing the examination paper. As for the election, the vote held up in our electorate in the face of large swings generally. This made me feel dreadfully guilty, still does when I think about it, for I would have preferred to have done without that.

Here we are thirty years after Michaela's death and while Dallas wishes we could talk about her at times, I find I still cannot, which I know is unfair of me. If I attempt to do so an old and painful wound, deep in the psyche, opens up and my composure falls apart. I cannot shake off the conditioning of a lifetime, the imperative that 'real men don't cry'. Accordingly, the resolution of the problem has, I confess, been quite one-sided. We found the most enduring emotional scars affected our other children, for they witnessed the accident and the appalling, immediate, aftermath. One of our children especially, who was closely bonded as a sibling with Michaela, has never fully recovered from the experience. Grieving parents, in spite of the crushing load of bereavement they suffer, should be aware these tragedies can have a long-term effect on other family members and their consequences can often be difficult to correct. Life goes on and in spite of the trauma. You make a recovery of sorts, but it is never the same. All I can hope is this account of our experience may help someone.

The Whitlam ascendancy

Gough Whitlam was the saviour of Labor. He virtually transformed it, rescuing it from its own grim determination to inflict self-destruction. He effected the third of the three reifications of Labor since its beginnings in the early 1890s. The first had been wrought by Fisher and Hughes in response to a strong nationalist sentiment prior to World War I, and found expression in the establishment of such national symbols as the Australian Navy, the Commonwealth Bank and the railway connection across the Nullarbor Plain. These undertakings were facilitated by the support of Alfred Deakin, leader of the Fusion Party, the legislative programme itself 'merely a completion of the Barton–Deakin [the preceding Fusion Government] programme'.[36] The second covered the creative period of postwar reconstruction under Chifley, as backed by outstanding public service policy-makers like 'Nugget' Coombs and Fin Crisp. There was no serious obstruction to these undertakings either. Each of these periods was a feat of government drawing on the great reservoir of talent available in the bureaucracy. Neither was radical in the ideological sense. Whitlam's was distinguished by being both creative and a radical ideological performance. It was virtually a solo achievement, made against the general limitations that being in Opposition imposes, and those difficulties particular to that time. In order to save Labor from itself Whitlam had to fight key power barons in control of the Party every inch of the way, as well as blunt the hostile attacks of the Coalition Parties. It is not too far-fetched to declare that Labor's survival depended on Whitlam's success in this battle. His was by far the greatest achievement in creating the conditions for, and many of the outcomes in, that period of significant change.

Labor long regarded itself as the repository of social justice; as the Democratic Socialist Party of Australia, it was the sole creative powerhouse of ideas and ideals for Australian society. In practice, prior to Whitlam, its response to national needs and ambitions was largely piecemeal, and too often opportunistic; it was also developed from within the same very limiting conceptual framework which boxed in the thinking of the conservative coalition. There was no exposition of Democratic Socialist ideology. To the extent there was any element of social justice guiding its actions, this was a product of instinct rather than the exegesis of a coherent, intellectually sustainable ideology. *Socialism sans Doctrine* was how it was dubbed in a work by the French observer, André Metin, in 1901.

Labor's problem was one of long-term attrition. Its traditional blue collar electorate base was contracting. The Party burdened itself with a form of collective political paranoia. Many of its setbacks—like the conscription 'split' of World War I; or that of the Great Depression over economic management; Chifley's humiliating defeat of the late forties over a raft of unwisely selected policies on bank nationalisation, medical services, petrol rationing; the negative effects of Communist-led industrial strife in the forties; or the sectarian 'splits' of the fifties—were very much self-inflicted. But these were always rationalised as the product of conspiracies by powerful, secret malign forces rather than largely the outcome of the Labor Party's own decisions or deficiencies. That is not to say that others did not take advantage of the opportunities Labor created whenever it gave free rein to its often clumsy, elemental passions. The more Labor failed the more it tended to live off slogans and cling to a sentimentalised, mythical golden past. The greater the disasters, the greater the propensity to rationalise these humiliations as the price of principled conduct: 'Better to lose and keep our principles intact than win office by selling out on what we believe in'. A defeatist psychology permeated the Party. After 1949 we could not win government because of our errant conduct, but instead of confronting that factor honestly we adumbrated various fictions, which we declared to be matters of principle, and which we asserted would not allow us to accept government. It boiled down to the unstated assumption that we were just too good for the general public and until they woke up to this fact they would be deprived of our services. Swallowed whole in this credulous fashion by a sizeable part of the Party, such assumptions only protected incompetent leadership.

Whitlam shattered the warped mould in which Labor culture had cast itself. Almost single-handedly, he was responsible for a wholesale rewrite of at least two-thirds of the party policy at the 1965 National Conference of the Party, the first I attended as a delegate. It was a virtuoso performance. It had some of the old-timers shaking their heads disconsolately as he irreverently slaughtered one rickety old sacred cow after another. The hitherto bipartisan commitment to the White Australia immigration policy was unceremoniously dumped; no matter the heartburn this caused for some of the 'old brigade'. (This allowed Prime Minister Holt to move decisively against its practice by the following year, confident of bipartisan support for the change.) Aboriginal welfare was run to the top of the masthead of Labor's concerns, a precondition for the bipartisan support necessary to that later successful referendum of 1967 which allocated responsibility for such matters to the Federal Government. This change irreversibly transformed not just the welfare commitment of the nation to our original people, but also the way in which Aborigines were understood by the wider community. It has been one of the most positive outcomes of our national political processes. Labor's tendency for ultra-nationalistic sentiments in defence and foreign policy had become extreme, with our attitudes to such an important ally as the United States reflecting nothing more than the hostility borne of an inferiority complex.

Whitlam began stressing Australian national confidence but, as a true internationalist, linking Australia with world concerns for peace and development. A sober approach ensued, replacing the shrill and uneven fixation on strategic tensions between East and West, and allowing the Third World to enter the political agenda, not just as a recipient of development aid but as a political force and a potential ally at international fora. Few seem to have noted that Whitlam set down enduring foundations, which Andrew Peacock later reinforced, thus creating a welcome bipartisanship to Australia's foreign policies which sustains itself to this day. More comprehensively, he evolved policies on education, national health insurance and health services, on welfare, housing, urban and regional development, the creative arts, and a wide range of other areas of public responsibility. He abjured colonialism and accordingly fathered the cause of independence for Papua New Guinea, forcing the Coalition Government eventually to adopt this principle. The Party's platform of policies was starting to look like a blueprint for the nation's future.

Whitlam actively courted the new middle class—paradoxically, many the products of Menzies' major initiatives in higher education—by stressing that advancement in society should be merit-based, and this was coupled with material commitment to the less well-off. That is, his strategy reinforced Labor's traditional base while enlarging its heartland. He aggressively sought educated, professionally qualified people to reinforce that appeal. Barry Cohen, a man of delightful charm and wit, often entertained his friends with clever mimicry of Whitlam's introduction of candidates in the Sydney Town Hall to an overflow 1969 election campaign audience. That occasion had been Cohen's first outing as a Labor candidate. The great man, with the assurance of a divinely consecrated pontiff, illuminated the crowd with the virtues of 'his' team: 'There's Bill Morrison, senior diplomat, Deputy High Commissioner to Malaysia, graduate of Sydney University . . . then there's Dr Bob Wann, Doctor of Philosophy and Deputy Head of the Bureau of Agricultural Economics . . . Major Peter Young, Vietnam veteran, intelligence specialist'. . . and on and on, the candidates basking in the glow of this new found public adulation. He at last came to Cohen. 'Then there's Barry Cohen . . . ', a pause which throbbed with perplexity, '. . . ah, ah, . . . [inspiration] . . . he lives on the North Shore'. As Cohen tells it, this experience provoked him to undertake part-time study and earn a good BA at the Australian National University. Whitlam proudly attended the graduation ceremony as Cohen's guest, behaving as if he was master to Cohen's apprenticeship.

Whitlam welded together previously neglected interest groups: the migrants, Aborigines, the education lobby, architects, planners and engineers, women; he also sought to co-opt the armed services, which had generally been ignored by Labor as too hostile. Allied to this wide-ranging vision, the spread and depth of policies was as enormous as the policy-making was prodigious. Small think-tanks involving academics, professionals and the more thoughtful political representatives were put together on an ad hoc basis to search out new ideas, better alternatives for realising society's goals and ideals. I recall it as probably the most exciting and inspiring period in my long political life. The haphazardly functioning Federal Parliamentary Executive became a 'shadow cabinet', whose members were given specific portfolios to cover and were expected to expertly cover the appropriate minister. The parliamentary committee system was structured to cover ministerial portfolios too. From this came formidable competitive pressure to perform well in order to remain in the 'shadow cabinet'. There was an astonishing improvement in the parliamentary performance of Labor. The general emphasis on merit began to seep into the Party as well, displacing the old Labor culture of herd conformity to the lowest common denominator.

In spite of my being known as a consistently committed Cairns supporter and mostly voting with the Left on major issues, Whitlam involved me in many of these processes. More than that, he went out of his way to encourage my political ambitions, and was particularly supportive when he saw I was persevering with my university studies. Perhaps he was confident that sooner or later I would reason my way through Labor's predicament —which I did, to discover it was my big predicament also—and move to support him. In any case he was right, but it involved a drawn-out, anxious struggle with my conscience before I was able to stand completely alongside him. Certainly much of the policy-making was derivative. The National Health Insurance Scheme was lifted directly from Canada. The Health and Hospitals Services concept had its genesis in Sweden. The inspiration for the onslaught against poverty came from the United States, as did the Urban Improvement Programme. The vague notion of an Australian Assistance Plan for welfare services derived from an even vaguer understanding that something like that was being done in Canada. The Schools Commission was, conceptually, the offspring of Menzies Universities Commission. The radical notion of regional and national government replacing local and State governments was lifted straight out of the postwar reconstruction papers of Chifley's minister for that portfolio, John Dedman. No matter, for these ideas for Australia, whether they were new or renovated, linked together to form a coherent pattern. It was a comprehensive vision for the future offering so much promise to so many, especially the new middle class. This was a new constituency for Labor—relatively well-off people who held in common a number of ideas, if self-interested ones, and who were in the habit of talking a great deal about them. They understood readily, if not admitting it to themselves, that the Labor Party was indeed helping promote their own material welfare; what was more, in offering middle-class reform, Labor would be creating interesting jobs for at least some of them. The benefits of siding with Labor were numerous, not the least being that many in the new middle class could so readily cloak themselves in the language of high social ideals and national vision, while promoting their well-developed notions of self-interest.

On the economy meanwhile, not only would we plan the thing, we would steer it with the finesse of an advanced jet aircraft pilot. We would use the range of economic data flowing into government much as a pilot uses his instrument panel to tack and trim the aircraft's balance and direction. A steady, on course flight and 'Hey Presto!', there would be steady economic growth of 6 per cent. This would pay all the bills for the big ticket spending, with no need for increased taxes, what is more![37] Here was a beautiful economic vision in which we all gain, and painlessly. That was derivative too, from the Crosslandite Socialists of the British Labour Party. No wonder the new middle class talked so much about these new and inspiring directions and with such ready approval. We would socially re-engineer the structure of society, and guess who would be commanders on the control platforms guiding these brave new advances? Why, no-one else but representatives of the new middle class. We were opening up new frontiers for humanity. Sweden spent close to 45 per cent of its GDP in the public sector while Australia almost completely trailed the field of industrialised countries at 26 per cent. Don't worry, was our view, it was just a matter of time. We would overtake Sweden as the brave new social laboratory of the world. Our enthusiasms were infectious just as our ambitions were boundless—just the right mix of ingredients from which to blend the new age. The reality that there were a number of fundamental economic principles which needed to be considered never really bothered most among us. Few of us stopped to think about the issues of savings, investment and what constituted real economic growth; these things were just not exciting enough.

Labor was dedicated to the Democratic Socialisation of the means of production, distribution and exchange. This credo was qualified by the proviso which could mean anything or nothing: 'to the extent necessary to eliminate exploitation and other antisocial features'. A hard core of the faithful believed in the commitment to a Democratic Socialist society. I was one of them. Few among us had even a rough understanding of the implications of our faith, some even imagining its roots to be in a confused, bowdlerised

Marxism. Even fewer were able to propound a specific exposition of the Democratic Socialist alternative, although some tried.[38] In the electorate the 'Socialist Tiger' was a disaster for Labor. Labor's opponents successfully presented ours as a programme for wholesale nationalisation; according to their script, even the 'Mum & Dad' corner stores were at risk of expropriation. Before Whitlam, Labor's response was pretty much to duck for cover, using the provision 'to the extent necessary', which by *reductio ad absurdum* established that there was no need for any socialisation of commerce. The clear but elusive implication of this sort of backtracking was *ipso facto* there must be, near enough, a total absence of exploitation and antisocial features in Australian society. Accordingly, the *raison d'être* for Labor's existence as a democratic Socialist Party had vanished. It was then, in reality, little different in its objectives and commitments to its conservative opponents.

Whitlam killed this toothless Socialist Tiger stone dead with a series of well-aimed sling shots. He forthrightly defined this commitment with a detailed exposition of society's injustices, outlined how Labor's various policies were designed to redress this unfairness, elaborated the role of government as a mechanism for transforming society to achieve these ends, and stressed the goal was equality of opportunity. His persuasive reasoning convinced a great number of people that they were Democratic Socialists too, especially members of the new middle class. Whitlam offered a continental variety of Social Democracy with powerful intellectual appeal to the middle class, or at least, that is how many of them saw it.

Whitlam was a winner to boot. He won the Dawson, Corio, Capricornia and Bendigo by-elections from the Coalition Government. The 1969 national election result, his first, was a spectacular boost to Labor's self-confidence, as were the encouraging results at a brace of separate half-Senate elections. All were tough challenges and all were won with impressive swings to Labor. At the same time Whitlam was waging a determined campaign against the toughest of his enemies, certain key oligarchs with considerable control of the Party. These were men who could not afford Whitlam's rise or his reforms, as these would eclipse their own authority. Better to be a noisy big toad in a small stagnant backwater than having to compete as a small toad in a big pond. Whitlam's great achievements would only be accorded grudging acknowledgment by these people—usually in the terms of, 'He was lucky that time'. Though he continued to chalk up his successes, they waited in the hope he would fail. One major stumble and they would set upon him.

Thus, in the midst of the 1966 Dawson by-election, a formidable test for Labor by any measuring stick, the twelve delegate National Executive decided Labor should test the constitutionality of State Aid to non-government schools before the High Court. At that stage in our history the issue was controversial and divisive in the community, and even more so in the Labor Party. To use one of Bob Hawke's favourite phrases, this decision was 'an act of sheer bastardry'. While many in the party, like me, harboured genuine worries about State Aid, the political timing of this decision was diabolical. The aim of the main strategists behind this ploy was to cripple Whitlam in Dawson and hopefully bring him down totally afterwards. Although Deputy Leader of the Parliamentary Party at the time, Whitlam took charge of this campaign, virtually living in the electorate for its entirety. The Leader, Calwell, made one brief appearance. Commentators saw the election, and its possible outcome, as an ultimate test of whether Whitlam would succeed or fail in the long run. The extraordinary local appeal of the candidate, Dr Rex Patterson, was of course a potent force. Whitlam's response was magnificent if imprudent. He publicly and accurately described the Executive as a 'factional and unrepresentative controlling group . . . [of] incompetent and irresponsible men that most of the States sent to be their delegates'. With great flair he added, 'I can only say we've just got rid of the thirty-six faceless men stigma to be faced with the twelve witless men'. Not even a 12 per cent swing to

Labor in the by-election could save him. His head was on the block. He was charged with gross disloyalty to the party.

Joe Chamberlain, President of the Executive and from Western Australia, was now in hot pursuit. He was, in his disapproval and punitive prosecutions of 'revisionists' like Whitlam, a sort of contemporary Vyshinsky of Labor politics. He relished the prospect of at last 'breaking Whitlam on the rack' of the supreme authority of the National Executive. To boot, Chamberlain could not abide 'silvertails', among whom he included Whitlam, for they were a parasitic class. Nor, ironically, could he abide politicians, who by their nature and occupation were untrustworthy. The fact that he had earlier campaigned energetically, but unsuccessfully, as a Labor candidate for State Parliament in Western Australia in no way diluted his righteous distrust of parliamentarians. Whitlam meanwhile was in free fall from a great height, crashing towards disaster. Suddenly, however, like a cat with a natural instinct for survival, he spun right way up, landed on his feet and bounded off.

Good friends at court materialised like *deus ex machina*. Whitlam's hero status with Queensland Labor had been reinforced by the Dawson outcome. The State organiser, Tom Burns, now Deputy Premier of the State, came out belligerently defending Whitlam. He brought the State in behind him. A 'confidential' letter from Whitlam to the South Australian Executive, undertaking to abide by the decisions of the Party and to work within it, 'fortuitously' surfaced. He was mildly reprimanded, more a flick with a feather than the slash of the stockwhip Chamberlain had been hoping to take to him. His *mea culpa* was meant—but not for the long term. Labor was a long way off being saved from itself. This, incidentally, is one of many instances where Whitlam displayed the good common sense to back off in order to fight more important issues on firmer grounds on another day. It is misleading to characterise his tactics as exclusively 'crash through or crash' when confronted with a major obstacle, for he was too intelligent to be unimaginatively stubborn. Where he was obdurate, as he some-times was, he had mostly already made a shrewd calculation that he would win. Thank goodness he did.

The historical background to Whitlam's drive to reform the Party is in itself fascinating. After the 1963 setback, the NSW State Executive of the Labor Party had requested Federal members and Senators to present written submissions on the condition, functioning and in particular, defects of the Party. Whitlam's report was highly critical and potentially explosive. Rather prudently, the executive declined to circulate it. The report, among other things, candidly canvassed leadership weaknesses: lack of community representativeness among Members of Parliament; insufficient professionally qualified members; lack of discipline among parliamentarians, the extra-parliamentary organisation, and affiliated unions; defective functioning of the National Conference and the National Executive; the need for adequate full-time staff and a professional Federal office instead of an amateurish shoe box scale operation; full media coverage of National Conference as standard practice. With this succinct document he put numerous self-interested groups off side—not the tactic recommended by the ordinary garden variety of time-serving politician of the times. He foundered somewhat in proposing that ALP members actively engage in the internal affairs of trade unions to ensure they were under Labor control (this later exposed him to the spurious charge of wishing to reinvent the Industrial Groups). However, the critical observation that 'he couldn't hold a glass of beer properly' probably did Whitlam most harm with sections of the party.

The late Alan Fraser, the MHR for Eden-Monaro then, rather artfully, proposed to Whitlam they exchange copies of their respective submissions to the NSW Executive for background information. There was mutual agreement and in this Whitlam was being just as crafty as Fraser. The contents of Whitlam's submission were published in some newspapers with a Canberra date line on

14 April 1964 as Whitlam had to have anticipated. Fraser had leaked the report. Alan Reid, a close friend and former press gallery colleague of Fraser, ran the report in the *Daily Telegraph* under the trouble-making page one headline, 'Calwell Hit in Report to Executive'. A long-standing and often bitter opponent of Whitlam, Fraser was not exactly inspired by lofty motives. In giving Fraser the provocative document Whitlam had decided to make a fight of it. So his confidential sketch of Labor's problems became a very public agenda for party reform which he could honestly say had not been leaked by him.

Public as it now was, Whitlam in any event began to move decisively on his long campaign to breathe new life, to create fresh electoral appeal, to inject self-confidence and self-respect into the Labor Party. He pursued this agenda for change vigorously from then on. After several arduous years, his goals were achieved and more besides. In this respect the National Conferences of 1965, 1967 and finally 1969 were triumphs of policy and party reform for him and the party. No-one else but he could have done it. There was no-one else anywhere in the Party with the tenacity, energy, vision, courage and capacity for that achievement. Whitlam was one of the greatest fighters for ideas in which he believed I have ever come across: probably the greatest.

Nor was Whitlam without guile in pursuing an ambition. He employed this quality at the 1967 National Conference when he sought to break the control which the Left exercised over the National Executive. He proposed, reasonably, that that body should be democratised and made more publicly acceptable by automatically including the Leader and the Deputy Leader of the Parliamentary Labor Party. In fact the inclusion of him and his deputy, Barnard, would have tilted the numbers on the executive away from the Left, giving a narrow majority to the Right and moderates, which was his real objective. The Left seethed, for Whitlam had built up high public expectations on this issue. For the Left to repudiate it would have been extremely disruptive. Labor appeared to be readying itself for another damaging round of internal brawling when Clyde Cameron brought to bear some of his own tactical craftiness. Cameron's proposal to the Left was simple, ingenious and thoroughly effective, outmanoeuvring Whitlam completely. Not only should Whitlam and Barnard be included as delegates to the National Executive by virtue of their offices in the Party, but so too should the Leader and Deputy Leader of the Senate, Murphy and Cohen. The Left applauded, while the public welcomed this apparent display of improved representation within the Labor Party. Meanwhile, Whitlam fumed for Cameron had demolished his well-laid plans: Murphy and Cohen consistently supported the Left and their inclusion negated the votes of Whitlam and Barnard, maintaining Left control of the executive. At least he got the four Federal and all the State parliamentary leaders onto the National Conference, which took control of that body away from the Left, and a good part of that 1967 Conference was opened to the media. In respect of the latter matter the effects were extraordinary. The conduct of delegates underwent a sea-change for the better. With the media watching, ready to pounce at the first sign of unseemly conduct, the behaviour was generally immaculate. The public impression was most favourable.

With extraordinary resilience Whitlam maintained his campaign unabated into the 1969 National Conference. Many of the Left regarded him with fear and loathing; he did not conform to those long-standing rules which obviously advantaged them. Instead of debating within the closed confines of the Party, in which their control was pre-eminent, he canvassed the issues widely in public. He built up a formidable electorate of open-minded public support and extensive committed party rank and file back-up. Without that security he would have been destroyed by his party opponents. The State parliamentary leaders were present as full delegates at this Conference and lifted the quality of discussion greatly. Tiny little

Canberra with a party membership of about four hundred, a few more than had voted for me at my first preselection, was admitted to National Conference, as was the not much larger Northern Territory. These were more votes for Whitlam, even if they unquestionably came from pocket boroughs. Whitlam's strategy was even more long-term and larger scale than I had imagined at the time. He was preparing for a huge showdown with those controlling the sectarian ridden Victorian State Executive whose destructive influences constantly reached out to disadvantage Labor. Victoria was held in the iron grip of a team of oligarchs who were more interested in exercising their power than working moderately for government.

One of his toughest fights was to have a nationally co-ordinated election campaign controlled from the Party's national office. This opposition was queer for a party which sneered at the States' rights commitment of the Liberals. The blatant pork-barrelling quality of policy speeches ended. They became carefully crafted documents outlining national strategies. He used the now open forum of National Conference as an educative platform to reach the public and the policy documents were detailed blueprints of how the new vision for Australia would be reached. He was a tireless political evangelist, restlessly, interminably moving about this large nation seeking to persuade and convert. And, as mentioned earlier, he would fight relentlessly for causes in which he believed. One day in a shadow Cabinet meeting he was challenged on his urban improvement policies. Whitlam was told there was no electorate support for his proposals as they were not considered an issue. He responded acerbically, 'If that's true, it's about to bloody well change. I'm going to make it an issue. Don't slavishly follow opinion polls, Comrades. Get out there and make the issues which are important to the future'.

He was as good as his word. That was impressive. Less so was a lecture on the merits of Federal administration as against State administrations. 'The Federal Government runs the best railways in Australia. If it ran all the railways they would be of a similarly high standard . . . The best hospitals in this country are the Repatriation Hospitals. If the Federal Government was in charge of all hospitals they, accordingly, would be of the same high standard.' I made a timorous interjection, 'But hang on, if the States had the same money relatively as the Federal Government to run these things wouldn't they do just as well?'. The finely etched features of Whitlam's aristocratic face flushed with impatience. The eyes hardened and stared resolutely ahead. The most dangerous sign of all, he commenced to tear small strips from the top of his fingernails. This usually preceded a major eruption. Would he dismiss me the way he dismissed all lesser mortals with the pejorative, 'Pissant!'? (Pissants, it seemed, were the blight of all great men of imagination.) A long pause . . . was it coming? . . . no; we went on to the next business, I could relax.

What was my role while all this action was under way? I entered the Parliament with an oversized, lower social order chip on my shoulder—and made great efforts to ensure it was not easily dislodged. I was against the system and against compromise with it. Yet, without recognising it, I had thoroughly compromised myself by going into Parliament, the institution which more than any other represents and maintains the system. I was no Whitlamite at first. For much of the early years I suppose I could have been described as independent left. I was opposed to the over-arching role of imperial powers like Britain and the United States. Like some of my colleagues, I resisted pressures to be caustic on communism. In many regards this was a reaction against Menzies' extraordinarily uncomplicated, monolithic view of world communism, a view which never distinguished the tensions between the Soviet Union and China, or comprehended the nationalist forces impelling that doctrine in developing countries. I was appalled by the crude power principles of 'real politics' in international relations. I was for big government and government enterprises. If it was government it had to be good, especially if there was a chance I might share a role in it. In spite of that, bit by bit I was moving towards Whitlam. I admired his spunky tenacity, his willingness to fight for worthwhile causes. He was an unflinching civil libertarian, and that was inspiring too.

There was another influence. I had come to tertiary education late in life and like so many mature age students I constantly discovered exciting new insights. Younger students I imagine would have taken these experiences in their stride as part of an unbroken continuum of learning, stretching from school through university. But with many years of meagre intellectual sustenance behind me, when I *was* finally subjected to these influences a mind locked behind the doors of various prejudices began to open up. I commenced to discover what Whitlam was really about, and that most of all he was a profound humanist. In the circumstances, I shall owe an eternal debt of gratitude to Roland Hill, who 'founded' the modern postal service back in 1840, for without correspondence study through the Queensland Secondary School of Correspondence and then the External Studies Department of the University of Queensland this opening up of a narrow mind may not have happened.

As a first-time delegate to National Conference in 1965 the force of many of Whitlam's arguments compelled my support. By the time of the 1967 Conference there were few differences between us. While I may have been too passionate and not reflective enough about how we handled the Vietnam War issue, my biggest stumbling block was State Aid for non-government schools. Apart from a generally dismissive and not very original attitude towards religion, believing as I did that it was the 'opium of the masses', I had far bigger problems of principle. My view was that Church and State should be kept separate, as history held many sad illustrations of what happened when it was otherwise. Equally, I firmly believed that it was the duty of government to provide a good standard of public services and utilities in areas such as transport and education. If, however, some people wanted something different or better, then the obligation was on them to pay for it themselves and not ask taxpayers to do so. Nonetheless, my principles aside, we were tearing the entrails from the Party with the State Aid dispute. The risk of another nasty split, one which might be terminal given our poor morale, was growing all the time. There was no question, the dispute was becoming more and more rancorous and sectarian for Labor.

Though a Presbyterian in good standing with his Church, Menzies, apparently oblivious to the divisive disputes of the 1860s and 1870s over State Aid (or perhaps more characteristically attuned to short-term political expediency), did the very thing his Church had counselled against. In publicly funding science blocks and libraries for non-State schools, Church and State were hand in glove in a way they had not been for some ninety years. Menzies' tactic was to propitiate the DLP and hold their preference votes, garner Catholic support for his party, and divide Labor. With the State Aid debate—always near the surface of public concerns for Catholics—taking off seriously, Menzies seemed to have miscalculated. The Catholics wanted more, and after initial travail, Labor regrouped to eventually become a cohesive electoral force on the State Aid issue. The full ambit claim of the Catholics was eventually brought to bear; in New South Wales Catholic schools began being closed down in the early 1960s, imposing an intolerable strain upon the State school system. Labor, with its traditional Catholic support, was sorely tried by Menzies' initiative. Whitlam, as much to save the Labor Party and its constituency, fought doggedly to establish broad community support for State Aid and he was certainly successful, but it was the Presbyterian, Menzies, who was the initial architect.[39]

I agonised greatly over the issue. In 1968, at York, Western Australia, I attended a Fabian Society Conference at which I was one of several speakers. Jim Cairns was another. Peter Walsh, later of the Senate and subsequently a Hawke Government minister, was present too. Cairns was asked a question about State Aid. His response was to this effect: 'Children do not have any say in choosing the place of their education. Their parents do that. Many parents exercise the choice because of a deep religious conviction. Unfortunately some of those schools are not up to an acceptable standard. No child should be handicapped throughout its life because its parents chose an inferior education system. Therefore the case for direct State Aid on that principle is unchallengeable'. That was it. Simple but incisive and incontrovertible. I had found the principle to justify what others would describe as my apostasy. I went back to Canberra irrevocably committed to Whitlam. The last barrier was down. To my surprise, Cairns went back to Canberra and opposed State Aid, which left me rather more confused about him.

By 1968, Whitlam was in full 'crash through' mode following a good Senate result the year before; the Party was performing well under his leadership, he was also once again taking the National Executive head on. As a consequence, Gorton was ahead in the opinion polls throughout the year. The Victorian State Executive charged Whitlam with making damaging public criticisms of its affairs and Calwell, determined not to allow his tired and shaky generational view pass away decently and quietly, charged him with 'debauching' the Vietnam policy, and of 'disloyal and untrustworthy conduct' in doing so. The charges went before the National Executive which conducted a show trial worthy of one of the now defunct East European regimes. Whitlam, as ever, convinced that intellectual prowess, cerebral argument and facts well-mobilised should win the day, accordingly entered this test with distinct disadvantages. What he came up against was the prevailing Victorian philosophy, best summarised in the immortal words of the late Pat Kennelly, 'You can keep yer principles. Just give me the numbers, that's all I need'.

Whitlam was totally unprepared for the onslaught within the National Executive. His opponents launched an unexpected attack against the fitness of a Tasmanian delegate, Brian Harradine, to sit on the Executive. Harradine was easily discredited. All the 'objective' evidence was against him in so far as Whitlam's oligarchic opponents were concerned: devout Catholic, ex-DLP, ex-Passionist Order Seminarian, official of the Clerks' Union anathematised as a 'Grouper' industrial organisation, and worst of all, a Whitlam supporter. Harradine was subjected to punishing questioning for a day-and-a-half. The grim charges were, even though not proven, upheld. He was excluded from the Executive. Doug Lowe, the second Tasmanian delegate, stormed out in protest. The oligarchs could not have prayed for a better result as they were now clearly in control of the meeting. They then turned on the 'Big Bastard', as they used to call Whitlam unsentimentally. Neither of Whitlam's leadership associates from the Senate, Lionel Murphy or Sam Cohen, both barristers, did a jot to try to ensure due processes, fair hearings and restrained conduct by that inquisitorial bench the Executive had made of itself. I worked with Murphy over many years and am much less impressed than some by the Murphy legend, or inclined to the view that he was an unwavering civil libertarian and a high-minded fighter for good left causes.

Whitlam, ever one for the 'grand gesture'—as he once put it to me—stormed off too. He resigned his leadership to '. . . permit Caucus . . . with least embarrassment to endorse their leader or substitute another'. Cairns responded simply and unemotionally, but with devastating effect in the Party, '. . . whose party is this— ours or his?'. Whitlam was in diabolical strife. At this point his situation was somewhat akin to the prelate Beckett, altogether too turbulent. There was to be a ballot on Whitlam's future. The night before, there was a meeting of the Left caucus to which a few outsiders, such as me, were invited. I expect it was meant to be a subtle backbone stiffener for us, in case we might have been wavering towards Whitlam. I went away early and uncommitted. On the one hand, Whitlam had overplayed his hand dreadfully and had been doing so intermittently throughout the year; I was certainly hostile towards him over the way he had behaved publicly on this issue. On the other hand, I grudgingly recognised that while his tactics might have been excessive, he was right in principle. It was a worrying matter. Uren of the Left saw me shortly after the ballot, inquiring, 'Did the right thing, Billy?'. 'Yes, I certainly did.' I had voted for Whitlam. Cairns received thirty-two votes to Whitlam's thirty-eight. In the light of Cairns' performance in government later I clearly 'had done the right thing'.

Gorton was quite evidently preparing for an early election. A smart move in that he was unlikely to lose now that we were in dreadful disarray. In an unsettled mood I went back to my electorate to campaign. My final university examinations were also imminent. In the course of any year my opportunities for study were episodic and quite inadequate. I used to depend on high-pressure cramming over the last few weeks before examinations. My electorate was large with many 'soft spots'. It required constant attention. The polls looked threatening. On the other hand I did not wish to repeat these subjects over another year. I could only do one or the other adequately—a tough personal decision. To try both would be fatal to each. Not surprisingly, the instinct for survival took over. I hurtled about the electorate in early campaigning mode.

As I drove into the Linville timber mill yards, well up the Brisbane Valley, the midday ABC radio news reported that after discussions with the DLP leadership Gorton had decided not to call an election. Thank God, I thought, but what a fool! If Gorton had proceeded with that election he would have been Prime Minister for another term, while Whitlam and Labor would have headed for an uncertain fate. Gorton should have called the DLP's bluff. They had nowhere to go with their preferences but to the coalition. The first time they delivered preferences to Labor, even selectively, would be the beginning of a very rapid end for them. They would have compromised the anathema with which they had stigmatised those who voted Labor. With a bound and a leap Whitlam was back in the race the following year. The man had more narrow escapes than Harry Houdini, and like Houdini, compulsively returned to these death-defying performances. A near brush with disaster seemed to whet his appetite for a return bout with even greater risks than last time. At the 1969 national election Labor won seventeen seats, needing only four more to form government. In fact, five of the seats won by the Coalition Government had been attained with the 'donkey vote'. It was a close run thing. The good news for me was that Gorton's retreat allowed me to return to my books and study, allowing me to get a satisfying High Distinction for far eastern history and a Distinction for trade economics. It was a happy moment when the last of that grind was behind me.

The precursors

The postwar forties were about the serious business of getting the country working again as a civilian society, harvesting together the fruits of peace. The fifties was a straight-corseted decade, much as we were trying to relax in a new age of prosperity; if there was more individual freedom, we were also inhibited by collective, hypocritical hang-ups left over from the Victorian period. Strict sexual morality was propounded in public but promiscuity was on the rise privately. The back seat of the increasingly ubiquitous FJ Holden was probably more responsible for courtship, conception and marriage and the subsequent baby boom than were any abstract notions of romantic love, or the appeal of a chaste wedding bed and a white picket fence around the conjugal home. Understandably, values were changing as the experiences of depression and war receded.

This process of greater personal freedom was probably most emphatically evident among women. With effective contraception and legal abortions giving women almost absolute control over their fertility cycle, reproduction rates eased back. At the same time, pressure was on housewives and mothers to re-enter the workforce to maintain the economic momentum and sustain prosperity. Now, having children represented a clear monetary penalty for a woman in income foregone (estimated by one source at some \$400 000) not to mention the burden of restricted individual freedoms.[40] Modern woman is the freest woman has ever been, possessing a more individualistic outlook and enjoying a higher degree of personal independence than in times past.

More generally, with increasing prosperity, and as more people could afford to buy a motor car, came greater mobility. This in turn allowed a greater diversity in the rising generation's interests, something particularly reflected in recreation. An earlier almost exclusive preoccupation with team sports, dependent on a form of collective discipline and commonly available transport, gave way to the decidedly more individualistic pursuits that greater personal income could provide—abseiling, windsurfing and surfboard riding, hang-gliding, scuba diving, and other activities scarcely known before the fifties. A growing proportion of the rising generation undertook tertiary education, in which positive values based on the merit performance of the person were stressed and low common denominator conformity was dismissed. This added to the growing sense of the importance of the individual. The practices of learning by rote and didactic teaching were replaced with a process of exploration, analysis and questioning of propositions. As the old orthodoxy of swallowing 'received wisdom' declined, so too came a steady erosion of the influence of certified authority figures.

Menzies was congenitally incapable of responding to these changes, if indeed he was ever aware of them; for not only was his personal style embodied in the notion of a reassuring authority figure, his whole vision was fossilised in a long-departed past. How else can the cloying highlight of his greeting to Elizabeth II on the occasion of her 1963 visit to Parliament House, Canberra, dredged from the sixteenth-century doggerel of Barnabe Googe, be explained?

I did but see her passing by
And yet I love her till I die.

As a sign of the times even the Queen gave a mild, elegant shudder of embarrassment at so much treacle in one dose.

Harold Holt, Menzies' successor, tried to break out of the obsolete social weave and warp as bequeathed by Menzies. He ended the White Australia Policy, promoted Aboriginal welfare, and initiated an independently administered national arts policy, something which Menzies had steadfastly resisted. Retrospectively, it all looks a bit timid in contrast to what was expected by the community and in comparison with the enormous accumulation of changes which have taken place since. Conservatives of the period, of course, regarded it all as rather radical. Less wisely, Holt beefed up the Australian military commitment to the Vietnam War and enforced conscription. His successors would pay a price for that, a big one. Holt's problem was that he had been under Menzies' shadow for so long that the authentic Harold Holt never emerged. On one occasion a senior Hansard reporter whispered to me as he was exiting from his shift in the House of Representatives, where he had covered Holt in a major debate, 'For Holt read Menzies'.

Holt's declaration, while visiting President Johnson of the United States in Washington in 1966, that Australia 'would go all the way with LBJ' in its military and policy commitment to the Vietnam War shocked and insulted many Australians. Its seeming servility was an embarrassment and a worry. (As an aside, Washington had a strange effect on many visiting Australian prime ministers. Gorton promised to go 'Waltzing Matilda' with the United States to 'resist aggression' in Vietnam. More unfathomable, or perhaps unravellable, was Billy McMahon's sustained solecism when, in the same city on a later occasion, he said, '. . . there comes a time in the life of a man in the flood of time that taken at the flood leads on to fortune'. There was a break from prime ministerial gaucheries out of Washington until Hawke arrived and promised that 'Australia and the USA would be together forever' and 'There is no country that the USA will be able to rely on more as a constructive ally than Australia'.[41])

Within a year of his record postwar electoral success of 1966 Holt was in serious trouble with his own party over his leadership. Then came John Grey Gorton, a most underrated Liberal prime minister. Such is the insularity between the Senate and the House of Representatives, he arrived in the House scarcely known there, although he had been in the Senate for nearly twenty years. He was tall, angular, good humouredly lackadaisical in the manner of a likeable larrikin from the bush. He had been a fighter pilot during World War II. His crumpled face bore testimony to an aircraft crash he had survived. In the 'seat of the pants' manner of so many fighter pilots, he would respond to a challenge instinctively by being airborne, ready for combat the instant the battle alert sounded. Unfortunately, this was often his response as Prime Minister, instead of a steady focusing on the wider issues involved. He was very Australian in his egalitarianism, his lack of pretension, his directness and his refusal to truckle to any person. The Gorton persona resonated well with many Australians. Gorton was brought down eventually by a conspiracy orchestrated in the Melbourne Club, played out within his party room at Canberra, and stage-managed by media magnate Frank Packer from Sydney, a former pugilist who seemed to think that human relations were conducted in the same way people behaved in the boxing ring. Packer used his hatchet man, Alan Reid of the *Daily Telegraph,* to write a damaging biography of Gorton. The aim was to hoist Packer's little pal, McMahon, euphoniously dubbed 'Billy the Leak' by Gorton, into the prime minister's office by tumbling Gorton out. Early into the work Reid disclosed that Gorton was 'a bastard by birth'.[42] Gorton responded with a nice turn of phrase pointing out that Reid had achieved exactly the same status 'by applying himself assiduously to that task for many years'.[43]

Gorton had to come unstuck with his conservative colleagues. He was a case of too much shock of the new altogether too quickly. He was an unabashed centralist while his party was dedicated to federalism and States' rights. It was Gorton's view that Canberra should have sole control of the economy. He flouted the mystical belief in market forces, establishing the Australian Industries Development Corporation as a public sector risk merchant banker, and flirted with establishing a government overseas shipping operation. He rejected Treasury advice and prevented a foreign takeover of the MLC Insurance Corporation. Pale-faced business-men in grey suits from the 'big end of town' were flummoxed by this heresy. Gorton made it clear that issues like the environment, education, health and housing should be led from the national capital, and that the States would be reduced to disbursing the funds. The States fumed. They unbridled their dudgeon when he clashed with them over Commonwealth–States finances and the takeover of potentially remunerative offshore mineral resources. He sensibly warned of the dangers of the 'forward defence' policy once Britain had withdrawn from the near region. More outrage, this time from the 'Colonel Blimps' who seemed to attach themselves so readily to the Liberal Party. Then his Foreign Minister, Gordon Freeth, made the perfectly sane observation that there was no need for panic every time a Soviet naval vessel appeared in the Indian Ocean. The DLP and Liberal Party backbenchers dependent on DLP preferences were staggered beyond belief, for their political existence depended on this demonology not being even faintly demythologised, and so more strife arose for Gorton. He advised his party its tenets had been in place for too long without review, were fustian, might not be relevant to contemporary needs and accordingly should be reassessed. This was shocking for a party whose members were content to hanker after the golden years of their past, rather than confront the mounting challenges which would determine the nation's future.

The forces of destruction—particularly in the form of Premiers Bolte of Victoria and Askin of New South Wales—were by now unappeasable and were closing in on Gorton. Even the great Menzies emerged from a usually discreet retirement to advise publicly in Perth that the Liberal Party was a federal party not a centralist one. Oblivious to the dangers, Gorton ploughed on with a purposeful tread, later informing the National Executive of his party that 'we had all paid too much attention to Liberal principles over the past ten years, and it was now time we moved towards socialism'.[44] Men of great self-importance in exclusive places, like certain habitués of the Melbourne Club, no doubt choked on their tumblers of Scotch or gasped over their long planters' gins when they heard this. By now Gorton was riding on a wild tiger's back.

In the way of these developments in politics, anything which could be used to Gorton's discredit was aired publicly with much tut-tutting by his own party members. His lack of discipline in private matters left him vulnerable. His tortured syntax was a matter of scorn. (Yet Hawke, a recent successor of his, fractured the Queen's English with great diligence and was loved for this common touch.) If Gorton had a quick eye for a stylish female ankle, the Liberals, however, felt this sullied their reverence for the institution of the family. That was the public stance. Privately there was consternation, at the Melbourne Club of course, that Gorton's real problem was he fraternised with uncouth 'downstairs' females:

> . . . if one behaves oddly with people in the establishment, there's not much trouble. If, on the other hand, one conducts the same sort of behaviour with people outside of the establishment . . . then the world gets to know and nothing can be done to prevent trouble.[45]

Perhaps his critics erred grievously in counting these things as flaws, for a later prime ministerial aspirant, Hawke, only increased his popularity every time he publicly flaunted his innumerable sexual liaisons, and also boosted his standing among some women when he treated females with dominating machismo tendencies. (Later again, as Prime Minister, Hawke would of course periodically prime his popularity with confessions of his encounters of an illicit kind, tearfully begging public forgiveness.) Perhaps that suggests that Gorton may have been instinctively in tune with the Australian people's love of a political larrikin. His personal peccadillos to one side, Gorton was very much in touch with strongly emerging issues and contemporary attitudes in society.

His customs minister, Don Chipp, was a genuine small 'l' liberal and as such the object of suspicions from his more numerous and influential conservative peers in the Liberal Party. He was seen as soft on drugs when in fact he was cautiously attempting to introduce a more humane and supportive attitude towards drug addiction, rather than rely exclusively on punishment. He believed people had a right to read literature like *Lady Chatterley's Lover* (a boring, poorly written work the demand for which and its notoriety were created by it having been banned). Censorship reached its ludicrous nadir with an enthusiastic customs official confiscating a work entitled *Fun In Bed*. The work was returned when it was discovered to be a book of stories and games for ill children. By the time it was discovered that Chipp had single-handedly brought about the most radical and extensive reform of our censorship practices, the new standards were firmly in place. The DLP never forgave him.

Chipp was not totally alone in implementing reform. The eccentric Billy Wentworth also helped uncap within his party a social conscience, previously not much in evidence. With Gorton's encouragement Wentworth undertook the greatest range of initiatives up to that time in social services benefits, community welfare policy, and later in Aboriginal welfare.

The point of these observations is that while Whitlam as PM sought to introduce a wide-ranging programme, radical in its departure from the constrictive style of the Menzies era, there was a link between his goals and some of the activities of his predecessors. Whitlam's major policy initiatives were anticipated by quite a few of Gorton's actions. Gorton's problem was he was in the wrong party to consolidate understanding let alone support, behind his objectives. Nonetheless, his forging ahead with a number of radical initiatives made Whitlam's programme of sweeping changes less alien than otherwise would have been the case.

The political assassination of John Grey Gorton

The 1969 election result was excellent for Labor. We were starting to see a way out of the wilderness of Opposition in which we had been flailing about for so long. For Gorton, the elegies were being rehearsed but he was not listening. To the indictments his party opponents were secretly preparing against him, was now added the claim that he was an electoral loser.

The next step in the plan to demolish Gorton was resolutely undertaken by Malcolm Fraser. Frank Packer's media outlets were fully mobilised for the onslaught. A story was leaked to the *Bulletin*, and it also appeared in the *Daily Telegraph*, accusing the army of subverting government civic aid policy in Vietnam.[46] Fraser denied responsibility for the leak and was immediately charged publicly with the 'lie direct' by the journalist Maximillian Walsh and also the editor of the *Bulletin*. It transpired that Fraser had even vetted the article before it was published. The leaked account was quite damaging to the junior army minister, Peacock, though this was a matter of no account to Fraser. Peacock was expendable, as was anyone else who ever stood in the way of Fraser's remorselessly pursued ambitions.[47] The sordid little incident grew out of all proportion to its importance. The Canberra journalist, Alan Ramsay, wrote that Chief of the Army General Staff, Lieutenant-General Sir

Thomas Daly, had complained to Gorton that Fraser was guilty of 'extreme disloyalty to the army and its junior minister, Mr Peacock' by leaking this story. Gorton and Daly denied this report. Ramsay declared Gorton had seen and cleared his article before publication. Gorton repudiated this. Packer's *Daily Telegraph* kept the issue on its front page for several days, steering the thrust of developments away from Fraser and directing accusations at Gorton, until Gorton was finally destroyed.[48]

What was an unedifying, squalid attempt to manipulate the media for grubby personal political ambitions suddenly boiled over into the Parliament. Gorton accepted a resolution by Whitlam proposing that Fraser, who by now had resigned from the Ministry as a matter of 'principle', be allowed to address the House. Fraser artfully skirted around the central issues, seemed to imply a denial, but then dexterously qualified those comments with the breathtaking disclaimer of any responsibility for truth: 'comments on the article are related to perspective and interpretation rather than denial'. Fraser had the gall to add the self-righteous claim, after the damage he had gratuitously done Peacock, that Gorton 'would prefer to allow a false and damaging report to be publicised about a senior Minister [Fraser]' by not convincingly denying Ramsay's article when shown it, an allegation Gorton denied.[49]

Fraser's response was 'skilful' and 'clever', answering nothing and evading all the important accusations. Gorton's statement in reply seemed a reasonable and convincing riposte to Fraser. In his comments Gorton denied the Ramsay report. Ramsay interjected from the gallery 'You liar'. The interjection ran through the chamber like the deadly shot of a skilled marksman. Gorton was finished. No-one listened to him after that. Later, Ramsay passed a personal note to Tony Eggleton, National Secretary of the Liberal Party, stating that Gorton had been 'unfair', that 'there was no question of you [Gorton] being a liar'. But too late. This devastating interjection had killed Gorton stone dead politically. No apology could breathe life back into his prime ministership, least of all a private one. Fraser's unscrupulous conduct did him no harm. His reputation remained intact. But then so many of the important moments in Fraser's public life seemed to involve unscrupulous exploitation of an opportunity. With his mixed Oxford accent, Fraser always put me in mind of what an English public school bounder is probably like.

The rest is a sordid political account of certain of Gorton's party colleagues conspiring to remove him from the prime ministership, and of secret deals of expedience with the Labor Party to bring this about, and in the House if necessary. Gorton left the prime ministership but surprisingly re-emerged as deputy to his successor, McMahon. Packer publicly declared that Gorton 'would be the next one for the chop', after several of his supporters had been ejected from the Cabinet by McMahon. Packer was right. Three days later Gorton was gone. This political massacre appears to have been the culmination of extended plotting between McMahon and Packer, with the willing connivance of Packer's hatchet man in Canberra, Alan Reid. The momentum began to gather towards the end of the previous calendar year with Reid confidentially advising selected sources there would be a change of prime minister by March 1971, a prescient prediction as it happened. Gorton was sacked as Deputy Prime Minister as a result of a series of articles he authored in the *Australian*. Stating the truth, if unwisely under the circumstances, he alleged that some Cabinet ministers leaked; they canvassed issues before Cabinet outside of that body, he said, including with their wives. Everyone knew he was fingering McMahon whose propensity to leak was legendary. Even Menzies and Dick Casey joked about this proclivity of McMahon's. The media baron, Rupert Murdoch, later, personally and mercilessly pinioned McMahon for this sort of behaviour in one of his newspapers.[50] There was an imposing cast of 'big names' which ensured the downfall of Gorton: Fraser most of all because of the ruthless way he wielded the broad axe; Menzies and Casey (the latter not without some relish at the prospect of evening up the score with Gorton for reputedly easing him out of the governor-generalship to make way for Hasluck);[51] various members of the Melbourne Club; most decidedly Packer but also Reid who regularly stiffened the backbones of Liberal MPs.[52] Indeed, Reid was eventually 'thanked . . . for all the help that he'd given' those in the Liberal Party who had conspired so successfully against Gorton.[53]

The last mile to government

The 1969 election was over and at last I was elected to the Parliamentary Labor Party Executive, the shadow Cabinet. Crean was first with seventy votes and Hayden and Beazley Snr were listed as equal second with forty-nine votes each, in that order because, I expect, I got a few more primary votes. At the risk of being immodest, my sudden elevation had much to do with a couple of effective television debate appearances during the campaign. Television was still a daunting medium for the older politicians, so they tended to exaggerate the value of 'good' performances by younger people. It was a heady moment. I had crashed through the left and right wing redoubts to make it. Eight years to arrive, but I was there, part of the great tradition of Labor. Moreover, I had preserved my independence: I had not lobbied for one vote. I suspect it impossible to convey to many what that experience meant to someone like me from what would now be termed an 'old Labor' background. I very much looked forward to my shadow responsibility, hoping for something with a strong economic content. I had come to believe the transformation of society would be determined by economics not draft resolutions on legal reforms—which is why, early in my studies, I had changed my university course from law to economics.

I was standing in King's Hall. The Caucus elections were just behind us. Whitlam whirled past. He suddenly pivoted and came over. 'What portfolio would you like, Comrade?' he inquired with appropriate solemnity. With more cheek than hope I responded, 'Treasury . . . ?' 'Sorry, Crean,' he replied. 'Transport . . . ?' 'Sorry, Charlie Jones.' I tried a few more. There was always a name to each I raised. 'Well . . . what's available?' I queried with some sense of despair. 'Health and Welfare. Comrade, it will make you. Grab it.' 'What else?' 'Comrade, I am afraid Health and Welfare is all that is available.' The great man's patience was evidently wearing thin. 'Hell, that's no big deal.' 'Comrade, we're going to do great things in this field.' I was dumbfounded. 'It's yours for the asking!' he added like an indulgent uncle handing out presents to relations he had inherited by marriage rather than by choice. In the event I began to learn about the detail of health and welfare rather quickly.

I made contact with large numbers of dedicated people in other capitals, particularly in Melbourne with its broader and deeper intellectual tradition. This contact was extremely helpful for a crash familiarisation course. As I commenced to come to grips with the area, I became aware of potential pitfalls. Some people had pet projects which they promoted with passion. That did not necessarily mean they were the most desirable welfare priorities. I soon learned one had to say 'No!', and that was never popular. The worst problem was trying to convince people that boundless compassion was not sufficient foundation alone on which to base sound welfare planning. Fiscal disciplines, the principle of progressive redistribution, the need to establish priority areas of commitment were important too; arguably more so. I also discovered that elements of the welfare industry were quite capable of seeking to organise the political agenda so as to get their ends ahead of others. And this sometimes through furious conflict and not even moderate attention to scruple.

I was participating in a think-tank gathering one day when the leader of the group, a young man of strong personality and with a keen personal following in the welfare industry, declared emphatically, 'We have to get rid of means tests and all of the stigma which goes with them. Needs tests are what is required'. . . His decisive, authoritative manner discouraged any querying of this welfare profundity. I asked uncertainly, after a few seconds of rising doubts, 'But what is the difference? Surely your means determine your needs. Don't you end up with the same thing?' I was assured in a stammering response that 'Ah . . . ah . . . well, yes and no . . . ah . . . ah . . . there is a qualitative difference . . . you'll . . . ah . . . pick this up with experience'. Other heads sagely nodded confirmation of this wisdom. 'Self-realisation', 'personal dignity', 'empowering users,' were terms much loved by welfare practitioners. There was never any lucid definition of what was meant, a mere mantra-like repetition of these terms being the sole justification for whatever was being proposed.

I addressed a large audience of emerging leaders of trade unions and professional associations at a residential college at the Australian National University one evening. The function had been convened by the ACTU and accordingly the invitation to attend was not the sort of offer one easily ignored in the Labor Party. I outlined an earnings-related contributory national superannuation scheme I had worked up. Representatives of the unskilled workforce told me bluntly that the income level at which contributions commenced was too low. In other words their members deserved exemption from contributing but should draw full benefits as a matter of justice. Then the skilled blue collar representatives, just as directly, made it clear that benefits should stand but that the income cut-in point for contributions should be even higher again. Their job was to get the best deal they could for their members. That was obvious. The white collar and professional representatives were totally against any contributions as a matter of high 'principle', although they applauded higher benefits for higher income earners. Exasperatedly I inquired as to where the money would come from to fund the scheme. 'Why . . . why . . . BHP . . . and . . . er . . . the big companies . . . yes, make the monopolies pay!' This phrase was enunciated with a rising triumphant cadence, the sentiment proving very popular all round. Thus I was introduced to the BHP redistribution factor. Something else was also confirmed: better benefits are always welcomed but someone else should be made to pay. That was the golden rule of progressive redistribution for many.

I also quickly learnt the difficulties of getting a new idea across, even to people who would benefit from a proposal. I worked up a paper in which I proposed that the outlays on the flat payment rates of child endowment and the total cost of income tax concessions for dependent children, which favoured higher income earners, be aggregated and paid out as a new means-tested children's benefit. An employee at the Launceston mail exchange was one of the many who wrote abusive letters to me accusing me of wanting to reduce families' living standards. He was just the sort of person who stood to gain handsomely from the proposal. I dropped it as too politically risky to persevere with.

The AMA gave me some of my most valuable lessons. Behind those comforting stethoscopes lurked some of the toughest and most unscrupulous trade union officials I ever met. When I used one loose word, it would be wrenched into a new shape to imply something sinister, and off they would streak to misrepresent what I was proposing. For a well-educated, generously remunerated professional group who functioned according to a lofty ethical code it was disappointing to observe that all they ever wanted to talk about was money, more precisely how much they were determined to earn. Discussion of better health care through a comprehensive development of integrated community health services, or the notion of preventative care, was congenitally uninteresting to them. They were preoccupied with our universal health insurance programme, and even there they had a narrow, almost pinpoint focus. Behind certain buzz words, like 'doctor–patient confidentiality' and 'patient privacy' loitered a very well-developed sense of personal greed. In closed session it came out nakedly. Their biggest fear was that I would cap their income. On one occasion in Melbourne, addressing an AMA meeting in the Clunies-Ross Building I became exasperated and sarcastically spat out, 'Stop complaining. When I'm finished your pockets will be stuffed with gold', for the funding arrangements of the programme were quite generous to the profession. With these unwise words, joy, boundless joy was experienced by many of the profession. Regularly after that I was accused of trying to bribe them at the expense of taxpayers. The fact that they were already heavily into the taxpayer's purse through subsidies from government and the tax system did not worry them one iota. They feared, correctly, that if I got my way I would endeavour to control their overcharging and overservicing. The tragedy of this debate, as with so much industrial politics, was that certain of the leadership groups were not well-representative of the doctors who beavered away at their various practices looking after people.

The last big battle

In 1970 Whitlam accepted his greatest challenge in taking on the doggedly confrontationist Victorians. Like all autarchic oligarchies, they had become besotted with their unfettered power. They had seriously over-reached themselves. In Queensland, the party was directed by the tough, redoubtable Jack Egerton who, in contrast to the Victorians, always made sure that reasonable dissent was accommodated. That is not to say he did so delightedly. To a group of colleagues and me, moderate lefties and products of the Depression such as Norma and Hec Chalmers, Joy Guyatt and George Georges (the latter somewhat less moderately left than others) Egerton once commented in exasperation, 'The only bloody reason we put up with you bloody lot is if anyone says we're like the Victorians I point to the bloody lot of you to show what we tolerate up here. J . . . . C . . . . ., you're a first class pain in the a . . . e, the lot of you. You don't know when you're on a bloody good thing'. It was a cameo Egerton performance, given for our benefit during a Queensland Central Executive Committee meeting (or in practical terms the State Executive). It will be noted nonetheless how we warmed to the idea of monolithic organisation: it was no ordinary State Committee, but the *Central* Committee.

On another occasion at the 1971 State Conference at Surfers Paradise I moved two resolutions, one to ban professional boxing and the other to legalise homosexuality. I lost the first resolution but was fairly convinced that the second had been carried on the voices. Egerton ruled otherwise. There was a groan from the respectably large group of civil libertarians among delegates. I called for a division. Egerton was furious. 'Gawd, I can't follow delegate Hayden. He's opposed to a bloke getting a punch on the nose but doesn't mind if he gets a punch in the bum. Those supporting the chairman to the right, poofters to the left!' Egerton's humorous, if rough and ready, response defused a fair bit of tension, for support for homosexuals' rights was in its infancy back then. Representatives of the clean-cut working-class were not too sure about homosexuals in those days.

Egerton knew when it was advisable to lose, even if he could force the numbers to win, and although he sometimes lost with ill-grace it was short-lived. He had a delightful wit, very Australian, very working-class. Even his staunch opponents were responsive to it. He knew when he had to be tough and when to jolly a meeting along. Most endearingly, he would provide genuine help for someone experiencing personal difficulty, regardless of whether they were opponents of his or not. 'Jack's never afraid to put 'is 'and in 'is pocket to help a bloke whose doing it 'ard,' was the kind of generous testimonial he would evince in the culture of old Labor. And he was tough. One night as he walked in the darkened streets near the Brisbane Trades Hall a thug slashed his face open, a reprisal for some sort of union conflict involving Egerton (there were one or two tough unions about then). He knew the assailant but was totally unhelpful to the police. 'You never scream copper because you're having a bit of strife. The workers aren't impressed with that.' Of course, one hopes this old creed has had its day.

In Victoria there was no give and so a rigid, brittle structure fractured under pressure to which it had been unaccustomed. In April 1970 the Victorians confronted the National Executive over the issue of State Aid. This was not smart, for the numbers on the National Executive had discreetly moved against them. They were unaware that Whitlam's implacable foe and long-term arch opponent of State Aid, Clyde Cameron, had allowed his head to be gently turned in the direction of self-promotion. Whitlam had whispered into his well-tuned ear, 'A dubious footnote in political history or the Minister for Labour in the first Whitlam Government after the 1972 election. The choice is yours, Comrade'. Cameron's superb organising skills and his methodical hunting down of quarry were, as assets, a prize beyond measure for Whitlam. Whitlam clung to his belief in principles and reasoned argument, but now he recruited a 'numbers man', one with plenty of political savvy; a person who understood that numbers were the crucial element in any power struggle and who knew how to mobilise them. The Victorians were crushed. One of their number, George Crawford, had referred to the National Executive after it had temporised with the State Aid policy, as the 'Mad Hatter's Tea Party'. Such palpable contempt of this august body was intolerable. If this conduct was not nipped in the bud it would be only a short step to even worse, like describing the Executive as a body of 'twelve witless men'.

After one tiring all-day session on this issue the redoubtable Joe Chamberlain retreated to his motel room. The telephone rang. Chamberlain spoke one word into the mouthpiece, 'Yes?'. 'Clyde [Cameron] here Alan. I can give you a good run down on what went on today [in the Executive meeting].' Chamberlain replied dryly, 'I'm sorry, Clyde, it's Joe Chamberlain here. You've got the wrong room. Alan Reid is in room. . .' Cameron, never one for being fazed in embarrassing circumstances, coolly responded, 'Oh, is that you, Joe? Cracker meeting today, didn't you think?'. 'It depends on your point of view, Clyde. Once you wouldn't have said that,' and hung up. The Executive went on to purge the Victorian Executive, appointing Mick Young as full-time administrator of the affairs of the Party in that State—no enviable task for Young but one done exceedingly well and paving the way to victory in 1972. Hawke, then in thrall to the Left for his elevation in the ACTU, implacably opposed this intervention but, curiously, quietly and promptly accepted a position on the appointed administration committee once the intervention was completed. Some union representatives who muttered about 'taking Cameron on' in Young's hearing provoked him to respond, 'Go ahead and take him on. You'll only need four things. A bottle of No-Doze tablets, a Trent memory-training course, a barrow-load of bayonets and a lot more bloody brains than any of you blokes have got,' and that was the end of that little mutiny. For Whitlam, meanwhile, this was probably his most singular victory in the long war to reform the Labor Party.

I was eating my breakfast cereal when the ABC news reported that Whitlam was preparing to visit the People's Republic of China, or Communist China as it was generally known. I nearly choked. What wizard had dreamt up this disaster in the making? The new prime minister, McMahon, predictably denounced this collabo-ration with the 'Reds'. With a nice turn of phrase, which for once he got right, he declared Chou En-lai 'had played [Whitlam] as a fisherman plays a trout'. Most of us only saw trouble ahead. The importance of luck cannot be ruled out in politics, although it is dangerous to base one's moves on the hope that a stroke of it will fall into place at the right moment. But Whitlam was indeed lucky. Unbeknown to the rest of the world, United States National Security Advisor, Dr Henry Kissinger, had been in China at the same time as Whitlam preparing a visit there by President Nixon. Suddenly Whitlam's move was much more than respectable and acceptable, it was a stroke of genius and so many who had earlier harboured grave doubts about the enterprise now bathed in the reflected glory of Whitlam's triumph. Whitlam was generally seen as coolly and calculatingly cerebral. Yet there were occasions, like this one, where, like a riverboat gambler, he could wager all on the chance turn of a card. 'To dare is to win' was often his tactic.

About the same time another nasty problem arose. The ACTU declared support for demonstrations against the 1971 South African Springboks' rugby tour. There was a collective groan of despair from the Parliamentary Executive when this was announced. We knew that while the ACTU liked to carry 'feel good' political resolutions it did little to back them up practically, its members being almost exclusively preoccupied with industrial issues. Moreover, the conflict would not be in the AFL capital, Melbourne, home of the full-time ACTU leadership, but in Sydney and Brisbane where rugby is played. There certainly was conflict in Queensland. The Bjelke-Petersen State Government declared a state of emergency and extra police were drafted into Brisbane 'in the face of the threat of real violence and defiance of law and order, with subsequent dangers to life and property'.[54] The Premier's fears were well-grounded. In the evening, after the test match on 24 July 1971, the police, many of whom had been earlier fortifying themselves with rum, charged into demonstrators quietly standing about outside the Tower Mill Motel where the Springbok team was accommodated. Commissioner Whitrod, greatly honoured and respected in the community, was present and tried to control his officers. They ignored him, running a rampage among the orderly crowd. It was distinctly unpleasant. Dallas and I, who had been with the demonstrators throughout the day, fortunately left about an hour before this incident, satisfied that all was quiet and uneventful.

Earlier that day a large crowd of demonstrators had assembled in Victoria Park, near the Exhibition Grounds where the Test was to be played. There was not a senior union official within coo-ee of the grounds. There was Jerry Jones, party organiser, Senator George Georges, who loved martyrdom for lost causes, a few other party members and Dallas and me. The students and their followers marched onto the grounds in ragged formation, with beards, long hair and longer military-style coats from disposal stores, headbands, hippie beads and Aldermaston peace badges prominently displayed—all the armorial badges of rank of alienated youth of the time. There were large banners boldly proclaiming obscure groups, 'The Spartacus Society', 'The Young Hegelians'. Peace banners proliferated. This was the height of anti-Vietnam War sentiment. The young gurus of this rather tattered band, Dick Shearer and Brian Laver, marched at the head of their ragged formations.

A tabletop truck with a public address system provided the dais for the occasion. The ardent leaders of the young stoked up the fires of their passions. One stormed, 'This meeting is directionless. I move that there is only one of two alternatives available to us. March down to Ballymore Park and tear the rugby headquarters down brick by brick, tile by tile'. There was thunderous applause. 'Or we can march on the gates of the Exhibition Grounds and confront the police there!!!' Excited peals of 'Yes! Yes! Yes!' from the half-hysterical youth. Those of us who cared for the welfare of the youth and the reputation of the Labor Party argued for a calmer response. It was hard, emotionally draining work for we were few and were jeered and scorned by the radicals. Fortunately older heads among the crowd, moderate lefties who could always be counted on to turn out in support of 'good' causes and who sensibly recognised the limits of prudent conduct, as well as the handful of us taking the strain of the debate on the back of the old truck, eventually prevailed. Stewart Harris, a Canberra-based journalist, later wrote this 'intervention was courageous, because it was open to so much political misrepresentation by . . . political enemies. It was an example of the best kind of leadership'.[55]

The situation was well under control, so several of us went off for tea and sandwiches nearby. When we returned we were shocked to find the crowd forming up to march off in the direction of the Exhibition Grounds. The mood of high-pitched excitement was electrifying. In our absence the radicals had brought in their reserve forces, as it were. Georges took the lead, to our consternation. It turned out a master stroke for which Georges has never been sufficiently thanked by the Party. To lead, sometimes in difficult, emotionally charged conditions, requires a fair bit of following of the crowd just so long as at critical points developments are brought back into control. At the Exhibition Grounds turnoff Georges, probably for the first time in his life, did not turn left. He got the strung-out procession to sit down as he harangued them through a portable loud hailer. Those towards the middle and at the rear were confused as to what was happening among the leaders up front. The more confusion, the more control Georges established. Then onto their feet and marching again, past the turnoff down which the police were deployed and on towards the city. Georges was condemned by some of his State parliamentary colleagues, and quite wrongly. Without his intervention an awful confrontation would have occurred for the police were spoiling for conflict, as they displayed later. There are a number of middle-aged people today who participated in that demonstration as youths who have every reason to be grateful to Georges. Georges saved them from police convictions and perhaps the stripe of a baton across some part of their anatomy. For Bjelke-Petersen the provocative tactics were well worth the effort. He won two important by-elections that day, Merthyr and Maryborough, on the nasty law and order stunt he had been running for the preceding few weeks.

In 1971 Whitlam was ahead in the polls. We were going full steam ahead when suddenly we were grounding ourselves again. Whitlam and Freddy Daly had a very public clash over the White Australia Policy, a clash which Daly spontaneously acknowledged in later life was unwise and wrongly informed on his part. Back then it convulsed the Party. The Caucus revolted against Whitlam and Cameron, who were at that time seeking to force the pace on radical industrial relations policy changes. Whitlam was on the back foot. Other interest groups, noting his unsteadiness, moved in too. He was forced to retreat on industrial relations, as well as on tariff and abortion reform; further, he had to promise to ease back on immigration, especially coloured immigration, and undertake there would be no fines imposed on union strikers disputing an agreement. He also pledged to consult Caucus more closely in future. This last was a nuisance for Whitlam. There is great popular appeal in the Labor Party to the notion of 'consulting the rank and file', of 'continuing dialogue with the grassroots'. Most of it is humbuggery, particularly when it is being promoted by some faction leaders. What is usually meant is that they are not in control of the process under way and they are running a blocking operation, manipulating the process in an effort to impose their control. Such calls for democratic participation are more often than not fake. Of course, this observation would rarely, if ever, apply to the NSW Right, for as Graham Richardson once explained of that group, 'all decisions are democratically taken at a meeting of one; me!'. Consultation undertaken with legitimate motives can be a rewarding experience; the process, nonetheless, can be extremely time consuming, offering little leeway for getting things done. That was Whitlam's predicament. Whitlam did go on to honour his commitments, all of them—for a little while. Once again 'crash through or crash', as a tactic, had been prudently and temporarily parked somewhere out of the way.

Somewhere towards the end of 1971 several of us on the caucus Health and Welfare Committee had spent a couple of solid working days trying to construct an equitable formula for the abolition of the means test on age pensions. Every one of us opposed the notion as absolutely regressive in that it would provide benefits for better-off people at the expense of greater need elsewhere. That principle mattered nought, however, for the abolition of the means test was enshrined in the party platform and was, accordingly, binding holy writ. The formula we were working up was complex, but within the limits of what was imposed on us fairer than the alternatives considered. We broke just before 6 p.m. for a beer and dinner. The ABC news announced that Opposition Leader Whitlam had committed an incoming Labor government to abolish the means test for all over seventy-five years in the first year, over seventy years in the second and so on. We were furious. There was nothing we could do. The Leader, who had obviously got wind of what we were up to, had engaged in a little successful pre-emptive play. So much for consultation.

Suddenly we were in the heat of the lead-up to the December 1972 national election. A one hundred dollars a plate fundraising dinner for the Liberals was organised by Peter Abeles and Sir Ian Potter at Abeles luxurious mansion in Sydney. McMahon was the star for the night. It all went exceedingly well, except that after the guests departed it was discovered that no-one had bothered to collect the plate charge! In order to straddle the political divide, as a prudent matter of insurance, Abeles also held a fundraising dinner for Whitlam. At fifty dollars a plate it was obvious that the market rate for Labor was a lot lower, but at least this time the levy was collected. Demonstrators at one of McMahon's rallies hurled jelly beans at him. They were gathered from the stage and held as evidence to be handed over to the police. Unfortunately, again, when the police came to collect this critical forensic evidence it no longer existed. Campaign office staff had innocently eaten them.

Whitlam held his key Brisbane rally at the Homestead Hotel, Zillmere. There were threats of police action by Premier Bjelke-Petersen. Under the Queensland Criminal Code it was an offence with provision of a severe fine and/or imprisonment of up to one year for a candidate to convene a meeting on licensed premises.

Whitlam flouted the Premier's authority, standing on the platform before a huge crowd, and to their delight lampooned the Premier. He pointed out with much pantomime that he was a candidate, but he had not convened the meeting. He ran through the names of the other candidates present, but neither had they convened the meeting. As Jack Egerton, President of the Queensland branch of the Labor Party had convened the meeting, it was *he* who was impaled on the legal spear. There was only one technical problem, Whitlam pointed out: Egerton was not a candidate, thus he *too* was just as quickly off the hook. The crowd loved it. At last the overbearing tactics of Bjelke-Petersen got their comeuppance.

McMahon was not making a good fist of his campaigning at all. At first his confused utterances on the campaign trail were put down to tiredness. Then as they persisted it became clear that there was an intellectual breakdown there, something which registered with and disturbed the electorate. He went on to criticise his ministers for incompetence in the administration of government.[56] More confusion. Suddenly it was a case of 'It's Time'. Labor won the election. With this success so much dead wood of the past was swept out, not the least was the sad division of the community over the Vietnam War. Whitlam's struggle had been long, often causing him great personal pain and uncertainty, but fortunately he never flagged. In the process of achieving this victory, Labor was regenerated and the style of politics in Australia, more generally, was radically transformed. That is why Gough Whitlam remains significant in the political history of Labor and this country.

PART III

THE FLAWED
YEARS:
1972–1975

Economic Incompatibilities

L abor entered the 1972 election campaign well-prepared for the contest. No party since Federation had gone into an election with as comprehensive a range of policies as Labor did in 1972. We took to the electorate a set of proposals which were the culmination of more than a decade of detailed development, skilful refining and persuasive presentation, the product of unrelenting dedication and hard work, mostly by Labor's charismatic leader Gough Whitlam. The electoral worth of our programme was convincingly demonstrated. Labor won and, on the basis of its performance in the lead-up as well as the actual campaign, deservedly so. This is not to neglect the bonus of the wobbly record of the incumbent coalition government, nor the fragile mental state of its leader Billy McMahon, whose age seemed to be catching up with him. Nevertheless, it was a tight result, with marked swings against Labor in some States and in some regions.[1] Labor entered government yet, paradoxically, after so much preparation and effort to get there, soon found itself inadequate to the task of governing.

It is one thing to have policies, which are expositions of the general intent of a party seeking election to government, even where these have been drafted in detail. It is another to possess the ability to *govern*, by which I mean having an understanding of the proper management and administration needed to enact and make those policies work in practice. It is important to be able to anticipate the pace of rapid reform which the public is prepared to bear; to accept the rigorous discipline of setting priorities; to be able to rebuff over-enthusiastic ministers urgently pushing to get on with their jobs after so many barren years of Opposition; to instinctively sense in Cabinet, not just the political marketability of a set of decisions, but the wider ramifications of their administrative and economic consequences. Theoretical specialists, whose abstractions could be truly prodigious, as well as certain articulate and impatient supporters, most of whom we had never seen before, suddenly converged at the doors of shadow ministers. As 1972 had unrolled and the opinion polls gave more hope of a Labor victory, various and sundry 'experts' came to warmly embrace these shadow ministers. In government there were some sound, practical advisers and in the public service too, a number of experienced administrators were available to advise and help. Some of these tended to be comparatively glum company for those among our ranks who wanted to pierce exciting new frontiers. Our people were shooting for the stars and did not care to be held back by prudent restraints. That is why, unfortunately, some preferred to listen to an enthusiastic greenhorn who had attached him or herself to a minister's office and who believed that an excitable interest in Labor was a substitute for administrative and policy-making experience and knowledge.

There was a complete absence of anyone with Cabinet and ministerial administrative experience within the ranks of the new government. This left many ministers hostage to their own suspicions about the motives and commitment of a public service which had served the conservative coalition so well for so long. That was unfortunate, for there was widespread goodwill towards the incoming government and, generally, an evident keenness on the part of the public service to faithfully serve it. The fact was that the public service, as much as the general community, was tired of the Menzies heritage, which practically everyone agreed was exhausted anyway. Labor did not always harness the goodwill, excellent resources and human skills within the public service to further the objectives of the Government. The Government would ultimately pay for this alienation, as would the community.

Perhaps the electorate should not allow governments to stay in office for too long, as the notion of a 'natural party of government' may not be a healthy one for a democracy. Extended periods in office make governments stale and foster hubris. Some of the Whitlam Government's major problems were the obverse side of this coin. Many of the disabilities arose because the coalition parties had been in government for so long that Labor members, who had languished for just as long in the desolate gullies of Opposition, had lost touch with the practical art of government. Too many tended to be frozen in the self-righteous language and declamations of Opposition, unable to distinguish between rhetoric and working solutions to real problems.

The Whitlam Government set about its task of governing the country as if fundamentally incompatible economic forces would automatically reconcile themselves in deference to the unmistakable virtue of the new government. With the single-minded enthusiasm of a team of tyros the incoming government conscientiously embarked upon its wide-ranging programme of social reforms, most of which represented large increases in public sector expenditures. That was a sacred commitment to the electorate and accordingly, the government absolutely rejected any attempt to deflect it from this course. The *sine qua non* of keeping faith with the electorate made it determined to maintain the campaign promise of no tax or interest rate increases. Those undertakings might have been inviolable, but they were also unsustainable. This collection of inherently incompatible objectives would have represented trouble for any government in the best of economic times. The economic circumstances prevailing when Labor entered office in 1972, compounded by the more difficult conditions which unfolded rapidly thereafter, were the ingredients for a political disaster. The promised 6 per cent annual growth in the economy, essential to provide the resources with which to pay for the reform measures without tax increases, never materialised. Growth of the order of 4 per cent was the best achieved and in fact there were instances of negative growth.[2]

Labor, moreover, inherited an economy already primed for overheating due to a grossly expanded money supply. These influences were aggravated by a huge increase in international liquidity in the form of US dollars sloshing about the globe, seeping into any weak points in national economies and infecting them with inflation. This was a consequence of America funding the Vietnam War and President Johnson's *Great Society* welfare programmes with external account and domestic budget deficits, rather than responsible revenue increases and expenditure cuts. A good part of the over-stimulation of the Australian economy also came from panicky expansionary measures initiated by the outgoing McMahon Government in a futile effort to fend off its own extinction. Such factors, plus the outgoing government's failure to make a full-blooded revaluation of the Australian dollar, left an economy over-ripe for an inflationary boom. The nascent volatility of the situation in 1973 was further compounded by a world commodity boom. There could not have been a worse time imaginable for a government dedicated to a comprehensive and expansionary reform programme to assume office—unless of course, the Government was prepared to concurrently take other firm and predictably unpopular countervailing measures. The responsible options were expenditure cuts, tax increases, tighter monetary policy, and larger exchange rate appreciations. Because of inexperience, the Government lacked the understanding and the will to act decisively in these spheres.[3]

Against a background in which fiscal restraints had been ruled out, Frank Crean, Jim Cairns, Bill Morrison and I argued for tax increases in the 1973 budget Cabinet discussions. We were spitting into the wind. My view was a simple one, namely that the more we deferred corrective action to the economic imbalances we had inherited from the earlier coalition government, the more those imbalances would become aggravated. This would mean increasingly fierce corrective adjustments in the future. My experience in public life had taught me that the pace of change is all-important. To stampede the process of change can only be counterproductive. Our vulnerability was clearly illustrated by an opinion poll at the end of our first year of office in which 'nearly three-quarters of people polled agreed, either strongly or in part . . . that the Government was trying to do too many things at once'.[4]

Because appropriate fiscal measures were shirked, the adjustment inevitably had to be by means of the much less equitable, blunt mechanism of monetary policy. That was a curious preference for Labor, which had traditionally prided itself on the equity of its intended aims and measures. Monetary policy was eventually adjusted but with a faint heart. After so many years in Opposition, posturing against the use of those sorts of measures, the Government now lacked the conviction necessary for decisive action on that front. True, in an effort to increase imports and, accordingly, soak up the inflationary pressures of excess currency in circulation, the Australian dollar was revalued early on by 7 per cent but this was not enough. For similar reasons tariffs were cut by 25 per cent several months later. The latter measure, curiously enough, was vigorously opposed by a normally free trade Treasury which declared that tariff reductions should only proceed on the basis of an industry-by-industry examination. This would have been a thoroughly impractical approach for the Government, given the urgency of its need to make adjustments to economic pressures. Similarly, Hawke at the ACTU unambiguously supported this policy initially; but then, when pressure was applied from some sections within his union constituency, he promptly rolled over, and opposed it, wanly justifying this apostasy on the fortuitously discovered grounds of 'failure of adequate consultation'.

These measures alone were not enough to correct the distortive forces seeping into the economy. In fact, for some time after February 1973 the Australian dollar, which had been linked to the US dollar by then, was devaluing with the fall of the US dollar. This was pro-inflationary and countered the effect of the earlier revaluation. Permissive fiscal and, later, wages policies aggravated the underlying problem. Minister for Labour and Immigration, Clyde Cameron, decided to make the public service the community pace-setter with improved wages and conditions. Annual leave was increased and with it a generous additional pay loading was granted, the working week was set at thirty-five hours, long-service entitlements were improved, equal pay was implemented, while paid maternity and also paternity leave were introduced. Then, as if to join in the spirit of this frolic, the Public Service Board granted rather generous wage increases. Not much later, however, the pampering suddenly ceased and Minister Cameron condemned the public service as a congeries of 'fat cats'. This was all rather perplexing to much of the public service and most of the community for, after all, the Government had set the standard and established the pace for these advances.

What was unfortunately not recognised at the time was that Labor was pursuing economic growth policies which were unsustainable. The longer Labor delayed implementing counter-cyclical measures, that is contractionary policies, the more it guaranteed that precisely those sorts of measures would have to be imposed in an intensified form—and that is exactly what happened. There was some voicing of anxiety about these underlying economic trends and their consequences raised in Cabinet—I was certainly one of those who spoke up—but that concern was drowned out by the impatient discourse of action-oriented ministers. After twenty-three years of trudging, barefooted and rejected across the barren, stony wildernesses of Opposition, there was not a moment to be lost in the task of transforming society. Paradoxically, the more the Government rushed headlong into this undertaking, the shorter became the time available in which to attempt to fulfil its objectives.

Treasury and the Reserve Bank cautioned the Government on the economic predicament confronting it,[5] as did a number of economic commentators. Not that everyone counselled restraint: one commentator, Ken Davidson of the *Age*, incited the Government to continue on its chosen course, his opinions buttressed by the gung-ho views of the Institute of Applied Economics and Social Research, Melbourne.[6] So the options for travel through the economy were of only two kinds—austerity or luxury class. Labor chose the latter but eventually found it to be a meretricious fake.

Gradually it began to dawn on a greater number of ministers that the success of the Government in reducing unemployment had in fact converted one ill into another ailment. Although indeed lower, the unemployment level was still high by earlier experience, and it was understandable that Labor should want to reduce it even further. With the benefit of hindsight it became clear to me that after each major postwar recession a new and higher 'natural level of unemployment', consistent with the notion of a fully employed economy, seemed to be established. The Government failed to recognise this at the time. The consequence was that the full employment target being aimed at by the Whitlam Government was, in fact, an over-full employment level. That error had clear and unavoidable consequences, chief among which was the injection of additional inflationary pressures into an already overheating economy. Industrial disputation broke out like a virulent contagion. The force of inflation created a tax monster quaintly termed 'fiscal drag'. It was the descriptive term for the inflationary effect interacting between wages and tax whereby the income tax taken by government was increasing faster than wages. A wages break-out followed, resulting in the largest increases in wages and salaries in about a quarter of a century.[7] The Government sought to implement regular wage indexation to offset the inflationary erosion of incomes and in the hope of curbing the cost-push effect of excessive wage settlements. The unions unenthusiastically endorsed the principle. In practice they pursued whatever increases they could extract through whichever sources were available, in particular by the use of industrial power. ACTU leadership was mostly self-serving and unresponsive to national need at the time.

The remark that 'one man's wage increase is at the cost of another man's job' provoked howls of rage from the unions. Treasury's sound advice that wage increases less than the rate of inflation were necessary if the economy was going to be brought back into trim was ignored. While some among us supported the Treasury line, too many preferred to be comforted by irrelevant shibboleths from the past. From others there was evident suspicion about the ideological correctness of someone embracing a Treasury policy. Tax cuts as a trade-off for income restraint were unlikely to have been accepted by the unions given their irresponsibility and poor understanding of economic matters. In any case the tax cut option was ruled out by the Government's firm conviction that it had to maintain its spending objectives. This further restricted the practical tools available to it to bring the economy under control.

In recalling these melancholy matters two observations come to mind immediately. Firstly, this denial that rising wages had a cost-push effect in the prevailing economic conditions became widely accepted in the community as economic fact. Secondly, many ministers also genuinely believed there was no connection. Some others, who had their doubts, discreetly kept their noses to their ministerial grindstones rather than confront danger. Nonetheless, a few did challenge this wonky orthodoxy. Jim McClelland as Minister for Labour and Immigration did, sometimes with the characteristic panache of a modern-day Ginger Mick using the 'slipper'. I had been challenging this dangerous shibboleth for some time but more regularly after I became Treasurer. I confess to lacking the idiosyncratic flair of McClelland in doing so. These confrontations were a troubling experience for me as I had been reared within a family environment which venerated the trade union movement. In our household the unions were seen as the only thing standing between ordinary people and rapacious capitalist exploitation. Though understandable as a result of our painful family heritage from the Great Depression, it was, nevertheless, a faulty image. The leadership of the ACTU, meanwhile, was as good as useless as we struggled with these challenges.

I had a difficult time of it, discussing these worries of mine, particularly at Oxley electorate council meetings of the Labor Party, in Ipswich, a city of working people largely on modest incomes. The divergence of my views from the sanguine outlook of certain party spokespeople initially caused perplexity within the Party in my electorate. Faithful adherence to the officially declared creed is a powerful force in Labor culture. This is especially true among working-class people who have learned to depend on collective solidarity as a mechanism with which to protect their interests. On the other hand, my expressing an alternative viewpoint paid dividends later when our government's prospects began to disappear. Party faithful had been hearing from me what should be done long before it was embodied in the 1975 budget. They knew my strategy well, came to support it, and later worked hard to uphold it in the face of a determined onslaught against us in the electorate. Politicians who fail to build up that sort of understanding in their home base make a serious misjudgment. I had been moving away from those old Labor cultural influences which had been so dominant in my formative years and adopting new, more critical ones. Experience in office served to further demolish the residual influence of older myths.

Secondly, a convincing case can be made that the difficulties experienced between the trade union movement and the Whitlam Labor Government provided a learning experience for the trade union movement and for Labor. This educative process was a significant step towards the present situation, with its productive exchanges between government and unions. The biggest single influence on the unions in this continuing learning curve, however, came from the wage 'victories' of 1981. Then the ferocious wage settlements achieved by the Metalworkers' Union flowing on from the open-cut coalfields, combined with Malcolm Fraser's ideological short-sightedness and irresolute economic responses, caused great swathes of Australian manufacturing industry to be annihilated by excessive wage costs. A resource rental tax, as seriously proposed by Treasury,[8] applied to the large profits of the mining industry, as a redistributional mechanism, could have headed off this reckless wage push and saved thousands of those jobs destroyed by the so-called wage victory.

By the second half of 1974 the economy had performed a somersault. Unemployment was rocketing upwards, there was negative economic growth, bank credit accommodation was near enough to unattainable but inflation remained intractable. The commodity boom had collapsed even more rapidly than it had developed and oil price shocks were redirecting the hitherto excessive supply of international liquidity. Subsequently the second treasurer, Cairns, rocked staid business figures and surprised some of his former academic associates in economics departments by announcing that he was content to forbear more inflation rather than more unemployment. He appeared to have forgotten that more inflation inevitably generates higher unemployment as well as undermining the general performance of the economy. Capital inflows for investment in the mineral extractive industries had fallen back markedly, undercutting economic activity further. This was a result, to some extent, of the perplexing 'keep it in the ground until global mineral shortages push up prices' policy of the relevant minister, Rex Connor. His unconcealed hostility towards mineral developers, and especially towards foreign investors in this field, left many confused and discouraged.

Like the Grand Old Duke of York who marched his troops to the top of the hill then marched them down again, by late 1973 and into 1974 the Government was in reverse on a number of its earlier brave initiatives. The currency was devalued.[9] Industry protection, in the form of quotas, subsidies, temporary assistance, which tended to linger once introduced, and voluntary import restraints, were implemented in an undisciplined and ineffective effort to save jobs. Those very industries which were a burden on the performance of our more efficient productive industries were the ones which benefited from this largesse.[10] The motor vehicle industry exemplified the impact of this contrary policy-making. As a result of Labor's period of office, this industry enjoyed a higher level of protection and was more fragmented at the end of that period than at its commencement. In 1972 there were four manufacturers and three assemblers producing some 436 000 finished passenger vehicles and derivatives. By 1975 there were three manufacturers, another two preparing to commence production, and four assemblers producing fewer than 404 000 vehicles; in other words more effort was being generated to produce less![11] The public impression of a government in confusion was not modified in any way by the internal bickering and conflict which had broken out in Cabinet, reports of which regularly spilled into the media. To an apprehensive public, this reflected a weakening purpose and a deteriorating morale on the part of a Cabinet under pressure.

Sales tax on motor vehicles was reduced to boost sales. All this did, as some at the time pointed out it would, was to bring forward the normal volume of sales and cause a later slump in demand. This and the other measures benefiting the motor vehicle manufacturing industry did not discourage one large motor vehicle producer,

General Motors-Holden's, announcing an intention to sack some 20 per cent of its workforce—and this after 'gratefully' pocketing the protection designed to stave off retrenchments. This blow was delivered just before Christmas 1974. The Leyland motor car plant was confronted with failure because it had produced a sedan, the P76, which had proved to be an incomparable dud in the marketplace. I was Acting Treasurer during some of this drama. I uncharitably harboured the suspicion that the Treasurer, Cairns, might typically react to this contingency by way of his heart rather than his head. I therefore sought to narrow his opportunities via some rather pointed criticisms about the vehicle's failure. I described it as a 'lemon', and made other criticisms which were widely publicised. The effectiveness of my ploy can be judged by the fact that, without the slightest qualm, taxpayers funds were forked out to buy a large number of the vehicles for government use, vehicles which in their wisdom the taxpayers themselves would not pay for as a matter of choice. As a further signal triumph, the Government also acquired the Zetland plant of the company. Once the decision to buy the plant had been made, in principle, there was a frantic exercise to discover how it could be credibly used. The navy lost out and the property was foisted on to the senior service. Incidentally, today one of the P76 sedans is proudly displayed in the Powerhouse Museum, Sydney. Perhaps as a fossilised example of its species, or of how expensively gold-plated a 'lemon' can become in the hands of a credulous government.

Whitlam was furious with much of this 'backsliding' by Caucus and the Cabinet. He disdainfully referred to the timorous revisionists as 'nervous nellies'. Unfortunately the Caucus was bolting, and the 'nervous nellies' were setting the pace of the panicky withdrawal. A major revision of economic management was justified. As mid-1974 approached, Treasury and the Reserve Bank were reading the wrong sheep's entrails to glean the hard material for their economic predictions. They were dolefully advising the government that the country was 'awash with liquidity', that 'the economy was in danger of sinking in all of this liquidity'. What was needed was a 'short sharp shock'. The Government was in no mood for violent remedies. By mid-1974 unemployment was poised to take off. This was intolerable for the labour movement generally. There were convincing indications that the country was in the midst of a severe money contraction and official data subsequently confirmed this.[12]

There was another powerful, detrimental inhibitor to adopting firm, but not necessarily popular, restraints. The Government had not long before just scraped back into office at the May election. The election had been provoked by the Opposition threat to use its control of the Senate to seize government and force an election at a time it presumed unpropitious for the Government. There was no doubt in the minds of Caucus members that the Opposition would use this power again and a firm belief that inducing a further sharp contraction of the economy would provide the circumstances for them to do that. The severity of the contraction made it clear that the Government had overcorrected for the economic conditions. What it failed to recognise was that in response to the severity and pace of this contraction the expansionary effects of eased restraints on capital inflows, a devaluation and several other accommodating measures all introduced a countercorrection which was excessive in pushing the economy in the other direction. Money supply soared once again, wage settlements exceeded price movements, company profits fell and business activity contracted with a further fall off in the demand for labour, while inflation spiralled. Labor was out of the pot and well into the fire.

As far as the Ministry was concerned, Treasury was thoroughly discredited by the time of the 1974 budget formulation. The Treasurer presented four papers to Cabinet. They were associated with the proposed structure of the budget and dealt with existing and prospective economic conditions. Three of the papers were distributed on the Sunday night, preceding the first meeting of the budget Cabinet on the succeeding day. On Monday the fourth paper was circulated at the Cabinet meeting. That paper outlined proposed budget parameters. After being read, the document was to be withdrawn from circulation. This was regarded as curious and immediately raised suspicions. The document did not assuage the doubters. Instead of a straightforward presentation of the budget parameters, with aggregate revenues and outlays figures and a balance of either deficit or surplus, the numbers were presented in an unusually complex way. Tom Uren's principal adviser, Dr Mike Keating, quickly illustrated that the figures implied a substantial surplus, that is, a fierce reinforcement of the contraction already underway.[13] There was near enough to pandemonium in the Cabinet as ministers revolted at what they believed was attempted deception by Treasury. Treasury, having failed to get its 'short, sharp, shock' in July was seen to be coming through another door for the same purpose. Its advice was doomed to be ignored from then on.

The budget in its final form was notably expansionary and fuelled a different set of problems. The outcome was fairly consistent with the principle of 'spend our way out of trouble', espoused by Cairns, whose views prevailed over the futile protests of Treasurer Crean. These problems were compounded by the arrival a little later of Dr Cairns as Treasurer, where he crafted his surprisingly relaxed attitude towards inflation into an art form. He was a policy administrator who relied on what his emotions said to him rather than being informed by rigorous analysis. It was not long after this point that I had a sustained argument in Cabinet about budget deficit effects on the economy and deficit funding. I entered into the debate with some passion expecting there would be a tough exchange. The ensuing discussion had its embarrassments. Cairns later came to my office to explain that he was an economic historian, not an economist, and that he found some of the principles of economics confusing.

Above: Unemployed on the track during the Great Depression of the thirties. For them, human dignity had been stripped away. As the verse on this photograph says, 'We are only humble bagmen in search of work in vain, In any kind of weather, in sunshine or in rain. When we get tired of walking, we try to jump the train ...'

Left: Brisbane, a garrison city during World War II, welcomes home the fighting 7th Australian Division returning from combat in Greece, Crete, Western Desert and Syria. An estimated quarter of a million people attended the parade, a huge number of people for Brisbane then, providing an indication of how strongly the community was affected by the tensions and uncertainties of war. (Courier-Mail)

Right: My father, George Hayden, crushed by the Great Depression, who literally worked to the last gasp of his life.

Left: My mother, Violet Hayden, on the rear steps of our residence, a battler's home, at 48 Mabel St, South Brisbane.

Above: Not quite a log cabin — but a modest start in life. The Hayden family home after some improvements I carried out once I commenced work and started earning some money. *(News Ltd)*

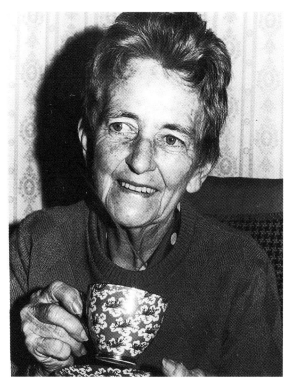

Left: My mum, Violet Hayden, in 1975 after I presented the budget as Treasurer. She never had any doubts that I would succeed in life. After all, she was my mother. (Courier-Mail)

Right: *With the King's shilling in my pocket — a naval conscript at Flinder's Naval Training Depot, 1951. I didn't see much of the world but I did see a lot of the sea.*

Below: *Rowing bow side in a four, behind stroke, Nick Carter, on the Brisbane River, circa 1953. St Helen's Private Hospital — of fond memory for me— is in the background.*

Left: Moving from upholding the Queen's laws in Queensland to making them in the national capital at Canberra. (News Ltd)

Below: A very pretty Dallas pasting up 'Vote Hayden' stickers in our first campaign, long, long ago (in early 1961). Coincidentally, that big gum tree is near the turn-off to the farm at Bryden, Queensland, which many years later we have made our home.

Right: *With Labor Opposition Leader Arthur Calwell at a public rally conducted from the balcony of the now demolished Trades Hall, Nicholas St, Ipswich, 1961.*

Below: *Dallas' father, Bill Broadfoot, from a Scottish underground coal mining family at Ipswich, is seated at left end, third row. Patron of the Ipswich Thistle Pipe Band, Dr D. Cameron, MHR for Oxley, and Minister for Health when I defeated him in 1961 (and who also medically supervised Dallas' birth!), is seated centre front.*

Left: *This photograph, taken at the steps of Old Parliament House, Canberra, 1963, was used for my first re-election pamphlet, headed 'Your Man In Canberra'. It was a heartfelt plea to keep me in Canberra as the member for Oxley. What's more, it worked too.*

Below: *Dallas in King's Hall, Parliament House, 1966, with our daughter Michaela, only a few weeks before Michaela's fatal accident.*
(Canberra Times)

Right: 'Hayden as the happy hooker', 1968. Undoubtedly Ian Sinclair and Doug Anthony would have dearly loved to get their arms around my neck like this later and to just keep squeezing. We were playing front row in the Parliament House rugby union team which easily defeated the ABC side 35–3, in spite of Mike Willesee playing full-back for the ABC. The referee was Doug Blake, deputy Clerk of the House of Representatives. Sounds a bit suspicious, doesn't it? (News Ltd)

Below: With Her Majesty, Queen Elizabeth II of Australia, after an Executive Council meeting at Government House with the Queen's Ministers of the Whitlam Government. Gough could scarcely contain his excitement at being called to sit at the Queen's right hand on this occasion. (CT)

Left: On TV with David Frost in Sydney, 1983, surrounded by a noisy audience of hostile doctors. The subject: Medibank, the first universal health insurance programme. When Frost asked me how I felt, I replied, 'Now I know how Daniel felt in the lion's den. Those doctors sound very hungry to me'. *(Fairfax)*

Below: Once were radicals – the 1973 Hayden Ministerial Office line-up with a youthful Paddy McGuinness as the token male. *(News Ltd)*

Right: In Canberra, late 1975, Gough and I signed the last of the Medibank agreements with the states, this one with NSW. A long, hard battle was won, which sometimes degenerated into a bitterly personalised campaign against me. For the first time ever in Australia the doctors had been bested in a political confrontation. (Canberra Times)

Below: With Drs Dick Scotton and John Deeble, the architects of Medibank.

Left: *The master and his apprentice. Whitlam as the recently retired Opposition Leader and me as his brand new successor in that role, campaigning in the by-election for Whitlam's old seat of Werriwa with the successful candidate, John Kerin, in late 1978.*

Below: *A happy break, from preparing the 1975 budget, with family at Burleigh Heads — Ingrid, Kirk, Georgina and Dallas.* (News Ltd)

Right: *Before Ben Chifley's portrait. In a moving 1948 speech on Labor's humanitarian ideals Chifley said, 'These things are really worth fighting for' — an inspiring statement of Labor's creed.* (Mitchell Library)

Below: *The three musketeers? Well not quite, perhaps. Bob Hawke, Mick Young and myself at the launch of Labor's Industrial Relations policy, 1980.* (News Ltd)

Left: Speaking at a Brisbane ALP rally.

Below: All good friends and jolly good company; for the time being anyway. With Bob Hawke, Neville Wran, Paul Keating and Michael Maher at a campaign function at the APIA Club, Leichhardt during the 1982 Lowe by-election campaign, which Maher won handsomely. *(Fairfax)*

Right: At Randwick Labor Club, during the 1980 election campaign. Warmly greeted by some of the tried and true believers of Labor whose faithfulness has sustained the party for so long. (News Ltd)

Below: In rather traditional campaigning mode in the Boothby by-election in 1981, with all-time cricketing great and State Labor MLA (S. A.) Gil Langley. (Advertiser, Adelaide)

Left: *Visiting the Pine Gap electronic interception base with Lionel Bowen, 1981. It was an invaluable asset for maintaining the balance for peace between the super powers.*

Below: *At King's Cross Homeless Youth refuge, during the 1981 Wentworth by-election. I attempted but failed to establish poverty and social justice as a community issue. The media were little interested: it was a casualty of the reaction against the overload of government activity in the Whitlam period. (News Ltd)*

Right: *Departing the nuclear-powered United States Navy cruiser* Texas, *Brisbane, 1983, and acknowledging anti-nuclear protesters nearby.*
(Courier-Mail)

Below: *This cartoon relates to my opposition to Labor's restrictive uranium mining and export policy at Labor's 1982 National Conference. I got metaphorically bitten by one of those poisonous snakes but recovered, briefly.* (Geoff Pryor)

For my part I had proposed a different tack with the budget, bearing in mind that additional severely contractionary measures would have caused a dislocating confrontation with the trade union movement. Yet wage growth had to be curbed. I proposed tax cuts as a trade-off for wage restraint with limited wage indexation—I had previously opposed the notion of full wage indexation—associated with substantial expenditure cuts. This proposal failed, I expect because it was seen as not exciting enough. Events had moved ahead rapidly and something which was practical had to be attempted to head off the economic waywardness opening up in the economy. My judgment of the time still stands, namely that the Treasury budget prescription was altogether too severe and the manner of its presentation to Cabinet allowed critics to accuse Treasury of deviousness. The inescapable fact is, however, that whether it was the Treasury 'hard line', some more moderate form of restraint of the kind I proposed, or more or less of either proposal, it had little chance of prevailing over the big spending 'fix' on which so many ministers were hooked. Whitlam, who by this time had become converted to the Treasury formula for remedying the economy, was isolated except for the support of Treasurer Crean. Whitlam fought tenaciously but he had no chance. He had arrived at that point of awareness too late. By that time play had moved on to another part of the field. For almost an entire year afterwards, he lost his zest for confronting the self-indulgences of ministers. His experience with the new, second treasurer he chose, Cairns, did little to rekindle his energies, leaving him deflated rather than recharged.

What this way of operating suggested to the public was an undisciplined Ministry, a Cabinet which met in private but whose differences were trumpeted to the media. Ours was a Cabinet with too much faith but not enough conviction. So when the time came for some sort of firm, decisive, but not terribly popular measures to remedy the economy, it squibbed the test with the fuzzy rhetoric of the past. Worse was to come. The Khemlani Loans Affair would swoop in on the Government like a giant, unappeasable pteranodon, tearing the limbs and gouging the entrails from its indefensible victim.

Meanwhile, down at social security...

The 1972 election would have been little more than forty-eight hours behind us when I received a telephone call: 'Comrade, Gough here. You've been working on health and welfare for several years. I know you have your heart set on the challenge of managing both but I'm in a jam. . . ' Whitlam was asking me to take welfare and also health insurance so that he could create a separate health services portfolio. He was short of portfolios. Caucus in Opposition had forced on him, very much against his wishes and unwisely in my view, a twenty-seven person Ministry. The Cabinet was to be comprised of the full Ministry. The decision was publicly justified on grounds of equality, a principle guaranteed to work within Labor culture. Some who supported this decision even believed in that principle; other, craftier aspirants with their own agenda, feared that if they made the Ministry they might not make Cabinet, and goodness knew what strange things a Cabinet without them might do. They accordingly worked with impressive energy to manipulate support for the decision (for the 'good of the party' of course). I sympathised with Whitlam's problem and co-operated instantly. Privately I was disappointed. Although health insurance commanded major public interest it tended to be a narrow subject, the main purpose being to arrange more efficient payment systems while combating the unsettling greed of *some* doctors. Unfortunately, the public usually heard the loud braying of greedy doctors—those who gave the rest and greater majority of the profession an unfair reputation—well ahead of what the minister might have to say on the matter.

My preferred interest was in dealing with the rearrangement of the health delivery systems, of integrating various professions and para-professional groups into effective community medicine, and in generally reordering the use of economic resources. Work on these aspects was intellectually provocative, stimulating and creative, as was policy development on preventative medicine—even if these also tended to be thoroughly uninteresting to most audiences. If you could always rely on health insurance to claim the lead, when it came to public popularity, a community health system was the long-odds plodder.

A little later I was sitting in a poky office in Parliament House, a room totally empty but for my presence. It had been allotted to me, for the time being, as my ministerial office. There was not even the slightest stir of movement; not from the scurry of frail mice nor the dull tread of frailer men. Not a single loose piece of paper nor even one unused paper clip was lying about. I sat there staring into the half-gloom. Soon, one unsettling thought irresistibly crowded out all the others: 'What the hell do I do now?!' But if I had any inkling then of all the action I was about to see, I would not have worried at all.

I was asked to attend the Department of Health at Woden, in Canberra, for a provisional briefing—provisional in the sense that I was not then sworn in as a minister. I complied, though unable to advise the bureaucrats that I would not be handling health as that was for the Prime Minister to announce. (For the moment, Gough Whitlam was too preoccupied as head of a government of two, of which he later jocularly commented that it was 50 per cent larger than was desirable for optimal performance.) I was joined by the Health Department officials. An extended finger, pointing like the business end of a pistol, indicated a pile of papers about half a metre high. 'There,' said a stern voice resonant with authority, a voice used to initiating fledgling ministers into the terrifying dimensions of a ministerial workload, 'is the Department of Health legislation and regulations which you will have to master'. I had never felt so threatened by a pile of papers in my life.

I suspected the performance had been well-rehearsed over time, as spent ministers went and novice replacements arrived. The air exuded by my public service inductors was quiet and deliberate. Though understated, they were abounding in confidence and gravitas. 'You can take it away and make yourself familiar with it,' the main voice of authority added. 'No . . . don't think I will,' I replied to various looks of surprise. Some eyes dilated, others narrowed. 'Of course, Mr Hayden. Just as soon as you're ready we'll arrange a series of briefings . . . '. The voice was now mellifluous and mildly deferential. A new reading was being made of the novice minister—the main theme being, 'We've got a troublemaker here'. 'No. It's not that. I've read all that paper over the past several years.' This was true, for I had assiduously prepared myself for this ministry, and that of welfare, over the preceding three years.

My two-and-a-half years as Minister for Social Security were, I felt, productive ones. The Department was transformed from being dominantly a bookkeeping manager of a well-established range of benefits to an active policy department and provider of a much wider range of services than hitherto. Some enduring policies were initiated. One such was financial support for refuges for homeless men, as conducted by charitable agencies. That programme was later expanded in its cover, and many of the homeless unemployed of the present are undoubtedly better catered for because of its existence. The sad pictures from my long ago police days, haunting memories of Eugene Ebzrey and others cursed by alcoholic addiction, I sometimes feel probably lie behind that early initiative. As my mother used to say of certain social casualties, 'No matter he's made a mess of his life. He's made in God's image. We can't neglect him'. Certainly I have always accepted that to some extent we have an obligation to be keepers of our brothers and sisters.

The Supporting Mothers' Allowance, now the Sole Parent's Allowance, was introduced despite moralising outrage from predictable quarters. One argument went that teenage females would be incited by the allowance and be induced to become brood cows, producing babies with an endless display of fertility—never mind that it was set at such an austere level![14]

Other critics condemned the proposal because they feared the modest level of independence it would give to lone mothers would reduce the flow of infants available for adoption. They preferred a practice where these mothers had few rights in respect of parenting their babies, where economic distress and narrow-minded social disapproval compelled the adopting out of infants. There was another consideration. Some married women living in an unhappy relationship, perhaps being physically abused by their spouses, were as good as domestic prisoners within their homes. This allowance would give them a real chance to exercise a choice for independence and freedom if they wished. Moreover, I also proposed a form of maintenance enforcement agency be concurrently established, in concept much like the present Child Support Agency. Curiously, I was advised by the Department that any attempt to set up such an agency would be unconstitutional.

A non-legalistic appeals system was set up in each State to handle complaints from users of the services and recipients of benefits provided from the Department of Social Security. (Unfortunately, but in the way of these things, the lawyers are now getting this system in their clutches.) Several welfare rights officers were appointed, after some training within the Department, to work as community welfare rights officers. Effectively they were to be advocates on behalf of users of the Department's services and benefits, in particular the non-English-speaking people who are marginalised in our society. There were twenty-one regional offices of the Department when I commenced in this portfolio. The annual report for 1975–76 disclosed that the number had risen to 120 regional and district offices. For the users of the services and the drawers of benefits from the Department, this was an overdue and essential advance.

All benefits were increased, in pursuit of the goal of raising people above the then-fashionable Henderson poverty line. The problem with this sort of concept is that a relative poverty line must always be with us. For instance, if it is set as a proportion of Average Weekly Earnings (AWE), as Henderson's methodology set it, then it will go up as AWE increases. That means that the recipient can be much better-off in material welfare over time, yet still said to be in poverty. In fact it is more misleading than that. Over time AWE has tended to increase at a greater rate than Household Disposable Income Per Capita (HDIPC)—HDIPC is what a person has to spend after tax—or inflation as measured by the Consumer Price Index. This means that over time benefits to the less well-off have, in real spending power terms, increased more relatively than the disposable spending power on average of income earners in the community. Yet, the official poverty measurement fails to acknowledge that material improvement. The so-called relative poverty thresholds, of which there is great variety, further amplifying the subjectiveness of the notion, are essentially a reflection of the differing values of the various people championing any one from among the several 'poverty' measurements in vogue. This is not measuring poverty at all. These measurements are really benchmarks identifying relative social disadvantage, and again subjectively. To use 'poverty' in this context, I feel, confuses the real issues at stake. I am deeply committed to redistributional policies to help overcome relative social disadvantage but I dislike the emotive description of these benchmarks as poverty lines when, incontestably, most people living below those lines are not impoverished. Perhaps to call this spade by its proper name might put at risk a lot of interesting jobs in various institutions which depend on the persistence of poverty in our midst?

For these and other reasons too Henderson's methodology was seriously flawed. Henderson's basic concepts were based on work of dubious quality done in New York some twenty years earlier. Its relevance to then-contemporary Australia was questionable. As the Department noted in a minute to me of the time: '. . . the definition of poverty chosen by Professor Henderson was determined in arbitrary fashion and is lacking any "scientific" base'. If he presumed that New York relativities were appropriate, there was 1972 data available from that source. Departmental work at the time on the more recent New York information disclosed that Henderson's methodology overestimated the poverty line for large families and underestimated it for smaller families. None of this solves the problem of determining an authentic poverty line, which in the end is a subjective measure. The reluctance of many in the welfare industry to acknowledge that basic fact undermines their credibility when it comes to defining poverty income levels.

By mid-1972 I was becoming increasingly dubious about the validity of Henderson's work. The McMahon Coalition Government in late 1972, threshing about in its terminal stages, appointed Henderson to conduct, solo, an inquiry into poverty. By then Henderson had become something of an icon in a community commendably moved by issues of social responsibility. There was no leeway but to continue the appointment once in government, especially as Labor, earlier in Opposition, had made so much of the running on issues of social concern such as poverty. To boot, it had invoked his name and work on many occasions in and out of the Parliament. By the time I discovered how flawed Henderson's methodology was, we were too deeply committed to the poverty inquiry process to be able to back off. In early 1973, by then Minister for Social Security, I had several discussions with Henderson. These confirmed my unease about some of his intended directions with the inquiry. On the other hand his determination to get his own way was understandable. It was quite evident that the inquiry report, if he prevailed, was to be the apotheosis of a hitherto long and steady career in Academe. I responded positively to his increasingly impatient demands to expand the terms of reference of the inquiry. To his chagrin I appointed four additional commissioners—he would not accept that this vastly expanded task was too much for one person to complete within a reasonable time frame. Each new commissioner would have a specific task: Education and Poverty; Law and Poverty; Health and Poverty; and 'Selected Economic Aspects of Poverty'. These covered the additional areas he had in mind. In this way I restricted Henderson to his figuring and neutralised his combative threat to me to go public if he did not get the expanded terms of reference and the necessary resources to support the wider responsibilities. He was angry and peeved at being thwarted. The additional inquiries and reports, I reckoned, would be valuable long-term guides for relevant policy-making. I saw little evidence that governments succeeding Whitlam's shared that view, until the Hawke Government made the most significant breakthrough of all: under the influence of Brian Howe, a genuine Christian Socialist, substantial assistance for needy families was provided via the means-tested family allowance introduced in 1987.

The Australian Assistance Plan (AAP) was another piece of social engineering in the grand manner. Welfare specialists in Victoria developed the concept of the Australian Assistance Plan, and through their close links with the Labor Party, had the notion endorsed as Labor policy.[15] I was initially quite attracted to the concept. In accordance with the plan, Australia would be broken up into regions. There would be Regional Social Development Councils representative of the regional community. Each of these would administer its own budget, provided by the national government, to operate a range of locally determined welfare programmes. As ideals go, a splendid concept. Unfortunately in practice it was found to be riddled with inherent flaws and difficulties.

First, there was an argument about territory and authority between the Department of Urban and Regional Development (DURD) and the Department of Social Security which engaged the respective ministers. Tom Uren was the Minister for DURD and an instinctive central planner. He was going to make 'new Canberras' at Albury-Wodonga, Orange and Monato in South Australia. In the upshot, quite a bit of land for this imaginative development, bought with public money, was later found to be surplus to needs. No-one should have been surprised when it was put back into the marketplace and often sold for less than it cost. Orange and Monato were lovingly tended as seedling cities but wilted early.

In any case Uren helpfully sorted out the argument between our departments and, as it transpired, between us. DURD already had the regional boundaries for Australia drawn up. There could not be two differing sets of regional boundaries. OK, he won that one. When it came to the question of who would be in charge of the plan, the answer to Uren was simple: he graciously conceded I was incontestably in charge of administering welfare policy and programmes, while he, as Minister for DURD bore the superior responsibility of exercising overall authority in the regions . . . Hang it all, someone had to ensure that all programmes were integrated and ran well! This was undoubtedly a burdensome degree of authority for Uren to shoulder, but he was not one given to shirking his responsibilities, I quickly discovered. But wait a tick, I replied, was I not the senior minister? The rejoinder came, patiently: yes, but only just. Among democratic socialists elitism wasn't permitted, I was informed with some evident sadness at my ideological ignorance. Uren seemed surprised that I would even try the crude little number of pulling rank; we were all equal in the new order. It was just that some, of course, had to assume more responsibility over their kinfolk than others.

Several pilot projects were set up to trial-run the AAP. Before too long, the process of men and women of goodwill coming together as members of the regional administering committees, as per the desired model, somehow became transformed into squalid little factional power struggles. There were notable instances of strife between the committees and office staff over the conduct of programmes, or more precisely, who would be in charge of them. Tensions occurred between the established positions of community groups, local government and State government representatives. Some important, established, charitable organisations suspected the plan would regionalise them, which they equated with dismemberment, and so they opposed the idea. Protests were also soon directed at the Department of Social Security when it scrutinised budgets to ensure there was effective accounting of taxpayers' money; this was excoriated as a meddling violation of the regional councils' sovereign independence.

The last straw for me was a report from my Department that the budget of one region had been used to lease expensive shopfront premises, acquire a brand new Statesman Holden sedan, electric typewriters when those contraptions were not that common, and a range of other well-padded items, of more comfort to providers than users of welfare services. I protested. I received a prompt response from this regional AAP office, its thrust being 'Welfare users have put up with second-rate conditions for too long. That is ending'. This was put to me by welfare providers with great conviction, as they doubtless detected the almost limitless career opportunities appearing before them. Whitlam had heralded such possibilities in his 1972 policy speech when he stated that 'Australia needs more social workers, and we will set out to provide them'. However, it seemed as though some of his listeners were determined to give him more help than he or many others of us wanted. More help than he or any of us bargained for in fact.

The problems with the AAP concept were numerous. First there was a collision over the basic philosophy behind the proposal. There was a view among some active—and endlessly talkative—welfare providers that the AAP would be a universalist-type project, reaching the middle classes as well as the needy and the marginalised. I was then attracted to the idea of jettisoning the pre-existing incrementalist approach to developing services, because of its lack of comprehensive planning and integrated services. I accepted the case that Regional Social Development Councils would need to be established in regions which were predominantly middle class, as well as in the obviously lower socio-economic areas. There was never any doubt in my mind, however, that their mission was to aim at more effectively helping the needy, the vulnerable, the marginalised. I acknowledged that some of these lived in areas peopled predominantly but not exclusively by higher income groups. The universalist approach, at least as proposed by some, seemed to imply an intention to convince many among the better paid middle classes, that they really had unmet welfare needs. Should this philosophy have prevailed, the welfare industry growth prospects would have been almost infinite. For the brave new social order heralded here meant that society would be organised simply according to two classes. First, a relatively small elite of wise and certain welfare providers in charge of our destiny. Then there would be the many more numerous and dependent welfare users who would draw succour and inspiration from the omniscience of their providers. I hyperbolise to make an important point of principle—one over which I frequently had heated exchanges, for it exemplified the lack of fiscal and practical rigour in the training of some professionals from the social sciences.

On reflection, the concept, and more generally the overall outlook among many of the welfare providers, could be best described as a form of welfare colonialism. Middle-class providers would come and occupy the territory of the users, creating in the process a vast range of delivery systems, an extensive order of dependence and an occupier's system of administration. As always with colonial systems, the occupying powers would do best out of the arrangement. The AAP was based on middle-class values and created by middle-class welfare planners, while it was supposed to be largely used by the marginalised and working-class, people for whom these cultural values were rather alien. The theory was that users were to become articulate activists defining welfare goals, engaged in supervising regional functions and participating in lengthy meetings, where they would cerebrally masticate complex issues. It was a great load of nonsense on high stilts. What the users want, in the nature of their direct and practical common sense, is services and cash, preferably quickly, and with as few questions as possible asked.

As if this wasn't enough, there was the torrent of words, of meetings, of reports, of conceptualising of services and assessment structures. On and on it went and while it lasted the welfare industry was having a ball. So much stimulating discussion with so many interesting people; people who thought and talked just like themselves. It had never happened before and on such an impressive scale, and best of all, the government was paying. I had been quite wrong in moving into the programme too quickly, on too wide a front, and endeavouring to hasten its full implementation. The imperative of the parliamentary cycle requires concrete and quick results from policy. Also, the preoccupation of most MPs is to serve the sauce from the public gravy pot in their electorates, and to do so generously. Adding impetus was the mostly undiscussed but ever-present thought that after so many failed years, a double dissolution might be forced at an unpropitious time. There was little enough leeway, therefore, in which to repair what we saw as the accumulated neglect from the past; in these circumstances we felt enormous pressure to produce quick results.

With hindsight, the pilot projects should have been restricted to a very small number and they should have been tested over several years. If this had been done with rigorous monitoring, we would have established much earlier that the concepts behind the programme were deeply flawed. Users could not be integrated into these sorts of systems at the level of responsibility and involvement conceived by the planners. There are insurmountable cultural barriers which make that as true today as it was then and earlier. State and local governments should have been given the management of the programme with fewer presumptuous, but more practical, expectations about user participation. I came to regard the concept of 'instant' regional administration replacing States and local governments as fabulous wistfulness. The States remain well-entrenched. When it came to political conflict, most usually provoked by a Whitlam Government effort to take over or subordinate a State responsibility, the States almost always outmanoeuvred us. The immediacy of their functions to the daily life needs of their populations and their more effective access to the media of the capital cities gave them great advantages over us. While there had been much criticism made of their administrative skills, Federal bureaucrats with whom I worked had a generally high regard for the professional skills and, in some cases, wider practical experience, of their State counterparts. I learnt to share much of that respect. State boundaries were the price of nationhood and I believe at that price nationhood has been a good buy. The people's good sense have made them work tolerably well since. If there is need to tighten up processes or to experiment with new forms of co-operation and administration between States and the Commonwealth these can be achieved generally, as we have witnessed, by joint planning and other agreements.

I like to believe there was much which was good and lasting in what I did as Minister for Social Security. Some of my dealings with the welfare industry, however, left me feeling rather jaded. Too many welfare practitioners approached the interaction between complex social and economic issues as though the economic part of the equation was irrelevant. Their view was that the proper role of government was to hand over the money and let them, the experts, get on with the technical tasks unhindered by bureaucratic concerns for accountability. There was often an unstated but obvious presumption that feeling strongly enough about some human predicament was all that mattered; and an observable tendency to want to plan comprehensive, neat solutions, stuck together with layer upon layer of committees, welfare deliverers and, of course, administrators and managers. Complexity was ubiquitous and fascinatingly, its functioning and delivery required evermore practitioners. Most of all, there was the demand for more. No matter how much was provided, there had to be more. Well before 1974 I was disillusioned by and increasingly alienated from much of the welfare industry; the negative experiences were many, but I found the lack of rigour, discipline and balanced conduct especially galling. The fact is, the welfare industry, like some teachers' unions and other public sector activist groups, destroyed splendid opportunities for advancement of their causes by the irresponsible behaviour and extravagant demands of some of their representatives.

Where I am on much shakier ground is justifying the plethora of commissions and advisory bodies set up within my portfolio. The first annual report of the Department of Social Security for 1972–73, enumerated eight such bodies with fifty-seven representatives manning them, and of course, many supporting staff.[16] A crop of commissions and the like blossomed as I prepared for the Great Leap Forward in social welfare. Some of these bodies were well and truly justified and some contributed sterling service. Overall I rushed the task. I have to accept that some of what I undertook was ineffective and an injudicious use of taxpayers' money. For that I deserve severe criticism. As Disillusioned of the Canberra suburb of Chifley, observed anonymously but pungently in the Canberra Times, of 29 January 1975:

> The Commission of Inquiry into Poverty continues to alleviate poverty among the academics with the amount of money it is spending on its research reports, will shortly do the same in the printing industry.

Should I have proceeded more slowly so that programmes would bed down, so that the transfer of resources could be successfully absorbed within the economy and to allow us to function more effectively? The answer to that is yes. The pace of change was too rapid, not just where I was working, but everywhere within the government.[17] There was the over-riding fear that we were in government for a brief spell only and accordingly we had to hasten the implementation of reform programmes on as many fronts as possible to leave an enduring mark of our efforts. The rest of this point is too obvious to require further development. Moreover, it is not an alibi. It is further cause for criticism of our, specifically my, conduct.

Long before I had finished my term as Minister for Social Security I had become sceptical of the canvassers of comprehensive welfare plans with their all-embracing solutions to the problems of society. As I have argued, their remedies, no matter how well-intentioned, were at the least unconscious patterns for assuming power; power over other people, political power more generally, and non-accountable power over how money was to be distributed. The Social Welfare Commission was established and given extraordinary authority to plan welfare priorities and recommend welfare policy to government. The Commission was cobbled together in the mistaken belief welfare should be removed from the established political processes. This was justified on the ground that after so many years of Menzies, and the downgrading of welfare, the policy processes had been discredited. As an attempt to lock future governments into a new, open and public process which would keep pressure on them to meet welfare priorities, the objective was well-meant but ill-conceived. But it was also the product of that unhealthy suspicion of the bureaucracy with which we were burdened when we entered office. Dissatisfaction with the performance of the Commission came to a head in the first half of 1974 with a report on child care. This report was regarded as extravagant in its claim for resources, particularly at a time when the government needed to apply certain fiscal disciplines. It was impractical too, with the trained staff required to make it function just not available. The minister responsible, Kim Beazley Snr, and I opposed the proposal. The derision and contumely of the then nascent feminist movement fell thick and fast around our political hides. Yvonne Preston, a prominent journalist noted for her ready adoption of fashionable middle-class causes, condemned me for 'putting on the mantle of the man of "economic responsibility"'.[18] Presumably a carefree dash of economic irresponsibility was preferred.

From a practical point of view, as this case illustrates, the commission suffered the defect of having power to influence community expectations, especially among well-organised, articulate groups, without the restraining responsibility of meeting the bills. This imposed considerable pressure on government to respond to those community expectations. The politicians were confronted not only with the pressure of heightened expectations of the political constituency, but the conflicting squeeze of fiscal reality. That is when the Commission began to founder. I proposed to Whitlam that it should be wound up, conceding it had been a major mistake by me. He demurred. But when in 1975 it publicly criticised Whitlam's much beloved National Compensation Scheme, an idea he had been fondly promoting since the 1950s, the Social Welfare Commission effectively sunk itself; Whitlam was thereafter impatient for the Commission's dismantling. Paradoxically, and to Whitlam's chagrin, criticism of the National Compensation Scheme by the Commission was something with which I agreed. I had come to fear that the quite evident hypochondria spawned by the Repatriation Benefits system—now Veterans Affairs benefits— would become a kind of contagion and spread more widely, given the concepts behind this proposal.

I was able to pursue one of my long-term projects, a national superannuation scheme in which contributions would be invested in a national development fund. This would boost national savings, fund national development projects and return the long-term bond rate on investments. Good thinking for a young socialist but not an ambition I now harbour, being rather more cautious about the political administration of public enterprises. The prospect of politically motivated 'raids' on the funds for pork-barrelling for political advantage, fiddling the rates of return, downwards of course, came to worry me. The country could be loaded down with dud 'visionary' projects like the Ord River Dam and irrigation works. The option of using private superannuation funds taken by the Hawke Government is superior. The final reports of the National Superannuation Committee of Inquiry, which I had set up, were produced in 1976 and 1977, proposing something different to what I had preferred, by which time we were back in Opposition.

Academics and professionals can be helpful, superbly so as I discovered with the introduction of Medibank. My broader experiences had shown me, however, that the wise politician's old saw—that experts should be on tap, not on top—had much to recommend it. I had also learnt that the best policy, planning and implementation of services came from the much but unfairly reproached professionals in the bureaucracy, and so worked closely with them from an early date. Some officials, of course, will try to install their own agendas within processes, as I also discovered early on. When I arrived as a raw, stripling minister I was soon confronted with a huge pile of outwards correspondence requiring my signature. I was solicitously advised that the Department had a great tradition of personalised responses to the public. Ministers had enhanced this tradition over many years, I was further counselled, by responding personally to inquiries directed to them from some of the several hundred thousand clients of the Department. It was hoped that the rights of the clients, ordinary people out in the suburbs as it were, would continue to be respected. Well, how could I, as a Democratic Socialist, refuse? The pile of letters remained daunting; though a fast reader, I was obliged to develop a system of flashing a sort of zig-zag scan across the pages, picking up the gist of the seemingly less complicated cases.

Even so, getting to the correspondence as my last chore, often at midnight and later, was keeping me at the grindstone through the early hours of the morning.

It happened that one day, in conversation with senior officials, I was rather chilly about something or other I discovered the Department was doing. 'It's established policy,' I was confidently told. 'Policy? I make policy on behalf of the Government. I don't recall this one and as I don't like it I don't see how I would have agreed to it.' Backsides were rolled uncomfortably from side to side on chairs. 'You signed a letter endorsing this line of action. . .' was the eventual response. The defence was that there had been an earlier minister who would never decide on policy submissions, or so it was put to me. A practice had been developed, I was given to understand, of slipping short but substantive comments into his letters, which he therefore tended to sign without reading. In this way policy development rolled on agreeably, public servants were covered for their actions by a discreetly organised ministerial commitment, and the minister's life flourished in blissful ignorance. Needless to say, the whole process of handling correspondence was altered radically.

A very senior officer would call on me with his colleagues and in a polished and well-practised manner, pass over a voluminous submission requiring urgent attention: 'If only you would be so good as to go over the matter immediately. Terribly sorry, urgent matter and all of that . . .'. All this was put solicitously and with just the right degree of unctuous regard for my lofty position. Being a fast reader however, still did me no good: I would read the document while the officer, who had drafted the submission and gone over it several times before it reached me, would read the paper too; irritatingly he would turn each page about a quarter to half a page ahead of me. Then the penny dropped. The blighter was putting psychological pressure on me to rush, to not take in the detail of what was being put forward. He was, I suspect, preparing the prototype scripts for a version of 'Yes Minister!'. I curtly brought that to an end. Later, I learned he had been using this device successfully over many years. Unfortunately, we had a major clash when I discovered he had been double-dealing with me, telling me only part of what he had been doing on a major undertaking, but not the part to which I would have objected. He retired shortly after this fiery *contretemps*, as a result of serious health problems.

My experiences with the welfare industry convinced me that omnibus social planning generally does not work and that we should not attempt it. Human behaviour and needs are far too complex and there is too much individualism in our make-up for large and expensive global responses, as it were, to effectively cover all or most of our welfare contingencies. What were once derisively rejected as bandaid responses, as incrementalism—that is hard-headed, practical, pragmatic responses to a particular set of social problems—is a more effective way to proceed. Nor should government try to fill in all the social potholes that can make some of our rites of passage through life a little rough. There are not the resources with which to do that and, far from it doing us great harm if we are left to struggle with some of the less catastrophic forms of adversity that arise in our lives, we may be doing ourselves a favour.

The most important thing I learnt from my experience of government was the limits to government—not just the limits to what it was capable of doing, but more importantly, what it should be allowed to do. The more government expands and intrudes its functions into our private lives, the greater the tendency for the free expression of human will and creativity to be inhibited. Absolute libertarianism is too neglectful of reasonable human need. Absolute State authority is too stifling of individual rights. The trick is to get the balance right. I also learnt another important truth. As an impatient young idealist I believed in the perfectibility of humankind. That I now acknowledge to be a potentially dangerous illusion. The inherently flawed condition of humans, their variety and frequent unpredictability, are among the most important bulwarks we have against an 'ideal', conforming State; a grey, boring servile State. I am no longer a Democratic Socialist nor even a Social Democrat, but I am dedicated to operating, as a liberal humanist, within a democratic, pluralistic State where we work to maintain a healthy trade-off between collective responsibilities and individual rights.

Medibank: a bit of shock treatment

I was deeply involved in the creation of Medibank as a functioning universal health insurance scheme. That was the Mark I version, as it were, of what we now have as Medicare. A rather fuller account of the original design and introduction of Medibank has been amply documented elsewhere;[19] the following comments, accordingly, are more in the way of notes from the battlefield. The existing health insurance system, prior to the introduction of Medibank in 1975, was designed foremost to entrench fee-for-service payments for doctors: a payments system which encourages providers of the services to over-provide those services, thus causing an excessively costly national health bill. The system was too expensive for most of the community and beyond the resources of the less well-off. It also disadvantaged non-English speaking members of the community and, because of its inadequate attention to our great teaching hospitals, adversely affected the quality and range of experience provided by practical teaching from our medical schools.

The struggle associated with this programme commenced for me when I became shadow minister in 1969 and it continued with little abatement until mid-1975. It was indisputably the most furiously fought domestic policy issue at any time since the politically unwise and terminal nationalisation and health services battles of the Chifley Government in 1949. Finally we prevailed; we literally won a long, drawn-out, hard-slogging political battle pitched over nearly six years. It was a struggle played out against the Australian Medical Association and certain fringe medical groups; against the unremitting ideological bitternesses of the non-Labor governments in Victoria, New South Wales, Queensland and Western Australia; the sustained opposition of the profit-making private hospitals and some of the religious charitable hospitals; and the bloated and inefficient private health insurance funds. A hostile Senate resisted our endeavours every step of the way, ignoring the mandate for this change which followed the success of the 1972 House of Representatives election. Implacable Senate opposition led to a double dissolution in 1974, a major ground for which included obstruction to Medibank. In spite of the Government's success at the 1974 election, the coalition parties insisted on forcing a vote on the issue at a joint sitting of both Houses of Parliament, a historic first, and then only after an unsuccessful appeal against the legislation had been taken to the High Court. The opposition with which we had to contend from various well-organised quarters was bitter, unrelenting and often cruelly personalised. To eventually overcome this formidable, combined opposition and in particular to succeed over the hostility of the AMA, was a relief indeed. Organised medicine had not been bested before.[20] For the twenty-six years from 1949 to the introduction of Medibank in 1975, organised medicine rather much got its own way from successive coalition governments.

The outcome of the struggle to introduce Medibank was never certain. There were several key points when I thought we could go under. The public service was convinced we had been defeated when the enabling legislation was rejected by the Senate in late 1973. Although I had seen this as an inevitable prospective result, I had not regarded it as the end of the struggle. The public service kept working away at the programme, nonetheless, even if convinced I would fail. On occasion, in a desperate effort to open up some headway in the face of intractable opposition, I either asked my advisers for or prepared options myself according to basic principles. Sometimes, to the despair of a couple of my advisers in particular, who generally preferred to keep the integrity of the package intact, I offered important concessions to our opponents.[21] Unwisely, only a few were accepted by these opponents; they misjudged the strength of their strategic position at crucial points.

There were some lessons I learnt in my lengthy political career, which are handy working generalisations for those attempting to create some positive achievements through the political processes. Australians feel uncomfortable with extended public conflict and expect reasonable people to work out compromises. They tend to reject people they see as rigidly clinging to a point of view to the absolute exclusion of other views. It is therefore imperative to respond to seemingly reasonable offers with seemingly reasonable counter-proposals. Sometimes this can involve giving ground, proposing an alternative, or, in certain circumstances, an offer reasonably cast but which you know your opponent cannot accept. It all depends on how important it is to move the process towards a comprehensive agreement at that time and what effect genuine accommodation will have on the functioning of and the key principles implicit in the programme. The strength of your tactical position also has a major bearing on your decision. Your opponents do exactly the same; the AMA, on this occasion, also engaged in a massive, well-funded, extremely effective campaign which distorted many of the programme's objectives.[22] I usually preferred a modest compromise if it was possible, for to give a little ground can allow your opponent to save face and is likely to produce a better mutual working arrangement. Notions of absolute victory, of demanding unconditional surrender, are overbearing and unwholesome in a democracy.

Nonetheless, the process of establishing compromises can create particular difficulties in the Labor Party. There is an articulate and quite audible group in the Party and a similar, equally active group at its fringes, generically identified by Paul Keating as 'Balmain basketweavers'. This push is quick to denounce compromise with issues which engage their self-interest. Fortunately, most of the party faithful, with great practical wisdom, understand and support the need for compromise, as that is at the heart of democratic political processes. I developed considerable personal and political respect for the AMA representatives with whom I dealt. They were tough, unrelenting proponents of their association's policy and in many respects their role was no easy one to discharge. They headed up an industrial association which was one of the toughest trade unions to manage in the country. Leaders of blue collar unions could always rely on an appeal to collective discipline in the face of a challenge, a quality deeply embedded in the culture of the trade union movement. Not so the AMA. Its leaders had to deal with a membership of well-educated, questioning, tough individualists.

The Government was doubly blessed in the quality of the personnel and the commitment of the people who backed it. Doctors Dick Scotton and John Deeble, creators of the Medibank health insurance concept, were remarkably adept academics, endlessly bouncing new policy ideas off difficult problems; what's more they were able to develop practical working systems with which to implement the ideas. The commitment and application of the unparalleled skills of Department of Social Security officers— Laurie Daniels, Dennis Corrigan, Bruce Holgate and a host of others—ensured the practical success of the Government's policies. In the case of Medibank they overcame seemingly impossible odds to have systems, in particular the computerisation systems, in place for the scheme to go ahead on 1 July 1975.

Rather early in 1975 I began to insist that we had to make the target date with the medical side of the insurance plan. As official documents of the time record, I anticipated that the Opposition would force an election before the end of the year. After so much work and the promises we had made to the public, I wanted to see the medical insurance side of Medibank functioning at least. On all their past experience, and with their practical knowledge of what had to be achieved with the computer programming, the officials doubted that the systems would be in place by the commencement date. Somehow they managed it, under the inspired leadership of Ray Williams. There was little room to spare, but they got there. It was a magnificent achievement. Nowhere in the world has such a huge computerisation programme been undertaken so successfully, recording every individual in the population for health file purposes and all in a relatively short time. One serious flaw in any major aspect of the process and I would have been on the back foot again, trying to ward off fierce attacks from my opponents. There were a lot of fingers crossed moments as we pushed the process to the very outer limits of performance to reach our target.

Generally, I much admire and feel greatly indebted to the numerous officers of the public service departments in Canberra with whom I worked. They functioned both apolitically and at the same time loyally to the government of the day. Contrary to popular opinion, these dedicated individuals work as hard, if not harder in many cases, than many in the private sector. I always experience a surge of annoyance when a former colleague complains that the public servants failed him or her. In most cases where this has been put to me, the fault had lain in shortcomings of the person making the charge. If you knew what you wanted and made it clear, my experience was that the public service would do its level best to deliver for you. There was never, at any stage while I was in Parliament, a public service conspiracy against any government. Claims that there were, and I have heard some from a few former Whitlam Government ministers, are fatuous.

At the heart of political life there is still much in the way of enjoyable hype—even when one has been under extreme pressure and taking a beating. Years later, recollections of the big engagements can still give a buzz, although the actual processes were sometimes lonely ones. Medibank had me away from home for extended periods, often visiting some of the most out of the way places to spruik the case for our health insurance proposals.

Memories abound of soulless motel rooms, the standard of which would have appalled Sadie Thompson and her clergyman friend, Mr Davidson;[23] of bare, freezing meeting halls in winter; of the mixed cheers and groans of audiences made up of friendly supporters and hostile opponents. At the same time, lodged at the back of my mind was the thought: 'Fail in this and you're a loser politically; political losers are has-beens'. Then there was the exhaustion of being in seemingly perpetual motion. One night, though dead tired, I found myself addressing a crowded hall of people at Bundaberg. As usual the front rows were taken by local medicos, all sombre and ready for hostile engagement. The supporters were further back. I opened my pitch with a little of the usual harmless chatter of how pleased I was as a Queenslander to be back in my home State, in particular to be visiting the progressive city of Maryborough . . . A doctor's voice, which surely could have won the sneering championship of the world, cut in like a steady, deadly laser, 'But you ain't, are you? You're in Bundaberg'. Mirthful titters about the room; embarrassment for me.

Early in the debate I was making my way through a Brisbane airport terminal when I was noisily and good-humouredly greeted by my colleague and friend, Jack Egerton. 'Hey, Hayden! A Wickham Terrace specialist told me last week that you don't like doctors because you had a nervous breakdown and failed third year medicine—you've been having shock treatment ever since . . . I always defend a mate though . . . I told him you didn't have enough brains to have a mental breakdown.' Egerton chortled his way out to his aircraft. Well, that explained a great deal. Such as the regular questioning of my health history by doctors at meetings. This had perplexed me. Apart from bouts of depression—for which I have never sought treatment, for the simple reason that until fairly recent years I laboured under the misapprehension that my experiences were normal—I had and continue to enjoy good health. The canard about my mental state apparently gained great currency in the medical profession and elsewhere. At its most specific and excruciatingly painful, this breakdown was supposed to have been a result of my grief in 1966 with the loss of our eldest child, Michaela. What the experience did teach me was how dangerous it would have been to my political career had I ever actually been to a psychiatrist.

A journalist, a female with whom I had once kept company many years earlier when we were single, contacted me and threatened to 'expose' the 'fact' that I had undergone regular shock treatment at the Royal Brisbane Hospital. It would, she said, be a better story for me if I made a clean breast of my condition. I responded, offering full authority for that person to have access to any medical files held on me at that or any other hospital. The journalist retorted that I had used my influence to have the files destroyed! The fact was, there were no, and never had been any, files to destroy. This was a no-win situation if ever there was one. On another occasion my wife received a telephone call late one night advising her that I had had a breakdown on an aircraft travelling to Brisbane and had been hospitalised. She was stunned and relieved when I arrived at our front door, literally minutes later, hearty and well. Yet another time, while shopping at the local supermarket, Dallas found herself being commiserated with by some ladies who had heard a report that I had deserted her to live in some sort of commune with homosexuals at Kingston, near Brisbane. These nasty fabrications, of the sort termed 'black propaganda' or 'disinformation' by State security services, went on and on.[24] They stung and distressed Dallas but we could not afford to confess that; the whole purpose of the campaign was to wear both of us down, to break our resolve. I should add that while much of this nastiness was sourced to some members of the medical profession, the AMA as a formal body, and its leaders, were embarrassed by it. The experience left a mark on me. One of the first things I did after becoming Foreign Minister in 1983, and on being acquainted with the terms of reference by which ASIS functioned, was to instruct that 'black propaganda' could not be used while I was the responsible minister. Later in the eighties, when Justice Hope was conducting his inquiry into intelligence services, I urged that he formally recommend that this practice be eliminated from the terms of reference of that organisation, forever. He reported accordingly.

Meanwhile, as if these and other obstacles in the way of a national health scheme were not enough, Gough Whitlam opened up another front for us. In July 1973, he had a brainstorm and decided that Canberra should take over the public hospitals of Australia. Alternatively, the national government would construct its own public hospitals in the States and impose financial conditions on the States' hospital systems. His purpose was to establish de facto control over them from the national capital. I froze with terror. We had more than enough difficult battles with States and organised interest groups, in trying to advance the Medibank concept. Yet those conflicts would seem trifling compared with what would confront us if this was attempted. I demurred, a task fraught with some difficulties for Whitlam abjured 'nervous nellies' and 'pissants'. It was Dr Sid Sax, a distinguished public health services planner and administrator who, with a polished display of elegant and persuasive problem-handling, shifted Whitlam. We were back on course; but that iceberg had come close.

Whitlam had a fancy for inspired undertakings of this nature, what he described as the 'grand gesture'. I recall sitting in his office with some other ministers and officials from various departments in readiness to discuss just one such project. The Treasury officials were, as usually on such occasions, sitting stiff-backed and looking doleful. The Whitlam proposal was to buy the UK-based Furness Withy shipping line. The Treasury officials outlined deficiencies in the proposal, all good and sound observations. Whitlam was impatient. He had heard them before—when he had first raised the project with me, for one. He had also heard similar demurring from the Treasurer, Crean. After my initial objection and through some sort of oversight, I expect, I had not been invited to many subsequent discussions until this concluding meeting. Whitlam wanted this meeting to comprehensively and finally endorse his proposal. He expostulated at Treasury 'negativeness', at the dismal absence of imagination. What he wanted, he said with forceful emphasis, was the 'grand gesture';'it was everything in politics'; 'like Disraeli buying the Suez Canal!'. Usually, in the face of the most fearsome provocations, Treasury officials could maintain absolute inscrutability. Not this time they didn't, no fear! They all reacted as if an unexpected electric charge had struck them through the seat of their pants. Fortunately, the unimaginative won the day.[25] The intermediary in this instance was the redoubtable Peter Abeles, who sought a spotter's fee of something like $1 million or $2 million should the undertaking proceed. He had other joint enterprise options, his most favoured of course having him in control of the operation. Abeles always did have an extraordinary capacity to be around at the right time and to know the right people.

The processes associated with the introduction of Medibank, the confrontation, debate, negotiation, restructuring of position papers following new developments, and a plague of other procedural requirements, relentlessly ground on. Moreover, the harder we tried for a mutually acceptable compromise, the more elusive the goal seemed; as if it was all doomed to go on for ever and ever. As the debate became more complex, and more prolix too, the consequence was that only a few in Caucus managed to keep up with the evolving detail. The sense of isolation I felt at this time was quite strong; then, to top it all off, Whitlam and I managed to fall out over the 1974 budget. Among other things, I wrote to him explaining what I thought of the quality of economic management; it was not a well-received missive. At around the same time Dallas and I returned to Parliament House one night from a meal at the nearby Lobby Restaurant. I was a little tired and sombre. Although we had just scraped back into office at the 1974 election, the prospect of another run at a double dissolution by the Opposition seemed very real to me, especially as I could see no convincing evidence that we were ready to reform our ways. I remember that evening well: a crisp, clear winter's night with a flawlessly beautiful, star-spangled sky.

There was a small group of Australians, from the Baltic States, opposite the Parliament. They were standing, holding candles, in a lonely, pathetic little protest, demonstrating against a decision taken for the Australian Government to recognise the incorporation of those States within the USSR. The scene added to my emotions. So little gained from the gesture, yet so much pain gratuitously created for those unfortunate people. It was impossible to dismiss their feelings even if, as was said of them, they overwhelmingly voted anti-Labor. It is regrettable that Whitlam was the first person I ran into in the Parliament. I commented on the foolishness of the decision. Unfortunately, the observations were rough-hewn. The combination of these two incidents, the budget and this matter, badly frayed the communications system between our two offices. I could get an out line from my office but not an in connection to the office of *numero uno*.

Now I found myself, of necessity, taking important, operational decisions on the implementation of Medibank unilaterally, decisions which might have benefited from slightly wider consultation. There was something of a replay of the Baltic States messiness in early 1975, when Foreign Minister Willesee and Labour and Immigration Minister Cameron were over-ridden, by fiat, in their efforts to bring more Vietnamese to Australia in an effort to help those people escape reprisals in their homeland.[26] It was on that occasion that the memorable, but unfortunate, comment was made in justification of the prime ministerial rebuff to Willesee and Cameron: 'We're not going to create ghettoes of Asian-Balts to vote anti-Labor'. Yet the Vietnamese came and settled, the 'ghettoes' flourished and, in spite of this hostility and Labor opposition to Western involvement in the

Vietnam War, they continue to strongly support Labor. The Liberals were politically inept to an unparalleled degree to have let Labor poach this 'natural' constituency for them so quickly and easily.

At some stage in 1974 my Department suggested I visit Britain, Canada and the United States to observe the functioning of the various health systems in those countries. I demurred, pointing out that I had all the facts I needed from authoritative sources. 'Of course, Mr Hayden, and you handle the material superbly, no doubt about it. But . . . well . . . we rather feel that if you make this visit and return, drawing on concrete examples from your observations when responding to the exaggerated claims of the AMA, it will have more persuasive effect with the public.' I wanted to object that if I was performing superbly why in blazes should I go overseas. I went. The bureaucrats were absolutely right to suggest I go. Thereafter, I would respond to some outrageous challenge from the AMA, the private health insurance funds or the private hospitals with: 'Hang on a bit; I've just come back from there and you're dead wrong'. . . Such riposte usually put an end to the latest bit of misrepresentation. Similarly, for quite some time into the debate on the health reforms, I would trundle into radio and television studios, fully armed with annual reports, tables, quotes and a range of other paraphernalia, ready to do detailed battle with any claim or query which came up. Another new lesson started to seep in: people are soon bored with detail, especially with a mass of statistical data; overwhelmingly, they want to be reassured on simple little things. 'Yes, you will be able to choose your private doctor', 'No, madam, you will not be forced into a public ward to have your baby', and so on. In spite of its comprehensive complexity, we reduced the selling of Medibank to a simple set of reassuring propositions, a key one of which was 'three out of four taxpayers will be better off'!

Going overseas in 1974 brought other interesting experiences, besides enhancing my knowledge of health affairs. During our travels we were able to go to Scotland, a welcome break. In Edinburgh we made some purchases of lovely, softly woven cashmere woollen garments, from a quaint, antique-looking store, perhaps some centuries old. There were clan ties. 'Do you have a Menzies?' 'We have a Mingies', was the reply, in glorious Scottish brogue. I purchased it—explaining, slightly embarrassed, for my late father's hovering ghost definitely would have been twitching with disapproval at my behaviour—that it was for a former prime minister. 'We know of Sir Robert Mingies here,' she said in tones which I could only explain as understated Scottish imperialism. I sent it to the old boy, then retired by several years. I penned something to the effect, 'I am sending you this small gift as a token of respect; from the land of the Lion in the North to the lion of Australian politics in the South'. Menzies eventually sent back a nice little note, thanking me and giving some explanation of the family tartan—an unusually civilised exchange for two Australian politicians who had had some notable, heated exchanges.

Back in Australia, suddenly there was a memorable moment when a sea-change occurred in the seemingly irresolvable Medibank process. There was nothing gradual about the transformation in our fortunes; what rolled in felt like a luxurious, surging breaker that suddenly sweeps over, larger and better than anything before or after. A message was relayed to me on about 10 April 1975, from my Department. A few officials of the AMA, led by their president, Keith Jones, wanted to meet with me. The AMA would not mention over the phone the topics they wished to raise. They also wanted absolute confidentiality about the meeting. In my office we briefly indulged ourselves; while wishing that we might have a breakthrough, our suspicions were of another impossible ambit claim to further complicate proceedings. At the session which soon followed, in the department meeting room at Woden, Jones wasted no time with preliminaries. He said simply that most members of the AMA Federal Council saw no further point in opposing the introduction of Medibank. I was stunned! However much I might have wished for this, it was more than I had a right to hope for, given our experiences to that point.

We drove back to Parliament House—my Principal Private Secretary, Gae Raby, and I—in a rented car. On the local ABC radio station, Stephan Grapelli and Yehudi Menuhin were joyfully fiddling away in fast jazz-waltz beat: 'I can't believe you're in love with me. . . ' which was immediately followed by the Andrews Sisters singing *Boogie Woogie Bugle Boy* with full, brassy big band backing. We were free spirits at last, the first time for years and years, it seemed. We had won! In the privacy of the motor car we indulged an understandable display of elation, with me beating out the tempo of the tunes on the accelerator pedal, so intoxicated were we by the sudden turnaround in our fortunes. My office staff and Department were a remarkable group of talented and dedicated people. We had fought as a team and the victory, so long in coming, was very much due to their collective efforts. I was and remain grateful to them. Though it was an appropriate time for a huge celebration, we instead went back to Parliament and the routine grind that demanded our attention there. Later that same day I bought vinyl records with those two tunes. I still play them from time to time. Even now I can nostalgically recapture a little of that sense of elation on that happy day; that exquisitely happy, happy day so many years ago.

The non-Labor States remained a major obstruction. As July quickly closed in, it looked as though the hospital side of the programme would be decidedly difficult to implement. Labor in South Australia and Tasmania would enter the programme by the commencement date. Victoria, New South Wales, Queensland and Western Australia, all anti-Labor, were, apparently, unappeasable. The Victorian Health Minister, Scanlan, even passed a law providing for the dismissal of any State-employed medical practitioner who in any way worked with Medibank. Then some useful developments occurred. Charles Court, the wily Western Australian Premier, let it be known discreetly, that, in effect, there was a time for politicking and a time for the transaction of the serious business of State. The latter had arrived. Western Australia would join the programme: but, please, this is just between the two of us, as gentlemen of good standing . . . being Court's further implication.

I should confess that a little earlier I started dragging my feet quite deliberately in dealings with the States on public hospital funding. I wrote to Whitlam as early as May 1975 pointing out that if I wore 'lead boots' in the course of these negotiations I could save the budget as much as $285 million in outlays in a full year. In this I would be greatly assisted by the non-Labor State governments' intemperate opposition to everything I sought to achieve. I was concerned about our fiscal situation. The Melbourne *Age* threw a spanner into the workings of this little ploy by publishing an article in June, disclosing how much that State would lose, in additional revenue for its public hospital system, by not entering the Medibank scheme.[27] The Victorian Premier, Rupert Hamer, was on the telephone to me in a flash, deeply troubled. Was the report correct, he inquired? He knew that if the *Age* report was accurate, he could be in diabolical political trouble. He was advised the report was soundly based and, moreover, his health ministry had held the information for some time. Nothing could deflect him. He was promptly on a plane to Canberra.

By now I was less dedicated to the 'lead boots' delaying tactics. Having become Treasurer, I was running that portfolio while cleaning up the Medibank arrangements, which was a somewhat messy and burdensome experience. I was also certain that Malcolm Fraser would be tempted to force an election because of the Khemlani Loans shambles. Hamer turned out to be the quintessence of co-operation. He would pull out every stop necessary to accelerate the entry of his State into Medibank he explained, adding, 'The more I look at it, the more I recognise that we do not differ at all'. It was all rather surreal. For some years I had been on the receiving end of some most stubborn and ill-informed obstructionism and personal denigration, while I fruitlessly tried to make headway with the idiosyncratic Scanlan. Scanlan's superior was now sitting before me, effectively telling me that broad grounds for agreement had always existed! Victoria entered the scheme earlier than I had intended, even if after the commencement date. This entailed a cost, but not as a form of punishment; their entry date was the earliest we could manage logistically.

I knew Queensland was near enough to sewn up; to the extent there would be further delays, there was nothing I could do about them. I had met State Treasurer Gordon Chalk and Health Minister Llew Edwards at a secret meeting, one Sunday in June at Chalk's Brisbane office. Chalk's electorate and mine had overlapped for many years and we had established a good personal and working relationship. Llew Edwards' electorate was, like mine, based on Ipswich; moreover, we were family friends. Chalk and Edwards were keen to enter the scheme but their coalition partner, in the person of the Premier, was making it difficult for them. Bjelke-Petersen was relentlessly stalking the Liberal Party, seeking to split it over a number of issues, in particular Medibank. His ambition was to entice a small clutch of defectors from the Liberal Party to join his party so as to form a government in his own right, something in which he was to succeed, but not for a few more years. In the meantime Queensland lost $10 million in Medibank payments for its hospitals because of Bjelke-Petersen's bumbling attempts to destroy the Liberal Party with the pointed bone of Medibank. This only left New South Wales—whose Premier, Lewis, was in Canberra condemning the scheme at exactly the same time Hamer was in my office pressing his case urgently for entry into the scheme. Suddenly Lewis discovered he was isolated by the 'apostasy' of the other non-Labor States. Seven days later, on 25 June, Lewis ran up the white flag of surrender. He begged entry from 1 July. His request fell upon sympathetic ears; unfortunately, a similar delay, as for Victoria, would be unavoidable, as was the attendant cost.

I look back on this extended display of obstructionism, of wooden-headedness from the medical profession and the non-Labor States, and I marvel at the futility, the irrationality and the cost to them. The medical profession could well have achieved a range of concessions beyond what was finally implemented, concessions which would have been agreeable to them. If only they had allowed their leaders more flexibility. If only they had recognised, as had Court, there is a time for politicking and a time to transact important matters of State. The greatest damage they did was to themselves, for the level of public respect for doctors fell away dramatically during this episode. Their great blunder was to behave in such a way as to suggest to the public that avarice was their main motivation. As for the States, most of the non-Labor States succeeded in inflicting substantial fines on themselves, for no more reason than their being so blindly hostile to the national government. Their opposition was simply and foolishly based on the fact that it was Labor. The days of that kind of numbskull party politics, thank goodness, appear to have gone. The experiences with Medibank contributed a good deal to that change.

Medibank was touted by many as a socialist health scheme. It was nothing of the sort. It was middle-class welfare reform and it favoured the medical profession. It was based on private medical practice, fee-for-service payments, patient's choice of doctor. What it did more than anything else was to efficiently collect and distribute funds for medical and hospital care. To the extent that doctors bulk bill government for services to patients, where the payments are set at fixed rates, the practice of overcharging will be diminished.[28] Of course more needed to be done about doctor overservicing, another major source of excessive costs within the health delivery system, but there was not enough time. Whatever criticisms might be made of the cost of Medicare, the successor to

Medibank, it is an indisputable fact that it has more effectively controlled overall health cost in this country, compared to the experience of most similar, developed countries.[29] More than that, the greater the public sector share of health funding, measured as a proportion of GDP, the lower total health spending tends to be.[30] In other words, efforts by governments to make the public pay more of the cost of health privately, inflate the comparative cost of services rendered.

The curious irony at the heart of this great struggle was that, while I believed Medibank a vast improvement on the costly inefficiencies of what it replaced, it was not my preferred option. I would rather have had a system of free public hospitals, adequately funded, as then in Queensland, and there backed by the development of self-administered community health centres, staffed by salaried medicos and para-professionals. The cost of operating these centres, including staffing salaries, would have been funded by per capita subscriptions from voluntary subscribers supported by a government subsidy. Such a system was to be developed according to areas of established welfare need. Unfortunately, elections are not won and governments do not hold office by offering and developing policies which are too complex in their structure, and time-consuming in their practical development, even if they offer better health care and cost containment. In the upshot, Medibank shone gloriously and briefly. Fraser promised to preserve the scheme but immediately the 1975 election was out of the way set about dismantling it. Later, with the staying power of the Hawke Government to assist him, Neal Blewett introduced Medibank's successor, Medicare, which continues to flourish today and, I trust, will do so long into the future.

Treasury: and trying to slow the printing presses

My appointment as Treasurer was made as the Khemlani fiasco was at its peak. Whitlam, presumably, reached the conclusion that

Cairns would have to go as Treasurer as his involvement in unorthodox loan raisings was being exposed. I had flown into Sydney airport by commercial aircraft during this period and, while in transit, received a message that Whitlam wanted to see me at his RAAF VIP aircraft not far away. He told me that he felt compelled to move Cairns as Treasurer because of these adverse developments and inquired if I would accept the vacant portfolio. My answer— which I think I gave equably, but with heart pounding, for this was the ministry above all others I had hoped to occupy one day— was 'yes'. And that was how it happened. By the next week I was Treasurer of Australia, the big welfare spender now converted into an austere bean counter.

I was appointed Treasurer and Jim McClelland became Minister for Labour and Immigration on 6 June 1975. Neither of us had held those roles long enough to have any impact on either the June Quarter Consumer Price Index or Average Weekly Earnings statistics. These were released within weeks of our taking our respective offices. The Average Weekly Earnings (AWE) statistics for that quarter, reported a sharp reduction in the rate of increase. The easing in the rate of increase in the Consumer Price Index, comparatively, was extremely modest. I was talking with Whitlam in his office the morning of the release of the AWE statistics, when, referring to those statistics, he said rather pointedly, something like, 'Comrade, Jim McClelland is already rolling back the wages front. You'll have to pull your socks up. You made no impact on the last inflation figures'. They had been released in mid-July.[31] I made ready to laugh at this jest. But no: as I gazed at him I realised laughter was not appropriate. This was a serious moment; I had been rebuked, and properly so, it would seem.

I had watched the management of Cabinet decision-making for nearly three years by this time. An Expenditure Review Committee had been instituted to sort out the scheduling of minutes for Cabinet consideration. Before that, minutes used to arrive at the

Cabinet office directly from ministers and it seemed their existence was enough to justify their scheduling. It all appeared to proceed according to the old boarding house rule: first in, best fed. As a consequence, when the dinner gong went there was a rush for the best pickings. Sometimes we arrived at Cabinet with a pile of submissions from various ministers a third of a metre, or more, in height. A long tiring day would ensue, as we picked our way through the mass of paper. More commitments, more spending, more problems with the economy. Whitlam, mostly, would move along the pace of decision-making at a rapid clip. At the end of such a day, during which general weariness would lead some of the ministers to lose interest in the seemingly endless process, Whitlam would expansively comment to the effect, 'Well, Comrades, we've had a very productive day. A number of historic decisions were made. Thank you'. I would mutter in my mind, 'Productive! Historic! We're sinking under the weight of decisions. This is another nail in our collective coffin'. It was a point I argued during appropriate debates in Cabinet, but not with much effect.

If, in the course of one of these marathon efforts, there was opposition to some proposal much favoured by Whitlam, and it looked as though the opposition might be successful, he would resignedly suggest that there be a full debate on the matter. Then, the democratic process really bloomed, like some invasive weed in endemic proportions. Any of the twenty-seven ministers present could participate but, he would stipulate firmly, they could speak only once and for a maximum of five minutes. Then the affair would unroll endlessly. Some would speak for much more than five minutes, and often several times. There were a few notable windbags who savoured these occasions. Opponents would start to drop out of the process, hammered into surrender by exhaustion and frustration at what was going on and the time it was all taking. If at some late stage it was apparent that the opposition was looking for mercy and ready to surrender, the matter would suddenly be put to a vote. This tactic would most often succeed. Curiously, the fractiousness of the Cabinet, so unused to the disciplines of collective responsibility, reduced the practice of consensual decision-making to a minimum. If, however, the opposition in Cabinet persisted, the matter would most likely be held over to another day. More often than not the opposition would surrender, rather than go through the punishing charade again. Even masochists have pain thresholds.

I had not been entirely unprepared for my stint as Treasurer. Once when I was Acting Treasurer, it so happened that I requested access to the Treasury's economic forecasts. There was stonewalling. I was then informed by John Stone, Deputy Secretary of Treasury, with whom I was speaking on this matter, that they were only available in computer printout form, that the presentation was in technical, coded style, incomprehensible to the layman, including to Stone. Eventually, in the company of another officer, Stone did bring these printouts across to Parliament House. Not before we acceded to Treasury's stipulation that the meeting had to take place, not in my office, but in that of the absent Treasurer. These little psychological advantages, it would seem, were important to some. As the venue was immaterial to me, I concurred. The printouts were indeed incomprehensible. I left to go back to my office, accompanied by my chief adviser, Paddy McGuinness. McGuinness was in a fury. 'You've been snowed, mate,' he said. 'They bloody well have those printouts processed and they produce a literary statement of what the forecasts contain.' 'Wouldn't do that, Paddy. Not in their interests,' was my reply. Some few months later I discovered, speaking with the Government's resident, independent economic adviser, Professor Fred Gruen, that there was in fact a literary presentation of those forecasts. I took the opportunity of my next stint as Acting Treasurer to explain to Treasury why it was in their interests to provide the forecasts to me, pronto. They responded with amazing promptitude. When I became Treasurer I had arrangements well advanced to have the literary presentation of the forecasts made public. There was evident discomfort among certain Treasury officers at the notion that the mumbo jumbo of the Treasury forecasting divines would be out in the marketplace of ideas. Kerr's intervention, in November 1975, ended that enterprise.

There is a sequel to all this. As a member of the Cabinet Economic Committee of the Hawke Government, I argued for access to the same forecasts. Matters came to a head somewhere around December 1985 when the argument, literally, raged over two days. Treasurer Keating finally conceded, not enthusiastically but with evident exhaustion and greater indignation, that we could have that access at the next committee meeting. He was as good as his word. After that, it happened that I was absent overseas a great deal. I inquired one day, out of curiosity, of the Cabinet Secretary and Head of the Department of Prime Minister and Cabinet, Sir Geoffrey Yeend, as to when the Cabinet Economic Committee had last met. It seemed there had been a long gap since our last, argumentative meeting. Yeend checked his records and reported, 'Just on twelve months ago!'. I was somewhat flabbergasted, to put it mildly. The committee had never met after that confrontation over the economic forecasts; it was replaced by the Structural Adjustment Committee in August 1987 of which I was not made a member. But then the NSW branch of Labor lives by what ought to be termed the Jack Lang principle: 'Knowledge is power, the more it is shared the more power is diluted'.

In the last year of the Whitlam Government, however, the real test for me would be the budget formulation for 1975–76. The cavalier indifference to economic disciplines had to be expelled, ruthlessly if need be. The budget deficit had to be forced down. I discussed with the Treasury Secretary, Sir Fred Wheeler, my preferred level of domestic deficit of $1000 million to $1500 million. He expressed concern that it represented too severe a turnaround and that a figure of $2000 million to $2500 million would be more appropriate. I accepted the advice, settling for the lower figure. By way of a guiding principle and because of Wheeler's advice, the following lines were penned for the budget speech by Treasury, and accepted by me:

> There is nothing sacrosanct about the particular public and private sector shares of G.D.P. But sharp movements in these shares can be disruptive . . . [32]

Cabinet greeted the strategy with one of its exasperating displays of internal contrariness. In general the Cabinet was happy with my declaration about the budget deficit and the need to cut back the rate of spending. Many ministers, however, felt their mission so critical to the qualitative improvement of society that their portfolio demanded an exemption from these disciplines. Before the Cabinet process commenced I outlined my objectives to Whitlam, stating matter-of-factly that if I failed to achieve the deficit target I would resign. There was no glory in being a lame duck treasurer. By arrangement with Whitlam the first portfolio to be addressed was Education, that of Kim Beazley Snr. On my figuring, Beazley Snr would be the most formidable opponent with whom to grapple. He had a capacious intellect, argued a well-constructed and detailed case cogently, and could be devastatingly effective with his use of language and analogy. His style was not emotional, hectoring or bullying, the typical tactics of many politicians, especially when they have a weak case. I was successful in achieving a marked cutback in Beazley's claims. A good start, but I was uneasy. Beazley had stated emphatically that spending reductions in one of his programmes, which I had badly mauled, would cause a large-scale retrenchment of schoolteachers, well beyond anything reasonable. Further, this would occur in a very short time after cutbacks took effect. I respected Beazley greatly and still do. He was a member of Moral Rearmament and tried to live by their moral code, in particular their commitment to absolute honesty. While I do not believe that anyone can be absolutely honest, Beazley consistently tried and he persistently came closer to that objective than just about anyone else I have ever known. At the morning tea break I rang the relevant group in Treasury and instructed them to convene a meeting with Beazley's officials to make sure there was no error on the part of Treasury, on whose assessments I had to rely. What came down the line, however, was pained offence: the omniscience of Treasury in those days was unchallengeable. Lesser departments, meaning all departments other than Treasury, made mistakes—but not Treasury! Later, a somewhat deflated official reported that Treasury had indeed been in error. I restored the programme shortly after receiving this information.

The expenditure-cutting experience was fascinating. I started with items at $5 million and above, for in terms of national expenditure amounts below that sum looked like 'teapot' spare cash. Nevertheless, it was not long before I was down to $1 million, and then it was a matter of raking over the 'petty-cash' items below $1 million. Once the momentum was under way the resistance of most ministers moderated and the fiscal reductions were mounting quite nicely. There were still a few ministers who behaved in Cabinet as though they were delegates from their departments. They would doggedly argue their department's brief with neither wit nor imagination, they lacked both flexibility and the good sense to recognise that persistence would not be rewarded. Quite the reverse in fact. Some of these ministers could be awful windbags and wasters of precious time. There were not a few of these in the Hawke Government too—I expect every ministry has had its share of them. In any event, I was able to advise Parliament that outlays were estimated to increase by half the rate of the previous year, and receipts at a faster rate than outlays. We were starting to slow the printing presses at last. As for me, I felt I had reached the pinnacle of a parliamentary career. To be the economic manager of the nation was an overwhelming privilege. It was in many ways a more significant role than that of prime minister, although some former treasurers, who have moved on, clearly would not agree with that assessment. In days past, the Treasurer covered what are now the ministries of Treasury and Finance, as well as being responsible for the Taxation Department. He had to master every other submission before the Cabinet, have a grasp of its detail at least as competently as the portfolio minister and had to handle the process alone. The workload was heavy and the tasks demanding. The job has also often required one to be quite tough, even rough, in rebuffing a good friend in Cabinet.

Shortly after the budget for 1975–76 was introduced, the deficit grew beyond the desired level. Unemployment had begun to increase more rapidly than forecast by Treasury, leading to additional payouts of unemployment benefits. Also, this increased unemployment led the rate of wages growth to ease more than had been expected, causing a drop off in PAYE revenue. In terms of economic management the result was welcome, as the inflationary forces which had been let loose in the economy were clearly easing. A major innovation in that budget was to eliminate concessional deductions within the prevailing income tax system. These were atrociously inequitable as they allowed deductions to be claimed at a person's maximum marginal tax rate. So a rich man's dependent spouse, dependent children, health insurance charges and so on were more generously subsidised by the taxation system than those of the middle or working classes, or those poor who paid tax. A flat rebate was substituted, the first change to this policy in sixty years. Being a Democratic Socialist committed to principles of equity and fiscal progression, I was rather pleased with myself at achieving such an important equity reform. The Fraser Opposition condemned the initiative. Later, Fraser, as Prime Minister, abolished the dependent child rebate and integrated it, with child endowment, into a new family allowance. I was at first absolutely despondent that my lovingly created arrangement had such a relatively short life, yet soon realised that Fraser had built an important advance on my change. Later again, through a series of steps, Fraser's changes were integrated by the Hawke Government into a means-tested, single, family payment, one of the most important welfare reforms undertaken since Federation. As I look back on those developments I see a consistent trend of improvement, each step an advance on the earlier one. Naturally, when the earlier steps were quickly forgotten, one's ego suffered. On the other hand the community is better off through this evolving process, and there is a great privilege in having been a part of it.

Before the budget process was completed a committee headed by the late Professor Trevor Swan, a distinguished economist from the Australian National University, was established to review the structure of personal taxation. I instructed members that I wanted a fair and equitable reduction in marginal tax rates on average and lower income earners by applying a progressive reduction in the tax burden within the income tax system. At the same time the budget deficit had to be reduced. In short, issues of equity were to be the guiding star.[33] This committee was vigorously opposed by some senior Treasury officers led by Stone, and the display of personal hostility towards it by at least one individual was quite breathtaking. I subsequently endorsed and implemented its findings, even though these too had been condemned and resisted. Eliminating tax concessions and replacing them with deductions, it was said, would destroy the insurance industry, a criticism vigorously taken up by the Coalition Opposition. But as Treasury itself had made written submissions to a government committee proposing far larger reductions in subsidies to the insurance industry, subsidies provided directly through the income tax system, I thought their position was most intriguing and perplexing. My perplexity was eventually made unambiguously clear to the officers concerned. Malcolm Fraser, subsequently, is reputed to have said of Stone that, 'he believes in the deregulation of everything he does not regulate'. That probably sums up a great deal of the contrariness experienced with Treasury over time: free market in principle, opposing the 25 per cent tariff cut of 1973 in practice; open market in theory, opposing the Australian dollar float and deregulation of the money market in the early eighties. However, territorial defensiveness is just as or more likely to explain this sort of inconsistent behaviour than any recondite theorising about monetary and fiscal principles.

It happened as the committee was winding up its work, that one of the committee members who was then a junior Treasury official, Daryl Dixon, was vigorously criticised by Stone in the presence of Whitlam, Crean and me. The gist of the criticism seemed to have been provoked by a feeling that Dixon had deserted the Treasury culture by collaborating with the committee. Dixon, though, was a young man of great personal integrity and Stone's discontent was squelched on the instant. Not that this did Dixon much good; he found it best to move on to another department later. Treasury then was a toughly disciplined organisation with little patience for those who moved outside its narrowly defined culture. Wheeler, with whom I became personally friendly and with whom I would have a Scotch or two and a discussion late at night in my office at Canberra, confided in me that he had run afoul of this exclusivist culture. He had returned from several years of service in Geneva to take over the Public Service Commission before moving to Treasury. At Treasury he was treated as an outsider and at a certain high level in the Department an almost impenetrable barrier was spread between him and most of the rest of his Department. Direct contact with various areas of his Department was made, only with difficulty, through a tight-necked funnel, as it were. In other words, there was a determined attempt to regulate his control of his own Department.

During this budget presentation period, Hawke, wearing his ACTU hat, came to me in Canberra. He sought and got assurances on a strictly confidential basis that there would be income tax cuts, and that they would benefit lower and middle income groups. He went directly to the outside staircase of Parliament House and reported this information to the assembled press as a coup for himself![34] Thus I was introduced to the Hawke style of self-promotion, a style impressively effective in illuminating its sharply focused personal goals and one with which I would become entirely familiar over the years.

Suddenly, after the budget presentation, I was feeling the full blast of the blow torch on my hindquarters. On 22 October 1975 I had categorically stated in Parliament, in response to a question, that only Whitlam, Crean and I had been aware of the taxation measures in the 1975 budget before its presentation. When I returned to my office I was advised that Hawke, who must have been listening to question time, had left a telephone message before the end of question time to the effect that he had been given a briefing on the budget, including the tax measures, before its presentation. Hawke went on to say, in a very forceful manner as it was repeated to me, that if he were asked a relevant question about the matter, as he was certain he would be, he would have to disclose this as a matter of integrity. I had forgotten that I had arranged the briefing in an effort to head off a repeat of the vigorous, negative and very damaging criticism of the 1974 budget by Hawke. Nonetheless, the implications of Hawke's warning— or perhaps it was much more than a warning—were clear enough.[35] With all the strife we were experiencing in other areas, this was an undesirable development. My foolish oversight had created a potentially serious problem for the Government.

The implication of Hawke's message seemed clear to me and I was worried. Accordingly, after this discussion with him, I arranged with Whitlam's press secretary, David Solomon, to appear on Richard Carleton's 'This Day Tonight' TV programme on Monday 27 October. I would make a full disclosure ahead of Parliament. The weekend was a less than exquisite experience as I waited for what might be my political demise. I saw Whitlam before I went on the programme. I had cleared the briefing of Hawke with him beforehand. I outlined what I was going to do. I said to him, effectively, 'If it goes bad, there's no point in both of us going down. I'll take the blame by myself. The Party can't take many more disasters, least of all at the top'. I was gratified when Whitlam responded to the effect, 'One thing I have always admired about you, Comrade, is your tough self-discipline'. I savoured that compliment more than most I have received. To me self-discipline, taking the strain under pressure without crumpling, is one of the most important qualities a person can have. In the event, I was a bit battered by the experience, but made it safely out the other end.

One day in the midst of those turbulent post-budget days I was sitting at the luncheon table, at Parliament House, with Clyde Cameron, his young research assistant, John Bannon, and my principal economic adviser, Dr Peter McCawley. Cameron began denouncing the burgeoning leaks from Cabinet. When he made the point that ministers should be able to trust colleagues with secrets, I knew I had him snookered: 'Come off it, Clyde. A Cabinet submission from you was leaked into the newspapers a few days before it was circulated to ministers'. Cameron looked genuinely disappointed. 'It's awful when you can't even trust people in your own office,' he said with a straight face. 'Clyde, you and I know better than that, don't we?' And like a compulsive sinner who genuinely regrets his human weakness, he responded penitently: 'Well, it's true . . . sometimes you can't even trust the author himself! That's when it's really bad'.

In the political processes of our parliamentary system one cannot win on everything. Sometimes, in Cabinet, you might lose a case to which you are passionately committed, only to then have to go forth as a minister and argue for the one you had previously opposed. In Opposition, in the period leading up to the 1972 election success, I had opposed Labor's proposal to provide university education free of student fee charges. I did not believe this was an equitable policy. I had also pointed out that we would find the cost burden increasingly difficult to bear and would only be able to persevere with it at the cost of other programmes, perhaps programmes more equitable and more important to Labor culture, such as the means-tested Tertiary Education Assistance Scheme (TEAS)[36] allowances for needy but able university students. There was little support for my view. In our desperation to find more expenditure savings, and in order to meet the determination of Cabinet to preserve free university education—a thoroughly popular commitment with most ministers—we froze TEAS university students' allowances in the 1975 budget. Shortly after the presentation of the budget I sat in the meeting room of the Labor Party office in Adelaide. Here, on the usual selling the budget circuit to the various States, I was suddenly confronted by about a dozen or so angry young university students. They were TEAS recipients. Needless to say, I did not relish the paradox of justifying an action to which I was totally opposed in private. It was embarrassing and discomforting to find the youngsters were angrily making many of the same points I had earlier made in Opposition, fruitlessly, to my colleagues. These young people were the very ones to whom we should have given first priority, according to the Labor values in which I believed. But political life is nothing if not full of ironies.

And anti-climaxes. Great moments savoured in the prospect, often turn out to be fizzers. After the budget had been presented I went to Washington to attend the International Monetary Fund conference. In the way of these sorts of high-level international conferences, there was much *brouhaha* about the significance of this annual gathering in the media. Also in the way of most high-level international conferences, most of the work had been done by the full-time officials before the arrival of the minister. The 'political masters' typically arrive late on the scene of these events, promptly walk to the spotlight at centre stage and accept kudos for all that has gone right. But what happens if the exercise goes badly wrong and who suffers as a result? It is because of the potential for such consequences that public servants are present—and why they work so exactingly for successful results. What became quickly clear at this conference was that IMF officials had pretty much written off the Australian Government. Representation from the fund at our official reception at the Australian Ambassador's home was rather low-level and the interest displayed was perfunctory, to put it generously.

The return flight on Qantas seemed to encounter almost consistent, low-level turbulence. As a result, by the time I arrived at Sydney airport, I was tired and slightly distressed. I held a press conference and got through it safely enough, quite something for those times as I was fearful that some new and damaging disclosure, arising from the Khemlani loans affair, might have been made while I had been away. Had that been the case, I would have walked into the media event, totally ignorant and unprepared. Later, I arrived at the domestic airline terminal to discover a TV camera crew had positioned itself against one wall of the gangway with a young interviewer at the opposite wall, and a microphone cable stretched across the walkway. Feeling as if I had given the 'vultures' their due already, this was irritating in the extreme. There was no escape, however. If I were to retreat, the story would be: 'Treasurer flees media'. I could only go forward, which in the event was probably the poorer decision. I erupted ill-temperedly, swung my suitcase at the interviewer and exclaimed, 'Out of my way, you bastard'. It was a wonderful feeling, briefly. Then as I settled into the flight to Canberra self-recriminations flooded in. In the end, I certainly got a lot of publicity, which I lived to regret. But I also received much supportive mail. One missive went: 'Good on you, Bill. Next time don't miss the bastard and make sure your case is full of building bricks'. Several years later I received a courteous letter from the young TV interviewer. He advised me that, until that incident, he had been unknown and more or less going nowhere. As a result of this encounter though, he had become a national identity overnight, promotions followed, and he was by then enjoying unparalleled professional satisfaction. It was nice to know that my conduct, which was inexcusably boorish, had contributed a most welcome boost to his fortunes.

In late 1975, a time when it was clear from public opinion polling that the Whitlam Government was inexorably lumbering towards a huge election defeat, Princess Margaret visited Australia. There was a black tie formal dinner for her at Government House on the night of Wednesday 22 October 1975. This was followed by another black tie dinner in her honour at the Prime Minister's official residence, The Lodge, the following night. Here would be a welcome diversion from some of the gloom, or so I thought. On the Wednesday night I was seated at the dinner table beside, and on the right of, the wife of one of our defence force chiefs. This lady was favouring those to her right with a lengthy, animated and somewhat detailed monologue about how, being short of cooking brandy with which to cook a Christmas pudding, she rather 'naughtily' used her husband's best Napoleon brandy for the task. He was not amused I gathered. She had what was regarded in those times, in some circles at least, as a 'cultivated' upper class Canberra public service accent. It was a style of speech, forced out over a fixed lower jaw, which gave a strange effect, as though she were chewing rather than speaking her words. The crushing effect on the spoken words was fondly presumed, by its practitioners at least, to be the way the British upper class spoke. At a certain point, the lady in question generously turned her attention to me and inquisitorially demanded, 'And which of the services did you serve in during the war, Mr Hayden?' I explained I was too young to join the armed services during World War II. She fixed me with a cold and, I thought, disapproving look, 'But you were not too young to serve during the Korean War; surely?' This was a challenge rather than a question, the rising cadences of which should have warned me I would be squelched if I gave an inappropriate response. Rather lamely and not very originally I responded, 'By then I was too frightened.' That was all it took. A fierce, dismissive look followed before she turned her back on me, keeping it that way for the rest of the evening, and re-commencing her discussion with her more congenial neighbours to her right. That back was ample and inhospitable, reminding me much of the wide and daunting bulwark walls of a medieval fortress. I daresay that my behaviour was regarded as an intolerable *faux pas* by the lady next to me who, through her husband, bore an imperial title and who also, undoubtedly by great personal diligence over the years, had developed a matching nature.

The next night I fared no better. This time I was seated on Princess Margaret's right. A waiter accidentally dropped the red hot contents of a gravy tureen over my shoulder as she was serving me. I sat there confused, wondering what the devil one did in the circumstances and, in particular, in the presence of royalty. My shoulder started to smart as the sauce soaked through my coat. 'Get that coat off,' came the imperative in that distinctive accent of the royals. Her Royal Highness helped me as I fumbled out of my jacket to reveal a not terribly elegant pair of trusty but tiring braces. 'Good Lord man, do they still wear those things down here?' she expostulated in genuine astonishment. Unfortunately, as a lad from South Brisbane and Ipswich I had somehow missed out on the opportunity to refine the social graces, and I guessed it showed at crucial moments like this.

My social *faux pas* aside, at least I was making progress in my treasury job. As Treasurer I stressed the need to restore profits for business in the public accounts sense. If that's run-of-the-mill stuff these days, it was rather radical for a Labor representative then. Such views of mine created a great deal of suspicion in certain circles in the Labor Party and the trade union movement. I emphasised the limits to growth of the public sector. The theme I stressed over and over with my colleagues, as much as the community, was that the days of imaginative big spending were over. The fiscal and monetary affairs of the nation, henceforth, would be managed much more cautiously. No longer could we practice 'levitation economics'—the equivalent of trying to ignore the laws of gravity. All this was set out in some detail in the Arthur Calwell Memorial Lecture, at Monash University, in September 1975. The speech was well received by economic commentators. It was condemned in predictable quarters as an apologia for the 'bosses'. There is no doubt that the 1975 budget provided the foundation for rational, disciplined fiscal management.[37]

If we had served out the remainder of our term, another two years, I have no doubt that as Treasurer I would have turned the economy around. The 1975 budget stood up well. Fraser adhered to it with only minor modifications. In fact, the discipline embodied in the budget and the correct direction it took shocked Fraser, for he recognised that once it commenced to take effect his best opportunities for defeating Labor would recede. Furthermore, the 1975 budget provided the foundation stone on which the development of rigorously responsible economic management evolved thereafter. I courted hostile responses within sections of the trade union and political wings of the Labor movement for condemning excessive wage increases, for pointing out that through this pressure profit levels, in the national accounts sense, were being eroded, and with that erosion investment levels contracted. Even if others didn't want to believe it, I knew that this would finally cost jobs. I criticised the belief that Labor could spend its way out of trouble, ridiculed the notion that deficits did not matter, and initiated an emphatic concern about the level of money supply being released into the economy. This was all rather novel for Labor in those days. The postwar situation of relatively simple, uncomplicated economic management where, generally, sustained economic growth, low inflation and unemployment rates predominated around the developed world (including Australia) had been crumbling away for some years. As the problem was becoming even larger, the McMahon Government ran into it without recognising what was happening. Labor was confronted with the same problem, at least until that 1975 budget. Cairns as Treasurer, probably more than anyone, sought to manage the economy according to compassionate responses influenced by the experiences of the Great Depression. I too had come out of the Depression, but was able to realise that kindly sentiments only made the problems worse. The 1975 budget was the signpost which brought to economic management a new and rigorous approach; we now know that as much as some may not care for it, there is nonetheless no substitute for those economic disciplines, unless of course one is content to watch economic disaster compounded by more economic disaster.

The flak I received for my trouble mostly came from articulate sources in Labor branches in higher-income suburbs and from their middle-class hangers on. The presumption of these people seemed to be that the role of government was to provide an ever overflowing cornucopia of 'goodies' through the public sector. These were the sorts of people who had an uncanny ability to be in the right place at the right time, with a sufficiently large pail to generously fill from the overflow. They were great believers in policies of low taxation and increased government spending. Some of them still hanker after the good old days of big spending, of generous government handouts, and regard the sort of disciplined fiscal policies I initiated then as an act of high apostasy against Labor principles. Fortunately, I was able to further develop these fiscal disciplines as Opposition Leader, and to see them eventually adopted by the Hawke Government.

Alas, we were our own worst enemies. Through egregious foolishness on the part of some of our colleagues we gave Fraser the alibi he needed to turn the government out of office, and unceremoniously so. This came in the form of the bizarre Khemlani loans affair mentioned earlier. What followed was blazing history— at least for some years after—and to which I will turn in the immediately succeeding sections.

The late Australian historian, Professor Manning Clark, once commented that Whitlam would be treated more kindly by history than by many of his contemporaries. When I now reflect more rigorously on our record, I am less sure that will be so of his government. Yet, having said that, I have to confess, contradictorily, that the most fulfilling, exciting days in my life were with Whitlam. I would not exchange them for a crock full of gold. It is rather presumptuous of me to say this, but I wish we had teamed up earlier in economic management. The way would have been rocky at times, for great men like Whitlam are not always comfortable travelling companions. But let there be no doubt about it, Whitlam was a great man. Together, we would have made the score card on our government's performance a considerably better one than what we in fact ended up with. More than that, the pair of us might have durably set in place more elements of his inspirational vision, for the long-term benefit of Australia.

PART IV

1975:
A HERETIC'S
VIEW

Prelude to the Dismissal

Remembrance Day, 11 November 1975, was a day to remember in more ways than one. It marked the spectacular end to an extended, increasingly bitter parliamentary confrontation, an end brought about by the swift, decisive intervention of the Governor-General, Sir John Kerr. Around Parliament things were quiet enough, but beyond that building the nation's political processes had became an inferno of bitterness and hatred. By the time the fury had subsided, the reputations of all the key participants had been severely scorched. In these relatively more detached times it is difficult to believe that this normally calm country had been so badly fissured and riven by mistrust and tensions as it was then. It was a condition in which it remained for quite a time thereafter.

Tuesday, 11 November 1975, was the day on which the fate of the Whitlam Government was ultimately determined, with tragic consequences for Labor. In the lead-up, the coalition parties had increased their numbers in the Senate, establishing control of that chamber, through a number of discreditable political ruses. These numbers were used to obstruct the passage of the 1975 budget through the Senate, a tactic which seized up the processes of government. The Governor-General invoked his extraordinary reserve powers under the constitution and dismissed the Whitlam Government. He then appointed the minority Fraser Government, and granted it an election in which it convincingly trounced the

Labor Party. While the end result of the political drama was the humiliating loss of government by Labor Prime Minister Whitlam, insult was added to injury when incoming coalition Prime Minister Fraser seized that office with the finesse of a nineteenth-century Yankee freebooter. Fraser succeeded by stubbornly persevering with the most extraordinary, brutal, political opportunism. In doing so he lost much moral authority, an essential ingredient for a prime minister whose duty it is to govern for all the nation. Elections may proceed according to a degree of contrived division; government, however, can only be sustained by general consent. Sir Robert Menzies was able to confidently administer the affairs of this country for many years because he indisputably had consensual support and with it the moral authority of national leadership— which is not to say Menzies was beyond criticism. By comparison, Fraser's lack of moral authority diminished his opportunities for wide-ranging, decisive administrative initiatives, of the sort that naturally produce controversy, because he feared that they would open up the old wounds. Instead of becoming more imposing and expansive in wielding the authority of his office, he became more timid and ineffectual as time passed. It was almost as though the ruthlessness of his conquistadorial tactics of storming and taking the office of government had left him unnerved. This weakness was to be noticed even by his own people, including some of his successors, such as John Hewson.[1]

Fraser was not the only one to suffer as a consequence of the events of November 1975. Governor-General Sir John Kerr was jeered to his grave and beyond. And the institutions which had previously been held high in public esteem as the pillars of our democratic system—the Parliament, the High Court, the vice-regency—having been stained by those events, also came into disrepute. Paradoxically, the man who was stalked as the quarry in this affair, Whitlam, so savagely excoriated and abused by his foes in 1975 and after, seems now to have been rehabilitated as a sort of icon in Australian society. At least this is how he appears to innumerable Australians. Perhaps popular sentiment has cast him into the role of a noble martyr destroyed by a conspiracy of dark and malign political forces. The Australian public love what they see as an honourable victim of ill-fortune, deceitfully destroyed by a ruthless and malevolent force. Popular folklore has probably already placed him beside Ned Kelly, Les Darcy and Phar Lap, in the national iconography. That is no small achievement for one Australian in his own lifetime. Fraser, cold, aloof, humourless, continues to be denied that public esteem and the affection which he craves.[2]

Kerr, lauded as a decisive man of history by so many in 1975 is now more recalled for his unfortunate appearance at a Melbourne Cup Day than for a remarkable life of achievement as a scholar, advocate, jurist and head of State of this nation. Poor Kerr: so quickly discarded by so many who earlier had incited and lauded him, once they had concluded his presence had become a liability. For anyone closely involved in the unfolding of events in 1975, in particular for someone active politically, it would have been an understandable conclusion that our system had been permanently disabled. Such were the divisions and bitternesses then. Yet since the departure from politics of the main actors in those extraordinary events, the sky has not fallen in. Parliament appears to have shrugged off completely what hitherto had been an unfortunate and socially unhealthy overload of contumely and vindictiveness.

For a rising generation of young Australian voters the constitutional crisis of 1975 belongs to history, if in fact they are aware of it at all. Even the key antagonists, Whitlam and Fraser, have left behind the strained frosty civilities they reserved for one another in public, to be seen as recently as November 1991, campaigning with a common viewpoint and from the same platform on the issue of the uncertain future of the Fairfax media empire.

This leaves only Kerr on whom to comment or rather because of his demise, on history's assessment of him. I hope that what I have to say will help restore some of his reputation. But as much as I am concerned with Kerr's reputation, as a recent incumbent of the same office and having learnt much about the nature and potentials of that office, I consider it important to offer some observations on the man's actions in 1975. In a number of important respects Kerr was harshly dealt with for trying to resolve an awful conundrum. Mine is not an uncritical viewpoint for there were some things which Kerr did which he did not do at all well; I of course also accept that this begs the question of whether in similar circumstances I would have done any better.

My proposition is a simple one: Kerr sought to do what he believed was right and proper. If his judgment was flawed, I believe it was not as gravely so as many claimed. It could be that his logical analysis of the situation broke down at critical links; additionally, he was perhaps handicapped in handling the unfolding crisis by a faulty political 'feel' for the situation. These, however, cannot be categorical judgments. What can be said categorically is that Kerr had few options and had to function in stifled, difficult conditions. Even a saint, operating under divine inspiration, would have despaired at trying to successfully handle this vexatious situation. It should be added that, even after twenty years, absolutely no concrete evidence has been adduced with which to impugn his motives. The gravamen of my criticism of Kerr is that he should have allowed the political process to have worked itself through to a greater extent. Had I been in Kerr's place, at that misbegotten time, doubtless I would have done a number of things differently. I can state, however, that if those two powerful, stubborn, conflicting personalities who led the Government and the Opposition, respectively, should have persevered with their dogged confrontation, then—at some point later than that at which Kerr acted—I would, as Governor-General, have been forced to have intervened much as he did. A governor-general could not sit idly by as the country plunged deeper and deeper down a sinkhole of economic chaos, while two titans slugged it out in a personal battle over who was to control government. Nor could a governor-general remain detached from a situation where countless ordinary Australians were also sent reeling with every blow those giants threw at one another. Kerr allowed Australia to decide the issue of its government—that much was his right and duty and that, as much as anything else, was endorsed by the people on 13 December 1975. Too many of his detractors forget that.

If a similar situation arose in the foreseeable future the options for a governor-general would be even more restricted. The objective conditions under which he would have to act have altered dramatically. A clash between the Houses of Parliament deadlocking authority to finance the daily functioning of government would have immediate, chaotic effect on our exchange rate and our foreign currency reserves. Our floating exchange rate and open money markets now mean what we do domestically, in our economic management and political processes, can feed almost instantly into the international money markets. A replay of the sort of confrontation we witnessed in 1975 would almost certainly lead to a huge, immediate run on the Australian dollar. Short-term, footloose, foreign capital in this country would flee. Foreign holders of the Australian dollar would attempt to dump them. The consequences would be chaotic. A governor-general, confronted with conditions such as these, would be handling a major national crisis. He would have to act early and decisively, invoking his reserve powers to do so.

In the case of Kerr it should have been his judgment not his motives which was challenged in the end. He was not an arch villain but rather, at its worst, perhaps someone miscast by history. Though who is to say who would have better played the role at that time. The larger question is, how did the political process decline to such an extent as to have created conditions in which the brute force of an Opposition-controlled Senate could be mobilised safely to force the dismissal of the Whitlam Labor Government? No British monarch has dismissed a government of that country since 1783. Kerr's action was by any measure a sensational event. The experience was and remains unparalleled in our national history since Federation. The dismissal of Premier Lang of New South Wales, by Governor Game in 1932, is distinguished as a State event and because, as some suggest, it probably involved an illegal intervention by the State Governor.[3] There can be no serious quibble about the legality of Kerr's intervention.

One thing that is a given about politics is that a crisis or a scandal cannot be created and sustained when there is nothing at issue. It is, furthermore, quite rare for a government to be brought undone by one issue alone. For that to happen there must be the most egregious evidence of incompetence or dishonesty, or both, and its substance must be such as to sustain the case against the government over time. The final act of 1975 was not confected from nothing. There was certainly the bad music of the Khemlani affair discordantly twanging away through most of 1975 but this was merely by-play to a more general theme. The real question was the adequacy of the government's management of the affairs of the nation and the way in which some ministers conducted themselves in office. We should have been more alert to the fact that our opponents would not allow slip-ups to go unchallenged and that major blunders would be used by them to fashion the instrument with which to crucify Labor.

The Opposition had set about a strategy aimed at destroying the Whitlam Labor Government from soon after the initial election of that government at the end of 1972. For instance, Reg Withers, then a Liberal Party senator, divulged in early 1974 that twelve months earlier his party had embarked on a course designed to force an election. His press secretary of that period, Russell Schneider, disclosed that Withers outlined this strategy to his leader, Billy Snedden, in October 1973. The plan reputedly proposed deferring Supply rather than rejecting it. In this way the Opposition would keep control of the Appropriation Bills and meanwhile the process of delay would maintain pressure for intervention by the Governor-General to resolve the deadlock. This was precisely what was threatened in early 1974 by Snedden, almost a test run for the big event of late 1975. By the latter part of 1975 this cloacal plan was being relentlessly bedded down.

Labor certainly called foul in February 1975 and with good reason when, on the retirement of Senator Murphy to join the High Court the coalition government of New South Wales ignored long-standing precedent and replaced him with a non-Labor nominee, the independent Cleaver Bunton.[4] An even louder protest was raised nearly seven months later, when a largely unknown Labor Party branch member, Patrick Field, was nominated by the Queensland State Government to replace the deceased Labor senator, Bert Milliner. Field importuned the position by making it clear to the State Premier, Bjelke-Petersen, that he would be a willing tool in the hands of that government. It will be recalled that Premier Bjelke-Petersen was a man of notable spiritual devotion who never allowed religious scruple to stand in the way of his extracting advantages from blatant political chicanery. These mean-spirited acts were designed to tilt the balance of power in the Senate. Before Milliner's death the Labor Party could marshal thirty votes. This included that of Bunton, who, by the pattern of his voting with the Government in the Senate, disabused any hopes the coalition parties might have harboured about capturing his support. It also included the vote of Independent Liberal senator Steele Hall. A tied vote in the Senate according to the standing orders of that chamber would not have allowed the Appropriation Bills to be passed but neither would it have permitted the coalition tactic of deferring Supply. This would have drastically altered the game plan available to the coalition.

On the other hand, in righteously protesting about the questionable conduct of the coalition parties, Labor did not do so innocently. The 'Gair affair' of 1974 was carefully engineered by Labor. Gair had been roughly ejected from the leadership of the Democratic Labor Party in a manner which left him smarting with resentment. By a dubious arrangement with Labor, he was to resign from the Senate before the then imminent Senate election, his vacant seat to be then contested at a forthcoming half-Senate election. This would have meant six Senate positions were to be contested rather than five in the State of Queensland. Labor believed this would have increased its prospects of winning three Senate seats, rather than the maximum of two it otherwise could have expected. It was part of a strategy by Labor designed to gain control of the Senate. Gair's DLP Senate compatriots objected, provoking a typical comment from him: 'I've carried you bastards for years, now you can go to buggery'. If Gair had resigned after the election, a replacement would have been chosen by the Queensland State Government to complete the unexpired three years of his elected term. Unfortunately for the government, its foray into political skulduggery fell apart even before it started. The Queensland Government issued writs for the Senate election before Gair resigned, meaning there were only five instead of six Senate vacancies to be filled at that election. The State Government action meant a higher proportion of valid votes would have been required to elect a senator than if there had been six vacancies. Thus, this political 'counterinsurgency' tactic demolished Labor's ingenious but certainly not innocent tactic to gain extra representation in the Senate. Labor was understandably outraged by this brazen manipulation of the political process. Bjelke-Petersen was not playing the game according to the rules. Labor simply forgot that, in these sorts of cases, in Australian politics, each side tends to write the rules as opportunity suggests.

Snedden, equally, became infuriated by what he felt was undisguised political knavery involving the government and Gair— as if such tactics were somehow new or forbidden. He threatened to block Supply. Whitlam responded by calling a double dissolution. The 'curse' of Gair soon claimed its victims: all the DLP 'roosters', who had been in the Senate, were converted, unceremoniously, into Freddy Daly's celebrated political 'feather dusters'. Every one of them was defeated. In any event Labor won the election with a reduced majority in the House of Representatives and at the cost of its credibility. The Government gained no advantage from the Senate election outcome in Queensland, while Ireland received a fascinating new Australian Ambassador in Vince Gair. The personal tragedy of Snedden's fate as leader of his party was sealed. And while the DLP abjured Gair for his apostasy, the Labor Government condemned him privately for his double-cross; in the meantime Gair contentedly made his way to his small pot of gold in Dublin. Although there was no hard proof, there was a general suspicion within Labor that Gair had double-dealt, communicating with the coalition parties as a matter of prudent insurance in case there was a change of government in the near future. He was not keen to have to make the return journey to Australia at any early date.

There were several other unfortunate misadventures for Labor, the raid on ASIO headquarters in 1973 not least among them. Whitlam described it as the single most damaging incident to the public reputation of the Labor Government in its first term of office. It was also beyond any responsible justification. Then Ms Junie Morosi arrived in the office of the Treasurer, Dr Jim Cairns. She was a sensation, regrettably, and Dr Cairns was never to be the same after her arrival. Together their impact on the Labor Government was unfortunately dramatic. A story about her, popular at the time but perhaps apocryphal, began with Cairns having a hard time in the House in an economic debate and gathering a great deal of criticism. In the course of the parliamentary exchanges his opponents frequently referred to 'Keynes', the celebrated late English economist, John Maynard Keynes. Morosi was then reputed to have returned to the Treasurer's office where she was in charge.

The reason she was in charge of the office of the minister responsible for managing the economy of the nation, no doubt, was because her mind was uncluttered by even the simplest principle of economics, such absence giving her a greater confidence in choosing economic management policies than otherwise would have been the case. In any event, on her return to the office she supposedly demanded angrily of the staff, 'Quick, go through our files and see if we've got anything on this guy Keynes who's causing so much trouble for Jim!'.

Before the presentation of the 1974 mini-budget there was much public dismay at feuding in Cabinet and the lame document it spawned. There were constant leaks about conflict in Cabinet between the Treasurer and most of the rest of the Cabinet. The government appeared to be a shambles. By this stage, as detailed previously, inflation had well and truly taken off, unemployment had climbed and the world trade boom collapsed. The general public was, not to put too fine a point on it, startled out of their collective wits by the trend of events. All these experiences were deeply shocking to an Australian electorate hitherto used mostly to steady economic growth, low unemployment, nominal inflation, and the uneventful government of their public affairs. The contrast with the steady, predictable days dominated by that patrician figure, Menzies, was startling. Suddenly it seemed as if the roughriders were in town, whooping it up.

Enter Mr Khemlani

Then came the Khemlani loans affair, which was how that unconventional loan-raising sortie came to be known. I am quoted approvingly elsewhere, by Whitlam, in a way which some may mistake as an endorsement by me, implied at least, of this unconventional loan-raising activity: '. . . France, England, Japan and Denmark have already trodden that so-called unorthodox, unconventional path'.[5] The quote is accurate as far as it goes, but it does not go far. Certainly not so far as to claim that the Khemlani exercise was on a par with what had been done in the countries referred to. My statement was made in defence of the team, the Labor Government, of which I was a member. It was made at a time when the team was under *damaging* attack for *insupportable* loan-raising efforts. A re-reading confirms that it was a defensive statement, one honestly expressed as to content and avoiding extravagances of rhetoric in what was a fairly torrid session. It did not claim to exculpate and it certainly did not endorse the extraordinary Khemlani loans affair. Nothing could do either credibly. As I re-read it, it struck me again just how carefully I had phrased my comments.

The Khemlani loans affair became central to the downfall of the Whitlam Labor Government later in 1975—certainly the Australian public was staggered beyond belief when it learnt of our seemingly bizarre behaviour in the matter. This uniquely ambitious undertaking was not something I would have embarked upon, and had I been consulted I would have firmly warned against becoming involved. On the first occasion I was Acting Treasurer, during the absence of the Treasurer overseas sometime in 1973, I received importuning cables from people with unusual names and usually despatched from exotic places. They offered me on behalf of the Commonwealth of Australia dazzlingly large amounts of money, remarkably low rates of interest and incredibly easy repayment arrangements. A zoot-suited spiv selling the Sydney Opera House on a quiet Sunday afternoon for a month's salary would have been capable of making a more convincing offer. My instincts told me that these communications were some sort of con job, the suspicions soon confirmed by Treasury officials who assured me that such cables were commonly received from people they referred to as the 'men in green glasses'. There were successive experiences of these kinds of communications whenever I was briefly Acting Treasurer and all were rejected; all ended their short days of review going into Treasury's so called 'rogues' gallery' or 'carpet baggers' file.

The first attempt at one of these unconventional loan-raising forays, involving Khemlani, by the government was authorised by an Executive Council decision and was for an amount of $US4000 million. The enterprise was put into the hands of the late Rex Connor MP, a man whose fiscal instincts were reflexively guided by the principles of Social Credit theory and whose political beliefs proceeded according to an unshakeable faith in international conspiracies perpetrated by the capitalist system. Through the influential offices of Clyde Cameron MP, Connor and one Tirath Khemlani were eventually brought into contact with one another. Cameron was a man whose economic theory was derived exclusively from the simplistic philosophies of the Henry George Single Land Tax League and whose life-long political creed was to never forget a slight no matter how small and, further, to never miss a chance to get even.

There was a degree of argy-bargy as the small cabal of ministers secretly engaged on the 'Khemlani exercise' shuffled Executive Council minutes back and forth, extending and withdrawing approval for various levels of borrowings. All the borrowings were to be exclusively managed by Connor. All were authorised for 'temporary purposes'. There was an eerie, prophetic quality to the commencement of this process, almost as though disaster had been written all over it from the start. Connor was introduced to Khemlani, according to Whitlam, on 11 November 1974, a year to the very day before the tragedy of the Whitlam Government struck its desperate climax. Recalling some of the high-water marks of this grand venture into unconventional loan raisings will give some understanding, to those for whom these matters are buried in dusty historical archives, of why the political atmosphere ignited the way it did once the public disclosures commenced.

Connor, who was Minister for Minerals and Energy, was given Executive Council (Exco) authority to hunt for a $US4000 million loan to, according to the explanatory memorandum, (a) deal with exigencies arising out of the current world situation, (b) deal with the international energy crisis, (c) strengthen Australia's external financial position, (d) provide immediate protection for Australia's supplies of minerals and energy, (e) deal with currently and immediately foreseeable unemployment in Australia. The authority which Connor obtained was something of a first—Exco authority to pursue loan funds is the prerogative of the Treasurer and for very good reason. The established practice was that once the Loan Council had set the borrowing programmes for the Commonwealth and the States each year, 'these programs constituted the final borrowing programs for each authority for the year . . . '[6] I might add, Loan Council borrowings were always through conventional funding sources. Officers of the Treasury Department, who were strongly opposed to what was proposed, were excluded from the team which drafted the Exco document. It was most unusual for overseas loan negotiations to proceed without there first being consultation with the Loan Council.[7] There was no such consultation in this case. The second point to note is that of the five heads justifying this loans hunt, only two, (b) and (d), fell within Connor's ministerial authority.

There were clear economic consequences to Connor's loan offensive, should it have succeeded. It was to be an addition to the Loan Council approved overseas borrowing programme which had been set at $A2000 million for 1974–75. Interest was to have been accumulated on a compound basis, and capitalised into a lump sum payment at the end of twenty years. At the prevailing exchange rate at the end of 1994 the proposed borrowing would have increased the total borrowing programme in Australian dollars from $A1507 million at the end of 1974 to nearly $A12 000 million at the end of 1994. A $US4000 million borrowing at the end of 1974, when Connor obtained Exco authority for this escapade, represented 8 per cent of then GDP according to calculations by the Treasury Department; it would have more than trebled our existing external debt and would have nearly doubled our level of external reserves. All at the stroke of a pen! For Fiscal Year (FY) 1994–95, 8 per cent of GDP exceeded $A36 000 million, which gives some comparative measure of what was being undertaken. That is one reason why, possibly, the Treasury noted on one occasion with ironic understatement that the exercise was 'not to be compared with any previous borrowing or loan programme in Australia's history'.

If it had been obtained, the borrowing would have put upward pressure on the Australian dollar to the disadvantage of our export industries with inflationary consequences; it would have greatly expanded money supply forcing monetary policy adjustments such as interest rate hikes; the lump sum settlement would have represented a large withdrawal of this nation's international liquidity (unless, of course, the debt was rolled over, adding to the woes of our chronic current account deficit) and the lengthy time before settlement would have exposed the undertaking to massive exchange rate risks. Let me further illustrate one point in relation to exchange rate risk. The devaluation in the Australian dollar against the US dollar from the end of 1974 to the end of FY 1994–95 was 41 per cent! The borrowings were to be at an effective cost of 7.92 per cent when the market rate in New York for loans over seven to ten years then was between 8.75 per cent and 9 per cent; that is, it was expected that lenders in a capital hungry world would penalise themselves to provide the loan. Then there was the small matter of the commission. Between 0.5 per cent and 1 per cent was the rate in dealings with conventional sources; the Connor project involved a rate of 2.5 per cent. In other words, there was an extra cost of between $US60 million and $US80 million as a premium for the 'quality service' offered by Khemlani on the $US4000 million borrowing.

The loan was for twenty years and was for 'temporary purposes'! In 1958 the Attorney-General gave an opinion that 'a borrowing for temporary purposes is a borrowing the proceeds of which are to be repaid during the financial year during which it is effected'.

Thenceforth, that advice was the guideline adhered to for temporary loan borrowings. That was about to be swept aside though. In December 1974, Attorney-General Murphy impatiently asserted that it was 'intolerable' that the Australian Government should experience delays, necessitated by the requirement to consult the States through the Loan Council, when borrowing opportunities arose. The Australian Government should be able to borrow 'at the stroke of a pen', he declared with his usual impulsiveness.[8]

Connor was just as robust and no less impatient with the cautious verification and procedural systems adopted by the bureaucrats. On 9 July 1975, Connor, in the course of the special one-day sitting of the House of Representatives convened to address this loans fiasco, gave great insight into his character as he quoted expansively:

Give me men to match my mountains,
Give me men to match my plains,
Men with freedom in their vision,
And creation in their brains.

He accordingly made no bones about his views. If lenders did not need legal opinions he could not see why as borrower he had to be delayed by legalistic quibbles. He should be able to proceed to sign the relevant documents and have the proceeds of the loan paid into the public account, thereby avoiding any constitutional problems. Connor was a man for crashing through barriers; even ones erected for safety purposes. The reaction of the public service advisers was not recorded but, can probably be faithfully summed up in a word—stricken! Connor imagined he was cursed to travel like Gulliver in a land of Lilliputians, little men who struck and tugged at him, trying to hold him down.

The Attorney-General expressed the opinion—orally, as seemed to be the prevailing practice—that the funds were to be used to assist in reducing unemployment, which was described as a temporary phenomenon. The fact that the unemployment problem of that period was recognised within the ranks of government as being one which would last for an extended period appeared to have been immaterial. Murphy's opinion was that the borrowing 'could probably be regarded as a borrowing for temporary purposes within the meaning of the Financial Agreement'. The Solicitor-General, Maurice Byers, confirmed to Kerr in mid-December 1974 that the Attorney-General felt 'the loan contemplated could be regarded as for temporary purposes . . . and that he [Byers] thought the Attorney-General's view was an arguable view but it was a long bow'.[9] A notable QC of the time, a Falfstaffian figure who had some interest in these matters, is reputed to have chortled to colleagues that the proposition was certainly arguable before the High Court; that is for about two minutes before the presentation was stopped dead. Despite the serpentine twists and turns in the cobbling together of the Exco and the subsequent justifications of those actions, 'temporary purposes' loans arose for one reason alone: to avoid the scrutiny of the Loan Council, of the States and of Parliament. Eventually, those bodies would have to consider the undertaking. It was all a great deal of self-defeating trouble. If obtained, it was considered that the funds could be channelled through the Pipelines Authority, the Petroleum and Minerals Authority, the Atomic Energy Commission, the Commonwealth Trading Bank, among others, to avoid the scrutiny mentioned. This was indefensible deception. Jim Cairns to his credit, at an early stage, warned that it was 'foolish to try to hide this proposal from the States'.

There was certainly freedom in Connor's vision and creativity in his brain when it came to the matter of identifying where the borrowed money would be spent: projects included 'Palm Valley ($100 million), Dampier ($350 million), offshore oil ($210 million), a national pipeline grid, a coal liquefaction plant ($450 million), doubling the size of the Ranger proposal ($150 million), the Redcliff project ($170 million), and the Cooper Basin project (unstated amount)'.[10] Connor was satisfied that 'the loan could be fully utilised within a period of three years'. I recall writing much later in the margin of the submission in which I read this, 'Crikey . . . !!!', but, then, I lacked imagination and daring. Perhaps it was more than daring for it was noted that Connor expressed the opinion that all the proceeds of the borrowings would be spent on imports within the three year timetable.

The case had even more bizarre aspects. In early December 1974 when initial discussions got under way about the $US4000 million borrowing, certain 'agents', presumably Khemlani or his associates, urgently whispered into the receptive ears of the ministers involved that absolute secrecy had to be maintained. Otherwise, they were cautioned, loose talk might imperil a further $US5000 million which 'would be available in a month's time'. Later, in 1975 after the Exco for the $US4000 million borrowing had been withdrawn, and a little later again, on 27 January 1975, another Exco authority was issued for borrowings of $US2000 million. Notwithstanding this Connor made an abortive attempt in April to obtain yet another Exco for another $US8000 million borrowing. It appears Khemlani received a letter from Connor in March authorising him to seek this sum also.

Connor was obviously untrammelled by the guidelines set for ordinary mortals whenever they were to search for borrowed funds. He would pursue the faintest whiff of borrowable funds uncorked by the least credible financial carpetbagger who happened across his path, even when he did not have authority to do so. Such occurred at one point in January 1975 when his Exco authority had been revoked and with no new one, at that point, to replace it. The same thing happened again in May when he said there would be no more waywardness on his part, only to proceed to tic-tac with Khemlani on the prospects of further borrowings. This last binge proved to be the fateful one which brought him down. Nor was he ever discouraged by Khemlani's obvious dissembling. Khemlani was always, at critical points, on the verge of stitching up the deal and then unaccountably he would miss an aircraft, it would be delayed, or it would be out of action. He would sleep in; or arrive at a Swiss bank with which he was to seal the arrangement, after it closed; or turn up at its office on Saturday perplexed that the principal, with whom he was to do business and whom he always claimed to know well, was, like the bank staff, not at work.

If we needed to hear any more alarm bells, the Government should have been listening when the Union Bank of Switzerland advised the Government, in late 1974, that it had never heard of Khemlani, that it would not handle the kind of business he was seeking to hustle along, did not believe the proposition was genuine, would not proceed with it and advised the Government not to dally with it. The Swiss National Bank, with an impressive capacity for understatement, suggested that the proposed enterprise might have an adverse effect on Australia's credibility in banking quarters, and the Federal Reserve Bank of New York, which was to be the repository of any funds obtained, was concerned and sceptical about the size of the proposed loan. More than a fortnight after that the Exco authority to borrow was rescinded. Three weeks later Connor had a new Exco licensing him to loan hunt again. The men in those conservative banking institutions were no match for the magnificent vision that flourished in Connor's fertile mind.

Connor might have been a bluff, impatient and suspicious man by nature, but not in his dealings with Khemlani. He hung on and on, in spite of a total lack of performance by Khemlani. Khemlani's was a masterful *tour de force;* he played the ministers with all the skill of a king angler who has hooked a marlin on light fly tackle. As a Labor senator excitedly claimed on one occasion, 'We got nothing but good reports' on Khemlani. The truth was that, at best, the reports were equivocal and for the prudently wary they were a warning to be extremely careful. Scotland Yard knew of nothing detrimental about Khemlani but said of his company that it 'has no known capability or experience in overseas loan transactions and therefore caution should be exercised in "loan" transactions with the company Dalamal'. The Bank of England considered the proposal a funny money one. Dalamal & Sons, of which Khemlani was manager, was 'a relatively new company' with a capital of £100 sterling. Morgan Guaranty came up 'with nothing negative' but reported Khemlani's company had no real 'track record' in the field of international finance. In spite of these massive reservations Connor stuck to Khemlani, like a crab clinging to spinning seaweed in a desperate bid for survival in a treacherous sea.

On about 21 December 1974, only a week after the authorisation of the Exco authority for Connor to go out hunting for loan funds, Cairns unmasked Khemlani's duplicitous behaviour. Cairns pointed out that key statements by Khemlani had been checked and found to be false. He had not been delayed at London Airport en route to Switzerland, he did not know the Chairman of the Union Bank of Switzerland, the Chairman never had any intention of working on a particular Saturday nominated by Khemlani, and so on. Connor was forced to concede that he would cease contact with Khemlani. One can only guess at his mood at this sudden collapse of his grand plan but 'sullen' would probably be an understatement. Never mind, for Connor even the darkest cloud had its silver lining and within a few weeks he was happily off on the chase again with Khemlani. Fresh spoor of the elusive quarry had this time been picked up on the path to the Moscow Norodny Bank.

There was something of *la grande geste* about the noble proportions of this borrowing, reported at the time as being the largest funny money proposal thus far recorded in Zurich. Here was another first for Australia under Labor! Scotland Yard reported that up to that time the largest loan raised in the Middle East was a

$1200 million loan to the United Kingdom and the next largest a $1000 million loan from Saudi Arabia to Japan. This elusive $US4000 million petro-dollar loan being stalked by Connor was an ambitious undertaking to match the vastness of his vision. With the loan moneys he could level mountains and build on plains, creating prosperity and a patrimony for the future, using the resources God had given us.

Connor's understanding of economics was always in inverse proportions to the size of his dreams. In a Cabinet discussion one time about the size of the deficit and measures to bring it down, Connor intervened, displaying once again not so much his lateral thinking but his limitations. He advised that the Government should include in its budget the value of assets as a credit item. Any business is run that way, he advised. He had been a small businessman and brought the same breadth of outlook that he used there to management of the national economy, as he was about to illustrate. There was a stockpile of wool held in store as part of the Market Support Fund then in operation. This was worth in excess of $300 million. By a stroke of the pen the deficit is reduced by this amount, he then announced magisterially. I was a little surprised. I had always imagined the national budget as an economic regulator of some greater significance than a small shopkeeper's book-keeping record. I recall muttering to someone nearby, *sotto voce,* 'My God! Milo Minderbinder personified!'[11]

It was not until late April that the Opposition finally bestirred itself on this loans fiasco. Curiously, the late Phillip Lynch had first raised a query about the $US4000 million loan on 21 December 1974. Then the matter had gone into limbo for four months. Perhaps the dimensions of the borrowings and the roguish characters commissioned to pursue them staggered the Opposition's credulity. But now, in late April, the questions finally came thick and fast. The non-Labor States began querying the details of the loans efforts and by late May were requesting that the matter be listed for the forthcoming Loans Council. The game was up by then. A grim destiny was closing in rapidly on the Labor Government. Then came the confessions, promises of never again, sackings, new ministerial appointments; but such desperate efforts merely served to emphasise the vulnerability of the Government and at best gave only a brief respite before the political Armageddon.

With events building to a crescendo, a curious thing happened one day as I prepared to enter the chamber of the House of Representatives for question time. I was Acting Treasurer at the time. The Secretary of the Treasury, Fred Wheeler, and a team of heavies from that Department suddenly emerged through the large swing doors at the King's Hall end of the lobby. Their arrival had been unheralded. There were two signs that something big was up, to cling to the vernacular: first, Wheeler was smoking, which by itself was not worthy of notice for I suspected that he had been born with a cigarette in his mouth, even if this time the smoke issued from his nostrils with the force of a volcanic cloud; the second sign was the number and seniority of his team. I have noted over many years that public servants only gather a large team of top people around them to call on their Minister when something quite serious has gone wrong, or because they are aiming for the psychological advantage of numbers and gravity.

Wheeler's demeanour made it clear the former was his concern. He explained briefly that the international credit rating agency, Standard & Poor, had completed a review of the credit worthiness of Australia and had downgraded it from the top rating of triple-A to double-A. Question time was under way when I got into the House and so it was too late to speak with the Prime Minister. I sent a note suggesting he and I have a talk behind the Speaker's chair at the conclusion of question time. 'Gough,' I said as we stood behind that magnificent old piece of towering, hand-carved furniture, a gift from the House of Commons, 'we've got problems'. I explained our predicament. Whitlam stood silently, reflecting on our dilemma for

a matter of seconds and then said soberly. 'Comrade, this is terrible
. . . absolutely terrible . . . But tell me, what the f . . . ing hell does it
mean?' Whitlam always had a marvellous sense of humour; or was
he dead serious? In the event, Treasury adroitly headed off the
downgrading.

Ignoring such efforts, some of my colleagues publicly aimed a
fair amount of criticism at Treasury, in the belief that that department
had conspired against the Labor Government. However, most of the
documents which materialised in the media and Parliament had *not*
previously been seen by Treasury, such was the hermetic
effectiveness of Connor's secrecy, and it therefore seemed unlikely
that Treasury was responsible for anything in the way of leaks.
Goodness knows, there was enough incriminating paper plastered
about Europe and New York to sustain the media and the
Opposition attack on the Government for an extended period.

Why did others in the Cabinet fail to challenge Connor and his
fellow loan planners? First, bearding Connor unscathed was like
trying to pass safely through a crocodile pen at feeding time. In any
case few among us knew what was happening until it suddenly
exploded in the Parliament. At first there was mystification as to
what it was all about. Later, in late May 1975, I stumbled across a
new set of developments as Acting Treasurer after a damaging
allegation of further unorthodox loan-raising efforts were aired on
the television current affairs programme, 'This Day Tonight'. A
senior staffer from the prime minister's office, David Solomon,
contacted my office at Parliament House and advised that the Prime
Minister wanted me to issue an immediate and categorical denial of
the damaging contents of that report. I declined unless I was first
fully briefed on the matter. The discovery I made was that there was
a mini-remake of the loan fiasco in existence—the shadow of
Connor, as played by Jim Cairns. It required some fairly blunt
talking to Treasury officials before I extracted what had been
occurring. Their attitude, perhaps defensible in itself, was that as

Acting Treasurer it was not appropriate for me to become involved in a major, ongoing matter being personally handled by the Treasurer. It would not be fair to the Treasurer and it would not be in my interests. It was a point put with consideration and helpfulness and that I appreciated. On the other hand I was under orders to act and the television programme seemed to require some response. Treasury would have preferred to await the return of the Treasurer from overseas. In the event, after a testy exchange with Wheeler over the telephone, in the presence of Moss Cass, officers of that Department arrived at my office. They were obviously disheartened. They briefly but unenthusiastically sketched the Cairns fiasco and suggested that, as I had forced the point, it would be best for a full briefing to be given to the Prime Minister and me simultaneously. This was the first time Whitlam had learnt of Cairns' initiatives in this field. The Australian Broadcasting Commission had taken aim at a decoy bobbing in the water, for their story was wrong in fact, and, in effect winged the Treasurer flailing about elsewhere. He threshed about for a short while trying to get airborne again, but he was done for.

Bit by painful bit the Opposition extracted from a grudging Government more and more detail of this fantastic undertaking. The hedging, the concealment, the evasiveness of the Government made it look nothing but untrustworthy. The whole process was a remarkable vindication of how the open parliamentary process can make government accountable for any serious offences of commission and omission. Pinioned by its own fatuous behaviour, the Government squirmed about looking for an escape. A royal commission of inquiry was proposed, something I opposed vigorously. The Government desperately needed to inter the remains of this disintegrating enterprise quickly and get on with the business of governing properly, while royal commissions can take on a life of their own, airing all sorts of sensational hearsay accusations but doing little to prove anything. But I should confess, with the safety of twenty years between the event and these writings, that I quietly harboured suspicions. I was not entirely convinced that all the sorcerer's apprentices who had been stewing up this rancorous brew had made a full disclosure of what they had been about. I felt that if there were any such matters they could be sorted out privately. I never thought for a moment there was any intentional illegality or personal cupidity involved in this enterprise and subsequent events have established that beyond any doubt. Their sin was far more serious than that: behaving like prize fools in high public office. After twenty-three years of Opposition, which had its own debilitating effect on the political psyche of Labor members, we had to make a fresh determined effort at disciplining ourselves and trying to make a respectable fist of government. The thought of another long spell in Opposition overwhelmed and depressed many of us. In the upshot we opted for a one-day sitting of Parliament.

In the meantime, the amateur loan-raising activities of Cairns' son in Fiji, involving the unauthorised use of official stationery from the office of the Treasurer, had been disclosed publicly and the Prime Minister acted decisively in an attempt to try to contain the damage. During the one-day sitting of Parliament the Opposition had its chance to lash the Government for its extraordinary behaviour, while the Government did its *mea culpa*. For my part I kept my fingers tightly crossed. Eventually Connor and Cairns were caught misleading Parliament, for their inexactitude in handling what was purported to be the truth, and were sacked. Well that was that, the worst was behind us. The passage would still be a bit rough but we were heading for calmer waters and better sailing. A few weeks later Fred Wheeler called on me. He was in a mild state of shock. He had learnt that the prime minister's office had had contact with a well-known Australian figure, Sir William Gunn, then in London and incidentally exploring an unorthodox $US4000 million loan raising for the Australian Government—without its authority—in the company of one Dorothy Denton, whose registered professional qualifications for major international financial forays, according to Treasury files, were that she specialised 'in charities concerning foundation grants'. Gunn at this time was a member of the Reserve Bank Board of Australia and his involvement would have given considerable respectability to any efforts by Denton to raise an unorthodox loan. Which goes to show how gullible some of our most experienced, leading citizens can be. Here it was, as soon as our back was turned, clambering out of its coffin to haunt us, as if we were living a remake of an old Dracula movie.

The prime minister's office assured me that the Gunn approach had been exclusively one-sided and had not been encouraged. This was too much for me; I now felt obliged to use the ultimate sanction that no minister should use unless he means it. The surreal paper-chasing of foreign loans around the globe, in the company of people who would make the picaresque characters of Agatha Christie's *Orient Express* look like staid gentlefolk, had to end immediately. If it did not, I would be compelled to resign from the Ministry. I would then advise Parliament that my position as a minister had become intolerable because solemn undertakings of the Government to that body had been violated and I could not be party to that. The point was put with moderation, but not so much as to blunt its thrust. This time we finally buried the monster; and if I'd had my way, it would have been with a stake made from cancelled loan authorities mercilessly driven through its heart.

Men to match whose mountains?

Let me start with the atmospherics of the downfall of Cairns and Connor. On 9 July 1975 the national Parliament assembled for one day to hear the confessions and assess the contrition of the Government. In the manner of our parliamentary processes, a style surprisingly widely accepted in the Australian community, admissions of error were modestly few and aggressive justifications for curious acts prevailed. In the course of events a lonely, deflated Jim Cairns rose to vindicate his actions. It was probably one of the sadder days in my life. What this forlorn and devastated man was really about to do was to confront the failure of his lifetime mission to become a great reformist Democratic Socialist minister. He stared into the ghastly face of his own failure. He stood before us all, a pitiful, shrunken figure. I recalled then, as I still do, the affection I had felt for him for so long and the inspiration he had given to much of a whole younger generation of Australians by the high principles, the ideals, the firmness of his resolve to fight for the marginalised and for justice and truth—that at least was the way so many of us had seen it. I remembered also my first encounter with him. With great courage he had addressed a meeting at the Teachers' Union Building in Elizabeth Street, Brisbane, in 1961. The subject? A severely critical analysis of the White Australia Policy. It was the stuff of an impressive humanist, the commitment of a civil libertarian, the principles of a courageous and thoughtful Democratic Socialist.

Cairns suffered quite adversely within the parliamentary party, and for some time after, because of that speech. He never complained and he was never deflected from the course he had charted then. For a long time afterwards I was greatly influenced by Cairns. In Parliament he was an outstanding debater. His was not a pyrotechnic style; his strength lay in a steady, convincing passion, a well-constructed and carefully researched point of view. He had compelling presence and an excellent speaking voice. Most of all he did not flinch from putting forth radical views on reform regardless of the scorn of others. His greatest triumph was the way in which he had inspired people, eventually mobilising huge congregations in opposition to Australia's involvement in the war in Vietnam. He was a folk hero. Few people managed to stand for so much that was good and to do so as decently as he did. These are some of the reasons why I said in the House of Representatives, on 9 July 1975:

*. . . I do not believe that this House can easily press on to other issues
without fairly acknowledging the valuable and honourable role of the
honourable member for Lalor Dr J. F. Cairns to this institution over
many years and his honourable and unyielding commitment to the issues
of personal rights, civil liberties and the freedoms of a democratic society.*

Then suddenly there was Morosi and his head was turned.
Moonlight walks holding hands in the rose gardens near Parliament
House. Morosi feeding him dessert from a spoon in a very public
restaurant. Inevitably the newspapers zoomed in to score direct hits
and do him great damage—'My Love for Junie' went the headline in
the now defunct *Sun*, over an article purporting to be an interview
with Cairns. The tragedy of this was, in my view, that Cairns'
relationship with Morosi was purely one of psychological
dependency on his part.

It was extraordinary that on reaching government, after such a
long and gut-breaking forced march over so many years in
Opposition, the moment for which Cairns had worked so long, the
moment when he should have sought to transcend an already well-
burnished reputation, to rise to even greater heights, he started to fall
apart. It was as though he had always stood on feet of clay and
suddenly the weight of public adulation proved too much. Those
brittle feet started to crack and splinter under the strain, while his
involvement with Morosi raised critical questions about his judgment.
It had already become apparent in Government, that his great strength
was in his rhetoric and the support he afforded worthy causes. He did
not take easily and certainly not naturally to the detailed but essential
humdrum of developing policy or, later, of the disciplined
administration over marathon hours expected of a minister.

So there stood Jim Cairns in the House of Representatives on
the night of 9 July 1975. His address should have been one of
contrition for his shortcomings but also one of defiance in
rededicating himself to important causes for humankind, and a

reassertion of the great humanist spirit for which he had been respected. In this way he could have rallied his own not inconsiderable number of personal admirers and gone out with his honour high. For the Morosi incident was a trivial human failing, of no consequence in the battle for human progress in which Cairns had been so long engaged. Such a peccadillo would have been quickly forgotten, as eventually would have been the loan matter also. Instead his speech was self-exculpatory, self-indulgent and capped by the tabling of a document that seemed to infer a young woman, a former personal staffer of his, was the cause of his downfall. For many of us that was just too much. The faults that bring us down must be found in the fragile material of our own character. No-one else should be blamed. Leaders in particular are in a special category of responsibility and accountability.

Rex Connor was of a different cast. Not for nothing was he known by the sobriquet of The Strangler. His practice was to enter the Cabinet room shortly before a submission from him was to be considered and to leave shortly after it had been dispatched. His presentation of the item was nearly always brief. His treatment of anyone who disagreed with his submission was sharp and brutal; somewhat reminiscent of a large professional wrestler landing a nasty forearm jolt on the mouth of a much smaller opponent. Having disagreed with him on several occasions, I know from personal experience what it was like to be on the receiving end. I resented the way he would bluff and bulldoze to get his own way and very much objected to his ill-tempered bullying of more gentle and thoughtful souls, such as the then Minister for Environment, Dr Moss Cass. For my pains he once described me as 'an interfering little bastard', before telling me 'You should mind your own business! . . . I don't interfere in other ministers' submissions! . . . I don't want anyone interfering in mine. Unerstan?'. He had a habit of punctuating his sentences with this 'unerstan?' as a threatening interrogative. If those well-known members of the Sydney demimonde, Lennie McPherson or Tim Bristow arrived at my doorstep to give me some summary advice and concluded their presentation with that same sharp interrogative, I am sure I would understand perfectly the full import of their message, in spite of its brevity. In such a way, Connor, too, was an effective communicator.

He would enter Cabinet with a heavy, measured footfall, his weathered head swivelling about the room as he took in the appearance of his Cabinet colleagues; he would sum up the mood around him as he went, and judge the tactics he might need to adopt for that day. His eyes, always half-hooded, unblinking in a saurian fashion, gave him a baleful appearance. He was a large man with a wide girth and he looked—as he indeed was—tough. He wore loose-waisted trousers held up by wide fireman's braces and usually left his suit coat in his office. My impression was of an ill-dispositioned Barney Bear entering the room. In moments of whimsy I sometimes wondered why he ever bothered to open the door. Why not just knock it in, walk over it, clean up any opposition and retire while the dust from the commotion was still settling? Eventually I saw another side of him when he was cornered for having misled Parliament on the loan-raising issue. Along with the Prime Minister's private secretary, John Menadue, I was deputed by the Prime Minister to go to Connor's Canberra residence and confront him on the matter. Connor had been ill and at that time was recovering. I accepted the task without demur but on reflection it scarcely seems the sort of duty a prime minister should delegate, especially with respect to such a senior minister. It was 8 October 1975. That day, more dreadful reports appeared in the *Melbourne Herald* claiming that Khemlani was still actively searching for loan funds with Connor's authorisation.

Connor denied the reports. His demeanour was milder than I had ever encountered; he was not his usual confident, combative self. Though evidently unwell, this too did not satisfactorily explain the change. Somehow, in some indefinable way, it seemed to me that he was physically smaller than he used to be. It is often noticeable with men of strong and dominant character in positions of authority that when they are at the peak of their influence, they actually do seem to be larger than life—the buoyancy which comes with the exercise of power, of decision-making, of ordering things and people about seems to enlarge them physically. When their authority is ebbing they seem to shrink to more normal human proportions, and something like this seemed to be happening to Connor as I watched him. I invited him to sue the newspaper for damaging his reputation with false allegations, as, after all, he had claimed that the articles were false and damaging. He declined, stating he did not believe in suing. A few hours later he released a public statement, proposing that he would sue. His responses were vague, even perhaps a little confused. I suspect he was enduring great inner turmoil as he struggled to work out how he would handle this latest disaster, especially as the well-tried and proven tactics of the past, the bluff, bluster and bullying, would hardly work in this case. I returned to Whitlam's office, reported Connor's denials and told Whitlam that I believed he was not being truthful. Five days later there were more disclosures in the *Melbourne Herald*. These sealed his fate.

The next morning Whitlam stood at the lectern before the Caucus at its usual weekly meeting and explained to members that their colleague Rex Connor was at that moment on his way to Yarralumla to hand in his resignation as a minister to the Governor-General. I was told earlier that Whitlam was trying to extract a resignation from him but the process had taken a perplexingly long time. Maybe Connor sought to exert some form of leverage designed to evade the inevitable. Was the fulcrum friendship? Was it something less pleasant? With that knack of his for dramatic effect and his somewhat didactic preference for precision as to even the smallest facts, Whitlam paused in his delivery and stared reflectively at the large wall clock in front of him. Suddenly the wide swinging, blue-baize covered doors to the Caucus room dramatically burst open. Connor entered with that curious short-stepped gait of his, so odd for such a big man; after his imposing bulk had passed through, the doors seemed to quiver with fear as they shuddered closed. I could have sworn then that, although not as big and buoyant as in his heyday, he was bigger than when I had seen him at his home a few days earlier. It was clear he was going to fight back and give it one last go. At that moment I found some grudging but spontaneous admiration developing for the man.

Connor was popular with many of the Caucus, especially among older members who had been through the Great Depression and who, as trade union officials, had engaged in some bruising encounters with bosses. They believed in solidarity and, like Connor, that the real enemy of Labor was a capitalist conspiracy against it—and that was what the loan fiasco really represented. They also saw in Connor another important aspect which bonded many of these people to him: he was a fighter for Labor principles and this demanded of them the loyalty of mateship, one of the most commendable qualities one could ever display. They were in their own way entirely admirable people. 'Let's hear from Rex,' Senator Reg Bishop called out, for Whitlam's announcement of his impending resignation had been greeted with some hostility. Connor breasted the lectern with his familiar opening of, 'Boys'—one always received well by the troops—and went on to the effect of 'I have a letter in my hand addressed to the Governor-General. It's my resignation as a minister. I was on my way out the front door to drive out to Yarralumla to hand it in, but it occurred to me that I shouldn't do such a thing without first hearing from you. We're a team and a decision like this shouldn't be taken without con-sultation'. This was a clever intervention, plumbing some deeply felt emotions and traditions in the culture of Labor. One in, all in. Do not act without consulting the rank and file. To top it, conspiracy theories about our predicament were rife and 'poor old

Rex' was not going to be a scapegoat. No matter that over many years Connor's practice had been to carefully ration out the opportunity for his colleagues to participate in what he was doing. Nor that when he did provide such chance, it was more often than not related to a need to broaden support for a proposition likely otherwise to fail in the Cabinet.

This unexpected turn of events converted the meeting into a scrappy affair. I was one who spoke early calling for Connor's resignation. I could not honestly see any other course open. It was a task of some discomfort for I was putting myself forward as a pall bearer to Connor's political ambitions. As I regained my seat I noted Connor's piercing dark eyes, almost pitch black, aiming a look he had directed at me before but never with this intensity; it was not a pleasant moment. Mick Young quickly moved a clever and subtle resolution accepting Connor's resignation with regret, while expressing admiration for his work and general approbation of him. Young usually had brilliant political instincts and this was such an occasion. The resolution was put and carried 55 to 24 votes, with Connor voting for it. There were few things on which Connor and I agreed, the only constant between us a mutual dislike. Somewhat contradictorily I expect, I found at that moment of humiliation for Connor there was much to admire in him. He took this awful personal setback with a grace and nobility of character, of the sort I hoped I too would be able to muster, should I ever be placed in a similar position. In his short statement to Caucus he seemed to hint of there being something more to the loans affair than had thus far been divulged. Another minister of that time, the late Frank Stewart, also knew what Connor knew. He had been present, as the third person, at a discussion from which Connor confidently departed believing he had support at the highest level to persist with his restless pursuit of large loans—despite solemn undertakings to Parliament to do nothing of the kind. Stewart shared this secret with Governor-General Kerr. As a Catholic with deep religious convictions, aspects of what Stewart knew caused him some moral concern. Kerr, a High Church Anglican, sympathised with him, but as a prudent layman of that often subtly political Church declined to act as a father confessor and advised him he would have to sort his dilemma out himself. The Governor-General never publicly repeated what he had been told, although he must have felt greatly provoked at times by some of the vituperation to which he had been subjected.

Pathways paved with good intentions

On 15 October 1975, Malcolm Fraser as Leader of the Opposition announced to a joint meeting of Liberal and National Party parliamentarians that he intended to use the numbers available to him in the Senate to in effect block the budget. This was the second occasion in as many years when Labor had to confront such a threat. In April 1974, when Opposition Leader Billy Snedden announced he would block Supply, Prime Minister Whitlam acted promptly and decisively, taking the country to a national election with a double dissolution. The public was made aware that patience had been exhausted and the Government would not tolerate the threat of wanton obstructionism of 'the Programme', as Whitlam liked calling it, by the Liberal–National Party in the Senate. 'The Programme', which tended to have a consecrated ring to it whenever Whitlam invoked it in public addresses, was the rack of reform policies Labor had put forward successfully at the 1972 general election. In 1974 the declaration of going to the people was redolent of strong national leadership. The reality was otherwise, as the Government had received good news and bad news: while inflation for the March quarter, contrary to the trend to that point and also quite unexpectedly, had fallen impressively, that 'good' inflation figure was a false dawn. In any case, Treasury had warned the Government that the economy 'looked bad' for the whole of 1975 and the implied message was unmistakable: go to the electorate now and there was a fighting chance of survival, ignore the challenge and it would be too late.

If Billy Snedden had not been so weakly opportunistic in 1974 as to allow his coalition partners to push him into that 1974 election and had held out, contesting the election at its normal time in late 1975, I have no doubt he would have won. Labor was beyond electoral salvation, even with a dramatically disciplined change of economic management and, in general, greatly improved ministerial performance. Conceivably, it would have been Snedden rather than Malcolm Fraser who would have become the twenty-eighth prime minister of Australia. Speculating even further, he possibly would have enjoyed several years of successful management of the country; certainly he would not have been dogged and distracted, as Fraser was, by significant sections of the community questioning the legitimacy of the measures by which he had assumed that office. If events had unfolded that way, the life of Governor-General Kerr at Yarralumla would have been distinctly more congenial, and his name and work quickly forgotten by the public.

As it turned out, in late 1975 Fraser, true to his word, relentlessly used the Senate to jam up the budget process in the Parliament. The two Houses engaged in a paper war of 'resolutions'. The Senate invited the Government to resign as a precondition to its passing the Appropriation Bills. Unsurprisingly, the Government declined the offer and was instrumental in having a resolution carried by the House of Representatives condemning the Senate tactic and upholding the House as the seat of government. Several resolutions of a similar nature followed from each of the Houses. In late October the Government introduced and passed Appropriation Bills similar to the first Budget Bills. Unlike in 1974, the Government knew it had no chance of surviving an election in late 1975 and it resolutely resisted the notion of a general election as a simple matter of survival. The Bass by-election in Tasmania, at the end of June, had already provided a chilling warning of what was ahead for Labor, with a swing in excess of 17 per cent against the Government. The result cut the majority of the Government to three and left it traumatised with fear of an early election. The message of Bass was clearly read by both sides of the Parliament. Fraser was emboldened because of healthy omens like this and a fear that if he did not act then to force an election the flood tide of opportunity might very well be at its peak. The only cards the Government had to play were its improved economic management and better disciplined industrial relations policies; we also felt that at last we were regaining some credibility with the electorate.

There were other lesser, but important, inducements for Fraser to force an early election. Various pieces of legislation aimed at improving democratic rights and processes were treated as if they were a conspiracy against the coalition: provision for enrolment quotas in rural electorates to be increased so that they moved closer to those of non-rural seats was regarded as an unfair plot against the National Party; optional preferential voting was seen as something designed to favour Labor; compulsory public disclosure of sources of funding for political parties was regarded as a conspiracy which would imperil financial support from business to the Liberal Party; Senate representation for the Northern Territory and the Australian Capital Territory was objected to as the coalition thought it would increase Labor representation in that chamber. None of these measures were congenial to the coalition parties, all were treated as if part of a great plan to undermine them, yet experience shows that neither of the major parties was either advantaged or disadvantaged as against the other. The measures did, however, commendably improve the quality of democracy within our political system.

The Government cobbled together a financing formula, as a sort of makeshift crutch on which to hobble along as Supply ran down in the wake of the Senate obstructionism. Essentially comprising a system of vouchers, these would serve as a form of IOU on which it was proposed the banks would extend credit to cover, for example, the wages of public servants and members of the defence forces. These credits would also pay for goods and services. The Solicitor-General advised that the process was legally valid. Perhaps so, but as Professor G. Sawer succinctly put it, was it practical? As Treasurer I had large doubts, although I could bear with the proposal as a political bluff, a legitimate political tactic. I am afraid I would have retreated from any effort to have it go much beyond that. In my view, this system could only function briefly and not happily and would have broken down in the early New Year; I also recall Senator Wriedt expressing somewhat similar concerns. Wriedt and I registered our reservations on the matter clearly enough and we were prepared if necessary to demonstrate our convictions later. I accepted the need for as few as possible to share in Whitlam's thinking at this stage, for we were at a critical moment in the confrontation and loose talk is always dangerous in Canberra.

How far the tactic was to be taken was never explained. As Paul Kelly illustrates in *November 1975*, Whitlam's failure to discuss this with Kerr, his misreading of Kerr's character so as to presume him weak and compliant to Whitlam's wishes, and his failure to develop any contingency planning in case his attempt to bluff Fraser into allowing the budget to pass through the Senate failed (if indeed it was a tactic of bluff—I believed it was); all of these were serious flaws and contributed greatly to his downfall.[12] In any event, the enterprise was doomed before it started. State governments were ready to take injunctions against the Federal Government to test the legality of the proposal once it was in place and functioning. Similarly, depositors and shareholders of banks, reputedly, were poised to take legal steps against the mechanism on the basis that their funds were insufficiently secured. Some of this was prudent self-interest and some was political manoeuvring. Kerr has written that a number of banks, at least, had received legal advice before the sacking of Whitlam questioning the legality of the system. This is certainly correct. One opinion I have seen, provided for the

Australian Bankers' Association by eminent counsel, baldly states the scheme was 'legally incapable of implementation as proposed'. Some other private banks, at least, also sought opinions for their own use from eminent counsel. To my knowledge some of those categorically declared the proposal to be 'illegal'. For all I know, all the opinions sought could have given this advice. I might add that this information came to me many years after the event. Kerr's own background as a leading counsel and jurist also allowed him to make a well-informed, personal judgment on this matter. In the circumstances, this advice about the government's proposed funding arrangements, passed on to Kerr, and his own conclusions on the proposal, must have worried him. The thought of his being complicit in an unlawful act would have been greatly disturbing. As far as I can judge the matter, Kerr might have arguably made some errors of judgment, but he was a moral man.

For the record, formal advice to the government was that 'Officers of the Attorney-General's Department are of the view that it, the temporary financing scheme, would represent a lawful exercise of the powers of the government,' and that the scheme 'involves no offence against any law'. Kerr was given clear advice of this opinion well before the various opinions supplied to the banks would have reached him. By 11 November 1975 none of the private banks had agreed to work with the proposal. One of the largest banks in the country was in fact becoming restive at the prospect of participating in these rather hastily prepared arrangements. On the day of the dismissal of the Whitlam Labor Government there was a minute from the Treasury to me exploring this development and how perhaps it might have been handled. Time and events prevented a suitably considered response from me as Treasurer. A more relevant question was whether it was any sort of practical arrangement, when what the Government was proposing was access to unsecured credit. In their duty to their shareholders and to their depositors to act prudently, the banks' concerns were genuine ones.

The view from Government House

For Kerr, pacing the extensive grounds and commodious passages of Government House in grand isolation, the worries of this mounting chaos must have been extremely troublesome. Kerr conceded this when he wrote of 'The loneliness of the decision I was making . . . was a time of intense mental solitude.'[13] Having spent seven years at that establishment in the office of Governor-General, I can emphatically confirm the nature of the isolation and the sense of loneliness. It is not that one does not meet people, nor have them visit, nor move about the country among many people. On the contrary, all those things occur regularly. It is the nature of one's association with other people which changes. One has to be guarded about discussion which could be misunderstood as breaching conventions about the non-partisan role of the office. If that is restrictive enough, one has also to contend with changes in people's attitude. The office and the establishment at Government House with all its staid style and ritual appears to erect a protective veil between the occupants and visitors, even friends. A distance tends to open up which is difficult to bridge. It is a sobering fact that, despite Australians' reputation for a dislike of ceremony, a surprisingly large number who visit prefer the formal embroidery of the contrived arrangements.

Then there is the glorious atmosphere of Yarralumla itself. The way the grounds are hedged in and screened by forest and plant life, it can feel as if you are hundreds of kilometres from the next place of civilised habitation. Indeed, one beautiful Saturday morning when I was alone in the grounds there, except for the armed guards at the main entrance, and looking along the driveway, out through the firmly shut wrought iron gates and up Dunrossil Drive, it struck me how similar the place was to the lovely garden estates around the public psychiatric hospitals in Ipswich. It suddenly seemed as if those heavy gates were shut and guarded not to keep the public out but me in!

If the Labor Government had been more perceptive about these factors, we might have thought more carefully about the impact of some of our tactics on that lonely man out at Yarralumla. When I now re-read various parliamentary statements by Whitlam, or ministers such as Morrison, myself, et al., on how the system of public administration was on the verge of seizing up, of how public servants and defence personnel would cease being paid, of the corporate sector grinding to a halt, the economy fizzling out, because of the obstructionism of the coalition, I am struck by the stark and dramatic implications of our utterances. For Kerr, used to the less rumbustious atmosphere of the courts, the impact must have been like a gratuitous course of high voltage shock therapy. For anyone in that position with any sense of responsibility, the instinct to do something would have been great.

In assessing what he might have done, I expect that he felt hobbled because the Labor Government had adopted the view that the governor-general did nothing, absolutely nothing at all, unless advised by his responsible ministers. Such an extreme whig view (with which Queen Victoria would not have been amused) meant that where Kerr required a legal opinion, he was advised it would come to him through his chief minister—but only if the chief minister approved of him receiving it. In retrospect, this was unwisely stifling. Nor was the provision of a critical opinion for Kerr on the reserve powers of the governor-general handled as skilfully as it should have been by the Government. The Government undertook to provide the Governor-General with a joint opinion from the Government's first and second law officers. This should have been an important document. It dealt with, *inter alia,* some views put forward in another opinion, by a previous solicitor-general and a then current Liberal MHR, Bob Ellicott QC. Ellicott's advice was that the reserve powers did exist and that '. . . it would be within the Governor-General's . . . duty to dismiss his Ministers and appoint others'. A document was presented to Kerr by Attorney-General Enderby, on 6 November, only five days before the dismissal of the Whitlam Government. There was only the Solicitor-General's signature on it. The signature had been scratched through, thus voiding it, and the word 'draft' was scrawled across the top of the document; Enderby was responsible for both of these amendments. It was pointed out to Kerr by Enderby that there was disagreement between the two law officers over the way in which the opinion conceded the existence of the reserve powers and these differences were yet to be resolved. I am not sure how reassuring Kerr found this or what confident guidance he derived from it—I expect less than the Government would have wished and much less than Kerr sought. Certainly one suspects that it would have increased enormously the subsequent influence of the opinion of Chief Justice Barwick, which Kerr received on 10 November and which, it seems to me, was similar in import to the opinion of Ellicott. This was a consultation, incidentally, expressly forbidden by the Prime Minister as chief adviser to the Governor-General.

Based on his calculation of how long existing Supply would last, Kerr concluded he had to act soon. I must admit that from what he has written he did so with a clearly imperfect understanding of what the true position was, including the rough crutch of the temporary financing arrangement. He correctly acknowledged that some 60 per cent of government expenditure, including that for sensitive areas such as pensions, is off-budget and is appropriated automatically. Annual approval of Parliament for these items is not required. For the remainder, there was sufficient Supply for several more weeks and the jury-rigged temporary financial credit arrangement would have lasted until about the second week of January. In other words, there was still quite a deal of time left in which the bluff and manoeuvre of the political processes could have been legitimately played out. He received government advice that the last date on which an election could be held, until well after the new year was under way, was 13 December. He calculated that all these factors meant he had to act by 11 November. One of the critical influences in striking on the 13 December election date deadline was related to the unavailability of school teachers once the Christmas vacation period commenced. This claim, I have always thought, was quite overdrawn. There are other people as responsible and capable as school teachers, able to take charge of polling booths on election days. Kerr accepted this government advice. I suspect it was presumed this time-limitation factor would shock him into an early resolution of the impasse and in favour of the Government. This was a classic case of the dangerous consequences of gratuitously dismissing a proud and educated man's respect for his own intellectual independence and judgment.

Nor was Kerr helped by the two determined, larger than life personalities with whom he was dealing: Whitlam, a patrician figure, a sparkling orator, mercurial, headstrong and full of pluck; Fraser, a dour, stubborn Scot who would resolutely plod through the fires of Hell, tearing apart with his bare hands any attacking furies in the way of his goal or ambition. Each had staked too much of his future to be able to back away credibly from the course he had set for himself. A course that would destroy one and deliver a flawed triumph to the other. Each was adamant their numbers were holding solid behind them, that there was no wavering. Both were convinced of the righteousness of their cause. How could Kerr make an informed judgment on these claims and counterclaims? Yarralumla is only ten minutes away from Parliament House by car. For a governor-general locked into the solitude of that establishment, the internal machinations of Parliament are beyond reach and a comprehension of unfolding political developments probably even further away.

Then there was the issue of Kerr's character: his was just not strong enough to fortify him in confronting Whitlam. Kerr was unable to forcefully present the options as he saw them and outline for Whitlam the inevitable consequences of various courses of conduct. There were occasions when he chose to be entertaining and loquacious, when he should have been given to serious counselling, conduct which only caused misapprehension of his intent and led to much bitter recrimination later. He was silent when he should have offered warning. In his autobiographical work, *Matters for Judgement*, Kerr stated he had doubts about the legality of the loans for 'temporary purposes' but felt this was a matter that properly belonged to the courts. He was correct in conceding this role to the courts, but given his eminence as a jurist he should have warned his ministers, as a matter of prudent advice, of his doubts. That is a duty on important matters such as this, of the vice-regal representative. Walter Bagehot's stipulation of three duties for the Sovereign in a constitutional Monarchy—the right to be consulted, to encourage and to warn—holds also for vice-regal representatives.

This was, I should have thought, a clear case where the duty of the Governor-General was to warn his responsible ministers. Kerr makes a savvy enough observation in his autobiography when he refers to the duty to warn: 'A wise man would not be volunteering it often'. Like all precious specie, this important right would be debased if put into circulation in too great a volume too frequently. But it would seem from Kerr's autobiographical account, that, having drawn this sensible conclusion, he practised a course of thorough prudence in spite of harbouring many serious doubts about various government actions. This was Kerr's fatal flaw—a detachment, a lack of resolve in his dealings with his ministers. His conscience warned him of pitfalls ahead in the conduct of his responsible ministers; his instincts, however comprised, took control of him and he remained mute. I suspect the trigger was finally pulled, while the political gun was held against the temple of the Government, by a telephone call by the Prime Minister to the Governor-General on the morning of 11 November. My hunch was and still is that Kerr had decided to act several days before 11 November. It is my belief that this telephone call absolutely clinched the fate of the Government, putting an end to equivocation on Kerr's part. Whitlam announced in that call that he would be coming out to Yarralumla to notify the Governor-General that he would be seeking a half-Senate election. As Kerr wrote of that telephone call, 'the issue crystallised finally'.[14] I was convinced, along with many others, that the simple arithmetic of the electorate meant a half-Senate election would solve nothing for Labor, even if the non-Labor States were prepared to issue Senate election writs, which they were not. Adding to our woes, as mentioned, the credit financing facility plastered together by the Government had got nowhere with the private banks and would be instantly immobilised by a raft of injunctions should it have become operative. Then there were the dire predictions of an economy seizing up and coming to a dead halt.

I saw Kerr in his study at Yarralumla on 6 November 1975. I had twice earlier discussed the sorry state of political affairs with him, albeit briefly. The first time was on 22 October, at a function at Government House when, in response to a question from him, I acknowledged that the political situation was messy and I rather expected that he would have to act firmly in an effort to right it; I had in mind that he would defend the Government's right to govern, a misbegotten conclusion if ever there was one. The second occasion was eight days later when, at his invitation, I called on him at Government House. He was only able to make the most cursory references to the then running problem as Fraser had arrived too and he had to, quite reasonably in my view given the circumstances, divert his attention to Fraser. My meeting with Kerr on 6 November had been occasioned by Enderby, who advised that Whitlam wished me to call on the Governor-General and give him a 'warts and all' account of the interim financing arrangement we had put together. 'Don't worry,' I was assured. 'He's one of us. You can trust him. He's on side. Tell him the lot, is Gough's view'. When I eventually did so, he did not seem notably interested in what I had to say on this scheme. Enderby had exactly the same experience during his discussions on certain legal matters with Kerr the same afternoon. In my case, Kerr was more interested in soliloquising about Whitlam's extraordinary fighting prowess in an election: 'Like a lion with his back to the wall . . . he can win . . . if not this time next time around'. Now if you want to sink terror deep into the heart of a politician you have only to talk of an early election when it is obvious that his party is headed for disaster. My demurs were good humouredly put to one side.

I should record here that all Kerr's comments about Whitlam were expressed with unfeigned cordiality and admiration for the man, although they displayed a shallow comprehension of political moods and processes. I departed hurriedly, not for the airport where I had a tight timetable to catch an aircraft home, but to Parliament House. I left strongly suspecting that Kerr had concluded he would have to force an election. I deviated from my route to the airport to inform the Prime Minister of this suspicion. I said, 'My old copper's instincts tell me he's going to sack us'. He dismissed the advice. He stood outside his office, pressed against the corridor wall, twirling his spectacles thoughtfully between thumb and finger of one hand. After a few seconds' reflection he pronounced with finality, 'No, Comrade, he wouldn't have the guts to do it'. With that decisiveness one of the great moments of our history went unanticipated. If the Prime Minister believed Kerr to be a man of putty, this was a regrettable miscalculation.

Prepare to meet thy doom

On the afternoon of 11 November 1975, I was working in my office jotting down notes for an anticipated urgent debate on economic issues. Miss Gae Raby, my amiable and always forbearing principal private secretary ambled in to make the following announcement: 'Guess what? You've been sacked. Malcolm Fraser is the Prime Minister . . .'. Raby beat a hasty retreat as imprecations and expletives suddenly showered down around her. The key, and repeatable, point of what I said to her, as she disappeared through the doorway was that I was sick and tired of hearing mindless gossip from the lobbies of Parliament House—oh yes, I put Miss Raby straight on a thing or two.

The bells rang, summoning members and senators to the afternoon session of Parliament. I entered the chamber and was met by an unsettling atmosphere of stillness. It was awful, the mournful silence of the death watch. It felt as if I were entering a mouldering necropolis. I sat down beside Joe Berrinson who said 'Well, it's all over. Kerr's sacked us,' in his usual matter-of-fact way. My short fuse began to activate again, before I remembered that as Berrinson did not have much of a sense of humour, the statement had to be true. Later that day, still dazed from the collision with so many political catastrophes in such a short period, I spoke on some radio current affairs programme with the late Phil Lynch, Opposition spokesman on Treasury matters. The presenter opened proceedings with, 'My first question is to the Treasurer; What. . . ' I forget the actual question, but as soon as it was asked I opened my mouth to respond. Before I could get a word out and to my dismay Phil Lynch began answering. Then the full impact of the whole sorry sequence of events of that afternoon struck me. I was no longer Treasurer. It was all over. We really were finished as a government. I only finally comprehended this stark new reality, and in an extraordinarily wrenching fashion, at the very moment Lynch answered the question ahead of me.

Then, on the afternoon of 11 November 1975, and even more dramatically, a number of unexampled events occurred at Canberra. The budget was unexpectedly passed by the Senate. In the House of Representatives Fraser announced that he had been appointed Prime Minister and had formed a government with the authority of the Governor-General. Whitlam countered with a successful no confidence motion against the Fraser minority Government. The same afternoon, Official Secretary at Government House David Smith read the proclamation dissolving Parliament from the front steps of that institution, to howls of anger and outrage. Following a practice consistent since 1963 (long before he had commenced working at Government House), Smith did his duty as a public servant according to standard guidelines. If someone else had occupied Smith's position at that time, they too would have done exactly as he did. It is a sad commentary that Smith, his wife and family suffered a great deal of unfair criticism after that occasion; these very fine people never deserved the indignities to which they were afterwards exposed, although they have borne them with stoicism.

Immediately after Smith's reading of the proclamation dissolving Parliament, Whitlam stood at the front steps of the Parliament House and angrily made a comment which has lived ever since: 'Well may we say God save the Queen, because nothing will save the Governor-General'. Many at the time, including some in the Labor movement, expressed concern that these words might ignite dangerous political passions. I thought and still believe it was Whitlam's most magnificent moment. He indisputably knew, as so many of our trusty foot soldiers were aware, that we were about to go out and engage in a pitched political battle where just about every feature of the battle plan, in particular the slant of the media, would be against us. Only a political naif would fail to recognise the electoral disaster looming ahead of us. I wrote at the time, in my erratically kept diary, that at that moment Whitlam was inspirational, like a lion carrying the scars of many battles, roaring defiance as its fate remorselessly closed in on it. The distinguishing mark of a great leader is, for me, the ability to rally his followers in circumstances where an honourable peace is not an option, and, thereafter, to fight with all his heart an unequal battle where he knows he is doomed to defeat before the first blow is struck. That is what real fortitude in the face of adversity is all about.

That night on the ground floor of the old Parliament House, in the lobby near where I had my office as Treasurer, various Labor MPs and senators were wandering about looking stunned. One group, arms linked around one another's shoulders, went by singing, off-key, 'The Internationale' and 'The Red Flag'. A remarkable moment for here were some of the most right wing people in the Caucus singing songs that belonged to more radical causes than any to which they had ever been able to commit themselves before. But this was no more than the bravado you might expect before the shadow of the gallows. I entered the office of a fellow defrocked minister. There was also a meeting under way involving about fifteen or so serious-minded Caucus members intently discussing 'mass mobilisation of the workers', from which flowed some silly talk of a great national strike, of the workers taking to the streets. I immediately withdrew. I become impatient with those who, while privileged to exercise leadership on behalf of others, are ready to collapse on to soft pillows of sentimentality at times of crisis. My sojourn at Yarralumla aside, I have lived with the working-class culture all my life. It was perfectly clear to me that Australian working people were not going to seize up the operation of their country over a political imbroglio, putting at risk the limited security they had been building up over the years for themselves and their offspring. Not for an unpopular government. Nor for a political party that appeared to have forgotten how to behave with the personal propriety and discipline the working-class apply to themselves and accordingly expect of their representatives. This was the sort of romanticised waffle that sustains the cheap red push on lazy Saturday afternoons in various upmarket, inner-city areas of Australia. The chattering types presume to speak for the proletariat while knowing very few if any genuine working-class people. The workers with soundly based common sense ignore them. The President of the ACTU, Bob Hawke, enhanced his reputation by calling for calm from the 'workers'. Well-intentioned as his words were, they were also unnecessary; noisy hotheads speak for few in the community.

A futile fight

After the sacking of the government, on the campaign trail in Melbourne, I attended a rally at Nunawadding High School, where a warmly responsive crowd packed the hall. At first the enthusiasm was heady and then within five minutes I detected something that caused me a little edginess, for public speakers can 'feel' an audience. There was a brittle tenseness to the noisy barracking. These were loyal Labor supporters who rallied to the Party's cause at a time of crisis; they would put on a brave front, but privately they feared for Labor. At that moment I knew beyond any doubt that we were in deep and dire trouble. Every other meeting confirmed this. The economic content of Fraser's policy speech did not withstand simple critical analysis yet it was warmly approved by many editorials. While out on the hustings I telephoned the editor of one important newspaper in the Fairfax chain, a personal friend, to complain at the uncharacteristic lack of rigour in the editorial analysis of Fraser's economic statement. 'Sorry, you've got to put up with it. There's been a policy decision by the paper. Labor's had it and Fraser's being supported. It's Labor's fault. It squandered support and goodwill prodigiously.' This seemed to be the official policy of just about every major daily through the cities of Australia. These newspapers did not manufacture the causes of public disenchantment with Labor—that was all our own work—although they did their best, and very effectively, to fan the flames of discontent.

On 24 November 1975 there was a huge midday rally at the Sydney Domain, billed as the official campaign opening. To that time I had not, and still have not, ever seen such a crowd. People's passions lashed about noisily and some thought the response of Labor supporters ominous. This was not so: if they had listened closely they would have detected only tension, even fear, rather than aggression or the threat of it, as the dominant mood behind the noise of the cheering and heckling; certainly it was very similar to my experience at Nunawadding High and at a host of other places in the course of the campaign up till then. Meanwhile, people streamed into the parkland in their thousands. Was there hope in this of a favourable turn in our hitherto dismal fortunes? The opinion polls were by then focussing on the political parties and Labor was in diabolical trouble. Freddy Daly, the eternal optimist, looked out over the crowd. 'I saw this happen once before,' he said soberingly. 'Even bigger crowds when Lang was sacked. The following Saturday he was turned out of office by a huge majority. This is a bad omen for us.'

Daly was right. We were in trouble. The campaign dragged into its closing stages. Except for a few brief hours when I could return home to change clothing, I was continuously on the trail. So were most other former ministers. Campaigning is a wonderful experience, but it has its awful side too. The parry of the press conferences, the glad-handing around electorates, the warm, friendly support and the company of complete strangers to whom you were bonded by the tribal culture of Labor—these represent the high points. The nights however are something else. Nothing to look forward to at the end of the day but a cheerless motel room, the boredom of your own company, a complimentary bible from Gideons—often aged but always in a pristine condition—and a glass of room temperature tap water to cool down any steamy tendencies. The spectres of doubt and insecurity, which have hung about in the background all day, are hard to lock out at such moments. The only relief for me in '75 was a telephone call home to talk to the family; just to talk to Dallas about everyday things over thousands of kilometres of telephone cable was a lift to a flagging confidence; or to lecture the children fondly, if they were still awake, on why they should be asleep at that late hour but, privately, being pleased to speak to them. And so would end another day on the campaign trail, with another and another and more after that to come until that final, cold, grey dawn of election day. To wait and role-play while the inevitable lumbered onwards, heading straight at you like a grim, unstoppable juggernaut.

While in Perth between commitments, I had a call from the then Queensland assistant organiser for Labor, Bob Gibbs, now a State minister there. 'You'd better come home pretty quickly. We've just had some polling results and it looks as though we'll lose every seat in Queensland. Everingham may hang on in Capricornia. It's dicey. It doesn't look good for you. You certainly won't make it unless you get back to Oxley, right away. The electorate's unsettled and fairly unhappy with us.' I mumbled a protest about commitments. 'Please yourself. Stay away and you're probably done. Come back and campaign and you might be lucky. You might scrape in. I wouldn't count on it though.' I was due to stop in Sydney that night and go on to Queensland, but not my electorate, to campaign early the next day. In Sydney, where I would arrive late in the evening from Perth, I was scheduled to visit a fundraising dance, of all things, for a Labor backbencher who had got me to agree to this arrangement very much against my better judgment. For the life of me I could not see what good arriving there at something like 10 p.m. was going to do. The NSW Party machine had pressed this member's request also in their characteristically 'persuasive' way, and as it is usually the better part of discretion to humour that body, I had agreed to attend. Gibbs' message was sobering; I liked to believe I was brave, but it was a bit early for martyrdom. I made arrangements to return to my electorate and withdrew my acceptance to the Sydney function. Not much later, as I waited in the office until it was time to go to the airport, the Sydney backbencher rang in. In a wheedling voice he said, 'Bill, how could you do this to me? Don't you realise if you don't come to my dance I will lose lots of support and be defeated . . . [slight pause] . . . Would you want that on your conscience? That you caused my defeat?' This was not a time for subtly letting him down. 'My friend, do you know what will happen to me if I go to your dance instead of going home to my electorate? I'll be defeated. Now I don't know whether you want my defeat on your conscience or not but I'm damned sure I don't want it on mine. I'm on my way home!'

Dallas and I moved out on the morning of election day. We expected the worst and had prepared a positive statement in such an event, for then the media would most likely descend on us. As we went around each of the booths according to the well-worn practice for such days, we tried to keep our spirits up for the sake of our 'troops'. They were apprehensive too. At our local polling booth people whom we knew well greeted us quietly as they stood in queues waiting to vote. They were obviously embarrassed. As they shuffled how-to-vote cards from the various parties, our how-to-vote was going to the bottom of the pile they were holding, a clear give-away that we were in trouble. Many sought to look away casually but the movement was stilted, self-conscious. Still, it was good to know that this was not so much a judgment of us personally, but rather a conclusion as to what they had to do with their votes—as worrying as the latter was.

That night as the votes were counted, our booth workers would telephone the Labor Party figures through to our central campaign office. It was disastrous. With as few as half-a-dozen booth results in, I knew I was in trouble. Under the circumstances every figure was going to be important to our calculations of possible outcomes. Eventually I had a call from the booth captain (as we called the person in charge of our scrutineers at each polling place) at Dinmore State School. An unmistakable Australian working-class accent came across the telephone line like a heavy truck struggling up a sharp grade in low gear; it was his first time working on a booth, let alone being in charge of our group there. ' 'Ow's the vote goin', Bill?' 'Not too good at the moment,' I said without any private confidence that anything was going to change. 'How's our vote there?' I didn't pretend to be hopeful. 'Oh, bloody good. You got [quoting a number] . . . ' My heart sank. It was much worse than the previous election, where there had already been quite a swing against Labor—in itself an early indicator that Labor was becoming increasingly unpopular in Queensland. I suspected that we would be forced to preferences in Oxley. It was therefore important to know how all the vote was distributed. 'What did the Libs get?' I queried my loyal supporter. 'Ah bugger them, Bill. I'm not going to count for them bastards. I'm a Labor man through and through. Won't have anything to do with them mongrels.' I implored silently 'Oh, God, make me strong,' and, knowing there was no way of reversing the result, thanked my friend for the help and said, 'Don't forget there's beer and a bit of tucker on at the Trades Hall tonight'.

The aftermath

On the following day, Sunday, I was taking telephone messages at home from party workers at the central counting office for the electorate; they were scrutineering a check recount by the electoral officer and his staff. Their task was to count the distribution of preferences. The telephone rang for the umpteenth time, disturbing my dark meditations. It was Gough Whitlam. 'Comrade, how's it going in Oxley?' I was not in the happiest of moods nor ready to be on my best behaviour, 'F . . . ing awful like everywhere else'. The only news Whitlam had was like a roll call of the brave and the bold, bodies fallen all over the country. 'Comrade; you're still certain you don't want to have the leadership of the party?' I was livid. 'J . . . . f . . . ing C . . . . . Gough, I don't even know if I'm going to be in the bloody Parliament. We look like going to preferences. Leadership is the last f . . . ing thing I'm interested in.' The expletives were triggered in part by my general agitation; I was after all a trifle edgy. In response, Whitlam sounded wounded. 'Oh, very well, if that's the way you feel. I'll talk to Hawke. He's the only other prospect. After this setback I'm prepared to hand over the leadership.'

Uncertainty as to the election result was the immediate reason for my reaction to Whitlam's approach to me, but there were two other causes for that abruptness. Whitlam's indisputable talents aside, it was not for him as Leader or any other individual to offer someone the leadership of the Labor Party; that remains a privilege that rests exclusively within the provenance of Caucus. Leaders who have tried to publicly bulldoze the Caucus into supporting one of the leader's favourites, where the anointed son did not stand as high in favour with the Caucus, have been humbled before. Whitlam's amanuensis, Graham Freudenberg, has acknowledged this same point:

> ... the independence, even the waywardness of Caucus is such that a leader's intervention would be likely to ensure failure as success for his candidates. Curtin and Chifley were never able to guarantee success for their protégés or exclude those of whom they disapproved.[15]

His reference to my 'still' not being interested in accepting the leadership related to a proposal he put to me in late 1975, which was that I should take over that role. Whitlam apparently contemplated retiring from Parliament in the then near future to take up an appointment as Chairman of the Interstate Commission. Though it lacked enabling legislation at that stage, he seemed sanguine about being able to set it up and, as his speeches showed, it was an organisation about which he had thought a great deal, a notion to which he was deeply devoted. On that earlier occasion, I had declined much more gracefully than on 14 December 1975. I had a niggling feeling, the first time round, that the chalice offered might turn out to contain a draught of bile rather than the sweet wine of success. The transport minister of the time, Charles Jones, who recalls the incident, was present on the earlier occasion.

The other reason I did not respond affirmatively was that, while I respected the sense of sacrifice which undoubtedly motivated Whitlam's offer, I also detected in his tone such regret at the turn of events that he felt compelled to make such a proposal. So many hopes dashed, ideals shattered, so much faith and commitment invested in the transformation which Labor in government could bring about in society, now about to be liquidated by the political repossession agents who had taken over; it was a period of despair and doubts. Yet for all that, it had been mainly our own work, and despite the anger I felt at our own foolishnesses, I could not shake off my affection for Whitlam. In any case I survived, by 112 votes.

The developments in late 1975 had many repercussions. Debate at the time must have been confusing for the general public. Academic lawyers were popping up all over the place confirming or rebutting the validity of Kerr's actions. With great conviction, experts quoted what delegates said at the pre-Federation Constitutional Conventions, arguments which could be used to bolster or deny the assertion that the Senate could exercise the sort of power it did. This conveniently ignored the fact that the record of those debates, in any event, was not admissible in justiciable cases. The Senate has always had the power to legally act in the way of 1975, and Labor had itself exploited the fact to gain political advantage on a number of occasions.[16] Without the provision of the Senate power, it is doubtful whether Federation could have been brought about. Federation was a tricky exercise, which had its moments when the whole notion might fail, such were the suspicions of the smaller colonies about the motives of the larger ones. That the Senate had not acted before in the way it did in 1975 means nothing; in acting as it did in 1975, a precedent was established which could be used to justify that sort of action being taken again. The great irony would be that having a precedent to give respectability to a repeat of that sort of action, a Senate controlled by Labor, the Democrats and other minority forces, for instance, might collude opportunistically at some future time to turn out a Liberal–National Party government in the House of Representatives.

In a 'scissors and paste' compromise, the architects of our Constitution sought to integrate two fundamentally contrary systems of government into our parliamentary process; responsible parliamentary government of the Westminster type, and some of the separate powers of the United States federal congressional system. At times of stress like 1975, these contrary principles can clash destructively. The legality of the use of the so-called reserve powers of the governor-general has also been called into question. The Australian Constitution is quite distinctive and different to that of other Commonwealth countries in the powers it invests in the governor-general in his own right. The governor-general can dismiss ministers as he can appoint them. The Constitution is unequivocal on that point. Kerr acted within his authority in withdrawing the commission of the Whitlam Government and in commissioning the Fraser Government. He acted properly by taking the advice of his responsible ministers in the Fraser Government in calling an election, a double dissolution, and in dissolving Parliament for the purposes of the election. He was wrong, however, when he declared that in Australia if a prime minister 'cannot get supply he must resign or advise an election . . . [and if he fails to do either] . . . my constitutional authority and duty require me . . . to withdraw his commission'. [17] In stating this in his written reasons for the dismissal of the Whitlam Government, Kerr closely followed the written private opinion of the Chief Justice, Barwick. [18] There was however a critical difference. Whereas Barwick gave an opinion that the Governor-General 'has constitutional authority to withdraw the Prime Minister's commission' Kerr transformed this into an inescapable obligation by saying that he was 'required' to withdraw the commission in the relevant circumstances. Curiously, eight years later Barwick wrote more imperatively that Kerr had '. . . a constitutional duty . . . which he was bound to perform'. And that Kerr '. . . did what he was constitutionally bound to do'. [19] In varying his advice in this way Barwick was acting as the advocate for his client's case and not as the disinterested jurist determining a difficult case. His credibility suffered accordingly.

Of the general thrust of these opinions Professor G. Sawer has written:

> On no previous occasion in Britain, Australia or any British-derived
> parliamentary system has the Monarch or a Governor dismissed a

> ministry having a majority in the Commons, Representatives or similar
> House, because that ministry has been denied supply by the Lords,
> Senate or similar House.

and,

> Not, so far as my reading goes, has it ever been suggested by
> constitutional writers that there is a rigid rule requiring advice to
> dissolve or action by the Crown to procure dissolution merely because of
> denial of supply by an upper House.[20]

There was much speculation at the time of the approaching climax to this crisis that several Opposition senators were distinctly uncomfortable with Fraser's budget-blocking tactic. It was widely reported that some would not support this tactic, which of course meant the blockage in the Senate would have been terminated. Laurie Oakes mentions eleven Opposition senators who were believed to have been opposed to what Fraser was doing.[21] The late Phillip Lynch was concerned enough that some of his Senate colleagues might desert that he and Reg Withers 'exerted great pressure on them to hold on a while longer'. One of them was the late Senator Missen who had been proposed 'more than once' for the Ministry by Lynch but who was rejected as being 'too intellectual'.[22] At the time of the 1975 crisis I accepted the prevailing wisdom, shared quite widely in the community, that a number of coalition senators were on the verge of breaking away from Fraser's discipline and would refuse to support further obstruction of the budget. I am much less certain of that now. On this matter at least, if I am correct, Kerr may have had a better feel than some of us who were there at the heart of the political storm in 1975.

While Missen was an outspoken critic of Fraser's obstructionist tactics, he did declare that he would not cross the floor to 'rat' on his party. He was not prepared to provide Fraser with an excuse to retreat from his confrontationist tactics at the cost of his own integrity within the Party. Missen rationalised his attitude as one of high principle. At the same time there was a prudent feel about these rationalisations. Recent experience within his party back then would have reminded him that persisting with his opposition would bring terminal repercussions for his future as a senator. If he had proved impossible to budge, other coalition senators opposed to Fraser's tactics may have been less tractable.[23] The fate, shortly after these events, of Liberal Senator Bussel of Tasmania illustrated that cold-bloodedly enough. His outspoken criticism of Fraser's tactics cost him his Senate preselection.

Chief Justice Barwick was unwise to act as adviser to Kerr and thus cast the High Court into the seething cauldron of political bitterness and debate. High Court justices would do well to keep clear of such political entrapments in future. Markwell has set out precedents to Barwick's action and says '. . . a Chief Justice—State or Commonwealth—has given advice on almost every exercise of reserve powers in Australia this century.'[24] As well-stated as Markwell's case might be, nonetheless the interventions of 1975 establish the imprudence of justices of the High Court acting in future as informal sources of opinion during constitutional crises, especially as action taken on the advice may be justiciable. Similarly, Barwick's disclosure in early 1994 that another Justice, Mason, later a Chief Justice, had given confirmatory advice to his own, compounds these dangers for the Court. Kerr has acknowledged in his autobiographical work that he had talked to someone in Sydney, while the crisis was current, about the dilemma with which he was grappling, who 'was not and never had been engaged in politics'. These discussions 'tempered' his 'solitude'. The person remained unidentified for nearly two decades until Gerard Henderson, Director of the Sydney Institute, divulged that Kerr informed him his great 'consoler' in his 'pre-Remembrance Day 1975 solitude' was indeed Sir Anthony Mason of the High Court. Kerr acknowledged he had spoken to Mason 'direct' and that there had been 'more than one contact'.[25] That was quite uncharacteristic of the normally prudent Mason—and, as circumstances unfolded, thoroughly unwise.

The most serious charge that can honestly be levelled against Kerr is that he denied Whitlam natural justice by denying him a fair hearing. On 30 October Kerr raised doubts about the authority of the Senate to block Supply over a convivial lunch with Whitlam and James McClelland. He referred to the written opinion of Bob Ellicott QC and with Balmain working-class robustness allegedly dismissed it as 'b . . . . . .t'. Yet, when Kerr acted, the written opinion he produced to justify his actions very much paralleled Ellicott's opinion. Kerr did not candidly discuss with Whitlam the problems he saw; though he mentioned it in his published work, he did not reveal his apprehension about time rapidly running out for the Government in which it could govern legitimately. Nor did he canvass options, outside a brief flutter at the prospect of a delayed half-Senate election. Without any warning at all, on the morning of 11 November 1975 Kerr pounced on Whitlam, sacking him.

A man in Kerr's position acting with consistent firmness and fairness, open and direct to all parties, demonstrating his capacity to act decisively, would have etched an indelible and respected place in our history texts. What a difference this conduct would have made in the record that counts. But Kerr feared dismissal by Whitlam, a possibility which he claimed was made apparent to him on more than one occasion. In mid-1975, discussing the ejection of New South Wales Premier Lang by Governor Game, Whitlam reputedly said to Kerr, that in such circumstances 'It's a race to see who gets rid of whom first'. And then later again, at a dinner at Government House in early October to honour the Prime Minister of Malaysia, Tun Abdul Razak, Whitlam stated in the presence of Kerr and Razak, during discussion on the current political situation, that 'It depends whether I get in and sack him before he sacks me'. An article 'planted' in early October in the *Melbourne Herald* through a journalist sympathetic to Labor, speculating on Kerr's early recall, also heightened Kerr's paranoia as he grappled with these momentous problems—if the attention he gives this in his memoir is anything to go by.[26]

To frighten Kerr further, there was also Whitlam's peremptory and justifiable dismissal of Queensland Governor Sir Colin Hannah, as one of the three State Governors commissioned to act as administrator of Australia on occasions of the unavailability of the governor-general. Hannah had made a strident, almost hysterical public attack on the Whitlam Government as Governor of Queensland. A former military officer whose training equipped him to respond to difficult issues in a reflexively, physical way, Hannah's transgression was not so much that he suffered from an excessive notion of his own importance, which he did, but rather in the intemperate manner he assailed the national government at a public function in Brisbane. In doing that he soared dangerously above his natural level of pomposity. Kerr has declared that he was concerned to save the Sovereign from embarrassment and protect her from the turmoil which would arise were she to have been drawn into this turbulent antipodean hootenanny. That is a thoroughly commendable objective, as the Queen would doubtless have been grateful to have been insulated from the rough and tumble of a major Australian political crisis by her Governor-General. On the other hand the royals and their advisers have had a great deal of experience in handling sticky problems, including some rather rough customers at the frontiers of their far-flung realm. The Queen's private secretary's letter to the then immediately retired Speaker of the House of Representatives, Gordon Scholes, of 17 November 1975 is redolent of the way they would have handled any attempt to draw them into the conflict:

> . . . but it would not be proper for her [the Queen] to intervene in person in matters which are so clearly placed within the jurisdiction of the Governor-General by the Constitution Act.

In other words, it is up to us to fix those things we have broken, especially where the Constitution explicitly imposes that responsibility on Australia. Similarly, if Whitlam had sought to dismiss Kerr I am certain the palace would have taken a deliberately careful and long look at the proposal, by which time the crisis would have been well and truly sorted out within Australia. This, incidentally, is something Whitlam acknowledges more or less in his autobiographical retort to Kerr, *The Truth of the Matter*. The relatively uncomplicated sacking of Hannah as a stand-by administrator took about a fortnight to finalise. In the meantime, the political lunacy of such a heavy-handed attempt to cower and enfeeble the office of Governor-General, especially at a time of great political crisis, would have generated a whirlwind of resentment in the electorate. The political consequences for the perpetrator of such foolishness would be fairly self-evident, I should have thought.

There is no excuse nor mitigating factor for Kerr's failure to act with directness and clarity in his dealings with Whitlam. It may well have been, as I have argued, that his judgment and strength of personality under pressure were flawed. There is another observation I should make here: Kerr should have recognised that his decision would have become thoroughly unpopular with a large section of the community and that hostility would have endured long after the event. I believe it would have been proper for him to have announced at an appropriate point that he recognised that his decision, as essential as it was in his view, would be misunderstood and resented by many; and that, for the sake of the reputation of the office he occupied and for the comity of the Australian community, he would therefore step down as Governor-General as soon as it was clear a government had been elected. Had he done that, there would have been widespread respect for the quality of his character and many of his critics would have been inclined to be more respectful, even if grudgingly, of his actions. Kerr did seriously contemplate this option, but after retiring to his private quarters to cogitate, another view apparently prevailed and the option lost all savour.

And that is about all that there was to 1975, at least as far as I am concerned. A stupendous happening at the time; but now, as our history has continued to unfold, an event of more recognisable proportions. I only hope that today, when just about every person and institution involved and buffeted by those events has been rehabilitated, that Kerr will be looked upon in a kinder and less subjective light. After all he did not create the crisis, as it has been described. As the vernacular has it, he was on a 'hiding to nothing' whatever he did. Had he dug in behind a set of principles whose consequences were to uphold the Whitlam Government, he would have had just as much obloquy heaped upon him as he received for supporting those principles which, in their effect, favoured the Fraser-led coalition. There may have been weaknesses in his character and defects in his judgment, which is to say he was human, but I have no evidence that his motives were sinister. I believe John Kerr was a good man who, at worst, erred on this occasion; it would be a mark of maturity if more of us would acknowledge that he was far from an evil man.

My judgment in this matter has changed little over the years. I always sought as much as possible to avoid direct *ad hominem* criticism of Kerr; several other senior members of the Whitlam Government adopted the same attitude. Our criticism was directed more to constitutional weaknesses, as we interpreted them, those which conflicted with the principles of responsible government and which allowed this event to occur. When our own sore blunders were added in, the right atmosphere was created for Fraser's stubborn, opportunistic and eventually successful drive for government. The one exception to my policy of avoiding public criticism of Kerr occurred in 1979 when he was made Australian Ambassador to UNESCO. The manner of his appointment was interpreted by many—most notably in the newspapers—as evidence of a 'favour', as it were. Fraser's handling of this appointment was so appalling that I had cause to wonder briefly whether the relationship between Kerr and Fraser during the dramatic events of late 1975 may not have been as straightforward as I had presumed, doubts which I also referred to in Parliament. But those concerns came and went quickly as I became convinced that this was a Fraser blunder and that there was never a conspiracy.

Conspiracy theories were pandemic in the wake of 11 November 1975. None has stood the test of time. Though much was made of them, Kerr's addresses to the Union Club in Sydney and the Indian Law Institute in 1975 are unexceptional and enunciate orthodoxies which should be followed by any governor-general faithfully discharging the duties of his office; furthermore, they had been enunciated by many authorities before. There is no menacing hint in either, as some seemed to find, of what was to happen in November 1975. Neither Fraser nor his official motor vehicle were concealed about Government House as one story had it. An innocent comment by a military aide about that aide's successor was misunderstood.[27] The offices at Government House are still not soundproofed, contrary to a claim that they were at about the time of this crisis. The military was not engaged in discussions about a potential call-out, but more appropriately, given the priorities in peacetime, there was a discussion about a farewell banquet for a retiring defence chief. No doubt the CIA had quite a number of clever operators working for them in various parts of the world, but as an organisation it was not smart enough to orchestrate this extraordinary event. Let us be fair and give credit where it is due—these events were all the work of local politicians. A more comprehensive and effective rebuttal of many of these somewhat overwrought speculations from that time has been set out by the former Official Secretary at Government House of the time, now Sir David Smith.[28]

Oakes, Kelly, Buckley, and many other commentators at the time, were aware that discussions had occurred between Kerr and another person. They claimed the gist of the talks had been relayed to the

Liberals. To paraphrase Buckley, 'word had been passed on down the line' to Lynch. This loose chatter of Kerr's was undoubtedly a product of the isolation and loneliness he experienced at Yarralumla; not the evidence of a conspiracy but of a lonely mind and a loose tongue. Nonetheless, one cannot excuse this indiscretion. It was also uncharacteristically imprudent, given his eminent public position, to have been so indiscreet. As to the controversy over whether Kerr telephoned Fraser on the morning of 11 November 1975, and if so what he discussed and was that proper—we know he did telephone Fraser at about 10 a.m. that day. He stipulated that if made Prime Minister Fraser would first have to agree to (i) a double dissolution immediately, (ii) no legal persecution of members of the Whitlam Government from matters arising from the Khemlani loans affair and, (iii) no new policy and no new appointments before the election. In the circumstances I feel Kerr's contact and his stipulations were prudent and proper. Stipulation (ii) led to Attorney-General Ellicott's downfall. Ellicott resigned rather than follow Fraser's direction that the government would take over a private citizen's prosecution for conspiracy (initiated by one Danny Sankey, arising from aspects of the unorthodox loan initiatives) against Whitlam, Murphy and Cairns in Queanbeyan Petty Sessions Court, with a view to ending it. In setting (ii) as a precondition Kerr, it seems to me, considerately sought to prevent any vindictive persecution of Whitlam and his colleagues. Denied the enormous resources of government in defending such a prosecution, they could all have been financially broken by the experience. That was a decent and proper act by Kerr and an honourable discharge of a solemn undertaking by Fraser. There were a number of senior coalition members present when this telephone call was taken by Fraser, including Senator Reg Withers who was standing opposite Fraser at Fraser's table. While Withers could not hear what Kerr said, he was able to read the points outlined above, for Fraser wrote them on a piece of paper as Kerr spoke to him.

What if there is a next time? The late J. R. Odgers, former Clerk of the Senate, has suggested that on 11 November 1975 the Labor Government could have moved a resolution in the House of Representatives, while stalling in the Senate, 'rescinding all votes on the Appropriation Bills and sending a message from the House of Representatives acquainting that House of the decision of the House of Representatives and desiring the return of the Bills'. If the Senate ignored this resolution the 'House could have instructed the Speaker that the Bills (when returned to it from the Senate according to parliamentary procedure) were not to be presented to the Governor-General for assent'.[29] Had this occurred chaos could have ensued. The Fraser minority government would then have been without supply. On Kerr's interpretation of a legitimate government being one that could deliver supply, it would have been without that legitimacy. This could have left the parliament jammed in grid lock, the community startled and confused and Kerr's plans in tatters. Odgers' solution was to propose a permanent appropriation for Supply to cover any election, a very practical suggestion which, in the way of so many worthwhile ideas from within our political processes, has never been acted on. Without a permanent appropriation for Supply to cover election periods, should there ever be a re-run of the Senate conduct leading up to 11 November 1975, the Kerr approach would have no chance of resolving the dilemma such conduct would create once more. The political processes could then again enter an unprecedented period of turmoil and anarchy.

Whitlam failed to anticipate the course of action Odgers outlined for two reasons: his failure to have at hand and consult with a reliable, small group of trusted and experienced advisers to develop options as events unfolded (as Fraser did); and his single-minded presumption that the Governor-General would pliably behave according to his will. What Whitlam did do, and for which he seems to have got no credit, once his bluffing tactics had been brought to a dead halt by Kerr, was to properly accept the constitutional processes and go to the people. Some of his speeches might have been fiery, and with every justification from his viewpoint and that of a host of his fellow Australians, but his conduct was impeccably constitutional and correct.

In the end, however, it was what Kerr did that mattered. It is my view that his actions were legal and proper, although somewhat hasty. We in the Labor Party may not have cared for this fate of ours, and we protested long and loud. Our anger, and the angst caused by this experience, however, does not make our removal invalid. Its rightness, I restate, was confirmed by the overwhelming public endorsement of the Governor-General's actions, implicit in the subsequent election result.

PART V

RETURN TO
OPPOSITION:
1976–1983

Demoralisation and Defeat

We re-entered Opposition—that role with which we were sadly all too familiar—badly demoralised and infected with disabling bitterness. Fraser was detested to a point where the judgment of many among us was distorted on too many matters of importance. There was too much preoccupation with the personality and insufficient attention to real issues. Governor-General Kerr was reviled and there was much hostility to the institution of the Crown.[1] The confused republican response which evolved from this ignored the fact that our downfall had been executed by the novel application of Senate authority and the Governor-General's reserve powers; all the handiwork of full-blooded Australians. On these things our responses were largely elemental, with a good dose of vengefulness too.

So many of our best human resources had been sacrificed at the election, that the task of rebuilding would have to be undertaken with limited materials. Yet, the Caucus was in no condition to robustly re-assert itself as part of any tough fightback; it was thoroughly demoralised. Labor had just returned from a national election where it had suffered one of its most humiliating defeats ever. My own rueful meditations probably exemplified this generally prevailing mood of sombre defeatism. The Labor Party with which I had grown up was an institution proudly conscious of its achievements. There were even Labor historians in academia who polished impressive Labor achievements from the past. No other party had this sort of systematic, scholarly structure for chronicling and embellishing its accomplishments. The remarkable thing about Labor was not so much that it had produced a volume of history of which it was proud and which firmly nourished its spirit, although that was impressive enough; the curious thing was it had done this with such little experience in government, which is where history is made. The Labor Party, however, used those brief opportunities to good effect; ideologically it was interventionist and redistributionist and initiated many reformist policies in government. The conservative parties, philosophically, believed in small government and minimising interventionist policies. But, as the Menzies record displays, their faith found little expression in practice.

Yet behind that facade of institutionalised confidence there was a private fear shared by many. Was Labor a party, by its nature, largely condemned to Opposition? A party only rarely and briefly permitted to hold the reins of government? To the time of the Whitlam Government the Labor Party had spent fifty-six of the first seventy-two years of nationhood in Opposition. Nearly half that Opposition was endured in the period between the 1949 defeat of Chifley and the election of Whitlam. Moreover, there was the knowledge that Labor had a propensity to self-destruct at times when it should have been reinforcing its claims to remain in office or relishing the prospect of coming into power. This time Labor's propensity was not for Greek tragedy but bathos. No national government had launched itself into its commission for government with greater confidence and enthusiasm than the Whitlam Labor Government. None had brought its period of government to such a humiliating close and after such a brief period, by its own bizarre conduct.

How long was the servitude of Opposition to be endured this time round? Ten years? Twenty years? More perhaps? The situation was absolutely horrid to contemplate. Then, when things were so bad it was inconceivable they could get worse, the unbelievable happened. Reported on the front pages of Rupert Murdoch's newspapers was a new scandal—an abortive attempt by Whitlam, incited by Bill Hartley of the Victorian 'old left', to negotiate a $US500 000 (about $1.75 million in current money values) donation to Labor Party campaign funds in late 1975, from official Iraqi sources. The disclosures came in early 1976. Whitlam's shaky position was further undermined when it appeared that the national secretary of the Party, David Combe, was being left isolated as a scapegoat in this fanciful escapade. Had this distasteful exercise been exposed before the election, Labor probably would have lost another 3 to 5 per cent of its vote. Reputedly, Murdoch personally wrote much of the copy detailing this exposé, but regardless of who wrote the material, the style was overkill and that saved Whitlam's political hide. There were Caucus members, I was one of them, who did not approve of what Whitlam had done. On the other hand we cared even less for the notion that Murdoch's newspapers could depose and choose our leaders for us.

At the time, I steadily resisted urgings from colleagues, Jim McClelland, Mick Young and John Button among many others, that I should challenge Whitlam for leadership of the parliamentary party. I had and retain great personal affection for Whitlam, despite the problems we had in government between 1972 and 1975. I was, nonetheless, so devastated at the foolishness which unceremoniously flung us back into Opposition, that I fretted about the future of the Party and for my own career prospects. I was traumatised to be the only Labor survivor in the whole State of Queensland, and then by a very narrow margin. What were the alternatives? As much as I might not care for it, I was a professional politician, locked into an occupation that gave a high public profile but low employability elsewhere. Others have had this experience too.[2] The sorts of things I might do well and which were immediately available to me were unappealing to my temperament and perhaps more so to my sense of fastidiousness. All this at a time when our dependent family were at their most expensive to support and at a stage in their education critical to their future career prospects. My options were massively limited; restricted to going onwards in politics and trying to make the best of it, or else to exit the lifestyle completely and confront dubious alternative career prospects.

My confusion and irresolution were added to by an unfortunate event in September 1976. Dallas was assaulted at the front door of our home in Ipswich by a young man who, we later learnt, had been surreptitiously loitering about the local area for a few days judging which home would be the most vulnerable to his criminal purposes. Ours it proved to be. The house was on a large battleaxe-shaped corner block on the crest of a rise, unfenced on the two boundaries opening onto the public thoroughfare, and set well back in the midst of a dense thicket of native trees and shrubs. The children were at school and I was in Canberra. Dallas struggled fiercely for she genuinely apprehended her life was at risk as she was wrestled to the ground. Her assailant attempted to strike her head with a largish piece of river rock, part of an ornamental garden at the house entrance. Her screams were effectively stifled as the collar of her frock was twisted tightly about her throat. Somehow, through a combination of Dallas' desperate resistance and miraculous luck, her assailant ran off. She was admitted to the Ipswich General Hospital for several days with acute shock, various bruises and a nasty back injury which even after all these years causes her disability. She was thereafter also prone to periods of tense apprehension and insecurity. The police were extremely efficient, and quickly apprehended the offender, a juvenile, who was detained for psychiatric treatment by order of the court.

Some weeks later, one of our children discovered a long carving knife with a synthetic ivory handle hidden in the base of a thick clump of golden cane palm, close to the front entrance of our house. It had not been seen by any of us before and speculation about it being there leads one to a fairly obvious conclusion. A few years after this event, and well short of the period of the attacker's sentence, we were stunned to read in the *Courier-Mail* that the young man concerned, who had gained early release from his counselling, had been convicted of the violent sexual assault of a mother at her home in a not too distant suburb of Ipswich one night. He had been working there as a painter during the day, during which time he had coldly calculated the most effective method of his assault.

With this distressing experience for the family I continued to worry about what to do with my future. Life in national politics has its compensations but it can be selfishly demanding. Dallas and I found about half of our matrimonial life was spent in occupational separation. Of the remainder, a high proportion required intense joint electoral activity from both of us, particularly as we represented a large marginal electorate with a sizeable rural area. Was it worth persisting with? I ruminated that had I persevered with law studies perhaps I would not want to contest the 1977 election. I could enter the practice of law—to no doubt eventually profit from running a real estate conveyancing mill during the booming eighties, probably on the Gold Coast, while making 'interesting' associations with squat men in white shoes and tropical suits. Those unappealing meditations aside, I decided to resume part-time law studies with the intention of not recontesting my parliamentary seat at the next election and instead completing the course full-time thereafter. But as I lingered about the Parliament, the infectious influence of politics reasserted itself. I jettisoned this gloomy reverie. Instead, I trod a narrow path which eventually wound its way to Yarralumla.

I re-entered the Federal Parliamentary Labor Party (FPLP) Executive when a vacancy occurred, after having not contested a position following the 1975 election. By mid-1977, when all FPLP office bearing positions were automatically thrown open to caucus preselection, according to then recently adopted standing orders, I contested the leadership. I spoke with Keating earlier, suggesting I was contemplating contesting the deputy's role occupied by Uren. Privately I was half-hearted about the prospect for in spite of the many differences now separating Uren and me, the difficulty I had with his rigid ideological attitudes and his impatience with other points of view, I admired the way he made a notable success of his life. Like me, he had only had a modest full-time education and came from a battler's home. He was a war hero to me and a great sportsman. He had driven himself to success as a branch manager with Woolworths, overcoming his educational limitations. He had other difficulties to overcome including, I discovered, a reading problem. (He was not alone in possessing this defect; there were others who made it into subsequent Labor ministries who also sought to compensate for their disability the way Uren did.) To overcome his reading defect he took oral briefings from advisers, retaining sufficient of the detail to satisfactorily meet any challenges later in the Parliament, from his bureaucrats and elsewhere. Keating, meanwhile, quickly outlined a persuasive case as to why the deputy's office was a consolation prize and not to be seriously entertained by anyone with genuine leadership claims. I was influenced by the cogency of his presentation—but only because I wanted to be. I called on Whitlam as a courtesy and we amiably discussed this prospective challenge. I told him I would not be organising numbers for myself nor encouraging others to do so, an undertaking I absolutely honoured. He mentioned that while he had not been keen about resuming leadership after the 1975 election debacle, necessity forced him to and having gone that far he felt he had to finish off the task.

Clyde Cameron, a superb political plotter whose congenital Machiavellianism had destroyed as many ambitions as it had made (often doing both to the same person over time), urged me to visit Gordon Bryant, who was hospitalised at the time, to sew up his vote. Bryant and I, previously long-standing friends on the Left, had fallen out after I became Treasurer. He regarded me as an unimaginative economic manager standing in the way of progress. I acknowledged he was immeasurably more imaginative than me but I feared the national economy could scarcely afford his sort of luxury. I declined to visit him, believing the gesture would not be sincere. Whitlam, who reciprocated Bryant's distaste for him, was reluctantly pressured into visiting him by his backers. Bryant voted against me. When the challenge came, and as dictated automatically by the rules, I opposed Whitlam. Keating, as it happened, contested the deputy's office! I was beaten by two votes and Keating was defeated by three votes. I had hitherto dismissed any suggestion of leadership ambitions, very sensibly ruling myself out on the grounds of deeply ingrained personal deficiencies.[3] It may seem perverse, but I was glad that I did so well yet did not win. A firm claim for the future had been lodged should it ever be needed, while Gough had been spared a humiliating defeat. He certainly did not deserve that.

One colleague who had not shared my doubts about my leadership potential was Jim McClelland of the Senate. After the 1975 election debacle he became extraordinarily bitter towards Whitlam and was frequently lobbying me to oppose him for the leadership at the 1977 mid-term ballot. This I eventually decided to do, but no thanks to McClelland's importuning, for I had seen enough of him to conclude he was something of a political gadabout whose loyalties could move mercurially. The only thing certain about his moves was that they would not damage his interests. McClelland started his youthful political involvement as a Trotskyite, but soon moved from that left extreme to well across to the right of the political spectrum. There, he collaborated with the Groupers in the trade union movement, a source of particularly lucrative industrial law practice. Next he garnered support from the right wing NSW Labor machine to enter the Senate. In the Senate, with the election of a Whitlam government becoming a more realistic prospect every day but his prospects of becoming a Cabinet minister in it rather slender, he mobilised vain Caucus ambitions to impose a twenty-seven member Cabinet on an incoming Labor government. This was an absolutely stupid decision, damaging to the interests of the subsequent Labor government, but beneficial to McClelland's aspirations. Then, much later he denounced the foolishness of this decision as though he had always been opposed to it. In the Caucus he made another characteristically dextrous move in courting much affection and support from the Left to become a minister. Subsequently, as another Senate preselection approached and with no winnable place for him on a left ticket, he quickly got back in favour with the NSW Right. As Labour minister he caused the Left much heartburn by adopting tough industrial policies characterised by them as 'union bashing'.[4] By then it did not matter—he was back in favour with the Right.

In actively conspiring to undermine Whitlam's leadership in Opposition in 1976 and 1977, he attacked Whitlam's character. On the day of the 1977 ballot for the Caucus leadership McClelland repented and announced that he would have to 'stick with his principles' and support Whitlam instead of me. He personally apologised to me after this public announcement, explaining that 'on principle' he could not walk out on an old friend like Whitlam. I casually advised him not to worry, I had not been counting on his vote. Although my vote increased in Oxley, something of a spin-off from my narrow loss in the leadership vote, the 1977 elections were a worse result for Labor than that of 1975. Kerry Sibraa of NSW and a Sussex Street favourite lost his Senate berth, an outcome anticipated by the Party. Shortly after the election, Premier Wran appointed McClelland a judge in NSW, promptly creating a Senate vacancy for Sibraa to fill within a matter of days, while also amplifying McClelland's career satisfaction at a time when the latter deemed that further interesting parliamentary prospects had disappeared. Not long after that, he would animatedly discuss Wran in various unworthy ways. Later, in the golden and hoary days of his retirement, he wrote a number of newspaper columns in which he seemed to fret about the loss of a true left vision and principle by Labor parliamentarians. By now he was embracing various popular radical stances of the chattering classes. McClelland was an extraordinarily agile politician. The only problem was when he moved you could never be sure whether he was going to zig or zag. His was a particularly hard act to follow and an even more dangerous one to stand in front of.

A new Leader of the Opposition

I became Leader of the Opposition after the 1977 election, having proceeded to that Caucus election with certain misgivings. I knew only too well my shortcomings for the task. Media analysts put them forward cogently enough once I was elected to this position: a natural diffidence of character some described as an inferiority complex, caution about others, a tendency to personal remoteness, a conviction that as I could adequately lead myself, others too should be able to lead themselves—all very much products of a disturbed childhood or so I was informed by the commentators. Above all, I knew I did not have an abounding and undentable faith in my own infallibility or in my providential selection above all others to lead my colleagues to salvation. And I knew myself to be a worrier, as I still am. When I cobbled the 1975 budget together I spent endless moments worrying. A mistake on a major item could cause untold harm elsewhere; to the economy, to ordinary people in the community who trusted me, to my party as a government. More than that, my tendency to worry showed and was interpreted as a lack of personal confidence. Perhaps, and yet it seems to me only fools and megalomaniacs could be devoid of doubts in such onerous positions of public responsibility where miscalculations can so adversely affect others.

There was also my voice: thin, high-pitched, reedy, even whining, or so I was informed after my election. I took to reading aloud randomly selected tracts from the Bible, alone each morning at Canberra, before my burnt muesli and skim milk, in the interests of putting a bit more timbre in my voice. Senator Susan Ryan at a later stage arranged for one of her contacts, the theatre director George Whaley, to give me voice control lessons. Whaley is an inspired theatre director but he surely counts me as a case too difficult for even his great talents. These physical exercises, to relax me, had me crouching half-forward, swivelling at the hips from side to side, rumbling guttural noises in the back of my throat, my head lolling about. I was not sure whether I was supposed to assume the persona of someone half-demented or identify with some early link in the primate chain of evolution. I felt uneasy being remade in such a way. Whatever my defects the flaws were the authentic me, while this was a process for creating artificiality. I soon terminated this fudge, if somewhat arbitrarily.

Then the matter of my dress seemed to cause others a lot of heartburn. One had to dress the part of success, I was counselled by personal staff, to impress the 'movers and shakers'. But on dress I drew a rigid line. As I put it more than once, at the time—I dressed for bodily comfort in a given climate and to keep out of gaol. I had no intention of togging up like the head male floorwalker in ladies lingerie at David Jones or Myers. I am proud to say the most I have ever paid for a suit is $400, even then regarding myself as having been considerably overcharged. Barry Cohen, fashionable men's clothier from ritzy parts of North Sydney, confirmed that I had certainly not been overcharged, but he was not at all sympathetic to me. Long experience in public life taught me that the time dandies spend admiring themselves and worrying about how they look leaves too little for hard, creative work. When I employed male research staff, speech writers and journalists, I favoured the casual to unconventional dressers, as indifference to dress fashion seemed to go with lateral problem-solving, an important element in reformist policy development. The best dressed person I ever saw in my office was Alan Ramsey, the journalist, and that was only once when he wore a suit to a friend's wedding. But as my father used to say, it's not the cost of the suit, it's the quality of the person in the clobber that counts.

How was I able to recognise these harsh truths as matters of fact? Any self-respecting journalist will tell you that if something appears three times in cold typeset print, it has to be true. And as I saw my failings catalogued many more times than that, on this principle alone I stood irrevocably condemned many times over for my transgressions of manner and style. I should try to be as critically candid about myself, as I can be about others, which is never an easy challenge. On that basis I acknowledge that even if none of those criticisms had ever been made publicly, it would have made them no less true. Certainly, I was the best equipped on ability to be leader of those making themselves available, but that does not say much in favour of any of us who were available.

The role of Opposition Leader must be the toughest job in the country. There is only one tougher; namely being Labor Opposition Leader. Opposition has no executive power. When it speaks on policy it is discussing the equivalent of a wish list. An Opposition has two very difficult tasks: firstly, to develop policies, and that takes quite some time; then, before it can execute its wishes, to win government, when the next election may be some years away. In the meantime, Government speaks on a daily basis, if it is so inclined, with the decisive authority of executive power. What Government says and does is sought-after news. To gain attention, Opposition has to create news angles; yet the artifices and gimmicks needed to be fashioned to attract media attention to a proposal, given the imperatives of television coverage, can be very risky. The dividing line is fine. Oppositions, furthermore, are expected to oppose, yet the width of a human hair separates acceptable criticism from whingeing. Where the actual crossover point lies tends to vary with the views, and in some cases the party political disposition, of particular public affairs commentators. There is another important factor: a leader has to surrender some of his intellectual independence if he has strong views on particular subjects which have the potential to open up differences within his team. This does not, or at least should not, mean he settles for the lowest common denominator of popular appeal; rather, the outspoken independence of the past has to be curbed and more tactful methods adopted.

Both of the major parties have structured factions, and with Labor these are more tightly organised and disciplined now than when I was Opposition Leader. They have been thoroughly formalised by the voting system used for Caucus elections. There is an advantage here for a leader in that this makes dealing with the internal organisation easier and more predictable. On the other hand, because of the authority of the Caucus to appoint ministries and more particularly shadow ministries in Opposition, a leader's authority can be undermined by the power of the factions, especially where he is attempting to exercise some discipline. In spite of that, a surprising degree of self-discipline is in place in the Labor Party; not only are the factions themselves disciplined, but a notion of fair play is also evident and exercised. Political power barons wheel and deal with one another, clash with opponents, form temporary alliances as faction interest requires, and defend their group's political territory fiercely when challenged. A successful faction leader effectively assumes a full-time role. Usually, a skilful faction chief is rewarded with election to the Ministry or shadow Ministry, at which there should be little wonder, for these people control the ubiquitous 'numbers'. Occasionally the personal stimulation of exercising notable power is all the reward a faction chief wants; but that alone is rare. Not surprisingly, these heavy numbers controllers are rarely effective at developing and persuasively propounding creative policy ideas, doubtless because they find themselves fully extended physically and intellectually in organising, or perhaps more properly 'fixing' the numbers. A Labor

Opposition leader has to tread his way through this uneven field gingerly, set as it is with political bearpits and mantraps. He cannot afford to be part of a faction. On the other hand he cannot remain too apart from them. It is a tricky balancing act. Even factions can have several substrata, which makes dealing with these entities an even more intricate affair. If he misjudges the extent to which he can confront a faction, the leader can unravel the splicing which holds together that extraordinary heterogeneity. While Labor is a single party in name, in fact it is an exceptionally complex coalition—and it cannot be Labor if it is not also emotional. That is why individuals entering the Party with no familiarity of its culture and symbols can experience so much difficulty coming to terms with the manner of its conduct.

Then there is the extra-parliamentary Labor Party. In government the leader as Prime Minister has considerable authority; as he distributes much favour and authority, the cost of his displeasure can be high. Moreover, indiscipline can put a government at risk, the possibility of losing power being a large restraining factor on conduct. In Opposition meanwhile, the leader frequently has to struggle to maintain authority. There is much interfactional jockeying for power, especially the power to determine policy and to lock the Party into favoured initiatives which will be binding in government. Factions will war over such issues at party conferences, while the conflict is consecrated as pursuit of high principle. Sometimes that is the case but often it is about faction barons imposing undertakings, extracting commitments, requiring demonstrations of faithfulness from their foot soldiers, in support of the faction's cause in combat. Paradoxically, there is a common righteousness in defeat among the more ideologically driven factions which irrevocably binds them together. 'We were right. We stand for principle. The opportunists had the numbers . . . ', is a shared language which sustains these tribal groups in a manner, I suspect, redolent of the way in which early Christian groups clung to their faith when confronted by adversity. As well, there is evident careerism developing within the ranks of the two major factions. Factional apprenticeships in them often tend to be served faithfully, albeit uncritically, as a way of proving entitlement to advancement. Non-conformity is treated like an incipient contagion, such are its latent dangers; non-conformists usually have short political lives in the two major factions whereas in Centre Left, alas a declining force now, this quality once flourished handsomely.

In this tortuous process the leader has to be ever alert and ready to confront efforts to lock the Party into policies which would be damaging electorally, no matter how much they might be preferred by a particular faction. A dicey business this, for a leader cannot survive without factional support from some quarter; but exclusive reliance on one quarter is divisive and limits the independence of the leader. In rare instances, the need can arise for the reformulation of a standing policy which has developed into a major electoral impediment. If the issue at contention has become a rallying cause for a particular faction, as was the case with the excessively restrictive uranium mining and export policy of Labor up to 1982, any confrontation proceeds with an overload of politically lethal dangers. It might be that the disability it presents has reached such proportions that it has to be confronted and either changed or leadership relinquished. There is no point in being leader while held hostage to a policy in which you have no faith and which you believe will be a liability to the country if it is imposed on your party in government.

Whitlam sought to short-circuit many of these obstructions to the achievement of his objectives. Yet even he had to retreat from this device on a number of celebrated occasions, as mentioned in an earlier part, for the dominant factions had cut-off points beyond which they would not tolerate violations; not even from so celebrated a leader. After Whitlam, there was no disposition by the

Party at any level to forbear confrontationist tactics from a leader; furthermore, the factions were becoming much more structured, disciplined and intelligently purposeful to be easily pushed about in that way. The days of pre-emptive strikes through unilateral public declarations were largely finished. For my own part, I was jealous of my personal independence. On macro-economic management I was and remain a conservative. On micro-social reform I had and retain liberal redistributional values based on deeply held principles of social justice. The extent to which such ambitions can be fulfilled is determined by the success of macro-economic management. Many of the objectives I wanted to reach on that broad macro-canvas could only succeed with support from the Right. On the other hand, I held my position through the support of the Left. The Left did not so much admire me as despise Hawke. They never forgave him for organising and using them to win the presidency of the ACTU from Harold Souter (the choice of the Right) before, as they had it, deserting them, to join the Right as one of their most energetic opponents, and hammering them remorselessly thereafter.

My act was a tricky one. It meant that neither side was able to embrace me for very long and consequently both sides had reservations about me. As much as I was able to preserve my independence, my role was built on a loose foundation. The NSW Right in particular resented my lack of 'trust' in them—their idea of trust was of course like being asked to settle down with a boa constrictor as a bedmate. Shortly after my election as Leader, NSW President of the Trades and Labour Council and of the Party John Ducker, and NSW Party Secretary Graham Richardson, dined and wined me generously at some expensive Sydney restaurant. With coffee and liqueurs came the offer, too good to knock back—or at least Messrs Ducker and Richardson seemed to believe. Yes they had worked hard to defeat me, and yes they acknowledged I had succeeded with support from the Left; but the Left were embarrassing baggage in the electorate. If I detached myself from the Left, entrusted my future to them, they would shower me with honours. They would make me Prime Minister! I remained reserved through all this, a reaction they regarded as crass and ungrateful and at which they were accordingly pained. Would the guarantee stand up when Hawke arrived in Caucus, I asked, as he certainly would? Well, that would be a new situation, they replied and as it was a couple of years off I was rather getting ahead of myself; and so the discussion went. Ducker announced with the complacency of a successful exponent of the use of raw power, 'We are the biggest, strongest, most successful branch of the Party in Australia. What we say will happen, happens!'. I was to hear variations of that boast many times over the years ahead. Such talk always alienated me for I believed Labor was about the constructive use of power for the benefit of the weak, as much as anything else—not the raw exercise of power for its own sake, or as a means of grabbing any available plunder.

We parted warily. The fate of Geoff Cahill in 1976 instructively dwelt in my mind. Cahill was NSW Branch Secretary in 1976, a shooting star in the party firmament. He had all the right credentials for success in that environment: he was a good Catholic, a sound family man with several children, an active sportsman and effective administrator, and in possession of an appealing personality. In short, a favoured son destined for higher things. He had, however, made a fundamental error. He had commenced thinking for himself, and worse, starting to say what he thought to the party faithful. The people who had made him concluded this independence was dangerous heresy. His views often clashed with the prevailing orthodoxy declared by the New South Wales chiefs. This sort of thing was taken to be dangerous, for it could well prove contagious; therefore it had to be expunged with a strong drenching of full-strength political disinfectant. Cahill was warmly farewelled by some of his sponsors when he left for an extended overseas visit in 1976. When he returned he was met by a lone, stony-faced colleague in an overcoat, hands shoved deeply into his coat pockets, projecting all the charm of a dyspeptic undertaker—none other than Barry Unsworth, later to briefly become Premier of New South Wales. Cahill was then taken to the Trades and Labour Council offices in Sussex Street where, with a total concentration on the task before the several assembled officers seated about a table, a piece of paper was pushed across the table towards him. There was no ceremony, as this was work of a special kind and had to be executed precisely and tidily. Cahill had thus met his date with destiny. The sheet of paper was his resignation, which he was expected to sign without demur. He signed the paper. A little later, the people who had presided over his fall from grace generously praised him for his loyal services to the party faithful and wished him well on his future chosen career path. Little wonder I preferred to have ample open space about me when these people were in my vicinity. The fact is I never had the commitment of the NSW Right. As Graham Richardson has clearly stated in a moment of uncharacteristic candour:

> The truth is that we were always going to challenge [Hayden]; the
> research made it legitimate.[5]

Later I added to my perverse reputation with the Sussex Street power barons by determinedly avoiding entanglement with their fast and flashy business friends. Or maybe it was just a case of me not being able to recognise them—in Queensland those masters of the universe would have been wearing white shoes. I preferred more pedestrian company. The more important reality was that there were fundamental differences of principle separating us. And there was an added complication in that Sydney retains its own peculiar cultural characteristics, its own way of doing things; it remains the larrikin capital of Australia long after the rest of Australia has evolved in other directions. Richardson often lectured me that the art of politics was in giving people what they wanted. From observation that meant catering to the needs and responding to the pressures of the rich, the powerful, the well-connected, of conceding to well-organised, articulate, and often minority interest groups and of then lining up for political kickbacks. Too often the cost of favours, met by taxpayers, exceeded the value of the kickbacks. I preferred to believe that while the art of politics requires some giving, and in a very public and accountable fashion, the over-riding objective is to set national goals based on resource redistribution. In setting such priorities, chief among which in my view are creating a more just society and better attending to community needs, there has to be public consultation and the people's support. The less powerful and poorly organised, that is the greater majority of people, also have rights. Conceding to the demands of the powerful, the well-placed and the articulate too easily might well be to the disadvantage of most people and of the country itself.

As far as I was concerned, the least appealing aspect of the role of Leader was meeting certain expectations of the media. 'Feeding the chooks corn,' as Bjelke-Petersen used to slightingly refer to the process. If you fail to meet a media expectation of providing 'hard copy', at best you will be ignored. More likely you will be publicly birched in their columns. The news media of the Western world thrive on combative news copy. In Australia it has assumed excessive proportions, and among other things helps nourish that peculiar, exaggerated, hectoring form of parliamentary rhetoric which, too frequently, energetically embraces *argumentum ad hominem*. The style is not unique to Australia but the excessive use of it appears to be a characteristic of our parliamentary systems. Excess is more likely to succeed in capturing media attention than understatement. Subtlety and allusion are for wimps, and irony involves the risk of literal interpretation, conveying the opposite impression to that intended.

An incident in early 1978 is an illustration of the expectations on politicians to 'play the game'. I had not long been Opposition

Leader, when I noted that Fraser had intervened in a computer tendering process. This seemed improper and he was challenged. We put Fraser under sustained pressure for several days over his actions. The fact that he was an extraordinarily uncomfortable, even ungainly, parliamentary performer under stress allowed us to exploit standing orders and his own limitations, to keep the issue alive well beyond what should have occurred. Fraser was obviously rattled. After one notably energetic parliamentary exchange a senior journalist, then in the parliamentary gallery, came around to my office to discuss the issue with me. He said effectively, 'The Opposition's going great, but you won't really make this as big an issue for the media as it should be unless you brand it with "scandal", or the "smell of corruption"; you've got to understand what makes a story'. In the upshot, Fraser's personal intervention could only have been described as unwise rather than improper.

Necessity steeled me to do many things as Opposition Leader I had hitherto been able to avoid. I learned to be my own 'bastard' in the Parliament, as Whitlam used to describe the function, even if there was a line beyond which I found it difficult to proceed. Nonetheless, the message from my journalist acquaintance partly reached its target. We became quite effective at making a story for the media, as it were, by exploiting standing orders, drawing out the issue at contention and selecting the more appealing adjectives for the commentators, without quite engaging in the excesses recommended by my media interlocutor. We had a market to reach—the electorate—and our medium was then as it is today, the media. What the media was prepared to carry determined, and still does, the manner of presentation. Professionals in that business might like to deny it, but there is an overarching principle to their practice: no news is good news unless it is bad news. It was a practice which I was glad to leave behind me in the wake of events in early 1983, but not before I had overstepped the mark in late 1982 and attracted a severe media opprobrium for the way in which I raised a tax issue.

Rebuilding

After the spectacular way in which the Whitlam Government had breached the outer limits of prudent economic management, our most important need was to re-establish public trust in our ability to manage the economy soberly. On this score the Party stood almost totally discredited. Ironically, however, the cautious approach I endeavoured to bring to economic management was soon to be condemned by certain Party activists and fringe dwellers. These were people who had soaked in the sweet ambrosia of government spending earlier and who wanted a commitment that Labor would maintain this fiscal lifeline. Our task would be to persistently hammer away and create a credible set of measures over many months to demonstrate that the new management would be different and reliable; a range of other policies relevant to the needs of contemporary society would have to be developed. This would take the best part of a normal parliamentary term, as time-consuming procedures were involved. The task was eventually completed and for the first time careful costings were made, credible revenue measures adopted, and policies selected on the basis of economic and social priorities. We rejected the old haphazard method of policy determination through personal muscle rather than community need. Consequently, when the 1980 election was fought our expenditure and revenue figuring, although initially attacked by Fraser, withstood the brief onslaught convincingly. The joint issues of foreign affairs and defence, in particular, had been an Achilles heel for Labor over decades, although Whitlam had established a rational and acceptable basis for proceeding with them. It was essential that we attend to them in a consistently sober and constructive way, preventing more excitable, self-appointed spokespersons taking the initiative away from the leadership. Most importantly morale, discipline and purpose were restored after the electoral setbacks of 1975 and 1977.

The most immediate task was to deflect elsewhere the hostility towards Kerr and the resentment towards the Crown evident within the FPLP. If the bitterness towards Kerr continued to dominate the conduct of the Party we would make no headway in seeking to restore our credibility in the electorate on the material issues which counted with the community. Though Labor hated Kerr, it did not follow that the rest of the community shared that view, or at least as intensely as some among us did. Republicanism was a confused response to the 1975 crisis and irrelevant to the restoration of Labor's credibility. To lead the troops away from Kerr and the Crown, one had to make the right sorts of noises sometimes in order to encourage greater engagement elsewhere. Where was elsewhere? Malcolm Fraser was the most obvious and legitimate target. He was in the Parliament and able to defend himself. He was also widely disliked, even by many of those who had supported him against Labor. His harsh, unforgiving personality as a public figure we felt might well make this a successful tactic. The trick would be to successfully link Fraser to issues but then to focus more on the issue itself rather than his personality.

There were bonuses. Fraser's poor strategic sense resulted in a number of ministerial casualties being bagged by the Opposition. In 1978 Finance Minister Eric Robinson was required to stand down as a result of questions about the conduct of an electoral redistribution. Opposition tactics forced a judicial inquiry, but Robinson was cleared. Senator Reg Withers, Government Senate Leader, however, was winged in full flight, to be forced out of the Ministry by Fraser following the findings of the inquiry. Withers, as the minister responsible for electoral matters, had been found guilty of an impropriety by the McGregor Royal Commission of Inquiry in having sought to influence a change of name for an electorate without declaring his motives to the electoral redistribution commissioners. Then it was Ian Sinclair's turn to stand down as a minister. He was to face a trial in the Supreme Court concerning

private business dealings which had been aired extensively in the
Parliament. After Sinclair there were more to come: damaging
matters were raised in the Parliament about the management of
another minister, Peter Nixon; and then later, Michael MacKellar
and John Moore, two more ministers, had to depart the Ministry
over a faulty declaration in respect of property of small value
brought into Australia by the former as accompanied luggage.

A more adroit leader would have avoided most of these
problems. Fraser's vulnerable point was that he was an uneasy
rather than spontaneous parliamentary performer. He was also an
unconvincing moraliser whose punishments meted out to errant
ministers were usually excessive. For instance, Withers'
transgression was rather trivial, yet Fraser sacked him. The
punishment was so out of proportion to the offence that we were
stunned. As Withers later explained to me, his offence had been a
long-standing one, namely successfully protecting Phil Lynch in
1977 when Fraser sought to sack him in relation to some of Lynch's
business dealings. Whereas these had been criticised publicly,
Fraser's hostility to Lynch was as much as anything of a highly
personal nature. As a close family member of Fraser's put it,
discussing Lynch in Withers' hearing: 'That little man . . . Irish
Catholic . . . father a railway fettler . . . had no place in *our* [my
emphasis] party.' There was a far worse aspect to Fraser's conduct.
While Fraser severely punished Withers and subjected Robinson to
great stress, he did not disclose he had been told by Robinson once
and Withers three times, in the period before he (Fraser) set up a
royal commission into these matters, that Withers had spoken to
Pearson, the Chief Electoral Officer, about the electoral name
change. After the adverse findings of the inquiry, Fraser, who did
not appear before that body, unsuccessfully pressured Robinson to
sign a statement, effectively an alibi for Fraser's dissembling
conduct. In sacking Withers, Fraser excluded from the meeting
several ministers—Killen, Guilfoyle, Viner—who might have

opposed him. Fraser, later, was evidently mystified with Robinson's public characterisation of him as a 'bastard'.

We also developed the tactic of moving censure or no confidence motions in the Parliament over some issue which had become known to us, concerning ministerial propriety most usually. Fraser would be flummoxed by these sudden developments. Instead of grasping the debate by its tusks and hurling it back at us, he would move to gag discussion. This suited us fine. We would exploit the standing orders sufficiently to get some of the essence of our charges out, enough for the media to be streaking off with the issue, leaving question marks all over the place. The then Speaker, the late Sir Billy Snedden, who wasted no affection on Fraser after being deposed by him in 1975, was agreeably tolerant of our points as we struggled to get something telling on the record. Then, another round would follow on the morrow. If we were lucky we could keep the matter before the public for the sitting week; very occasionally we would manage to keep it running into the succeeding sitting week, depending on how Fraser handled the matter. We could always rely on him being his own worst enemy. Some may look askance at these tactics, but the Parliament, as it presently functions and with incessant demands from the media for a headline, is a forum which provides its own form of theatre. In that context these were legitimate tactics.

I had learnt a major lesson from observing the unfolding of the Khemlani loans fiasco. If Labor had been candid when that matter was initially raised in the Parliament, it would have fared much better. Arguably, that issue would have had a short life, provided further overtures for funds had been terminated on the instant. But by engaging in evasive and less than full responses, and by being overbearing in some cases, a never ending impression of sleaziness, even of dishonest conduct was created. In the end, those impressions were exploited to the full by our opponents. The other thing I learnt from Whitlam—something which was confirmed by the reactions to Fraser's dogged efforts to defer resolutions critical of his government—is to always take on a major censure or no confidence debate immediately and do it with the serious style Menzies inevitably adopted on such occasions. If it is not disposed of promptly, the issue swings menacingly above the government until more often than not it comes crashing down on its head. Meanwhile, the unsubstantiated charges also tend to monopolise commentary at the expense of attention to the government's legislative programme.

My first national conference as leader of the FPLP was in 1979 at Adelaide. For me, this was a test of wit and will and of course the numbers, holding the Party to moderate, workable policies acceptable to the community. It was during that conference that Hawke and I had a celebrated falling out. Hawke was convenor of the economics committee. He sent a message that he could not attend the conference to steer through his committee report because of a major industrial dispute he was handling; the report proposed, beneath a thin cosmetic layer, a referendum on prices and incomes. I thought this rather strange because in 1974 when, as a result of irresistible Caucus pressure, Whitlam had reluctantly put such a proposal at a referendum, Hawke had vigorously opposed the incomes proposition as a matter of 'high principle' and 'social justice'. His passionate opposition had helped defeat that referendum. I did not care for the proposal as I do not believe you can fix prices or wages by fiat, except perhaps over a fairly short time frame, and any such attempts can have dislocative economic effects. A proposition was put to me by John Ducker that the New South Wales delegation had organised the numbers to carry the referendum proposal. He invited me to a 'broadly representative' breakfast comprising luminaries from the Right, who met each morning of the conference in this way to map out their tactics and strategy for the day ahead. There I would hear their views and 'surely they were entitled to have their views heard by the Leader'. New South Wales was after all the biggest, the strongest and so on.

Uren got wind of the breakfast and that morning buttonholed me in the hotel foyer. He kept stabbing me in the chest with his large, pointed forefinger as he issued a stream of threats about what would happen to me if I voted for the Hawke proposal. It was an inelegant exchange for, like anyone else, I cannot stand people trying to push me about, especially if they use physical intimidation—at least Uren was left under no illusion about what I thought of his tactics. At that stage the Left was prepared to support a referendum on prices but wages were sacrosanct, an impossible option. His *sine qua non* was quarterly wage adjustments, and little else, something which left me as cold as the dual referendum proposal. There was not much to choose from but as I had started my push on a prices/wages policy, I felt I had to take something away from the conference. I could of course have made a stand on principle with a few like-minded supporters, opposing both proposals, then depart the conference with a profound sense of righteousness. In those circumstances, however, I would be leaving completely repudiated by the Party and thoroughly discredited before the public. A stand of that kind is an extravagant luxury for a team leader who wants to make as good a fist of his task as possible. When only frail materials are available, the leader has no choice but to crimp together the best result he can; he can always make a suitable re-run at the issue to try for a better result later. I thought about the alternatives, reasoned that if we were to win the next election and the dual referendum was part of the party platform, it would be an item at the end of the 'never to be got to list' of proposals. I would ignore it in any policy speech. The general pitch of the resolution otherwise was quite saleable. Thus did I attend the breakfast and unenthusiastically agree to support the referendum proposition.

The party president, Neal Batt, at some early stage of the conference had been telephoning Hawke and urging him to attend, as he believed the numbers were tight on this issue. I was asked to go to the room, just off the conference floor, where Batt was talking to Hawke. Batt said to Hawke that he would pass the telephone to me to allow me to reinforce his message. Hawke immediately explained why it was impossible for him to leave the industrial dispute to come to Adelaide and further, that he could not get a seat on a commercial flight to get there. By then I was persuaded that with my support as Leader the numbers would be there to carry the item. I told Hawke that under the circumstances, which I outlined, there was no need for him to come across from Melbourne. Hawke's immediate response was along the lines of, 'Well, that's interesting. Let me have a look at the plane timetable. I just might be able to get across in time for the debate,' and that is exactly what he did.[6] I was not so much mystified by this rather rapid change of attitude, although that was part of my response, as thoroughly suspicious. In the meantime the 'collective left', as Uren describes certain numbers to distinguish them from their excommunicated brethren and other heretics who have drifted away from the true faith in order to think for themselves, commenced parleying with me about an acceptable form of words on a prices/incomes policy. Suddenly, and very quickly as it transpired, the absolutely non-negotiable position of Uren was replaced with a more acceptable proposal; the only item on which they would not budge being quarterly wage adjustments.

I discussed Hawke's instantaneous change of travel status, from impossible to can do, with a friendly contact at the conference, Eric Walsh. He gave simple and direct advice, to the effect of: 'Don't be a mug. You're about to be set up. Hawke will come in and do the Left over with a blistering attack. The item will be carried. The newspapers will report the event as a Hawke triumph. The Left will be hostile on you and they'll be after revenge. The NSW Right are offering you a one-way ticket to disaster'. My developing suspicions confirmed, this issue assumed a different and sharper focus. A major factional struggle was brewing over a few words; but these were very important words in terms of future power. It was also a critical part of the strategy to determine leadership in my time.

I knew as Leader I could carry enough votes to determine which proposal succeeded. If I remained with the Right in the circumstances I would be facilitating their tactics to promote their man Hawke to the leadership, at my expense. I would also certainly destroy my influence with the Left. The more beholden I became to the Right, the less independence I would generally have and the more limited my future as Leader would be. The Left had no designs on the leadership and the more intelligent of their leadership accepted that I would baulk at many of their proposals. With them on this issue my overall independence of movement was preserved. The Right are pragmatists on most things. I knew therefore I could muster their support on most issues provided I pitched the appeal in an appropriate manner. On the other hand, I anticipated occasions when I would want to take the Party further in the direction of radical changes than many of the Right might countenance, and in that Left support would be critical. Being Leader can be a high-wire balancing act over the tiger pit. Exhilarating certainly, but a major slip-up and you are a goner. I supported an amendment hammered out with the Left, advising Ducker of my intention before the vote. He was not amused. The final resolution, proposing that a prices/incomes policy would be developed with the unions, encompassing prices, wages and non-wages incomes, taxation reform, termination of tax avoidance and the notion of a social wage, was well received by the media and the public.[7] That resolution, minus the wage adjustment component, was to be later pursued by me, and others such as Ralph Willis. Its final form, however, always proved elusive while I remained Leader. Ultimately, and ironically given Hawke's bitter denunciation of the proposal at the time, Hawke was the major personal beneficiary of this policy, frequently describing it as 'my prices/incomes accord'.

By 1980, the objective evidence was compelling: we had succeeded on just about all the tasks we had set ourselves. We had become credible on economic management and taxation and issues such as foreign affairs and defence, areas where the electorate had previously considered us weak. There had been intervention in the State branches of Queensland and Tasmania and the installation of interim administrations, followed by new and democratic rules and later the election of a representative party structure. It did not take long before those new party structures were in fairly good condition. The intervention processes had been turbulent and painful, especially in Queensland. There I had to face down some old cobbers whose important personal friendship to me had to be subordinated to the good of the party. It was unpleasant business and some still will not speak to me, such is the depth of resentfulness. The rebarbative word used to describe me is 'grub', a term which superseded the equally rancorous 'Grouper' once the latter had lost its potency with a rising generation unfamiliar with the vitriol of the earlier Labor split. The unpleasantness aside, those interventions gave a solid foundation on which to build for the notable improvement in Labor's fortunes at the 1980 national election, that of Hawke in 1983, and the Queensland victory of 1989.

In one of those delightful ironies of politics Hawke, in spite of the advantages he personally derived from these positive changes, actively undermined my efforts, notably in Queensland. There, he sought to weld together a structure of personal support for his larger political ambitions from among those disaffected by my actions. The Queensland intervention could have been avoided by the simple expedient of incorporating some of the intellectual leadership from among the dissidents; people like Denis Murphy and Peter Beattie. The Party had serious commercial problems with its radio station, and performance difficulties in the electorate. Murphy and Beattie would have helpfully added their creative and physical energies and their presence to re-absorb the dissidents into the mainstream of the Party through some sensible compromise. I offered to stand down as a member of the Inner Executive of the State Executive, which managed the detail of our business and electoral concerns, to make room for at least one of them. I hoped in vain it would be seen as an example someone else might like to follow. But I copped loud abuse instead, and beefy forearms thumping the table top intimidatingly— something I was to witness two years later with the ACTU on the eve of the Flinders by-election. And so, quite dispirited at the knowledge I was falling out with good friends, I resigned my position to join the push for intervention. There is a real life lesson in this: the 'old guard', unable to recognise their weakening position, would give no ground and in the end their unimaginative stubbornness left them with nothing. Compromise and accommodation with foes, in a principled fashion, can be important virtues for holding a democratic structure together.

At roughly the midway mark of my term as Opposition Leader I contested the 1980 election. We polled 49.6 per cent of the two party preferred vote. The swing to Labor was the largest in the preceding twenty-five years. I had said to a few people, well before that election, that if I did not win and failed to get reasonably close to victory, say within about 2 per cent, I would not remain in the leadership. In the upshot, after the 1980 election we required only a fraction over 1 per cent of the vote to win government. By 1980 we were doing better than most would have believed beforehand. In the last week of the campaign we snagged ourselves on the issues of wealth and capital gains taxes, which were from National Conference established policy. It was obvious this was an area where the Government could manufacture a fear campaign to Labor's disadvantage. An injudicious comment about a capital gains tax by a candidate, Peter Walsh, during an interview with a remote radio station in that last week set the issue alight and the polls showed we lost ground in that closing week. Perhaps I should have resisted the fear campaign even more strenuously than I did. If so I was recreant. Yet all we had to fall back on in the way of counter-policy was a meaningless proposal to hold an inquiry into wealth. The shadow Treasurer, Ralph Willis, and his Caucus Economics

Committee had failed to cobble together a policy on these issues in spite of regular prodding to do so. My own view, based on experience, was that at such a late stage the fear campaign would have minimal impact as most voters had firmly decided their voting intention by the middle of the last week of campaigning. However, with political processes in such an extraordinary state of flux these times, and old certainties suspect, I expect I got it wrong.

I started the formal election campaign seething with anger and humiliation. The campaign committee had decided, on prompting from party pollster Cameron, not to promote me as Leader but to include me in a troika with Hawke and Wran, the latter both active, public pretenders to my office. The decision was cut and dried before it went before the committee. Hawke supporters, especially in New South Wales, saw to that. Cameron's proposition was that qualitative polling disclosed public perceptions of weakness in my leadership and the presence of Hawke and Wran, seen as strong leaders, would strengthen my position. At the least, I thought it more likely their presence would reinforce any impressions of weaknesses on my part, which would hardly then escape the attention of the key forgers of this tactic. It would be no disadvantage to the ambitions of Hawke and Wran but harmful to my prospects, unless I could distance myself from this stunt. Lionel Bowen was furious about the proposal. My view was more cautious; rancorous debate would be counter-productive for me but potentially useful to others. I was certain though that once the campaign got under way the troika gimmick would disappear under the weight of issues which would inevitably focus on the leader, as in all campaigns. That is exactly the way it went and within a week or so the luminous troika of that year shone no more.

'It is a knell that summons thee...'

The most popular man in the country, Bob Hawke, arrived in Caucus after the 1980 election. Hawke had been in Caucus no more than a year when he came around to my office to talk to me one night. He entered, walked past the table where I was seated, across to the far side of the room and comfortably settled back into a large lounge chair. The body language, his mood, were unmistakable. This was his office! I remained seated at the table and adopted a formal manner, contrary to my normal disposition, and prepared to do a little game-playing. I knew from press gallery contacts what Hawke had been peddling about the gallery. He apparently never entered that sanctified territory without being armed with a brace or two of personal opinion polls, whose selective brandishment was hardly aimed at promoting my best interests. I suspected his visit might be an elaboration of this conduct. Suddenly the play got to him, and, flustered, he quickly heaved himself across to the straight-backed, business chair in front of my table. Children should never be teased, we were told when we were young, but I couldn't help myself that night. We were, after all, competitors. Sure enough, he produced a poll and suggested I should stand down for him. He was nothing if not direct. With an equal disregard for preliminaries, and with impressive clarity, I told him he could 'go and get stuffed'. I then outlined several reasons why I believed he lacked certain important leadership qualities. He left, obviously miffed. It was staggering to think he presumably expected that I would agree to his invitation! He regarded his mission to unseat me as entirely virtuous and ethical. Keating's ambitions in 1983, on the other hand, Hawke was to later see as basely driven:

> It was left quite clear that this man's (Keating's) naked ambition and arrogance was (sic) leading him to a total perversion of the history of the Labor movement.[8]

Now my act had become even trickier: not only had I to keep the factions happy, at the same time as combating Fraser—I also had to watch my back, behind which stood Bob Hawke and Neville Wran, open pretenders to my office. Wran rolled off the bandwagon when his confrères in New South Wales made it clear he was wanted there and there would be no support to take him to Canberra. Then there was the ACTU, publicly professedly neutral, but some of whose leadership was nonetheless discreetly but very actively working against me. In a television programme, Hawke once described Keating's drive to take the prime ministership from him as 'treachery'; once in the same programme it was disclosed he and some of his ACTU cronies were plotting to unseat me as Opposition Leader from 1980.[9] My problem was I had to perform every day. My act was getting ragged—like that of a threadbare juggler, or a fortune-teller in baggy pants. Hawke, in contrast, had only to be there and wave the latest popularity poll ratings. As with Rin Tin Tin or Michael Jackson at their peak, he was always a long way ahead of anyone else in popular affection. As a parliamentarian Hawke was out of his *milieu* and it showed. It was this grave flaw which brought him down when Keating left the Ministry in 1991 as a prelude to taking over the whole shop. Keating's departure made those deficiencies starkly obvious. With the people it was a different thing and he was top of the pops. All that public adulation must have caused his natural modesty considerable discomfort, but somehow he managed to conceal any sign of embarrassment.

In July 1981 there was a special national conference to consider a report on party reforms. A determined effort by the Socialist Left to encumber the party with a mandatory nationalisation policy was narrowly defeated after much lobbying, calling in of old IOUs, and tough debate. I said in debate, '. . . we are . . . as too often happens with the Labor Party, in danger of confusing the politics of the warm inner glow with the inspiration of the light on the hill . . . ', advice still relevant to the role of some party members.[10] There were pluses which included: National Conference to be enlarged, women to comprise 25 per cent of delegates; an affirmative action campaign by which women would comprise 30 per cent of Federal and State

MPs within ten years; the number of delegates from States to be determined proportionate to membership. My strong commitment to proportional voting was referred for further study, but only in so far as it might be appropriate for application within the Party.

I believed and still do that we would have a more representative and democratic House of Representatives electoral system with multi-member electorates with candidates voted into office by proportional representation. A minimum vote as a precondition to election would cut off most of the thin and unsteady tail end which might otherwise clutter the parliamentary processes. Protests from the major parties that proportional representation would lead to an unstable and unworkable parliament are largely a reflection of their wish to continue exercising an oligopolistic control over the political processes. What is missing is a concern to foster as much healthy pluralism as possible in the public interest. A proposal to enlarge the executive was defeated by the power brokers who feared dilution of their control, and with this defeat went an undertaking to guarantee female representation on this key body. Another proposal, for direct election of branch and union delegates to National Conference, was defeated for similar reasons. Those changes endorsed in 1981, including proportional elections, now operate within the Party. The results represented major reform within the Party, an achievement for which many of us had worked extremely hard. The personal triumph, however, belonged to Neal Blewett whose elegant drafting and capacious intellect is evident throughout the document which he, essentially, compiled. Button's efforts in organising and jollying along party members, encouraging their participation in the process, was a key ingredient of its success.

The key to success in Labor politics is not so much that you had prevailed at the last challenge, but that you succeeded at the next one. In this highly competitive environment, solid results in the Lowe by-election in March 1982 meant nothing. It was the next test which counted. At the end of the year, on 4 December, the Flinders by-election was held. We needed a 5.5 per cent swing, following a swing of 6 per cent in 1980, to snatch this traditional Liberal electorate of Flinders to the Labor fold. Early published polling showed we were just short of winning.[11] Then, at the last moment, a solid chunk of the support evaporated. Curiously, support for Labor nationally held up well during and well beyond the Flinders by-election.[12] The reasons for the vote loss were localised. The Labor candidate, a local real estate agent, had been selected through the vigorous application of numbers by Bob Hawke's Centre Unity faction, which caused some obvious tensions within the Labor Party in that electorate. Three days before the by-election the *Age* published a page one story accusing a company of which the candidate was a partner of being involved in some dodgy real estate dealings; it was alleged these transactions had left some home buyers over-geared and unable to pay mortgages. Deep in this very damaging story the *Age* mentioned that 'it did not allege that the candidate was directly involved or that he was even aware of the sales where inflated prices occurred', but by then all the damage had been done and the article ran on to add further to that damage. The *Age* made it a masthead story replete with a photograph of him. The report gave substance to a nasty 'whispering' campaign against the candidate in the Flinders electorate. A few years ago, I was informed by a former senior executive journalist with the *Age* that the story had been supplied by a prominent unnamed Labor figure, an influential member of Hawke's Centre Unity faction. He dropped sufficient tantalising clues, however, to make that person's identity unmistakably clear.

On the Thursday preceding the by-election, the deputy, Lionel Bowen, Bob Hawke, Ralph Willis and I met the ACTU in Melbourne to discuss wages policy. We had been trying to work out a prices/incomes policy with the unions, based on the notion of a social wage, for quite some time. If this could be achieved it would form a key part of our next election platform. The meeting had been called by the ACTU on rather short notice. I was on a break at the Gold Coast. Bowen warned me by telephone, in his rather cryptic fashion, that the arrangement was a 'set-up' and maybe I should not cut short my holiday to attend. As I saw it, if I attended and it was a 'set-up', I could be damned as a result of what occurred there; but then, at least, I would have a chance of defending my interests. Bowen's instincts proved correct—it was a classic ACTU machination.

The ACTU officers proposed a six months wages pause, followed by a catch-up as the basis for a wages/prices agreement.[13] This was an impossible proposition; Hawke and Willis were opposed to it as were Bowen and I. On the earlier, strong, recommendation of Hawke, the FPLP Executive and later the Caucus had endorsed opposition to a wage freeze recently announced by Malcolm Fraser. Now we would be left out on a limb with our wage freeze opposition, finding ourselves set against the ACTU proposal. This turn of events raised pointed questions about the quality of the contact between the ACTU and the FPLP, especially as Hawke, the former president of the ACTU, was the go-between for the two bodies. Regardless of that personal factor, if the process went wrong, as it did, I would wear the blame. How this breakdown in fundamental understanding occurred, given Hawke's deep grounding in ACTU culture, was perplexing, to say the least. Or perhaps the explanation is perfectly straightforward, if one is suspicious by nature. In offering Fraser a form of wages pause the unions, moreover, would be seen as tacitly accepting the principle, no matter if somewhat qualified, of a wages freeze which Fraser had announced. Finally, it would be made to seem that Fraser's tough, confrontationist tactics with the unions worked whereas the tactics of the FPLP, which had become protracted and inconclusive, appeared to proceed from a basis of weakness in its relationship with the ACTU. Ralph Willis, a former ACTU officer, had been negotiating inconclusively with that body on behalf of the FPLP for something like two years seeking a prices/incomes agreement.

A vigorous disagreement ensued in which I inferred fairly directly some of my suspicions about motives. This was not conducive to a productive outcome. Hawke's contribution was to float an idea for a wages structure consisting of a basic wage automatically adjusted for cost of living movements, with a further component adjusted according to other principles such as productivity. Actually, I thought it a rather good concept in equity terms but, strangely, it was tangential to the issues before the meeting. The proposal irritated the ACTU representatives. Curiously, on this they directed their anger at me rather than Hawke or both of us. The fact of the matter was the ACTU had no intention of delivering any advantages to the Labor Party while I remained its leader. This would be made crystal clear to me a few weeks later, with an intervention in Sydney in January 1983 by that body's president, Cliff Dolan. Nor, it seemed, was that body unduly disturbed that this set-back to the FPLP was occurring on the eve of the Flinders by-election. The *Age* headlines of this fiasco, next morning, just twenty-four hours before the by-election, were lethal. Journalists had been well backgrounded. Senior Canberra-based political correspondent for the *Age*, Michelle Grattan, flew especially to Melbourne to cover the event, such was the level of anticipation among some journalistic sources. As I had already publicly described the prices/incomes agreement as the 'lynch pin integrating our policies', this rebuff left me dreadfully exposed at the hands of both the Government and my competitors within the Party.[14]

Flinders was always a long shot, not the certainty some people in the Party had expected. In the event, we failed to win that seat; but whatever our other failings, history was against us. Since Federation and to this by-election Labor had won Flinders only twice, in 1929 and 1952. This voting record illustrated the difficult task we were taking on, and some of my office staff believed it should have been highlighted. Any such attempt, however, would have been depicted as mere defensiveness. The rules of engagement were being written by the numbers in control of the information, including some handling our polling information. In the past twenty years the Labor Party two party preferred vote in Flinders has exceeded that of the 1982 by-election on only two occasions. The first was in the full flush of enthusiasm for Labor led by Hawke in 1983, when the seat was won. The second was in 1984 when the vote was marginally ahead of 1982, and the seat was lost. Since then the vote has been well down.

The adverse consequences of this by-election for me within the FPLP were probably containable. The second half of 1982, however, was a time of political stumbles—which were, incidentally, much my own work. They added up to a disaster waiting to happen, as it did in early 1983. In June 1982 I declared, after consultation with and having obtained an explicit agreement from Lionel Bowen, our Foreign Affairs spokesman, that USA warships carrying nuclear weapons would not be able to use Australian port facilities under a Labor government. This was effectively the policy of both the New South Wales and Victorian State Labor governments; there was strong support for it in the Party; and it was consistent with the principle behind opposition to USA B52 bombers flying over Australian territory or using Australian land facilities. This latter had been urged into policy by Bowen with single-minded determination. To me it seemed that if, as Fraser declared publicly, the Americans had guaranteed the B52s would not be nuclear armed, then they had varied their neither confirm nor deny principle. As far as I was concerned, they could then go one step further and apply that variation to naval vessels. On 14 June 1982, Bowen qualified my comments.[15] I was alerted to this by a staff member, Alan Ramsey. I contacted Bowen whose characteristically elliptical explanation was, to the extent I was able to follow it, that Kim Beazley Jnr had expressed alarm to him that with my statement as it stood, he would have trouble holding his electorate of Swan, in Western Australia. Bowen claimed he accordingly made a mild qualification, one which he assured me would cause no trouble. Next morning I discovered the media had interpreted his comments as a repudiation of what I had said. The sky fell in a great big heap on top of me. I was forced to retreat. By itself this problem, too, was containable. The trouble was I was not smart enough to limit the mistake to this case alone.

In late June, Deputy Secretary of State, Walter Stoessel, and his Assistant Secretary, John Holdridge, in Canberra for the ANZUS Council talks, met with me. My position was now thoroughly vulnerable; within the Party it had become untenable and the Americans knew it. The pair of them did the old, good cop/bad cop routine, with Holdridge giving me the tough stuff. Later, as Minister for Foreign Affairs in the Hawke Government, I was told by a senior Foreign Affairs Department official who had travelled with them on the flight which brought them to Australia for this visit, that the pair had discussed with some relish how they would carve me up, as it were, when they met me in Australia. They certainly had the whip hand and they knew it. I had earlier conceded to a contact in the USA Embassy in Canberra that I was in strife on this issue and needed to ease my way out of it, which may not have been wise. I countered lamely to these two that if an exception to the neither confirm nor deny rule could be made with the B52s it could be made elsewhere, as with ships. 'Mr Hayden, we don't make any exceptions. If your government wishes to declare there are no nuclear weapons on a particular aircraft, that's their business. We won't make such a declaration in any circumstances. No exceptions!' I toyed, briefly, with the idea of making another run at the issue over this disclosure of Holdridge's; the implication of what he said being that the Fraser Government's claims were misleading.[16] I quickly dropped the idea. It would be interpreted by the media as a desperate and unconvincing effort by me to escape the pillorying I deserved. Fraser would certainly run that line and the debate would become ragged, confusing, and I would be the only loser. What was evident, moreover, was that generally, the public regarded ANZUS as the equivalent of the holy grail of national survival. This was a delusion, but a beloved one.

No sharp and alert politician should allow himself to get into that sort of jam. Once having got into it, an able and experienced political figure should move quickly to extricate himself. I stumbled in, then floundered around in the political bog for too long. It was a major blunder and I deserved the reproaches coming in my direction from colleagues. Why did I do it? It was partly due to strong views which I then held about nuclear weapons; partly also a less reverential attitude to ANZUS than was more commonly accepted in those days. If I am brutally frank with myself, however, I suspect some of the motivation came from an unconscious and not terribly credible desire to wrong-foot Hawke. His uncritical support for the USA, developed after he became President of the ACTU and sought to consolidate right wing support behind him, was well known. In any event, the consequences of my behaviour were similar in effect to someone pulling the pin on a hand grenade but neglecting to throw the device away before it explodes.

I do not think, on my record, I could be accused of having devoted undue attention or favour to one faction at the expense of another. I was next violating one of the sacred symbols of the Left, the policy on uranium mining and exports. As the flagship of left wing causes, this was a dangerous issue with which to tamper. Additionally, a large part of the mainstream of the Party had come to embrace it emotionally. Emotion is a fundamental influence within the Labor Party. The smallest, most tattered league of people comprising a freedom movement in some remote part of the world, scarcely heard of before, can always rely on someone in the Australian Labor Party to be promoting its causes. The same with human rights, civil liberties, social justice, and many other issues. This is not to suggest that the Labor Party has a monopoly on concern for human beings, for I generally have too much respect for the genuine plurality and liberalism of Australian society, regardless of individuals' political persuasions, to even faintly imply that. What I am distinguishing is the passion and sense of shared pain with which so many Labor members will take up issues. The Party also importantly provides a medium for changing policies, influencing the direction of social values and affecting the shape of society. Unlike the Liberal Party, ordinary branch members of the ALP can make influential inputs in this process—another feature of the Party which has always made it so attractive to me.

I recognised the emotional commitment behind the ALP's restrictive uranium policy, but I never understood the justification of that policy in any rational way. When Whitlam accepted the policy at the 1977 Perth National Conference, courting Left support for his leadership in the process, it was a foregone conclusion that we would have this smelly albatross strung around our neck for years to come. Only a little earlier Jim Cairns, as a minister in the Whitlam Government, a leading figure of the Left, confidently announced to an eager Caucus that he was heading for Iran to tie up contracts for the sale of uranium; he had the keen backing of Whitlam at the time. This seemed forgotten and lost in the mists of the distant past as the 1977 conference addressed this issue. Tom Burns, State Parliamentary Leader in Queensland, made a fiery intervention in the debate, making it clear that his State would not be bound by the prohibitive policy in so far as the Mary Kathleen uranium mine was concerned. To appease him and head off fissionable tendencies appearing in Queensland, the Mary Kathleen mine in that State was given a special exemption from the policy. The principle hammered repeatedly in the debate was that all uranium represented an unacceptable lethal hazard and accordingly mining and export of the mineral had to be prohibited. Rather mystifyingly 'all mining and export' exempted Mary Kathleen. It was never made clear why the unacceptable lethal hazard was tolerable in the case of Mary Kathleen, except in terms of the great political factor—votes. If that was so then the issue was capable of being addressed from a variety of facets on the political prism and not locked within inviolable moral boundaries defined by the Left. But then it is a common mistake with Labor, to confuse moralising with morality.

By 1982 the policy was becoming an electoral liability. The South Australians, with their large Roxby Downs project under way,[17] and Labor in the Northern Territory too, saw the policy as a handicap to their winning government. I regarded it as a serious handicap to our winning nationally. Besides, I did not at all believe in the policy. Between national conferences I was obliged to support existing policy. In 1982, however, I signalled my intention to seek to alter uranium policy in an interview with Michelle Grattan published in the *Age*.[18] The Left were furious. One prominent member of that faction warned me that the Left had been unable to dominate the Party policy agenda since the days of the Vietnam War, until the issue of uranium mining came along. They were not going to let their hold on this issue within the Party slip away without a fight.

A few weeks later, in July, at the national conference in Canberra, one of my staff reported to me that Laurie Oakes, the well-known public affairs commentator, was heard announcing over television that the Left had deserted me over the uranium issue; they were now supporting Hawke and there would be a challenge within a matter of a few weeks. I was exasperated. I was confident I would have learned of this before Oakes if it was correct, and moreover Hawke was anathema to the Left. They regarded him as a cynical apostate who had used them to achieve his own ambitions. They believed he had then cavalierly dumped them to form an even more personally productive alliance with the Right, and, in so doing, had turned on the Left. He had, furthermore, frequently denounced the uranium policy and this patently left him no leeway—especially as he so often invoked the word 'integrity' when describing himself—to cut deals with them on the issue in terms acceptable to them. I marched up to Oakes and told him in no uncertain terms what I thought of his story. Journalists were altogether too prone to scribble damaging gossip: how disgusting! Oakes, with what I should have recognised was false meekness (always a danger signal with him), said that if he was wrong he would apologise. He preferred to wait a bit, however, before doing so. I should have sensed immediately that there was trouble about.

Within twenty minutes I found Oakes had been correct. Uren had pledged Left support to Hawke as retribution for my threatening the inviolability of his restrictive uranium mining and export policy. I also suspected that the numerous amendments to his beloved urban and regional development policy paper—a blueprint for revisiting his leftover dream from the Whitlam period—as drafted by close colleagues Button and Walsh, triggered much of his fury. This paper greatly pegged back his big spending ambitions. From what he has recently written, this probably provoked him more than my opposition to the uranium policy. In the lead-up to the Whitlam victory of 1972 Uren had plastered the party policy document with numerous, precise commitments in regional and urban development; thereafter in government he would brandish this document at Cabinet, and in particular the Treasurer, asserting his right, by decision of the 'supremacy' of National Conference over all organs of the Party, to full funding for his grand design for a new Australia. I was alert to preventing anything of this sort happening to any new Labor government. I had calculated I would lose Left support but hold Right support on the uranium issue and should win. It was hazardous but the issue was important enough to justify the risk. I had not expected Left defection to Hawke. A far bigger shock came when I discovered that Hawke had given Uren an 'unequivocal' pledge that should the former become Labor Prime Minister, he would support the existing restrictive uranium mining policy, were it to continue as such. The sting in the tail of Hawke's undertaking was that, 'If the Victorian delegation decides to vote as a bloc in support of the existing uranium policy, I'll vote with them'. His faction caucused on Sunday, 27 July, where an unsuccessful effort was made by some of his closest supporters to lock it into supporting the restrictive uranium mining policy. Hawke reputedly also told Uren, 'I can't imagine anyone being so stupid as to make such a statement as made by Hayden'.[19] This conveniently missed the point that up until then Hawke was on public record as a passionate opponent of the policy. I was in real strife. Too bad. I had not faltered in my purpose and, having made my decisions, was prepared to accept the consequences.

The leadership situation could not be allowed to drag on this way. The constant undermining was damaging to the Party and had to be stopped; there was also the matter of my self-respect. One way or the other it needed to be sorted out. My press secretaries, Alan Ramsey and Dominic Nagle, had previously pressed me to make a stand against Hawke's white-anting of me, although to this point I had declined. I now took their advice. I went around to Hawke and told him I was going to convene a Caucus meeting on 16 July at which I would declare open my leadership. If I said he was overjoyed at this seemingly unexpected bonus to his ambitions, I could not be accused of hyperbole.

Concurrently, I was taking on the most determined fight of my political career over an issue, making it clear that I was seeking substantial change to the uranium mining and export policy and would not settle for less. This forthright challenge worked. The conference that year saw the policy change markedly, a major breakthrough. I would have wished for more but what I got came with a fiery, bruising and very bitter contest—the Party could not have given more without a major eruption in its ranks. In these sorts of Labor Party contests one must know when to call 'enough'. The resolution which eventually carried the day was drafted by Bob Hogg, Victorian State Secretary. It was an extremely prolix and convoluted piece of drafting, and attracted some criticism. But critics misunderstand political processes and in particular Labor culture: the drafting had to contain a myriad of points to which those giving ground could cling, to display to their supporters that they had fought for some important specific principle or other. Button's Senate preselection was coming up in the weeks ahead and he would succeed or fail in that according to whether he was supported by the Victorian Left. Those of us at the centre of the push for the change accordingly accepted his contention he would have to vote against us to remain in the Senate. With a fine margin of luck, we felt we should be able to get the resolution up without his vote. But before we succeeded in our enterprise, we had to experience the turmoil of an emotional division called for by an angry Uren. At one stage in the debate my Principal Private Secretary, Michael Costello, advised me that he could only find thirty-five votes for what I was doing and other number specialists agreed with his count. He reminds me that my response was philosophic: 'Well, if we go down, we go down. This is too important to back away from'. Unfortunately, several people who urged me along on this enterprise, stressing its political importance to their electoral interests, went on to vote for the existing restrictive policy, later explaining they only did so because of duress from colleagues.

Subsequent conferences made scarcely detectable adjustments to what was achieved in 1982 in changing Labor's uranium policy. That year the decision allowed Nabarlek and Ranger mines to continue and Roxby Downs to go ahead under a Labor government. The 1984 conference, benefiting from the bruising clash of 1982, was able to make these commitments more explicit, but that is about as far as it went. In the immediate lead-up to this issue at conference Hawke had retreated to his room, remaining there for some time, reportedly in a state of agitation. He was struggling to sort out, not so much a great personal moral conundrum but, rather, whether he could get away with a little bit of political chicanery. His problem was simply this: could he risk supporting a resolution which defeated my proposal—thus creating a major setback for me while hopefully promoting his ambitions—or would that be too obvious and consequently damaging to his reputation? Here was a great dilemma for any man of integrity. A trade union colleague reputedly gruffly told him to stop being a fool, to get back to the conference and support me, which he did.

Hawke's people, meanwhile, were busy. In the lead-up to the special Caucus leadership vote they had access to party polling conducted by Australian National Opinion Polls (ANOP), well before it was available to me. Caucus members were being contacted and certain poor results concerning negative personal perceptions of me were given an emphatic presentation; meanwhile, the fact that the poll had the party running some 4 per cent ahead of the government fairly consistently, well ahead of the 1.4 per cent required to win government, was not mentioned. At about this stage the director of ANOP, Rod Cameron, who was not averse to directly involving himself in some of these sorts of machinations, was stressing that the personal readings on the leader were what determined the outcome of an election. My response—that Maggie Thatcher had been rating 32 per cent approval against Jim Callahan's 60 per cent at the time she walloped him and the Labor Party, that Lange of New Zealand was scarcely into double figures of public approval prior to his successful election, and that Mitterand of France had not been scoring well at 18 per cent on the eve of his victory—was dismissed as defensive drivel. The term Cameron used to others was 'paranoia'. Well, as the saying goes, even paranoiacs can have reason to be suspicious. More recently, with Prime Minister Keating whom he favoured and who did not rate well in the popularity stakes, Cameron, remarkably, appeared to have adopted a different tune. I could now write his patter for him.[20]

In the final days before the Caucus election, there was much high drama with the Left holding highly publicised private meetings to decide whether Uren had acted with authority or not. Paul Keating relates an incident from slightly earlier, during the conference, which began when he heard loud insistent pounding on his hotel room door while he was showering. Only partly dry, he headed for the door with a towel wrapped around his waist. When he opened the door, Uren rushed in, fell on his knees before him and then clasped Keating's hands, imploring him to support Hawke. Uren was having his problems within the Left for the unforgivable sin of 'unilateralism'. The Victorian Left, in particular, were outraged that Uren had pledged Left support to Hawke without consulting them and probably not genuinely consulting anyone else. With Keating on board Uren might have been able to avoid an embarrassing rebuff from his faction. Keating did not join him. On Sunday, 11 July, the telephone rang at home in Ipswich. Dallas answered it. She came to me looking slightly puzzled; 'Tom Uren's on the phone. He's crying and saying he's been talking to the "little people" who tell him he's treated Billy badly. He wants to ask for your forgiveness'. I immediately had images of Uren at the bottom of his garden, in dialogue with those little white and brightly coloured concrete gnomes, so beloved of some people in modest, well-ordered suburbs. Not that one should scoff—discourse with the 'little people' saved my bacon on that occasion. I won by forty-two votes to thirty-seven. The margin was too narrow. I knew immediately that there would be fresh activity against me and reasonably soon; I was not far enough ahead of the pack to cause them to lose interest in their quarry.

On the announcement of the result, I momentarily debated with myself the results and the consequences. Should I stand down and avoid further turmoil and, without wishing to be misunderstood, thus also retain my dignity and self-respect? We did not have much in the way of worldly goods when we were growing up in South

Brisbane, but great store was put in those abstract, personal qualities. There was, after all, little else to cling to. There was a spontaneous round of applause, cheers from supporters and good humour from opponents. The die seemed to have been cast by my momentary indecision, and I rather think that the way it worked out was in Hawke's interests. If he had won, Fraser would have delayed an election for as long as possible, a year and more, by which time the economy would have been performing strongly and the severe drought broken. Hawke himself acknowledges the economic pick-up was gaining strength by May 1983, indicating it was under way before the March election that year as a result of earlier stimulatory measures adopted by Fraser.[21] Whatever Hawke's strengths have been, not even his staunchest supporters would seriously claim that he was effective in the Parliament; an extended stint as Opposition Leader would not have done him any additional good. Nor would another year of critical analysis of his performance from the media. No politician wears media rebukes well, least of all Bob Hawke. Whether his extraordinary popularity with the public would have allowed him to survive another year of the typical setbacks of an Opposition leader is a matter for speculation.

I observed, with wry good humour, that the combined pledged vote for Hawke and me, before the ballot, was greater than the total vote balloted. That is consistent with experiences of this nature in the past. Paradoxically, it was Hawke's and Keating's experience too in the Keating leadership challenges of 1991.[22] The first and only time in my many years in Parliament that I lobbied for votes was in 1982. In the past I had relied on my performance as a minister or shadow minister to gain the votes I needed. This time I was fighting for my existence as leader. I needed help and I got it. I was surprised actually, for I could think of no special reason why people would be prepared to work hard to help me and, even more so, to take the risk of retribution, should I have lost. Peter Walsh, John Dawkins and John Kerin threw themselves into the contest with gusto and several others including Button helped too. I found it all a bit humbling and overwhelming.

In any event why fight so hard for a position about which I had initially not been particularly enthusiastic? I had worked hard, extremely hard, in the position for several years and had helped bring about the much better than anticipated 1980 results. As I look back on the experience of that earlier election, it was probably one of the most enjoyable in a lifetime in politics. I was surprised at having come to like the job of being Leader. The combative nature of the office, the constant stress and unslackening pace, the intense pressure of work, a multitude of personal challenges by which you stood or fell, each day of each week, made it a uniquely fulfilling experience. In the upshot we were within 1.4 per cent of winning after the results of that election were finalised. Policies of substance and electorate appeal were coming on stream, and more were to be released in the near future. It seems to me that my life has been a case of taking on increasingly more demanding challenges while privately worrying about how well I would discharge them, and in the final result discharging them quite well. A case of challenges making the man. The 1983 election was close at hand and I felt, still feel in fact, that after so much effort it was not unreasonable that I should have wished to have a final shot at the top job in the country. Final in the sense that if I won I would become Prime Minister; an honourable ambition for anyone. If I failed, I would not necessarily want to spend more time in the most demanding and punishing role of Opposition leader.

No sooner was the ballot over, than the pantomime started. Uren lumbered into my office. He was sad-faced and close to tears. He grabbed my head, pulled it downwards, kissed me on the forehead and said, 'I've been a bastard, Billy. Forgive me'. I flinched. He then awkwardly made his way out. Physical proximity with people, female or male, with whom I do not have a close relationship generally leaves me feeling uncomfortable. A kiss from a man was even more difficult, although Tom has a tendency to plant kisses on his male colleagues, either as a sign of sorrow or approval. That sort of thing between men, however, was *infra dig* when I was growing up in South Brisbane and it is always hard to throw over your upbringing. Then, an even more amazing thing happened. Hawke came to my office, unremarkably enough. He shook hands with his left hand firmly gripping my right upper arm, and making direct eye contact; I then felt that magnetism for which he is justly renowned galvanising me with a transfer of energy, with a strength for life, provoking a confidence and a goodwill towards him. Such a memorable moment suddenly made me feel that he was a 'good bloke' to be with. There was something more than the relief of surviving in this; rather, it was an instance of that extraordinary, indefinable personal quality of his that I experienced on that occasion, the same quality he was able to transmit to the public in a great variety of ways. 'Love me, trust me, you know you can depend on me . . . and most of all you know I can't live without your love,' seems to be its message. The great personal love affair between Hawke and so many of the Australian public scarcely seems understandable on any other basis.

Unfortunately, the warmth between us quickly cooled. In spite of firm pledges of loyalty from him and some of his key supporters, within a few weeks they were all energetically back at work—and theirs was not a labour of love on my behalf. We were back on course towards our goal of winning government, with allowance for the different ambitions being pursued by Hawke and me and our respective supporters. Graham Richardson, NSW Branch Secretary and the genial wielder of political broad axes and heavy cudgels, personally contacted me to reassure me of the undivided loyalty of that branch now that the Caucus vote on the leadership had concluded. 'Don't worry, Bill, try to trust us for a change. We're all standing squarely behind you now.' I froze. The nape of my neck tingled. This sounded dangerous. Within weeks of these solemn pledges, Hawke's minions were energetically campaigning for him in the Caucus lobbies and around the press gallery. In less than a month Hawke was overheard in the Lobby Restaurant, where he was entertaining a journalist, expressing his despair at being prevented from acting as saviour of the Labor Party through my selfishness; he was, of course, armed with a poll report of some sort. By early November he had tossed discretion to one side and proceeded, in a not too subtle way, to publicly white-ant my leadership in a radio interview during which 'he refused to rule out the possibility of a leadership spill . . .'[23] This caused an uproar against him in the Caucus. Another apology came, written this time, but within days he was again actively campaigning against me.[24] Now politics is rough and I accept all of this without complaint. I do think, however, it is a bit rich in the light of all this to indulge in such a sustained bitter and righteous denunciation of Keating's prime ministerial aspirations, as he set down in his autobiography of 1994. Bob Hawke after all wrote the original script for getting rid of an exhausted leader who, he felt, lacked his talents.

A few weeks later Max Walsh, writing in the *Australian Financial Review*, reported that the NSW branch was out again, actively working against me. I was not surprised, for they are a tough bunch at Sussex Street—which probably explains much of their success. I had to telephone Richardson on some mundane matter the same morning as the article appeared. He was absent from his office but his secretary undertook to contact him and have him telephone me back. He did that within the hour. I would not have raised the article with him. The reported manoeuvrings were par for the course in the circumstances. To mention the report would have signalled insecurity on my part to the delight of my opponents. Richardson explained he was calling from a pay telephone at the side of a busy highway out at Parramatta. He seemed to be breathless and his speech was delivered in staccato bursts, punctuated by heavy, fast breathing. Immediately I answered he launched into an extraordinary patter. 'Mate . . . I know what you're phoning about . . . It's that bloody awful article . . . of Max Walsh's this morning . . . Bloody awful, mate . . . bloody awful . . . Not a skerrick of truth in it . . . mate . . . Lies . . . all bloody lies . . . mate . . . didn't we tell you we're standing behind you now . . . [a cold shiver ran down my spine again] . . . when we say something like that . . . in the New South Wales branch . . . believe me . . . mate . . . we mean it . . . I'm telling you the truth . . . mate . . . you know I wouldn't tell you a lie, mate . . . '. I interrupted this entertaining little soliloquy: 'But Graham, last time you told me you were backing me, I trusted you and look what happened!'. His voice dropped to that of the penitent who cannot deny his sin but wishes understanding, forgiveness, and, most of all, the embrace of a loving return to grace. 'Ah, mate . . . I've got to tell you the truth . . . that time I told you a lie . . . this time I'm telling the truth . . . try to trust us for a change, mate.' Richardson declared on numerous occasions that he always 'came through the front door' announcing his intention to get his victim as he entered. He has also ebulliently confessed that he has never hesitated to lie where that served his ends. In my case he exclusively adopted the latter tactic, which somewhat demolishes his claim of always coming through the front door to commit political homicide.

Some time early in 1983, as Minister for Foreign Affairs I was invited to be the visiting guest speaker at a NSW State Labor Conference. I was warmly welcomed. As much as anything, I expect, the delight of many delegates was to see that I was really alive and there were no obvious scars which could be used in evidence at a later date. I related the Richardson dialogue, to the immense gratification of delegates, especially those of the Left. The Left were used to bruising experiences at the hands of the ruling junta in Sussex Street, as the party headquarters in that State is colloquially known. I added, 'So you see, when a high-ranking official of the New South Wales branch of the Labor Party calls you "mate": BEWARE! It's like the Mafia sending you a bunch of white carnations. You're in trouble'. A little later, a very large bunch of white carnations arrived at my Parliament House office with an effusive card declaring something like, 'I never forget a good mate' and signed by State Secretary Steve Loosley. I had it framed on a deep red background and kept it on display in my office for some time after.

Interspliced with these party developments, the major issue of extensive illegal tax evasion and contrived tax avoidance arose. The McCabe–Lafranchi report exposed bottom-of-the-harbour tax rorting. This was followed by the report of the Costigan Royal Commission which declared that revenue lost to government by this practice was measured in 'hundreds if not thousands of millions of dollars'. The report was a double-edged sword. A classified volume made available to me detailed money laundering and criminal activities of certain members of the Painters' and Dockers' Union, a body affiliated with the Labor Party. I promptly and very publicly took steps to break that affiliation. A few Caucus members, some with close political contacts with the Union in Victoria, and even stronger links with Hawke, vigorously opposed my action. From a discussion I had with Fraser at the time I was left in no doubt that he was speculating on ways in which this fraternal association could be put before the public to disadvantage Labor. He made a strenuous but ham-fisted effort to get this calumny under way in the Parliament.[25] Had he succeeded, the consequences would have been diabolically bad for Labor. The Costigan material on the union was indeed ugly. My disability was that I could not detail the information provided to me confidentially and I had to move fast. As I was unable to give a detailed justification of the action I took, my critics' activities in and out of the Parliament thrived. So did Hawke's prospects. My distancing exercise was successful, nonetheless, even if rather bluntly executed. Fraser was left on the defensive on the tax issue. Later, after becoming Prime

Minister, Hawke congratulated me on the speed, determination and effectiveness with which I had distanced the Party from the Union. By then he had read the report and, of course even better from his vantage point, he was in charge.

A Taxation Department report tabled in the House of Representatives by Treasurer John Howard disclosed, to the discomfort of the Government, that the Taxation Office had long urged the government to act against these rorts. The report divulged that insufficient had been done.[26] These developments, coupled with Fraser's penchant for high-minded moralising about the solemn duties of public office bearers, left the Government looking incredibly soft on the tax evasion and contrived avoidance industries. In the course of all of this a rather kinky development occurred, according to the report of the Costigan Royal Commission. The Perth Crown Solicitor's Office had 'lost' a file recommending prosecution of a bottom-of-the-harbour case, only for the material to eventually turn up in the bottom drawer of a senior legal adviser. Costigan reported it had been left there intentionally to avoid proceeding with a prosecution. As if that was not enough, an officer in the Perth branch of the Attorney-General's Department and his wife decided to engage in a little private enterprise. They began a prostitution business, rather unimaginatively entitled, Kim's Introductions. As further recreational diversion, the wife engaged in bottom-of-the-harbour tax dodges, while the husband used his Crown Law Office telephone number to take business calls for his partner's flourishing little hospitality business. There were hoots of derision and howls of outrage publicly at this disclosure.

Tax avoidance and tax evasion activities had become lucrative growth areas for some of the new rich in Australia. The Opposition had been making quite a damaging impact on the Government on these tax issues when the office of NSW Attorney-General Frank Walker made contact with mine. It urged on one of my staff, through several telephone calls, that I should take up immediately the particular case of a businessman who, it was said, was engaged in certain tax activity. Walker had announced earlier, and with great fanfare, a State government inquiry into this subject.[27] I eventually spoke with Walker. Walker informed me that details of tax offences by various people had been compiled in this report which would soon be released publicly. One such person, a prominent businessman, whose appointment to head up a Federal government inquiry into tax malpractices had been announced quite recently, was among them. This appointment was inappropriate and should be stopped, and it would be when his report was published, Walker said. If I would raise the matter in Parliament that week he would have the detail in a copy of the report to me by early the next week. This would be a major story to my credit. If I did not raise the issue in the closing days of that week then the report was going to be published, probably some time in the next week, and I would have forfeited a great opportunity to further promote our campaign against tax malpractices. I agonised over this matter and finally did one of the more stupid things I have ever done—I raised the matter in Parliament. The person concerned then vigorously denied the charge. I was in deep trouble. The report never arrived while I was in Parliament. As a result of some persistent contact, Walker at last provided a limited number of papers in March 1994, which were purportedly the report promised those many years ago. There was no reference in any of the papers to the businessman concerned or any company with which I am aware he is or was connected. I am still waiting for Walker to provide the material promised, even after all this time. In any event I was bleeding again and it was all my own work. The decision was made of my own volition and I accept the consequences, but it was a silly decision.

By early 1983 I was physically and mentally exhausted and fairly demoralised personally. It is curious how one recalls particular experiences at significant times, things which seem to have an influence on one's judgment or fortunes. I saw Klaus Maria Brandauer perform brilliantly in the film *Mephisto* at the Schonell Theatre at the University of Queensland. I drove home to Ipswich, lost in morose and probably self-indulgent reflection. Had I, like the character played by Brandauer, compromised too much with principle to serve my own ambitions at the expense of my younger ideals? Every time I turned the question over in my mind the answer was a brutal 'yes'. A leader of a political party, especially one comprised of such an extraordinarily complex set of demands and expectations as is the Labor Party, has to give ground, to surrender some of his independence, to ensure an effective accommodation and coalition of interests. More independence is lost in appealing to the wider electorate, seeking to attract and retain its commitment to the Party. Around that time I also happened by chance to buy Joseph Conrad's *Heart of Darkness*—a novel I interpreted as a sustained metaphor for how a man, civilised and decent, subordinated his values to live with and profit from jungle savagery, the savagery of raw capitalism. Kurtz, in his death throes at the closing stages of the narrative, reflecting on the crude, self-serving compromises which advanced his ambitions, cries out in disgust at the horror of it all. I found that cry spinning about in my mind like a fiercely ricocheting piece of hot metal. Now that I look back on those events, I was clearly falling into a state of self-pity as I set about unconsciously preparing for my fate.

Too many things had gone wrong. My judgment, frankly, had become faulty. In this condition I reshuffled the FPLP Executive, a typical 'damned if you do, damned if you don't' situation. I should have done it the previous year for we were, in particular, not making the impact we should have been making on economic policy. The Left energetically opposed my earlier proposal to replace Ralph Willis with Keating as shadow Treasurer.[28] Although I was by now beholden to them for my narrow survival, the reshuffle could no longer be deferred. Those who felt they had been unjustly treated were predictably angry and their support was consolidated behind my opponents. Hawke sympathised with them, fuelling their discontent, encouraging their sense of injustice. Paradoxically, while he indulged them in their disappointment he, for instance, later told me in government that making Keating shadow Treasurer was the best thing I had done. There was more to come. I was attending a meeting of the election campaign committee in the Labor Party offices at Sydney on 21 January 1983 when Mick Young came over to me to advise that the President of the ACTU, Cliff Dolan, who was Melbourne-based, wanted to see me in an office a couple of floors lower down. Dolan's message was as crystal clear as it was brutal. He informed me that our prices/incomes accord policy paper had been deferred to a special unions' conference for the third week in February. He added that there was no chance of its getting through the conference. I understood the message clearly. Here was an extension of the Flinders by-election experience with the ACTU: there would be no prices/incomes policy while I was leader. I went back to the meeting and mentioned this latest obstacle. I noted some exchanged smirks of satisfaction. The noose was tightening.

A little later John Button, Deputy Leader of the Senate and a close confidant, visited me twice in Brisbane, to urge me to stand down. The first meeting was on 6 January 1983. Surprisingly, the proposal for the first meeting had been reported in the *Australian Financial Review* a fortnight earlier, long before I knew it was to take place.[29] Button put his points directly. At the second meeting he said, 'Now understand clearly what I am saying. If there is a move in Caucus to declare your position open I will not move it or second it, but I think you should stand down'. I interpreted the further implication to be: 'But I will vote for it'. It is strange how long-forgotten incidents come back to mind in a flash because of some startling development. As I drove home to Ipswich I suddenly remembered an account of an incident of many years earlier, probably apocryphal, and reputed to have occurred during the visit of President Lyndon Johnson to Australia in 1966. He was in Brisbane. An American secret service officer went over to the local police motor cycle escort waiting outside Johnson's hotel. The motors of the bikes were running. He instructed the sergeant in charge, Eddie Brosnan, a giant of a man, superbly fit, a front row forward for the Kangaroos, to switch his motor off as it was too noisy. When Brosnan declined to comply, the American switched the key to off. Brosnan effortlessly threw a punch from his seated position, spread-eagling the American. When he recovered, the American went over to complain to the head of his detail. His senior officer's response was, 'If your own side is knocking you down, you must be doing something wrong; it might be better to stay down'. I turned to thinking that maybe I should start taking such advice on board myself.

The task of approaching me must have been difficult for Button. He was doing what he believed was best for the Party, of which he had been a member for many years. He had experienced some quite difficult times in the strife-torn State of Victoria as he sought to assist party reform there. Button's record for persevering with what he believed in was impeccably consistent, no matter what others might think. He had been a loyal Whitlam supporter until after the 1975 election, when he became a faithful supporter of mine. This support never wavered until late 1982, just after his Senate preselection in Victoria (for which he was dependent on Left support) was successfully out of the way. Towards the latter part of 1982 he threw his influence in with the Right and behind Hawke; again he was unwavering until the approaching Keating challenge for leadership in late 1991, when he committed himself to Keating. Back in 1983 Button wrote me a letter in which he said that five of the six State branch secretaries believed I should stand down. One of us was confused, for four of the six—Queensland, South Australia, Western Australia and Tasmania—had recently pledged their support for me in personal conversations. By this time, however, I did not care. Incidentally, the prompt and discreetly arranged briefings in which he related these confidential discussions between him and me to Richardson and Hawke, including at Hawke's home, put a bit of fast spin into the pace of the contest. They did not concern me for I was then unaware of them.[30]

I too had to think very seriously about my situation. Labor was ahead of the Government by a fairly consistent 4 per cent in the opinion polls, more than enough with which to beat the Government. This convinced me I could win the forthcoming election. In the early part of the week in which I resigned, I discussed the opinion polls with Button, no doubt in a desperate effort to buoy my sinking self-confidence. He responded with unmistakable conviction, advising he had been reliably informed that the Morgan poll to be published that week would show a slump in Labor's support. Prepublication details from the Bulletin polls, at that time, were often available to one or two Caucus members so I was not surprised that he claimed to have this information. Another hole had been punched in the frail, leaky tub in which I was trying to keep afloat.

I had to consider a wide spectrum of concerns, without becoming egocentric. It was clear the constant erosion of my position had to be weakening Labor. This latest move to eject me from the leadership would unquestionably reach the media with damaging consequences, and it would be followed by more moves and more speculation. There was a self-fulfilling momentum to what was happening. Dominating my thinking was the unrelenting toughness of the ACTU on the incomes accord and social wage policy, on which I had been trying to get agreement for far too long. After my meeting with Dolan there were a number of stark considerations. There was no doubt that organisation would hold back from an agreement, or offer a diluted and politically unappealing alternative, in spite of the fact of an election looming.

Even in the unlikely event it proved otherwise and the ACTU conceded the prices/incomes policy, and Labor won the election, the forces in that organisation masterminding this opposition would also undoubtedly make life at the top unbearable. This too would be destabilising for government.[31] My sense of responsibility to the Labor Party left me grieving at the mess that was being created around me. In my demoralised frame of mind I had little left with which to resist the relentless sniping and undermining to which I was being subjected.

I had substantial obligations to the Party, to the ordinary folk in the branches whose trust in the Party was touching in its sincerity—and whose faithfulness I'm not sure politicians always repay anywhere near the measure they should. People like my late parents, like so many ordinary, decent, working-class people with whom I grew up in South Brisbane and lived with in Ipswich. The sorts of people I constantly met with in my many journeys about this vast country of ours. Hawke's popularity with the public was greater than mine. I was not blind to my shortcomings. My defects were too regularly catalogued in the media for me to be anything but well aware of them. My opponents, mostly those in the Labor Party, made sure they were regularly brought to notice in the right quarters. Hawke's extraordinarily close personal involvement with people from 'big business' proved invaluable. While I dealt with such people out of necessity I largely kept myself at arm's length to more easily rebuff any unwelcome policy claims from them. It was a case of not standing so close as to be taken over nor so far away as to be forgotten by them. Hawke drew down on some of these friendships. He and his 'little mate' Peter Abeles undertook a pilgrimage to the residence of 'Rags' Henderson, chief executive of the Fairfax dynasty on one occasion. They did this to ensure that an opinion poll of uncertain validity but of damaging force to me was fully reported in Fairfax newspapers.[32] Hawke told me Larry Kornhauser, another of his rich 'mates', paid for the production of an expensive, glossy publication of Hawke's speeches which he circulated in great numbers. A newspaper reported the undertaking rather breathlessly as a secret weapon designed to undermine me further, though when I scanned the speeches I quickly concluded there was no threat in this.

On another front, there had already been a break-in of the premises occupied by the Party's advertising agent. The burglar was extraordinarily perspicacious on political matters as far as break-in artists go; apart from a few other trivial items, he grabbed the party opinion polling. More than that, he must have been a true blue Liberal supporter, for the polling results turned up in the hands of the National Secretariat of that party fairly promptly, who then had a ball waving the results about to all and sundry. With leaked poll results at least, it seems I was a trendsetter: a similar thing happened to John Howard and John Hewson respectively when a determined move was under way in the Liberal Party to get rid of them.[33] Their successor Alexander Downer has been a more recent victim of the leaking of detrimental Liberal Party confidential polling. That, incidentally, is one of the Liberals' great problems these days—they are incapable of doing anything original.

I recalled something my late mother used to say periodically: 'Never hang around where you're not wanted. Remember you've got pride'. Then there was, most importantly of all, my family. The unrelieved demands of the job and the personal abasement from disparaging commentary reached into our home to exact some toll. It hurt Dallas, for so much of it was personal and some quite vindictive. Our children, as the local member's offspring, were frequently teased and taunted at school; not only was this talk nasty, I was concerned it could affect their personalities. I announced my intention to stand down as leader at a FPLP Executive meeting in Brisbane on 3 February 1983. It hurt. It hurt like hell revisited several times. To surrender is, in its effect, to abase yourself before someone else and acknowledge their superiority. It is an awful experience. Because of our cultural conditioning I suspect, it leaves one feeling discredited and unmanned. The latter is the worse feeling.

I negotiated certain commitments in the following descending order of priority: first, a guarantee that my staff would be found jobs; second, that my key supporters in the Caucus would not be penalised because of their support for me; third, that I become Minister for Foreign Affairs; fourth, that I be appointed High Commissioner, later, to London. The last I dropped subsequently. I announced my impending resignation to the FPLP shadow Ministry, adding that at least there is always some silver in the lining of the darkest clouds. Mine would be that I did not have to attend any more National Executive meetings which were the most boring meetings in the world. I added that I did not recommend my escape route to anyone else wanting to avoid those meetings. At an unwanted press conference shortly after, I mentioned in passing that 'a drover's dog' could lead the Labor Party to victory in the forthcoming election. Hawke always resented that metaphor, taking it as a personal slight. It was not meant that way. I just was not going to walk out like a sheep heedlessly scurrying along the race to the slaughterhouse floor. A bit of defiance before the axe fell was justified. At the meeting of the Caucus where I formally resigned—an act so overwhelmingly popular that it seemed at last I was getting something right—I mentioned towards the end of my brief comments that after my experiences as Leader of the Labor Opposition for five years, I felt qualified for immediate appointment as Patron of the Society of St Sebastian. Only Michael Duffy, a regularly practising Catholic, appeared to understand the imagery. Perhaps others kept po-faced because they thought me too self-indulgent.

In very quick time thereafter the ACTU convened specially to consider the prices/incomes accord, which they then speedily endorsed. Presumably the sticky, technical hitches which had held it up for so long and which Dolan made clear were irreparable had suddenly self-corrected themselves. For the life of me I could see no change in the before and after documents. Perhaps, on the other hand, I am afflicted by an obscure form of dyslexia. Most fascinating of all was the way someone had misled Button. On the day of my announced intention to stand down, the expected *Bulletin* poll was published which, contrary to Button's earlier assertion, revealed an increased Labor lead over the Government, a lead of five points. That, however, was immaterial. On the last occasion when I spoke to Button, I know now, I had already made the irreversible decision to stand down. As of that time, nothing would have deflected me from my course.

Fraser, meanwhile, had made the most disastrous decision of his whole political career. He rushed out to Government House, without a prior appointment being made, to call a double dissolution. If only he had waited, the course of our political history might well have been quite different, something he has acknowledged to me in private conversation. He should have realised that once I had accepted that I should stand down there was no way I could step back—not even if he had obtained his request for an election immediately on its first presentation to the Governor-General, which was before I had announced my intended resignation. I received a very early telephone call on the morning of 3 February, the date I announced my intention to resign as leader to the FPLP Executive in Brisbane. Laurie Oakes informed me that Fraser had taken the decision to call an early election that day, having heard of my imminent resignation. Perhaps if I held back with my resignation Fraser's action might save my leadership? My response was, 'No, I've gone too far. There is no room to turn back'. As Leader, I was totally and permanently disabled politically once I had acknowledged privately to a few within the Party that I would resign. No matter how few knew of it, it could not be concealed for long. It would have been the major issue of the election. Interestingly, Fraser's advisers were divided on their advice to him. His office was urging the election option but at least one of his outside advisers, the

Melbourne academic, and now Federal MP David Kemp, counselled the dangers of that sort of opportunism. The foolishness of Fraser's decision to call a sudden election was best summed up in the comment: 'The turkey called an early Christmas!'

How good was my leadership? Some media commentators, distinguished only for being preoccupied with advanced primary school studies at that time have cursorily dismissed it. Perhaps they make a sound judgment but some have been kinder. I draw comfort from the remarks of Paul Kelly, who was there then, even if he was undoubtedly too generous.[34] The fact is that the Hawke Labor Government ran on the policies drawn together as a team effort under my leadership, for some years after its initial election. Similarly, the ministerial appointments remained rather much as I had made them in early 1983, in spite of Hawke condemning them at that time and of course mustering support from those disaffected by the changes. Fraser, I seem to recall, had a similar experience with the 1975 budget. After damning its introduction he administered it pretty much in its original form once he had snatched government. Always the bridesmaid, never the bride, might well be applied to my political history. Hawke went on to a landslide win at the 1983 election. Labor achieved a primary vote of 49.5 per cent with the Democrat primary vote at 5 per cent. This was consistent with the trend which the opinion polls had been recording for some months before. Hawke's period of service was the second longest of any prime minister and the longest of any Labor leader. To set the record straight, he was in my view a very able and an evidently successful prime minister.

Finally, Graham Richardson and I buried the hatchet, if that is not an unfortunate image. This happened a couple of months after the 1983 election. I had made a decision to stay on in Parliament and that meant I had to give a maximum work effort for the Government in my new role as Foreign Minister; I do not have much time for parliamentary slackers and therefore could not allow myself to become one. For the sake of a healthy psyche and a collaborative effort with the team, I had to do my best to rid myself of any bitterness. It was not easy but it was necessary. I had seen how, in their last years in Parliament, Arthur Calwell and later Clyde Cameron poisoned their souls with resentment of past foes, for wrongs done or thought to have been done long ago. This was a shame for it had a pickling effect on what had normally been breezy personalities. I resolved to do my best to avoid the same thing happening to me.

I saw Richardson at the Canberra Trans-Australia Airlines terminal one day. We had been civilised but distant until we crossed paths this time. It suddenly occurred to me how contrary my behaviour was to my resolution and, to be candid, how immature it was. I went over to Richardson at the baggage collection area and said something like, 'This is a bit bloody silly. We've got to work together from now on. We'd better get a better personal working association'. 'Couldn't agree more,' he replied. I commented, 'There's got to be something symbolic to honour the occasion. You triumphed. You can send the vanquished a bottle of good red with which to toast the new arrangement'. 'Yeah, OK,' he said, but looked rather dubious and perplexed. 'Remember the symbolism, Graham? The blood of Christ? You're a good Catholic; you'd understand.' 'Yeah. Yeah. I'll do that. . . ' He was better than his word. He sent me a dozen. Later, as a friendly working arrangement was established, we dined together at Le Rustique restaurant in Canberra, an excellent Provençal-style French eatery now sadly gone. I was host, meaning Graham allowed me the honour of paying the bill. We consumed good food and a too-ample supply of fine wine, all over quite a period.

It was probably the glorious wine which relaxed and encouraged Richardson to entertain me with many anecdotes at my prompting. I was treated to the fond recollections of a connoisseur of his craft, an account of the little ploys and plots his team set in my path: of the co-option of several national press gallery journalists who happily printed 'slanted leaks' supplied by Richardson and patently designed to damage me, on the basis that these journalists would be kept on the 'information drip' with other important leaks from the Caucus and Party as a *quid pro quo*; of how the energies of the National Party Secretary, Bob McMullan, were harnessed to dribble selected 'confidential' polling results, chosen to disadvantage me, among elements of the Party; of a deliberate working on the nervousness of candidates trying to win marginal seats; of the recruiting of named defectors from my camp, all the while encouraging them to remain actively involved with me so they could secretly report back on my doings. In this expansive mode, Graham went on to disclose he even had a 'plant' in my office, reporting on my doings, reactions, mood under pressure. Yes, of course I had been set up in the Flinders by-election, but that had been the work of Hawke's people, not Richardson. He seemed impressed with the ruthlessness of that performance yet had reservations on overall form: it lacked the polish of his cultivated style. My most damaging foes, he reflected, were a small coterie of ACTU officials who decided to collaborate with Fraser's wages freeze in late 1982 after the FPLP Executive had decided to oppose it on advice from our Industrial Relations shadow Minister, Hawke. Hawke had consulted with the ACTU first. 'Bill, you were smart to recognise that there was never going to be a wages/prices policy with the ACTU while you were Leader. C . . . . ., I've done some tough things in my life for the good of the Party but that was sheer calculated bastardry of proportions I could never duplicate.' Later, recalling Hawke's outraged denial on a television programme when he was accused of having 'blood on his hands' because of the machinations which brought about my fall, Richardson reported colourfully, 'he [Hawke] had more blood on him than the entire stage at the end of Hamlet'.[35]

I marvelled at the things he had done or been party to without even the slightest hint of conscience. In particular, the way in which he was able to use contacts within the ABC radio programme 'AM' to regularly air views through a young academic who had been primed by 'Richo' to say things not exactly helpful for me. Fascinatingly, the academic concerned told me much later these performances greatly helped his career as a scholar. It was presumed by his superiors that his appearing so often and speaking with such conviction and scholarly detachment on political issues on a 'quality' current affairs programme must have meant he was a reliable and informed researcher. It did his political prospects no harm either. Through the grace more generally of Sussex Street, he is now Senator Tom Wheelwright and undoubtedly, as I assess his abilities, a young man capable of making a valuable and constructive contribution to Labor in politics.

When the bounty hunters brought in my scalp they did not settle for peanuts—furthermore, a lot of debts were cashed in over the years after the 1983 election. Ironically, as Foreign Minister, I had to authorise many of them with my own signature. Of the several political appointments of heads of overseas missions made during my term of office, most were initiated by the Prime Minister as an expression of gratitude for personal services rendered at a crucial time. I recommended one only—Whitlam as UNESCO Ambassador— for, as I mentioned to Hawke on several occasions, as a Labor principle I thought we should stick fairly closely with the professionals who had invested their careers and established their expertise in the diplomatic service. The last goodwill appointment by the Prime Minister, as I recall it, was former Western Australian Premier Brian Burke to Dublin. 'This will be a popular appoint-ment, Bill,' the Prime Minister crackled. 'I'm sure it will go over well with a lot of influential people, Bob,' I recall replying. 'Ahh, more than that, Bill. He's widely respected, lot of credibility. He's the next Labor Prime Minister. New South Wales will support him. I wanted him to stay in State politics and make a clean changeover. His view is he's tired and wants a break before he comes back into Federal politics.' I silently remembered how Burke had sought a conference with me when I was Opposition Leader, wanting Susan Ryan sacked for 'causing trouble' by speaking out on Aboriginal welfare issues in Western Australia. I pointed out this would be unfair. Ryan, as our spokesperson on Aboriginal Affairs, was faithfully expounding National Conference policy. Burke's response, to the obvious consternation of his deputy, Mal Bryce, whom he had brought along for this discussion was: 'Well you can't expect me to know all the policy. My strength is I'm a presenter, not a policy man'. Federal politics, I hoped, required other attributes in addition to presentational skills. Though I had reservations about most of these diplomatic appointments, I did not resist them, as I preferred not to expose myself to the disabling criticism that I harboured bitterness and sought revenge at the expense of 'good blokes'! Labor loves its good blokes, and if its women learn to conform to the traditional male ways—as they seem to be doing despite proclaiming a desire to do things their own way—Labor will come to embrace its 'good girls' too. In politics I found long ago that you cannot expect to win on all issues; you save your energy for the important issues you hope you can win, or the ones so important in principle that you are prepared to go down fighting for them. As this issue fitted neither criterion, I had to forbear in silence when the public criticism was periodically aired—usually complaints from retired old shellbacks in the Department of Foreign Affairs on behalf of their serving colleagues—that I was consciously politicising the diplomatic service.

Richardson was and remains a thoroughly entertaining scallywag and we kept that working association in good order while I remained in Parliament and after. Politics is riddled with its ironies and paradoxes. Hawke succeeded with the support of the NSW Right. His prime ministership prospered under their patronage, until they decided it was time for a change. In *Whatever It Takes* Richardson has written an epic folktale on this and other subjects in which, not surprisingly, he always seems to hold centre stage.[36] There is also something of Swift's 'That Which is Not' when he declares 'It was evident that Hawke's leadership had entered its terminal phase, and that it was in the interests of the Party to make the transition to Keating as smooth and as painless as possible',[37] and that Hawke's fate then rushed in to claim him. The fact is Keating forced the pace against an unwilling Richardson who desperately sought to sit on the fence, with a slight self-insurance tilt towards Hawke, in a contest with a very uncertain outcome. Richardson would certainly use the impressive array of numbers available to him without remorse when it suited him and provided he was certain of winning. In doing this he drew down heavily on the Ducker legacy, for it was Ducker who had built up and welded this organisation together. What Richardson failed to do was something Ducker never neglected: listening to, jollying along, flattering, and generally keeping up the morale and commitment of the foot soldiers. The result was that the NSW Right was falling into disarray at the time of Richardson's retirement from Parliament. Had he not departed there would have been a serious revolt against his methods, as a new generation with different views about participatory rights was emerging in the ranks of the NSW Right. This is a story as old as politics.

I like to think that I was a good craftsman but acknowledge I was not a virtuoso performer. One of my defects was that I was a very ordinary, run-of-the-mill representative of the community. While most ordinary folk in our community live their lives out faithfully and steadily in the suburbs, according to a predictable cycle, life is rarely ever as exciting or eventful as they might wish. To them, a grey personality such as mine was discomforting, reminding people of the ordinariness of their existence, a condition they would much prefer to escape; this view seemed to also have the support of the political commentators back then. Hawke, on the other hand, had glitter and offered excitement—his performance a new and diverting experience for the physical senses. Whitlam's appeal was provocatively intellectual, conjuring up images of an inspiring future to succeed a dull and regulated past. Fraser was different. Stolid and grim, determined like an austere boarding school headmaster, he promised discipline and predictability after the heady and wayward years of the Whitlam Government; just what the country wanted. McMahon was too inconstant and Gorton, perhaps, too headstrong and headlong for the people's comfort, especially after the steady plod of Menzies. Menzies was grandly seignorial, a sage father, an authority figure out of the stifling fifties, a period when people kept in their places. Menzies met the rising, unchallenging demands of the *petit bourgeois* for conforming respectability—a constituency which Menzies adored and Barry Humphries lampooned mercilessly. Keating's appeal was that of a gutsy street fighter who would slug it out, toe to toe with his opponent, asking no quarter and giving none. At other times he was witty and charming, obviously intelligent and not afraid to make difficult decisions in difficult times. He invoked the strong impression of a respected, if disliked by some, leader of the corner push: a leader who was tough but who had style. This is an image with deep roots in our culture, in particular among Sydneysiders.

In all the circumstances, it was remarkable I got as far as I did and, to be immodest, performed as well as I did. I was, after all, to use boxing jargon, fighting above my division and beyond my class; at least if the assessment of my performance by some at the time is to be believed. For my part, I have neither regrets nor recriminations at any of my experiences as Opposition Leader. Those years were an unparalleled highlight of my life. Something recalled with fond remembrance and a sense of privilege. My opponents within the Labor Party had their goals, which they were entitled to have, and the fact that I was excluded by them was unimportant in principle. I tried to combat them, but they had the heavy artillery, and the more effective strategy of unrelenting pressure. They won because they were better at what they were doing, which was not quite the thing I was doing.

PART VI

INTO EXILE – THE REASON WHY

The Reason Why

On 5 March 1983 the first Hawke Labor government was elected with a comfortable majority of twenty-five. It was a remarkable event. Less than eight years earlier Labor had been written off, condemned to long years in the wilderness of Opposition. For all the popular satisfaction with the result, I would be neither honest with myself nor convincing to anyone else if I denied that I felt a certain deadness inside. I experienced an understandable sense of personal failure. The policies on which Labor fought the 1983 election had been elaborated and refined, largely, during the previous five-and-a-half years of my leadership; I had chosen Recovery and Reconstruction as the leitmotiv for the 1983 campaign itself.

We had worked hard to develop a set of unified policies designed to promote recovery in the wake of a severe economic contraction, one imposed by the Fraser Government in a desperate effort to combat serious trade and current account deficits. The short-term, stimulatory proposals were to be interlocked with a number of major capital development programmes of longer term benefit to the nation. In the course of this deliberation my successor made his major contribution to the elaboration of these election policies with measured solemnity. He urged that Recovery and Reconstruction become Recovery, Reconstruction and Reconciliation, reconciliation having been the theme of his slightly earlier Boyer Lectures on the ABC. I was certain the addendum added nothing but neither did it do any harm. It was, therefore, easy to accept and wiser to do so rather than having a snarl over small beer being served in a big pot. This being Hawke's sole contribution to the election policy-making process, the campaign theme was adopted without much fuss. There was not the slightest evidence of anyone having additional, let alone alternative, views of substance to those already worked out. My long-held suspicion was confirmed that whatever my vulnerabilities might be elsewhere there would not be any serious challenge based on competing policy ideas.

I was next preoccupied with something I did not care to confront, but something which I had to. By relinquishing the leadership my clout in the Party had well and truly peaked. I was vain enough to believe that by dint of hard work and performance I would justify my berth as a minister. At the same time I recognised there would be a finiteness about this, for there is also a matter of generational change in the values of a society much as there is evolution of the various social organs which maintain its viability. In a biological sense organs which do not evolve, atrophy and disappear; so too with individuals who are linked too much to the past, rather than instinctively operating at the cusp of the future. In public life, one must know when one's time to depart the stage has come and, hopefully, do it decisively and with grace. This was the sober reality I understood I would soon face. I was a product of my values and my times. These, increasingly, would distance me from many of a younger generation of ministers who indisputably were first-rate managerialists. They would strive for outcomes measured by values of the new age to which they belonged. I was a product of the Great Depression, and remain such.

In the fundamentals of my political beliefs I remain very much a collectivist in an age which enshrines individualism, which emphasises rights where I stress duties. The two are not mutually exclusive, quite the contrary, but the imbalance, for me, has tipped too far in the direction of new age selfishness. Thus success is most usually measured by personal, material acquisitions, achievements and the sensual fulfilment these give. Pure market force ideology in this consumer age emphasises and reinforces this trend. To the extent that members of the Gimme Generation are concerned at all for communitarian goods and services, of the order of the built environment, education, health and the like, it is a concern for the situation in their immediate area and a determination to get the best for themselves. That their superior quality of life may have come from public sector sources and be at the expense of others is an immaterial consideration; for many such people, this is only their due, much in the way they also expect personal success. So many of the great liberalising movements of our time, like gay rights, feminism, animal rights, environmentalism, are single-issue commitments distinguished by a lack of relationship to or much concern about the condition of the broader community. Such causes make many of us uneasy in their means, if not their ends, when they are promoted ruthlessly and through unscrupulous misrepresentation. It is more fashionable and presumably more fulfilling to hug tree trunks and provide an outpouring of compassion for our overnumerous kangaroos than to worry about human beings, but people were and should remain, in my view, the central concern of left wing political speculation and action. That is if the Left still presumes to lead the cause for social emancipation and the uplifting of the human spirit through the pursuit of inspiring ideals and practical goals.

I had another more immediate problem. In the Whitlam Government I often vigorously disagreed, sometimes even warred, with Cabinet colleagues because of important differences on policy. Those differences could be understood as the impatience of a young man of socially radical disposition. My engaging in robust argument now would be interpreted as a case of the vanquished striving to assert some authority or vindicate himself, a dangerous outcome.

The less that happened the better for the Labor Party, for the Government and for me. It was the dominant reason I opted to become Minister for Foreign Affairs. In freely chosen exile, as it were, by working hard and hopefully productively, I would be doing a service to the Party and the nation. I would also be avoiding the potential for easily misunderstood conflict.

Overall, it was a wise choice, made all the more sound by the way in which Hawke and I, mostly, complemented one another on many foreign policy matters—and often on issues where commentators had predicted major conflicts between us. That mutual restraint resulted in a productive, overall balance. It was something which came instinctively to two people of mature experience who readily understood what was good for their party and country, and what was politically feasible. Our approach to Middle Eastern questions makes a useful illustration: while Hawke had an oddly passionate commitment to Israel, my sympathies for the rights of the Palestinian people had also been made clear. Because of this I had to use care in dealing with these matters or risk being declared partisan. I was, after all, referred to as 'that well-known anti-Semite' by a local media representative during my official visit to Israel in 1984. Paradoxically, it was Hawke who made the really tough commentary about Israel's handling of these problems. In a speech in Melbourne to representatives of the Australian Jewish community he castigated Israel stating that 'after thousands of years we may be witnessing a giant eyeless in Gaza'. 'Is there not emerging,' he asked, 'the danger of Israel being blinded to the threat to its very soul and the vision of its founders'? There was a predictable outcry when he also linked the experiences of the Palestinians with, among others, those of 'the black in South Africa'.[1] Because of his emotionally expressed commitment to Israel's cause, the effects of his statements were electrifying among the Australian Jewish community. If I had said the same things they would have been dismissed as the eructation of prejudice.

When I was Foreign Minister, Mark Leibler, a leader of the Australian Jewish community with whom I became friendly, suggested my criticisms of Israel may have owed something to my earlier competitive hostility towards Hawke. I think Leibler was partly correct; if so the impulse was unconscious. I am also certain a large part of my attitude was learnt at my mother's knee, listening to her talk about the mystical cause of Ireland, its freedom, and the sacred land occupied by a foreign power. There were potent messages in this childhood conditioning, through which evolved certain universal principles in me capable of being triggered emotively: a people's right to liberty, freedom from occupation by a foreign power (especially an imperial one, hence my later anti-Vietnam War activity), the sovereign right of a people to their land. From such values the cause of the Palestinian people was warmly embraced to the point of gross and unfair simplification of Israel's situation. I have matured beyond those simplifications. Israel, small, surrounded by hostile forces for so long, her right to exist regularly challenged, has survived because of her determination to do so. Some of Israel's actions have been excessive and some of her policies towards others, for whom she had certain responsibilities and duties, have been intemperate. But in the conditions in which that nation seeks to survive, while excessive responses are not excusable, they are also often understandable. I have sometimes wondered how we Australians would have behaved in similar circumstances to those endured by the Israeli people.

On Indochina, it was Hawke who proposed in 1983 that I initiate dialogue, as Foreign Minister, with the countries of that region. The list of characters on the playbill included not only the non-communist Cambodian coalition partners warring against the communist government of Kampuchea, the ASEAN countries and China, but the USSR and the USA as well. The proposition was that Australia should encourage contact between parties who, mostly, had their own good reasons for not wanting to speak to one another. The aim was to facilitate a process of dialogue leading to a peaceful settlement of the warring inside and near the borders of Kampuchea. I regarded the proposal with some caution. There were a great number of differences between many of these parties and some had large political interests at stake. Australia strolling into this particular pastry shop and upsetting the wares so carefully if unsteadily arranged, could well be disastrous.

There were many complex interests at stake. The USA seethed at this intrusion into its carefully arranged interests in that part of the globe; they saw me as tossing another anti-American straw into the wind, missing entirely of course Hawke's strong pro-American disposition and his role as initiator in this. The Australian interest in China was larger and more important than any interest in Indochina. China and Vietnam, meanwhile, were tensely divided and in regular military conflict at their borders. Humiliated by a major military reverse at the hands of the Vietnamese in 1979, China was still smarting. The irritation was added to by a tendency of Vietnam to provocatively swagger, off-handedly proposing to 'teach China another lesson'. This was a rather tricky situation to handle.

The outward position of the ASEAN countries was to be uniformly hostile to Australian contact with the Vietnamese. Privately, there was considerable variation of opinion among them, but Singapore 'rode herd' and rode it hard on them. That country took a loud, strident moralising approach, a characteristic role for some of her leaders. As Singaporean-registered cargo boats dumped kilotons of consumer goods at harbours in Kampuchea, Singapore noisily denounced any propensity by other countries to have contact with Kampuchea. Thailand had its own agenda. The resupply of arms, from various sources, to the different Cambodian factions militarily opposed to the Heng Samrin administration in Kampuchea, flowed easily and without hindrance through Thai territory. There were advantages in this for Thailand. While Chinese arms flows to the Khmer Rouge safely reached their destination through Thailand,

Chinese support for the indigenous Thai Communist Party concomitantly dried up. That was more or less the end of that organisation as an effective force. In rather peculiar ways, moreover, Thailand derived a goodly supply of state-of-the-art military equipment by illicitly tapping into some of this flow of military hardware. Indonesia and Malaysia mouthed criticism as required, but privately had more sympathy with what Australia was doing.

I registered my reservations to Hawke when first discussing this proposal, pointing out that the complexities in this were 'much more difficult than those involved in resolving a domestic industrial dispute'. In his characteristic, crackly voice, with its strong Australian accents—so suggestive of another Australian prime minister of renown and of similar physical proportions, Billy Hughes—he responded: 'Ah . . . I don't know that that's right . . . same principles you know . . . just a bigger canvas'. I drew in a deep breath and wheezed slightly. There would soon be more instances of Hawke's tendency to want to fine tune the major trouble spots of the world.[2]

As I turned the proposal over in my mind, the inherent dangers in it fascinated me. Carefully handled we might puncture some of the pompous posturing coming from some of our friends and associates, perhaps even make some worthwhile advances towards easing conflict in Indochina. I happily took on the task. The risk of total failure, and the dismissive hoots which would inevitably follow such a setback, were no justification for fudging the challenge. It also occurred to me that should the Australian role be appreciated by the Indochina Peninsula countries, there could be, over time, a beneficial commercial spin-off for this country. That is the way it has proved to be. There is a caveat. We had to get into the Vietnam market early to get a good commercial toehold. Once the 'big players', the USA and Japan, normalise their relationship fully with Vietnam, conditions will change dramatically. As a sprat in international commercial terms, we will be struggling to hold our position in a large commercial sea full of voracious predators. In international relations, especially commercial ones, there is little sentiment at the end of the day; mainly self-interest, a lesson we Australians have to learn.

I also suspected then, and became firmly convinced over time, that Hawke had encouraged the Indochina initiative as a red herring to distract the Party, especially the Left, from the vexatious and difficult to manage issue of East Timor. The suspicions were well-grounded. He never conceded this but the implications of his conduct were clear enough; he was satisfied to let matters roll once I began work and took little direct interest thereafter. I pursued this issue without any distraction from Hawke, for his preoccupation was with the big power equation, in particular our relationship with the USA. The Left followed my initiatives avidly and paid less attention to East Timor. This was not my game plan but rather the way things worked out.

We managed to keep out of major trouble. Our persistence mostly wore down regional critics, and eventually they began to show a more receptive attitude towards our urging for increased dialogue. At the beginning it was all rather rough going. On the occasion of my first post-ASEAN conference in Bangkok in 1983 I was subjected to much heavy-handed pressure from several ASEAN foreign ministers, in a way clearly indicating they had caucused beforehand. Then George Shultz, USA Secretary of State, moved in to capitalise on this earlier attempt to soften me up. He delivered a stern and irritatingly patronising homily about how unwise our Indochina initiative was, in the course of which he referred to certain expectations on Australia's part—by which he clearly meant the Government but me in particular—as 'stoopid'. He used this offensive adjective emphatically several times, and each time my blood pressure notched up another several points. I have never claimed to be a diplomat, consistently making it clear my background was in politics; I was a product of the broad and open forums of the Labor Party where if you do not learn early how to successfully defend yourself and your views in often vigorous debate, you do not survive. I responded with notable asperity. Shultz later complained to Hawke about my 'prickliness'.[3] Happily, a breakthrough on the Cambodian issue came after I moved to Yarralumla. The collapse of communism in the USSR, a realignment of China's strategic interests, and a reduction of USA hostility permitted major advances. Pre-eminent among those pursuing these opportunities were Australian Foreign Minister, Gareth Evans, and then Deputy Secretary of the Department of Foreign Affairs and Trade, Michael Costello. They did so with great commitment and skilfulness. The deficiencies of the Cambodian Government and the poor standard of its armed forces nevertheless caused difficulties for the process. After visiting Cambodia in 1995, however, I came away with more confidence about its future prospects.

Vietnam, once the annual object of passionate excoriation by ASEAN conferences, is now a member of that body, is active in the ASEAN Regional Forum, receives high-level visits from Chinese officials, and is receiving official US aid through a recently established US embassy in Hanoi. Her former mentor and provider, the Soviet Union, no longer exists and Russia is too preoccupied with her own survival to be of any use to Vietnam. Cambodia and Laos are welcome to join ASEAN as soon as they demonstrate they have the will and can mobilise the resources to allow them to do so. They, like Vietnam, are no longer political pariahs. Things do change in politics, especially in international relations. It was all worth the risks and the difficulties and perhaps I even got a bit of it right.[4] I was regarded in some circles as being anti-American. I could more correctly be described as having been less flexible with them than Hawke. I recognised that the relationship between our two countries was not one of equals, but one in which we, as the smaller partner, suffered certain clear disadvantages—which is not the same as saying we had no leverage. I came to believe that in the interests of deterring nuclear conflict between the superpowers, we were obliged to support America. That commitment was morally driven: it would be immoral to claim neutrality and non-alignment on such an issue when most life on the globe could have been extinguished by a major nuclear conflict. In those circumstances one has to choose and I chose, but with the important rider that our support for deterrence was committed on the explicit basis we would vigorously push ahead with our arms control objectives. Our support for America did not come cheaply either, for it exposed Australia to serious risks; in the event of a nuclear clash the joint facilities at Nurrungar and Pine Gap would be high priority targets. I also never understood the view, and still do not, that the joint facilities enjoyed isolation from any trade or commercial policy considerations. In 1984 I publicly floated the idea that Australia might use them as leverage to extract more willingness on the arms control issue by the USA. Later, in about 1986, I raised the possibility that we might use their presence as a means of securing better commercial treatment for our farmers.[5] On both occasions I was rebuked by Hawke for my impulsiveness.

The Americans expressed irritation when, in Japan in 1984 and again in 1985, I criticised their attempts to force domestic economic adjustments on Japan. These would have resulted in Japan importing more American products. It seemed to me the unstated agenda of the Americans was bilateral trading arrangements which could be at the expense of countries like Australia. I pointed out quite accurately that most of the economic adjustment needed to be carried out by America. With a US dollar overvalued by perhaps as much as 30 per cent, America needed to apply corrective measures in its own economy rather than unfairly expecting the Japanese to impose all the hard disciplines on themselves.[6] America's preference for living in continuing economic comfort, maintaining its excessive consumption levels while others did the belt tightening and saving, was unreasonable and in the longer term destructive of its important global leadership role. It was mortgaging its future with this economic slackness and the liability could become irredeemable. (Observant readers will recognise this general problem is not an experience exclusive to the USA.) By 1995, a decade later, my analysis was largely well borne out with these long simmering differences coming to a head in a major trade clash. America's weakening economic influence was evidenced by the resolute way Japan confronted the American demands, something from which, earlier, she had always shied. To the Americans' chagrin, I also disagreed with their demands that Japan increase its defence spending and extend its defence capabilities. Should Japan have done that there would have been widespread apprehension through East and South-East Asia and the South Pacific region. This would have been detrimental to Japan's interests and unhelpful to the sense of regional security, leading to increased levels of arms spending.[7] In each of these matters Australia had a direct major national interest, different to that of the USA, and which the Americans were unwilling to acknowledge.

In spite of these differences, I learnt to cautiously admire America and what it generally represents as a free, liberal society. I could not, however, take an uncritical view. Some of the things the USA has done in various parts of the world have been clearly imperialistic and inappropriate for a country professing the values of freedom and democracy. Instances of this sort justify criticism. I also put Australia first, as much as I could. Perhaps a misunderstanding of this background led the USA State Department senior official, Paul Wolfowitz, to move about Asian capitals spreading some unpleasant accounts as to my motives and allegiances in pursuing Indochina conflict settlement policies. A national foreign affairs commentator, the late Peter Hastings, discovered what was happening and disclosed what he learnt.[8] But no matter how crabbed a companion I might have seemed to our major ally at times, once the New Zealand Labour Government got into full swing after 1984, the situation commenced to change rapidly and much the better for me. When New Zealand set about implementing its prohibitions on nuclear-powered and nuclear-capable warships, I suspect that to the Americans I suddenly started to look almost as wholesome as Mom's homemade apple pie.

Putting foreign policy together: at the workface

The fundamental objective of our foreign policy is, more generally, to secure and promote our national interests globally, and specifically to do so in regions of particular importance to us, especially within our geopolitical region. Those national interests embrace political, commercial and strategic concerns, and in addition matters of moral duty. These moral duties might be said to be based on Western universalist values, requiring us to act in areas such as human rights, world poverty and underdevelopment, arms control, disarmament and peace, the resolution of conflict. In doing these things we should proceed with a confident but unexaggerated sense of national confidence.

We are not a superpower, not even a great power. As a small country we lack the sort of leverage those powers have. But we are not without influence. Much of it is the product of good diplomatic relations mostly based on any of a range of shared interests and ambitions as well as a concrete basis of shared understandings. Some comes from our reputation as a good global partner respecting due processes through established agencies, in particular the UN, its sub-bodies and the International Court of Justice. In certain situations, our long-standing record for being territorially non-threatening and non-acquisitive has advantaged us. A willingness to disagree with our most powerful ally, the USA, on matters of important principle where we believed it was justified, attracted respect elsewhere for our sense of what was right and fair and for our evident independence. We demonstrated that although aligned we were not a slavish client State. In some circumstances,

Left: *The headline said it all, but not for long. This was taken after the 1982 caucus election confirming my Opposition Leadership.*
(Fairfax)

Below: *A pale green Hayden on the Gordon River, Tasmania, 1983.*
(News Ltd)

Right: *I told the 1983 NSW State Conference of the Labor Party that being called mate by its controlling right wing officers was like receiving a bunch of white carnations from the Mafia. You knew you were in trouble. That night a dozen white carnations arrived from NSW Secretary Steve Loosley with a message on an attached card, 'Thanks for the memories mate'. Actually, Loosley and I had always been good, if at times somewhat uneasy, mates. That has been true of Graham Richardson, too. (Fairfax)*

Below: *A Cambodian refugee camp on the Thai–Kampuchea border, 1984. Remarkable medical services were provided by volunteer western doctors and nurses in quite primitive conditions. (AP)*

Left: *A decade after Vietnam's victory in the war in its country I greet Vietnamese Foreign Minister Nguyen Co Thach on Australian soil in 1984. Some were noisily opposed to the visit; now, associating with Vietnam is quite fashionable.* (News Ltd)

Below: *Meeting with Afghan refugees who had fled Soviet military occupation of Afghanistan, at Peshawar, Pakistan, 1985. Australia provided generous aid for these refugees.* (AP)

Right: *The Shanghai Public Park sign from colonial days which says, 'Dogs and Chinamen prohibited'. My father told us about this sign as children — my blood still boils at the indignity of that statement.*

Below: *'Lots of kangaroos in Australia. You know, I've even got a kangaroo street-crossing sign a friend brought back from Australia for me.' This was part of the private dialogue when President Reagan and I got together in New York in 1986 as eminent international statesmen.*

Left: *Speaking at the welcoming ceremony, San Francisco, for the 1986 Australia–US bilateral talks. Flanked by Australian Defence Minister Kim Beazley, US Secretary of State George Shultz and US Defence Secretary Caspar Weinberger.* (AP)

Below: *With Soviet Union Foreign Minister, Eduard Shevardnadze, Canberra, 1987. These were important talks and were the product of the positive manner with which we dealt with the Soviet Union, instead of lapsing into shrill, Cold War name-calling.* (News Ltd)

Right: With the
irrepressible and enduringly
likeable David Lange,
Prime Minister and Foreign
Minister of New Zealand.
Often engaging as a good
humoured scamp and scally
wag, Lange is always a fine
boon companion, especially
as he is a teetotaller.

Below: The last hurrah, literally. Bob Hawke with Dallas and me launching the 1987 Oxley
election campaign at Ipswich, the last of the twelve I contested in twenty-seven years in the
House of Representatives. (News Ltd)

Left: *Bob Hawke welcoming me on my arrival in Canberra on February 15 1989 as Australia's twenty-first Governor-General.* (News Ltd)

Below: *Shimon Peres, then Foreign Minister, greeted Dallas and me on the occasion of an official visit to Israel, 1988. I admire Peres greatly as a social democrat and a committed humanitarian.* (Reuters)

Right: With Dallas, Ingrid, Kirk and Georgina at the private entrance to Government House days after our arrival there in 1989. Ingrid is an accountant and Georgina a lawyer, both practising in New York. Kirk is a lawyer practising in Canberra.

Below: With the Hawke Ministry which I had just sworn in at Government House, April 1990. (NLA)

Left: *With Bob Hawke at Parliament House, 1989, for the swearing-in as Governor-General.*
(Fairfax)

Below: *The monarchist thorn between two not quite blushing but good humoured republican roses. With Donald Horne and Tom Keneally at the launch of Max Suich's* New Independent Monthly, *Sydney, 1989.*
(News Ltd)

Right: As Commander-in-chief of the Australian armed services, with the ship's company of HMAS Hobart. *(Fairfax)*

Left: *Talking with Peter Mikhiel of Bankstown over morning tea at Admiralty House, 1990, after launching the ACTU's youth magazine.*
(Fairfax)

Below: *Paul and Annita Keating, and George and Barbara Bush, with Dallas and me at a state dinner, Government House,1992.*
(NLA)

Right: Kerbside camaraderie with Bishop Challen, Melbourne, 1993 at the Brotherhood of St Laurence headquarters.
(News Ltd)

Below: Handing over Warapa (NT) Land Trust Deeds to Tony Wray.
(News Ltd)

Left: *With Prime Minister
Paul Keating outside
Parliament House, 1995.*
(Fairfax)

Right: *I met with President Suharto on my first official visit as Governor-General to Indonesia, 1995. Suharto's success in managing the economic and political life of Indonesia has contributed greatly to regional stability and has been invaluable for Australian interests. (AP)*

Below: *Me and Graham ('learn to trust me mate') Richardson on a convivial occasion.(News Ltd)*

Left: *Attempting to improve on Bill Leak's art work. Leak was much less than amused. Mercifully, all evidence of my handiwork has been removed as the reproduction on the jacket of this book shows.* (Fairfax)

Below: At Government House, 1995.
(Stuart Spence)

Above: *Beside Lake Burley Griffin with Dallas at Government House, 1995. According to folkore, the original idea was that when parliament was to be formally opened, the Queen, or the Governor-General when Her Majesty was unavailable, would depart from the Yarralumla jetty by boat to the pontoons adjacent to the Parliamentary triangle and then proceed to parliament, perhaps in an ornate, open horse-drawn carriage to maintain the tone of the ceremonial occasion. Whenever I hear this drollery (as I hope it is), I have visions of purple silken, square-rigged sails languidly powering an elegant, clinker built vessel of flawless Huon pine, with diaphanously gowned maidens manning long oars, providing additional power. The concept was never proceeded with, perhaps because of the cost of purple silk or maybe a shortage of vestal virgins in this modern age.*
(Stuart Spence)

paradoxically, a degree of regional influence emanated from our formal treaty ties with the USA. Lee Kuan Yew of Singapore saw us as too small to be militarily important; but our presence in the region was welcomed, nonetheless, because in his view the ANZUS ties would have worked as a trip-wire bringing in the USA should we be attacked there. On the other hand, Vietnam's Foreign Minister Nguen Co Thach saw the formal link as giving us influential dialogue standing with the USA and therefore even greater status with regional nations (in particular on the vexatious question of Kampuchea), without which our initiatives on that issue could not have been taken seriously. But ANZUS is effectively gone and we stand on our own feet now.

At the global level, it was seriously put to me by some officers of my department on the occasion of Australia's election to the UN Human Rights Commission in 1985 and to the UN Security Council in the same year that it would be unhelpful to our national interests for Australia to serve on those bodies. There, we would be required to make decisions on issues and support determinations which could cause resentment from a national party or from parties affected by them, and this might be disadvantageous for us elsewhere. Better to accept our limited influence as a small power, keep our head down and beaver away, according to this view, promoting a narrow and restricted notion of national self-interest. The point is not without some validity: there was no doubt on the part of the Department of Foreign Affairs in its advice to me later that a major reason that Australia was rebuffed when it canvassed for re-election to the Human Rights Commission in 1987 was that some countries saw us as having been too energetic in pursuit of human rights issues. This lost us support second time around.

Soon after arriving as Foreign Minister in 1983, I detected a preference among some to be overly agreeable towards certain outside interests and accordingly not independent enough in catering for the national interest. At its worst this could manifest itself in a severe infection of 'localitis', where a diplomat serving too long at an overseas post came to be more identified with the host country's interests than Australia's. Others held to the attitude that ANZUS was our most important relationship, in particular regionally, from which it followed that we be a slavishly faithful and predictable ally. To me, this kind of deference could not only be discomforting but could weaken opportunities for the expression of a confident and independent statement of our national ambitions. ANZUS was important, but the reality was it always remained a link in the international strategic chain of communist containment. Its regional importance was mainly restricted to that role as Australia should have learnt from several rebuffs when it sought to invoke its provisions locally. To exaggerate our power would have been foolish and damaging of course, but to underplay our influence forfeited opportunities to promote our national authority more effectively. The USA was a very big and influential part of our world but there were a number of other centres which, I felt, were suffering some degree of neglect, including in the then communist world, because of this.

Despite reservations, and regrettably, I once accepted a speech written for me which contained remarks that the USA was a shield between Australia and communism in Asia. This was too uncomplicated a view, distorting as it did the real nature of our important relationship with that country and what we should seek from it. Again, there was a theory that energetic international action on peace and disarmament would only irritate our powerful ally, and thus be disadvantageous to us. Further, that active concern on human rights in our region would provoke hostility from important neighbours and, pursued in other forums, would have us regarded as meddlers seeking a role in this field with neither influence nor credibility. There is some truth in these opinions, but it is the place of careful technique to minimise the effect of damaging reactions. Arms control and human rights are too important to the future and quality of civilisation to neglect due to concern for less than crucial sensitivities. In any event, we weathered whatever tensions arose because of initiatives in these fields, which in itself is a good illustration of how excessive the cautions and restraints were.

The Department tended to fare poorly in those important battlefields of bureaucratic territory and power, known as inter-departmental committees. In negotiating disputes, there was a softness of manner which some from the department mistook for a smooth diplomatic style. It was obvious to me that Australia's foreign policy had to be securely intertwined with the promotion of our global commercial interests but this seemed to pain some of the purists and other well-rounded products of the older, lingering culture in the Department. Their love of playing with words without saying anything much itself created a problem. This was a style which tended to generate similarly agreeable but empty responses from foreign associates, while the hard heart of the matter at contention remained glossed over. I demanded that graduates from a broader range of disciplines, in particular, economics, be recruited. With them came more rigour and attention to the detail of our commercial interests. After lobbying Hawke over several years, trade and foreign affairs were amalgamated in 1987, the most obviously sensible amalgamation of all those made that year and probably the only sensible one in administrative terms. Similarly, some officers in Australia's overseas development aid agency (now known as AusAID) had allowed aid project assessments to be influenced too much by sentiment rather than rigorous cost-benefit analysis and critical technical justification. Thus, inadequate projects in various recipient countries had taken on a costly, self-perpetuating life of their own, sometimes running for years and constantly being returned to Canberra for generous fiscal top-ups. The prevailing attitude seemed to be that, having made a bad decision in the first place, there was no alternative but to keep sticking the flawed undertakings together with more adhesive made from Australian taxpayers' paypackets—to do otherwise would be embarrassing for our bilateral relationship, seemed to be the view. My approach was to disengage as quickly as creditably possible, while employing more of the sort of people who would bring rigour and discipline to the assessment processes. This worked admirably.

There was a tendency among some departmental staff to try to escape the responsibility of presenting unambiguous advice to the Minister by taking cover behind a heavy barrage of equivocation. The most notable examples of this were displayed in early submissions to me on important policy issues. Such submissions would cogently argue a case up to the point of a seeming conclusion; but then the next paragraph would literally commence, 'On the other hand . . .' at which the contrary case would be just as coherently and convincingly presented. Then, with the completion of this would come the heading, 'Recommendation', under which and without exception would sit the brief and succinct notation: 'For decision by the Minister'. As anyone may note, this process put the Department in the remarkably privileged position of never having to make a decision and with the Minister to blame if something went wrong. If, however, all went well, as mostly it did, the Department stood modestly forward to claim its bit of glory for having advised the Minister so well. There were groans of despair when I demanded hard conclusions and clear recommendations. But by and large my eccentric request for plain advice was accepted and acted upon, at least up until the closing stages of my Ministry in 1988 when I noted a new twist from the past seeping in. Contrary views would be explored, properly enough, but after 'Recommendation', a new formulation commenced to percolate into the process: 'For information'. With so little time left to serve as Minister I bequeathed this to my successor to tidy up, which he did.

In practice, the preference for agreeableness could sometimes take on a dissimulating quality. At one time I learned that the Americans had received briefings out of Washington on our arms control and disarmament policies which were somewhat at odds with the seriousness with which the Government, and particularly myself, regarded those policies. While the Americans might have been inclined to see and welcome this as indicating revisionism on our part, it effectively undermined the genuine force of what we were trying to do. I was then able to establish that Washington was following a line developed during bilateral discussions by a senior representative from the Department in Canberra. After a robust discussion in my office at Canberra that officer left rather shaken to prepare a typewritten *mea culpa*. Back it came, several pages long, appropriately abject, and confessing to having 'engaged in special diplomacy'. 'Special' was typed over a long lump of white-out which, when the page was reversed, showed the word 'deceptive' had been covered over.[9] Oddly enough, the Minister suddenly found himself expostulating. Mostly department officers were diligent, resourceful, able and sought to serve the Government well. Many, especially some of the younger ones, were exciting company when they were tossing around ideas free of the old and tired baggage of past generations.

In the very early years of my foreign ministership there were several major advances in the cause of peace and disarmament. The Labor Party has, of course, always had a deep commitment to these causes and I had been a long-time activist on them, from well before I entered Parliament. Hawke was much less enthusiastic about broadly initiating policies of this kind, I suspected because they would not be welcomed by the USA. As the early months rolled by, a potential threat to the Government's arms control policies arose domestically with an efflorescence of support for the traditional Palm Sunday peace marches in Sydney and Melbourne. Huge crowds spontaneously participated in what, in the immediately preceding years, had been modestly supported, desultory affairs of negligible impact on the public consciousness. In 1983, and for the next couple of years, that changed dramatically. Conflictive rhetoric directed against the Soviet Union by President Reagan left many with the fearful impression that Washington was spoiling for a stoush which would surely end up nuclear. At the 1984 election there was so much concern about these deteriorating atmospherics that a Nuclear Disarmament Party, led by a then young rock star and supporter of some self-interested causes, Peter Garrett, fielded candidates in the election.

I instinctively recognised that we would have to move quickly and decisively to establish our ascendancy on peace and disarmament issues. Through my long association with the Left, whose social commitment I have always respected, I had a good idea of how they thought and developed tactics when they saw an opening to achieve an important objective. In full zealous mode, they could operate with deadly effectiveness. I saw Hawke and outlined the steps of the strategy I expected the Left to unroll. Nuclear arms control would be promoted to begin with, leading to demands for neutrality and non-alignment for Australia. Following this would come demands to close down the joint bases at North West Cape, Nurrungar and Pine Gap as nuclear war-fighting links. At some stage also, visits by USA nuclear-weaponry capable and nuclear-powered naval vessels would be made untenable as a result of aggressive protests. And eventually, even if only a good portion of this succeeded, there would be demands that the ANZUS Treaty be abrogated unilaterally by Australia following the New Zealand Labour Party's example. All of these and a range of unpredictable associated results could produce an unsatisfactory overall political outcome for Labor. While there was undoubtedly concern at the then sudden, sharp slump in relations between Moscow and Washington, I was confident the general public would arrive at different responses to those guiding the Left.

Hawke was distinctly unimpressed by my analysis. Clearly, he saw me as something of a wimp at the fringes of the peace movement, and accordingly not as resolute in my support of our powerful ally as I should be. In the light of the mounting protests, however, Hawke suddenly reassessed things and I was off and away with a raft of arms controls policies. The initiatives and activities included: the appointment of an Ambassador for Disarmament; pressure for the negotiation of an effective comprehensive nuclear test ban treaty; work on a treaty outlawing all forms of chemical and biological warfare; an energetic contribution to the disarmament activities of the United Nations; condemnation of French nuclear testing in the Pacific; the successful pursuit of a nuclear-free zone for the South Pacific; funding of $1.7 million for the foundation and operation of a Peace Research Institute at the Australian National University; and, later, funding of the 1984 International Year of Peace. This was a comprehensive program which allowed us to streak ahead and stay there. The Nuclear Disarmament Party disappeared and Peter Garrett was able to devote his energies to what he did best: singing roughly off-key, closing down jobs for timber workers of modest means in NSW forests, and trying to keep cheaper CDs out of the hands of consumers.

As much as I took satisfaction in our peace and arms control policies, the situation in South-East Asia, properly enough, continued to claim my attention. There was an occasion when I advised the Secretary of the Department, Peter Henderson, of my firm view that, with the acquisition of FA18 fighters as replacements for the obsolescent Mirage, we should end the permanent garrisoning of a squadron of fighter aircraft in Malaysia. To do otherwise, and at a time when there had been several unpleasant tensions in our dealings with Indonesia, could easily leave an important element of our defence capability isolated and immobilised. Keeping our aircraft there was more a status symbol for elements of the defence forces, meeting an exaggerated but unwise sense of our own importance in some quarters in Australia. In the event of hostilities, however, they could become an easy target to internal insurrection or the symbol of hostility in the event of across the border attack—admittedly an unlikely event, but if so why have them there? Worst of all as a prospect, in certain circumstances Australia could find a key part of its defence capability immobilised by the arbitrary decision of the host government. Henderson strongly endorsed my views. On later reading the notes of discussion between secretaries comprising a defence committee, I found that Henderson energetically opposed my views, arguing that any withdrawal would greatly damage our diplomatic relations with Malaysia. Here, I felt, was another case of 'soft' diplomacy, more concerned with winning favour elsewhere than protecting important elements of our national interests. Henderson's defence of his contradictory actions was that when he was dealing with me he had to accept my policy instructions, but when participating in this sort of statutorily independent committee he could express his personal views, which was correct in fact. That is, when with me, his practice was apparently 'Yes, Minister', but when away from me he performed according to a different tune. As perplexing as this behaviour was, his views on the above matter, as far as I was concerned, were decidedly faulty anyway. The committee in question has apparently not met since this fateful experience. In the end my view largely prevailed: the aircraft were not permanently deployed in Malaysia; there was no consequential damage to the bilateral relationship.

It is not that I had or have an exaggerated notion of Australia's influence in world affairs. Rather, underlying my attitude was a simple belief that Australia must arrange and pursue its national interests with a fundamental recognition that in certain circumstances, and in spite of great goodwill from allies and friends, we might have to battle alone and hard with our own resources to defend our interests. At some given moment of difficulty, good allies and friends might have seriously different priorities to ours and this could leave us exposed and vulnerable. We would do well to recall the experiences of World War II in this context: the continuing disputes over Britain's defence, or lack of it, of Singapore; the arguments of the time over whether the Australian 7th and 9th divisions should return from the Middle East for the defence of Australia; Britain's turning to the USA for foodstuffs to Australia's potential trade detriment; Australia's extreme difficulties in obtaining aircraft, arms and ammunition from the UK and the USA; Churchill's endorsement of a USA proposal to shift its Pacific fleet to the Atlantic; not to mention the Curtin Government's belated discovery of the UK–USA secret understanding in document 'WW1' of fighting Hitler first, with Australia's needs rated well down the priority list, after the Middle East, India, Ceylon and Hawaii. Respectable cases could be made for such wartime priorities from the point of view of the UK and USA. But for Australia, with its own pressing set of priorities about its national defence at a time when it felt vulnerable and threatened, these priorities could scarcely be termed reassuring. That is why an important degree of confident independence has to guide our foreign and defence policies.

This carefully crafted national confidence is not served at all well by any overweening nationalism. In some quarters there is a tendency to presume we stomp the world stage with the authority and influence of a great power, big-noting ourselves as the saying goes. The Labor Party has not been immune from this syndrome. Similarly, some major newspaper commentaries on these matters often proceed with an underpinning of some grand notion of our own significance. Among the various illustrations available, two telling ones come to mind; the first concerns Labor's approach to East Timor. In 1982 the Labor Party National Conference adopted a retributive policy towards Indonesia for its occupation of East Timor. I expressed reservations about such a policy to Labor's spokesman on Foreign Affairs, Lionel Bowen, at that conference. The policy proposed the suspension of all defence aid to Indonesia until it completely withdrew from East Timor, and its tone was in all respects unambiguously confrontationist. Our total defence aid to Indonesia, at that time, amounted to a minuscule 0.32 per cent of

Indonesia's defence spending. It will be readily appreciated, therefore, how embarrassingly empty this threat was. If implemented, any effect against Indonesia would have been inconsequential, but relations between Australia and Indonesia would have deteriorated quickly and markedly, leaving Australia at a clear disadvantage. Any opportunity for Australia to attend to humane concerns about people in East Timor would have been notably weakened. It was, unarguably, impractical as foreign policies go, and the sort of policy ultimately inimical to Australia's interests.

Bowen's explanation was that it was necessary to accept the policy to placate the Left on the foreign affairs and defence policy committee. If we won the election he would, he said, have no trouble diluting it to avert problems. I had serious doubts. I also had other problems: changing the uranium policy and handling the mounting confrontation with Hawke were completely preoccupying me at the conference. There are limits on how many political battles one can wisely fight at the one time. The East Timor policy I would get to later—and so it proved, in quite unexpected circumstances. As Foreign Minister I would have the uncomfortable task of battling to change it at the 1984 National Conference. In the meantime I had to steady the Party on this volatile issue. Thus, nearly two years later I was standing on my feet for close to eight hours at National Conference, fighting a sustained battle to pitch out, or modify into more reasonable terms, a clutter of impractical or imprudent foreign policies written into the party platform in slacker times. Among the jumble, East Timor policy was one of the major pieces to be deconstructed. While all this was going on I had to try to maintain a solid *modus vivendi* with Indonesia. Failure in any of these challenges would have meant trouble.

It might help to have some understanding of Indonesia's situation: after four centuries of totally unenlightened colonial occupation of East Timor, Portugal pre-emptively walked out of the territory leaving it to its own quite inadequate devices. Murderous armed conflict broke out between the East Timor factions, Fretilin, Apodeti and UDT. Fretilin was only one of these and certainly not the universally acclaimed faction as many of its thoroughly partisan supporters would have. East Timor was a 'vacated' non-self-governing territory devoid of any identifiable, credible admin-istration, being torn apart by internal civil war. It was moreover quite non-viable economically. For Indonesia, a disturbing political vacuum had opened on its flanks. In terms of international relations, power vacuums inevitably create instability and sooner or later a national interest concerned about the implications of this instability will move to fill the vacuum, one way or another. Indonesia had its revolution in 1965 when a perceived communist plot to take over the country was crushed by the military. Indonesia worried that East Timor was perhaps now open to external communist influence, or of even having a communist government.

In late 1975 Australia was in the grip of a politically paralysing constitutional confrontation, followed by a divisive election, and in no condition to take any constructive initiatives. From Indonesia's point of view there had to be decisive action to resolve the dilemmas she foresaw. No-one else gave any indication of being interested in the issue. East Timor was consequently occupied by Indonesia in that year. There are ways, other than bellowing through a bull horn, to register our concerns on human rights, and in the case of East Timor we adopted sensible procedures and effective measures. Thus, we were able to deliver humanitarian aid into East Timor. It should also be recalled that East Timor has benefited from more social and economic development in the past twenty years under Indonesian administration than it received through four centuries under the dead hand of Portuguese colonialism. In fact much of the dissidence occurring in East Timor today is a product of exaggerated expectations of what the new economic order could provide and not of sympathetic responses to Fretilin's sporadic and limited insurgency activity. None of this is to ignore abuses of human rights when they occur, some of which have indeed been grave violations. It might, however, serve the cause of fairness to acknowledge that considerable advances have been made in an attempt by Indonesia to curb such abuses and to punish offenders, while recognising more needs to be done.

This brings me to my second point: maladroit media conduct, based on exaggerated opinions as to where we sit in the world, has also caused severe strain in our bilateral relationship. The media has a duty to inform but it cannot divorce itself from the responsibility of avoiding unnecessary damage to our national interests with other countries. There is more at stake for Australia than the level of circulation and the profits derived by newspapers. In 1986 the *Sydney Morning Herald* published a page one exposé, as it was put at the time, of corruption at the top in the Indonesian Government.[10] Indonesian reprisals were prompt. They inconvenienced Australian holiday-makers and set back the bilateral relationship enormously in many ways. The author of the article, David Jenkins, called on me shortly after its publication, concerned the article had caused a political firestorm for Australia. He seemed to be suffering some kind of nervous spasm, as he twitched compulsively while speaking to me. However, Jenkins went on to explain himself on the grounds that: he had been instructed to write the article by his editor; there was a sense of urgency about the project as his editor wanted to scoop the publication of a book on this topic by a West Australian academic; he conceded there was nothing new or needing urgent disclosure in the article as distinct from the wish to scoop; his editor felt that as Marcos of the Philippines had been brought down by disclosure of Marcos' nefarious personal peculations, this article could be the beginning of something similar in Indonesia; the sensational headlines and introduction to the article had been written by the editor to 'harden up' the story! I have every reason to believe what Jenkins told me was true.[11]

All that was achieved from this blatant attempt at self-promotion by the *Sydney Morning Herald* was considerable disadvantage for Australia and for Australians—though not for that newspaper. Certain media commentators suggested that the bilateral relationship must have been fragile in the first place to buckle as it did over this matter. There was no denying that, or that the fragility was largely a result of being subjected to regular stress by the unconscionable conduct of some of the media. Elements of the Australian media have been the cause of the greatest strains in bilateral relations between this country and other countries of the region. Certainly, when I arrived in the department in the early eighties some senior officers advised me that news broadcasts from Radio Australia were frequently inaccurate and provocative, causing unnecessary strains for our political relations in the region. Incidentally, I would be interested, as I am sure would many others, in a rigorous opportunity cost assessment of Radio Australia and other inflated media exercises such as the ABC's Asian television venture; I am certain the money could be spent with greater community benefit elsewhere.

Australia and regional stability

The reality with which Australia has to contend is relatively uncomplicated and benign compared to that confronting many other countries in our region. Indonesia as an archipelagic nation comprises 13 000 islands, with 300 distinct ethnic groupings and 365 languages and dialects. Because of this extraordinary heterogeneity, the Indonesian authorities are constantly alert to any regional centrifugal tendencies. Although dominantly Islamic, the authorities are quick to curb inclinations towards fundamentalist Islam. Indonesia's economic growth is now strong and hopefully will be sustained but there remain major challenges to broadly enhance the condition of its people. It will be a newly industrialised economy within the first decade of the next century and perhaps, by one estimate, the world's fifth largest economy by 2020.[12] Imagine, that Indonesia, for whatever reason, were suddenly cast into fissionable, internal turmoil, with the potential for heading towards social breakdown. At the very least the flow of boat people to our shores, fleeing this dislocation and collapse, could dwarf anything we have seen before. Suppose some future Indonesian head of State, keen to continue in office beyond his best years and no longer confident of the support of the military, ABRI, courts Islam as a counterbalance and this leads to a high-pressure distortion in the domestic power balance. In such a scenario, should the military actively seek to regain their authority as a secular force guiding Indonesia's destiny, there could follow serious internal ructions of potentially great concern to Australia. Again, would we remain indifferent if an aggressive, zealous, proselytising strain of fundamentalist Islam spread like a contagion in Indonesia? Then we have important interests in Papua New Guinea, which shares a land border with Indonesia. Strains between these two countries arising from border difficulties have caused problems in the past. To what extent could we remain uninvolved in such a development? As a further illustration, would internal turbulence in Indonesia, caused, say, by uncertainty and challenges arising from a leadership succession vacuum, vent strains across this border? Perhaps not, but we cannot be absolutely sure. These are powerful reasons why we need to cultivate our role as a good and influential neighbour of Indonesia, a constructive partner not a strident public, carping critic. There is no influence for us in that role, although there are many noisy groups in the community who, unlike government, can afford to behave with indifference to the broader national interest.

About 60 per cent of our valuable export trade in mineral products and LNG is shipped through the Malacca, Sunda, Lombok and Ombai-Wetar Straits. It is worth noting that Indonesia is one of Australia's major competitors in the export of bauxite and LNG. After nearly forty years of effort Indonesia only finally achieved archipelagic status under the November 1994 implementation of the United Nations Law of the Sea Convention. She is now moving to limit and regulate sea lane passage through these waters. Australian shipping commonly uses five north/south routes and two east/west routes in the Indonesian archipelago. Indonesia is offering only three north/south sea lanes through its archipelagic territory. This could add considerable distances (and costs) for shipping commodities to certain destinations. Given Indonesia's past record of attempting to close straits which are busy merchant marine and naval sea highways, there is cause for some apprehension about what she might do in the future. Consider, hypothetically, the sorts of hindrances to normal shipping movements that could follow if Indonesia treated these waters as a limited national resource. Suppose, having done this she then imposed a tax on approved passages, adopting any one of a number of justifications in doing so? Tensions could arise over the right to levy such a tax, the rate of the tax, the claim to restrict, regulate, even prevent shipping. This is not at all far-fetched. Many of the orthodoxies of public international law are Eurocentric in their origin. Indonesia looks at this issue from a different cultural perspective. The potential for regional tensions would be great, in particular major powers like Japan and China could be sorely aggravated by any inconveniences caused. China's unilateral claim to the South China Sea, which covers a number of important sea lanes and which extends to close by Indonesia's gas resources from the Natuna Islands, causes concern in Indonesia and has led to heated dispute with the Philippines. Similarly China's territorial claims to the whole of the Spratly and Paracell Islands, also claimed variously, in full or to some extent, by Vietnam, Taiwan, Malaysia, the Philippines and Brunei represent a possible cause of great tension in the region.[13] More potential regional strains mean more localised complexities. Given the effective military withdrawal of the USA from the immediate region with the fizzling out of the Cold War, American preoccupations most certainly would be elsewhere.

There are a variety of elements present in our region capable of producing major instability. There is the case of periodic Muslim separatist activity in Southern Mindanao, in the Philippines. Were it to lead to major strife, with the prospect of a breakaway from the authority of Manila, there would be a high probability that Indonesia would intervene forcefully to protect itself from a potentially destabilising source of Islamic fundamentalism, as was once put quite firmly to me by a senior Indonesian Government official. The decision to intervene would not be hindered by special regard for the Philippines people. Generally, the Indonesian ruling élite do not hold them in high regard. They are seen as having lost their true ethnicity, as being confused between the competing influences of the Malay, Spanish, Chinese and American cultural heritages of their past. While Australia is one of the most racially tolerant and openly pluralistic societies in the world, this is not true of most of the countries in the Asian region. The Malays in Indonesia and Malaysia are openly hostile to Chinese. Mahathir, who is of Malay and Indian ancestry, idiosyncratically plays the ultra-Malay nationalist card, often quite crudely, to emphasise the legitimacy of his claims for acceptance as a Malay.[14] Malaysia's Bumiputra policy of positively discriminating in favour of Malays at the expense of Chinese is officially sanctioned racial discrimination against Chinese, denying them places in business and higher educational institutions even where they possess greater merit and ability, and forces many Chinese students of notable intellectual accomplishment to study overseas. University education standards have been lowered to accommodate the objectives of this policy and meanwhile widespread impoverishment among the Indian population is a direct consequence of their neglect by government. Singapore is tolerant as long as non-Chinese stay in their place. China is confident of its racial and cultural superiority. Korea distrusts the Japanese and the latter are among the most racially exclusivist people in the world. When Foreign Minister, I once announced in an Asian capital I believed it inevitable that in the distant future Australia would be dominantly a Eurasian society. I was discreetly advised that the message was not well received among leading figures in certain Asian countries. This was seen as encouraging miscegenation, a distinctly uncongenial phenomenon to the more traditional-minded of them.

Countries in our region generally adhere to nuclear non-proliferation requirements, some, unfortunately, with varying degrees of faithfulness. The biggest, China, makes little and unconvincing pretence of honouring those controls. What of future leadership in parts of the region, specifically India's stirring visions of her role and influence, not in, but on the world? What of the potential shock-wave effect of that country's nuclear capability? We should perhaps recall India's expanding naval pretensions, in particular her slightly earlier proposal to build an island naval base in the Bay of Bengal, close by and west of Thailand, north-west of Malaysia and north of Sumatra, which caused some tense moments in and between those countries. That proposal, as with her enhanced blue water naval capability, is in limbo for good economic reasons— at least for now. The point, however, remains: developments such as this in the Indian subcontinent can reach into our immediate sphere of interest with extraordinary celerity. The playing out of national and ethnic identity on the subcontinent is a complex process, both creating and reflecting tensions between India and Muslim Pakistan. Pakistan, too, has its acknowledged nuclear weaponry capability— developed with Chinese technical assistance—and is deploying a nuclear-armed version of the MII missiles acquired from China. India is deploying Privthi ballistic missiles and is developing a nuclear warhead for them, and when she successfully completes her satellite vehicle carrying programme she will, in effect, have an intercontinental ballistic missile capability.

To take another angle: some of our near and important neighbours are dominantly Islamic. The prospect for Islamic 'togetherness' leading to closer economic co-operation, exchanges, even military provisioning of a sister country worried about a perceived challenge cannot be categorically ruled out. Why would a country like Indonesia, for instance, with ample coal, oil, and water resources, suitable for hydro-energy, want to enter a comparatively more costly, major nuclear power generation programme? A programme which, on present costs and rates of return, is an uneconomic undertaking. It is worth noting that Indonesia has installed three research reactors, the most recent and largest in 1987, with a total power generation capacity in excess of 30 megawatts. In 1996 it proposes to commence a major nuclear power generation programme with a 600 megawatts reactor, to be completed in 2003, in a seismologically unstable area at that. Twelve more reactors are to follow this between 2003 and 2015. Indonesia has also embarked upon a non-military missile development programme (but the missile has the capacity for conversion to military purposes) and will eventually far outstrip our level of nuclear technical competence. This is not to say we should make too much of such developments, but that there are many factors we need to consider in arriving at our foreign policy assessments.

Malaysia and Singapore, superficially, work well together. In fact they are deeply suspicious of each other and the structure and equipment of their defence forces have reflected this over a long period. Under the Five Power Defence Arrangements—a no longer relevant (if it ever was) hangover from the colonial period— Australia, New Zealand and the United Kingdom are formally associated with these two countries on defence matters. The Integrated Air Defence System, a central element in the arrangements and commanded by an Australian military officer, is due for technical upgrading, the outcome of which may leave the impression that its warfighting command and control capabilities will then extend well beyond the defence perimeter of Singapore and Malaysia, south as much as north. That could have unfortunate consequences for Australia and is a good reason, but not the only one, for withdrawing from the arrangement. As well, there is an extraordinary development of submarine capability, mainly conventional boats but not exclusively so, by various nations from India, through Southeast Asia, to East Asia including Taiwan and Japan. The submarine has many functions but above all it is a potent warfighting unit. This is scarcely a reassuring portent when the case for substantial cuts in our military spending is presented to us as a domestic fiscal discipline.

What the above set of references indicates is just how complicated foreign relations in our region is becoming and how 'hard' issues may readily arrive at our doorstep. Australia will have to learn to exercise its foreign relations with great skill, care and subtlety, a task for which the impatient and direct Australian character is not well-suited. Until now, the aggregate value of the Australian economy has exceeded the combined worth of that of ASEAN. That will not last much longer. Even with lower per capita GDP, the total value of some individual ASEAN economies will be larger than ours. As countries in our region develop their economies, our significance in the region will shrink, perhaps to comparatively tiny proportions. Our position and status in the region will be determined by how successfully we handle our national economy and our external political relations. Many of the advantages which gave us an edge in the past will no longer be there. Once we clung to the stabilising presence of the United States and, in security matters, compensated for lack of numbers with privileged access to leading edge military technology from America. The first prop has gone and the second is rapidly disappearing. Our Eurocentric disposition had been no disadvantage when European values dominated the political and commercial world. That could still be helpful; for instance, we could do more to promote Australia as a stable economic and political environment within which to establish European-owned industries to serve the Asian region, and as a link between the cultures of East and

West. In this regard we are achieving some success in having Australia adopted as the regional headquarters for various corporations. Our greater success will be determined by us acknowledging our differences, striving to anticipate the nature of change, understanding the immense cultural diversity of the region, engaging in energetic and constructive diplomacy, making sure we are competitive, and a reliable supplier of high-quality goods and services, and thus taking advantage of openings when they occur. The Asian market is not susceptible to sentimentality, especially from a country like Australia which is seen as the god-child of one of the greatest colonial powers in the region's modern history. But nor should we allow our preoccupation with Asia to become a fad at the expense of our important interests in Europe. Europe remains a substantial market for our exports and is a major source of investment in Australia.

This fluidity and change is not restricted to our immediate area. Three-and-a-half decades back Japan and East Asia accounted for 4 per cent of world GDP. North America with Mexico represented 37 per cent. Today those two blocs are level pegging at about 26 per cent each. More than half the world's current economic growth occurs in Asia now. With technology and know-how transfer plus Asian inventiveness, Asian economies will achieve economic maturity at a far faster rate than ever applied in the older, Western developed economies—though growth rates will eventually fall back as those economies mature. In Asia, Japan is now promoting the Japanese way of capitalist management and social development, one which succeeds while avoiding the community breakdowns which exemplify even the best of successful Western societies. That appeals to the orderly and ordered way of doing things preferred by so many people living in Asia, especially those with a background of Confucianism. This of course implies of necessity an increasing great power interest in the region by Japan. With American military power diminishing—and probably to be totally withdrawn in the event of a resolution of the Korean Peninsula differences—with pressures in America now escalating for the United States to turn away from Asia and towards Europe commercially, and with the high yen forcing much Japanese investment to go increasingly offshore, the pressure for Japan to oversight its interests will escalate. In these circumstances and in the absence of a dominant USA presence, should instability in the region appear as a threat to Japan's vast commercial interests, that country could be forced to elevate its military capabilities and presence to protect those interests, much as it would indisputably prefer to avoid this. China would be uncomfortable with such a response and would feel the need to react. Adding to these potential complications is the fact that China will be a full superpower some time early next century. To this should be added the risk that Taiwan, at some time in the future, overreaches itself by making it clear it regards itself as an independent nation–state and no longer a territory of China. Mainland China would be unlikely to let such a development pass without some major military response. This, in turn, would engage the interests of some major powers, not least the United States.

All these hypothetical situations contain ingredients for potential instability in regions of immediate, major interest to Australia, but with the stress on 'potential' not 'actual'. It is far more certain that the worst excesses of conflict will continue to occur within the old Warsaw bloc, parts of the Middle East and nearby, and sub-Sahara Africa. Asia, preoccupied with its economic developments and success, is fairly stable at this point. The nature of conflict elsewhere and its potential for this region gives no substance to the fanciful notion of a 'clash of civilisations'.

Finally, Australia has to jettison the assumption prevailing in some places that increasing prosperity in Asia will automatically bring increasing evidence of Western embourgeoisement of those societies, and with that the rise of a Western-type middle class in those countries. The appeal of such speculation is that with this sort of development it will all be so easy for the West to simply fuse with

Asia. As yet another unfortunate instance of cultural superiority, this also loses track of the fact that, allowing for some fusion with Western ways, the various parts of Asia will have their own and quite different cultural values by which they will want to live. That is an imperative we must learn. Australia will have to develop diplomatic skills in handling the balance of power as it develops and shifts in the region, a notion distinctly uncongenial to the uncomplicated perception of many Australians about our times and place in international relations.

The further presumption of some of our military leaders—one of long standing and stated periodically—that they are better able to promote our diplomatic interests than our diplomatic service through their close and growing involvement with the other military services of our region, leaves me distinctly anxious. Military personnel usually are unskilled as diplomats because their training is unambiguously to handle events of a different order, and in quite different ways, to those of a diplomat. My fear is that the nature of some of theses military entanglements with our neighbours may lodge the belief elsewhere that in the event of some tension between countries in the region, Australia will choose to support a particular country. We would do well to avoid any such impressions, by generally keeping clear of formally structured entanglements. Our best interests, in present circumstances at least, will be promoted by professionally based political engagement with our neighbours, not through military roles which, in some circumstances, might become bigger and more demanding than we would wish or could practically handle, or which, alternatively, could put at risk other relationships, or another important relationship, at some considerable disadvantage for Australia. By definition, a bilateral agreement creates a closer involvement with the agreement partner and excludes other parties. In some conditions this may tend to restrain options and diminish our flexibility in functioning more broadly in the region. We also have to bear in mind that some countries in our region do not share our fastidious concern about certain human principles. We do not jail political dissenters, there is guaranteed freedom of expression and freedom of the press, trade unions and their officials have the right to organise and to resist unfair treatment of workers and to publicly condemn government without being jailed; nor are we governed by corrupt ruling elites, and human rights generally and moral rectitude in government and its services to the people of our country, specifically, are key parts of our culture. These important cultural values of ours should not be compromised either by inference arising from formal military association with others or by the nature of obligation, explicit or implicit, arising from formally endorsed military-type commitments.

A literal interpretation of the Australia–Indonesia Agreement on Maintaining Security, signed in 1995, establishes there are no rigid obligations for Australia to become automatically engaged, militarily, in any developments affecting Indonesia. Prime Minister Keating, furthermore, has publicly defined its provisions as not covering internal developments in Indonesia. It is largely a document about consultation, closer dialogue and reinforcing confidence between the two signatory nations. Its negotiation and drafting stand as a glowing tribute to the undoubted skills and prudent nature of General Peter Gration, former Chief of the Defence Forces. I have to concede this case represents an important exception to my general stricture regarding military officers acting as diplomats. The conduct of Air Marshal Sir Frederick Scherger, Chairman of the Chiefs of Staff Committee, in 1965 when conducting delicate negotiations with American officials in relation to the war in Vietnam, was redolent of the sort of military attitudes which worry me when brought to the sensitive area of diplomacy. Scherger was keen for Australia to commit a battalion of troops to the Vietnam war and, in these negotiations in Honolulu, 'disregarded the terms of his instructions and came close to creating a *fait accompli* for his political masters'. Not that his political masters would have been discomforted greatly by such an outcome for, contrary to their subsequent claims in parliament, they committed Australian troops to that war without a specific request from the United States and with no request at all from the Government of South Vietnam. The Australia–Indonesia Agreement is, however, more than I would have cared to embark upon, as foreign minister, at this stage of Indonesia's development and given the nature of our other interests in the East and South-East Asia region. It should also be added that the ANZUS Agreement is prudently drafted and gives no absolute guarantees. That is not the way in which it is often interpreted by observers in Australia, as some newspaper commentary here at the time of the signing of the Australia–Indonesia Agreement on Maintaining Security demonstrated. In other words, hopeful expectations can lead to interpretations of the nature and extent of our commitment to another country under a formal agreement which extend the literal text of the document.

The capacity for misunderstanding motives when new regional security policies are announced can sometimes be great. For instance, ASEAN's 1995 declaration of support for a South-East Asian nuclear-free zone, allowing for the current strains between China and some ASEAN member States, and the inclusion within ASEAN membership of China's historic opponent, Vietnam, could be interpreted by some as an effort to politically hem in China. Australia will have to skilfully avoid being drawn into any such strategies should they evolve, for their consequences may not be in our national best interests.

The ideal world and reality

People who follow a one-dimensional perception of moral values in foreign relations pursue a misleading caricature of reality. They confront no complexities, experience no difficulties arising from a range of considerations of the sort which often restrict action to second best, or even lesser order, solutions. For such individuals the issues always embody universal, absolute, and straightforward principles. They enjoy another advantage: they are free to denounce and criticise publicly without having to worry about the consequences of their actions on the foreign political and external commercial relations of their country. The working foreign minister is denied that luxury, being required to balance a number of considerations before initiating action. Temporising on an issue of principle is a matter of great and binding common sense if an alternative hasty act or assertion of abstract principle provides a net result much worse than a temporised outcome. To do this is not necessarily to discard moral objectives. It is far more difficult to be consistently moral in the superintendence of a country's foreign relations than to be a moralising commentator.

There is no room for rigid or doctrinaire modes when dealing with issues in the practice of foreign affairs. For just as the successful art of politics in an open pluralistic society often requires a degree of compromise, the same also holds for international relations. National or public opinions are well and good, but there are limits to their efficacy beyond our borders. The practical options available, the degree of acceptability of outcomes and due concern for what are conventionally regarded as moral values, create a bedrock on which those charged with the responsibility of making policy and decisions must stand. It is a fact of life, however, that what is bedrock to one person may be shifting sand to another; which is another way of characterising the differences between realists and idealists. Those who believe in pure realism for example, tend to accept the role and use of superior force if it is available and necessary to achieve an important end. This is a perspective as old as history, a famous instance to be seen in the way the Spartans crushed the Melians in classical Greece. For practitioners of Realpolitik, power is the international political determinant, meaning that smaller States for instance shall be clients, perhaps even servile satrapies of the central power.

Pure idealism, by contrast, is based on a code of absolute ideals to which all outcomes have to conform. Compromise with these ideals is shunned. There are no nuances acknowledged, no recognition that when it comes to relations between nations, especially where domestic opinion is stifled in one of them, the choices available may all be far from idealistic. To salvage something positive from a process of dialogue, to create some practical if limited outcomes, might require compromise. Not to compromise in such cases is a victory for doctrinal rigidity and a setback for a worthy cause. As suggested earlier, practical policy alternatives on the vexatious issue of Indonesia's incorporation of East Timor were few and low on any measure of pure idealism; yet they were relatively quite effective. We must have ideals by which we are guided but we must be practical about what we wish to achieve and how far we can advance in that direction in any given set of circumstances. This at least was the orientation I endeavoured to bring to my own work as Foreign Minister.

I have previously also argued that while the tensions between Moscow and Washington prevailed until recently, averting superpower nuclear conflict was the great moral imperative. Australia would not be immune from the consequences of that sort of conflict even if it were neutral and non-aligned. People of moral conviction and courage as a matter of practical necessity will accept an uncongenial option if the alternatives are worse in their likely result. To ignore that responsibility is to be immoral. In those circumstances the moral option was to adopt policies which maximised restraint on the potential use of nuclear arms while pursuing the objective of nuclear arms control and ultimately disarmament. To have been a non-aligned critic, which many urged to be the more moral role, would have sidelined us as an ineffectual carper, much as Sweden has been regarded at international fora. We actively supported deterrence, justifying the presence and role of joint facilities at North West Cape, Nurrungar and Pine Gap, and providing various facilities for nuclear-powered and nuclear-capable naval vessels. Nurrungar and Pine Gap in particular gave greater world security because of the accuracy with which they provided information about the conduct of other powers, thus diminishing the dangers of belligerent responses to false alarms. And as the joint bases indisputably would have been high priority nuclear targets in the event of such a conflict, Australia took serious risks in the deterrence of nuclear conflict. This gave us an important degree of leverage with the USA, allowing us greater freedom to pursue our many independent nuclear and conventional arms control measures. I constantly reminded our American allies and other powers of this when they questioned our right to aggressively pursue other arms control measures, as they often did. The Americans frequently became cross at our independent actions, claiming they were a weakening of Western resolve. Our persistence, however, could not be ignored. Eventually we were hosting important meetings on these matters with representatives from the USSR and the USA at Canberra. Such actions meant that at last Australia was being treated seriously by the superpowers.

Our role was one not without other perils. In 1985 we confirmed an earlier decision of the Fraser Government to provide landing and refuelling facilities on Australian territory for USA military air and sea craft engaged in an MX Missile testing with a splashdown in international waters in the Tasman Sea. We moved the splashdown point away from Australian territorial waters. The decision leaked out through misadventure from my office,[15] immediately setting off a series of problems for the Labor Government, and especially within the Party. Hawke was leaving for a visit to several foreign countries, but the full fury of this tempest had not yet arrived. He and I were in his office discussing his trip. He moved to leave—but not before firstly gripping my hand in a strong shake, his other hand firmly taking hold of my right forearm. His eyebrows beetled down, hard, and he looked me full in the eyes, tough and resolute. 'Keep in there fighting while I'm away. We'll win this. We'll win because we're right.' 'Oh . . . I hope so,' I said with some inner uncertainty. It would not help us much to be convinced we were right when the Party had other ideas, in particular on something where its feelings were extraordinarily strong. We just had not prepared the Party, or the community for that matter, for this sort of development. It was a classic illustration of not being able to make a difficult policy stick because it had not been sold first within our own organisation and to the electorate. The attitude of party membership, generally, was that the Government should in no direct way be engaged in testing nuclear weaponry capabilities such as missile carriers. Perhaps the quaver of uncertainty in my voice unsettled Hawke. A corner of his mouth tightened, and turned down disdainfully, as he uttered one word, a single imperative, in my direction: 'Fight!'.

Hawke soared aloft in the comfort of a RAAF 707 aircraft, no doubt contentedly reflecting on the satisfying challenges waiting ahead—running repair work around the globe is always a great tonic for prime ministers who have overextended themselves on the unavoidable but humdrum domestic agenda. Meanwhile, on the ground back in Canberra quite a number of people, including me, were preparing to re-enact our version of the typhoon scene in Conrad's *The Nigger of the Narcissus:* hatches were battened down, portholes blocked, and the bilge pumps were being cranked up. Careful note was also being taken of where the lifeboats might be. Over the next few nights on national television, Kim Beazley Jnr, the Minister for Defence, took the full blast of the developing gale of opposition from within the Labor Party, for it was the Labor Party that came furiously roaring in on the Labor Government rather than the Opposition. I rationalised that as the weekend would soon be with us, with a bit of luck, the issue might die down during the break. Therefore, without valour but with much discretion, I saved myself for later, in the hope that the flux of events would be such as to not need my intervention; in the meantime young Beazley could take the early force of the protest. On Monday, 4 February, the issue was not only still raging, but approaching political gale force. I chose to go public, appearing on the Mike Willesee current affairs television programme to declare myself in support of the decision. After its screening I knew I was in trouble with the Party. A senior American official at the USA Embassy, suspected of being an undeclared CIA officer, telephoned my office to say some complimentary things and to offer his public assistance, if it would be of help . . . 'Dear Mary, Mother of God, save me from well-intentioned friends!' I muttered quietly to myself.

At about 5 o'clock next morning the telephone rang beside my bed in our then home at Belconnen. It was Hawke. The belligerence had gone; his mood was instead submissive and contrite and the voice came through unevenly like radio static: 'Bob here, Bill. I've just announced to a press conference that we won't be offering facilities . . .'. I muttered a relieved 'Thank goodness . . .'. I still believe we were right but to have persisted would have put much more at stake, which was an unacceptable cost. Contrary to the statement in the press release issued under his name at Brussels, this was the first time I had spoken to Hawke since my farewell discussion with him in his office earlier. Failure to prepare the Party for the decision, however, was a blunder, as was the way it became public knowledge prematurely. Dramatic as it was, the incident had its lighter moments. As the storm raged with greater ferocity, Hawke, in machismo mode, was initially disposed to fight. Then, an adviser to him raised a frightening possibility at Brussels, when he reportedly said, 'Very good, Prime Minister, and if it goes to your party conference and you win it will be a celebrated victory which will confirm your dominance of the Party. If, however, you were to lose . . . it would be, Sir, I suspect, the end of your prime ministership'. As quick as a lightning flash, Hawke apparently responded, 'How do we get out of it?'. His principal private secretary, Graham Evans, later remarked jocularly that the time it took between Hawke being told he could lose his prime ministership, and his response, 'is the definition of a split second!'. This major snafu did a lot of damage to American confidence in the Australian Government.

To return to my earlier theme, an objective may be morally right, but its handling may still require the greatest care. For instance, it was morally right to oppose the Apartheid policy used by the minority white population to dominate South Africa. I was always aware, however, that there were weaknesses in our support base which maladroit moves could easily fracture. During earlier years when sporting sanctions were imposed against South Africa, public opinion polling in Australia revealed over 70 per cent of the Australian public supported closer sporting ties with South Africa. I had therefore to engage in a discreet balancing act, working on the issue in a way satisfactory to the Party, at the same time as trying to hold it under careful control to avoid alienating the electorate.

Hawke was impatient to accelerate the pace of this policy on a broad front. Being more cautious by nature, I countered that we move ahead with a code of conduct covering Australian business functioning in South Africa. Hawke was delighted. The ACTU had proposed that there should be a tripartite body comprising government, business and union representatives monitoring any such code. I offered business a loaded choice: it could voluntarily participate in the code of conduct, to be monitored by an independent observer who would publicly report on his findings; or, as an alternative, have the imposition of the dreaded tripartite body. Business fell into a deep funk, going on to accept my proposition with alacrity but without enthusiasm. Australian business interests in South Africa had an impeccable record in their labour force dealings, something substantiated by the independent observer's reports. Why then resort to such arrangements? Partly to ensure it remained so, and to provide a modest response to impatient demands for more action, thus reassuring the community that Australian business behaved ethically. With Hawke mollified into the bargain I was able to maintain control of the pace of policy development. Symbols and the reassurance they can give are important in any society; so too is political savvy in judging the pace of political change.

It was sometimes said I maintained inconsistent, hypocritical standards on certain issues such as human rights; that while I could be voluble on human rights in distant Central America I was more cautious on the same issues in the countries of our more immediate region, such as East Timor or China. An argument ran that in all instances of violations of human rights, the cases should be pursued uncompromisingly and with equal intensity. It was very clear to me, however, that in our more immediate region, the opportunities for others to respond punitively against Australia were far greater; this particular circumstance therefore required of us a different approach to the one we might take in handling, say, a Central American case. Local critics aside, others saw us as far more active. In 1984 while in New York, after visiting Central America, the lugubrious USA Secretary of State, George Shultz, growled at me, 'Why don't you Australians keep to your own backyard and let us look after ours?'. We had taken issue with illegal mining of Nicaraguan harbours by the United States; I had also been directly critical of Sandinista violations of basic rights while I was in Nicaragua, not that Shultz was interested in such independent thinking.

The situation with our near neighbours, with whom our political and economic interests are quite large, is qualitatively and quantitatively different. Were they to launch effective reprisals against us, we would be condemned by our electorate for the cost and bother caused to Australia, much of which ordinary citizens and local businesses would have to bear. Meanwhile, we would not have advanced the particular cause involved one iota. In certain circumstances, the human rights of the very persons about whom representations have been made may even be further diminished, with their well-being compromised through retaliation for our clumsy intervention. The embarrassing backdown forced on the powerful United States after it threatened China on the issues of human rights in early 1994, is a powerful lesson that international relations is a vastly different game to that of domestic politics in a plural, democratic society.

This is not to suggest that human rights issues should be neglected for the sake of a quieter life. On the contrary, I raised the issue of East Timor with Indonesian authorities persistently, and registered Australian concerns on human rights with Chinese authorities on a number of occasions. Oft times these interventions were not well-received but hostile reactions were contained, a useful result of itself. Journalists travelling with me were sometimes irked that there were no good slanging exchanges to report home. But the journalists and I had different agendas. The journalists' task is to write an arresting if not sensational story; they yearn for acerbic remarks to contribute flavour. My agenda, however, was to strike whatever blows I could for human rights, and concurrently keep our other interests in good shape—that is, to build the best balance between idealism and realism, and to achieve the best outcomes, that I was capable of. The sort of story some journalists wanted was not compatible with my objectives or the highest interests of Australia.

The paramount priority given to individuals' human rights by Western countries is resented by many developing countries. In the latter countries greater stress is laid on social and economic rights. That I understand, as I also accept the simple maxim that first comes bread then comes morals. A starving man not only has the right to steal bread to feed his family and himself; in such circumstances moral sanctions against theft are negated.[16] The two concerns, of individual human rights and social and economic rights, should be linked and our failure in the West to do this resolutely leaves us open to justifiable criticism. Equally, I accept that the consequence of some developing countries' exclusive assertion of social and economic rights is often a sham cover for abuse of human rights in their countries. I have yet to meet anyone, including in developing countries, who was amiably indifferent to the arbitrary deprivation of any person's liberty, of their imprisonment without a charge being levelled or a fair trial, of their being subjected to torture, or of facing the prospect of summary execution. Nonetheless, it is well to recall that the notion of universal human rights is relatively new and it is not universally endorsed. Even for so-called western nations the principle of human rights is relatively novel, its slow and sometimes painful development often resisted by some of the privileged who controlled state power.

The idealists remind us there is a code of moral conduct at the heart of civilised societies without which there cannot be respect for life, and thence, without which order and fairness break down into injustice, tyranny and repression. In the absence of this, at its worst existence becomes barbarous. Therefore, they argue, those moral principles by which a civilised society conducts its internal affairs should be enshrined in positive law to regulate the conduct of affairs between nations. That is very good, in principle. But nation–states are generally cautious about the extent to which they will allow themselves to be regulated by some supranational body—an understandable caution, for who sets the rules and by what standards?

It has to be acknowledged that much of what has been defined as morality over the centuries has been Eurocentric in its values and origins. Let us not forget that until fairly recent times it was a moral duty for 'civilised' nations to take civilisation and profitable trade to heathen nations with the sword and the word of God. Thus, what is moral and what is self-interestedly expedient can become mightily entangled. Many in the West tend to regard the principles of democracy as a moral right which should be imposed wherever it is absent. We conveniently neglect the fact that there are, relatively, only a few democracies in the world, that democracy generally came slowly, and sometimes painfully, to those nations. Further, that in its functioning it is a complex and difficult system, and that culturally, a great many nations are incapable of embracing it successfully at this stage, or may not want to at any stage, of their development. Finally, too, democracy is a relatively recent historical phenomenon for those countries in which it does flourish.

The weakness of the positivist's position is that nations are sovereign States and sovereign States are not necessarily bound by some form of supra-authority. In 1986 the International Court of Justice found against the United States on a number of complaints brought before it by Nicaragua, including mining of Nicaraguan harbours. The United States refused to accept the authority of the Court for the ruling on treaty obligations was inexpedient to its regional interests.[17] Thus we again arrive at the realist view of international relations as the exercise of raw power; of powerful nations dominating inferior States; of inequality between States leading to imposed balances of power, of spheres of interest, and of hegemonic relationships. Sovereign States are run by people, and people mostly wish their actions to be seen as right and fair in some moral sense. Leaders wish endorsement from their own people and approbation from elsewhere for their actions, desires which tend to restrain ruthless conduct, though they do not absolutely prohibit it. But whether moral values come from some notion of an unvarying universal natural law, or whether, as I believe, they are the product of the needs of organised and especially advanced societies, expressed as rules by which we may live together with maximum harmony and personal freedom, is not really at issue here. The theory of how international relations functions derives from the practice. There is, more generally, a psychological divide between the idealised principles of both politics and international relations and their practice. The difference is between what people want to believe and what they have to do. It happens that some things have to be done which fall far short of the standards and principles we like to believe in. Yet to acknowledge this could often be unpleasantly discomforting, personally and for the body politic. Most societies, including our own, cope with this disjuncture by developing and maintaining a variety of symbols and comforting reductionist assertions—symbols of nationalism, evil external forces, the godlessness of others, our inevitable virtue, God is with us, and so on. In this way unpleasant acts, and sometimes mean self-interest are justified; not only do these cease being uncomfortable, they can even become defined as virtues in support of a higher goal than what the reality otherwise suggests. We all live our lives in this way to a greater or lesser extent, with the exception maybe of saints; and there is no company less tolerable I would propose than that of a saint.

Practical experience as Foreign Minister, together with various theoretical analyses, have convinced me that national interests and the use of power cannot be totally divorced from the ethical. As Niebhur has acknowledged:

> *Politics will, to the end of history, be an area where conscience and power meet, where the ethical and coercive factors of human life will interpenetrate and work out their tentative and uneasy compromises.*[18]

If pure idealism can take us but a short way, pure realism is no panacea either, for the latter 'can offer nothing but a naked struggle for power which makes any kind of international society impossible'.[19] By contrast, my aim has been to show that there is an alternative to either muddled idealism or stark realism. It is to pursue practical policies, accepting the limitations of realism on one's options to act, but to be guided by a deeply ingrained sense of what is morally right. That is, what will best serve the interests of humankind and preserve civilised values. Because of such an approach and views I have never found anything inconsistent in my long-standing support for the concerns of the peace movement where they have been lucidly stated on the one hand, and my commitment to an adequate self-defence capability on the other. The velvet glove might not work. The mailed fist has to be ready just in case. The notion of adequate self-defence includes the capability to project force well beyond our shores to demonstrate our resoluteness in protecting our national sovereignty or our major interests should necessity require.

This position backgrounds a set of proposals I floated within a very small group of ministers, including the prime minister, in November 1984. I was and remain curious about the need of some of our near neighbours to vigorously proceed with nuclear power generation schemes. It seemed to me, and remains my view, that allowing ourselves to fall behind in nuclear technical competencies is not in our national interest. We should therefore support an active and reasonably broad programme of nuclear technical research and development in Australia, for two reasons at least: to allow us to maintain a level of skill and knowledge which would equip us to hold a position at the leading edge of technical awareness in the arms control debate; and to be able to sell appropriate nuclear technology and intellectual property and services for civilian use and to commercial advantage. I accordingly proposed that government should boost support for nuclear physics and engineering at the University of New South Wales, which had an established nuclear engineering department. The Atomic Energy Commission, as it then was, I argued should be further enhanced with new equipment, including a new reactor. All reactors produce weapons-grade neptunium, from which neptunium 237, suitable as a nuclear explosive, can be extracted. The process is costly but technical advances are reducing costs and the material is not regulated by International Atomic Energy Agency safeguards. Russia has tonnes of this material which it sells commercially under slack controls; in addition, there is no evidence of nuclear explosives being made from this material to date. I further proposed we consider developing one nuclear power generator as part of this integrated project, at the same time recognising that the latter would have had little chance of proceeding given the level of community emotion on nuclear matters.

There was a third reason for my making these proposals: to be inadequately prepared to defend ourselves should the need arise is a very short-sighted policy. I contemplated Australia reaching such a level of know-how in this broad area that if an effort to develop nuclear weaponry capability was under way or had been achieved by others in our region of immediate interest and in circumstances which gave Australia reasonable security concerns, then having reached the threshold of being able to assemble nuclear weaponry, Australia could do so in the shortest possible time. As the situation currently stands we would be looking at ten years, at least, in which to reach that technical capability. I am talking only about necessity, of supreme emergency, requiring this grave step. After all 'to be sane in a world of madmen is in itself a kind of madness'.[20] I left the meeting referred to feeling that my views had been accepted. Obviously a misapprehension on my part, for nothing was subsequently done about the proposal. I have acknowledged these sorts of views publicly on several occasions.[21]

The United Nations: promise of a better world?

The United Nations, like the League of Nations before it, was welcomed by many as an organisation that would avert wars, administer international justice and ensure that peace would prevail. That is not how things have worked out. The United Nations has performed better than its progenitor; but the League suffered, as the United Nations still suffers, an inherent deficiency— the workings jam up with the pressure of conflicting political interests. Countries represented in the UN frequently tend to pursue a self-interested political agenda, and often form blocs to do so. The UN can be highly politicised and become fragmented and ineffective on important issues, as is all too evident in the Security Council when a major interest of one of the permanent members has been undesirably challenged by some proposal. In such a situation the member nation can then exercise its veto power.

This may happen less frequently now that the older bipolar structure of world politics, as dominated by the superpowers, has effectively crumbled. The permanent membership of the Security Council reflects the immediate postwar importance of the countries which had prevailed in the war. Half a century later this representation is rather unreal. The continued inclusion of Britain and France, both of declining importance as world forces, while the great powers of Germany and Japan remain excluded, creates an undesirable balance. Yet I suspect the chances of changing this so that influence symmetries are restored, remains quite limited. As soon as any such attempt is made, other power blocs, with Third World, or black African or other bases, are likely to lodge strong claims for representation. The wrangling within those groups and between them, as well as within the UN generally, would be interminable, faction-ridden, and in the end most likely self-defeating. We are stuck with a poor arrangement, but the consequences of attempting to do something about it would appear to be worse. Imperfections in ourselves and our institutions often lead to diminishing returns—especially where the surrounding human environment has over a lengthy period undergone radical change in social, political and economic structures.

The excited commentary and strained media images of the New International Order, following the swift and successful Gulf War in 1991, was nothing if not redolent of the vaunted (but quietly aborted) New International Economic Order of earlier. Too many of the constituent parts go too much in their own directions to allow the UN to work well as an entity. Nation–states, especially the more dominant ones, are simply not going to hand over to the wayward mechanism of the Security Council the sort of political authority, or the disposition of their human, technical, fiscal and military resources, which would be needed by the UN to fulfil some New International Order role. It could well follow that a major national interest of one or more such countries might be seriously compromised when their forces are used by the UN to quell a problem of conflict. The earlier notion of peace-keeping forces was meanwhile supplemented to become so-called peace-making forces—a euphemism for war-making, or imposing peace against the will of either or both or more of the combatants. This was tried in Somalia with disastrous results in circumstances where an attempt at a political and not a military resolution would have been more appropriate, if by no means certain of success. Peace-making of this kind requires far more heavily equipped forces and more formidable rules of engagement than were permitted in Somalia. And to call it for what it actually is, war-making seems an entirely inappropriate activity for the UN.

The difficulties which have bedevilled UN operations in former Yugoslavia are salutary: of language barriers at command level, of different military doctrines, incompatibilities of logistic practices and equipment between national forces, the dreadful necessity for the UN to make staff command appointments on the basis of national representativeness rather than on military merit.[22] Neither the USA nor the European national forces as such became engaged in the turmoil in former Yugoslavia, where lightly armed UN peace-keeping detachments performed nobly but with limited effect. A wise attitude on the part of the USA and the Europeans, for becoming involved on the ground in the Balkans would have required a military commitment more appropriate to a full-scale war with difficult terrain, and the irregular enemy forces hard to identify, the number of personnel required being disproportionately higher than the opposition forces, probably by a factor of seven to one or more. Some NATO estimates of the ground troops required for an effective intervention were in the range of 300 000, with high risks in terms of casualties and potential duration of the conflict.[23]

By contrast, the UN military commitment to the Gulf War benefited from a stroke of good fortune. It was predominantly an American undertaking and America had all the equipment and forces it required in the right places, in the right quantities, at the right time and held in such a way they could be moved to the field of war speedily. It is not cynical to say that if oil supplies as critical as those in Kuwait and Saudi Arabia had been at stake in Somalia and if a key balance of regional power important to Western interests was in imminent danger of being upset, as was the case when Iraq invaded Kuwait, the responses there would have been far more robust.

To be credible, UN peace-making forces would have to be ready to respond to larger scale problems. One suggestion is to cache of large numbers of personnel, cash and *matériel* ear-marked and readily available from member States for exclusive use by the UN. Given the difficulties the United Nations has in getting some of its member States to pay their bills to keep the institution solvent, I would not be at all sanguine about the prospects of the military force being able to pay its way. Peace-keeping forces are supposed to help contending factions or countries, who genuinely want peace, arrive at that end. These forces are not really equipped to handle full-scale, determined hostilities between combatant forces whose notion of peace is an outcome where one group prevails over its adversaries, stays there, and expects the UN peace-keepers to maintain the new status quo. The conflict in former Yugoslavia starkly illustrates this point. It also demonstrates how embarrassing the failure of UN peace-keeping commitments can be for that institution and for the national pride of participating countries. The fact is the UN cannot impose peace where peace is not wanted by all participants; to propose it can do otherwise is to create cruel illusions. Former Secretary General U Thant explains how the UN finds itself in this unfair predicament thus:

> The United Nations is a last-ditch, last-resort affair, and it is not
> surprising that the organisation should often be blamed for failing to
> solve problems that have already been found to be insoluble by
> governments.[24]

This is not to dismiss the effectiveness of the UN; there are many things which the UN does and does well, particularly through some of its specialised agencies. The UN also provides an important platform for small nations like Australia, allowing us to more effectively express our concerns internationally and permitting us to play an important role on a wide range of global issues. It also allows a platform from which aggrieved nation–states, especially smaller ones, offended perhaps at the clumsy behaviour of a large or larger power, can vent their concerns. Many of its specialist agencies have made profoundly important contributions to humankind in famine relief, disease control and health in the developing world. In particular, in recent years the UN has mediated the withdrawal of Apartheid South Africa from Namibia and established the latter's independence; negotiated agreements between Iraq and Iran, ending eight years of fighting; mediated the withdrawal of Soviet forces from Afghanistan; established a broadly representative government in Cambodia; and ended El Salvador's long-term civil war. These are enduring achievements which reflect nobly on the organisation, but none involved a peace enforcement process.

Without the United Nations the world would be a much less pleasant place in which to live. It was an important organisation during the bipolar domination of the superpowers. It will, conceivably, be even more important in this age of multipolarity, when nation–states are working out new relationships with each other, and in a world environment where footloose mega-global firms and entrepreneurs otherwise go unregulated and the powerful take advantage of the weaker in matters of commerce, communications, finance and banking. It has made us much more aware of a great many profound issues: racial discrimination, torture, disappearances, the rights of the weak or of minority or disabled and other disadvantaged groups, of fair and just treatment of refugees; the protection of the cultural heritage of mankind; the global effects of environmental issues; of international crime, in particular the illicit narcotics trade; and of how we manage international resources, such as the deep-sea bed and outer space. The UN is rightly condemned for the proliferation of its bureaucracy but without it we would be creating a plethora of ad hoc bodies to manage these issues. The situation would be worse, the inefficiency compounded, and the coordination between programmes with links almost impossible.[25] My hope is that we maintain reasonable expectations about what the United Nations can achieve and go on to support it. This would seem far more sensible than our present habit of creating fond and unreasonable expectations and then condemning it—but not its constituent members—for failing to achieve them.

The special case of development aid

Overseas development aid, too, is an area where idealism and realism collide. The debate on guiding principles often proceeds from incompatible positions with each side claiming to hold the high moral ground. The libertarian position has been succinctly put, thus:

> Economic differences are largely the result of people's capacities and motivations. . . A disproportionate number of the poor lack the capabilities and inclination for economic achievement and often for cultural achievement as well.

On the other hand idealism has it that:

> The same duty of solidarity that rests on individuals exists also for nations: 'It is the very serious duty of the developed nations to help the underdeveloped'.[26]

These incompatible attitudes illustrate that one person's morality can be another's anathema. As a matter of justice and personal obligation I accept we have a duty to redistribute resources from the rich to the poor nations, just as I justify the case for a similar redistribution between individuals within our own society. I do not, however, accept I should feel any guilt for the condition of people in developing countries, no matter how much some of the politically correct in our community might argue that one should.

Perhaps the great paradox of the aid is good for recipient/bad for recipient countries debate is that some on the doctrinaire right oppose it because they see it as an indefensible extension of centralised state power against the interests of economic development, while the equally extreme doctrinaire left considers it a perpetuation and enhancement of international capitalism and backing for the political objectives of the neo-colonial powers.[27] Aid, nevertheless, should be the subject of rigorous performance criteria. The fact is for a great many countries the blight of long-term poverty is substantially the fault of their governments; particularly so when they are reluctant to act to increase their domestically sourced tax revenue because such policies are unpopular. They nonetheless expect governments of developed countries to bear the very same unpopularity in funding greater flows of aid from their taxpayers. Corruption too is often a problem in many recipient countries, to the point where it is a way of life; public administration is frequently irresolute and incompetent; oppressive or crude local political practices and intrusive economic policies lead to bad development decision-making, squandering resources and hindering economic development; and in some instances local politicians prefer to remain popular by avoiding tough but essential decision-making, conjuring up external straw men to blame for the adverse consequences of their deficiencies. Meanwhile the economies of those countries careen out of control. Population growth rates are too high in some cases and effective control programmes are inhibited by cultural attitudes, religious beliefs, or political timidity, to the cost of improved living standards. If population growth rates exceed economic growth then, in spite of aid, which in some cases might be quite generous, the measurable per capita living standard of a recipient country will fall. The economic resource base of an aid recipient country might be limited, producing one or only a few primary products. The sale of these resources can be subjected to intense competition on world markets and disrupted by sharp cyclical movements caused by oversupply of similar produce from other developing countries.

Aid can obstruct structural reforms and accordingly impede sustained economic growth and the development of social justice. There have been governments, Kenya and the Philippines come to mind immediately, which have steadfastly avoided genuine, extensive land reforms benefiting the farm workers and the peasant class. The largest and best tracts of productive land remain in the hands of the representatives of a rich and influential land holding class who resist major reforms out of self-interest. In 1988 the Government of the Philippines initiated a ten-year agrarian reform programme by which 10.3 million hectares of privately owned farm land was to be redistributed. After six years only 1.6 million hectares had actually been redistributed. The greater the aid effort to relieve rural poverty arising from this inequity the more the pressures for land redistribution are modified, and the less the local rich feel required to make sacrifices for the benefit of their own impoverished. Aid in these circumstances can be as much and probably more a subsidy to the rich and privileged as it is of service to any other groups. It is money that stays in the pockets of the privileged middle class. Aid donor countries should band together and demand certain domestic policies such as redistributive taxation and land reforms, some advances in the human condition measurable through commonly used social indicators, as a condition for the continued receipt of aid. Many of the rich and privileged in aid-accepting nations are insensitive to the condition of their impoverished masses, in some cases callously so. I think it worth attempting, nonetheless, with suitable, adverse international publicity for countries which unreasonably refuse to comply.[28] If we don't tighten the rules, in the end all we may achieve is the punishment of the poor.

Most of Black Africa is another problem. Poverty is on the gradual decline in Latin America and Asia; yet much of sub-Saharan Africa continues to become poorer. Africa's share of world trade is under 2 per cent and declining. Tanzania, Zaire and Sudan remain poor in spite of generous aid outlays; Zaire and Nigeria in particular have earned billions of dollars from minerals, including oil, but determinedly remain poor. Zambian President Chiluba condemned African leaders who he said have 'raised sky-high monuments to themselves instead of putting up grain silos and planted [military] mines instead of seed'.[29] One commentator has observed that 'Virtually all indices of economic progress have performed miserably since the 1960s, when black Africa gained its independence from colonial rule'. He has pointed out that nominal GNP per capita, for black Africa, grew by an unimpressive 1.4 per cent in the 1960s, 0.5 per cent in the 1970s, followed by further declines in the 1980s. Population grew by an annual average of 3 per cent but food production per person fell by 7 per cent in the 1960s. It fell further, by 15 per cent, in the next decade, and continued to fall in the 1980s. Close to 45 per cent of black Africa's food is now imported, in spite of the UN Food and Agricultural Organisation claim that the Congo Basin alone was capable of producing enough food to feed all of black Africa. More than $US80 billion has been spent on aid since 1960.[30] All of this reflects a development fiasco expensively underwritten at cost to donor countries' taxpayers.

These sorts of disasters should not be blamed solely on a colonial past. True, the problem of corruption in Indonesia and the

Philippines has its roots in the way in which tax gathering was practised by the earlier Dutch and Spanish colonial administrations. To acknowledge that, however, does not fix the problem. While corruption persists it will be an impediment to efficient development. It is sometimes alleged that the national boundaries of some black African countries, arbitrarily drawn by white colonial powers, are the cause of tribal tensions. This conveniently ignores the reality that in most cases, the tribal tensions pre-date colonialism. There is even some evidence that colonialism restrained those violent tendencies. On the other hand many developing countries or States have become impressive success stories: Singapore, Hong Kong, the Republic of Korea, Taiwan. The development of Japan after the devastation of World War II is the most remarkable of all development stories. New countries are currently busily recruiting themselves to this band of successes— Thailand, Malaysia, Indonesia, Brazil, among others. Could it be that some cultures are prepared to drive themselves harder to achieve success? Consider the case of Japan and what it has achieved, with its only natural resource base being its people, their intelligence and a respect for personal industry.

One of our immediate neighbours, Papua New Guinea, runs the risk of forfeiting splendid opportunities to promote its economic development and social improvement. From independence in 1975 until 1992 Australia provided A$8000 million in aid (1990 prices) to Papua New Guinea. In spite of this aid and a hefty boost to per capita income from mining developments (albeit through the enrichment of an enclave), GNP has grown at about 2.4 per cent per annum while official population growth, which almost certainly understates the real rate, is 2.7 per cent. That means simply that the country is getting poorer. The population, estimated at 3.9 million in 1992, is expected to reach 6 million by 2010. A projection of no more than 0.5 per cent growth per year in formal employment growth is plausible, giving a total of only 234 000 wage jobs in

2010 at a time when the economically active population will have reached over two million.[31] A social and political time bomb ticking away on our doorstep and the cause rests squarely with Port Moresby. These sorts of problems extend to several other developing countries of the South Pacific, all relatively substantial aid recipients from Australia, provoking the following conclusion:

> . . . there can be little doubt that . . . in most countries of the South Pacific . . . On even the most approximate calculations . . . it does not seem unduly alarmist to note that a scenario of very low economic growth and a failure to create many more private sector jobs than hitherto will lead to unprecedented economic and social strains.[32]

We do developing countries no favours by remaining uncritical of these shortcomings. Silence excuses the failures, not to mention the injustices their incompetent and self-serving ruling elites impose on their less well placed peoples. We heap fiscal injustice onto our taxpayers, too, if we remain mute. They have to forego a degree, small as it might be, of enhanced personal security in their paying for aid used ineffectually. In the circumstances, the case for Australia making increasing amounts of its aid rigorously performance based is not seriously challengeable. That is why, as Minister for Foreign Affairs, I introduced the notion of 'project aid' for part of the budget of Papua New Guinea. This aid was performance rated. The only reason a much greater portion was not subjected to this discipline was simply that neither Australia nor Papua New Guinea, at that time, had sufficient skilled people to supervise a more extensive performance rating system than the one we implemented.

In the final analysis, a substantial benefit arising from aid donoring is a 'feel good' experience for many people of donor countries. Aid contributes only marginally to economic development. As the *Economist* has reported, an extensive review of ninety-six countries spread over 1971 to 1990 found:

In almost all cases aid is spent entirely on consumption . . . practically
nowhere is there a big increase in investment . . . Overall, though, aid
has little impact on economic growth. [33]

Open trade regimes are much more important to the growth of
developing countries than aid. In fact much of the international aid
vote can be characterised as 'hush money' paid out by rich
countries to moderate the tendency for complaints about lack of
access to their markets for the products of developing countries.
The case for humanitarian aid is incontestable, as is the case for
development aid based on notions of ethical obligation to one's
fellow human beings. But the governments of developing nations
have a duty to apply aid according to ideas of social justice and
public responsibility and of how to best promote economic growth.
In my view, the elites in developing countries must impose greater
redistributive burdens on themselves and their 'well-heeled'
supporters for the benefit of their people in the same way in which
we oblige Australian taxpayers to accept sacrifices to progressively
fund our aid programmes.

ANZUS: myths and reality

The years 1983–88 saw an extraordinary, sustained effort to preserve
the integrity of the ANZUS Treaty as a fractious New Zealand set
about unravelling it. Then, due to totally unexpected influences—
the sudden collapse of the superpower contest between Moscow and
Washington—this strategic arrangement quietly laid down and, to
all practical intents and purposes, expired. No-one seems to be
grieving over this fact. The Australia, New Zealand, United States of
America Alliance, the ANZUS Treaty as it became known, was
effectively drafted and agreed upon *ad referendum* in February 1951.
With it was created one of the great myths of Australian public life.
Through skilful manipulation of some facts, concealment of others
and persistent repetition of a simple message, the ANZUS Treaty

became consecrated territory for Australia. Its sanctity was the touchstone of our citizens' patriotism. To criticise it or question the real nature of its implications was treated as heresy and angrily denounced by the high priests of conservative politics in Canberra.

ANZUS was, we were assured, essentially an American guarantee to protect Australia in a very uncertain world. This was a potent message, plumbing deeply embedded fears in the national psyche of the downward thrust of the 'Yellow Hordes'. This cultural insecurity was added to by the ubiquity of communism: in control of the vast Soviet Union; subjugating Eastern Europe; China in its thrall; wars of 'liberation' being fought in its name in numerous countries but especially Asia. More broadly, politics around the world were being played out against the threat of communism, real or imagined. While militant demands for decolonisation were being mistaken for communist subversion by colonial expropriators, anti-communist McCarthyism rampaged in the United States, with its own variant in Australia intimidatingly promoting the Communist Party Dissolution Bill. These ingredients and many similar ones created a political atmosphere scarcely conducive to rational and reasoned discussion on the big issue of that time and after—international strategic security. To question American actions was to be un-Australian. It was as simple as that. In the face of this coercive atmosphere many genuine liberals muted themselves, disappeared into their studies, retreated to their gardens, or became lost in other community activity rather than risk their reputations and destroy their careers.

As a regional security guarantee for Australia ANZUS was extremely limited. Essentially it was an important link in a chain of treaties and agreements which John Foster Dulles, Consultant to the USA Secretary of State, was ambitiously hammering together to contain worldwide communism. Contrary to the self-serving account of Percy Spender, External Affairs Minister, who presided over its drafting for Australia, the Americans willingly gave us ANZUS, but at a high price in firm global commitments to USA strategic objectives. The British were not churlishly opposed to the notion of this agreement, as was often claimed; they, more than any other source, were responsible for it being offered to Australia by the USA, seeing it as a means of easing Australia's sense of insecurity about Japan in the Pacific and putting Australia in a position to fight in distant lands, protecting British interests if necessary. Australia, moreover, was isolated and without leverage to extract anything from the USA against American inclinations, as a *quid pro quo* for accepting a 'soft' peace treaty with Japan. We got ANZUS because America wanted us to be in it, to be a bit player in the big competition against world communism and for the 'free' world.

I had long harboured suspicions that more extensive obligations had been assumed by Australia on the basis of the preambular clauses of the Treaty than had ever been acknowledged by either Australian or American spokespeople on the subject. As Foreign Minister I set my department the task of exploring the implications of those preambular paragraphs. This helped somewhat in confirming my suspicions, although investigations of relevant sources had 'not yielded an authoritative explanation for the inclusion in the Preamble of the second recital . . . '.[34] I had found preambular paragraph two a curious inclusion covering the Philippines, Ryukyu Islands and Japan, which superficially seemed superfluous in the light of Articles III, IV and V declaring the liability of other pact members to respond in the event of an attack on one of them in the Pacific. In addition, these are scarcely the sort of places Australia would choose, it seemed to me, to flutter at the top of the masthead of its trilateral treaty guaranteeing its regional security. Preambular paragraph three specifically mentions military obligations for Australia and New Zealand outside as well as within the Pacific area as members of the British Commonwealth of Nations. In the light of relevant official documentation, some now declassified, it is clear the first reference was and is meant to act as a memory jogger for Australia and New Zealand—in case of any tendency towards backsliding later—that ANZUS is an inescapable part of a greater strategic network of commitments, just as the second reference was to brace them to their wider duties to be ready to fight for the colonial and political ambitions of the British Empire, such as in Malaya and the Middle East.

Article thirty-one of the Vienna Convention stipulates the preamble of a treaty should be included in any interpretation of it and is one of the principal formal parts of a treaty or convention.[35] In spite of their importance, Minister for External Relations, Richard Casey, made no reference to these preambular paragraphs when steering the Bill through Parliament.[36] Presumably this was thought wise as any elaboration of the extensive commitments secretly entered into by the Government would have further inflamed an already enraged but misdirected Labor Opposition, not to mention fuelled public outrage so soon after the defeat of Japan on discovering that Australia was committed to the military defence of that country. The Government cunningly planted a story in a newspaper prior to the parliamentary debate on the draft treaty in 1951 that Evatt, when Minister for External Affairs, had been responsible for preventing the USA establishing a major postwar military base on Manus Island, then in Australian mandated territory. Labor was effectively charged with being anti-American and therefore un-Australian, according to the political lexicon of the time. In consequence Labor parliamentarians largely spent their time kicking, prodding and shrieking at this dead cat instead of analysing the Bill.

Evatt's contribution was defensive, rambling and largely irrelevant. In the meantime government spokesmen took the noisy, patriotic high ground, peppering the parliamentary chamber with a sustained fusillade of chauvinistic platitudes.[37] Two exceptions to this unenlightening performance by Labor were W. M. Bourke and Kim Beazley Snr. The latter said with characteristic insight, '. . . the chances the United States of America will be called upon to honour this pact in the event of an attack being made upon Australia are at most only one-tenth of the chances that Australia will be called upon to honour this pact in the event of the United States of America becoming involved in a world war'. He added, 'No country is in a position to attack Australia in the first instance without moving elsewhere on a scale that would inevitably cause war'.[38] It would be thirty years before Parliament, through the Joint Committee on Foreign Affairs and Defence, endorsed this commonsense conclusion as conventional wisdom.[39] It was also a view that Menzies shared privately but, as with certain other important issues of principle embraced by Menzies, what he said publicly was often what served political expediency. For instance, during the early part of World War II he publicly supported Winston Churchill's leadership of Britain. Privately, however, he was a Chamberlainite, actively seeking to erode Churchill's position with great and powerful sponsors in England and according to one account had ambitions to replace Churchill as wartime Prime Minister of Britain. Churchill responded with dislike and distrust, regarding Menzies as 'an inveterate defeatist'.[40]

Spender has baldly but unhelpfully declared the second preambular paragraph states a 'factual situation'. Of the third, he said it 'merits particular attention', but only because it was not added to the Treaty after the Canberra drafting meeting of 18 February 1951.[41] Spender delphically concedes that with the Treaty Australia assumed obligations 'far beyond the shores of Australia', which does not tell us much at all.[42] Watt, head of Spender's department at that time, did not discuss the preambular paragraphs at all in his *The Evolution of Australian Foreign Policy*, although he radiates enchantment at other aspects of the Treaty. Elsewhere he gave the game away, in secret session with New Zealand External Affairs officials in early 1951, confessing the objectives sought by the Australian Government through ANZUS were security protection (i) against a re-armed Japan (ii) against communist imperialism in Asia and (iii) against Asian expansionism generally.

The last, which signalled the ever-pervasive fear some Australians had of the threat of 'Yellow Hordes', was the most important Australian expectation according to Watt, but because of its sensitivity could not be acknowledged publicly.[43]

Later, Casey in *Friends and Neighbours,* and Menzies in a journal article, both alluded to these broader commitments. But in the absence of specific background material, which of course was classified and therefore restricted, they provided inadequate evidence to allow informed conclusions about the depth and breadth of Australia's commitments assumed under ANZUS. Starke QC in a forensic analysis of the Treaty concluded preambular paragraph two implied the 'general intention of interdependence of [ANZUS with] the arrangements and treaties safeguarding the offshore island chain'. This analysis was not taken further.[44] Dulles, however, had previously confessed all in private. Before arriving in Australia for the February 1951 Treaty negotiations, he advised Macarthur the second preambular paragraph established treaty liabilities towards Japan, Ryukyu Islands and the Philippines 'in the event Japan and the Philippines are not initially members of the pact'.[45]

America was always interested

The popular Australian notion that ANZUS reflected and cemented a 'special relationship' with our 'great and powerful ally', was fostered from the start by conservative political figures. They variously declared: that it grew out of the close kinship established between our two countries as allies in the Pacific during World War II; that it was an open-hearted response for the prompt commitment of Australian armed forces in support of the USA during the Korean War; that it was also a concession wrung from the Americans for Australia accepting, unenthusiastically, a 'soft' Japanese peace treaty when the public was decidedly hostile to the idea, thus assuring the treaty's acceptability with the broader community of wartime allies.[46] There seems to be a contradiction between the first two points and the last. The former imply willing USA concessions to Australia as a warm expression of appreciation for past services. The last unmistakably implies a reluctant yielding after forceful arm twisting. Indeed, the heart of Spender's account is how ANZUS was fought for and won in spite of steady USA resistance.

It was not a case of greater Australian endurance, skill and determination overbearing the Americans. In fact the United States blew hot and cold on the notion of some form of Pacific pact from 1949, but even when cool she was never hostile to the notion. A draft policy planning paper of the State Department of July 1949 proposed the USA '. . . should sound out the Philippines and Australia on the desirability of a Three Power Defence Treaty, along the general lines of the Atlantic Pact, composed initially of the USA, the Philippines and Australia'.[47] While Dulles had some early reservations about a treaty with Australia, these were more concerned about its nature than with opposition *per se*. Soon after his appointment as Consultant to the Secretary of State in April 1950 he was doubtful about an Atlantic Pact (NATO) type of treaty but was keen on something conceptually similar to a Monroe-type doctrine—and that was exactly the basis of the subsequent ANZUS Treaty.[48] A working paper of November 1950 prepared for Dulles proposed, 'It would seem important to accelerate some understanding with Australia and New Zealand, the only two dependable countries in the Pacific area'.[49] It is clear that the weight of support for the concept picked up as the year advanced and by the time Dulles was heading for Australia via Tokyo in early 1951 he had firmly committed himself to the idea of a tripartite pact between Australia, New Zealand and the USA.[50] In between times American affection for the new Menzies Government was enthusiastic and the USA Ambassador in Canberra was keenly urging the case for the tripartite treaty.[51] Goodwill towards the Menzies Government was enhanced when it refused to follow the British lead and extend recognition to communist China, an action the Americans interpreted as designed to garner kudos from them for the treaty proposal.[52]

Spender complained, and with good reason, that Menzies was undermining his efforts to forge the Treaty with the USA. Menzies privately believed there was no need for a treaty as the USA had demonstrated its willingness to defend Australia in World War II, a view he was not afraid to confide loosely and to Spender's chagrin.[53] As Spender regarded the same view expressed publicly by Eddie Ward, Labor MP for East Sydney and a firebrand of the Left, as half a hobble short of treachery, his irritation with Menzies must have been palpable.[54] Nor was Spender inspired when he discovered his Prime Minister had described his treaty in Canada as 'a superstructure on a foundation of jelly'.[55] In the USA in July 1950 Menzies broached a maximum of three topics in official talks with various Administration representatives, including President Truman and Secretary of State, Dean Acheson. They were the Korean War, Australian immigration policy and access to a development loan for Australia.[56] He neglected to register even a mild interest in Spender's treaty proposal. In the world of foreign relations, official exchanges can convey a loud enough message by something not being said, and Menzies' omission was a communication of crystal clarity. The Americans would have been confused by this, especially when in September 1950 Acheson was briefed to the effect '. . . Prime Minister Menzies is understood not to believe a Pacific pact necessary now'.[57] Then, Menzies stuffed more lead into Spender's saddlebags when he told Acheson that, 'he [Menzies] favoured proceeding promptly with a Japanese peace treaty and he felt that it should be a generous and not a punitive treaty'.[58] Curiously, in spite of Menzies' opposition to ANZUS at the time of its conception, on the eve of his retirement from Parliament some fifteen years later he boasted the ANZUS Treaty was '. . . the best single step that has been taken in the time of my government . . . making the USA in substance our ally'.[59]

After this, Spender would have had negligible, if any, influence with the Americans to force them to act contrary to their wishes, something Watt frankly acknowledged.[60] Nonetheless, Spender's own advocacy showed a tendency to scorch the very ground on which he was trying to stand. Rather than being clear-sighted and well-briefed on his objectives, Spender sallied forth uncertainly on a number of crucial occasions, making contradictory presentations. In March 1950 the USA Secretary of State received a cable reporting an Australian External Affairs officer comment '. . . Spender plan still too vague for discussion and Australian Government "not ready" '.[61] A 9 October memorandum to Assistant Secretary of State for Far Eastern Affairs, Dean Rusk, advised that the Australian Government appears '. . . to be interested not so much in written assurances of military protection as in an opportunity to participate more closely in military and political planning', and less than three weeks later '. . . while Spender is still interested in the Pacific pact, what he really wants is closer participation in all stages of high level Washington planning which might later involve the disposition of Australian Forces or material'.[62] Much of this negative advice was feeding into the policy-making processes of the USA right on the eve of Spender's arrival there to commence preliminary negotiations on his tripartite treaty. It set the accommodating Americans on the wrong course. In an effort to meet these less stringent requirements they speculated that consultations might eventually result in 'some association of an acceptable type'.[63]

Why Spender was so disgusted with Ward and angry with Menzies is hard to fathom, for three days later in New York he committed the same sort of solecism as that of which he had accused them. An official record notes Spender '. . . stated that he personally realised that there was no danger of Australia being attacked without simultaneous attack on the United States'.[64] He attempted to get around this weakening of his own case by endeavouring to link the difficulties of the sale of a 'soft' Japanese peace treaty in Australia with the Pacific pact as a 'sweetener', as it were. He forgot, or perhaps his prime minister had not told him, that Menzies had blown this leaky little tub out of the water during official talks when he had passed through the USA a little earlier. In opposing the Japanese peace treaty, New Zealand and Australia stood alone among the developed Commonwealth countries and among the allies who had fought in the Pacific, but New Zealand's opposition was half-hearted. At the London Commonwealth Prime Ministers' Conference of 1951, New Zealand Prime Minister Holland was clearly equivocal about declaring his country's opposition to the proposal.[65] Holland further loosened the ground under Spender in Washington in mid-February that year, advising Administration officials '. . . New Zealand would not give [the USA] trouble on a Japanese treaty but Australia probably would'.[66] Thus Spender had to contend with three important figures actively eroding the foundations he was supposedly trying to establish: the Prime Minister of Australia, the Prime Minister of New Zealand and Australia's Minister for External Affairs—that is, himself.

It is difficult to discover in the relevant official records evidence of Spender's reputedly noble and indomitable struggle to woo and win USA endorsement of an ANZUS-type pact. ANZUS was negotiated from go to whoa in approximately ten months, which is remarkable expedition for concluding such a treaty.[67] The afternoon of 14 February 1951 was all that was required to complete the draft Treaty, agreed on *ad referendum*, at the Australia–New Zealand–USA trilateral conference in Canberra. Dulles immediately conceded that 'We are . . . prepared to consider all possible suggestions . . . I want to make clear there is no hesitation or reluctance on our part as regards the substance of what you want'. It is relevant to note, given earlier comment, that the Americans prepared a new preamble which was accepted, although I have been unable to locate the working papers behind this process.[68] Nor would this open-handed, co-operative American attitude have been a surprise for the Australian negotiating team. The official record of Holland's meeting with the State Department in February reads: 'Mr Dean Rusk then inquired whether a tripartite arrangement among Australia, New Zealand and the United States would not suffice to meet their security requirements' and it is further recorded that Holland 'wholeheartedly agreed to this approach'.[69] In all the circumstances New Zealand would have promptly shared this important information with its negotiating partner, Australia. More generally, Dulles' initial enthusiasm for a Pacific pact was earlier conveyed formally and in some detail to Australia by John Allison, adviser to the Dulles mission to Australia.[70] Spender alludes to this mysteriously as if it was a secret leak, which is a rather elaborate and oblique way to present a simple, straightforward matter of fact. Perhaps this was another element of the myth-making, conscious or unconscious.

Contrary to Australian claims, the original draft Australia submitted was drastically amended by the Americans. Articles VII and VIII provided for a substantial ANZUS Council. It would have had authority to set up 'such subsidiary bodies as may be necessary to accomplish its purposes . . . The council shall also co-ordinate its planning so far as possible with that of other regional organisations and associations of States of which one or more of the Parties are members.'[71] This accorded with Spender's stated aim that there should be 'effective consultative machinery on the political and technical level through which our countries could have a say in both regional and global discussions which affected our destiny.'[72] The priority he gave such a consultative and planning process earlier in the USA, as quoted, would imply this objective was amongst the most important, and possibly *the* most important, he had set himself. It was an objective he failed to achieve. The USA Joint Chiefs of Staff had other ideas, fearing these provisions would allow Australia to 'demand knowledge of and to participate in planning by the North Atlantic Treaty Organisation and the Organisation of American States and vice versa . . . resulting in . . .

impairment of secrecy through too wide disclosure'.[73] Australia got the 'brush off', being treated as 'small fry', to use Spender's phrases.[74] The result was a much less substantial, more ambiguous and relatively anodyne redraft of Articles VII and VIII, which Australia had to accept. What else could 'small fry' do in the circumstances? Spender got his tripartite treaty, but in a notably attenuated form to that he desired, while the USA got all that it wanted. Dulles had stooped to conquer, as it were.

Australia got its treaty in large part due to Dulles' personality and the political climate, national and international, of the times. Dulles believed in a Manichean battle for survival between the civilised and freedom-loving West as the embodiment of virtue, and those evil empires in the East, the Soviet Union and China, where tyranny and injustice prevailed. He conveniently ignored the tyranny and injustice of several nasty little dictatorships which hung in with the West. He was instrumental in redefining the Cold War as a moral challenge rather than as an ideological–political contest. His stern, Calvinistic temperament in such things was summed up by Sir Oliver Franks, British Ambassador to Washington at the time:

> Three or four centuries ago, when Reformation and Counter-
> Reformation divided Europe into armed camps, in an age of wars of
> religion, it was not so rare to encounter men of the type of Dulles. Like
> them he came to unshakeable convictions of a religious and theological
> order. Like them he saw the world as an arena in which the forces of
> good and evil were continuously at war.[75]

This righteous zealotry for the anti-communist cause, set against an actual firestorm of communist agitation and encroachment, disposed Dulles to energetic action and to commitments designed to contain the Marxist–Leninist incubus. The times were of course conducive to such a man: there was fear of a thrust into Iran by the USSR, internal communist threats to France, Italy and Japan, a guerilla war in Greece, unrest in Turkey, the Berlin Blockade, the USSR was in possession of the atomic bomb, and the USA infected with the hysteria of McCarthyism. As if this were not enough, there were also fears of a communist Chinese attack against the Nationalist Chinese in Formosa, and internal communist insurgencies disabling the political and economic development of several South-East Asian countries. The last provoked General Macarthur to fretfully observe of Indochina in late 1950 that French forces should be able to 'clean up' the communist forces in four months, their inability to do so raising doubts about their 'capacity and caliber', a simplistic judgment which came back to haunt the USA less than a generation later.[76] Then, paramountly, the Korean War unexpectedly broke out on the eve of Dulles' departure from Tokyo for the Philippines and Australia, a war that initially went badly for American and later UN forces, and the shock of which had wider ramifications.[77] To Dulles, and many others at the time, freedom was in peril. In the circumstances Dulles' vision of the world was bleak indeed, moving him to comment in the Philippines '. . . [there was] a real danger of attack on the Far East and the Pacific', and he did not know 'whether the danger was greater [in the Far East and the South Pacific] or in Europe'. He further warned that 'We have to drive with a light rein [in drawing up a Japanese peace treaty] because the temptation for Japan to go over to the other side is great'.[78]

When the notion of a Pacific pact was addressed, as 1950 ran over into the new year, Dulles, because of his temperament and the nature of the times, drew down a very large menu of commitments for Australia and other USA allies. The objectives were sharpened, to include:

- fighting in defence of Japan if she were attacked;
- securing Japanese skilled labour, industrial resources, and political and military support for the West in the East–West contest;
- shoring up Japanese confidence in the event of her being cut off;

- having military bases available in Japan for the USA;
- saving Japan from falling to communism internally;
- preventing Japanese revanchism;
- providing for Japanese membership of the Treaty immediately or subsequently;
- committing pact members to defence liabilities in the Pacific;
- linking Japan, the Philippines, Australia and New Zealand, and perhaps Taiwan and Indonesia with the USA through the pact to form an 'island chain' of defence in the Pacific;
- assuring Australia and New Zealand of their security should they be required to fight in the Middle East or Malaya;
- mollifying Australian hostility to a 'soft' Japanese peace treaty;
- avoiding absolutely any commitments to Hong Kong and consequently to exclude the United Kingdom from any pact; and
- avoiding liabilities involving exhausted colonial powers in the Pacific generally viz., the UK, France, the Netherlands and Portugal, which of course excluded them from any consideration for treaty membership.[79]

These extensive obligations had to be understood in the context of the Vandenbourg Resolution of the USA Congress, according to which allies were expected to make efforts to be militarily credible of attending to their own defence.[80] This was reinforced by the later 'Guam Doctrine' of President Nixon;[81] and this probably explains why American Administration representatives were usually mystified at Australia's preoccupation with its regional security within the ANZUS Treaty. The USA was on a global holy mission. If we too had the faith, seemed to go the implication, we would unerringly recognise that. Local sideshows unrelated to that millenarian mission were largely our own business. The larger priorities were quite explicitly announced by the Americans: to fight against communism in Malaya and the Middle East, to defend Japan, to fight China or the USSR. That was an extremely impressive list of obligations for Australia to accept for the sake of a security treaty to protect her territorial integrity when in the words of Spender, '. . . there was no danger of Australia being attacked . . . '.[82] In locking Australia into all this, Dulles revealed himself as 'a curious cross between a Christer and a shrewd and quite ruthless lawyer', so effective was he that he was able to comment to Macarthur that under Article IV of the Treaty the 'United States can discharge its obligations against the common enemy in any way and in any area that it sees fit'.[83]

Whether long or short, it's all the same

When Dulles set out for Australia in early 1951 he had in mind a 'major island chain' treaty covering Japan, the Philippines, Australia and New Zealand with the USA. At one stage there was some thought of including Indonesia, but this was discarded early on. After discussions with the British Ambassador in Tokyo and a formal UK Government submission to the USA Administration in Washington, his priorities changed, as he confessed. The British made firm representations for a trilateral USA treaty with Australia and New Zealand.[84] Consequently Dulles settled for bilateral treaties with Japan and with the Philippines and a trilateral arrangement with Australia and New Zealand. As he reported rather artfully to the Joint Chiefs of Staff in Washington in April 1951 '. . . the total effect of these pacts would be the same in substance as the single pact which had been contemplated originally'.[85] Acheson confirmed this interpretation.[86] So did President Truman.[87] In 1952, in testimony before the Congressional Foreign Affairs Committee, Dulles said if there were armed attacks on the USA Trust Territory, the Ryukyu or Bonin Islands or upon USA bases in Japan, the ANZUS Treaty 'would be invoked'.[88]

The concession of a trilateral arrangement was not benignly made to ease the domestic difficulties of the Australian Government as it entered into an unpopular 'soft' Japanese peace treaty. In the first place, Britain was not talking about her responsibilities nor gratitude towards a former colony which had shed much blood in two world wars defending her interests. Nor was the USA doing anything similar with regard to an ally and friend which had stood with her in the war in the Pacific. These countries were engaged in Realpolitik considerations, talking about the big global game and how their interests would be best served as important world powers. Britain feared an 'islands chain' treaty could leave the impression that her exclusion meant she would be denied security protection by the treaty members in the event of aggression against her, which might incite communist expansionism at her expense. Britain was no doubt concerned about her status and that of other colonial powers in the Pacific; she was exhausted and discredited by an ineffective defence of her colonies during World War II, and concerned that any substantial presence was no longer sustainable in the postwar period with its different values. She was not asking to be included in any pact, but in effect for treaty-making to be concluded in such a way as not to broadcast her vulnerability.[89] Thus she strongly urged the alternative of 'a tripartite pact—United States, Australia and New Zealand—on the basis of which each would go to the aid of the others in the case of hostilities occurring which would effect the interests in the Pacific of any one of the parties'.[90] Moreover, she clearly expected additional benefits to this from a tripartite treaty. She was concerned that an explicit obligation to fight for Japan might interfere with the ability and willingness of Australia and New Zealand 'to send forces to the Middle East in case of need'.[91] That is also why the USA Joint Chiefs of Staff, shortly before the Canberra negotiating conference, wanted some 'sort of Pacific Pact as it was their belief that if Australia was reassured as to its defense in the Pacific area it would be in a position to give more assistance to the general cause in the Middle East'.[92] Spender acknowledged that ANZUS facilitated Australia discharging 'responsibilities outside the Pacific area'.[93]

Neither Britain nor the USA needed to have worried in the case of New Zealand. In early 1951 Prime Minister Holland informed the USA Administration 'that New Zealand already had a commitment to furnish within seventy days of the outbreak of war an augmented division of some 33 000 to 50 000 men—for the Middle East—that these would be volunteers, but the replacements would come through conscription . . . and She intended, as a matter of fact, to strip the country of all forces, not even reserving elements for anti-aircraft or port defense'.[94] When it came to fighting for the Empire, New Zealand had no peer. Australia, meanwhile, revealed its faint-heartedness only in private. In the course of confidential tripartite negotiations in Canberra during February 1951, Australian records note the USA observing the 'United Kingdom would have no objection to a tripartite arrangement' and Spender responding 'the United Kingdom objections were met by a tripartite arrangement'. There was forceful advocacy on behalf of Australia that a tripartite treaty would give Australia the security to allow it to fight in the Middle East, just as background notes for the Australian negotiating team instructed them that 'we must insist on a firm defence guarantee from the United States if we are to be expected to play a substantial part in a global plan for resisting communist imperialism'.[95] Dulles' view was that Japan should be allowed to enter the ANZUS Treaty at some later, suitable time and Spender and Doidge for New Zealand agreed.[96] Six months later a 'Mutual Defense Treaty' was concluded between the Philippines and the USA. The following month a Japanese Peace Treaty, a Security Treaty and a Treaty of Mutual Co-operation and Security between Japan and the USA were in place. The links in the Pacific Islands Pact were rapidly forged together. Given the real intent behind this treaty-making and subsequent experiences, Australians were continually misguided by conservative politicians as to its purpose and encouraged to view ANZUS in isolation as their 'special' defence agreement. In a much more sanguine and accurate way, the Americans saw it as one of several links through the Pacific providing her with significant commitments in the global challenge to contain communism.

Now that the Cold War is over and America is realigning its strategic and foreign policies giving priority to particular regions and interests rather than striving to cover the globe, the region in which Australia is situated is lowly rated. That is why after strenuously resisting Philippines Government pressure to quit that country, America evacuated its hitherto strategically essential military bases there fairly quickly once the East–West confrontation ended. As the SEATO Treaty quietly slipped into ineffectiveness, so too has ANZUS.

Australia received certain tangible advantages from the Treaty, namely access to advanced military technology available to few countries. This important edge in military hardware was being eroded in the region even while I was in the Parliament, and has subsequently weakened further. We cannot complain. We are trying to become arms manufacturers and salesmen in the international market place, which is an unhappy development according to my values—and also a wasteful exercise absorbing large amounts of taxpayers' money as large, implicit subsidies to keep these projects fiscally afloat.[97] As for other benefits, there were valuable exchanges of intelligence material; on regional matters however, the quality of what we got was uneven, its supply occasionally hindered by mistrustful USA agency officers. Where we were effective, as in many instances through ASIS, the quality of what we exchanged was often superior to what we received. If ANZUS was seen as an insurance policy for Australia then we certainly paid our dues fully. We risked being a nuclear target by hosting joint military type installations at Nurrungar, Pine Gap and North West Cape. As a government, we forbore considerable dissatisfaction from elements in the community by providing airfield facilities for nuclear-capable military aircraft and porting and resupply backup for nuclear-powered and nuclear-capable naval vessels. Australia was also one of the United States' most reliable supporters internationally. All these things were morally justifiable if one accepted, as I came to, that they helped deter the threat of nuclear conflict.

On the other hand, on the occasions when Australia sought to invoke ANZUS obligations in the region the USA gave us a polite but firm rebuff. In 1956 Australia was pressed by the USA to commit troops for clandestine military operations against and sometimes in Indonesia, then seen as a potential communist threat. In 1958 as Australian concerns mounted about the future of Dutch-colonised West Irian—now Irian Jaya—and the possibility of it being taken over by Indonesia, Menzies privately recorded his fears that 'the United States would not support the Dutch and Australia in a military sense'. Nor did they. Undeterred, he continued to hammer publicly the message that, despite these rebuffs the Treaty and 'great and powerful' friends gave us protection. The Government's Defence Committee in June 1963 concluded the USA might not always support Australia 'and may even counsel compliance in order to avoid reactions on the part of countries with which they wish to retain influence'. Ordinary people who said that publicly were labelled and condemned as subversives. External Affairs Minister Garfield Barwick sought a clear and comprehensive commitment from the USA in 1961 to respond with broad military support in the event of armed attacks against Australian military targets in Malaysia. He did not get it.[98] He got a *bout de papier,* something which 'cannot be claimed by either side as possessing any official status'.[99] In private Barwick commented:

> *In practice, each of the parties to the Treaty is going to decide whether or not to take action under the Treaty according to its own judgment on the situation that exists . . . The Government is of the opinion that discussion of the Treaty's meaning is almost certain to narrow its meaning . . . we will only tend to embarrass each other if we try either in public or private to explore such topics and in the Government's view*

*such exploration is bound to weaken rather than strengthen the reliance
we can place of (sic) ANZUS.*[100]

A strange comment indeed. The more we knew about the Treaty the less we would discover in it for our regional interests. In 1965, when the Menzies Government volunteered the commitment of a battalion of Australian troops to the war in Vietnam, it expressed the view to the US that because of the dispersal of its military forces at several points in the region, it would be looking to Washington and London in dealing with any 'special difficulties' which might arise for it. Washington's response was a bland, unreassuring comment to the effect that the US was aware of its commitments under ANZUS.[101]

Strategically, the country which stood to benefit from the Treaty most was the United States. Article V obliges us to respond to armed attack on the 'metropolitan territory' of the USA—such as an attack on the Atlantic littoral—which at the height of the Cold War was a feasible scenario. It is especially interesting to note the way in which the annual ANZUS Council meetings were subtly transformed. I wondered why, as a minor partner—'small fry' as it were—we were frequently asked by the Americans to lead discussion on the communist threat in Europe, the Korean Peninsula, and a host of other trouble spots where our involvement was minimal to non-existent and where the American policy concern was huge. These responses were spelt out in public communiques, a 'practice which could be called in aid by a Party seeking a broad interpretation of the area of application of The [sic] Treaty'.[102] As stated, I accepted that Australia had a moral duty to resist communist-inspired international provocations as part of the Western Alliance which resisted global communism, but to do so according to our own reasoned judgments. What is unacceptable was the calculated dishonesty adopted by certain conservative politicians in declaring what ANZUS did for Australia, as well as concealing its real purposes and the extraordinarily broad commitments Australia assumed with its advent. Equally unacceptable was the manner in which the good character of many decent Australian citizens was wantonly traduced and their loyalty questioned when they expressed reservations about the stated nature of the Treaty. My reservations dating back to my early years in the Parliament have been proved justified; the passage of time, plus access to once classified documents and other sources, indicates so many of them to have been correct.

New Zealand: the mouse that bit an elephant

In 1984 one of the smallest and hitherto most inoffensive of the world's nations brought the mightiest military and commercial power in the history of civilisation to a dead halt. In that year New Zealand prohibited nuclear-powered and nuclear weapons-capable naval vessels entering and using her port and harbour facilities. In effect, this was a blanket prohibition against the United States of America, preventing her naval vessels visiting New Zealand. Never before in the postwar period had any Western ally so directly and unambiguously confronted the strategic defence and foreign policies of the United States. Officials of the United States of America were stunned and perplexed. It was unheard of. It was irrational. Not even the temperamental Gauls postured with such hubris. For Australia, this development had the potential to create some nasty incidents. We had foreign policy and defence interests invested in the ANZUS Treaty and in our relationship with the United States of America. There was also our commitment, far from quiescent, to strategic policies aimed at achieving a balance between East and West. There were major commercial, political and security interests of ours in which New Zealand featured centrally. And the matter flared at the time of some regional uneasiness in the South West Pacific. This small fistful of issues alone bristled with the potential for a reaction dangerous to ourselves.

At home, media commentators, working on their old and trusty principle that no news is good news unless it is bad news, were romping about at their equivalent of a Teddy Bears' Picnic. One infelicitous step and the happy little teddy bears of the press would tear limbs off the hapless blunderer. There was also the Opposition, the venerable temple keepers, as some saw themselves, of the true faith of the ANZUS liturgy who upon infringements of the sacred texts would always bring down priestly imprecations of the worst forms of punishment. Then, too, there was the domestic electorate littered with traps for the unwary. On the right were those who seemed to think that we could bark at New Zealand as though it were a rookie private on the army parade ground needing to be licked into shape by a tough sergeant major. These people obviously had little personal knowledge of New Zealanders or their character. On the left was a very large and agitated peace movement, augmented by a recent sizeable influx of ordinary people from various backgrounds. To all these potential complications could possibly be added the strain of my own private belief that the issue certainly justified some concern, but nowhere near the fuss that had been generated. This would have been a politically lethal attitude to acknowledge publicly.

Australia and New Zealand have a lot in common; to a significant extent, if perversely, we are bonded by shared disadvantages. Similarly situated culturally and geographically, it makes good sense for Australia and New Zealand to become even more closely integrated in trade matters, and more generally in our social, economic and political policies. With a combined population of a little over twenty-two million people and stranded at the 'arse-end of the world', as one wit put it, Australia and New Zealand amount to no great significance on the world stage but at least do function more successfully together than apart. Our strategic outlook, nonetheless, is different from that of New Zealand. Australia abuts the South-East Asian region whose modern history is one of instability and the breakout of war at various points and different times. Further instances of that sort of unsteadiness to our north and north-west cannot be categorically ruled out. New Zealand, in contrast, has a different national security perception; by the time any aggressor got to New Zealand the rest of the world would more than likely be out of the main play. About the worst our neighbour across the Tasman might have to concern itself with, short of Armageddon, is the threat of a baleful brood of angry penguins landing on their shores.

While New Zealand did not see itself as having a role supporting the strategic policies of the United States of America, Australia did. The fact is that New Zealand was and is unimportant within the strategic designs of the United States. What troubled the Americans was the stark possibility that other countries more central to their strategic concerns, such as Japan, might be forced by domestic reaction to follow the New Zealand lead. This was a genuine concern of the USA. In turn, several of us in the Labor Government feared the Americans might have been tempted to react strongly and give New Zealand a sharp 'cuff' as it were, which would have been disastrous. Over-muscular reactions by the Americans would have created 'underdog sympathy' for New Zealand, generating hostility towards America within Australia. Therein resided potential for serious domestic political problems for the Australian Government. In the upshot the Americans behaved with commendable restraint.

There was a quite evident feeling among some of the senior parliamentarians of the New Zealand Labour Party in 1984 that the handling of this foreign policy rupture with the United States could be somewhat tricky electorally. Because of this the Party played, soft pedal, the policy theme of 'no nuclear ships' and emphasised a loyal commitment to the ANZUS Treaty, during the election campaign that year. The New Zealand Labour Government sought to avoid being positioned as 'anti-ANZUS' before the electorate. There was frank acknowledgment among some senior parliamentarians that were that to happen the government would become a one-term government.

Right up to the point of rupture, and even beyond, when New Zealand remained a 'friend but ceased being an ally' of the USA, as the Americans put it, the New Zealand Labour Government maintained the two prongs to its strategy. It was adamant in public statements that the 'no nuclear ships' policy would be enforced, and at the same time emphasised its abiding commitment to ANZUS. Opinion polls in that country reported high levels of public support for both positions, with fewer than one in three people favouring nuclear-armed warships visiting New Zealand but nearly four out of five people supporting ANZUS. The Americans pointed out that these were contradictory positions and perseverance with opposition to those visits meant suspension of ANZUS for New Zealand. What the contradictory opinion poll results revealed was that the New Zealand public wanted nothing to do with American nuclear-propelled and nuclear weaponry-capable naval vessels, but expected the United States to provide military guarantees as and when necessary. It is worth recalling that opinion polls in this country then reported similar findings among the Australian public. As events unfolded Prime Minister Lange, who had bounced into office with all of the sprightliness and gloss of a new and rather well-rounded rubber playpen ball, was being featured by many of his followers as a sort of latter-day Roland holding the pass against the barbarians. For some of us who dealt with him privately it was clear that, initially anyway, he held the tiller on the set course with a slack and unenthusiastic hand. A change of course was undoubtedly attractive and the Americans went away from early discussions with him believing this would happen. He convinced them, wittingly or otherwise, that he intended to mobilise the force of the prime ministerial office to deflect party demands that the policy be proceeded with immediately.

Prime ministerial expectations of this sort were like the dreams of those who chewed poppy seeds recreationally. The fact was plain: the

Party had bolted on this issue and the politicians would find it impossible to make up the ground again. The time to have put the issue under control was before winning government. There was, already, clear warning afoot for New Zealand Labour parliamentarians that their party would obdurately oppose any backsliding. Lange early on entertained a notion that he would deny the party wish to close the South African Consulate; the Party made it clear it would force him to close it. Before Lange could respond, the South African Government closed its Consulate to pre-empt the forced closure. It was obvious the New Zealand Labour Party would not allow modification of its 'no nuclear ships' policy. Not for its powerful ally the United States. Not for its trans-Tasman neighbour and friend, Australia. Certainly not for any local, backsliding MP. The respective policy positions of the governments of New Zealand and the USA were mutually exclusive. What is extraordinary, then, was the way New Zealand strung out a process doomed from the start.

New Zealand embarked on a two-track policy, one of which could be characterised as the track of faint hope. New Zealand managed to sustain a worried and faint expectation with the Americans that something would be sorted out given some time and patience. We advised the Americans there was more drinking water to be had from a desert mirage than there was substance from this hope. Once their early days of uncertainty and settling into office were out of the way, our New Zealand parliamentary partners were candid with us. A satisfactory resolution for the Americans required some sort of *deus ex machina* being lowered into the midst of these two sets of irreconcilable positions at a critical point. We were agnostically sceptical about that. For all its size, might and influence in the world, the Americans were genuinely confused by New Zealand's tactics and were unsure how to handle them. An elephant could surely stomp on a tiny mouse gnawing at its ankle but in international relations that just did not seem right somehow. If the Americans were confused and puzzled, as they obviously were, in fairness it was as much because the messages coming out of Wellington were distinctly puzzling to them. I expect the English cultural influence, which is much more overtly apparent in New Zealand than Australia, has left its mark on the humour of that country, or at least on that of the personality of Lange. Spontaneous irony and fondly hewn epigrams would cascade from him without warning, in the midst of the most deeply serious negotiation. This could be mildly disconcerting for an Australian interlocutor. So it can be imagined how devastating the experience would be for very serious and literal-minded Americans who like their humour straight and at the right time and place. Americans were never quite sure what it was to which Lange alluded. Was that some kind of elusive humour or was it a personal jibe at one or other of them?

Lange gives an example of his sense of humour in his *Nuclear Free: the New Zealand Way,* a work which is less sustainable as history than as entertainment. Two American intelligence officers of military bearing called at his Wellington office to brief him on strategic matters, something they do very professionally and thoroughly. In noting there were a pair of these officers Lange nonchalantly quipped, 'Which of you two isn't to be trusted?'. With youthful zest he recounts how 'easily annoyed' they became. Then, innocently droll, he recalls going to sleep in the briefing. That would have left a lasting impression with the Americans! Quite early in the piece the Americans were working under the assumption the New Zealanders had sought a quiet period of six months in which to change the 'no nuclear ships' policy to one accommodating to American concerns. They eventually got seven months, but it was not long before the Americans realised it would take more than one parliamentary term to bring about that change. A shiver of despair ran through their officials.

Some New Zealanders began to feel that perhaps American impatience would settle down with some adroit stroking. An idea started to float about briefly, like a folded paper aeroplane too heavily weighted at the nose, that maybe nuclear-powered vessels could use New Zealand ports. What this was supposed to remedy was hard to fathom. All American nuclear-powered combat vessels are nuclear-capable. Then came the USS *Buchanan* incident. Early in 1985 Lange announced that if his officials could tell him a naval vessel 'is not nuclear-armed' he 'would be on the poop to welcome the thing'. There was a great flurry of exchanges between the Americans and New Zealand. The USS *Buchanan* was submitted to the New Zealand Government as an acceptable vessel for a visit. The *Buchanan* was a conventionally powered DDG guided missile destroyer of the Charles F. Adams class. The Australian Navy has three of these vessels which have been regarded as being at the cutting edge of our naval defence capabilities. By American standards the *Buchanan* was obsolescent. True, the *Buchanan* had a capability to launch certain nuclear weapons, but the New Zealanders on this occasion could have honestly declared that the vessel was neither nuclear-powered nor nuclear-armed.

It was difficult to conceive what help this ship's visit would have been for New Zealand, except as a very brief expedient for getting a little more breathing space. It would have been only a matter of time, after such an approval, before a nuclear-powered and nuclear-capable vessel suddenly steamed over the horizon, like Commander Perry's naval squadron in 1853 testing the resolve of the Japanese at Araga. The Americans were under the clear impression that the *Buchanan* visit would be approved. After carefully reading the relevant cable traffic, especially that out of Wellington, I understood why. In the event approval was not forthcoming. Attempts at modifying the 'no nuclear' policy in New Zealand were cleverly scuttled. In the case of the proposed visit of the *Buchanan* details of the class of vessel, but not its name, were leaked through the *Canberra Times* in Australia on 19 December 1984. This was before the visit request came to the New Zealand Cabinet; in New Zealand disclosing this proposed visit was like casually throwing a burning cigarette butt into the cargo of a fully laden petrol tanker.

This and other leaks, mass mobilisation of popular support for a 'no nuclear' New Zealand, extra parliamentary party pressure, and, as surreal as it sounds, a threatened chocolate trade war by Queensland Premier Bjelke-Petersen (of which more later), all worked to weld together a fracture-proof capsule preserving the integrity of the policy from any destructive actions by politicians. Popular parties of the Left, such as Labor parties, have a long history of rank and file suspicion of their elected representatives. The behaviour of the New Zealand Labour Party membership in enforcing the Party's 'no nuclear' policy, was consistent with a long tradition experienced in many other countries. Nonetheless this can be exasperating for members of Parliament and this no doubt provoked Lange to comment fretfully that the role of the party conference was to allow 'limousine liberals' to have a 'crack at their parliamentarians' and to 'scratch their politically erogenous zone'.

As the drama continued to unfold, a leaked account of a letter from Prime Minister Hawke to Prime Minister Lange which, very properly and directly, set out the differences and concerns Australia had with his government's 'no nuclear' policy was also published. A similar letter was sent by Secretary of State Shultz on behalf of the United States Administration. As is the usual practice, copies were exchanged between the two governments. Newspaper commentary, hinging on the leaked documents, interpreted the correspondence as an effort by Australia and the United States of America to bully New Zealand. It is unnecessary to expand on the obvious by giving an account of the outrage these provocative articles generated there.

The history of leaking by the Department of Foreign Affairs was unfortunately long and persistent. Mr Justice Woodward, former Director-General of ASIO, commented appositely, 'I regard this problem of leaking of defence and security information [by the Department of Foreign Affairs] as being just as serious as the work of hostile intelligence services in this country'. It should be stressed that this is a criticism of only a very small number of people as overwhelmingly, the staff of that Department is comprised of loyal and hard-working public servants. But even with only a few people 'leaking' the damage can be great; a comparison with another department such as Treasury, which is 'leak proof' and which is notable for the self-discipline and sense of corporate loyalty among its staff, is to Foreign Affairs' disadvantage. Another story planted in the media was a claim that Prime Minister Nakasone had sought to influence New Zealand 'no nuclear' policy during a visit to Japan in January 1985. This caused further resentment at what was conveniently interpreted by some as foreign interests attempting to manipulate the sovereignty of New Zealand. Lange seemed to deny this report but, wisely in the interests of his integrity, with carefully chosen words, for he could not categorically refute these claims.

Somewhere in this period Lange was proposed as a recipient for the Nobel Peace Prize, presumably for that part of his work seen and reported in public in support of the cause of peace and, in particular, for what was presumably seen as the faithful manner in which he had proceeded with the 'no nuclear' policy of New Zealand. Now, such a nomination is more than enough to certainly tilt, if not turn, the head of the most modest and humble of politicians. It must be conceded that David Lange was inflicted with no such personality defects. Any thought now of even a mild change of direction to established policy was something quite out of the question; with this nomination, the hasp of another padlock had been neatly snapped shut on the rather wide stable gate, if there was any thought of bolting. Then, as if there was not enough strife, the unbelievable happened, and it was orchestrated by the unspeakable. New Zealand-born Premier of Queensland, Bjelke-Petersen, declared a chocolate war against New Zealand. He resurrected a long-unused piece of health labelling legislation, invoking an import embargo against New Zealand chocolates; chocolates which were made with

Queensland sugar! It was never clear how this decisive 'leadership' was going to break the back of New Zealand stubbornness. Lange has pointed out that trade between Queensland and New Zealand at the time ran at about 2:1 in favour of Queensland. This blundering behaviour by the Premier caused much derisory snickering in New Zealand. Some there, however, characterised it as further evidence of the clumsy, heavy-handed outside interference to which that country was being subjected.

By this time there was no room for manoeuvre on the part of any New Zealand minister, least of all Prime Minister Lange. He was imprisoned by the mood of his party. His position in his Caucus was, at best, precarious. As Prime Minister, he may have been in office, but was not in power. The Left had made it clear that should he take one false step, they would replace him with their man. The numbers in the Caucus, roughly, were twenty-five to thirty Lange votes, twenty to twenty-five votes against Lange, and about ten uncommitted votes. The Left had obviously sniffed the scent of nervous sweat glands opening up on the part of some politicians. On the eve of Caucus consideration of the proposed *Buchanan* visit, the New Zealand Federation of Labour President Knox made an uncompromising statement on television indicating the fate of any politician contemplating modification of the 'no nuclear' policy. The same evening twenty-thousand people massed in Auckland, a huge crowd according to New Zealand experience, to demonstrate solidarity with the 'no nuclear' policy. The game was up, if indeed it had ever been on. The *Buchanan* would not be visiting New Zealand. And a salutary lesson had been learnt. Any groping efforts to test just how far the existing 'no nuclear ships' policy could be pushed had been wrestled into submission.

The teacup tempest

From the Australian end a little bit of spice had been added to the mix in the form of a smidgin of secret diplomacy. The clandestine operation involved the American Embassy in Canberra, Prime Minister Hawke and the New Zealand Prime Minister's Department in Wellington. It did not include me as the Australian Foreign Minister nor my department. To this day neither the Department of Foreign Affairs and Trade nor I have a clue as to what was transacted between the parties to this strange arrangement. It would appear that Hawke felt some personal, discreet diplomatic initiatives between him and Lange, involving the Americans as third parties, might resolve this disagreement between the USA and New Zealand. This was rather presumptuous given the evident personal hostility that existed between Hawke and Lange. A friendly official of another country hinted some facts about this arrangement to an Australian diplomat who recorded the information on file. I happened to come across the note somewhat later, when going through that file for other purposes. The Department had rather prudently decided not to bring the inflammatory report before the notice of its sometimes temperamental Minister. That nothing came of the exercise is probably adequate testimony on how cleverly the figures involved had thought out the undertaking. Perhaps it was just another instance of Hawke's egocentric presumption he could transfer his indisputable local industrial relations skills to the 'big canvas of international relations'.

The notes on file make it quite clear that it was not the behaviour of the Department of Foreign Affairs itself nor some other problem requiring a mandate of secrecy. It was me. There was a suspicion I harboured anti-American sentiments, which was and is untrue. Certainly, my admiration was not uncritical, which was something Hawke could not understand. As an Australian nationalist and one who was inclined to put foreign policy issues within an international framework, I had a tendency to sometimes see these as more complex than Hawke perhaps felt I should. I recall the 1985 bilateral meeting between Australia and the USA in Canberra, now that New Zealand had been tipped out of the cart of allies. It was bleak, cold, blustery winter weather. Key representatives from both sides enjoyed pre-dinner drinks and social talk in the lounge before dining at the Lodge. The flames in the fireplace crackled along at a heartwarming pace. USA Secretary of State Shultz lay back, large and expansive, next to the fireplace in a big, comfortable club lounge chair. He was looking down his spectacles at a scrawny little figure sitting on a very low pouffe at his feet. It was Hawke. Hawke emanated rapt attention and deference, intently staring up into Shultz's po face like a medieval apprentice at the feet of his master, as the latter delivered one of his characteristic monotones on some subject or other. I felt like shouting across the room, 'For God's sake don't do that, Bob. It's the wrong impression. You're our prime minister. Treat him as an equal. Don't be submissive!' Instead, I silently lived with my irritation.

To illustrate just how far this paranoia about my so called anti-Americanism had developed, there is evidence of a conversation which took place in the office of a very senior ministerial colleague, as related by one of his staff. A senior public servant, the quality of whose particular work I had questioned and criticised several times, reportedly explained that because of my anti-Americanism I was out to destroy ANZUS, in the process of which I also wanted to destroy the Prime Minister. That was some plot. Clearly, to some, I was capable of far greater things than mere suspicion. As mentioned earlier, Casey of the CIA had apparently found me too 'left wing' to be congenial company. The Caucus Left regarded me as some sort of Menshevik revisionist and treated me with caution. Not quite facetiously, these reactions were good reason for my helping to form up the Caucus Centre Left faction—to have someone to talk to. I dare say the announcement I made in the early part of 1982 as Leader of the Opposition, that port visits to Australia by nuclear-powered and nuclear-capable vessels would be prohibited under a Labor government, gave some good cause for suspicions about me. That was a blunder on my part. On the occasions I publicly suggested that Australia should use the joint facilities as leverage to get a better deal for our farmers from the United States, not only was there no support for the notion, but into the bargain I got a free lecture from Hawke on why I should not muddy the waters by mixing strategic and commercial matters. Earlier, in Geneva in 1983 at the United Nations Committee on Disarmament, I had suggested that the joint facilities in Australia could become an issue if they were drawn into the 'Star Wars' strategy and technologies, and if the USA was not more enthusiastic about nuclear arms control issues. An anxious telephone call from Hawke in Australia soon followed; he could not understand my tactic of applying a little creative tension on a friend or ally as a timely reminder that Australia maintained its independence, that it participated as an ally with rights and some importance and could thus not be taken for granted, not even by a large and influential ally. As previously mentioned, this is an approach I have occasionally also used in my personal relations, and one which has proved very productive.

While Australia's secret diplomacy in the shape of Hawke's 'Canberra Initiative' sputtered to a tired halt, before it even got fired up, there is no doubt the more pedestrian efforts of our orthodox diplomacy to gain more time for New Zealand by deflecting any American inclination for commercial retaliation were of some help. Why more time? It was always in my mind that the longer the United States was given to consider New Zealand's stance, one the latter could not possibly back away from, the better the prospects that the Americans would be able to adjust to it. They might not have ever come to like the situation, but that was another matter. Concomitantly, time was necessary to assess whether there would be any follow-on effect from other countries, that is, to establish whether the New Zealand policy might induce other governments to emulate her. This was something the Americans feared and very properly so. If there was no follow on, then the prospects for their living with the indigestible were actually quite good.

The Americans did forbear with what they regarded as a succession of irritating experiences. There were, for instance, accounts that Lange had been converted to the principle of deterrence, that he would work to change policy at the grassroots level, that a major statement would be made accepting the American 'neither confirm nor deny' principle. Although none of these stories were credible to Australia, they were grasped with some faint sense of hope by the Americans, much as we cautioned them on their implausibility. Then, as mentioned, there was the USA difficulty with Lange's sometimes elliptical manner of addressing an issue. Whatever the explanations, the rejection of the *Buchanan* visit request seemed to mark the end of American patience. ANZUS Council meetings of the three partners were suspended. Instead there would be bilateral American–Australian talks. In all it was not a harsh and damaging reaction and the American restraint in the circumstances reflected very much to its credit. This is said in view of the very large concerns the Americans had about potential consequences elsewhere of New Zealand's stance, in places of much greater strategic significance to them.

There was still a need to hold the ring, in a manner of speaking, between the United States and New Zealand. The New Zealand anti-nuclear legislation had yet to be introduced to its Parliament; when the time came, that would tear open slightly healed wounds for the Americans. I sought to register with our American allies that in spite of the differences of the moment there were fundamental commitments which New Zealand had carried out, and others it continued to carry out, which were of inestimable service to Western interests. For this reason I publicly developed several appropriate points to reinforce this view with the Americans. I stressed the superb fighting skills and the sheer courage of New Zealand troops who fought in the Italian campaign in World War II. I was convinced the New Zealand people could be counted on again should there ever be a real threat to freedoms in the West. I said the New

Zealanders were more experienced and influential in functioning in the South-West Pacific than we were and this was important to Western interests. I also mentioned the Soviets were 'fishing' about in the region and that the Libyans were unhelpfully active there too. I genuinely believed and still do believe in the first point. For the rest there was a degree of licence—to be blunt, of political opportunism—adopted in an effort to keep pressure off the New Zealanders. However, it was also my view that it was as much in the interests of the United States for that pressure to be kept off the smaller country, for reasons already gone over. I quickly regretted that excursion into opportunism. Apart from being inherently discreditable, such sallies have a bad habit of returning erratically when least expected and, like a boomerang out of control, clipping their launcher. Which is exactly what happened to me.

If it had been true that New Zealand had been more effective in operating among the small island States of the South-West Pacific than had Australia, it had ceased to be so once the ANZUS imbroglio began to heat up. Deeply religious, influenced by the missionaries, now guided very much by the Christian Church, the people of the island States mostly shunned radical ideologies like communism. They were accordingly quite apprehensive at the sudden turn of events between America and New Zealand. America was seen as a powerful and benign protector of the values which appealed to them; obversely, New Zealand lost some standing with them. Nonetheless there was a chuckle from the direction of New Zealand as Lange engaged in a little tail-twisting, suggesting that Australia was a slow learner wallowing in the slipstream of New Zealand in the region. Meanwhile, I could do little but seethe quietly. Sure, the Soviets were cruising about the South-West Pacific, but their conduct was very proper; they were eschewing political engagements and were only interested in sound commercial fishing ventures. My comment about them achieved a momentum of its own, as most Cold War comments tended to.

Shortly thereafter I heard Lange chortling across the Tasman that some people were inclined to over-react, revisiting the Cold War on the region. With good humour I reciprocated, alluding to the jerky policy movements of New Zealand on this matter, and observed that 'At times New Zealand is like the cross-eyed javelin thrower who doesn't win any medals but keeps the crowd on its toes'. Lange wrote to me deeply miffed at my comment—rather strange that his well-honed sense of humour should have deserted him so easily! An unexpected plus was that the Americans took the comments on board and lifted their presence in the region, with fairly regular and welcomed naval visits to the island States and Seabee working parties helping out on island projects. Instruction on the Libyan presence was generously saved for a later private discussion between Lange and me at the Royal New Zealand Air Force Base, Ohakea, on 1 May 1987. Lange, all smiling aplomb, pointed out that his government preferred to deal with the Libyan issue in a more measured and mature way to that adopted by Australia. More seriously, he confessed his approach sought to avoid provoking antagonisms among some radical Maoris who had contact with and received political education from the Libyans.

The story of my arrival in New Zealand for this meeting is entertaining enough in itself. I had presumed that Cabinet would make a decision to close down the Libyan People's Bureau at Canberra, for Hawke was single-mindedly opposed to its presence. My Department felt strongly that I should promptly, thereafter, fly to New Zealand to discuss the decision with Lange. I was opposed to the closure of the Bureau for several intelligence and security reasons advantageous to our interests. Subsequently, with some helpful support for my view in a Cabinet presentation from an influential agency, the Bureau was not closed. (It was closed a little later but that was a result of separate events.) The prevailing wisdom was, nevertheless, that the visit should still go ahead. There was also a strong feeling within the Department of Foreign Affairs that contact with Lange as Foreign Minister of his country and me as the Australian Foreign Minister was desirable for, by then, the prime minister to prime minister relationship across the Tasman had become badly unravelled. Hawke made little attempt to conceal his dislike of Lange.

I worked out a simple and diabolical plan for the trip. I would leave Canberra in the coal-pit darkness of long before dawn and get to the New Zealand Air Base where Lange and I would have our talks. Then, with less apparent presence than a shadow I would flit back across the Tasman, take my place at question time in the Parliament to hopefully bat back to the boundary a few fiercely bowled bouncers from the Opposition, and a good day's work would thus be done. It was an exquisitely clever plan. Alas there was one flaw, one wild joker in the pack for which I had made no allowance: the New Zealand love of a good practical joke. Or at least one New Zealander's love of such. I lay back in the cushy seat of the Royal Australian Air Force 34 Squadron BAC I-II as it prepared for another of the faultless landings for which the squadron is renowned. We banked gently to port coming on to final approach for a smooth and graceful landing. As the idiom has it, I was feeling pretty full of myself. I really had put one over on the media, and when you can do that, you are clearly having a nice day. Suddenly, my self-indulgent reverie was shattered by the anxious voice of a top officer, then of the Department of Foreign Affairs, David Sadlier: 'Hey, look at all of those people down there . . . Hey wait a minute . . . They're television crews down there!'.

On the ground David Lange was kind enough to explain that the media had got wind of the visit from a Canberra leak. I was mildly surprised—so few knew of it in Canberra that this was unlikely. At the end of our conference I got Lange to agree on a form of words we would both use about the visit now the media had cottoned on to what had happened. I scarcely need add that, contrary to earlier expectations, this had become a perfectly rotten day. He agreed that the words would not be released before my estimated arrival time in Canberra. As our aircraft started to wing its way aloft, a most uncharitable thought crossed my mind. I urgently unbuckled the seat belt in spite of cabin crew protests and switched on the cabin commercial radio which we had tuned in to the wave length of the New Zealand Broadcasting Corporation when we were landing earlier. It was there, being broadcast, loud and clear. My visit, and what sounded very much like the form of words upon which Lange and I had agreed, was a lead news item. I really was quite angry with those Canberra people. They had leaked to my discomfort once again and it was obvious they were getting very good at it. By then, quite evidently, they could anticipate the contents of a leak before they had heard or seen any of the relevant material! To finish off the whole sorry episode, I arrived at the foot of the front steps of the old Parliament House, Canberra—to be met of course by the serried ranks of the Canberra press corp. There they were before me, arrayed like solid phalanxes of fearsome Janissaries, all formidably armed with standard combat issue tape recorders and notebooks. And did they look angry! I had got away by myself, which as far as the gallery is concerned is unforgivable of any senior minister. For just as public servants feel uncomfortable if a minister is so foolish as to be determined to think for himself, the Canberra gallery feels the same way about ministers who do things by themselves. To sum up, it was not a nice day, it was a lousy question time, and by the end of it all I wished I had not been born so clever.

In fairness, Lange was a genial host. He saw me onto my aircraft for my departure, chatted amiably with me in the cabin, then, as he was about to take his leave looked around the cabin of the aircraft obviously taking in its comfort, its fittings, its impressive tone. His brow creased giving an impression of deep thought, an otherwise very serious look for his impish countenance. Some dreadful shaft was about to be unleashed. Then he said, solicitously, 'Not bad . . .

not bad at all,' his head nodding approval, like a metronome rocking in time with the cadences of his speech. In an instant, the seriousness was replaced by that characteristic wide, beaming, puckish presence as he chortled, 'Not bad at all . . . but not as good as our 727!'. He then trundled off with the self-satisfied, delighted rolling step of the youngster who has scoffed the last of the cream cakes, just ahead of the boy in the next row of desks.

There was another major effort initiated by New Zealand in the latter part of 1985 to negotiate some sort of mutually acceptable compromise with the United States. As with the earlier efforts, it struggled along like a rather overworked tramp steamer with a faulty engine trying to make way in foul weather. In late September 1985 David Lange delivered a tough, uncompromising speech to the Canterbury Regional Labour Council, unambiguously reaffirming the 'no nuclear' policy of the Labour Party. The USA and New Zealand were in the midst of New Zealand-instigated negotiations on the 'no nuclear' policy and here was Lange effectively declaring that the issue was not negotiable. This was more than the Americans could take. It was not a shot across the bows for them, but a bracket of high explosives fired right into the boiler room. The exercise was quickly scuttled as another futile gesture as far as they were concerned. Their sense of despair had been added to by the presentation of legislation to enforce the 'no nuclear' policy of the New Zealand Government. The consequence was quick in arriving; New Zealand had the final anathema pronounced against it—it was a friend, but no longer an ally. In the end, the outcome was as successful as could have been expected. Australia held its own interests together quite well. There was no attempt to abrogate the ANZUS Treaty; the separate Australian bilateral relationships with New Zealand and with the United States of America were in good shape; the effects of the break-down between New Zealand and America were minimised; no commercial penalties were inflicted on New Zealand; and there was no knock-on effect reaching other countries from the 'no nuclear' policy.

It was fashionable too, in some quarters, to portray the USA as a bullying ogre intent on imposing its will on brave, innocent little New Zealand. This was just not true and an unfair assessment, as I observed events. Of course, when a long-standing and previously well-functioning arrangement like ANZUS is proposed to be ruptured by one of the other parties, it would not be surprising if the other parties to the arrangement made their concerns plainly known. That certainly happened. My impression was and is, however, that at a certain point the Americans decided there had been no knock-on effect from the New Zealand policy and, as New Zealand was so unimportant strategically, the matter was not worth pursuing any further. If there had been a knock-on effect the American response might have been different, for then there would have been much more at stake.

The extent of apprehension around the world at the New Zealand action was extraordinary. Representations and expressions of concern were made by a large number of countries. The feelings ranged from uneasiness to general alarm at an action by New Zealand which was seen as having the potential to unravel the Western linkages strategically hedging in the communist powers. There is no doubt in my mind that if such an unravelling had occurred, these countries too would have reacted in some way or other. There was even concern raised in 'non-aligned' Indonesia, which fired its own shot against the New Zealand policy in the *Jakarta Post* of 7 February 1985 (a newspaper with a remarkable capacity to anticipate official government attitudes):

> But it is debatable whether Mr Lange's point is valid and worth making at the cost of his nation's alliance with the United States . . .

David Lange, however, should have the last word on this point. The British sent their Chief of Defence Forces, Admiral John Fieldhouse of the Royal Navy, to try to talk some sense into the New Zealand Prime Minister—or that was how the Admiral put it when I met him in a Sydney domestic airport lounge. He was on his way back from New Zealand and heading for home. Like the Americans, he too was a little flustered that he had not been able to pin down the mercurial New Zealand Prime Minister. The old seadog then gave me a stirring account of how he had attempted to straighten out the irrepressible Lange. With a delightfully plummy accent he recounted: 'I pulled myself up to my full height and I looked the Prime Minister straight in the eye. I said to him; "Prime Minister, do you realise by your conduct you are giving comfort to the Queen's enemies?" '. I remember thinking to myself, 'Strike a light, that was courageous, I hope you don't do anything like that while you are in Australia'. This encounter took place not long after a passenger liner of the USSR, in the hands of a New Zealand pilot, struck a rock and sank in Princess Charlotte Sound. I saw Lange shortly after my conversation with Fieldhouse and recalled it to him. He was in joyful, exuberant mood. 'Did he tell you what my response was to him?' he inquired. Without waiting for my reply he merrily continued, 'I drew myself up to my full height, but I couldn't stand too close to him of course,' he said confidentially and with a gentle, affectionate pat of his impressive girth. 'I looked him full in the eye and I said, "Admiral, do you realise that New Zealand is the only Western ally since World War II to sink a Soviet ship!".'

Lange and I worked together a good deal and I got to like him greatly as a person; but his was always a hard act to follow. More than that, it was an act that was impossible to keep up with. How important was this huge effort by Australia, the USA and New Zealand to try to salvage something from the ANZUS imbroglio? Indeed, how important was and is ANZUS? The answer is best summed up, perhaps, in Shultz's memoirs as USA Secretary of State, *Turmoil and Triumph*. There is no reference to ANZUS in the index and only one to Australia. In his single comment on this country, he refers very briefly to dealings he had with Hawke as a trade union leader and who, only incidentally it seems from his account, became prime minister.

The Hawke years, the Keating ascendancy

Managing foreign policy during from early in 1983 to mid-1988 was my task and I thoroughly enjoyed it. It was, however, only one part of a larger whole—the conduct of the business of national government—in which I also had some part to play. In length of service Bob Hawke was Australia's most successful prime minister, after the late Sir Robert Menzies. What makes the Hawke achievement more remarkable is that his successes came in straight-out election contests against united opposition parties. Menzies luxuriated in a succession of easy contests with a psychotic, self-mutilating Labor Party. Hawke's powerful appeal to the public was undeniable, just as it is indefinable. I wrote to Her Majesty, Queen Elizabeth II, Queen of Australia, on this very point in one of my periodic dispatches to her, in October 1989. I had seen a television news segment the night before covering one of Hawke's celebrated acts, in which he was 'tripping over television camera cables in shopping centres', as Keating once put it. There were hundreds of people closed in around him, most of them mothers and many with small babies. Some of the infants were held aloft by strong, proud, maternal arms to glimpse the great man—although, at the risk of being indicted for heresy for harbouring such doubts, the historic importance of the occasion seemed not to register with the poor infants. I puckishly reported to the Queen that the look on the mothers' faces seemed to be saying, 'Look son, at the great man—and watch his feet. They don't even touch the ground when he is walking'.

Hawke's evident charm aside, there were warning signals that all was not as secure as it should have been. Eighteen months after the triumph of the 1983 election when Labor's popularity should have been at its highest, the government lost important ground to the Opposition at the 1984 election. I was moved to comment in public, with all the solemnity of Robin Goodfellow, that 'the drover's dog had won again, but he was looking a bit clapped out this time'. I was in Melbourne, just after the comment became public. The telephone in my office rang. The handset appeared to be almost whirling and howling in a furious dervish's dance, thundering its summons to me. My premonition proved correct; on the other end of the line was a wrathful prime minister, who began barking, 'How dare you . . . '. I soon gathered I might be guilty of *lèse-majesté*, a dangerous offence. 'All good fun between friends, Bob. Besides, it's true.'

We were saved from defeat at the 1987 election by the inexcusably selfish thrust of Sir Joh Bjelke-Petersen's 'Joh for Canberra' campaign. This weakened the coalition's unity and sheared votes away and beyond the reach of John Howard to retrieve; that loss at least was not his fault. In 1990 Labor lost the national election on aggregate votes; it only gained a minority of the two party preferred vote but gathered a majority of seats because of a clever strategy of concentrating on marginal seats. Less clever was advising voters, in particular traditional Labor voters, that they could cast their primary vote for environmental candidates rather than Labor and then wooing preferences back to Labor. This most certainly inflated the vote of environmental candidates, but also sanctioned Labor voters casting votes for non-Labor candidates. Once done, easier repeated and life-long voting behaviour is thus liable to be broken down at a time when these are weakening generationally anyway, and rather quickly. There was a better way of handling the environmental issue than open surrender to the environmental lobby; for once they discovered how easy it was to collect, they never stopped doing so until the timber workers, quite properly, called enough in early 1995 and forced the government to consider other views. The environmental lobby has its own agenda which is not necessarily in the best interests of the country overall; in 1990 the government submissively met what seemed to be a maximalist claim, which is no basis for making national policy.

Prime Minister Hawke was exceptionally able as chairman of Cabinet and as an administrator. He was always well briefed by his department on items before Cabinet and his grasp of those briefings indicated he had digested their contents well. More than that, having absorbed his brief he stuck with it. His self-discipline and focus was so complete that he was rarely diverted and then only, but not always, by a most powerful argument. He conducted well-ordered meetings and was patient, I often thought too generously so, in allowing differences to be aired. No-one, at least in my experience, could ever fairly accuse him of not allowing dissenting views to be heard fully. He established and maintained a good sense of morale and discipline among the Cabinet members, although he did prefer to settle for consensus when there was contention, often accepting the price of a more modest outcome for the sake of comity in the Cabinet.

I found Hawke always accessible as Prime Minister, although I rarely sought to use this entrée. I proceeded on the basis that if I restricted entry requests to the barest minimum, based on a clear and pressing need to see him, then the restraint would be acknowledged and entry provided when sought. Thus it worked. Indeed, he probably sought my presence on more occasions than I requested appointments with him. These requests of his were usually related to issues likely to arise on one of his or my impending visits overseas; or sometimes were associated with internal matters. There were not many important differences on matters of principle between us. On several occasions I 'batted' hard for him to gain support for a position on an issue: for instance, in 1984 from the Centre Left faction on uranium policy at National Conference. Later, I defended him and worked hard to gather wide Caucus support for his public statement that the Hawke Government acknowledged *de jure* incorporation of East Timor within Indonesia. This had never been previously acknowledged publicly by the Labor Government and it was thus explosive stuff, capable of splitting the Caucus apart. Should that position have been repudiated, it might well have destroyed the bilateral relationship. The Fraser Government had acknowledged *de jure* recognition, and to deny that government's undertaking would have meant a major reverse, not just for the Labor Party, but for Australia. Hawke benefited incomparably from a key part of Labor culture: when the hard battles come up, members will rally, fighting the issues on behalf of the Party and to protect the leader. Labor, with its sometimes combative factions, is like a large tribe prone to clan conflict but which quickly unites about the leader to repel outside threats.

There is another example of my doing Hawke a big favour. In 1986 the Zionist Federation of Australia, led by Mark Leibler, proposed to my personal staff that Australia should take the lead in opposing the General Assembly resolution which equated Zionism with racism. I was initially unenthusiastic, though I had condemned this General Assembly resolution repeatedly as an obstruction to the implementation of desirable UNESCO policies. The practice had been that, on issues entirely unrelated to this General Assembly resolution, certain black African and Arab countries would collaborate to add its wording to UNESCO policy resolutions, immediately provoking a majority of countries, including most of the West, to vote the UNESCO resolutions down. My principle private secretary, Michael Costello, persuaded me I was scarcely being consistent with my past attitudes, and accordingly, I saw Hawke and proposed I should act on this matter. He was, understandably, a little uncertain of the political wisdom of such a move from Australia, fearing it could have international repercussions and cause internal party dissension. I quickly persuaded him the risk was all mine and went to work on the factions, in particular the Left where I called in some old IOUs and issued a few on myself for future redemption. The Left were hesitant but nowhere as difficult as Hawke and I had anticipated. To Hawke's surprise and delight I delivered party endorsement for the initiative, which was followed by keen support from the Opposition. Hawke suggested a formal resolution from the Parliament endorsing opposition to the Zionism is racism resolution. Because of the importance of the resolution he explained he would move it in the Parliament. I replied that I was happy to speak after him. He suggested it was better to restrict the speakers to one from the Government and one from the Opposition, and so it proceeded.

For a busy prime minister Hawke was extraordinarily generous with his time. I would enter his office, resolved to be as brief as possible and to the point to allow him to get back to the endless demands a prime minister has to meet. On just about every such occasion he had other views. He would encourage a wide-ranging discussion on various matters, from political tactics in the electorate, to objectives he had set himself or wished me to pursue in other countries or at international forums, to often mere chummy gossip. These encounters would sometimes last half an hour or so. Hawke would usually open up diffidently, or uncertainly. At that early point he would tend to be somewhat edgy, as though my presence discomforted him for some reason. Then he would settle down to whatever the task was he wished to pursue. Attempts to soften me up on some matter or other, I would always cotton on to quite early. My preference was for a swift and direct presentation, as this tended to save time, especially on matters of principle. Still, this was Hawke's preferred method of operating.

These sessions usually took place just before the dinner break or late in the night, as rising time for the House approached. The best part being a generously poured Scotch, the rich brown liquid caressing clear ice cubes which gently clinked as I amiably swirled the contents before savouring the next delightful draught. What a splendidly civilised way to treat another human being one might have thought; a pre-dinner drink or a night cap for a guest! Hawke would draw deeply on a big, fat, exotic cigar, blowing practised smoke rings which wobbled to the ceiling, the room pleasantly suffused with the rich, pungent scent of the slowly burning, tightly rolled, aromatic tobacco leaves. There was, by then, an easy, mellow atmosphere of warm camaraderie during which I would meditate on when he would raise the crucial issue and what it might be. Most often this would emerge casually, especially if it was something contentious or sensitive. It was common for these talks to last forty-five to fifty minutes before my leaving his office. I would often depart with mixed feelings: sometimes with a sense of peace and contentment, of work well done, of the enjoyment of an important intimate association with a warm fellow human being—having again recognised just how hard Hawke worked for that idiomatic stamp of approval; 'good bloke, 'awkey'. On other occasions I would be puzzled that a busy prime minister would spend so much time approaching issues so obliquely when directness would work as well and save time. Certainly he had a great reservoir of something I was short of—patience.

Hawke's office desk made for an interesting contrast with that of Gorton, McMahon, Whitlam or Fraser. Their tables were always littered with bundles of paper: files, letters, cables, memos; the jumble seemed endless. Hawke's was nearly always clear. On the occasions when there was paper there, it was minimal and in precise order and place. Yet he was always meticulously briefed by his public servants, and he was always on top of the detail of his brief. This was true in Cabinet, in talks with visiting government representatives, or with any other group. His was an impressive performance. He obviously required little sleep at night to get through so much work as well as he did—but busy ministers of senior departments with extraordinarily heavy workloads often have to master the technique of getting by on little sleep. This was my experience too, managing on as little as four to five hours' sleep a night, for many nights in succession, whether in the Whitlam Government, as Leader of the Opposition, or in the Hawke Government. (In fact, only in the less stressful role of Governor-General did I settle back into a normal sleeping pattern, and then it took some years to get back to a steady five hours a night.)

Hawke had a knack for quickly picking up what might be described as a good policy idea. Certainly, he skilfully administered the policies developed in the lead-up to the 1983 election success. Yet when those ideas had been set in place, there was a problem. As his former speech writer has it in his informative biography of Hawke:

> . . . the last term of his Prime Ministership lacked the overarching sense
> of cohesion and relevance, of purpose and direction and dynamism,
> which animated his first period in government.[103]

In the general running of government he was fortunate in the resourcefulness and quality of the key people upon whom he could depend in Cabinet. His Treasurer, Paul Keating, was a powerhouse for lateral thinking and for churning out new ideas. Moreover, Keating had the intelligence to argue his case persuasively and the courage to fight unflinchingly for things in which he believed. Finance Minister, Peter Walsh, relished the task of chopping up rhetorical humbug and of scourging sloppy ministerial arguments from the Cabinet Room. He took no prisoners, gave no sanctuary, recognised no neutrality. I am one of his best friends as he is one of mine, but I knew better than to ask for mercy or favour in the pre-budget processes. After he had combed through the spending claims of my ministry, I more than once withdrew at the conclusion of the experience, painfully wounded in the soul, peeved and sulking at his inhumanity to an old friend. He had a clever, incisive mind. If instead of going on to the family farm early in his life, as so many farm lads seem to, Peter Walsh had studied science at university, as I am sure he could have done with easy success, then I think that he would have gravitated naturally to vivisection. He was the quintessential Minister for Finance. Ralph Willis as Minister for Employment and Industrial Relations—quiet, steady but diligent and intellectually resolute, and with a profound sense of social justice—was the person who forged the links which gave the various incomes accords to the Government and the Australian workforce.

In April 1986 I found myself in an extraordinary position. In late 1982 Senator George Georges belligerently interjected during a Caucus meeting which I was addressing, 'Why don't you resign for the good of the Party?'. It was a savage psychological blow which I managed to withstand, but only by mustering a lot of inner reserve. Now the National Executive of the Party was to consider the expulsion of Senator George Georges for flouting a Caucus decision regarding the deregistration of the Builders' Labourers Federation. I wrote a two page letter to the national secretary arguing that while there was a case for discipline, expulsion was too severe. In spite of the differences Georges and I often had over the years—although paradoxically I worked hard within my electorate organisation to get him over 60 per cent of the local party vote for his first preselection—I still respected him, even if often grudgingly. I saw him as, I said in my letter to the executive, 'genuinely representing and leading an authentic and legitimate stream of opinion in the Party'. More than that, like me he had come from a deprived background in South Brisbane and because of his Greek background had to battle hard to make his way in life, There was probably a shock factor for executive delegates on receiving a supporting letter from me in defence of Georges, our conflicts being so well known. The Executive Chairman, Wran, later told me the letter had considerable influence on the decision not to expel him. But Georges wanted martyrdom at the time; about a year later he had well and truly overstepped the mark and was out of the Party.

There has been criticism of the accords from certain unreconstructable ideological economists who, in their confusion, believe the theory of perfect competition can be a practical objective in the marketplace. They have never understood the political or social limits to many processes. The alternative to the accord would have been strong economic growth, cost-push inflation injected by militant wage demands and even worse external account imbalances. Undeniably, the flexibility of Australia's centralised wages system with the accord has stood up well in international comparisons and 'was on the scale of that in flexibility in the United States'.[104] Australian industry generally is now far more internationally competitive than at any time in the postwar period because of the comprehensive changes wrought in the Hawke–Keating period. Keating and Bill Kelty of the ACTU hammered out the heads of agreement, but Willis was the person who sweated over the fine points in the back room as it were, producing the practical detail behind the working agreements. The irony of the accords is that Keating was not a willing disciple initially. Once converted, he embraced the new faith with a passion and an intelligence which ensured its success.

There were other outstanding ministers in the Hawke Government: Kerin, who handled the primary industries portfolio, always a difficult act for Labor; Beazley Jnr, arguably the most effective peacetime minister for defence, to name another. It was an impressively talented Cabinet all round. The key people to the success of the Prime Minister and the Government were, however, Keating, Walsh and Willis, but pre-eminently Keating. Another personality of great significance for the many welfare reforms he implemented was Social Security Minister, Brian Howe. Welfare reform is at the very heart of Labor commitment. One analysis of social security recipients has found that between March 1983 and September 1991, the vast majority of those beneficiaries had sharp increases in their real incomes. For instance, the real disposable income of a full-rate pensioner couple rose by 14.1 per cent; the increase was 18.7 per cent if the pensioner couple was in receipt of rent assistance; and for a sole parent pensioner with two children renting privately the increase was 24.9 per cent. The report concluded that these substantial improvements in benefits had reduced poverty markedly.[105] Another researcher using a more realistic poverty line than that of Henderson has concluded that 'no sole parents receiving social security pensions should be in poverty in April 1994' and, in a turnaround on earlier experience, 'The aged now appear to have lower poverty rates than all other types of families'. This research makes it clear that there is still a substantial level of relative poverty 'despite very substantial increases in social security payments'.[106] It is this last observation which reinforces my suspicions about the serious deficiencies of relative poverty measures. If a more rigorously constructed and relevant definition of poverty is not soon arrived at, the declining public confidence in this process will disappear completely.

Less reassuring was the attempt to impose patient co-payments for medical services under Medicare in 1991. This, as much as anything, finally sealed Hawke's downfall, shearing off critical Caucus support which went to Keating. Hawke's support was a deadly miscalculation for this policy was, in effect, an ill-informed and regressive effort to raise more revenue. It was not designed to remedy any problem of medical over-servicing. Analytical work demonstrates convincingly that while a patient initiates first treatment contact with a doctor, return servicing is largely initiated by the doctor. In short, over-servicing is a function of the supply of doctors and their wish to meet income targets, largely set by themselves. In such circumstances, to impose a penalty on a patient is unfair and ineffective in controlling costs. Moreover, as 'co-payments have a disproportionate impact upon the use of services by the poor and possibly the sick', the potential outcome was an intolerable proposition for Labor culture.[107]

The Hawke Government administered the most radical and remarkable range of economic transformations Australia has ever seen, and in one relatively compressed period. These changes continues to dramatically reconstruct our country socially and culturally, as well as economically. Extraordinarily, they were brought about by a Labor Government, many of them through close collaboration with the ACTU—programmes and policies which, in their principles at least, represented outcomes traditionally anathema to both bodies. The Australian dollar was floated, currency exchange restrictions ended, restrictions on the numbers of foreign banks trading in Australia were greatly eased, dividend taxation imputation was introduced which favoured the rich, and an ambitious industry restructuring programme was embarked upon involving a relatively rapid dismantling of most industry protection. A programme for privatising public enterprises was drawn up, capital gains and fringe benefits taxes were implemented. The credit for these measures is usually allotted to the Hawke Government, though my clear impression was that every one of them was successfully carried through Cabinet by Keating. In fairness, Walsh disputes this view and he spent more time in the Cabinet than I. But Keating was certainly the dominant personality fighting for every important issue coming within his broad portfolio, and for many others as well. To secure support for his proposals, he was always the one doing the early legwork and lobbying of people—quite unnecessarily in my case as I was generally in favour of them.

The tax summit following the 1984 election, however, was exclusively a Hawke initiative. The idea was thrown up on the spur of the moment during a radio talkback programme. It ended up looking little more than a stunt aimed at taking the heat out of the taxation issue, one area where Hawke did not have a good command of the facts. Although Keating completely disliked this proposal, he nonetheless faithfully took it on board, producing an impressive range of proposals in his white paper. It was my clear impression, from the Cabinet meetings I attended where the issue was discussed, that Hawke supported the concepts embodied in the white paper, in particular the sales tax option. Evans and Kelty have made it clear publicly that it was unambiguously their impression too.[108] Yet, surprisingly, when the heat came on that specific proposition from business and the unions at the summit, Hawke effectively walked out on Keating to leave him high and dry on the issue. Keating fought to the end, and when he could fight no longer, because Hawke had publicly determined the outcome of the issue against him, he accepted the pain of this unpleasant let-down with commendable grace. He commented, good humouredly, that he had crossed the line like Ben Hur, but with one wheel off his chariot.

I always liked Keating. He had style and grace, to add to his obvious intellectual talents. In this sales tax matter he also demonstrated the qualities of a great, unremitting fighter for things in which he believed and to which he had committed himself. My disappointment was not that Hawke retreated from the sales tax proposal—I had then been opposed to the concept myself, after all, as indirect taxes are regressive and this proposal would have boosted inflation. Rather, I was annoyed at the way Hawke went about dumping Keating in a humiliating manner. But Hawke was not the only culpable party on that tax issue. The tax summit saw organised business do one of its usual backdowns when the pressure was on. Business retreated from the indirect tax proposal, but has been condemning the pusillanimity of governments for not introducing such a tax ever since. Major elements of organised business did exactly the same thing in 1977. Those which had called loud and long for the withdrawal of payroll tax, a disincentive for the employment of labour, were struck dumb the instant it was proposed in Labor's policy speech of that year and remained silent until the election was over.

Keating shattered the ideological rigidities of the Labor Party with a series of well-aimed, muscular blows, some of which I confess left me a little uncomfortable. To put the facts baldly but fairly, it was a case of Hawke Prime Minister, but Keating leader. Traditionally, the philosophy of Labor was based on notions of egalitarianism, collective participation, co-operative undertakings. Labor's initiatives of the 1980s however, implied the very opposite social values: competition, individualism, rewards for successful personal initiative, and the inevitable consequences arising from these things, in particular encouragement of merit-based élites. In embracing these, Labor set a political course very much against the older one based on class. The 'them' and 'us' dichotomy, the notion of the 'class enemy', of the 'exploiting capitalist', which was the political diet of my youth, was being challenged or made irrelevant in the Hawke years through Keating's initiatives. Labor commenced transforming itself. The process had some of its origins in the Whitlam period, and the egregious mistakes of that era were instructive for Labor later. After 1977 the appeal to the electorate from Opposition on macro-economic management was measured, and consciously conservative in many ways, but at the micro-level we clung to traditional notions of Labor redistribution.

Once Labor was elected to government in 1983, a huge, radical movement gathered momentum under Keating's direction. Kelty's contribution to this process from the ACTU should not be underestimated. The way in which the trade union movement, under his leadership, participated consistently in key areas of government in the elaboration and management of wages policy, in the redistributive effects of the social wage, in supporting micro-industry reform, and more recently, promoting award contracts arrived at through enterprise bargaining, is unparalleled in its extent, duration and success. Frankly, if Hawke in leading the ACTU had been disposed to have been only moderately as helpful to the Whitlam Government as Kelty was to the Hawke–Keating Government, the economic benefits for Australian families in the Whitlam period would have been markedly greater. Hawke instead consciously pursued a wages break-out which proved crippling for the economy. Kelty, who undoubtedly had a better grasp of economics than any of his predecessors, worked with Keating to avoid that.

When, as Leader of the Opposition, I sought a prices/incomes accord with the trade union movement, I privately felt that on the basis of our experience with the ACTU under Hawke during the period of the Whitlam Government, once in Government we would be fortunate to hold it together for a single parliamentary term. The sustained success of the Keating–Willis–Kelty collaboration almost defies belief. Those accord arrangements have held together for well over a decade. Nevertheless, the accord is now looking over-mature. It limits the exercise of fiscal options in macro-economic management at a time when these tools should be more widely available for use by government, and forces greater reliance on monetary policy, which is blunt in its impact and regressive in its distributional effects, for economic corrections. The accord is primarily concerned about people in the workforce; to the extent its measures favour the employed, it creates limits on more extensive, progressive redistributional fiscal policies. The accord has probably exhausted most of its usefulness, yet something like it has to be in place if wage break-out is to be curbed and inflation thus contained at a time of strong economic recovery.

Two stout cornerstones were placed under the national economy shortly after Federation gave us nationhood: within two years industry protection was in place and two years after that the industrial arbitration system was established. There was enduring bilateral support for both from conservative and labour politics until the eighth decade after Federation. Suddenly the time for an old idea in the form of a new policy had come; firstly, there was a bipartisan repudiation of protection and the age of relatively free trade and competition was rapidly emerging. The undeniable fact was that Australia could no longer use the prosperity of our mining and farm export industries to subsidise uncompetitive secondary industries, through the protection mechanism. The workforce in the non-farming, non-mining sector had become too large for that to work satisfactorily any longer. Moreover, as a regressive redistributive mechanism, it was and is neither a practical nor a fair choice to cling to high levels of protection.[109] To a centralised form of industrial relations was then added the tool of enterprise bargaining. The considerable transformation which has occurred may not be as much as those who wanted an end to unions of course, but I remain a firm adherent to the view that without effective unions working people are highly vulnerable to exploitation, especially at a time of sustained high unemployment. The *quid pro quo* to that view is that unions should behave responsibly in their demands on employers and the economy.

In the mid-eighties photographs of Hawke being socially indulged by the newly rich 'monopoly money' multimillionaires, about to become billionaires, started bobbing up in newspapers. Some of us felt uneasy about this; it was the wrong image for Labor, especially as we were lecturing the public about the need for belt-tightening. There was also something 'fishy' about the huge accumulations of wealth being made so quickly by a number of such flashy, shallow individuals. A few of us suspected massive tax avoidance and perhaps evasion, for these were booming industries; little did we know we were right, or that this was only a small part of the smart tricks of these clever men. The same people are still with us today, though reduced to living the life which the relative austerity of a few million provides, rather than that to which they had become accustomed. Nor has bankruptcy seemed to have overly cramped their style. Some of us expressed concern in Cabinet about one memorable newspaper photograph of Hawke in formal dinner suit being 'duchessed' by his rich host on the deck of his host's luxury sea cruiser. Hawke impatiently dismissed the concern.

As the eighties closed and the nineties got under way both parties converged on the need for labour market reform. Keating, by this time Prime Minister, inspired by great challenges and ready for conflict in defence of his goals, was a contrary character to his predecessor. Hawke's style was generally to look for consensus where there was contention, to attempt to massage a resolution where there were strongly held differences. There can sometimes be virtue in this style. This is not an approach which Keating finds congenial, though, being less concerned with wooing popularity and more interested in maximising positive results. Ironically, when I appointed Keating shadow Treasurer in early 1983 he vigorously resisted the assignment, introducing me to some rather colourful assessments of what he thought I was trying to do to him and the questionable nature of my ancestry. He was half-right. As with everything Keating has done in his life, once buckled into the task he mastered it with extraordinary talent. Keating is easily the most seminally important peacetime leader this country has had, introducing in just ten years a radically different and comprehensive economic and political agenda for this country. To purloin Paul Kelly's apt figure, Keating has brought about 'The End of Certainty'.[110] That is to the good, for it was that very same certainty of the past which, were it still in place, would have guaranteed ultimate failure. The Labor Party is now more relevant to the needs of Australia and its future; and as we are probably at one of the most critical periods in the history of the country, this has been a crucial development. The Party has junked its past preferences for stifling controls and regulations, for the impedimenta which moved in lock-step with interventionist commissions and a strong inclination for detailed predictive planning. We should be able to escape the dreaded Argentine road because of the course we are now on. Keating and Kelty have largely weaned the trade union movement from industrial disputation as the first resort and most regularly used tactic in industrial relations. Business, too, has been deeply engaged in these processes, although some of its spokespeople prefer to pretend otherwise. The Australian experience is of a mild form of corporatism, one which has released a huge impulse for competition, for greater efficiency, to achieve cost advantage for this country in the global marketplace.

Nonetheless there are some dangerous temptations implicit within the corporate State, specifically a tendency for the relationship between the various parties to become overly comfortable. With closer involvement and better understanding also comes the potential for cosy deals and other arrangements that may allow economic flab to build up and efficiency to run down. The best way to guard against such a tendency is to maximise the public openness of government dealings with business, unions and other interest groups. A further measure is for government to limit its interventions, and where there are dealings between business or labour to require that these also are open. There is another supervening issue: the deeply etched, long-standing and fundamental commitment in the heart of our national culture to caring about our social casualties. We need to be vigilant to ensure this fine ethical commitment is not eroded through selfish materialistic preoccupations in what must become a more individualistic society.

To return to Keating: a notable failure of his was the recession of the early nineties. The monetary instruments were applied too severely, kept in place for too long, and excessively contracted the economy. It has to be said that it was a failure shared by just about every other economic forecasting outfit and economic commentator in the country. In a recession shared by all of the OECD countries, Australia, as a major exporter in relation to the size of its economy, could not sustain faster economic growth than the rest of the developed world without imports growing faster than exports. By improving productivity and competitiveness, radically altering the composition of our exports and tapping into the rapidly growing Asian economies, it may be possible for Australia to sustain growth faster than the OECD average. Keating took hard decisions and we are all now drawing on the benefits which flowed. Yet the flaw of his management has been that growth and prosperity have inextricably been bound to widening trade and current account deficits. To the extent this is caused by growth in consumption rather than investment in productive, value-added enterprise (and to a substantial extent it is), it seriously erodes the economy. I come back to this a little later, but it is a far more serious problem than can be cured merely by more flexibility in labour markets, of which we hear a great deal.

Enhanced productivity requires a hefty boost to investment. First, however, national savings have to improve significantly. One source of greater savings would be an improvement in the national account's profit ratio at the expense of wages and salaries, something which has occurred. The turnaround between wages and salaries on the one hand and profits on the other rectifies what had become a serious imbalance; it is unarguable that the redress of the balance between these factors was overdue.[111] Investment however remained very low, a major reason being that business had been using an improved financial flow to pay off injudiciously accumulated debt. As we now know, much of this was entered into blithely in the 'free and easy' eighties. That such excessive blunders occurred, and in so many large and conservative corporations, challenges the reputations of their directors and executive officers for prudence, wisdom and business savvy. The market, in all its glory, behaves in strange ways. Instead of penalties a great number of those people received handsome salary increases as inducements to try harder! In the period 1984 to 1992 total remuneration received by senior managers increased by 48.7 per cent while real average earnings declined by 1.9 per cent.[112] It would be desirable to publicly expose business to a greater degree of critical review; to require it in future to provide as much detailed justification of its general management as is common for the public sector. For what the eighties demonstrated is that if business blunders in a major way, the rest of the community become a victim of its failures. And nor is it good enough for business to attempt to limit its responsibility by simply repeating the sanctimonious claptrap of being accountable to shareholders and them alone. We have all seen reports of small shareholders being mowed down, as it were, by the juggernaut strength of institutional and large corporate shareholders who dominate voting at many annual meetings.

Another important method for increasing savings, so that private investment can grow, is for governments to eliminate budget deficits during upswings of the economic cycle. Based on grounds of improved efficiency, there is a strong case for government to sell many public enterprises. For those who still vaguely hanker to enter the paradise of a Democratic Socialist State through public enterprises, there are the salutary examples of Australian Airlines and Telecom to disabuse them. Far from taking Australia in that direction, these were merely examples of State capitalism. Telecom in particular was overbearing in its customer relations, reluctant to innovate, levied rather fierce user charges, and displayed little enlightenment in its workforce policies—not that the relevant technical union behaved with wisdom and restraint at key points over the years either. It was only when competition turned up that circumstances began to change for the better; if consumer rights really are to be sovereign, privatisation of such organisations does not deserve a tear from anyone from the Left. Public enterprises have been, generally, under-capitalised, inefficient as a result, and regularly plundered when governments needed cash to reduce the budget deficit. Labor governments were no better at resisting these temptations than non-Labor ones. The privatisation of such undertakings means at the very least there is no risk for taxpayers as the government does not have to meet the cost of losses. If there is a profit, then government cannot lose in that it collects its dividend in the form of taxes. There is one qualification. If the enterprise is a natural monopoly then it is better in the public sector, but with rigorous performance criteria imposed on it. I confess to being somewhat unsure what constitutes a natural monopoly these days, as many public enterprises I would once have described as such are now performing more satisfactorily for consumers as a result of outside competition. Nonetheless, merely to sell off enterprises to reduce the deficit is no real fix if there are structural defects in budgets.

The response to middle-class welfare has been mixed. For instance, assets of age pensioners were very properly means tested in the early eighties. In 1993, however, the Liberal Party was proposing child care benefits for beneficiaries with a combined family income of $50 000 per annum. At an income level a little less than twice Average Weekly Earnings, that was generous indeed! A person earning Average Weekly Earnings is among the top 35 per cent of income earners. This runs over the border of equity into regressive redistribution. Many were shocked when Labor offered a cash rebate 'positively related to income—the higher the income the higher the payment'.[113] There was no income ceiling on the entitlement to this benefit. John Hewson, then Liberal Opposition Leader, riposted: 'Labor wants to give taxpayers' money to millionaire families!'. He was right. Similarly, in 1993 Labor clung to a promise to cut taxes, when cutting the deficit should have been the priority if equity was not to prevail in the tax exercise. The restructuring of the tax scales over the term of the Labor governments shifted the tax burden from high to median and low income earners.[114]

To make any real impact on our present high levels of unemployment, government will have to induce sustained growth, over many years, of about 4.5 per cent to 5 per cent. An outcome of this order would cover expected slower workforce annual growth of about 2 per cent to the end of this decade, improved productivity of the order of 2 per cent, and allow annual growth in the employed workforce of about 0.5 to 1 per cent. On the other hand improved productivity is most likely higher than quoted above and, with increased workforce participation following economic improvement, will retard the rate of reduction in the unemployment level.[115] These ambitious growth targets will require unusually high levels of savings and investment, further micro-reform in industry and the labour market, and sustained low inflation, for which objective sustained wage restraint is essential. That is a fearsome set of ambitions to pursue and they all have to be achieved rather quickly. Furthermore, all these targets are set at levels well above the long-term experience of these things in Australia.[116] In fact our experience with economic growth over the past few years makes it clear growth in excess of 3 to 3.5 per cent is unsustainable and that means high unemployment levels are intractable. Keating's impressive record of achievements on so many other economic fronts is undermined by his failure to resolve the dilemma at the heart of this problem. The fact is, unless we reduce our consumption levels (i.e. lower our living standards) to allow these savings to occur (and this is done according to principles of equity of burden sharing), prosperity and growth will continue to spill into trade and current account deficits. In turn these will have to be restrained by contractionary domestic economic management. The consequence of that is that gains against extraordinary high levels of unemployment will be marginal and often temporary. Neither of the major political parties is prepared to publicly address this issue directly and in plain English for the simple reason they undoubtedly feel (rightly) that it is an unacceptable political truth. But unless it is candidly addressed, Australia's dependency on foreign lenders will worsen and its sovereign economic independence will be increasingly weakened. Employee contributions to compulsory superannuation and a realistic increase in the Medicare levy will also increase national savings.

The paradox for Australia is that our future could be one of comparatively strong economic growth, of impressive national prosperity, of comfortable affluence for those in the workforce, but all co-existent with a large, permanently unemployed, marginalised class. Unlike previous experiences, that marginalised class will include a relatively high proportion of well-qualified and experienced people who once would have been part of our middle class. Research by Professor Gregory of the Australian National University concludes there is a contracting middle class in Australia.

He reports one in three male middle earning jobs disappearing in the decade-and-a-half to 1990, with employees from the disappearing middle taking jobs from the unskilled.[117] These are some of the reasons why immigration should be geared to accepting only those immigrants whose job skills are really needed in Australia. Family reunion should be further wound back and better related to economic activity. Improved productivity is seen as important in hauling back our foreign debt. One economic analysis, however, states that to be effective in countervailing the pace of foreign debt accumulation none of that gain should be expended in extra consumption.[118] This, of course, re-emphasises the point of the unavoidable need for continuing downward pressure on wages and salaries. At the end of the day, my intuition is that unemployment will jam around 8 per cent as its natural level—a dreadful thought.

The end of it all

At some point in 1985, I believe it was, I advised Hawke I would be interested in being considered for appointment as the succeeding governor-general. As I mentioned earlier, my career as a politician had peaked once my leadership role came to an end. I believed it was time to get out and engage in an alternative role productively than risk sliding into irrelevance as too many do, in many occupations. Those who hang about too long as figures from the past irritate and obstruct a rising generation who have a mortgage on the future.

There was another reason for deciding to depart soon: my poor and deteriorating hearing. I discovered in middle-age that I suffer from irreversible nerve end deafness, probably a congenital condition, for which a hearing aid proves less than useful. I now realise a major disability for my schooling had been impaired hearing. The intense concentration of trying to hear clearly was too tiring; it was easier to slide off into a pleasant little daydream. This disability was a barrier between me and my teachers. That is probably why I later found correspondence study so congenial, though making sufficient time for it was always difficult. By the late eighties my performance in the parliament was being seriously restricted by this defect. At this stage, I realised I had unconsciously settled into a form of lip reading; of staring at people's mouths as they spoke, instead of making eye contact, which sometimes made them feel uneasy.

It did not occur to me at the time, but the position of Governor-General was a long way removed from the fiery principles of that old 'Wobbly', my father. I had a number of points I intended to make in support of my proposal. Before I could fully detail them Hawke warmly agreed to my assuming that position. It was a relaxed, good-humoured, almost casual discussion. The role of governor-general was an honourable one and generally accorded public respect. It was a role where I could serve a limited term, according to the practise in that office, and complete my long period in public life productively and with dignity; something my family would appreciate after all the years of separation and sacrifice that political life imposes, often harshly, on families. Because of the need for confidentiality, Hawke informed only a couple of very senior ministers of this arrangement. Confidentiality remained intact until certain events occurred in 1988. The prospective appointment was then leaked to Alan Ramsey of the *Sydney Morning Herald*.[119] It occurred in the context of a dispute within Centre Left as to whom the faction should support for election to the vacant office of National Secretary of the Party; a member of the faction, whom I preferred, or an outsider.

The Centre Left faction was formed after the 'hard numbers men', Robert Ray and Graham Richardson, of the Right from Victoria and New South Wales respectively arrived in the Caucus. We moderates occupying the middle ground could smell the threatening scent of these predators on the political breezes. Unprotected, we knew they would have us by the scruff of the neck in no time, shaking and jolting the political life out of us. So Centre Left was formed as an act of self-preservation for a gaggle of mild Fabian reformers. As Barry Jones once patiently explained to us at a meeting when we were anxiously exploring an identity crisis: 'We are a political lonely hearts club. What draws us together is that no-one else loves us'. A few seconds for the message to sink in, a few more of grave head-nodding agreement, and with that high crisis resolved we moved on to other, lesser business. In fact Centre Left was a powerhouse of ideas, of policy development and elaboration and most importantly it was consistently guided by principles of equity and progressive redistribution. In no time the irreconcilable postures adopted by the Right and the Left were bridged as they conspired at ways of depleting the ministerial numbers from our faction. Their justification was simple: they had more numbers than us therefore they were entitled to more ministers. 'You don't believe it's fair?', we were queried, 'then let's put it to a democratic vote to find out'. In that lay a lesson in genuine political realism, of a particularly breathtaking variety.

I attended my last national conference of the Labor Party in June 1988, at Hobart. I had just returned from Norway. As we winged in over the Derwent River estuary I marvelled for the umpteenth time at the sheer natural beauty of the countryside. Overhead a morose, grey sky, below us grey-green waters and lush, emerald green, rolling countryside made gloomy by the heavy cloud cover. Sunbeam shafts pierced through scattered openings in the storm-grey canopy, focussing irregularly on segments of the countryside, illuminating them with a sharply contrasting iridescence. It was as if God had decided to spotlight specific features in the countryside, to demonstrate the transcendental beauty of nature over the clumsy, artificial contrivances of us flawed mortals. Here was the typical, strong, brooding colouring of a half-grey Tasmanian winter's day. A moody, irresistible call to set one thinking, deeply and sombrely, about the shadows of life that lurk in one's unconscious, of things that could have been, or which have yet to be, good or bad.

As an urchin growing up in South Brisbane, I realised that we were different because of our father's personal problem, and in the many years since I have learnt to keep a straight face when confronted or provoked. In my case, the device has served as an effective mechanism for blocking the display of a wide range of emotions, including surprise and mirth at the bizarre and the ludicrous. When I arrived at the Wrest Point Hotel, where the conference was being held, I was summoned to Hawke's room. Through the door which was ajar, I heard the gravelly, good-humoured voice of the Prime Minister call out, 'Come in, Bill; be out in a minute'. I let myself into his suite, then sat down. There was cheerful chortling—or was it singing?—from the direction of the bedroom. Then suddenly Hawke walked out. I had heard about this memorable act before, but had never been exposed to it. Hawke was stark naked, bollickers. He was briskly rubbing his back with a towel held by one hand high above his shoulders and the other somewhere near his waist. He had evidently just showered. He looked reasonably fit, springing into the room with all of the bounce and confidence of a boxer from one of the lighter weight divisions. I suspected he harboured visions of himself as a Greek god, I saw only an extroverted quinquagenarian flasher. While his important appendage was dingling and dangling as he moved, I kept a straight face, trying to ignore the entertaining idiocy of the act, and talked about my recent trip; he meanwhile settled back, indolently, on a long sofa to listen. As I talked, I couldn't help thinking how far from impressive were the dimensions of the apparatus which he displayed with such evident pride and satisfaction—and him supposed to be such a lady-killer . . .

A revealing insight subsequently lit up my understanding of Hawke. Blanche d'Alpuget in her biography of Hawke relates how his mother had wanted a daughter when Hawke was born, that,

'Her craving for a daughter was immoderate'. D'Alpuget has Hawke recalling with some evident pain, 'My mother wanted me to be a girl. She used to say, "You were meant to be Elizabeth" '.[120] The boisterous, saloon bar camaraderie; the boon companion of the blokes; the accumulated lost weekends; the compulsive ladies' man with magnetic appeal for so many females; the virile cricketer and enthusiastic spectator of body contact sports played by others; the long practised combative style of rhetoric—all of these machismo images, so carefully cultivated, were adopted for one reason. As was this periodic flashing, in which I had been initiated now at Hobart. His progress through life had been dogged by the curse of Elizabeth, the girl who never was. To keep her at bay, it seemed he had to be, or at least act, excessively macho.

On 17 August 1988 I went into the Cabinet Room of the new Parliament House for the first and last time. It was a strange feeling. I was about to tear myself apart from a lifetime of gregarious contact and conflict with parliamentary and party colleagues, of wide involvement with people at an intimate and informal level. I was heading off to solitariness and formality, of impartiality and of distance from that active political life, things which had been the key constituents of my past. As Hawke began to speak, I turned to collecting my thoughts, expecting that I could leisurely put together a number of points while he and others spoke. I had not prepared beforehand because there had been such a torrent of distractions arising from the process of closing down my office and moving out of the department, and from a dozen other sources at least. Suddenly Hawke surprised me by speaking only briefly, then announcing, 'Well, we'll hear from you now, Bill'. I was jarred back to the present and the task before me. I made what I hope were some appropriate comments. At the end of these I recall thinking, 'Now for a cuppa with my old mates, chew the fat a little, and off on my solo voyage across Lake Burley Griffin'. As I was speaking Keating looked unusually introspective; Barry Jones meanwhile kept casting his gaze back and forth along the direction of the table. Both later remarked that they had wanted to speak but were cut off when Hawke stood up to move proceedings along. When I finished Hawke stood up, moved to the door, and said: 'Well that's it, Bill. We've got to get on to the Cabinet meeting'. Then it sunk in. I was no longer an insider, but on the outer. It also struck me how difficult it had been to get into that Cabinet Room and stay there, and what a privileged access it had been. I would never be able to get that door open again. A few such as Walsh, Beazley Jnr and Kerin stood and clapped, others looked confused, and that was that.

Keating came around and saw me later in my office. My departure had left him rummaging about in his thoughts, dwelling on the purpose of so much of our struggle in a frail and finite life. It was a moving insight into his personal philosophy—or more correctly, his teleological view—of life. It was not the first time he had shared this sort of thing with me but it was the most passionate exposition of his high sense of public duty and the competition that presented to his commitment to his family. It was one of those rich moments when the shared confidences that come from a deep, personal friendship add savour to the meaning of life. Several other colleagues dropped in over the next couple of days as I cleaned out my office. Equally rewardingly, several members from the Liberal Party and a few from the Country Party also called in to wish me well, including some of those best bowlers I talked about much earlier. And thus it all ended, those long years in Parliament, in the way so many things of personal importance end in the life allotted us—with a bit of a whimper.

I was privy to the tendering of another man's resignation, which had strange echoes of my own, a few years later. On the night of 18 December 1991 there was a happy, noisy celebration under way at Government House—the traditional staff Christmas party. A band was playing vigorously, the residence suffused pleasantly in the choruses of gaiety as delighted friends and workmates and their families met up for this eagerly anticipated annual event. The problem with real life is that, unlike art, it has no sense of the proper mood for the dominant historical event of the moment. I had received a message from the office of the prime minister. Bob Hawke was coming out to Yarralumla to formally present his resignation as PM to me as Governor-General. As he had just been defeated by Keating, this would be a sombre occasion. The celebratory atmosphere could not be avoided, however, for the building is too small. I felt distinctly uncomfortable as I greeted Hawke at the private entrance to the house. I wondered how he would comport himself under the enormous emotional strain he would be experiencing, in particular with this jarring background of evident celebration all around; his propensity to cry publicly at times of emotional stress was well known. Would he be able to contain his feelings tonight? Yes, he would, it proved.

In our discussion I recalled a proposition I had put to him after the 1990 election. I had then recently had a long talk with a senior diplomat from a country influential in the affairs of the UN, who was then passing through Canberra. I had become friendly with this man during my period as Foreign Minister. The office of Secretary-General was to become vacant in the then near future, and so I explored the prospects for an Australian successor to this office. He encouraged me to believe there could be support for an Australian nominee. The major powers, he went on to suggest, wanted to strengthen the role of the Secretary-General in the light of their then current experiences with the developing Gulf War and the general intoxication with the New International Order. Later again, in talking to Hawke at Yarralumla, I told him that in my reading of economic trends the economy would be severely recessed by the time of the next election and I doubted that Labor could win, regardless of who was leading the Party. I urged him to consider discreetly testing the prospects for himself going forward as an Australian nominee to this position within the UN.

My position was simple and non-party political: it would be an enormous honour for an Australian to be Secretary-General of the UN, and indisputably, Hawke could have fulfilled the task better than any other public figure I could then think of in this country. His personal qualities and skills in fact would have made him an even better incumbent of that office than he was a prime minister, and he was a most successful Australian prime minister. I had, much earlier as Foreign Minister, suggested to Hawke that we should urge Malcolm Fraser to nominate for the then coming vacancy of Secretary-General of the association of Commonwealth nations. Again, I saw great prestige and a positive influence in world affairs for Australia, should Fraser have been successful in this venture. Party political affiliations were an immaterial matter. Once Fraser nominated, I lobbied energetically for him during 1988. Unfortunately, I discovered that although Fraser was well known among Commonwealth countries this proved quite unhelpful for his candidature. In any event, discreet 'toe testing of the water' for Hawke, by our then Ambassador to the UN, Dr Peter Wilenski, was discouraging, as I was informed by him later. (I have sound reasons for believing that the Department of Foreign Affairs and Trade was excluded from any knowledge, let alone involvement, in this process—for good and obvious reason too, given its propensity to leak.) My own view is that Australia should have embarked on a more robust formal campaign before giving up.

It would have been the zenith of a scintillating public career for Hawke to have become Secretary-General of the UN, and would have avoided the subsequent humiliating closure to his public life. If he had honoured his clear undertaking of 1988 to Keating, to stand down after the 1990 election, 'in time to maximise Keating's chances of winning the next election . . .'[121], he would have departed the political stage, widely respected by the general public, and in Labor circles and the industrial movement deeply revered. He would have been elevated to an honoured figure, a national elder statesman, and eagerly sought after as such in the community. In Labor folklore he may well have become an enduring icon. But these things were not to be.

Hawke expressed the opinion to me that if only he had had another twelve hours, he would have talked around that handful of wavering votes which eventually served to elect Keating by a narrow margin, and gone on to have won the ballot himself. I believed him, such was his extraordinary power of persuasion when he decided to convert some waverer to his point of view. Yet this would not have profited him at all, but only prolonged the dying agony of his leadership. The challenger can afford to win by a thin margin. The challenged must win convincingly to stay in charge. I should say too that had Hawke survived as Prime Minister he could not have won the 1993 election for Labor. By then, new approaches were required, quite ruthless combative skills, and a relentlessly aggressive policy presentation. Only Keating met these demanding criteria. Hawke's special relationship with the Australian public would have survived the campaign but Labor would have lost the election. Keating won against the odds, contrary to the predictions of the opinion polls, most of the 'expert pundits' in the media, and the disbelief of most of his parliamentary party. It was a virtuoso performance in which he surmounted the huge array of problems and forces opposing him, in effect, single-handedly. There has not been an election victory to equal it in my living experience; nor can I discover one faintly like it at any earlier time.

To return to that night at Government House: this experience of meeting with Bob Hawke was a deeply emotional one. That I recognised it was time for him to leave the scene in no way diminished the vast reservoir of sympathy I held for him. I experienced an urge to put a comradely arm around his slightly hunched shoulders, an affectionate, supportive embrace during what was obviously an inordinately painful period for him. After all, we had been comrades together for many years, pursuing a common purpose and we had enjoyed a good working relationship once the competitive differences had been settled. Instead, it was 'No, no, you can't do that! The wrong thing! It's unmasculine!' Once more I listened to my head, not my heart. As a lame substitute, I held out my hand, commiserated, and wished him well.

I believed, and still do, that it is essential for us all to exercise self-discipline at times of great stress. If we all collapse when the heat is on, no-one is in a condition to respond to the cause of the problem, or to properly discharge their responsibilities and duties to others at time of peril—or that at least was what my early life and background taught me. Hawke's grace and composure in defeat were impressive. It is a pity it did not last. His bitterness towards Keating drenched his soul with bile, and there were numerous instances of hostility thenceforth directed at his rival—at a Zionist Federation dinner in Melbourne in June 1994, or in the form of a threat to destroy Keating mentioned to Malcolm Fraser, in the denigration of Keating's leadership expressed in a Canberra gambling parlour, and in the shrill vituperation against Keating in his autobiography.[122] This was an unfortunate aberration, in many ways understandable, and best forgotten, for Hawke was one of Australia's most successful prime ministers and that is how I wish to remember him.

There is a brief postscript I would also like to add, in view of some rather harsh things which have been said about Hawke. Hawke was a deeply committed Labor person; those who suggest otherwise, explicitly or implicitly, are being grossly unjust. If Hawke had moved his career into the courts as a private industrial advocate he would have earned a lucrative income; much more than he derived from the trade union movement or, later, Parliament. Hawke was and is steeped in Labor culture. He has established his right to be regarded as a great Australian prime minister as well as a great national trade union leader and a significant Labor leader.

As for myself, I am glad that in 1976 and 1977, when I agonised over the future of the Party, my own situation, and a host of related matters, I decided to pull myself together and cease being self-indulgent, as it were, and go forward once more. Accordingly, I had those unparalleled, enriching experiences of being the Labor leader for more than five years. In the Labor pantheon of honour that rates rather highly. It also means much to me personally for I am nothing if not faithful to the sense of service to the community as Labor has traditionally conceived it. Then there was an equally long period as Minister for Foreign Affairs and Minister for Foreign Affairs and Trade, a ministry different from any other. Noisy squabbles in the Parliament aside, foreign policy does enjoy a great deal of bipartisan support, for which we have the Whitlam–Peacock legacy to thank. A country seriously divided at the party political level on foreign policy looks immature and foolish to other nations. The conduct of foreign policy involves the practice of dealing with the broad canvas, of mostly handling large, general principles, which creates a different sort of pressure to that experienced by ministries such as Treasury, where small mistakes can have very large and damaging consequences. Whereas foreign policy has its own disciplines, of course, I also enjoyed very much its intellectually stimulating and exciting nature.

I have been extraordinarily fortunate, many times over, to experience the rich variety that life has to offer and to engage in the public service that those long years in public office afforded me. The golden ransom of Croesus could not have compensated for it. The remarkable and quite unfair aspect of the rewarding life I have had is that so many others, rarely heard of and inadequately acknowledged by me for too long, made the successes possible. The many men and women who served me as my personal and electoral staff, public servants, colleagues and branch members, and most of all my family, whose sustaining love and support was also generously extended, in spite of my many blemishes. I managed to undo their painstaking efforts to protect me from my own instinctive excesses too many times. They were dominantly the creative forces in my public life, a life which, frankly, was not terribly important when I consider that many others would have fulfilled the tasks I handled at least as well as I did. The discomforting thought is that some would have done the job better.

And so I made my way to the house at the edge of Lake Burley Griffin, Yarralumla. Sometimes the thought runs through my mind, 'If only you could see me now, Mum. I didn't let you down'.

PART VII

'THE OFFICE OF THE GOVERNOR-GENERAL'

I've Got the Keys
to the Door . . . !

Thursday, 16 February 1989: a most surreal feeling, to be standing there, at the State Entrance of Government House, Yarralumla, in the Australian Capital Territory. The large, gleaming, black Rolls Royce had come to an elegant halt under the *coche portière*, at the State Entrance, seconds beforehand. Three uniformed police motor cyclists, our escorts for this occasion, stood to attention beside their powerful vehicles, slightly ahead of the Rolls Royce. The butler at Government House, Mr James Heenan, a venerable institution in his own right, startled me. As I arrived at the State Entrance door from our upstairs suite he swiftly moved forward and, unexpectedly, commenced brushing me down. Dallas and I had occupied that suite for the first time the night before; today she was merely greeted, respectfully and good-humouredly so, but no more than that—for, through outmoded practise, spouses derive their significance from their partner's role as Governor-General. The former farmhouse at Yarralumla which became a stately Government House has also been a kind of amber, preserving various forms of fossil behaviour.

It was a rather strange feeling, being there, soaking in the specific atmosphere of my surroundings and anticipating the task immediately before me. I had lived through a great diversity of life's experiences in the preceding decades, but this was all so absolutely foreign to any of them. Of all the feelings at that precise time, the overwhelming one was: 'This is the beginning of the end'. It was an unsettling thought, but no less unsettling than the next, which was: 'However did I end up here?'. Much less than a decade beforehand I would never have dreamed it ever likely that I would be standing where I was at that moment. No-one who had grown up with me in South Brisbane, or with whom I had been associated in the Queensland Police Force, or who had worked with me in politics in Ipswich, could have predicted this outcome.

Twenty-nine years earlier Dallas and I had visited Canberra for the first time. We were young lovers, in a relationship much frowned upon by the conventional, narrow morality of that time. No matter, for we loved one another and that made us far bigger than any petty disapprobation from the larger society. Then, we stood before the daunting black, wrought iron gates of Government House, at the end of leafy Dunrossil Drive. By craning our heads about we caught glimpses of the House, a remote building in the distance. This could only be a place beyond our ken and eternally beyond our reach. It was there, surrounded by a high perimeter fence, buffered by a deep forest of trees and shrubs, protected by vigilant guards. What little of it that we could see stood grand in its protected isolation and foreign in its occupation and role, for an Englishman and his family then occupied this piece of Australian territory. We moved away quickly from something about which we knew so little and concerning which we never expected to know more; what was the point in dallying at the door of the inhospitable and the impenetrable?

Continuing our holiday tour all those years ago, we moved on to Parliament House. As we stood in the public gallery of the House of Representatives, gazing down into the empty, green-carpeted chamber, with its green upholstery and its ornately carved Speaker's chair, emotion excitedly gripped me by the heart: 'Oh, to stand there one day and denounce the injustices of a wretchedly unfair system!'. In my imagination I could see and hear great Labor leaders of the past—Curtin, Chifley, even Scullin, before them Hughes? No, not him, for he had ratted! And Labor can never forgive anyone who does that . . . Well it was all too much, to dream these sorts of dreams; you had to keep your life expectations within practical perimeters. To over-reach in personal ambition was to risk falling into a black pit of self-delusion out of which one might never climb. Back to Ipswich and the sober reality of an ordinary, everyday existence. The return to the steady plod of the beat.

Yet here we were Dallas and I, climbing up into the rear seating of the Rolls Royce—literally so, as it was inordinately high above the ground. The vehicle moved off grandly. The vice-regal ensign, of gold and red crown above a golden lion on a royal blue background—quite unantipodean—fluttered on the hood of the limousine. Ahead of us, the three policemen on their motor cycles, with little blue and white pennants busily flicking on the front mudguards of their vehicles, leading us on the route to Parliament House. Those huge gates, which had once kept us in our place on the other side of the wall, opened submissively to allow the new, temporary master and mistress of the grounds of Yarralumla to exercise their vice-regal right of way. The elms lining the long and distinguished setting of Dunrossil Drive gracefully reached across the driveway, linking to form a soft, cool canopy. The cycles of life playing themselves out, beyond that gleaming steel and glass cocoon in which we moved forward so sedately, were far out of reach, another world. We inspected that other world as aliens observing the pulse and throb of life of another existence from a remote and privileged platform. We were discreet viewers of the activities of others, but partitioned off from their reality. It all seemed so fanciful.

Movement somehow retarded, every instant and event as if in slow motion. The motor cycles moving forward, the pace of our vehicle, glimpses of golfers on the greens at the adjoining Royal

Canberra Golf Club, a few scattered pedestrians walking in the forested verges at the roadside, had all strikingly wound down. As Fauré's sublime *Requiem*—not quite appropriately perhaps for this occasion—played on the car radio, moving gently from 'Offertoire' to 'Sanctus', it was as though the whole process had been carefully scripted to create an air of unreality about us.

I mused that I had acquired a role dramatically different to any I had undertaken before. Throughout my life I had been in a process of change. In my parliamentary career I had ended up a long way removed from the political values of earlier days. Initially, my radicalism was an incongruous mix of naive Utopianism and class resentment, added to which was a burning sense of social injustice. The flame of social injustice I once felt still burns, but in a more even way. My understanding now of the causes of social disadvantage and what can be done towards its amelioration, has been tempered by a realism that comes from hard, practical experience. The most important thing any pluralistic political system can do is to accommodate those who speak out against injustice, and give them responsibility for participating in the administration of its correction. Then they learn the limitations to change and, in particular, the resistance to change among the very people they wish to serve with their idealism.

Oblivious to my ruminations, the gleaming Rolls Royce turned and rolled along Adelaide Avenue. The large, stainless steel flagpole atop Parliament House, ambitiously reaching for the heavens, was in full view. A huge Australian flag fluttered nobly from its masthead. Children shrieked, jumped and rolled happily on the lawns which run up and over the building. Adults leisurely walked the same territory. This was not a legislative building which rose up high on a hilly outcrop, overwhelming the people, imperiously demanding the submissiveness of its subjects. This was a place where Australians could walk and enjoy each other's company, while the legislators functioned beneath their feet. There was no awe here. Just a healthy interaction between the ordinary people of the country and an institution comfortably linked into their life. It all seemed so wonderfully symbolic and quintessentially Australian.

The vehicle finally halted on the Great Verandah paving at the front entrance of Parliament House. We were greeted by Prime Minister Hawke and his wife, Hazel. Next, a smart General Salute by the Army's first Recruit Training Battalion, accompanied by the band of the Royal Military College, Duntroon. Then a brisk march in double file, headed by the Usher of the Black Rod from the Senate and the Sergeant-at-Arms from the House of Representatives. Black hammer-tail coats, knee breeches and long, black, silk stockings with silver buckles on gleaming patent leather shoes, preceded us as these officers of high rank and antiquarian dress gave us passage through the Parliament. We were headed for the Senate President's suite. Some of the attendants winked broadly and good-humouredly as we went by—they had seen enough pomp and ceremony and, after so many years in Parliament, knew us too well to be overwhelmed by the occasion.

After some formal greetings we moved to the Senate chamber where, first, I received Her Majesty's Commission. Then, for the first time in the history of the nation, a governor-general made an affirmation of allegiance and an affirmation of office as an atheist, on the invitation of the Chief Justice, Sir Anthony Mason. The world did not stop spinning at this boundless heresy. More to the point, procedures in the Senate chamber did not falter, not even for a second. This was rather perplexing for some had publicly condemned my imminent appointment as a case of the heathen knocking down the sacred doors of the nation's citadel. I had received abusive letters challenging that my non-belief ruled me out as a fit governor-general. One such, seething with outrage that an infidel would grasp the helm as head of State, wrote indignantly that after retirement as a commander of the Royal Australian Navy he had become an Anglican minister. Now, with my advent at

Yarralumla the national thread was, presumably, unravelling fiercely and hopelessly. From the tenor of his missive, I fully expected him to fold his surplice and cassock, pack the lot in his old naval dilly bag and say an affectionate farewell to the choir boys—for he angrily declared his intent to head back to his native England. There, at least, the head of State could be relied upon to defend the faith. Others too were left somewhat confused: the Boy Scouts had to ponder this conundrum of my lack of belief, but resolved their difficulties by making me National Patron of their Association rather than, as tradition always had it, Chief Scout. Privately, I drew a large sigh of relief. The prospect of dressing in scouting clobber with short pants, thus exposing to quiet derision my hairy legs, skinny shanks and knobbly knees, had filled me with horror. For the sake of fairness, most people writing to me as Christians wished me well, and in kindly and not unwelcome fashion advised that they were praying for me.

The last duty this day was to review the tri-service Royal Guard of Honour in the forecourt area of the parliamentary precinct. Ceremonies over, a new life had begun. On our way back to Government House, as if to add to the occasion and my reverie, excerpts from Handel's delightful *Water Music* began to play on ABC FM radio. It was hard to believe that, as Governor-General, I had just stood at centre stage in command of the Senate chamber of the new Parliament House—for as long as the Senate Clerk and the Usher of the Black Rod had tolerated me, that is. Paradoxically, after twenty-seven years in the House of Representatives in the old Parliament House, I would now be prevented from ever again standing in the chamber of the House of Representatives, in session. I felt a little sad that so many links with the past had now been sundered.

What had I achieved in all of those years? Not as much as I might have liked, I confess, good intentions allowed. I cringe at the recollection of some of my angry, callow, early speeches. I was then a heavy-handed interventionist and protectionist making, for instance, emotional speeches about the dairy industry in which, in my electorate, there was so much poverty and where children milked cows morning and night with their parents, and were so exhausted by their labours they fell asleep in school classrooms. Rather quickly, a new dimension to understanding this problem opened up during my part-time study of economics. I remember a night when, fired with truth and conviction but not fortified with wisdom, I attended a dairy farmers' meeting at Mt Mee. The night was thoroughly cold and the meeting hall, which is all I recall to have existed at Mt Mee, was coolly inhospitable, the dairy farmers there to protest that margarine consumption was crushing demand for butter. Theirs was an age-old and simple solution: ban it from the marketplace! I rose confidently armed with tables irrefutably establishing that while margarine consumption had gone up, butter consumption had gone down by a much greater per capita amount! My explanation? Simple! Dietary changes were the cause of the dairy industry's woes. Now, there was a silly thing to say! The meeting exploded into disbelief and I was roundly condemned. I had transgressed a basic tenet of their industry faith, I had violated a code by which they lived. Margarine was the evil enemy! I was a heretic and would not be listened to; worse, I was a socialist from the Labor Party whose aim, or so they said at the meeting, was to provide cheap food for the city people by exploiting the farmers. I left the meeting sadder, but with a little better idea of how hard it was going to be to bring about the changes I wished to make in the world. Of the many lessons I was to learn during my political life, few were as telling as that early one.

After the whirl of that first day as Governor-General, Dallas and I had a chance to settle into our new accommodation. Government House is set in 53 hectares of bushland, lawns and formal gardens, breasting onto Yarramundi Reach of Lake Burley Griffin. There is now a large, attractive ornamental pond which Dallas had constructed out of an eyesore of a marshy, leaking old farm dam.

The building itself was a rabbit warren of rooms. The formal area downstairs was comfortable but tired looking, while upstairs was frayed and all faded gentility. The administration office area was tacked onto the main building in 1926 by someone whose idea of taste ran to replacing a graceful glass conservatory of the Victorian style with a flimsy timber structure.

What is called Government House was the outcome of unplanned development undertaken in fits and starts up to 1939. The core of the building, of three floor levels, was constructed in 1891. It is a twin-gabled Victorian-style building which, often in the way of these things, was even more attractive externally in its original bare clay brick finish than now with cream cement rendered surfaces. A two-storeyed extension to the east, now embracing the formal reception room, governor-general's work office and associated rooms, and the State Entrance was added in 1898 and further elaborated in 1939. The dining room was another afterthought, added to the northern alignment of the building in 1925. These additions, jammed incongruously against the staid and stately Victoriana of the original building, are in the delightfully extroverted Art Deco style. Further first-floor improvements above the reception room area were completed in 1939 to provide accommodation for the Duke of Kent; mooted to become Governor-General, his appointment was cancelled when World War II erupted. The 1939 work was presumptuously described as making the House 'fit for a king'. This was far from the truth. As a State residence, it really was quite ordinary and unmemorable. The pantry was a battered former residential-type building of the mid-twenties and the kitchen an add-on of grimly temporary construction. The deterioration in the latter was such that with heavy storms, ice-cream buckets and other vessels had to be scattered about to catch rainwater leaking through the roofs and running down the walls. Such was the state of these rooms that it was reported in 1991 that their continued use presented, 'a potential health risk to both the residents and guests of the House and to the people who work within it'.[1]

Dallas set about changing this, with a little help from me, and the enthusiastic assistance of the Official Secretaries, first David Smith then Douglas Sturkey, and the Official Establishments' Trust and Melbourne restoration architects, Allom Lovell & Associates. We rearranged budget priorities, scheduling main building restoration work at Government House ahead of any but the most pressing requirements elsewhere, in particular those at Admiralty House, the Sydney residence of the governor-general. Paul Keating, as Prime Minister, helpfully responded to an early appeal from me for more than $2 million expenditure for the construction of a commodious new kitchen and pantry of a standard appropriate for the residence of Head of State of Australia. A year later he approved a funding arrangement whereby a $2.3 million office block and a $0.76 million gardening complex were erected. The only part of the Government House Building not restored in our term was my office and that of my assistant. They badly needed restorative attention but it seemed undesirable to schedule my own needs as a priority ahead of other areas. In our second-last year in office Dallas, with the unflagging support of Douglas Sturkey, started the restoration of Admiralty House assisted by Sydney restoration architect, Howard Tanner. It was very fulfilling to be able to say we had left these important buildings in considerably better condition overall than we had found them. Most satisfyingly, the places from which staff worked, with the unfortunate exception of the Honours Secretariat, were made new. They were at last comfortable and a more conducive environment for people who are so critical to the successful functioning of Government House, with its public reputation for a consistently high standard of performance.

The residence of our head of State should be an appropriate showcase of Australian style. If it is frayed and neglected, visiting dignitaries and heads of State will conclude that Australia is a place of impoverished tastes and mean instincts, which is certainly not so. During our term, Dallas and I ceremonially received and banqueted the Queen of Australia, the President of the United States, and many other national leaders and distinguished citizens of this and other countries. Many ordinary citizens, too, from various parts of Australia were accommodated and enjoyed hospitality there.

State banquets are a highlight of the social calendar at Government House. These are marvellous opportunities for people to socialise but they are also occasions for the exchange of some very important business. On the occasions a distinguished visitor is to attend, guests are selected with a view to the access it may provide for them in their professional or commercial interests, or for the opportunity to present some of Australia's great range of creative talents. It is also an occasion for access to the thoughts and views of those same important visitors. Such functions are very much a showcase for the discreet promotion of Australian interests. Dallas and I were often encouraged to hear visitors remark on the warm, welcoming atmosphere of Government House. Commodious and graceful, with the air of a large, comfortable country house, it is the perfect setting for formal occasions without stiffness or overpowering ceremony. It is thus very Australian in its resonances. This is added to by Australian furnishings, some of it the property of Government House, other items on permanent loan from the Australian National Gallery, and additional items acquired by the Australiana Fund specifically for the residence. While some of the contemporary Australian artwork was acquired by Dallas and myself for the House, most artwork is on loan, and is periodically changed, thanks to the Australian National Gallery and Director Betty Churcher and her staff.

As the residence of the governor-general, spouse and family, Government House also accommodates many of the staff who work there. There are the several maids recognisable by their smart, custom-made uniforms in the form of either a neat floral two-piece outfit, or a well-cut one-piece green and white work dress, or on formal occasions, a navy skirt with either a plain white or a red, white and blue striped blouse, both with a loose red neck bow tie and a red jacket. These more contemporary and stylish outfits replaced outfits of a much earlier design. The footmen too have their distinctive clobber of blue jacket, dark tie and white shirt with dark trousers. The butler, meanwhile wears white tie and tails and the under-Butler Westminster rig on formal occasions. One has to adjust to the fact that private living in this establishment entails living with a lot of other people and sharing important elements of each other's lives, for such proximity brings personal closeness and a mutual involvement. The feeling is rather like that of a large, extended family, without being too invasive, something Dallas and I further encouraged during our time there. The building and its ambience, however, are only a small part, indeed the setting only, of the office of Governor-General.

More than cake and circuses

There are some in the Australian community who wish to dismiss the authority of the office of Governor-General. Lest anyone think this is a recent phenomenon, the view which sees the office exclusively as a ceremonial carapace strapped to the back of antiquated if quaint ritual, actually has a long history.[2] As Alfred Deakin put it with characteristic pithiness at one of the early Constitutional Conventions:

> We regard with little favour the title [of Governor-General] . . . which appears to the active politician to be little better than a glittering and gaudy toy.[3]

But such views belong to a less-complicated past: 11 November 1975 demonstrated beyond any doubt that substantial residual power was reserved to the office of Governor-General to act unilaterally and decisively. Although high drama of this sort thankfully rarely occurs, the more numerous day-to-day functions of the governor-general remain. Mundane as they might be they are also quite essential, and also represent much more than 'a glittering and gaudy toy'.

The functions of the governor-general overwhelmingly *are* procedural and ceremonial. In procedural terms, the office of Governor-General is, of course, not an executive one; it is not associated with policy development, although its workload is persistent. First and foremost, the governor-general represents the Crown in Australia, as provided by the Constitution. With some important exceptions, expressly provided for in the Constitution and dealt with later in this chapter, the governor-general discharges his duties according to the advice of his responsible ministers. This advice is most usually received through the Executive Council (which usually consists of the governor-general and two ministers) although there are other avenues. As a matter of strict legal interpretation of the *Acts Interpretation Act* the governor-general, '. . . is not legally obliged to follow the [Executive] council's advice'.[4] As a matter of prudent practice a sensible governor-general would not want to adopt this independent role except in the most extreme circumstance. It would be quite wrong for an appointed office-holder, most usually a person whose background reflects a very narrow spectrum of experience of the socio-economic values of our community, to have anything but the most restricted power to act contrary to the advice of a democratically elected government.

The governor-general usually presides over Executive Council meetings, although the vice-president of the Executive Council, or another minister, may preside in his absence. Government decisions about changes to regulations, defence force commissions and senior appointments, as well as judicial and senior public service appointments are considered at these meetings. If properly processed and in order, these matters are approved by the Council allowing the governor-general to authorise each item to proceed with his signature. It is here that the governor-general has an opportunity to 'consult, encourage, warn', as Bagehot put it. Should a governor-general ever have doubts about the legal authority of government to proceed with some matter before the Executive Council, then he may raise his concerns with his responsible ministers at the meeting of the Council before which the matter is properly scheduled for consideration. If his responsible ministers, on behalf of the government, advise that the government does not accept that view and intends to proceed with the item the governor-general, as a matter of general practice, is obliged to accept that advice and leave any legal action, quite properly, to the courts. The governor-general and his office are not set up to function as some sort of court of review, not even when there is a former distinguished legal advocate or jurist functioning in the vice-regal office. Any attempt to have it otherwise would be a disturbing usurpation of the proper role of the courts, in particular the High Court.

If there appears to be a blatant violation of proper processes by a government apparently bent on behaving with illegal intent, or from gravely dubious motives, the advice of the solicitor-general can be sought, as occurred in the case of the questionable loan raisings in 1975. If the solicitor-general advises, as he did in 1975, that the action is legal (or at least that it was arguably legal), it would be improper then for a governor-general to shop around for other opinions from the private legal profession. These can be as numerous and varied as leaves driven before an autumn wind. Nevertheless, if the Governor-General feels he has reasonable grounds for apprehending that the Solicitor-General in a particular case is too much the paid advocate for the government, he could— I certainly would have in such circumstances—seek an eminent private legal opinion. If the solicitor-general or the privately commissioned counsel advises the action is illegal the governor-general should refuse to authorise the intended action, expressing in writing to the vice-president of the Executive Council the explicit reasons for so acting. If government were to convene a ministerial meeting of the Executive Council without him in order to ratify the proposed questionable action, then the Governor-General should refuse to sign and therefore formalise the relevant papers when later presented to him for signature. He should also convey his explicit reservations to the Executive Council in writing at that time. If government persisted with its course of action, the governor-general should advise Parliament of his difficulties with the proposed action by communicating a message to the clerks of each of the two Houses for presentation to Parliament.

It is difficult to conceive of circumstances where such brazen disregard for proper processes and legal conduct could arise on the part of government. Should it indeed happen, then our democratic system would be in such grave disarray that something more than vice-regal intervention would be required to remedy it. In circumstances such as these where the government, very improperly in my view, additionally sought to prevent a governor-general from direct and independent access to legal advice on matters of government causing him anxiety, as in the 1975 loan raisings, then the governor-general would be justified in seeking the best private legal advice he could obtain. Sufficient funds from the Government House budget could be mustered for this purpose. In my case, should I have been presented with such circumstances, I would have advised government of my intention to so act. Candour and directness with government is essential in a governor-general's dealings with his ministers if he is to maintain moral authority and respect for his role among members of his responsible government. The possibility of dismissal should be no hindrance. Actual or threatened dismissal by a government would, as soon as disclosed by the governor-general, provoke instant and fierce public reaction; furthermore, such disclosure is justified in the interests of preserving the integrity of the process of government.

During my term, there was one minor instance where I discovered after an Executive Council meeting that legislation validating certain regulations approved at that meeting did not validly exist. This was due to an undetected error in transmitting the relevant Bill between the two Houses. Armed with a clear opinion from the Acting Solicitor-General I wrote a stiff letter to the Vice-President of the Executive Council, a minister, expressing my concerns. The matter was promptly remedied by an embarrassed government. As well, during my occupancy of the governor-generalship there were several administrative matters which came before Executive Council meetings about which I sought further information before allowing them to proceed. These matters were held over to subsequent meetings. Then there were some rare cases where papers had not been prepared properly, and which were accordingly returned to the Executive Council office for attention. In every one of these instances there was complete co-operation from the ministers attending the Council meetings and from the Council office.

In the period immediately before an election, following the dissolution of Parliament, I always subjected ministers to close questioning on items before the Council to ensure that they conformed with proper practice in executive decision-making at that caretaker stage of government. There were instances where I required the responsible minister to consult the Opposition spokesperson, seeking endorsement that a particular matter should proceed during an election campaign, before I approved it. In summary, the conventions which apply in this period are: no policy decisions to be taken which are likely to commit an incoming government, no appointments of significance to be made, no entering into major undertakings or contracts. There have been various suggestions that the role of the Executive Council could be assumed by the Cabinet. A variation of this procedure has been in practice in Canada for quite a long time and it reputedly works satisfactorily. Nonetheless, for reasons already outlined, the present practice in Australia functions as a more reassuring safety catch on the process of government. In the role described so far, the governor-general functions as the Queen's representative under the Constitution, as distinct from those other areas where authority is specifically defined in the Constitution as belonging to the governor-general alone.

Hasluck has also described a number of radical principles justifying a governor-general acting contrary to the advice of his responsible ministers:

> In abnormal times or in any case of any attempt to disregard the Constitution or the laws of the Commonwealth, or even the customary usages of the Australian Government, it would be the Governor-General who would present the crisis to Parliament and, if necessary, to the nation for determination. [5]

I am, however, concerned about aspects of this view. What is 'customary usages of the Australian government'? To the extent I have some feel for what it implies, my attitude is that this is a matter more properly addressed by the politicians and sorted out through political processes. To anticipate otherwise requires the Queen's representative to fulfil a role which it would never occur to the Queen herself to assume.

Nevertheless, there would be major difficulties in attempting to define this condition of 'abnormal times'. To try to do so would require speculation on circumstances where there had been a thoroughgoing breakdown of accountable government, and where the community was perhaps in riotous tumult and clamour. In such a situation of government disorder and civil revolt, notions of proper civil government and due legal processes, surely, would have gone by the board. A governor-general, so minded, might have a role in such developments; but it would not be according to the Constitution and customary practice and might well draw down on his role as the Command in Chief of the naval and military forces of the Commonwealth. It is also possible that in such extraordinary circumstances the armed services might well support the government.

Similarly, the view that a governor-general '. . . has a further duty to see that decisions of the Executive Council are consistent with government policy' is a mistaken one.[6] It is also dangerous, for what other authoritative source or account of government policy is there for the inquiring, vice-regal representative, except his ministers' advice? If I can invoke an American aphorism: 'Election platforms are for being launched from, not standing on!'. It is a fact of life that sometimes, after an election, circumstances related to governing the country are radically different from those presumed by an incoming government, or may else be in the process of dramatic change. Government may then wish to impose policy responses quite contrary to those proposed earlier.

Various hypothetical situations were put forward from other sources in earlier years to justify the independent exercise of authority by the governor-general. The reserving of legislation, it was argued, could occur where there had been a fundamental and unpopular shift in defence alliances without reference to the electorate, or changes from private to social ownership of the means of production. Such concerns, of course, reflect an earlier somewhat antiquated and strongly class-based aversion to the prospect of Labor in government, and the possibility this might bring with it quite different defence and economic policies to those of the conservatives. A third illustration is based on the introduction of a gross distortion into the electoral system giving one party a monopoly of power. The first and second are matters upon which, properly, the electorate should pass judgment at the next available election, in the unlikely event a government would be foolish enough to attempt either. There would be widespread consensus in the community about what would be an unacceptable 'fundamental' shift in alliances. Similarly, hostile responses to any attempted, unacceptable confiscation of private property for social ownership would be promptly forthcoming. It would also be justiciable. The people as electors are the best judges finally in such matters. The cautious performance of Labor in government for more than a decade since the early eighties certainly lays to rest cause for such exaggerated fears.

On the third matter, the question becomes, 'What is a corrupted electoral system?'. What sometimes seems to be the case superficially is much less so on closer analysis. At the Federal level there once existed a 20 per cent weighting in favour of rural electorates. In the view of some this was a vastly unfair advantage. For the National Party, the proposed reduction of this margin to 10 per cent smacked of disadvantaging rural electorates. The public was largely indifferent to the matter, in any event, which therefore scarcely justified vice-regal intervention. Again, there was a general belief up to 1989 that in Queensland the electoral system had been thoroughly corrupted, through malapportionment, to guarantee a monopoly of power for the government of Bjelke-Petersen. Labor complained that it was a victim of a huge rigging of electorate boundaries. The reality was that Bjelke-Petersen had exacted the greatest electoral boundary disadvantages against his allies in the Liberal Party. The private opinion of some better informed 'numbers people' in the Labor Party was that a fair and equal distribution of State electoral boundaries could have caused Labor to lose two or three seats from the total it held. The vice-regal representative would simply not have sufficiently clear-cut information to be able to intervene with a sense of certainty on such matters.

The role of Command in Chief of the naval and military forces is allotted to the governor-general by the Constitution. It is purely a nominal appointment and is exclusively ceremonial. Any authority exercised in this sphere is exercised on the advice of the government, through relevant ministers or by decision from Cabinet. It is on the same basis that judicial appointments and those of administrators of departments are made. Similarly, the appointment or dismissal of ministers, the summoning, prorogation or dissolution of Parliament, are, in general practice, acts taken by the governor-general on advice.

The governor-general is Chancellor of the Order of Australia, appointments to the General Division of which are made by him. Since 1994 these approvals are 'laid before the Sovereign' as a courtesy, and the appointments themselves made without ministerial advice. There is a solicitor-general's legal opinion, which I sought in the interests of resolving a difficulty I had with one proposed appointment that 'in an appropriate case the governor-general might reject or defer a recommendation of the Council without prior consultation . . . such circumstances would be unusual . . .' The procedure within the General Division awards is distinctly different from those made within the Military Division. The latter are made by the governor-general 'on the recommendation of the minister for defence'. Under the Australian Bravery Decorations system, Australian Gallantry, Distinguished Conduct, Conspicuous Conduct, Meritorious Conduct, are made on the advice of relevant ministers. Honorary awards to foreign nationals are made by the prime minister acting alone.

There have been some instances when appointments within the General Division, as recommended by the Council for the Order, have been referred back to that Council by the governor-general as Chancellor of the Order. Such action was taken before any public announcement of the awards was made because of the receipt of information which raised questions about the appropriateness of the appointments proceeding. An impending term in gaol, for instance, has amazing purgative effects on an impending honours investiture. In one notable case during my term, an appointment was postponed for some time, much to the chagrin of a very senior minister who had energetically backed the award. Contrary to the minister's suppositions, there was no personal conspiracy against him and his 'larger than life' little mate; more to the point it was felt that it would be inappropriate, in the circumstances of the time, for an announcement to be made—a decision which, indisputably, was to the ultimate advantage of the minister concerned. The decision was taken, however, for no other reason than to protect the reputation of the Order of Australia honours system. The General Order has established and maintains a high level of community support and respect because of its independence from manipulative political influences. The awards are for meritorious community service.

To move on to other aspects of the vice-regal role: not least among those duties are the requirements to engage in wide-ranging public speaking, and to travel extensively within Australia and occasionally overseas representing the Commonwealth as Head of State. The speaking engagements can be especially demanding in relation to important national and international conferences, although these undertakings are welcomed by the people with whom one comes in contact. In the case of travel to remote parts of Australia, the visits are quite evidently seen as an expression of interest in those people's welfare, and their contribution to Australia, the governor-general serving to represent the wider community. Rather than an exhaustive catalogue of the ceremonial and formal roles discharged by the governor-general, the above serve as an indication of their nature and ambit—some people will naturally continue to argue that all these vice-regal ceremonial roles could or should be eliminated.

Ceremony and ritual have deep significance in our psyches. The evidence that we humans need such ritual stretches back over the millennia of mankind's evolution and across all societies. The public expectation that the duties fulfilled by the governor-general, regardless of the designation of the office of Head of State, will continue unabated. Personally, Dallas and I very much enjoyed the range of contact we had with Australians from all walks of life. Some of our encounters ranged from the sublime to the humorous at least—from opening new scientific research centres, naming new buildings and inspecting colourful military parades to visiting the Marble Bar CWA ladies and being incredulously upbraided for declining a huge lamington with, 'What's wrong? Don't you like our

Marble Bar lamingtons?' I mumbled my embarrassed apology and scoffed the slighted lamington, a Marble Bar legend in its own right. Or having the celebrated Aboriginal painter, Rover Thomas, inquiring when visiting Canberra in 1992, 'How's that old fella Bill going at Yarralumla?' As I thought him to be older than I on our first meeting at Turkey Creek in the far north of Western Australia, my ego suffered a dreadful jolt.

The Governor-General must choose

When Parliament is racked by upheaval leading to the fall of the government, the appointment of a new prime minister, or the demand for a dissolution—the governor-general must be involved, to a greater or lesser extent, for he has a key role to fulfil. He becomes in effect the ringkeeper, ensuring that the process reaches a proper and just outcome. If a government in the House of Representatives falls because of defections, the first duty of a governor-general is to consult to establish if a new government could be formed. Despite claims to the contrary, it would not be appropriate in Australia, given the strength of party discipline over members of Parliament, for the governor-general to accept solely the advice of the prime minister of the fallen government as to succession. Aggrieved politicians would quickly take their revenge should the governor-general have been advised incorrectly. Nor should a governor-general accept the advice of the fallen prime minister to call an election if it appears, on sound grounds, that an alternative government can be formed. The governor-general would want to be quite confident of his grounds for taking initiatives in this sphere. A good example of a vice-regal stumble on the matter of prime ministerial succession can be seen in Viscount Byng's actions of 1926 in Canada. Liberal Prime Minister Mackenzie King, defeated in the Canadian House of Representatives, advised Byng to dissolve Parliament and call an election. Byng declined and appointed Conservative Leader Meighen who was promptly defeated in the

Parliament. The Conservatives were given an election, only to be trounced in a campaign where Byng was accused of partiality and favour towards the Conservatives. King, sworn in as Prime Minister, promptly sacked Byng. Byng should have withdrawn Meighen's commission when it was established that Meighen could not govern, and re-commissioned King allowing him to go to the electorate as Prime Minister. It is important that the governor-general should choose. It is equally essential that he choose wisely.

Governors-general are expected to be diligent and well-informed in making decisions about prime ministerial succession. In most cases, drawing from contemporary Australian experience, the selections are straightforward and are made by the majority party, or coalition parties, through their internal decision-making processes. From time to time, however, there have been thorny issues in the way of a clear cut selection; it is in these circumstances that the governor-general has to choose, even if his determination brings the risk of his being condemned out of hand by those who do not get their way as a result. To whom else could the task be allotted? Indeed who else in public office would enthusiastically embrace such an inherently difficult and risky process? Jurists would shun this potentially invidious role for the High Court. Apart from many other undesirable associations such a role would suggest, the connection thus established between Court, Parliament and its political parties would be thoroughly undesirable for a democracy. No wise public servant would want the task. The officers of Parliament, too, would cringe at the suggestion they accept the dubious honour. As for the Church, it would be more than any minister of religion, high or low in the hierarchy, would wisely contemplate, no matter how closely he might feel guided by divine providence.

There was some media speculation at one stage during my term as Governor-General that Prime Minister Hawke might seek to spike the prime ministerial ambitions of Paul Keating, one of his senior ministers, by seeking an election with much of the parliamentary term unexpired. The circumstances were that the Government had a comfortable majority in the House of Representatives; nor had any legislation been rejected or unnecessarily hindered by the Senate, or any dramatic change in policy contemplated which justified electorate endorsement. Hence there was no special reason for seeking an early election. It was not clear, moreover, whether the challenger would be a serious threat to the Prime Minister retaining his office. The nature of the speculation was clear enough: the electoral processes might be manipulated to short-circuit an internal party difficulty. Hawke made no such move. In such an event, nonetheless, should a prime minister present no reasons for seeking an early dissolution of Parliament, or reasons too flimsy to have credence, the governor-general would be justified in refusing that request.

It is far better to have politicians sort out their own political difficulties. In such hypothetical circumstances I would counsel the prime minister to obtain clear and evident endorsement from his party for his proposed dissolution. It is a course with its risks. If the challenger were to fail dismally and the Party and in particular the Cabinet to close ranks around the prime minister—who then renewed his request for an early dissolution, threatening the government's resignation if the request was not conceded—the governor-general would have to agree, provided the government was still in control of the House of Representatives. It scarcely seems a tenable hypothesis, however, for the party political reasons which caused the prime minister to seek to solve them with an early dissolution of Parliament would no longer exist. The public, alerted to the background to these manoeuvres by the Opposition and the media, would regard the case for an early election as suspect. If the government insisted on an election, such a course would almost certainly inflict unnecessary casualties on it in the electorate, perhaps even leading to its defeat.

It cannot be gainsaid, however, that if a government with a comfortable majority in the House of Representatives and a good part of its term to go were to seek a dissolution of the House early—and persist with that request, threatening to resign its commission if not granted—such action would eventually force the hand of the governor-general. There is nowhere for him to go in search of an alternative workable government. If no reasons are given for the early dissolution, or the reasons are weak, then one would expect that the Opposition and the media would highlight the unnecessary disruption and costliness of the tactic. Hasluck and Kerr stress the principle of the 'workability' of Parliament as the key criterion on which the judgment of whether to dissolve or not is made. I think, in practical terms, what I outline above is the more appropriate manner of handling this sort of situation. The governor-general ultimately has the whip hand in this exchange. In accord with normal practice he would release correspondence from the prime minister seeking the dissolution, as well as his response, disclosing that his hand had been forced and the view expressed that he would have preferred not to have been compelled to grant the dissolution. This would be done at the announcement of the dissolution or shortly thereafter. The course has its inherent dangers: it would almost certainly be portrayed as a highly political act, even with the effective granting of the dissolution. If the government was returned, the governor-general could start packing his bags at Yarralumla. No matter; in resisting political chicanery, he will have acted properly.

There is also the matter of prime ministerial succession where there is some uncertainty about who should assume office. In late 1967, for instance, when Prime Minister Harold Holt died through misadventure, Billy McMahon was Deputy Leader of the majority coalition party in government, the Liberal Party. He made a strong claim for the office, using devious stratagems to be appointed Prime Minister on an interim basis. The Leader of the Country Party, Jack

McEwen, was Deputy Prime Minister of the Coalition Government. Governor-General Lord Casey consulted widely, and properly appointed McEwen interim Prime Minister. At the subsequent party election John Gorton became Prime Minister. If McMahon had been appointed as Acting Prime Minister, this may have given him an unfair advantage in the subsequent party election which chose the prime minister; it would also have possibly caused much resentment and criticism of the actions of the Governor-General. Casey worked hard to avert this, even if he had a tendency to want to assist his old party in ways beyond the prudent and proper bounds of his gubernatorial responsibilities.[7] The fact is much of the consultations between Casey and McEwen reflected Casey's personal and political antagonisms towards McMahon. Earlier, in an extraordinary display of political intervention in the internal affairs of the Coalition parties, Casey had lectured McMahon, in Casey's vice-regal office, about McMahon's conflict with McEwen and his proclivity, bordering on compulsion, to leak confidential government information to the media, and reminding McMahon of his loyal duty to his party and the Coalition. Curiously, after leaving the office of Governor-General, Casey continued to play an active role within the province of the Liberal Party, helping bring down Prime Minister Gorton and having McMahon installed as his successor. Most of the plotting appears to have proceeded from the less than gaunt dinner tables of the Melbourne Club of which he was an *habitué*.[8]

With the exception of Casey, there is no evidence that the impartial discharge of office was in any way compromised by incumbents having past political party affiliations. Of the twenty-one governors-general who have served Australia, fourteen, or two of every three, had a background of active engagement in parliamentary party politics before accepting appointment. All except two of those 'political' governors-general served in non-Labor parties. At least one returned to active parliamentary politics after concluding his term of vice-regal office. In fact, there is quite a deal of documentary evidence that a past association with a political party in Parliament enhanced the working relationship between the vice-regal representative and the government of the day—even in instances where the government was of a party complexion other than that to which the vice-regal representative had once been politically affiliated.

A governor-general decides other matters too. For instance, no-confidence motions carried in the Parliament against a government. Contrary to some text book assertions, a motion of no-confidence against a government carried in the lower house of Parliament does not automatically require the government to resign; nor, should it fail to remove itself, is the governor-general or State governor required to dismiss it. A no-confidence motion was carried against the minority Field Labor Government in the lower house of the Tasmanian State Parliament in the second half of 1991, when certain independent conservationist Members of the Legislative Assembly withdrew their support from the Government and voted for the no-confidence resolution. The resolution related to legislation to which they objected as conservationists. At a subsequent adjournment vote the Government received a majority vote, demonstrating that the want of confidence was restricted to one matter. On other matters of business the Field Government could continue to govern successfully, and did so until early 1992 when a State election was called by the Premier. State Governor Sir Philip Bennett very properly did not intervene in the earlier parliamentary manoeuvrings although, not surprisingly, the major opposition group sought to encourage him to do so.

Other difficult choices remain to confront the vice-regal office bearer. A good example of this can be drawn from events in Queensland in late November 1987. The Premier of that State, Bjelke-Petersen, had become an intolerable liability for his Government. When met with a revolt by Cabinet ministers who wanted to rid the Government of him, the Premier retaliated by proposing to sack a number of ministers and reshuffle others in a desperate effort at saving his own political hide. Initially, Bjelke-Petersen believed he had the Governor's agreement for the sackings, but inside twenty-four hours of this presumed understanding it became apparent to Bjelke-Petersen he would be over-ruled by his Cabinet. When he approached the State Governor, Sir Walter Campbell, he was advised to first obtain majority support for his proposal from Cabinet. The Governor had adopted an entirely proper procedure. It was also the end of Bjelke-Petersen as Premier of Queensland.[9]

It is not the purpose here to catalogue comprehensively, if in fact it could be done, those instances where the governor-general has to choose. H. V. Evatt, in *The King and his Dominion Governors* and Eugene A. Forsey, in *The Royal Power of Dissolution of Parliament in the British Commonwealth*, as well as several other major authoritative texts on the topic, have attempted that already. I can only agree with a particular comment of Evatt's, that:

> Amongst the text-writers on the subject of constitutional conventions those interested will usually be able to find support for (or against) almost any proposition.[10]

But in the light of that, it is difficult to have much confidence in his contradictory recommendation:

> . . . it would save endless controversy and recrimination if the duties of the King's representatives were defined in a code which might provide for such cases as we are now considering.[11]

Unless, that is, it were possible to codify only those views congenial to oneself alone, which, of course, would have had intrinsic appeal for Evatt.

The Advisory Committee to the Constitutional Commission, comprising eight distinguished Australians, in 1987 ran into similar difficulties in its report, *Executive Government*. It unanimously recommended that the reserve powers should be 'systematically declared and written down by some authoritative body'.[12] It wisely avoided the question of naming that 'authoritative body' and whether government first and then Parliament generally would happily concede this role to any other body. Just as Evatt once conceded, 'I admit the difficulties of precise definition,' the Committee could not agree on the definition of an ironclad set of propositions. Two Committee members reasonably pointed out that 'well-qualified minds continue to differ widely on many significant issues'.[13] The only way in which this codification could be reached would be through bipartisan endorsement of a set of proposals, which would be most unlikely given their provocative and potentially explosive nature. More importantly, there are so many imponderables possible in the course of experience that codification would most likely build in the kind of rigidity which would have the potential to hinder flexible and practical handling of some complicated and unanticipated considerations bound to arise in our political system.

The reserve powers of the governor-general incontestably exist and have so since Federation. The powers are provided under the Constitution in the following sections: 5, power to summon, determining sessions, prorogation and dissolution, of Parliament; 57, double dissolution and joint sitting of the Houses of Parliament; 64, commissioning and terminating appointment of ministers, including the prime minister. But the codification of these powers, as urged by some lawyers and non-lawyers, is no simple matter. It is implausible to propose that legal draftsmen, or others, should define all the circumstances where these powers could operate. Much as we might define specific cases where they apply and may be used, the unpredictable case will arise and create turmoil. No-one anticipated the nature of the November 1975 constitutional crisis. If the reserve powers had been codified back then, but contained no specific provision for resolving such an affair, then the country might have been *truly* seized up by that impasse, as no-one would have had the power or authority to resolve it.

The case of dissolution

The advent of a strong, stable, two-party bloc in Parliament quite early in the history of our federation has minimised the need for independent vice-regal intrusion into the parliamentary processes. Prior to that consolidation, requests for dissolutions had been refused by the governor-general in 1904, 1905 and 1909. Since then there have only been two occasions when the governor-general has exercised authority in this area. First there was the defection— or perhaps more properly expulsion—of Hughes and supporters from the Labor Party, then in government in 1916. After forming a minority government with Liberal Party support, Hughes went onto coalesce his numbers with the Liberals to form a new majority Nationalist Party Government. Governor-General Munro-Ferguson deflected, rather than rejected, Hughes' request for a dissolution in the wake of those sensational events. The tactic worked admirably.[14] Then in 1941 there was the fall of the United Australia Party along with the Country Party in the coalition government led by Fadden, by a vote on the floor of Parliament, after the earlier exit from office of Menzies. A Labor government was then appointed when Fadden recommended, and Governor-General Lord Gowrie accepted, John Curtin as Prime Minister. This was a straightforward case where only Curtin could form a government. The issue of succession after Holt's unfortunate death could also perhaps be included here, although there are some notable distinguishing features about that case compared to the other two. In the first two instances cited, the role of the governor-general was brought into play in conditions less steady than usual, involving the transfer of government from one party to another without an election being involved.[15]

No request for a dissolution has been rejected outright since 1909, even though reasons put forward by prime ministers as justification for a dissolution over the years, frankly, have often been rather flimsy. The cases drafted to justify the dissolution of Parliament have, in some instances, been more a matter of *ex post facto* rationalisation. Prime ministers have been known to happily store a bank of Bills bottlenecked in the Senate to cover the contingency of an early dissolution of the Parliament. When they have subsequently moved, this has been less due to a sense of urgency about the legislative programme breaking down, than the judgment that an election at a particular time would be advantageous. Obviously, the decision to press on to a double dissolution in 1974 was influenced by certain political considerations arising from the prospective state of the economy, as explained earlier. The dissolution of 1975 was granted as part of the Governor-General's solution to a political crisis.

The double dissolution sought by Fraser in 1983 was an overnight, impulsive decision based on a different set of political circumstances. Fraser learnt of momentous impending changes in the leadership of the Opposition Labor Party scheduled to occur on 3 February 1983. It might be suggested that in those circumstances the Governor-General should not have given Fraser the dissolution he sought. But there was more to that instance than opportunistic timing on Fraser's part. Firstly, the Governor-General was presumably unaware of the sudden developments occurring overnight in the Labor Party; secondly, the document submitted by Fraser consisted of five pages of well-argued reasons—the best stated case I have seen—as to why a double dissolution was necessary. Indeed, Fraser had had his case ready in draft form from about September to October the previous year, as he had been contemplating an election late in 1982. He had been anticipating—wrongly as it transpired—a sharp downturn in the economy aggravated by worsening drought through 1983; the view he took was that this would worsen his party's electoral prospects as 1983 drew on, and so there was a need to go to the polls early. It would be quite a confrontation for a governor-general to advise his prime minister that, although he had no concrete evidence, he doubted the authenticity of the case being put and this was sufficient to justify rejection of the request. Although that is beyond contemplation, Sir Ninian Stephen *did* require more supporting information from Fraser which delayed his ploy by several hours and lost him important momentum. In the event, Fraser got his double dissolution. Crisp was alive to this very point. He wrote, drawing on Evatt's work of 1936, and after referring to several precedents:

> . . . *any Prime Minister with a majority in the House but a minority in the Senate must now receive from the Governor-General approval for a requested double dissolution, even if the measure which is the occasion of the deadlock were unimportant and 'manufactured' to bring the necessary situation about.*[16]

The tests justifying a double dissolution were laid down by Chief Justice Sir Samuel Griffith when the first double dissolution was sought in 1914. He made three points, following the presumption that the technical requirements for the exercise of the power as provided by section 57 of the Constitution formally existed. The points were: the power to dissolve both Houses of Parliament under section 57 of the Constitution is an 'extraordinary power' exercised on the discretion of the governor-general; this extraordinary power is to be exercised only where the proposed law is of such importance it should be referred to the electors, or the state of deadlock in legislation is such it can only be ended by a double dissolution; the governor cannot act except on the advice of his ministers, however, he is not bound to follow that advice but rather he has to make an independent judgment. The fact is only ministers can advise on the importance of legislation deadlocked and the nature of the deadlock. The governor-general is in no position to make an informed personal judgment on the situation as he is too far removed from the seat of action. He cannot consult Opposition members of Parliament and in any event would be unwise to do so, such would be the likely partisan nature of that advice. There have been six double dissolutions since Federation.[17] Requests for these all formally met the criteria laid down by Griffith, and, in the circumstances, the governor-general of the day had no choice but to approve them. He was not and could not be privy to the more important, unstated but thoroughly dominant political imperatives behind some of those requests.

On an important and not unrelated matter, we undeniably have too many elections. Without even bothering to include separate Senate, or State and local government elections, the increasing frequency of elections of a government at the national level is disturbing. From and including the first post-World War II election in 1946 to that of 1993, elections for government, that is in the House of Representatives, have occurred on an average of every 2.2 years. Of the double dissolutions held since Federation ninety-six years ago, two-thirds have occurred in a little over the past decade-and-a-half. Clearly, the procedures are being capriciously manipulated. The cost of a national election is huge and Australian taxpayers pay the bill. The election for the House of Representatives and for half the Senate in 1993 cost $63 million. Of this $13 million was paid to registered political parties and independent candidates under the public funding scheme. One way of getting around this problem would be to enact fixed terms of Parliament. A constitutional change would be essential. On past experience there is probably no chance of success for that undertaking.

The nexus between the Senate and House of Representatives should be broken. If it is not, the national Parliament will become top-heavy with excessive numbers of senators over time. The present formula determining the number of Federal electorate divisions provides for a total of 147 seats in the House of Representatives. The Constitution requires that the number of senators representing the States will be half the number of representatives coming from the States and there will be equal numbers of Senators from each of the States. Thus there are currently 72 Senators, 12 for each State. Present demographic projections have populations in Federal divisions 40 per cent larger by the year 2020 than is the case currently. If the populations within Federal divisions grow in line with population growth projections and the number of electorates is not increased in order to hold the number of Senators steady, providing adequate local representation for electorates would be extremely difficult. On the other hand, Federal divisions could be kept at their present enrolment level but that would involve a 40 per cent increase in the number of divisions and consequently in the number of senators, in conformity with constitutional requirements. Thus, in this way there would be about 102 senators representing the States, or 17 for each State by the year 2020.

That is absurd. Tasmania, for instance, has five Federal divisions guaranteed as a minimum for it by the Constitution and has 12 Senators. Even on the most optimistic population projections for the year 2020 Tasmania will still have only 5 members in the House of Representatives. It would, however, have 17 Senators! This sort of extravagance could not be justified in any responsible way. The number of senators should be fixed, either at its current level or, preferably, at a lower one. Multi-member electorates and proportional representation for elections to the House of Representatives should be implemented too as part of an undertaking to make Parliament more representative of the pluralistic political values of the community.

The reserve powers and reform

The fundamental defect of our parliamentary system is that the Constitution which guides it was drafted to function according to two scarcely compatible methods of government: a large bit of representative government of the Westminster kind, and a key part of federal government of the USA Congressional type. These, grafted together, were bequeathed to us as a political Bactrian camel; at times of stress like 1975, we find the twin humps confusingly unco-ordinated. The creation of the Senate was essential if Federation was to proceed at all; a Commonwealth of Australia was after all a most uncertain prospect right up to the mid-1890s. A Senate was to be the States' house, protecting the interests of the smaller constituents of the federation from any overbearing or predatory tendencies by the bigger States, although it has never really functioned as such. The dominance of clearly defined parties and the early emergence of strict party discipline ensured that it was, like the House of Representatives, an institution of party politics. The more clear-minded delegates to the Constitutional Conventions of l891 and 1897, such as Macrossan and Deakin, predicted this would occur.[18]

In November 1975, the imperatives of party politics and political opportunism asserted themselves in the upper chamber as successfully as always. Not that Labor has cause for righteous indignation; for it too has a long record of threatening to use the authority of the Senate, indeed *did* use that power on a few occasions to obstruct coalition government legislation, as discussed earlier. In the wake of events following November 1975 there were widely held fears that periods of unstable government would ensue, as political opportunism would prevail. That the Senate would function, as it always had, as the tool of the majority political party in that House, but more aggressively so than previously. As three former clerks of the House of Representatives expressed it:

> With governments perhaps often unlikely under proportional voting patterns to have power in the Senate, this risk [of blockage of supply] can arise twice in each year and thus give rise to quite unacceptable instability of government.[19]

Though I too harboured that anxiety for quite some time, looking back over the twenty-one years since that event, it has not happened. Parliamentary government has been very stable, remarkably so as it is a vastly different institution now than then. An unmistakable evolution is occurring in the functioning of the Senate, in that it is becoming more broadly representative of the community. Minority parties and groups as well as the occasional independent exercise the balance of power and are helping maintain the stability of the system through reasonably responsible conduct. One anticipates that this minority representation will not go away, but it will conceivably grow, and along with it the influence which such representation can bring to bear. This plurality may be uncongenial to notions of comfort and predictability which governments may have previously entertained if not experienced, but executive government is now more accountable because of it; and there is also community approval for such diversity.

The elaboration of the Senate committee system, particularly in the expansion of committee hearings on topical and important public issues, is also progressively redefining the role of the Senate. The evolution of the Senate committee system, in recent years, seems to be in the direction of making it an increasingly independent and powerful chamber. On the positive side, this has the prospect for offering a genuine counterpoise to impatient executive government in the House of Representatives. If this trend continues, the public may well come to look to the Senate as an essential check and balance, the bulwark defending its interests against executive government. If the Senate does take on this role of probing and challenging the executive on matters of accountability, not only will this mean a dramatic shift in the relative importance of the two Houses, it will also make the Senate an extremely influential institution in other ways. It will become a major focus of media commentary and public interest, as well as a meaningful avenue for airing major sectional grievances against government administration and policy. The House of Representatives will retain considerable importance as essentially the seat of executive government, but the opportunities to indulge in staged, noisy theatre will become fewer and fewer as the Senate forces it to justify many of its policies and administrative decisions. Provided the Senate exercises this developing role prudently and according to the national interest, the chances of another 1975-type crisis are negligible. That crisis erupted because Labor had handled so many things incompetently, and because the Senate had been hijacked by an Opposition using corrupt Senate replacement practices. The Senate now is in the control of neither Government nor Opposition and is likely to remain that way over the years ahead, a new environment which hopefully will only prove to be to the public good. If it might be vexatious for ministers, it will also require of them more skills and subtlety in managing government in future. A perspicacious delegate at the 1891 Constitutional Conference, Hackett from Western Australia, observed:

> . . . either responsible government will kill federation or federation in the form in which we shall, I hope, be prepared to accept it, will kill responsible government . . . [20]

I think Hackett was expecting too much, but the practical common sense of the Senate appears to be moving our parliamentary system in the direction he noted and in doing so giving us a more workable and better process of government.

Of course there is a weakness in the present situation, in that forcing a double dissolution may be rather attractive to minority groups at particular times. A double dissolution reduces the quota required for the election of a senator under the Senate proportional representation method of voting. Because of this, certain groups might have more of their representatives elected, or else some who might not otherwise survive could find themselves hanging on.

One possible way of combating this potential difficulty would be a constitutional change providing for a joint sitting of both Houses of Parliament, instead of a double dissolution, in circumstances where there is a persistent blockage of legislation by the Senate. Such a change would add a further useful improvement to the working, accountability and representativeness of our parliamentary processes.

But constitutional alterations are, of course, daunting undertakings, and experience is against major constitutional reform being achieved by referenda. Thus, this evolutionary process within the Senate is probably the community's best opportunity for change for the better. The modest constitutional alterations I mentioned are worth a try but only if bipartisan support is available or, better still, all elected parties to the parliamentary system endorse them—a difficult proposition in our adversarial political culture. Nor does inquiry, communication and education offer much hope of advance on past experience. Since the events of 1975 we have had six sessions of the Australian Constitutional Convention between 1973 and 1985; the Constitutional Commission between 1985 and 1988; the Constitutional Centenary Conference of 1991; and innumerable academic convocations, from which there has been a prodigious outpouring of creative thought on this very issue and associated matters. My impression is that for the most part the rest of the community, including the bulk of the Parliament, have been uninfluenced by the process. With a stock of other constitutional 'good ideas' from the Royal Commission on the Constitution 1927 to 1929, the Convention of the Commonwealth and State Parliamentary Representatives of 1942, and the joint Parliamentary Committee on Constitutional Review 1956 to 1959 long gathering dust, the more recent worthy reviews look destined to join them. A shame, as these various changes also have the potential to reduce those instances where the governor-general's reserve powers might be invoked.

On to the Republic?

In the debate about Australia's constitutional future, any fair-minded person might ask themselves, what is 'broke' in our constitutional arrangements, that requires republicanism to fix it? The predominant objective of the republican movement is to eliminate reference to the Crown in the Constitution and with that to change the title of the head of State from Governor-General to President. In this, it seems to me as if we are being asked to hand over our old car so that it can be taken away and given a fresh coat of duco and a new brand name—all preliminary to having it sold back to us as if somehow improved. For my part I can see no point in embarking on a spirited, time-consuming, resource-hungry hard-sell campaign to enable a bit of tarting up of a vehicle which not only do we already own but performs quite effectively. This country is not held in thrall to some foreign potentate because of provision for the Crown in the Constitution. If we became a republic at midnight tonight, merely changing the title of Governor-General to President, then when we rose tomorrow morning we would notice not a whit of difference in either the way we live or in the manner in which our public affairs are administered. The only alterations would be in symbols, none of which would be particularly apparent or offer any material or tangible advantage in our day-to-day life. Australia has as much independence as any other country in the world; indeed, it is a freer, more open, tolerant, liberal democracy, than just about any other country in the world.

The *Australia Act 1987* removed the last vestiges of imperial legislative authority, as once enacted by the Parliament of Great Britain. Prior to this, Britain anomalously had over-riding legislative authority in certain matters. These matters, more properly, should have been determined by Australia as an independent nation. Any powers which had rested within the Parliament of the United Kingdom to make laws having effect in Australia—appeals to the Privy Council from the Australian States; the extraordinary practice, hitherto, of State governors being appointed by the Queen on the advice of her ministers of her United Kingdom Government, following advice from the relevant State premier; and the power of the Queen to disallow State laws—were all ended by that Act. With the termination of these anachronistic provisions, the position of Australia as an independent and sovereign nation was consolidated.

But as those provisions had always been more phantom than real, their elimination would seem to fit into the category of 'nit-picking'. For as the eminent people, including Gough Whitlam, who compiled the *Final Report of the Constitutional Commission* have stated:

> It is clear . . . that at some time between 1926 and the end of World
> War II Australia had achieved full independence as a sovereign state of
> the world. The British Government ceased to have any responsibility in
> relation to matters coming within the area of responsibility of the
> Federal Government and Parliament.[21]

In my seven years as Governor-General neither the Queen nor anyone at the Palace contacted me, nor sought to reach me through any other means, to advise me or influence me in what I was doing in the discharge of my duties as Governor-General. Australia's right to attend to its own affairs independently was meticulously respected. The periodic contact between Government House at Yarralumla and Buckingham Palace in no way derogates from our national independence. Even in the matter of awards, those made under the Order of Australia are by instrument signed by the governor-general. The awards are invested on the recipients by the State governors in their State capitals and by the governor-general in Canberra.

The letters of credence of ambassadors from foreign countries, taking up appointment in Australia, are formally passed on to the palace once the ambassadors' credentials have been presented by the governor-general. Requests for royal patronage and the use of the 'Royal' prefix by various institutions are a matter for the sovereign to determine and are sent on to the Palace for appropriate attention. The governor-general compiles a periodic dispatch to the Queen, as a courtesy. Although there is no formal requirement to do this, these reports summarise various developments in the country and are aimed at keeping the sovereign up to date on events here. I personally found this task, engaged in about every quarter, most satisfying. In the isolation of Yarralumla it was the only real opportunity I had to frankly examine and comment on the important developments and *personae* in Australian public life. This chore, so happily embarked upon by me on each occasion, in no way diminished our sovereign independence as a nation.

The struggle for republicanism, in addition to seeming such a huge task for so little return, has the capacity to wound the community. On the evidence available, moreover, it is apparent that the republican activists are more enthusiastic about the prospects of their cause than is justified by available, concrete evidence. Public opinion polls show that support for a republic waxes and wanes, and has done so over a long period. Not only has the recorded public level of support varied greatly over time, it also varies between different polling organisations. There is also notable variation and confusion in the way questions are framed, some being quite leading and others plainly misleading.[22]

Analytic work by Professor Murray Goot meanwhile demolishes the assertion that demographic changes favour the republican cause:

> If demographic factors—generational change plus European and now
> Asian immigration—were the principal forces shifting public opinion,
> we would expect the polls to show a clear and continuing trend in that
> direction, from the 1960s to the 1990s. On the whole, however, they do
> not . . . the level of support for a republic in the late 1980s was not
> appreciably greater than in the mid-1970s or late 1960s.[23]

Interestingly, pro-republican sentiment rose with the election of the Whitlam Labor Government, to 41 per cent in 1973, and slumped with the fall of that government, to 28 per cent in 1975. Goot pungently observes:

> It was almost as if conservative voters had suddenly realised that if the Queen's representative could 'save' Australia from a 'bad' Labor Government—perhaps from any Labor Government—then the monarchy and its vice-regal representative in Australia was worth keeping.[24]

The campaign to achieve a republic has many difficulties with which to contend, not least of them being the problem of carrying a referendum or referenda. Since Federation there have been forty-two proposals to alter the Constitution put by referendum; with the addition of another two seeking endorsement of conscription for overseas war service during World War I, in all forty-four referenda. Of these, only eight have succeeded. Where there has been substantial opposition to a referendum proposal, that proposal seems always to have failed. As well, minority opposition cleverly presented and perhaps not terribly punctilious about facts can prevail, even when there has been combined support for an issue by the two major party groupings.

Then there is the ambit cover of the referendum proposal. One presumes that those seeking this change would wish to avoid a ridiculous result where the nation becomes a republic while the States retain their monarchical constitutions. The thought of my being a republican Australian but a monarchical Queenslander fills me with dread, but that is the way matters could end. The referendum proposition should accordingly include a proposal to alter the constitutions of the States to accord with any changed Australian Constitution, although this would of course open up several additional battlefields. The States, following the Australia Act 1956, cannot legislate to abolish their Governor. They either hold a referendum or there is a national referendum determining the future of the governors of the states as vice-regal representatives. There is another trap in this. On one view, section 128 of the Constitution would require a majority of votes in all the States as well as overall for this to be achieved. Such an outcome was achieved in respect of only five of the twenty-three propositions put to the electorate as referenda since World War II. The first, in 1946, was popular because it proposed the Commonwealth Government take over the payment of social service benefits. There was all-party support in 1967 for a proposition that the national government make laws in regard to Aborigines. Then in 1977, there was all-party support for propositions (a) to prevent the abuse by State governments of their power to appoint casual vacancies in the Senate following scandalous conduct in this sphere by the Queensland and New South Wales governments slightly earlier; (b) to allow residents of territories of Australia to vote in referenda; (c) to impose a retiring age for judges after some public controversy on the matter beforehand. The all-party support for these four referenda explains why they were carried successfully. The case for a republic has not and will not attract overwhelming, popular support, as those earlier propositions did; certainly all-party backing is unlikely. As a case to be put before the electorate, both difficult to justify and of uncertain benefit, it would prove to be even less appealing than those eighteen referenda propositions which were rejected soundly in a majority of States since 1945.

Perhaps that reading of section 128 of the Constitution which concludes that a majority of votes in all States as well as an overall majority would be necessary to create the Republic of Australia is erroneous. Regardless of whether this is so or not, I would hazard a political judgment that the referendum would have to be carried in all States to be at all credible. There are significant barriers to this: the proposed change would firstly be a huge jolt to large numbers in the community; then, parochial attitudes would cause some States to resent others trying to impose their preferences on them. I would go further and argue that a bare majority vote in all States would not be sufficient to comfortably bed down such a change. To have 40 per cent plus of the electorate alienated on such a fundamental change would create a lot of division in the community, all for the purposes of erecting and grasping nothing more than a symbol.

As if the foregoing is not enough to grapple with, imagine the question of wording the referendum proposal. On one view it can be constructed simply enough—a proposal to delete references to the Queen and Governor-General and replace them with the term President. In other words, after a long and bruising dispute that fissured the community, we would go on as before but for a change of name. On another, and I suspect better view, even to achieve as little as this would require a more complexly constructed presentation. It should be considered, moreover, that it is not just the framing of the question which voters would be required to respond to at the referendum, but the case presented to them beforehand in support of change, including the description of the principles under which the president would function in office, as well as his practical duties. If he is not to be bound, as the governor-general is, to act on the advice of his responsible ministers, these would have to be restricted in some substantial manner. The Constitution as now drafted provides extraordinary black letter law powers for the office of Governor-General, but these are curbed in practice by the manner of a governor-general's appointment and the enforceable requirement, not just a convention, that actions taken should be on the advice of his responsible ministers. The sanction is withdrawal of the commission of a fractious governor-general.

Once a president is chosen by some process of election such as ballot by both Houses of the Parliament or popular vote of the electorate as a whole, the independence of that office would grow. Meanwhile, those who believe that a president elected by both

Houses of Parliament would attract nominations from the 'best' people in the community, need to be reminded of the adversarial structure of our political system. The hectoring style of so many Senate committee hearings is illustrative of the sort of grinding and very personal inquisition to which a nominee could be subjected. The process here, in Australia, would make the Supreme Court confirmation hearings of the USA Senate, such as in the cases of Dinks and Hill, look like a suburban manse morning tea party. The prospect of such an experience at the hands of tough, partisan politicians would discourage all but the most stout-hearted. If the office is non-executive, the independence which the ballot nonetheless would provide is almost certainly going to ensure more frequent clashes between the office of president and the government. In those circumstances, an active, populist president who is strong on appealing 'vision' but weak on the practical implications or means of implementing his ideas, could become a first-class nuisance to a government which was seriously endeavouring to implement different, but sensible and workable proposals. Conflict of this sort would not be in the public interest.

A non-executive president elected by Parliament might quickly prove to be an instinctive populist politician by nature, even though the person may never have been formally involved with political parties before. This sort of person might then build up a personal constituency among members of the Parliament of sufficient strength, say in excess of 40 per cent of members, so that, in spite of his adopting tactics which obstruct the proper processes of government, the government could do nothing effective to remove that person. The Opposition might well incite such conduct, seeing itself as the beneficiary of such tactics. This prospect could be curbed, perhaps, by the insertion of a suitable provision defining the office bearer's obligations to act according to the instructions of the responsible ministers. Note that the operative word is 'curbed', not 'prevented'. If this president has a wayward nature and does not follow his ministers' advice punctiliously once in office but has ensconced himself within the sort of parliamentary protection mentioned, who makes the decision he has exceeded the limits of his office? More importantly, how is any such decision enforced, in particular if the president is elected by a minimum vote of say 60 per cent of the Parliament, the preferred option of the Keating Government? One can only presume the same size vote will be required to undo the appointment. The more power given to people the more they want to use it, power being the extraordinary stimulant that it is. The simple option of the non-executive president to one side, there are also proposals for popularly elected presidents; and this for the public is the *sine qua non* for endorsing the process. But before any sort of public endorsement is even conceivable, the role and functions of this or any other form of presidential office will have to be detailed to the electorate in ways so far not even attempted. Should that finally be undertaken, the opportunity for sowing confusion in the collective mind of the electorate would be at a premium for opponents of the proposal.

I would expect the Australian electorate in its canny way would want the ambit of change clearly defined and drafted into the Constitution. It might be suggested that a provision could be made in the proposed constitutional change which would allow Parliament to define this matter more precisely. I would counsel the public against entrusting politicians, including the greater number not in Parliament, with the disposition of too much authority over their rights—some politicians can prove thriftless trustees at times. Australians should demand a constitutional guarantee that any elaboration of executive power occurs only on the will of the people through a referendum. Questions about any presidential executive power, or the complete absence of it, should the office be restricted to a ceremonial role, will have to be settled early. The installation of an executive president would require specific alterations to the functions and authority of the Houses of Parliament, and before that, to the Constitution, adding further to the complexity of the referendum. The process of a national election and the resources and organisation required for such an undertaking would put the choice of the candidate for president into the machinery of the established parties. In practical terms, the office will be controlled by the people who control those organisations.

More to the point, a presidential system based on a national election to the office of Head of State will result in more, not less, friction in our system of political government. Co-operation between our political parties is not terribly good. In a myriad ways, our culture seeks to resolve dispute by assigning adversarial roles and providing a forum for combat; while this has the potential to resolve conflict, it can also too often manufacture differences. Parliament is merely among the more obvious of such processes in our society. A national election could frequently lead to a president with an affiliation to a political group totally different to that in control of the Houses of Parliament. Since World War II there have been four occasions, 1954, 1961, 1969 and 1990, when the party elected to government, with a majority of Federal divisions to its credit, had a lesser national vote than that obtained by the party relegated to Opposition. It is reasonable to anticipate that this would happen more frequently in a presidential system, especially where a strong national campaign was successfully mobilised behind a 'charismatic' presidential candidate by one party while strong local campaigns gave control of the Houses of Parliament to an opposing party. It could even transpire that the presidency goes one way, the House of Representatives is in control of another party, and the Senate divides between several interests. All of this could convert Parliament into a bed of indiscipline and unpredictability. For us to create a structure that allows this to happen will also be to create a mess for posterity.

At the time of the 1975 convulsion, and for some time after, many people demanded an Australian republic. They claimed what occurred would not have happened in a republic where Australians controlled their own destiny, conveniently ignoring the fact the Governor-General who acted decisively then was an Australian, hand-picked by the Labor Government of the time, only accepting the position after much persuasion by the man he would later sack. Now I do not pretend I understand this view about the sanctuary and comfort which an Australian representative occupying the position of Head of State would guarantee, so long as the office is dubbed President instead of Governor-General. On many occasions during the 1975 campaign Whitlam declared that if there had been a royal at Yarralumla that person would be too steeped in the traditions, too deeply committed to the conventions, to allow what happened to occur. The eloquence of the case was put thus:

> It is certain that, like the Queen, he [Prince Charles] would
> scrupulously act on the advice of his ministers who had the confidence of
> the House of Representatives. He [Prince Charles] would realise that if
> the monarch or the heir to the throne were to act as Sir John Kerr did, it
> would be the end of the monarchy.[25]

This comment seems to me to be a compelling case for keeping the connection with the Crown in the Constitution. Perhaps, to speculate further, the logic here also implies a succession of royals occupying the official residence at Yarralumla. According to such views a prime minister would be confident that the vice-regal representative 'would scrupulously act on the advice of his ministers'! It may have been this touching faith in the probity and fundamental decency of the royals which inspired the Labor Party to humbly petition the Queen in 1975 requesting she act to restore the Labor Party to government. The initiative was surprising to some, as Professor G. Sawer commented:

> The petitions to the Queen asking her to give direction to Sir John Kerr
> as to his exercise of the power to dismiss Ministers on 11 November
> 1975 were . . . futile as well as demeaning to Australia; on that matter
> the Queen had no power to give any such directions.[26]

The other symbol which seems to cause consternation to some is the national flag. I can see no compelling reason why we should change what we have. It has stood the test of time. Our people warmly respond to it. It has meaning for us, and nor do I mind the Union Jack in one corner of it. It symbolises part of our history, a valuable and fundamental past we should not try to escape or deny and which continues to enrich the present for us. My great worry is, once one party in government carries out a wholesale redesign of this emblem, the next party to enter government could reverse that decision or bring in an altogether new format. There is the danger then of periodic changes to the national flag according to fashion, with any one design having a short shelf life. One of our most important national symbols could become as disposable as an old tissue box and lose all national respect into the bargain. It is said that no-one other than an Australian instantly recognises our flag as our national emblem, to which there may be some truth. But my view is that it is not the design of the flag that causes this, but that we are not large and powerful enough to command that sort of international attention which would focus attention on our national symbols anyway. Most other lesser world powers have exactly the same experience—the test of this is to collect a brochure of the flags of the world and see how many you can identify. One thing is for certain, politicians will attempt to change the flag at great peril to their careers.

I do not consider that my sense of being a proud Australian nationalist, confident of our independence and of our ability to define further our Australian way of doing things, of refining our own culture, has been compromised in any way because of the monarchal provisions in our Constitution. I do not feel those values of mine were in any way diminished on the occasions when I declared my fealty to the Queen in the chamber of the House of Representatives, according to required practice—not after my initial election nor my subsequent eleven re-elections to that House. And nor did I have any such problems on the six occasions I accepted my commissions as a Minister of the Crown from the Queen's representative at Yarralumla. I might wryly add I did not see any of my colleagues, who are now declared republicans, fuming with any sort of rebellious feeling when they went through this process of solemnly declaring faithful service to our sovereign. Finally, my pride in the national independence of this country was in no way diluted when, once more, I declared that fealty in the Senate Chamber on 17 February 1989 becoming the twenty-first governor-general and the seventh Australian-born governor-general of Australia.

I am obviously not a militant republican. Neither am I a deferential royalist. I daresay a republic will come one day, but of its accord. Let it evolve. We should not waste time and energies trying to force-deliver it for there is a real risk that rough handling will only deform what we would otherwise want to be as whole and healthy as possible. If a republic is what is really desired then it will not be achieved by tactics which can only create political polarisation on the issue. Unless the coalition parties can be wooed to support the objective, it has virtually no chance of succeeding, for the electorate is likely to become confused and badly fragmented by anything other than bipartisan support.

PART VIII

THE ROAD HOME — THE LAST JOURNEY

An Epilogue

At midnight, 15 February 1996 I was transformed into a pumpkin, as it were. On the morning of the next day, no longer a public figure, I climbed into a RAAF VIP aircraft of 34 squadron for the final time to make the last significant journey in my life—to home, a private citizen at last. But on that day, I returned to a very different home to the one in which I had started out. My experience of life has seen me pass through a succession of destinations and changes—change being, paradoxically, the constant experience down the years. I have stopped at various points along the way, but not ever retreated, before moving forward once again on the basis of my evolving beliefs. I often agonised over the values I held at a particular period and the growing recognition that in some of these I was wrong. But it was always a case of going on, of developing and refining my values and political commitment.

I started as a firmly committed Democratic Socialist, subject to some pronounced neo-Marxist tendencies. The overarching role of government as an instrument for the transformation of society, providing freedom, justice and security was a constant: but, slowly, there was an awakening, in the manner of fresh growth opening up on old wood. The perfectibility of humankind was looking less certain, there was less confidence that a different economic superstructure would create liberty and generate love and co-operation between humans in some hitherto unparalleled way. My years in responsible positions in public life had been gradually teaching me not to expect too much from the crooked timber of humanity and to be cautious about the natural tendencies of political government, which are to aggregate more power to itself, to limit access to information and to become remote and often unresponsive to public expectations.

The period of absolute certainties was being edged out by healthy doubts, a consciousness of the seeming absurdity of the human condition, and positive scepticism about life and its meaning, particularly its ultimate objectives. Grand master plans for our salvation once inspired me. Now they worried me. There was no comprehensive new age to be achieved in one person's lifetime by demolishing wholesale what we had and replacing it with a completely new economic structure, expecting that this would lead to new and wholly desirable social and political values. Such a path was paved with the self-interest of autocrats and it ended in inefficiency and unfreedom. If the choice is between freedom or egalitarianism, better freedom; but there are choices to be made between these and combining elements of both, the trick being to find the balance. Within this overall context it is as well to recall Kant's observation:

> 'To yield to every whim of curiosity, and to allow our passion for inquiry to be restrained by nothing but the limits of our ability, this shows an eagerness of mind not unbecoming to scholarship. But it is wisdom that has the merit of selecting, from among the innumerable problems which present themselves, those whose solution is important to mankind.'[1]

The principles of sharing and co-operation, of replacing exploitative capitalists with friendly government industries had understandable appeal during the excesses of the industrial revolution and the Great Depression of the thirties, for instance. In the post-war period such principles became less and less attractive as capitalism's human face became more agreeable and community prosperity burgeoned in an historically incomparable way, especially in the developed world. This experience was associated with vastly improving discretionary spending power for ordinary people. More and more people wanted a greater say over how they spent their incomes, and for government to have less involvement in the process.

In these circumstances I progressed from a belief in Democratic Socialism to acquire a greater faith in social democracy. Government still had an important role as an instrument of social, political and economic change—a belief I retain to this day—but the emphasis on government enterprise was withering rapidly. I am no longer the person for the 'big picture' policy response from government, designed to fix all of society's flaws. I retain a profound commitment to society, a deep belief that the role of government is to assist in establishing the conditions in which people can be free and independent and society itself secure while striving for greater material prosperity and an improved quality of life, including in the built and natural environments. This sense of community duty is tempered by a recognition that great social advances are best made according to pragmatic, empirical responses, and require the sound underpinning of a well-managed economy; moreover, that government should not presume its role is to respond to every, or even most, of the consequences of the everyday adversities which affect us as individuals or social groupings. The experience of some degree of adversity is not necessarily a bad thing for it can better shape our character. Too much public assistance can lead to undesirable levels of personal dependency and weaken our capacity for initiative and resourcefulness, important qualities to foster in the development of all who aspire to greater personal freedom.

The effects of increasing globalisation of business enterprises, of foot-loose firms and skilled employees each prepared to quickly move elsewhere according to whether they found national tax policies favourable or not, the inescapable need to impose adequately disciplined national economic management or risk losing control of the value of the nation's currency, led me to eventually recognise that external influences would mean further substantial limits on the role and size of government. Clearly our national sovereignty, in the sense of the degree of control we had over our economic situation, was being circumscribed by globalisation.

A further mistake we have made in the past is to contrast the levels of government spending and revenue raising in Australia with those in Europe and conclude there is ample room to easily increase these levels when, in fact, we should have been making the comparison with our main competitors, who are in the Asia–Pacific region, where those levels are lower than Australia's. On the basis of that comparison our options become somewhat restricted, as the government has acknowledged by a number of its actions.[2] Such a recognition will present agonising dilemmas for social reformers and compel priority setting, I would hope, according to genuine personal and community need at the expense of certain forms of middle class welfarism. This of course spells the end to notions of the comprehensive welfare state. It will not be affordable, practically, under these external pressures. This unaffordability has been implicitly acknowledged with the stated objectives of the Hawke and Keating governments to markedly reduce the level of government spending as a proportion of GDP.

It has become evident to me that the time for rigid doctrinaire beliefs is spent. Pragmatism has to reign, but not pragmatism devoid of humanity. It is the human condition ultimately which determines whether our system is a desirable and satisfactory one or not. Efficiency, productivity, profitability and personal reward are important considerations in this newest of humanity's ages. But so too is the fair distribution of those rewards, the degree of social justice available to people, and a common concern that our social casualties should have some share in the community wealth.

Age and experience have taught me to be selective and more modest in the social goals I should pursue. Most of all I have learnt the most important attribute we have in our community, which flourishes in genuine liberal societies, is the unpredictability of humans. The community may be pulled in contrary directions by our individualism, which often presents impossible challenges, thank goodness, to those who want to comprehensively plan and order our lifestyles and engineer predictable outcomes as they lead us over the threshold of a new, grey age of conformity. I prefer to worship plurality, the right to be different, to succeed according to individual merit and choice, but to retain a substantial sense of community obligation so that the principle by which our society functions is not one based on the survival of the richest and the most powerful. It remains an incontestable truism for me: to some degree all of us (to a large degree for me) are our brothers' and sisters' keepers—that is, we have a duty of care towards others. The best outcome for our society will not come from some revelatory vision based on a universal truth, whether described in theological or ideological terms. Rather it will be achieved by society, through individual and community efforts, in the pursuit of many different, smaller but important truths which do not overwhelm and inhibit people.

I recognise that more than anything my values have been those of a secular, liberal humanist; above all else, it has been these values which have been constants in my belief system, through the changes I have undergone and which have underpinned my behaviour and actions. Secular, because I believe not in things ordained by a higher power but in the exercise of free will, and in that restless quest for knowledge which recognises that there is no such thing as absolute truth. That we must strive to try to find truth but that we will only do that through reason, observation, and error. Human understanding, like human beings more generally, is flawed and we cannot avoid error, but we should try to avoid fault as much as possible and by our efforts lead a better life based on improved knowledge and a demonstrated sense of community responsibility.

Even the best scientific theories are approximations to truth and periodically have to be restructured in the light of new facts. Liberal, because of my commitment to tolerance, a deep belief in the right of people to be different, of the importance of freedom—but that kind of tolerance which does not necessarily mean personal approval of one form of behaviour among others. A humanist, because of my great confidence in human beings, in their unique capacity among all life forms for being moral, for leading a good and noble life, for being committed to social justice among their peers. Sharing a faith in the latter, I believe in the principle of equality of opportunity, which is not the same as committing oneself to equal outcomes. For instance, everyone has the right to seek admission to a university but only those who have demonstrated an ability to capably pursue studies there should be allowed to enrol, and no-one should be allowed to graduate who has not performed up to standard in those studies. Thus it is with life's other pursuits.

Life is full of opportunities. If we apply our reason and take advantage of those which we are capable of handling, then we make our own life much more fulfilling. Society should provide access to means by which people may improve their abilities, so that they can add to the range of opportunities they can handle. It also means we should recognise that happiness and success in life for a well-developed adult is measured more by quality than quantity. The material rewards of consumerism have their place but not at the expense of a well-developed, thoughtful, responsible mind. We should not stop when we have defined our rights, but go on to acknowledge our duties to others, to our community and to the built and natural environment in which we live. That is what I mean when I talk about being a communitarian, not the vacuous nonsense of the new right communitarian movement in America and Europe. This fashion of the moment, somewhat restricted in its appeal because of its intellectual limitations, presumes we can escape the stresses of our modern reality by conjuring up some delusionary return to a form of quasi-feudalistic village life of the distant past. Impractical as it is, the reactionary illusion is only a cover for dreadful social stultification and an oppressively hierarchical way of life.

Our goal should be to try to help people become autonomous agents through the exercise of free will, to be capable of reflective judgment and to act according to moral standards and be responsive to their community obligations. We should strive to live our lives according to well-founded eudemonic principles, working for the nurturing of virtue and honourable and tolerant conduct, an ethic of decent and accountable behaviour towards others, as a community norm. By my standards, that rules out narrow-minded moralising, and bigotry. As is common with all of us, I have made too many mistakes and committed too many venal sins, at moments of human weakness, to ever be able to dress in the cloak of a moraliser. As much as I regret those lesser transgressions, they have not been without some benefit. They have made me more tolerant of others who have erred, as I have done, because they are human. We can always hope to atone. Hermann Hesse puts the point nicely in his novel *Siddhartha* when he says:

> *What I have so far learned from the Samanas [ascetic Indian holy men]*
> *I could have learned more quickly and easily in every inn in a*
> *prostitutes' quarter, amongst the carriers and dice players.*[3]

We have lived through the last fling of the last cycle of an ideology. Opposition to the Vietnam War was its high water mark. In retrospect, garlanded hippies sharing dope and sex in communes were probably the most significant features of a period when a lot of thoughtless nonsense was talked and accepted by too many as wisdom. It was very much a period of protest against an age of abundance, but in which the protesters drew down on the fruits of that prosperity. This was not the Great Depression of the thirties, when high unemployment, general insecurity and considerable impoverishment shaped people's values as a collective experience in reaction to extensive economic hardship. The sixties and seventies, the time of flower power, worry beads and kaftans, was the leading edge of a revolt of a new and distinctive form of individualism. Sartre and Marcuse edged out Marx and Engels. The puritans of the working-class movements of the thirties were overtaken by middle-class hedonists of the sixties. A bourgeois revolt of the younger against the tired bourgeois standards of their parents. A dropout generation repudiating the paternalism of home, school and government.

Labor, then the party of the outsiders, of the socially and politically discontented and alienated in our midst, embraced much of this dissent, attracting many of the discontented to its ranks. The consequence was that these largely better-educated and articulate new recruits with their particular form of middle-class values reshaped aspects of Labor causing it to shift ground, sometimes in dramatic fashion, to coincide more with the image of the good society shared by these people, one which was shaped around their self-interest. This moved Kim Beazley Snr to comment at the time, perhaps a little harshly, with words to the effect, 'Once Labor was led by the cream of the working class. Now it is under the control of the dregs of the middle class'. Thus Labor saw nothing incongruous in introducing free tertiary education and non-means-tested age pensions in spite of the quite evident consequence that this could only be done at the cost of the less well off, the battlers, Labor's traditional heartland. Of course Labor had to, and must continue to, appeal more to the middle class if it wishes to be a contemporarily relevant party with real prospects of becoming a government and of remaining in office. But at the expense of the more needy? I do not believe so. That is why non-means tested child-care allowances are wrong in principle.

Another age has come, swamping the indolence and self-indulgence of the slightly earlier period. This is the time of economic rationalism and free markets. These are all very good as long as they do not overwhelmingly govern our values, as we see happening in too many instances; for the nature of this ideology, sees individuals as solely the masters of their own destiny. The consequence of this allows the human casualties in our system to be ignored, for personal failure is considered by many who would be described as pure market force ideologues as the just and righteous penalty for not succeeding. This has an irresistible attraction for many of the proponents of this sort of view for it converts their self-interested preference for assuming no or little fiscal duty towards these human casualties into high principle. By my reckoning, that is a very non-humanist attitude.

Nonetheless, influences from the sixties and seventies linger. For instance, among today's early middle-aged middle class there are some, usually quite articulate and single-minded, who have a pronounced 'gimme' mentality. Such people display an extraordinary capacity to convert self-interest into national priorities. The old left principle of 'from each according to his means to each according to his needs' has been converted to 'he who hath will get more and he who hath not should pay'. Personal rights, often narrowly conceived, are emphasised at the expense of community duties. The organising mantra of so many during the sixties, 'the end justifies the means', is deeply entrenched in the conduct of many single-issue and single minded pressure groups. Political policy-making proceeds too much on the basis of appeasing the demands and threats of some of these groups. What is regarded in certain quarters as clever political campaigning, merely results in excessive concentration on marginal electorates by political parties, and giving in to minority manipulation and extortion for votes.

All of this leads to a growing sense of neglect, of the alienation from the political processes of a vast number of people. Labor's traditional vote reputedly is rapidly eroding as a reaction to this experience.[4] There is also, according to one recent poll, a surprisingly high level of voting intention uncertainty, even at the polling booth, further evidence of this community decoupling from the established political parties.[5] Disenchantment about the political processes is also notable among the young. As one young HSC student put it to me in late 1995 at a reception for students at Government House, 'None of the political leaders is speaking for us—none of them understands our worries about the future.' Or, as another of the students said it to me, 'There is a debate going on but it is conducted in the terms and experiences of the past. It is not about the present or the future.' This view was vigorously supported by others attending the reception. Little wonder that this view was popular, with unemployment jammed around 8 per cent (which incontestably understates the true level of unemployment because of the definition of work adopted by the Australian Bureau of Statistics in its workforce surveys), and unlikely to go down much. The proportion of the community which is defined as wealthy has grown, but the number of those at the bottom end of the socio-economic scale has grown too, by a much greater percentage than the wealthier. In the meantime there is a squeeze on the middle-class, the 'disappearing middle-class', as the phenomenon has been dubbed, a common enough phenomenon in the rest of the developed world also. It is speculated that many previously in the middle class have fallen into the lower socio-economic category, over-skilled for the tasks they have to do and pushing less skilled people out into unemployment. Today, university degrees are no insurance against their holders having to enter the low-skilled low-paid sectors of the workforce where employment is genuinely wanted. Another ingredient is thus added to the dynamic for social and political alienation in the community. This represents a radical and sudden collapse of long established social structures and requires radical and urgent responses.

The problem before us is not to preserve and foster the work ethic but rather to encourage people to become constructively engaged in our community in ways other than within the conventional notion of the workforce, a place where there are presently no jobs for a great number and where there will be no jobs for many over the whole of their lifetime. The major step in this direction is to replace most of the welfare benefit payments with a national dividend, as it was once called, or guaranteed income as it is often now described, paid in regular instalments. This payment becomes part of taxable income associated with a restructured tax scale, and is taxed away as one earns more income. That is, need is met and the aid provided is means tested, both through the taxation mechanism. It would remunerate important forms of currently unpaid work, like full-time parenting or part or full-time voluntary community work through appropriate agencies for small scale commercial, home-based child care services, and could make much part-time work more acceptably self-supporting. The commendable range of occupational training schemes supported by government would need to be enhanced by adding training for those sorts of activities, for full-time, life-time leisure activities, for the various arts and crafts, for gardening and landscape development, and in other areas too, where there is a prospect of earning some income. The alternative is to watch a large level of unemployment swell to greater dimensions over time and with it all of the dislocation and cost of alienation and social anomie for which the employed workforce has to pay. In the past, the response to those who sought greater government intervention to create jobs for the unemployed was that the only cure was a genuine economic recovery. We have been experiencing sustained, strong economic recovery for nearly two years to the time of writing this and unemployment, as in other developed countries, remains high and intractable.

The success of BHP Steel in becoming more efficient, competitive and profitable, of succeeding to the benefit of our economy and adding to our living standards, is part of the evidence of why this is happening and happening on a broad front in industry. Investment in new technology has netted vast advances in productive efficiency for BHP. Since 1983 the hours worked to produce a tonne of steel have gone down from ten to a little over three, output has increased by nearly 50 per cent, while the workforce has gone down by a commensurate proportion.[6] At the other end of the labour market, the more highly skilled job opportunities are associated with low aggregate labour inputs compared to high capital investment. For instance in 1995 Cathay Pacific Airline was contemplating investing A$110M to establish a flight training centre in Australia which would provide eighty new jobs; a capital to labour ratio of A$1.4M per job! Jobs for the unskilled and semi-skilled are disappearing while those for the skilled, in so many cases, are incredibly expensive to establish.[7]

As those youngsters implied at Government House in late 1995, the dialogue in politics is conducted in terms of a stale, old debate. It is not addressing the problems of their generation and of our future. To fail to respond radically to the radically different nature of unemployment in contemporary conditions is as irresponsible as persevering with the present policies of criminalisation and harsh punishments in response to the problem of illicit drugs. The depressing succession of disclosures from the Wood Royal Commission of Inquiry into the NSW Police Force in 1995 exposed how those policies are not only thoroughly deficient, but have failed. The unedifying images on television and in the newspapers of police, up to very senior commissioned levels, accepting bribes, fraternising socially with criminals, running dead on serious criminal cases for a crooked friend and a handsome fee, taking sexual favours from prostitutes, soliciting child pornography: there seemed no end to the decadence and moral squalor which appeared to have poisoned the standards of that force.

The common factor in most of this sleazy behaviour appeared to be drug money—in a word, greed. Greed is an evil, it was so in the eighties, was again in this case and always has been; greed drives behaviour which recklessly grinds over the decent moral standards of the community. In the meantime, the temptation for criminals and the danger of systematic corruption of officials, represented by drug money could be reduced greatly by the decriminalisation of current illicit drugs, with their supply to addicts being regulated under strict controls. Of course I worry that some may be enticed into hard drug-taking by this seemingly easier access to them. This suggestion has dangers, but I am sure of a modest degree compared to the arrangements of the present system. In the present situation, if someone really wants a supply of hard drugs, there is no difficulty in getting them, provided the purchasing money is available; and the dreadful measures some desperate drug addicts will adopt to get that money are, unfortunately, well known. This illicit trade also of course exposes addicts to lethal consequences from their habits when they are supplied with drugs contaminated with noxious substances or which are over-strength to what they have become used. What stops a greater number of people resorting to hard drugs is not their illicit nature but awareness of the personal consequences of drug-taking, and that comes through a measured drug education programme. That is why the current pilot project in Canberra trialing controlled access to hard drugs for addicts deserves careful support. Similarly, victimless police offences such as gambling and prostitution should be de-criminalised and, only as absolutely necessary for reasons of the public interest, regulated to diminish the tendency towards corruption of officialdom such as that which was exposed in Queensland recently by the Fitzgerald inquiry into the Queensland Police Force.

But the fears of the younger generation about the future are as much to do with confusion and uncertainty as anything else. When I was a young man, if someone then had said to me, 'Do you want to be a good family man?' I would have known exactly what they meant: supporting a wife who remained full time at home, two and a half children, a housing mortgage and paying off a second-hand car. Today, anyone young and thoughtful would have to respond to that question, first with the query, 'Define what you mean by family,' for the notion of family has many variants and presents a complex concept now days.

The single parent family, in particular headed by the mother, is commonplace today. So is the unwed mother who prefers parenting alone to a formal co-habitation with a male, and this preference is no longer the target of vindictive moralising and social ostracism, as it was when I was young. Once society decided to recognise people's rights to lawfully practise homosexuality certain inevitable consequences followed. It is no longer a violation of the law for a couple who are same sex partners to establish a stable, permanent domestic relationship. Many claim this, and others recognise it to be, a family relationship. As a matter of justice homosexuals should be entitled to enter a legal contract similar in its rights for and obligations upon those partners to that available under marriage contracts between heterosexuals. In the matter of child adoption, it is difficult to see how opposition to this right can be sustained logically. It can not be upheld on grounds of fairness. There are already cases of male homosexuals and also of lesbians having established custody rights, in the courts, in the matter of offspring. Lesbian women have conceived and are conceiving through artificial insemination. I have no doubt that some among these people prove poor parents—not because of their sexuality, but as a result of parenting defects also common among some heterosexual parents. Society does not propose seriously that the state should conduct a full-scale intervention to tear those children away from their natural and custodial parents, unless there is neglect or abuse of the siblings, as it would in the case of children in the care and guardianship of heterosexual parents. It is a logical conclusion from these cases that adoption should not be denied merely because of the sexuality of the applicant.

I agonised greatly over this issue and over some time, during my first exposure to it in the International Year of the Child in 1994. I was, in the first instance, deeply shocked. It was a radical proposition, for which I was totally unprepared, so I can understand community anxiety about it. Then, as I reasoned my way through the suggestion I realised it was highly likely that some middle-aged mothers, dissatisfied for whatever causes with a heterosexual association, would enter a lesbian relationship and take their children with them. The only test of their right to hold their children while they are in such a relationship is the same one applied to heterosexual partners: that the child is properly cared for.

These are important issues for they determine the rights of a minority to be treated fairly, consistently and with human respect within our community. They deserve more discussion, but mostly, our opinion leaders shy away from the controversy. Similarly, for those of us who believe, as I do, that we should have the option available of ending our lives with dignity when we feel we have lived long enough, that further living is an unacceptable burden, the present prohibition against voluntary euthanasia is quite unreasonable. It cannot stop someone engaging in voluntary euthanasia, that is suicide, who has soberly and responsibly reasoned their way to this conclusion. What it does is restrict our range of choices to acts of the most violent kinds against ourselves. It would be preferable to have available some small draught or pill, soporific in its effect, capable of inducing a contented passing from this realm of the living.

For many people, especially the young, the uncertainty of the modern age is added to by the effects of post-modernism, of the deconstruction fad. Past generations had forms of established authority to guide and reassure them and heroes to act as role models. In the nature of de-construction, these things are challenged. Authority is assailed for not being flawless or, more likely, for its lack of political correctness and, on similar grounds most often, heroes are toppled as base figures of scorn. For most people this process opens up a vast emptiness in their souls. Our superior courts seemed to be a last bastion for an accepted authority role. Yet many in the public have found themselves confused because of the foolish public statements of some who people the court benches, and this has diminished respect for, and confidence in, those bodies. Many worry at the extent of added authority over parliament (which, unlike the court, is both representative of and accountable to, the public) that the High Court has arrogated to itself by the novel discovery of certain personal rights implied in the Constitution (a discovery which the participants in the various conventions leading to the drafting of the Constitution never conceded). One gathers the impression that what the majority of justices seemed to be propounding in this case, when addressing this matter, was perhaps influenced more by a particular notion of natural justice. Now the principles of that theory are commendable enough in themselves (though not without their intellectual dissenters in the community), but it is difficult to see how they can persuasively create implied rights in the Constitution capable of being accepted by all or most of the community. Such developments would only continue at considerable risk to the reputation and autonomy of that court, and it would only be a matter of time, before the legislature, the parliament, accepted this challenge to its authority as the elected and publicly accountable representative organ of the people. Confirmation hearings concerning the suitability of appointees to this bench, at the very least, would be convened by the law makers and conducted with sufficient robustness, such is the nature of our parliamentary proceedings, that only the stout hearted and, I suspect in too many cases then, the less well equipped for the task would persevere with the humbling experience for the sake of an appointment which offers much status but relatively poor remuneration compared to that enjoyed by the best practitioners at the Bar.

Now, because of these various trends demolishing faith and confidence in our established social symbols, we are increasingly forced to stand alone, to make our own reasoned judgments, to act as free agents in a complex age. That is no bad thing, provided we recognise what is happening and equip ourselves to better handle these new circumstances. This is where those young HSC students I mentioned above come in again. They were clearly alienated from the major political parties which they condemned for not speaking for them and about their concerns. But what should those parties have been saying on their behalf? As strongly as those young people felt on these points, they did not know! What they did know was they felt insecure, challenged and accordingly confused about their future, about the sort of social role model they should adopt for they were treading about in this insubstantial emptiness of the present age. The millenarian 'isms' of my age and earlier generations, ideologies which could, no matter how incorrectly, inspire the young and idealistic with their declared principles of caring, of social co-operation, of working together for something more important than the self, have been de-throned. The influence of the established Christian churches is waning as they encourage more thought and reasoning from their congregations and less blind faith. But for those to whom such an approach is uncongenial or too hard, Christian fundamentalism increasingly fills some of the gap with its clear cut certainties. Through an appeal to emotions, and thoroughly unscientific fictions about human creation and personal destiny, through a willingness to do the thinking and the acting on others' behalfs, fundamentalism recruits those dependent souls who fear the emancipation of real freedom, the freedom to think and act for one's self. But real independence is frightening for many souls, beyond those potential converts to religious simplifications. Perhaps a charismatic populist will emerge, leading some new evangelical political fashion, meeting with a significant degree of popular acclaim, reducing complex social and economic difficulties to absurd simplicities, playing on fears and insecurity, a degree of ignorance and, worst of all, prejudices, to complicate our political processes.

There is no reason why we should presume that Australia would be naturally resistant to the intolerances of a Le Pen influence. Australia is one of the freest, most liberal societies in the world. It is also one of the most compassionate and socially concerned countries on the globe. Yet it was not always so: from the thirties through the fifties ours was a socially narrow-minded society offering a high premium for conformity and intolerant of difference in many areas, particularly in sexual matters. We emerged from these stifling influences only slowly and with much struggle. I still recall fondly the involvement of many people—Don Chipp among the pre-eminent, but I include myself—in the anti-censorship debate in the sixties. One would hope there would not be a relapse to those earlier social conditions, for Australia is now such a refreshingly open-minded society. Yet if one believes that human progress proceeds according to the dialectic, as I do, then it is possible we could lose that hard won, tolerant synthesis established in earlier decades and with which we have lived more or less comfortably ever since. I am confident, nonetheless, that we could preserve these relatively newly-established rights, but only by vigilance and an energetic defence of them.

A serious threat to some of our freedoms has emerged in recent years in the form of increasingly strident, authoritarian demands for new styles of conformity. Emanating from sources loosely and ironically described as 'politically correct', such strictures amount to a form of censorship predicated on the engendering of guilt. There are unfortunately those in the community who believe we are all guilty for the sins and omissions committed by others, even of those of long-departed generations. Relations between the sexes and relations between Aboriginal and non-Aboriginal Australians are two areas which have especially attracted the attention of latter-day guilt merchants. The more we have intimidation of the community by zealots with a penchant for limiting what can be said and thought, the more our freedoms will be eroded. In the end, I would rather have people making ignorant remarks and stating their ill-informed prejudices—on the basis that they are within their rights to do so, but also, more importantly, so that we can identify the sources, nature and proportions of these particular forms of bigotry needing attention. Our response should not be to legislate for enforced muteness on such matters. All that does, in cases of seriously distorted social pathology, is to bottle up ill-informed resentments, which are in themselves likely to generate increasing discontent and disaffection. Our concerns in such cases would be better served by our seeking to persuade the bulk of the community of the evil inherent in such attitudes through public information and enlightened argument.

For instance, like probably the majority of Australians, I am greatly concerned about aspects of the condition of the Aboriginal people. Their initial dispossession from traditional society and lands and their cultural exclusion from so much of contemporary non-Aboriginal society, with the well documented consequences which have followed those effects, worries me greatly. Whenever I have had the opportunity to do so, and there have been numerous such instances in my long public life, I have responded positively to their justifiable needs. I have never done this because I feel guilty, for I have aimed in my conduct towards Aboriginal people to be as blameless and constructive as possible. Similarly, while the behaviour towards our Aborigines by some people of our earlier generations was execrable by our standards, those not responsible should not be accused of guilt for the conduct of others, especially that of the long departed from this world. What motivates me is a sense of responsibility, of duty, care and concern towards my fellow humans, regardless of their race, who are more vulnerable through social disadvantage. While that is a positive response, guilt is a negative, uncreative one with the potential to be socially divisive leading to more differences and conflict rather than reconciliation. Moreover, the politically correct will not admit of the possibility of any causal explanation or remedy other than their own, where they have any.

I accept the case for more spending on aspects of Aboriginal health need, as in certain regular visiting specialist medical services and simple utilities such as clean, potable water where supplies are available. But after visits to quite a number of remote Aboriginal communities I have become convinced that many of the communicable health problems will only be overcome when those communities which have not already done so, come to consistently maintain much better standards of community and personal hygiene and appropriate dietary standards, especially for infants, and effectively do this through their own trained community health workers. This will not be achieved in one generation because the cultural blockages are very powerful. Yet these basic possibilities for positive change are submerged because too many are intimidated by the prospect of being accused of racial intolerance. There is another example. We non-Aboriginal Australians remain silent in the face of dreadful violence by numbers of men living in Aboriginal communities, especially the degrading and violent maltreatment of women and girls, as a result of alcohol abuse. It is clear to me that people with an alcoholic problem have to want to fix that problem themselves, and further that it will only be finally overcome by the exercise of their will and a change of conduct. Aboriginal women know this and are saying these things in places as wide apart as Central Australia and Cape York Peninsula. A sensible policy would see us refusing to indulge the selfish and destructive excesses of some Aboriginal men; by asking these men to take responsibility for their behaviour, we would be doing much to support Aboriginal women.

Far from being another example of white Australians 'oppressing' their black brothers, my argument is that alcoholism is not solely a function of cultural and racial alienation. This problem has a fundamental personal dimension and must be addressed on that basis—in addition to the provision of broader social and economic opportunities for the individuals in question.

It would do much to assist the desirable process of reconciliation between our Aboriginal and non-Aboriginal communities to display equal concern about acute social distress which affects both communities. For instance, there is, very properly, much media concern about Aboriginal deaths in custody. Yet I have not noted equivalent concern reported about non-Aboriginal deaths in custody, in spite of the fact that the Royal Commission Into Aboriginal Deaths in Custody found,

> The work of the Commission has established that Aboriginal people in custody do not die at a greater rate than non-Aboriginal people in custody.[8]

What the Royal Commission also reported, however, was that blacks were grossly over-represented in prisons and that this was 'totally unacceptable'.[9] I am quite certain that if we took a socio-economic profile of our prison populations we would find that non-Aboriginal prisoners from the lower socio-economic groupings in our community are also grossly over-represented in our gaols and that it is among these people that, overwhelmingly, non-Aboriginal deaths in custody are occurring. These people, I am sure, are not over-represented in prisons to the same extent as Aborigines. Nonetheless, the grave social disadvantages they suffer, culminating in gaoling and far too many deaths in custody, also demand the public's disquiet and the government's policy attention. The point is that the nature of our society gravely disadvantages many people, black and white, and that it makes insufficient responses to their deprivation which, in too many cases, causes them to lapse into anti-social conduct. Then, society often punishes those people harshly for what, in many cases, is fundamentally a social disorder.

Ranged against a problem of this order, governments can only offer generic policy responses which are often associated with complex administrative procedures. This can create confusion and misunderstanding, leading to dissatisfaction among the public. Labor, for instance, has in recent times been assailed for losing its 'heartland', with voters, as mentioned earlier, reportedly drifting away from the party they have traditionally supported because the party, they say, has forgotten the 'battlers'. But the hard evidence scarcely supports this view. In practice the Hawke–Keating Labor Governments have been governments of notable social conscience. The social wage they have implemented has benefited the less well-off, making Australia 'a more equal society in 1993–94 than in 1981–82.'[10] It is emphatically clear that Labor's social wage package has been relatively more generous to those lower down the social–economic scale. The fear of unemployment worries a great many, yet there are more people in jobs than ever before and the proportion of the available workforce engaged in work is higher than in the past when unemployment levels were quite minuscule compared to the present. This has been happening in spite of unemployment having stalled at around 8 per cent. There have been radical changes in the workforce patterns, and these have also had the effect of complicating people's understanding of what is happening. There is more growth in employment for females than males, more opportunities becoming available for part-time rather than full-time work; at the same time, the blue collar workforce is contracting while the demand for intellectual skills is growing and teenagers experience low labour marketability. As this proceeds, the trade union movement atrophies, partly because of the notable job growth in the services industries, industries traditionally poorly unionised. More particularly the contraction in the union movement is partly a result of the benefits of the social wage reaching the workforce without involving direct industrial action, and also partly as a consequence of enterprise bargaining where a role for the unions is rapidly diminishing. Remarkably, the trade union movement and succeeding Labor governments co-operated in these developments which diminished the relevance of traditional trade union representation. And thus another one-time anchor of certainty loses its hold.

Meanwhile, our political parties trenchantly assail one another, the decibel levels on Parliament Hill rising to higher and higher ratings as the policy gap between them ever narrows. The Liberals seem politically enfeebled in important ways, but mostly because of too much time in Opposition. They propose little at a time of great policy need and what they do put forward lacks passion or conviction. Labor seems to be riding high and powerfully, but has no reason to feel smug; instead, that party should be earnestly addressing itself to the matter of its role in the future. Labor has spent so long in government that when it returns to opposition it will have to re-invent itself. As Labor has been at the very heart of the establishment of our society as government for thirteen unbroken years, diligently applying itself to making the established system work better and enjoying many outstanding successes in doing so, it can no longer credibly claim to be the radical alternative, the party that challenges the establishment. Labor has been privatising government enterprises rather than adding to them, as its policy on socialisation once would have implied; furthermore, it has pledged that it will reduce the level of government spending to that which applied in the fifties, a period once excoriated by the very same party for its social neglect.

While Labor has become thoroughly pragmatic, and properly so, in more generally managing the country's affairs, it is not a pragmatism devoid of principle. Come as they might from tradition and instinct, these principles accordingly need to be re-burnished and perhaps, in some cases, re-shaped for contemporary needs. This can only be done effectively by thoughtful discussion and creative debate. Labor needs immediately to establish a think tank, quietly working out a clear and relevant definition of what sort of party it is now and what sort of value framework it wants to guide it in the future. If the party does not re-discover itself it is going to lose valuable time in opposition with wasteful internal battles and factional power struggles which may not be notably creative. At its worst the party could lock itself into myths of the past, pretending it can stand still while society rapidly evolves around it: a certain formula for atrophy and irrelevance. Labor would do well to remind itself of Whitlam's noble efforts in the sixties and early seventies when he saved the party from its reckless tendency to self-implosion.

The work of our political parties is, though obviously of great importance, only one element in the making of Australia's fortunes. The improvement of our fortunes also depends on the duty of the community to inform itself on community need, to do so on the basis of fair principles and generally to act according to notions of the common good rather than be motivated by narrow concepts of self-interest, of number one being the winner always. Overall, I am optimistic about our future. We have shown commendable grit and perseverance with radical changes and transformations in our socio-economic system, changes which stand to benefit us, even if there is confusion in many instances about the nature of change and its ends. Similarly, while there have been remarkable changes in the values of society which may have temporarily added to that confusion, Australia remains one of the most liberal societies in the world. Let us stick to the task before us of making the process of change work for the benefit of all. We should not waste time looking back to our earlier years for some imagined golden age. I believe the best years are yet to come, just so long as we work for them intelligently and diligently and with care for our fellow humans.

With thoughts such as these, I eventually made my way along that road to home, the last journey in a long and fulfilling public life. Dallas and I have retired to the country near Ipswich. We have retained our home in the town proper, and we move between the two addresses, for Ipswich is where our hearts are anchored. To a home which is the haven of so many fond memories, of bewitching hours and days as our children grew from infancy to maturity. A home where we constantly rediscovered ourselves as the duties of life moved us from one role to another. This is the place where we were young lovers, then parents, worrying about our children's education. We felt such pride as each achieved professional qualifications, we discovered that the virtues which go to make a good personal life, and the values of tolerance and social concern too, had taken a firm root in their personalities. Then, as our children moved away to make their independent way through life we discovered, living together and closely involved in one another's company in a way not before experienced, that we were mates, and always had shared a deep friendship and a mutual trust incomparably greater than any other relationship either of us had ever experienced. That is what we take into a retirement and it represents personal riches beyond material calculation.

LIST OF ABBREVIATIONS

AFR: *Australian Financial Review*

AGPS: Australian Government Publishing Service

ASRB: Australian Sales Research Bureau Pty Ltd

CUP: Cambridge University Press

DFA: Department of Foreign Affairs

FRUS: Foreign Relations of the United States

MUP: Melbourne University Press

NLA: National Library of Australia

OUP: Oxford University Press

PDR: Parliamentary Debate Reports

RBA: Reserve Bank of Australia

SMH: *Sydney Morning Herald*

UQP: University of Queensland Press

USGPO: United States Government Printing Office

PART I

1. Travelling by train, usually goods wagons, without paying any fare. Common practice during the Great Depression.

2. C. Foster, 'Unemployment and the Australian Recovery', and R. G. Gregory, 'An Overview', in R. G. Gregory & N. G. Butlin, eds, *Recovery from the Depression*, 1st edn, CUP, Sydney, 1988, p. 295 & p. 2.

3. R. Ward, *A Nation for a Continent*, 1st edn, Heinemann Educational Publishers, Melbourne, 1977, p. 163.

4. R. D.Edwards, *Patrick Pearse: The Triumph of Failure*, Gollancz, London, 1977, p. 329.

5. Personal conversation with P. Carlton, Canberra-based journalist and war historian.

6. 'War Notes Recall Our Darkest Time', *SMH*, 7 December 1993.

7. Personal communications from G. Brown, Defence Group, Dept. Parliamentary Library, Canberra, of 28 May 1992; and from the Australian War Memorial, Canberra, of 15 July 1992.

8. Curtin was submissive to MacArthur throughout the war. He acquiesced to the use of the 7th. Div. for a strategically useless attack on Balikpapan in 1945 where Australian casualties were high. He was warned of its pointlessness and the casualties expected by his Australian military chiefs. He did nothing. He was advised by MacArthur that Blamey's operations in New Guinea and Bougainville slightly earlier that year were 'not worth a single Australian life'. They served no strategic purpose. Again he did nothing and casualties were high. See P. Charlton, *Australians at War: War Against Japan 1942–1945*, ch. 5, in particular pp. 138–39, 149–155; *Courier-Mail*, 27 October 1994, 'The Bloody, Unnecessary War' by P. Charlton; *The Australian*, 5 July 1995, 'A Very Junior Partner' by D. Horner.

9. 'The Case of the Corrupt Commissioner', 18 September 1982, and 'Corruption in the Cabinet—and Bribery of a Magistrate', 21 September 1982, *Courier-Mail*.

10. A pseudonym.

11. R. Fitzgerald, *From 1915 to Early 1980s: A History of Queensland*, UQP, St Lucia, 1984, pp. 127–34.

PART II

1. *SMH*, 6 October 1961.

2. G. Souter, *A Company of Heralds*, MUP, Melbourne, 1981, p. 384.

3. J. Stubbs, *Hayden*, Heinemann, Melbourne, 1989, see photograph no. 6 between pp. 82 & 83, captioned, 'Taken by security services …'.

4. A. Dalziel, *Evatt the Enigma*, Lansdowne Press, Melbourne, 1967, pp. 120, 136.

5. P. Crockett, *Evatt: a Life*, OUP, Melbourne, 1993, pp. 221–2.

6. ibid. pp. 163–4.

7. P. Hasluck, *The Government and the People 1942–1945*, Australian War Memorial, Canberra, 1970, p. 742.

8. Crockett, op. cit., pp. 122–7, see *en passant* pp. 119, 131–9; see also B. Muirden, *The Puzzled Patriots*, MUP, Melbourne, 1968; K. Buckley et al., op. cit., p. 203, address to the Evatt Foundation, Sydney, 1993, by Justice R. Meagher.

9. P. Hasluck, op. cit., pp. 732, 736; K. Buckley, et al., *Doc Evatt*, Longman Cheshire, Melbourne, 1994, pp. 132, 177–8.

10. *New Catholic Encyclopaedia*, McGraw Hill, New York, 1967, vol. 14, p. 912.

11. B. A. Santamaria, *The Movement 1941–1960: An Outline*, Campion Press, Melbourne, 1993, p. 33.

12. B. A. Santamaria, *Against the Tide*, OUP, Melbourne, 1981, pp. 141–3.

13. *SMH*, 12 October 1954, 'Dr Evatt Faces His Enemies at Caucus Meeting Tomorrow'.

14. 'Split of '54 a struggle for Labor's soul', *Weekend Australian*, 1–2 October 1994.

15. Personal communication from former Labor MHR for Hindmarsh (SA), Clyde Cameron, 15 May 1994, including an extract from Cameron's diary entry for Caucus meeting Wednesday, 20 October 1954.

16. ibid.

17. Minutes of the Federal Executive ALP, 12 February 1954 to 12 March 1955, NLA, Canberra, Folder S4.

18. Based on conversations with Bob Santamaria and Clyde Cameron as well as correspondence with Cameron.

19. M. Hogan, *The Sectarian Strand*, Penguin, Melbourne, 1987, p. 191.

20. G. Henderson, *Menzies' Child*, Allen & Unwin, Sydney, 1994, p. 77.

21. For a lucid discussion of the evidence of this see G. Gray, 'Social Policy' in S. Prasser, J. R. Nethercote & J. Warhurst (eds), *The Menzies Era*, pp. 211–28.

22. Two notable exceptions were the 'horror budget' of 1951–52 and the 'credit squeeze' of late 1961. In each case corrective action should have been initiated 12 months earlier. Similarly, private consumption levels were high. The shortfall in household saving was offset by foreign investment. More rigorous long-term economic management was eschewed in favour of short-term popularism. It is a shame that the culture of low domestic savings and high consumption has been so deeply embedded in our culture for so long. It makes it hard to change unrealistic community expectations. We lived off other people's savings as investment in the Menzies era. Now we live off other people's lending as debtors, which in many respects is worse.

23. FPLP Caucus Minutes, 3 March 1943, held at NLA, Canberra, reflect Curtin's distress at Calwell's comment:

Dear Mr. Forde,

In view of the accusations made against me by Mr. Calwell, i.e. 'that I will finish up on the other side [the anti-Labor side] leading a National Government', I invite the party either to dissociate itself from the accusation or appoint another leader. Obviously if the charge has a semblance of justification, the party is in an invidious position in entrusting its leadership to a potential traitor.

Yours faithfully,

(sgd.) John Curtin

24. In 1951 Menzies was predicting a maximum of three years 'in which to get ready to defend ourselves ... there is an imminent danger of [war] ...' CPD, House of Representatives, 7 March 1951, p. 78.

25. *SMH*, 30 August 1940; A. W. Martin, *Robert Menzies: a life, 1894–1943*, MUP, Melbourne, 1993, vol. I, pp. 333–4, 237–8.

26. A. W. Martin, ibid., pp. 292–3, 338–43, 325–9, 345–7, 349–53; A. W. Martin & P. Hardy, (eds), *Dark & Hurrying Days: Menzies' 1941 Diary*, NLA, Canberra, 1993, pp. 13, 32, 59, 64–7, 99, 109–10, 112, 119, 140.

27. P. Crockett, *Evatt: A Life*, OUP, Melbourne, 1993, p. 91.

28. 'Cabinet Knew US Base was a Nuclear Target', *SMH*, 1 January 1994.

29. *Daily Telegraph*, 22 March 1963.

30. 'Packer the Power and the Legend', *Australian*, 18 August 1971.

31. 'A Sting for Ming', *Sun-Mirror*, 1 November 1964, reported 'Hayden mildly—but pointedly—observed that Sir Robert was about to undertake his thirteenth defence review'.

32. S. E. Ambrose, *Eisenhower, the President, 1952–1969*, Simon & Schuster, New York, 1st edn, 1984, vol. 2, pp. 208–11, 314–15.

33. ibid., p. 507.

34. B. M. Snedden & M. B. Schedvin, *Billie Snedden: an Unlikely Liberal*, Macmillan, Melbourne, 1990, pp. 109, 112.

35. *Australian Journal of Politics and History*, vol. XIV, no. 1, 1968, p. 3.

36. G. Sawer, *Australian Federal Politics and Law 1901–1929*, MUP, Melbourne, 1972, pp. 91–2.

37. 'Whitlam Pledges to Double Production—Aiming at 6 pc Yearly Growth', *Australian*, 27 November 1972.

38. W. G. Hayden, *The Implications of Democratic Socialism*, Victorian Fabian Society, Melbourne, 1968, as an early personal effort.

39. M. Hogan, *The Sectarian Strand*, pp. 98, 90–5, 251–5.

40. M. A. Jones, *The Australian Welfare State*, 3rd edn, Allen & Unwin, Sydney, 1990, p. 80.

41. *Australian*, 15 June 1983; *Age*, 20 June 1983.

42. A. Reid, *The Gorton Experiment*, Shakespeare Head Press, Sydney, 1971, p. 9.

43. 'I Did It My Way', *Sunday Australian*, 8 August 1971.

44. P. Howson, *The Life of Politics*, Viking Press, Melbourne, 1984, p. 696.

45. ibid., p. 507.

46. *Daily Telegraph*, 2 March 1971; *Bulletin*, 6 March 1971.

47. 'Mr Fraser and the *Bulletin*', *Bulletin*, 13 March 1971; 'Defence Row: P.M., Fraser Accused', *Daily Telegraph*, 5 March 1971.

48. *Sunday Telegraph*, 7 March 1971.

49. PDR House of Representatives, vol. 71, 9 March 1971, p. 680.

50. P. Howson, op. cit., pp. 645–6, 711–12; 'Mr Gorton and Mr McMahon', *Australian*, editorial 11 August 1971; 'Newspapers in the 70s', *Australian*, 16 November 1972. 'Publisher Says Gorton Should Go', *Canberra Times*, 10 August 1971.

51. P. Howson, op. cit., p. 508.

52. ibid., for extensive references, in particular pp. 588–89 on Menzies; 568, 672 on Casey.

53. ibid., p. 703.

54. 'State of Emergency', *Courier-Mail*, 14 July 1971.

55. S. Harris, *Political Football: the Springbok Tour of Australia 1971*, Golden Star Publishers, Melbourne, 1972, pp. 137–9.

56. 'PM's View of His Team: Stir on Report', *SMH*, 25 November 1972.

PART III

1. There was an overall two party preferred swing to Labor of 2.2% giving it a small majority of nine. There were swings against Labor in South Australia and Western Australia and in much of rural Queensland. In Western Australia Labor actually lost Forest and Stirling with Perth and Swan being closely run contests.

2. There was negative quarterly real economic growth in June 1973, June 1974, March 1975 and September 1975. Source: Dept. Parliamentary Library research section, statistical group, supplied October 1992.

3. 'Crean's Dilemma', warning of consequences of not reigning in expenditure: 'a sharp acceleration of inflation and a subsequent return to economic slump', *SMH*, 4 June 1973, editorial.

4. ASRB public opinion poll, *SMH*, 24 December 1973, p. 9.

5. Reserve Bank of Australia, report and financial statements 30 June 1973, see in *passim* p. 40 '... the basic need seems to be for a balanced application of complementary external and fiscal/monetary policies to achieve maximum growth and minimum inflation'.

6. *Australian Economic Review*, 1st qtr 1973 (8 June 1973) pp. 3, 7, 18, 19. ibid.; 2nd qtr 1973 (28 August 1973), Institute of Applied Economic and Social Research, Melbourne.

7. Australian Bureau of Statistics Average Weekly Earnings statistics, June qtr 1975 Ref. N. 6.18, annual change for September and December qtrs 1974 and March qtr 1975 were respectively, 25.3%, 28%, 27.3%.

8. Senate Standing Committee on National Resources report: The replacement of petroleum based fuels by alternative sources of energy, 1979–80, vol. I, AGPS, see pp. 589–90, Senator Tait & Mr J. Stone, Secretary of the Treasury, 16 November 1979, and report of Committee, Parliamentary Paper No. 222/1980, pp. 99–100.

9. 'Between December 1972 and December 1973 the effective Australian exchange rate appreciated by 20 per cent and between December 1973 and December 1974 it depreciated by approximately 15 per cent. The magnitude and frequency of exchange rate changes during this period were unmatched in Australian postwar experience.' Source: R. G. Gregory & L. D. Martin, 'An Analysis of Relationships Between Import Flows to Australia and Recent Exchange Rate and Tariff Changes', *Economic Record*, March 1976, vol. 52, no. 137.

10. See Industries Assistance Commission, annual reports, 1974–75, Ch.2, pp.15–20; 1975–76, Ch. 2 & App. 2.4—note in particular Ch. 2 Table 2 at p. 26 on the general competitiveness of the Australian import-competing sector disclosing a 14% reduction in competitiveness between 1971–72 and 1975–76.

11. Generally on motor vehicle industry see Industries Assistance Commission reports Motor Vehicles—Import Restrictions, 31 October 1975; Passenger Motor Vehicles and Components—Post–1984 Assistance Arrangements, 24 June 1981 in particular Ch. 5 and Table A5.5.

12. Reserve Bank of Australia, report and financial statements 30 June1975, at p. 43 '... in the September quarter 1974, money supply declined ... financial conditions became excessively tight ... Demand and output fell sharply and unemployment rose at a pace much more rapid than most had expected ... by late September, the emergence of clear signs that the intended monetary tightness was developing in the direction of substantial financial disturbances.'; op. cit. for 30 June 1976, graphs at pp. 17 & 35.

13. Budget submission No. 1245 was presented in a curious and unclear way. It outlined a proposal to cut spending by $600 million, and increase net revenue by $400 million. The presentation rolled on as though smoothly—when in fact it was disjointed—to point out that there was a domestic surplus of nearly $400 million already proposed, as though this followed after the cuts and revenue increases. In fact the the two propositions were sequential and aggregated a domestic surplus of $1400 million, equal to 2.2% GDP.

14. In fact, early statistics disclosed that nearly 90% of the beneficiaries were of mature age. More recent statistics reveal that the proportion of mature age female recipients has risen to 97 per cent, with an average age of thirty-three years. Moreover, 50% of recipients go off the benefit

within twelve months of first receiving it and 80% go off it within three years. Statistics supplied in private communications from Minister for Family Services Senator Rosemary Crowley dated 20 April 1995 and from Minister for Social Security Peter Baldwin dated 27 June 1995. Moreover, nearly 50 per cent of recipients go off the benefit within two years of receiving it and three out of four receive it for less than five years. Incidentally, the teenage birth rate from the late 1980s into the 1990s 'has been lower than any other period since records began in 1921'.

15. According to Mr Race Matthews, at the time private secretary to Whitlam as Leader of the Opposition, the commitment to the AAP was written into a speech for Whitlam by Matthews and another staffer, Dick Hall, in 1971 or 1972. It was the first Caucus had heard of the proposal.

16. The report mentions the following:
- Social Welfare Commission—11 representatives
- Working Party on Social Welfare Manpower—12 representatives
- Commonwealth Committee of Inquiry into Poverty—5 representatives
- National Superannuation Committee of Inquiry—3 representatives
- Committee of Inquiry into Rehabilitation and Compensation—3 representatives
- Advisory Council of Social Security and Welfare—11 representatives
- Medical Fees Tribunal—3 representatives
- Working Party on Homeless Men and Women—9 representatives

17. ASRB opinion poll: 'Nearly three-quarters [of people asked whether the government was trying to do too many things at once] either agreed strongly or in part!', *SMH*, 24 December 1973.

18. Yvonne Preston, 'Women and Children Last—Hayden and Beazley Back Away from Child Care', *National Times*, 29 July–3 August 1974, No. 182, p. 1.

19. R. B. Scotton & C. R. Macdonald, 'The Making of Medibank', unpublished manuscript, 1992.

20. ibid., p. 7.

21. ibid., pp. 79–80, 96, 105–6, 113–14, 116–32, 181, 190–5.

22. The AMA established a $1m 'Freedom Fund' with which to bankroll this disinformation campaign.

23. Refers to Somerset Maugham's 'seedy' characters in his short story 'Rain'.

24. See *Canberra Times*, 28 November 1979 editorial on this organised campaign, 'Medibank Revived' viz. '... Mr Hayden, who as Minister for Social Security was subjected by elements in the medical fraternity to one of the most vicious campaigns of denigration any contemporary politician has had to face'.

25. Discussion in PM's office night of 28 November 1973. What enthusiasts for this project kept losing sight of was that the finances involved in any such takeover would be quite large, would require legislative authority, hence would be subject to parliamentary scrutiny; very properly, I might add. This would have demolished the negotiating requirement for 'secrecy' proposed by the private sector 'spotter' who stood to do handsomely out of the deal on the basis of his proposals. There were a whole range of other valid objections to the project.

26. *SMH*, 28 April 1985.

27. 'Victoria Faces $50M Loss', article led: 'Victoria will lose at least $50 million of desperately needed Commonwealth cash for hospitals unless there is a dramatic political cave-in', *Age*, 17 June 1975, 'Insight' report, p. 1.

28. Program Performance Statements 1992–93, Health, Housing and Community Services Portfolio, Portfolio Budget Related Paper No. 9, 8A, pp. 95–6, Percentage of GP services direct billed is 71.9%, and 62.8% of all services; J. Deeble, The Health Proposals, paper delivered at the Monash University 'Fightback' conference, 1993, p. 6, 'over-schedule billing for non-cardholders is now only 7% of schedule fees'.

29. In 1991 Australia spent 8.6% of GDP on health. Canada spent 10% while in the USA, with a thoroughly unsatisfactory system similar to what the AMA is constantly seeking for Australia, it

was 13.4%. Source: *World Competitiveness Report 1992*, World Economic Forum, Switzerland, 1992, pp. 44–5. Long-run forecasts suggest health expenditure in the USA will exceed 20% of GDP in the next decade and on present trends rise to one-third of GDP by 2030; quoted in J. Richardson, 'Medicare: Policy Issues and Options', *Australian Economic Review*, 2nd qtr., 1994, p. 78.

30. Communication from A. S. Cole, Secretary, Dept. of Health, Housing, Local Government & Community Services, 26 July 1993; P. Saunders (quoting 1987 OECD report) in *Welfare & Inequality: National and International Perspectives on the Australian Welfare State*, CUP, Melbourne, 1994, p. 123, ' ... international evidence suggests that the higher the share of a nation's health bill which is paid by government, the lower the total cost of health care expressed as a proportion of GDP: for example, one OECD study has shown that for every 10 per cent increase in the share of the health bill paid by government, there is a 4.2 per cent decrease in the share of GDP spent on health.'

31. Technically the collation of CPI quarterly statistics was closed off mid-quarter. This meant the June quarter statistics were closed off mid-May, as was commonly known! The CPI index went up 16.9% compared to 17.6% for the previous quarter. The AWE index went up by 1.2% compared to 3.3% for the preceding quarter.

32. Parliamentary Debates Representatives, vol. 96, 19 August 1975, p. 54.

33. Daryl Dixon, 'Different Strokes', *Sun-Herald*, 18 October 1993.

34. 'Hawke Wins Cuts in Tax', *Daily Telegraph*, 17 July 1975; 'Tax Relief in Budget: Hawke', *Australian*, 17 July 1975.

35. P. Kelly, *The Hawke Ascendancy*, op. cit., p. 18 has an account on this matter slightly different in the chronology, but in the fundamental facts very similar. It makes some fascinating points.

36. TEAS was progressively changed and in contemporary terms has been replaced by AUSTUDY.

37. P. Kelly, *The Hawke Ascendancy*, Angus&Robertson, 1st edn, 1984, p. 16.

PART IV

1. 'Fraser Lacked Courage, says Hewson', *Canberra Times*, 26 September 1991.

2. 'Being out of office shouldn't mean being out of mind', *Sunday Age*, 9 February 1992, 'News', column by Malcolm Fraser, p. 15.

3. See G. Winterton, *Monarchy to Republic*, ' ... it is widely conceded that Lang's dismissal was probably improper because the government's alleged illegality was justiciable', OUP, 1st edn, Melbourne,1986, p. 46.

4. Evatt H. V., *Australian Labour Leader*, Angus&Robertson, Sydney, 1945, p. 429. Although a similar incident occurred in 1917 when, through collusion, a Tasmanian Labor senator suddenly resigned from the Senate to be replaced by a non-Labor State government with a Nationalist Party member.

5. G. Whitlam, *The Truth of the Matter*, Allen Lane, Melbourne, 1979, p. 45.

6. Treasury letter to me dated 23 December 1992, signed by John Fraser for A. S. Cole, Secretary of the Treasury, which says *inter alia*:
Under the 'Gentlemen's Agreement' ... the Loan Council decided the maximum aggregate amounts to be borrowed ... for the financial year for each authority within the overall limits decided by the Loan Council. Unless the Loan Council decided otherwise, these programs constituted the final borrowing programs for each authority for the year ...

7. ibid., which states:
Other than for certain trade credit arrangements, Loan Council approval was required before any approach was made to obtain overseas borrowings, and for the terms and conditions of borrowings subsequently arranged.

8. A letter of 28 September 1995 by Mr C. Neave, Acting Secretary, Attorney-General's

Department, Canberra, responding to an earlier query by me as to what written opinions might have been provided for that department in respect of the meaning 'borrowing for temporary purposes', states: 'Our researches have not disclosed any written opinion on this subject.'

9. J. Kerr, *Matters for Judgement: an Autobiography,* 1st edn, MacMillan,1978, p. 235.

10. Extract from relevant Treasury documents.

11. In Joseph Heller's anarchical *Catch 22* character Milo Minderbinder one of whose dazzling transactions was to buy the entire Egyptian cotton crop when no-one else would touch it, coat it in chocolate and sell it to the Germans during World War II.

12. P. Kelly, *November 1975*, Allen & Unwin, Sydney, 1995, pp. 74, 84–85, 160–61, 166–67, 200, 305–6.

13. J. Kerr, op. cit., pp. 347–48.

14. J. Kerr, op. cit., p. 357.

15. G. Freudenberg, *A Certain Grandeur: Gough Whitlam in Politics*, Penguin Books, Melbourne, 1987, p. 253.

16. Sir David Smith, former Official Secretary at Government House, Canberra, has reminded me that Labor in Opposition had frequently moved to block money Bills in the Senate, prior to 1975. See *Canberra Historical Journal,* new series no. 29, March 1992; Nan Phillips Memorial Lecture, Myths and legends—the stuff of history (or 1975 revisited)', by Sir David Smith, pp. 6–7.

17. J. Kerr, op. cit., p. 361.

18. Letter to Kerr from Barwick of 10 November 1975.

19. G. Barwick, *Sir John Did His Duty*, 1st edn, Serendips Publications Pty Ltd,1st edn, Sydney, 1983, pp. 114, 124.

20. G. Sawer, *Federation Under Strain*, MUP, Melbourne, 1977, pp. 145, 146.

21. L. Oakes, *Crash Through or Crash*, Drummond, Melbourne, 1976, p. 155.

22. B. Buckley, *Lynched*, Salzburg, 1991, pp. 93, 97, 229.

23. L. Oakes, op. cit., pp. 155–6, 187–8. Gerard Henderson writing in the *Courier-Mail*, 4 November 1995, 'Kerr: Facing the Rage', says 'Missen had no intention of crossing the floor in the Senate and passing supply.' His source is A. Hermann, *Alan Missen: Liberal Pilgrim, A Political Biography*, Poplar Press, Canberra, 1993, pp. 108–9. Hermann had personal access to Missen, his papers and diary.

24. D. Markwell, 'On Advice from the Chief Justice', *Quadrant*, July 1985, pp. 38–42.

25. G. Henderson, *Menzies' Child: the Liberal Party of Australia 1944–1994*, Allen & Unwin, Sydney, 1994, pp. 242–4.

26. J. Kerr, op. cit., pp. 255–6.

27. An innocent comment by a military aide, made to Whitlam during a visit to Government House in the course of these momentous events, caused some misunderstanding for Whitlam. Whitlam noted a door to the drawing room, opposite Kerr's study, shut which was unusual. The aide commented, 'My successor is in there,' referring to three army officers who were waiting in the drawing room and from among whom one would be selected as a replacement for that aide, according to standard practice. Whitlam thought the aide said, 'Your [Whitlam's] successor is in there,' and this gave rise to some conspiracy speculation among some Labor sources. Fraser was, in fact, then seated in a waiting room at the front of the House.

28. D. Smith, 'Myths and Legends: The Stuff of History (or 1975 Revisited)', lecture to Canberra and District Historical Society, 17 October 1991.

29. J. R. Odgers, *Australian Senate Practice*, 5th edn., AGPS, Canberra, 1976, p. 70.

PART V

1. It can be argued persuasively that Kerr's intervention in fact saved us from a far worse result before the electorate. Some polls registered 39% public support for Labor in July, 35% in August and September, rising to 43% after supply was blocked. This was the two party

preferred vote for Labor at the December elections.

2. *SMH*, 'Spectrum', 14 August 1993, p. 41.

3. J. Edwards, 'An Angry Man Who Blames the System', *AFR*, 29 June 1972; P. Bowers, 'The Reluctant Cassandra', *SMH*, 14 January 1976.

4. 'Left Hits Economic Policy', *Age*, 17 June 1975.

5. P. Kelly, *The Hawke Ascendancy*, 1st edn, Angus&Robertson, 1984, Sydney, p. 175. The ABC TV series 'Labor in Power', screened during June–July 1993, has Keating mentioning that Hawke was in communication with the NSW Right at least as early as 1980, working on my replacement. See *SMH* supplement, *Good Weekend*, 2 May 1992, pp. 11–17, in particular p. 12; G. Richardson, *Whatever It Takes*, pp. 65–70, Bantam Books, Sydney, 1994. See also F. Cumming, *Mates: Five Champions of the Labor Right*, pp. 124, 128, 207–9, 211, 216–18, 223–3.

6. I confirmed the content of this discussion with Neal Batt by telephone on Wednesday, 2 February 1993. He subsequently confirmed this with a handwritten note to me shortly after this date.

7. Transcript of proceedings ALP 33rd Biennial Conference, Adelaide, Tuesday, 17 July 1979, first morning session, see in particular pp. 200–4.

8. F. Cumming, 'Hawke, Keating Joined in Hatred', *Sunday Herald Sun*, 30 May 1993, reviewing the ABC programme, 'Labor in Power', referred to in footnote 5 above. See also B. Hawke, *The Hawke Memoirs*, Heinemann, Melbourne, 1994, especially pp. 500–5.

9. *SMH* supplement, *Good Weekend*, 2 May 1993, op. cit. See also *Good Weekend* 29–30 October 1994, pp. 12–22.

10. Official report of the proceedings of the ALP 34th National Conference, Southern Cross Hotel, Melbourne, 27 July–29 July 1981.

11. *Spectrum* polls published in the *Australian* recorded voting intentions as ALP 43%, Lib–CP 44%, AD 4% in October 1982. In late November the findings were ALP 42.2%, Lib–CP 43.9%, AD 6.1%. We required a 5.5% swing to win. The later poll reflected a 5%, two party preferred swing. The later poll showed the vote holding up to just a few days before the by-election. Australian National Opinion Polls polling for the party had us in by a whisker. This polling, for good and obvious reason I expect, was promoted energetically as a rock solid result, i.e. consideration of the usual margin of error inherent in all opinion polling was discarded. In the event the swing was a disastrous 1.4% for Labor.

12. Morgan polls had Labor running well ahead of the Government, nationally, throughout 1982. In November and December, at the time of the Flinders by-election, Labor's support had in fact increased nationally to 49–50%. See *Bulletin*, 1982: 15 February, p. 21; 3 May, p. 27; 12 October, p. 12; 26 October, p. 24; 7 December, p. 24.

13. 'ALP, Unions Split on Pay', *Age*, 3 December 1982, p. 1.

14. 'Labor's Prices/Incomes Policy is Economic "lynch pin" ', *AFR*, 17 May 1982.

15. 'ALP Leaders Split on Visits by N-Weapon Ships', *SMH*, 15 June 1982.

16. PDR House of Representatives, 11 March 1981, p. 667, records Fraser stating, 'Australia would need to know …in particular whether nuclear weapons are being carried. The Australian Government has a firm policy that aircraft carrying nuclear weapons will not be allowed to fly over or stage through Australia without its prior knowledge and agreement'.

17. *News*, 2 September 1982, reported the Roxbury Downs project would create up to 18,600 jobs and inject $640 million into the South Australian economy, with an imminent election in that State.

18. 'Hayden Under Pressure But Not Yet Under', *Age*, 30 June 1982, p. 11.

19. T. Uren, *Straight Left*, Random House, Sydney, 1994, pp. 336 & 327.

20. B. Jones, 'Policy Election Tipped', *Sun-Herald*, 22 December 1991, which says *inter alia*, 'Mr Cameron, of Australian National Opinion Polls, said that in any case Mr Keating's image problem did not matter' and 'A high popularity rating is a handicap, not an advantage, because you can't keep it up. When you start to decline you create a momentum'; *Sunday Age*, 22 December 1991, 'According to Mr Cameron, Paul Keating's unpopularity will not be a factor in

the [election] outcome, and the election will be fought on policies ... Mr Cameron asserts that it's policy, not charisma, that is now more important in deciding elections'. 'Carr's big problem: getting women to notice him', *SMH*, 16 February 1995. By late 1995 Cameron had revised his judgment much further *viz* 'Popularity is totally and absolutely irrelevant.' He was defending Keating PM against criticism about his lack of popularity as a national election approached in which Labor trailed the Liberal–National Party coalition; *The Australian*, 18 November 1995.

21. B. Hawke, op. cit., pp. 259–60.

22. S. Mills, *The Hawke Years: the Story from the Inside*, pp. 231, 244–7, 280–93.

23. 'Born to Rule', *Hobart Mercury*, 10 November 1982.

24. 'Hawke Blows His Cool', *Age*, 9 November 1982, editorial; 'Hawke v Hayden—Why the Fight Was Called Off', *SMH*, 9 November 1982.

25. *AFR*, 22 August 1982 gives an account of a torrid debate in the House of Representatives on this topic the previous day.

26. PDR House of Representatives, vol. 129, 22 September 1982, p. 1736, 'Documents Referring to Straw Companies and the Development of the *Crimes (Taxation Offences) Act*—Ministerial Statement, 22 September 1982'. See also pp. 1736–45 and question time pp. 1772–6.

27. 'NSW Will Name Tax Cheats—Top People', *SMH*, 13 June 1982; the article stated, 'Prominent NSW people will be named as participants in massive tax avoidance schemes, one of which involved 1000 companies ... Mr Walker said he intended naming the people and companies involved when inquiries were complete'.

28. 'Hayden Threatens to Move Willis', *SMH*, 26 August 1982.

29. ' "Kingmaker" Button Ponders Hayden's Future', *AFR*, 24 December 1982.

30. P. Kelly, *The Hawke Ascendancy*, Angus&Robertson, Melbourne, 1984, pp. 342–4, 354, 379.

31. G. Sorby, 'Threat to Hayden', *Sun-Herald*, 2 June 1991; while some claims are fanciful on my recollection of matters mentioned to me, there is a substantial kernel of truth in this article. I received a two-and-a-half page letter from Dolan, dated 15 December 1992, denying claims about his involvement in these matters as outlined in P. Kelly op. cit. I replied on 14 January 1993, pointing out *inter alia* that Graham Richardson had much earlier said that 'his people had [Dolan] and the ACTU sewn up and that I would never get the endorsement from [Dolan] or them on the prices/incomes accord. The *Age*, 'Button Exits Politics With Wit and Venom', 1 April 1993, reports Button saying 'I do not believe the Labor movement was going to let Bill Hayden win the election. People were threatening to take their bat and ball and go home ... there were too many ructions'.

32. P. Bowers, 'Leak set Hawke on Path to Lodge', *SMH*, 9 June 1991, p. 22; and 'Abeles was intimately involved', *Canberra Times*, 9 June 1991.

33. M. Steketee, 'Revealed: the Man Who Dealt the Fatal Blow to Hewson', *Australian*, 24 August 1994.

34. P. Kelly, op. cit., 1st edn, p. 431–2.

35. G. Richardson, op. cit., pp. 123–34.

36. G. Richardson, op. cit.

37. P. Hartcher, 'How Keating's Hit Men Got Hawke', *SMH* supplement *Good Weekend*, 2 May 1992, pp. 9–17, quote at p. 12.

PART VI

1. Speech by the Prime Minister, 'Celebration for Former Refuseniks', Melbourne, 17 May 1988, pp. 5–6.

2. Hawke was to say this to me again in 1988, before I departed for the Middle East. The advice in Israel was, 'Tell him to forget about it'. Undeterred, during the Gulf War he made a similar proposal to the US President Bush; S. Mills, *The Hawke Years*, Viking Books, Melbourne, 1993, pp. 142–7.

3. B. Hawke, *The Hawke Memoirs*, Heinemann, Melbourne, 1994, pp. 225–6.

4. My Indonesian colleague, Foreign Minister Mochtar Kusumaadmatja has said, perhaps too generously but nonetheless in a fashion I found agreeable: 'Bill Hayden, perhaps more than anyone else, did much to restore Australia's credibility as a potential partner for ASEAN in the politics of the Asia-Pacific region . . . [he] greatly contributed in re-establishing trust between Australia and South-East Asian nations, especially ASEAN and more particularly Indonesia.' 'A Tale of Hard Times and a Great Life', *Sunday Times* (Singapore), 14 May 1995.

5. 'Hayden Warns on Bases', *Age*, 8 August 1984; 'Hawke Facing Growing Party Unrest Over US Bases', *AFR*, 13 August 1984; 'Ministers Hint that US Bases May Be Lever in Wheat Fight', *Age*, 25 July 1986; 'PM–Keating Rift on US Base "Bargaining Chip" ', *Australian*, 25 July 1986.

6. Press conferences at Tokyo; 17 April 1984, Kyodo News Service; 17 June 1985 National Parliament Library Transcription Service.

7. *The Age*, 'Hayden Opposes Japan Build-Up', 27 July 1983; *The Australian*, 'Hayden Opts for Modern Approach', 27 July 1983.

8. Personal correspondence, dated 27 October 1983, received from the late Peter Hastings who at the time was writing for the *SMH*. The letter stated, *inter alia*, '[Certain officers of the State Department and Pentagon] proffered the view that you were ambivalent in your attitudes to the US. They did not say anti-American but on occasions seemed to imply it'. Some rather extraordinarily thin 'evidence' was offered by the Americans, according to Hastings's letter, to justify their concerns. In a succeeding letter dated 28 October 1983, Hastings said, *inter alia*, ' . . . the sort of questioning I encountered on the part of some in State and the Pentagon about Australian Labor Party, and Government, policies and attitudes indicates that we are taken far more seriously than we used to be, far more seriously than when I lived in the US many years ago or last visited there some time ago ... came to the conclusion that times have changed ... In a sense we have far more room for manoeuvre than most Australians realise'.

9. Most of the relevant papers are held in my classified records, file 203/3 'Disarmament', Australian Archives, Canberra. There are a few comments on files which were sharply sarcastic the barb of which, I suspect, was apparent only to the recipient and me. In spite of the differences on this issue after working closely with the recipient I came to respect him. I think this experience made a big difference to our relationship.

10. 'After Marcos Now for the Suharto Billions', *SMH*, 10 April 1986, p. 1.

11. *Australian Society*, 'Honesty Begins at Home', No. 12, June 1986, pp. 45–6, gives some confirmation of Jenkins's account to me.

12. Quoted in DFAT briefing for my official visit to Indonesia, 3–8 May 1995, p. 39.

13. 'Troubled Waters', *Far Eastern Economic Review*, 29 December 1994–5 January 1995, pp. 18–20.

14. See Mahathir bin Mohamad, *The Malay Dilemma*, Asia Pacific Press, Singapore, 1970, in particular Chapters 5 & 8, where he engages in racial characterisations which are racially offensive (see for example pp. 84–5) but in fact makes a strong case describing Malay ethnic inferiority compared to many other races; see 'Race is Central to Mahathir's Philosophy', *Canberra Times*, 1 December 1993, for an expansion of this point.

15. *SMH*, 1 February 1985, reported that an aide to Foreign Minister Hayden had 'confirmed yesterday that Cabinet had decided to allow aircraft to be based at Sydney to monitor [MX] splashdowns in the Tasman Sea'.

16. St Thomas Aquinas, *Summa Theologia*, 2a 2Æ, 66, 8, 'Theft and Robbery', pp. 81–3, viz.; '... when a person is in imminent danger and he cannot be helped in any other way, then a person may legitimately supply his own needs out of another's property, whether he does so secretly or flagrantly. And in such case there is strictly speaking no theft or robbery ... it is improper to say that using somebody else's property taken out of extreme necessity is theft. For such necessity renders what a person takes to support his life his own'.

17. Keesing's Contemporary Archives, vol. XXXII, August 1986, pp. 34548–9; Historic Documents of 1984, *Congressional Quarterly*, May 1984, pp. 3210–15; American Foreign Policy Current Documents 1984, pp. 1095–1101, 1986, Washington State Department.

18. Quoted in R. W. McElroy, *Morality and American Foreign Policy*, Princeton University Press, Princeton, 1992, p. 16.

19. E. H. Carr, *The Twenty Years Crisis 1919–1939*, 2nd edn (reprint), MacMillan & Co., London, 1951, p. 93.

20. J. J. Rousseau, 'Abstract of the Abbe Saint-Pierre's Project for Perpetual Peace', quoted in M. G. Forsysth, H. M. A. Keens-Soper, & P. Savigear (eds), *The Theory of International Relations*, Allen & Unwin, London, 1970, p. 156.

21. G. Robertson, *Geoffrey Robertson's Hypotheticals*, 'Should You Tell the President?', p. 277, Angus&Robertson in association with ABC, Sydney, 1986.

22. For an informative overview of some of these key issues see the paper by Brigadier J. B. Wilson, *Experiences in and Lessons from UN Operations in Yugoslavia*, delivered at the Chief of General Staff Exercise 1993, Canungra, Queensland, 22 June 1993.

23. Congressional Research Report for Congress, 'Bosnia: U.S. Objectives, Military Options, Serbian Responses', Library of Congress, Washington, 14 April 1993, p. CRS 6.

24. S. Touval, 'Why the UN Fails', *Foreign Affairs*, vol. 73 no. 5, Sept/Oct 1994, p. 46; quoted in U Thant, *View From the UN*, Doubleday, 1978.

25. R. C. Riddell, *Foreign Aid Reconsidered*, 1st edn, Johns Hopkins University Press, London, 1987, pp. 27–8.

26. R. C. Riddell, op. cit., quoted at pp. 17–18.

27. It has to be conceded that many aid recipient, developing countries willingly enter into performance guarantees in respect of these matters. In practice, they fail to meet their commitments because of political pressures at home. Bangladesh is a classic example; but only one among many.

28. 'German Assistance to Africa Shrinking', *Manila Chronicle*, 5 July 1993.

29. G. B. N. Ayittey, 'Economic Atrophy in Black Africa', *The Cato Journal*, vol. 7 no. 1, Spring/Summer 1987, pp. 195–6.

30. K. Gannicott, 'Population, Development and Growth', in R. V. Cole (ed), *Pacific 2010*, National Centre for Development Studies, Research School of Pacific Studies, Australian National University, Canberra, 1993, pp. 17–18, 33.

31. ibid., p. 35.

32. P. McCawley, 'Development Assistance in Asia: a Policy Survey', article for *Asia-Pacific Economic Literature*, Manila, 28 July 1993, p. 18.

33. 'Down the Rathole', *Economist*, 10 December 1994, p. 67.

34. Department of Foreign Affairs (DFA) file ANZUS Obligations, November 1984, No. 203/2/1.

35. *Vienna Convention on the Law of Treaties*, AGPS, Canberra, 1975, Treaty Series 1974, No. 2 reprint, p. 11.

36. PDR House of Representatives vol. 213, 13 July 1951, R. G. Casey, pp. 1708–11.

37. PDR House of Representatives vol. 216, 28 February 1952, H. V. Evatt, p. 595 and more generally pp. 592–617, 636–48, 722–32, 733–50.

38. PDR House of Representatives vol. 216, 4 March 1952, Bourke, pp. 773–6, Beazley, pp. 609–10.

39. *Joint Committee on Foreign Affairs and Defence*, 'Threats to Australia's Security—their Nature and Probability', Parliamentary Paper No. 349/1981, AGPS, Canberra, 1981.

40. A. W. Martin, *Robert Menzies: a Life Volume I: 1894–1943*, p. 238; D. Day, *Menzies and Churchill at War*, pp. 6–7, 10–11, 16, 136–7, 145, 152–3, 160, 162, 166, 171, 177, 179, 185, 202–4, 211, 219–23, 225–30, 235, 243–4, 252–3.

41. P. Spender, *Exercises in Diplomacy: the ANZUS Treaty and the Colombo Plan*, pp. 155–6, Sydney University Press, Sydney, 1969. *Foreign Relations of the United States* (hereafter *FRUS*), 1951, vol. VI pt. 1, USGPO, Washington, 1977, p. 177.

42. P. Spender, op. cit., pp. 188–9.

43. *Documents on New Zealand External Relations*, vol. III, 'The ANZUS Pact and Treaty of Peace with Japan', p. 663, GP Wellington, NZ; A. Watt, *The Evolution of Australian Foreign Policy*

1938–1965, pp. 117–63, CUP, Cambridge, 1967.

44. R. G. Casey, *Friends and Neighbours*, Michigan State College Press, Michigan, 1955, pp. 61–3, 66–7, 69–70 (although he somewhat throws the curious reader off the scent when he declares contradictorily, 'The Treaty is solely concerned with the security of the parties' (p. 66); *Foreign Affairs*, vol. 30 January 1952, R. G. Menzies, 'The Pacific Settlement Seen From Australia', pp. 188–96; J. G. Starke, *The ANZUS Treaty Alliance*, Melbourne University Press, Melbourne, 1965, pp. 93–8.

45. *FRUS*, 1951, op. cit., p. 177.

46. *FRUS*, 1950, vol. VI pp. 152, 200; R. N. Rosencrance, *Australian Diplomacy and Japan 1945–1951*, Melbourne University Press, Melbourne, 1962, pp. 111, 211–12; P. Spender, op. cit., pp. 41, 172; J. G. Starke, op. cit., pp. 30–1, 50–1; A. Watt, op. cit., pp. 121, 123.

47. *FRUS*, 1949, p. 1150, vol. VII, USGPO, Washington, 1976.

48. *FRUS*, 1950, op. cit., p. 1162, FRUS, 1951, op. cit., pp. 196, 200; AA A5954/1 cable No. 29 of 28 January 1951; cable No. 1 1305 of 21 January 1951; memo No. 27/1951 of 8 February 1951; AA A1209/23 57/5229 cable No. 1. 1305 of 21 January 1951; 'US Outlines Pact to Defend Pacific', *New York Times*, 17 February 1951, T. J. Hamilton, (Hamilton reported by Australian Embassy, Washington, to be a sounding board for Dulles [A4940/1]).

49. *FRUS*, 1950, op. cit., pp. 163.

50. *FRUS*, 1951, pp. 161–2, vol. VI pt. 1; AA A5954/1 ref 1819/5; P. Spender, op. cit., pp. 85–7, 101, 124.

51. *FRUS*, 1950, op. cit., pp. 65–7, 197.

52. *FRUS*, 1950, op. cit., p. 193; P. Spender, op. cit., p. 133 (where he denies this US attitude).

53. P. Spender, op. cit., pp. 39, 44, 54–5, 101, 109, 118, 126, 183.

54. P. Spender, op. cit., p. 183.

55. P. Spender, op. cit., p. 39.

56. *FRUS*, 1950, op. cit., pp. 121, 204–5, 209, 211.

57. *FRUS*, 1950, op. cit., pp. 219, 1308.

58. *FRUS*, 1950, op. cit., pp. 1261–2, 1308.

59. R. K. Rodan, The Prime Ministership of Harold Holt, unpublished MA history thesis, University of Queensland, August 1977.

60. A. Watt, op. cit., p. 123.

61. *FRUS*, 1950, op. cit., pp. 64–5.

62. *FRUS*, 1950, op. cit., pp. 67, 148, 224–5, 226–7.

63. *FRUS*, 1950, op. cit., pp. 67, 148, 224–5, 226–7.

64. *FRUS*, 1950, op. cit., pp. 151–2.

65. P. Spender, op. cit., p. 46; AA A1209/23–57/5229 cable No. 1.525/27; AA A5954/1, Divisional memo to Sec. DEA of 30 January 1951.

66. *FRUS*, 1951, op. cit., p. 155.

67. *FRUS*, 1950, op. cit., pp. 64–5 records 21 March 1950 'Spender plan ... vague ... "not ready" '. In one afternoon, effectively, in February 1951 at Canberra the principles of the treaty were agreed upon and the draft drawn up that night.

68. *FRUS*, 1951, op. cit., p. 68.

69. *FRUS*, 1951, op. cit., p. 149.

70. AA A12209/23 cable No. 1.1305 of 21 January 1951.

71. *FRUS*, 1951, op. cit., pp. 173–4.

72. *FRUS*, 1950, op. cit., pp. 218, 224–7; FRUS, 1951, op. cit., pp. 178, 202, 207, 210, 220–1, 228, AA A4940/1 C228 Cabinet Agenda No. 25 para 16; P. Spender, op. cit., p. 130.

73. *FRUS*, 1951, op. cit., p. 198.

74. P. Spender, op. cit., p. 42.

75. T. Hoopes, *The Devil and John Foster Dulles*, Little Brown, Boston 1973, p. 491.

76. *FRUS*, 1950, vol. VII, p. 957, USGPO, Washington, 1976.

77. *FRUS*, 1950, op. cit., p. 162; R. N. Rosencrance, op. cit., p. 183; T. Hoopes, op. cit.,

97–100, 114–16.

78. *FRUS*, 1951, op. cit., pp. 152–4, 160; AA A5954/1 1819/5, Rourke notes para 5; PDR House of Representatives vol. 213, p. 1710, 13 March 1951, R. G. Casey, on a similar theme.

79. *FRUS*, op. cit., pp. 1563, 1143–7, 1159, 1164–5, 1190, 1193, 1357; *FRUS*, 1951, op. cit., pp. 132–3, 135, 140, 144, 148, 154–5, 160–1, 165, 184, USGPO, Washington, 1976; Australian Archives (AA) A5954/1, 1819/5 Rourke notes.

80. *Congressional Record*, 11 June 1948, pp. 7791 on; *Congressional Record*, vol. 49 pt 6 p. 7792, ' "US" co-operation must be a supplement and not a substitute for the adequate and continuous defence activities of others', 11 June 1948.

81. *Congressional Record*, vol. 115 pt. 31, pp. 20958–61, 28 July 1969; *World News Digest*, June 24–30 1969, pp. 473, vol. XXIX, no. 1500.

82. *FRUS*, 1950, op. cit., pp. 1144, 1159, 1164, 1190, 11193, 1260, 1357, 1363, 1366, 1369; *FRUS*, 1951, op. cit., 133, 148–9, 152, 154, 184, 198, 780–1, 789–91; P. Spender, op. cit., pp. 118, 122, 189.

83. T. Hoopes, op. cit., p. 491; *FRUS*, 1951, op. cit., p. 177.

84. *FRUS*, 1951, op. cit., pp. 143–5, 154–5, 161–2; AA A5954/ 1819/5, Rourke notes para 15; P. Spender, op. cit., p. 124.

85. *FRUS*, 1951, op. cit., pp. 184, 195, 198; P. Spender, op. cit., p. 92 for delphic comment.

86. *FRUS*, 1951, op. cit., p. 185.

87. DFA file 203/2/1 op. cit.

88. DFA File 203/2/1 op. cit.

89. *FRUS*, 1950, op. cit., p. 1149; *FRUS*, 1951, op. cit., pp. 143–4, 154–5, 176–7, 185–7.

90. *FRUS*, op. cit., pp. 154–5, 185–8.

91. *FRUS*, 1951, op. cit., p. 194; AA A5954/1 E337/1/1; AA A5954/1 1819/5 Rourke's notes para 3 P M's ref E337/1/1; A 4940/1 C228 Cabinet Agenda item No. 25 from P. Spender, in particular para 9; P. Spender, op. cit., pp. 89, 225.

92. *FRUS*, 1951, op. cit., pp. 132–3.

93. DFA file 203/2/1, op. cit.

94. *FRUS*, 1951, op. cit., p. 148.

95. AA A5954/1 1819/5 Rourke notes, in particular paras 3 & 16–17; AA A4940/1 PM's file No. E 337/1/1 para 2; AA A4940/1 C228, Cabinet agenda item No. 25, para 12 (vii).

96. *FRUS*, 1950, op. cit., p. 1356; *FRUS*, 1951, op. cit., pp. 135, 139, 164, 177, 180; P. Spender, op. cit., p. 76.

97. For subsidies detail see G. Brown, *Australia's Security: Issues for the New Century*, Ch 3, 'Self-Reliance or Self-Delusion', ADSC/ADFA, Canberra, 1994, pp. 67–106.

98. DFA file 270/1/1 covering a *bout de papier* between US President Kennedy and Barwick undated and unsigned, and a covering letter to Menzies of 23 October 1963.

99. Lord Gore-Booth (ed), *Satow's Guide to Diplomatic Practice*, 5th edn, Longman, London 3, pp. 50–1.

100. DFA file 203/2/1, quoted above.

101. SMH, 1 January 1996, 'How We Blundered into 'Nam'.

102. DFA file 203/2/1, quoted above.

103. S. Mills, *The Hawke Years: the Story from Inside*, Viking Press, Melbourne, 1993, p. 303.

104. M. Coelli, J. Fahrer & H. Lindsay, 'Wage Dispersion and Labour Market Institutions: a Cross Country Study', RBA Research Discussion Paper, RDP 9404, June 1994, in particular p. 33.

105. A. Harding & J. Landt, 'Policy and Poverty: Trends in Disposable Income', *Australian Quarterly*, Autumn 1992, p. 44.

106. A. Harding, 'Family Income and Social Security Policy', paper presented ACTU Conference, Melbourne, 13 May 1994; A. Harding, 'Poverty and Inequality', in September 1994 paper presented ACOSS Congress, Brisbane, 27 October 1994.

107. J. Richardson, *The Effects of Consumer Co-payments in Medical Care*, National Health

Strategy, Background Paper No. 5, June 1991, quote at pp. 5–6.

108. ABC television series, 'Labor in Power', screened 1993, has Evans saying that 'a hole had been punched' in option C of the sales tax proposal, and Kelty confirming that he left a discussion with Hawke similarly convinced on the matter.

109. *Industry Commission Annual Report 1989–90*, AGPS, Canberra, 1990, p. 193, which points out that various forms of protection to industry increased prices and acted as a tax on consumers amounting to a consumer tax equivalent of some $650 per Australian or a total in excess of $10,800 million. This report also revealed, p. 194, 'the taxing effect on households is regressive, increasing from 4 per cent of income for the highest income group to 12 per cent for the lowest'.

110. P. Kelly, *The End of Certainty*, Allen & Unwin, Sydney, 1992.

111. See Budget Statements 1992–93, Budget Paper No. 1, Statement No. 2, in particular at pp. 2.27–2.28, graphs in panels A & B, in box 6, for an illustration of this and the immediately preceding points.

112. 'PS Chief Supports Better Pay for Workers', *Canberra Times*, 22 July 1992; 'Executive Salaries: Paying their Way?', *Australian Business Monthly*, October 1992; 'Executive Salaries Up 5pc, Workers' 0.9', *Canberra Times*, 27 November 1992; 'Bosses' Pay Rises Twice Average', *Canberra Times*, 26 February 1993; 'Inside a CEO's Pay Packet', *AFR*, 3 March 1994; see also transcript of ABC TV programme 'Lateline', 16 June 1993, covering executive salaries & fringe benefits.

113. P. Walsh, 'Child-care Rebate vs Cash', *AFR*, 18 May 1993, who made the telling comment, viz., 'And surely, on equity grounds, spare money should be directed to the families—and their 600,000 or 700,000 kids—who have no parents with jobs, rather than to families which have two parents with jobs'; P. Walsh, *Confessions of a Failed Finance Minister*, Random House, Sydney, 1995, table at p. 192.

114. P. Walsh, 'The Truth About Tax Rates', *AFR*, 25 May 1993, viz., 'At four and eight times AWE the average [tax] rate will have fallen by 9 and 11 percentage points since their peak in 1984–85. The average rate on one-third of AWE (about $10,000) has steadily increased from zero in 1977–78 to 9.8 per cent now. It will continue to rise.' [table supplied with article]. Imagine! Malcolm Fraser administered tax scales which were constructed around greater equity than those of Labor!

115. P. Kenyon & M. Wooden, *The Outlook for Labour Supply in Australia During the 1990s*, Work Paper 2/94, Institute of Public Affairs & Institute of Applied Economics and Social Research, Melbourne, 1994.

116. For a review of many of these tasks see F. Argy, *A Long Term Economic Strategy for Australia*, CEDA Information Paper No. 37.

117. R. G. Gregory, 'Aspects of Australian & US Living Standards: the Disappointing Decades 1970–1990', *Economic Record*, March 1993, pp. 62, 75.

118. F. Gruen & M. Grattan, *Managing Government: Labor's Achievements and Failures*, Longman, Melbourne, 1993, pp. 164–5.

119. A. Ramsey, 'ALP Shake-up Could See Hayden as Next Governor-General', *SMH*, 10 March 1988; A. Ramsey, 'When the Numbers Add Up, Or Do They?', *SMH*, 12 March 1988.

120. B. d'Alpuget, *Robert J. Hawke: a Biography*, Penguin Books, Melbourne, 1982, pp. 1–6.

121. M. Gordon, *A Question of Leadership—Paul Keating: Political Fighter*, UQP, St Lucia, 1993, in particular pp. 9–10; S. Mills, op. cit., pp. 219–21.

122. 'Keating Feud Strains Hawke's Relations with Jewry', *Australian*, 2 July 1994; 'Casino Staff Tried to Restrain "Noisy" Hawke', *SMH*, 28 June 1994; 'Hawke Predicts Downer Will Become Next Prime Minister', *Canberra Times*, 27 June 1984; 'Malcolm Fraser Recalls Pretoria Incident', *SMH*, 2 July 1994; 'Bob's Shout at the Mandela Inauguration', *SMH*, 1 July 1994; 'The Devil in Keating's Tongue', *SMH*, 25 June 1994; B. Hawke, *The Hawke Memoirs*, Heinemann, Melbourne, 1994.

Part VII

1. 'Government House Canberra: Strategic Plan', prepared by Allom Lovell & Associates, AGPS, Canberra, Melbourne, 1991, p. 30.

2. L. F. Crisp, *The Parliamentary Government of the Commonwealth of Australia*, 2nd edn, Longmans Green, 1954, p. 236.

3. ibid, quoted at p. 224.

4. G. Sawer, *The Governor-General of the Commonwealth of Australia*, Current Affairs Bureau, 1 March 1976, p. 25.

5. P. Hasluck, *The Office of Governor-General*, Queale Memorial Lecture, Adelaide, delivered 1972, MUP, Melbourne, 1979, p. 14.

6. J. Kerr, 'Address to Indian Law Institute', India, 28 February 1975.

7. A. Reid, *The Power Struggle*, Shakespeare Head Press, Sydney, 1969, pp. 22–30, 102–105.

8. P. Howson, *The Life of Politics*, 1st edn., Viking Press, Sydney, 1984, pp. 420, 491, 560, 567–68, 570–71, 573, 585–86, 588, 593, 645–46.

9. *The Canberra Times*, 'Sir Joh's Battle of the Bulge Lost in Cabinet', 26 November 1987, *The Age*, 'Sir Joh Faces Sack Today', 'Governor Has Power to Force Issue, Says Lawyer', 'Dumped Joh Calls Palace', 'How The Cabinet Crisis Continues', 26 November 1987.

10. H. V. Evatt, *The King and His Dominion Governors*, p. 268.

11. H. V. Evatt, 'The Discretionary Authority of Dominion Governors', in *The Canadian Bar Review*, vol. XVIII, no. I, p. 6.

12. 'Executive Government', in the Report of the Advisory Committee to the Constitutional Commissioner 1987, Canberra Publishing and Printing, Canberra, 1987, p. 138.

13. ibid., p. 38.

14. L. F. Crisp, op. cit., p. 231.

15. L. F. Crisp, op. cit., pp. 224–36.

16. L. F. Crisp, op. cit., p. 230.

17. They were 1914, 1951, 1974, 1975, 1983, 1987.

18. 'Constitutional Convention Debates, Sydney, 1891', p. 280, quoted in J. A. Lanauze, *The Making of the Australian Constitution*, MUP, Melbourne, 1974, p. 41.

19. Report of the Advisory Committee to the Constitutional Commission, op. cit., p. 22.

20. J. A. Lanauze, op. cit., p. 41.

21. Report of the Advisory Committee to the Constitutional Commission, op. cit., p. 22. Members were: Sir Maurice Byers, CBE, QC, Chairman; Professor Enid Campbell, OBE; Hon. E. G. Whitlam, AC, QC; Hon. Sir Rupert Hamer, KCMG; Professor Leslie Zines. *Final Report of the Constitutional Commission*, AGPS, Canberra, 1988, para. 2.128, p. 75.

22. Polling references in this and the immediately following section have been extracted/deduced from tables included in M. Goot, 'The Queen in the Polls', in *Out of Empire*, J. Arnold, P. Spearritt & O. Walker (eds), Mandarin, Melbourne, 1993, especially pp. 298, 307.

23. ibid, p. 304.

24. ibid, p. 306.

25. G. Whitlam, *The Truth of the Matter*, Allen Lane, Melbourne, 1979, p. 180.

26. G. Sawer, 'The Governor-General of the Commonwealth of Australia', *Current Affairs Bulletin*, 1 March 1976, p. 24.

Part VIII

1. Quoted in K. Popper, *The Poverty of Historicism*, Ark Paperbacks, London, 1986, p. 56.

2. Australia has already modified the taxing and financial regimes on banks in order to successfully compete against increasing numbers of Asian countries, otherwise it could have seen 'a large proportion of its financial activity go offshore to Singapore, Hong Kong or elsewhere in the region', quoted in J. Owens, 'Globalisation: The Implications for Tax Policies', *Fiscal Studies* (1993), vol. 14, no. 3, p. 28. Similarly, it has eased sales tax legislation in a keen

but uncertain effort to attract the siting of Cathay Pacific airline training operations in Australia vide *AFR*, 28 December 1995, 'Cathay May Cut Back on Aust Plans'.

3. H. Hesse, *Siddhartha*, Picador, London, 1991, p. 14.

4. *The Bulletin*, 10 October 1995, 'Blood, Sweat and Jeers', pp. 16–20; AFR, 'Labor Going the Wrong Way', 22 November 1995.

5. *SMH*, 'Week That Made the Difference', 27 March 1995.

6. Personal correspondence from J. B. Prescott, Managing Director and Chief Executive Officer, BHP, 23 November 1995.

7. AFR, 'Cathay May Cut Back on Aust Plans'. 28 December 1995.

8. Royal Commission Into Aboriginal Deaths in Custody, vol. 1, AGPS, Canberra, p. 1, par 1.31.

9. ibid., para. 1.3.3.

10. D. Johnson, I. Manning, O. Hellwig, *Trends in the Distribution of Cash Income and Non-cash benefits*, in particular pp. v and 1–4, report of the Department of Prime Minister and Cabinet, Canberra 1995; see also A. Harding, *The Distributional Impact of Social Wage Infrastructure in 1994*, in particular pp. 141–45, pub tract, National Centre for Social and Economic Modelling, University of Canberra, 1995.